A History of Engineering and Science in the Bell System

A History of Engineering and Science in the Bell System

National Service in War and Peace (1925–1975)

Prepared by Members of the Technical Staff, Bell Telephone Laboratories.

M. D. Fagen, Editor.

Bell Telephone Laboratories, Incorporated

Credits for figures taken from
other than Bell System sources
appear on page 721.

First Printing, 1978

International Standard Book Number: 0-932764-00-2

Library of Congress Catalog Card Number: 75-31499

Printed in the United States of America

Contents

Part I.   The World War II Period

I. Bell System Technology Enters Its Second Fifty Years, 3.   II. Bell System's Role in Military Research and Development, 4.   III. Events Leading to the War Effort, 5.   IV. Bell Laboratories Mobilizes for War, 9.   V. Scope of the Wartime Effort, 13.   VI. The Human Side, 14.

I. Background, 19.   II. Technology, 26: Radar Transmitter, 28; Radar Modulator, or Pulser, 30; Antenna, 34; Duplexing, 41; Radar Receiver, 42; Video and Indicator Systems, 48; Measurement of Angles: the Field-of-View Problem, 51; Range Measurement, 60; Radar Data Transmission, 62; Microwave Propagation and System Design Equations, 63. III. Radar Systems, 66: Shipboard Systems, 67; Submarine Radars, 75; Ground-Based Radars, 81; Airborne Radar, 89. IV. Magnetron Research and Development, 113: The British Breakthrough, 114; The Bell Labs and Western Electric Contribution, 115. V. Radar Test Equipment, 125. VI. Summary, 131.

I. Electrical Analog Computers, 133: The Dream, 134; Early Planning for an Antiaircraft Director, 137; Development of the T-10 Director, 139; First Tests and Standardization: M-9 and Its Companions, 145; Defense Against the Buzz Bomb, 147; Alternative Choices in the Design of Antiaircraft Systems for Tactical Situations, 150; Alternative Design for Army Use: the T-15 Director, 151; Fire Control for Coast Artillery, 155; Fire Control for Naval Dual-Purpose Guns, 158; Other Wartime Analog Computer Applications, 162; Postwar Military Applications of Electrical Analog Computers, 163. II. Digital Computers, 163: From Dial Sys-

Foreword

The year 1925 marked the founding of Bell Laboratories and also the first half century of the telephone. By that time there were 17 million telephones in the United States, 12 million of them in the Bell System. Alexander Graham Bell's vision that ". . . a man in one part of the country may communicate by word of mouth with another in a distant place" had already become a reality.

The engineering and science that made this reality possible have been recorded in the first volume of this series. Other volumes will describe the succeeding contributions of Bell Laboratories to science and to telecommunications technology. This volume tells the story of national service by Bell Laboratories and Western Electric from pre-World War II to the mid-1970s. The central subject is engineering for urgent national-defense applications—how the technology of communications, already richly endowed in the late 1930s was adapted quickly and in manifold ways to the compelling needs of a nation at war. The United States and its World War II allies gained decisive advantage from the circumstance that there existed this body of technology to draw from and build upon.

During World War II, some 2,000 separate projects for the Army, Navy, and National Defense Research Committee were pursued by Bell Laboratories. These projects, in addition to major radar and gun director systems, included an encompassing range of specialized communications equipment designed for aircraft, ground, and shipboard applications. The systems were also designed for use in areas from battlefield to worldwide, including global high-speed radio teletypewriter and telephone systems having a degree of message security never before known. Greatly improved sonar systems, a new magnetic airborne detector for locating submarines, proximity fuzes, and extremely sensitive and rugged magnetic mines were other innovations of the Bell System during the war years. Also related in this volume are such little-known stories as the origin of the bazooka, the development of an acoustic torpedo that during a critical period sank 39 German U-boats and seriously damaged 18 others, and the establishment of communications lines by paying out wire from aircraft. In the area of materials research, important contributions were made in the familiar fields of dielectrics, synthetic rubber, and magnetic materials, and a most signif.cant advance was achieved in the separation of the U_{235} isotope.

Based on Bell System operations experience, it was realized early that the outpouring of new and sophisticated military equipment would be effective only if its users were thoroughly trained. To this end, Bell Laboratories School for War Training was established, and thousands of officers were trained in the proper use and maintenance of communications and weapons systems. No less than 650 different instruction books were written and published for this educational enterprise. In this level of engineering support for work done for the Government, the Bell System matches what the Western Electric Company, Bell Laboratories, and the AT&T Headquarters staff provide for the Operating Companies of the System.

The World War II history, not surprisingly, places heavy emphasis on radar and sonar, two technologies firmly based on communications science. Similarly based is the technology of the real-time electrical control system. In the end, it is this technology and its related systems that dominate the history here presented. This volume also tells about systems engineering at Bell Laboratories and of the management at Bell Laboratories and Western Electric that expedited the fulfillment of wartime needs for electronics.

In 1937, the Navy asked Bell Laboratories to investigate the possibility of using radar for Navy fire control. To obtain the necessary sharp beams with small antennas, a development program was initiated aiming for much higher frequencies than those that were being investigated in the government laboratories. From this early work, which was based on Bell Laboratories' experience with microwaves for communications, a fire control radar for the Navy was developed and put into production by Western Electric before World War II—this radar was used in critical battles in the South Pacific early in the war. Continuing its research and development into the higher microwave bands, Bell Laboratories and Western Electric produced all of the fire control radar used in Navy ships—from submarines to battleships—during World War II. By war's end, over half the radars purchased by the armed services were units designed at Bell Laboratories and manufactured by Western Electric. But the design and production of radars as end products—as instruments, so to speak—are only a part of the radar story. The M9 antiaircraft equipment, designed by Bell Laboratories and built by Western Electric, used radars as direction-finding instruments, but each M9 was more than a radar. It was a functionally complete system: acquiring and tracking targets by radar, computing gun positions, and issuing control signals to the gun mounts. Late in 1943, shortly after the M9 was put into use, Lt. Gen. L. H. Campbell, then Chief of Ordnance of the United States Army, assessed the system:

> The M9 Director, electrically operated, is, we feel in Ordnance, one of the greatest advances in the art of fire control made during this war, and we anticipate from the M9 Director very great things as the war goes on.

And, indeed, the M9 system, which, as related in this volume, originated in a dream of a Bell Laboratories engineer, was decisive in winning the battle against the German buzz bombs that attacked London in 1944. And it was critically effective at the Anzio beachhead in Italy, elsewhere on the European continent, and at Saipan, Iwo Jima, and Okinawa in the southwest Pacific. Adapting the best technology of its day, the M9 system was designed not simply as a radar, but as a functionally complete entity for target destruction. It is an example of the kind of systems work in which Bell System people excel, being derived from our traditional practice of devising complex telecommunications innovations.

Postwar, this history continues by tracing, from 1945 through 1975, further activities in support of the nation's defense that Bell Laboratories and Western Electric were assigned—activities that were undertaken in response to continuing needs and that were often extensions of wartime research.

A new era in defense technology began in the early 1950s with the Bell System development of the Nike-Ajax Air Defense System, the heart of which was a computer-controlled guided missile. In 1953, early in the Nike system's service, General of the Army Omar Bradley wrote:

> Perhaps the most consistently successful of our guided missiles is the Army's new anti-aircraft weapon, Nike, named after the Greek Goddess of Victory . . . . It can reach higher than any known bomber can fly, and outward many miles beyond the range of AA guns.

Later systems—antiaircraft systems deployed in 1955, the Nike-Zeus antimissile system demonstrated in 1962, the prototype Safeguard antimissile system deployed in 1974—were all similarly functionally complete. Each design adapted the most appropriate technology of its day to the purpose at hand. Successive designs were augmented by whole generations of new inventions.

Included here also are accounts of work by the Bellcomm and Sandia Corporations—work done for the nation in a pattern different from that used in Bell Labs' conventional development of defense systems. These activities were derived from technical-operations practices of the total Bell System structure for research, development, manufacture, and use. Indeed, they were reminders that an integrated industry can be a strong national asset, to be called upon when needed. David Lilienthal, first chairman of the Atomic Energy Commission, stated in his book *Big Business: A New Era* that the Bell System was asked to manage the Sandia undertaking for the AEC because

> . . . capabilities of research, industrial techniques, and operation had to be combined on the same team, with experience working together as a unit.

Bellcomm is another illustration of the Bell System's ability to perform a specialized national service. When the United States space program was assigned the Apollo mission with its critical problems, NASA turned to the Bell System for assistance. In response, Bellcomm was organized, under Bell Laboratories' leadership, to provide systems-engineering support. Bellcomm resolved many decisive problems in the ensuing ten years, and when the Apollo program was successfully concluded, the Bell group was assimilated back into Bell Laboratories.

That the technical resources of Bell Laboratories and the large manufacturing capabilities of Western Electric could thus be mobilized to serve the nation's needs is encouraging evidence of the role of telecommunications as assumed by the Bell System. Each episode in this book illustrates the relationship of the broad science and technology of communications and control to national security and defense. Almost every case further shows how Bell Laboratories in the engineering of diverse systems has been able to assemble new, reliable resources out of novel, often untried, components. And also, almost every example shows how Bell Laboratories and Western Electric, together, manage the design, manufacture, installation, and continued support of complex systems and equipment. Dean Harvey Brooks of the Harvard Engineering School, writing in the Spring 1973 issue of *Daedalus,* the journal of the American Academy of Arts and Sciences, commented on this organization of research, development, and manufacture:

> The Bell System represents the best example of a highly integrated technical structure in a high-technology industry and is widely regarded as the most successful and innovative technical organization in the world.

We of the Bell System are proud of this judgment and the record it implies. We see in it further affirmation of basic principles of technical integration that have been built into the management of research and development in the Bell System since the time, in 1907, that the engineering forces in Western Electric and AT&T were consolidated. We are grateful that, in 1940, Bell Laboratories was ready to take on, and was given, tasks for the nation beyond even telecommunications services. Our part in the preservation of freedom is a proud chapter in the historic record of benefits that science and engineering bring to human progress.

W. O. Baker

W. O. Baker
President,
Bell Telephone Laboratories

Acknowledgments

Like the first volume of this history, subtitled *The Early Years* (*1875–1925*), this second volume is the work of many members of the technical staff of Bell Laboratories—active and retired. Their experience extends over a period of more than 40 years, going back for many to their first employment at Bell Labs in the early 1930s and covering their entire professional careers in communications engineering and research. The material in these pages was written by experts in their fields who made significant individual technical contributions while, at the same time, holding positions of administrative responsibility for planning and completing the technical projects described.

As in the first volume—and in the remaining volumes yet to be published as part of this *History of Engineering and Science in the Bell System*—we have tried to achieve an account that goes beyond the simple narration of events and to deal with the "how" and the "why," assessing the long-range importance of the technical contributions made by the Bell System.

The book is primarily concerned with Bell System achievements, but as is clearly evident, we recognize the immensely important scientific and engineering contributions to the national defense made by the M.I.T. Radiation Laboratory and many groups in other universities supported by the United States Office of Scientific Research and Development (OSRD), particularly during the years of World War II. There was close collaboration as well with the laboratories and engineering departments of the nation's leading electrical, electronics and military equipment manufacturers. Equally important were the independent contributions of, and the cooperative projects with, the technical communities of our Allies, notably the United Kingdom and Canada.

Mervin J. Kelly, a former president of Bell Laboratories, writing of the war years in his preface to *Radar Systems and Components*, expressed well this mutual effort and dependence.

> Since there was almost daily informal exchange of information between members of Bell Laboratories and other organizations, full acknowledgment cannot be made. Radar development, like substantially all of the war developments, was a most cooperative program. Scientists and engineers from all organizations involved in a program in our country and frequently those involved in England, Canada, and, on occasion, Australia and New Zealand worked as a single unit; information flowed rapidly through infor-

mal as well as formal channels. We are pleased to express our debt generally to all engaged in the radar development of the war period.

In the postwar period, there was much of the same spirit of mutual endeavor in the nation's defense effort. Thus the contributions of AT&T, Western Electric, and Bell Laboratories which are described in this volume were necessarily made as part of a larger technical community in which our own country and others are participants.

The nature of defense work is such that attribution cannot always be specific. Where outstanding developments and innovations are clearly due to an individual, we have tried to give appropriate credit. The selection of names is done with reluctance, since others may well deserve equal mention. Understandably, it is impossible to list the hundreds who participated in the team effort responsible for the successes achieved over the period of 50 years covered in this volume. We can only acknowledge the great debt owed to the many dedicated workers in the Bell System and elsewhere whose creativity, enthusiasm, and unselfish exchange of ideas contributed to a strong national defense system.

This history was initiated at the suggestion of Dr. James B. Fisk when he was president of Bell Laboratories (1959–1973). The first volume was published in 1975.

W. C. Tinus, W. H. C. Higgins and J. W. Emling collaborated with the Editor in the planning of the first six chapters. Most of the writing was done by W. H. C. Higgins (in Chapters 1, 2 and 3), W. C. Tinus (in Chapter 2), J. W. Emling (in Chapters 1, 2, 3, 5 and 6), B. D. Holbrook (in Chapter 3), C. F. Wiebusch (in Chapter 4), F. J. Singer, R. L. Miller, and J. G. Nordahl (in Chapter 5).

Supplementary material for Chapter 1 was provided by L. W. Morrison and G. N. Thayer; for Chapter 2 by L. R. Walker, who wrote the section on magnetrons, W. H. Doherty, E. T. Mottram, and A. K. Bohren; for Chapter 3 by W. A. MacNair, C. A. Lovell, H. W. Bode, D. B. Parkinson, and R. W. Benfer; for Chapter 4 by W. H. Martin, A. C. Keller, A. C. Dickieson, L. M. Ilgenfritz, R. J. Philipps, and R. R. Galbreath; for Chapter 5 by Doren Mitchell, W. R. Bennett, H. W. Dudley, Henry Kahl, J. G. Nordahl, and D. K. Gannett; and for Chapter 6 by F. J. Biondi who prepared the section on gaseous diffusion. J. G. Matthews was helpful in organizing the illustrations and captions for Chapters 1, 2, 3 and 7.

C. A. Warren collaborated in the planning of Part II and was its principal author (Chapters 7, 9, 13, and 14). He initiated this work while he was an executive director at Bell Laboratories in Whippany, New Jersey, where practically all of the military research and development had been done during and since World War II. R. R. Galbreath and R. A. Walker wrote Chapter 8; T. W. Winternitz did most of the work on Chapter 10 and, with W. H. MacWilliams, Jr., prepared Chapter 11; in Chapter 12, J. F. Kampschoer, G. H. Huber, S. E. Watters, and W. L. Cowperthwait contributed to the military communications section and H. J. Michael wrote the material on the importance of the Bell System network in providing communications for the United States government. B. D. Holbrook and B. McMillan were major contributors to Chapter 13. Supplementary material for Chapter 7 was supplied by P. L. Hammann and Ray Dungan; for Chapter 9 by R. C. Newhouse, L. W. Morrison, K. E. Gould, J. H. Hershey, and H. C. Braun.

In Chapter 14, the section on Bellcomm was written by J. A. Hornbeck, the first president of that organization and now a vice president at Bell Labs. The Sandia history was based on the account given in the *History of Sandia Corporation* by Frederick C. Alexander, Jr. and brought up to date by Morgan Sparks, president of the Sandia Corporation, and his associates.

Many of the experts mentioned gave generously of their time in correspondence and in discussions based on their intimate knowledge of the events described. They contributed greatly to the accuracy and completeness of the *History* by reviewing and criticizing the manuscript as it was being prepared.

There are people who deserve recognition for their part in the making of this volume: G. H. Baker and his associates in the Military Program Planning Center at Whippany, who provided essential historical data, Ruth L. Stumm, who worked diligently on sources for reference material and illustrations, and Jane K. Mitchell and her co-workers in the Technical Documentation Department, who were responsible for producing and publishing the book.

A particular acknowledgment must be made of the work of George E. Schindler, Head of the Technical Publications Department at Murray Hill, who, on my retirement from Bell Labs early in 1977, took over as editor of *A History of Engineering and Science in the Bell System*. The project is in competent hands.

M. D. Fagen
Editor

Part I

The World War II Period

Chapter 1
Introduction

World War II was a technological war. It is not surprising, therefore, that Bell Telephone Laboratories and its manufacturing associate, Western Electric, were almost totally involved with a wide variety of technology-based military weapons and defensive measures. This volume tells the story of Bell Laboratories involvement in the war effort of 1937–1945 and the follow-through in the period 1945–1975 required by the postwar situation to assure a strong defense posture for the United States. Bell Laboratories involvement was so varied that it is impractical to relate all the facets of Bell military effort, and it has been necessary to select only some outstanding examples. What is perhaps of greater importance than a description of the specific items produced for the military is the illustration of the extent to which a research and development organization, well grounded in the scientific method and using appropriate management techniques, could quickly be adapted for technological work in completely new fields of endeavor. The chapters which follow illustrate how this was accomplished despite the prewar public disinterest in military preparedness and the effects of a catastrophic depression prior to the war which seriously restricted the growth of United States industry.

I. BELL SYSTEM TECHNOLOGY ENTERS ITS SECOND FIFTY YEARS

As noted in the first volume of this history, the Bell System, as it entered the second 50 years of telephony, had every reason for anticipating great growth both in plant and technology. By 1925, the long-desired nationwide communication network was being realized. Technology had passed through the empirical stage, and a firm theoretical foundation was being established based on research, analysis, and measurement. Research and development had been consolidated in Bell Laboratories, and techniques of management had evolved which greatly enhanced the effectiveness of the organization through group effort and the promotion of internal intellectual competition. Finally, an integrated organization provided a means for efficient application of effort through close coordination of research, development, and manufacturing, all carefully planned to meet the needs of the user for a high-grade product under the overview of unique quality assurance techniques.

Principal authors: W. H. C. Higgins and J. W. Emling.

3

We shall see in other volumes of this history that the great hopes of 1925 were not only realized but exceeded in spite of two unforeseen catastrophic events of worldwide impact. One of these was the Great Depression of the 1930s. Even before the world economy recovered from this blow, clouds were gathering—a forewarning of the second war that was to engulf the world. In all, nearly 15 of the second 50 years of telephony were to be centered on these two events.

The effects of the Great Depression on the growth of telephone plant and technology will be made apparent in other volumes. For the present, it is only necessary to say that its impact was enormous, bringing about the only period in telephone history with a decrease in stations and traffic. In spite of this reversal of a 55-year trend, confidence in the soundness of the principles on which the system was based did not falter, and despite economic problems, research and development effort was continued at Bell Laboratories at a productive level. As a consequence, a group of knowledgeable people, equipped with advanced technology, was available when the onset of war brought great demands on engineering and science not only for a great increase in civil and military communications but also for the development and manufacture of new, technologically based military devices and systems of great sophistication.

II. BELL SYSTEM'S ROLE IN MILITARY RESEARCH AND DEVELOPMENT

The part played in serving the military needs of our country in the second 50 years of telephony is the theme of this volume of *A History of Engineering and Science in the Bell System*. Much of the volume is devoted to the wartime years when a major part of the Bell Laboratories and Western Electric Company effort was devoted to producing weapons and other military hardware of many kinds. However, the military needs of the country continued after the 1945 victories, and this volume also covers outstanding contributions during these later years.

We should note some significant differences in the work carried out in the two periods. During the war years, the prime objective of the Bell System, as it was throughout the country, was winning the war, and any task was undertaken by Bell for which there was a capability.[1] In the post world war years, the major priority lay in building up the general communications system needed by a strong nation with a prosperous and expanding economy. An obligation to serve specific military needs of the country was recognized and military R and D was continued in those areas where the Bell System seemed to be particularly qualified. This policy resulted in considerable emphasis on military communication systems but, because of the extensive and often unique experience of

---

[1] It has been estimated that more than 70 percent of American scientists were engaged in the war effort.

personnel in the fields of radar and underwater sound, much work was continued in those areas but it was very largely devoted to the design of defensive systems.

III. EVENTS LEADING TO THE WAR EFFORT

Those who participated in the effort during the war will have a vivid memory of the period, and the dates of the work to be described will readily fall into a well-remembered framework of events. However, it is roughly 40 years since the darkening skies provided the first hint of the deluge to come. The memory of some readers may not go so far back; and for these, Table 1-1 provides a list of some significant dates that will help to place the work in a proper time frame. We may add, as additional background, that in the 1920s and 1930s, World War I was remembered as the "war to end all wars." Expenditures for military preparedness seemed unnecessary to the majority of people and their representatives. The Great Depression made such expenditures even less popular, and in many western countries, by the mid-1930s, there were strong leanings toward isolationism and pacifism (the latter was particularly strong in England). Under the circumstances, it is not surprising that the few facilities we had for fighting a war at this time were largely those suitable for World War I conditions.

After World War I, there were some developments in aircraft, ship-building, and so forth that involved private industry, but most military development was carried out by the military organizations. For example, the application of electronics to weapons was carried out almost entirely by the U.S. Naval Research Laboratory and the U.S. Army Signal Corps Laboratory. It was not until the late 1930s, when the German expansion into neighboring countries caused misgiving to some farsighted people, that a few industrial laboratories were approached for assistance in advancing research ideas from laboratory demonstrations into manufacturable weapon systems. Radar, of which we shall hear much more later, was probably the first such case involving the Bell System. The involvement began in late 1937 when the Navy approached AT&T for discussions of a possible contract to expand the scope of research on this new concept, which had been in the exploratory stage at the Naval Research Laboratory during the previous three or four years. This ultimately led to the major wartime project of Bell Laboratories and Western Electric: more than half of all radars used by the United States forces in World War II were designed by Bell Laboratories and produced by Western Electric.

However, AT&T was reluctant to enter into a formal development contract on this project at that time. The Bell Laboratories research group at Holmdel, New Jersey, had been working for a number of years on projects that conceivably could be of use to radar development, but these

Table 1-1.   Significant Events in the History of World War II

Date	Event
Mar. 16, 1935	Hitler announced the institution of universal military service and the creation of an air force.
Mar. 7, 1936	German troops reoccupied the Rhineland zone that had been demilitarized by the Treaty of Versailles (1919).
Mar. 12, 1938	Germany invaded Austria. The union of the two countries was proclaimed a few days later.
Sept. 29, 1938	In the Munich Agreement, which the British Prime Minister believed would "bring peace for our time," Britain and France agreed to the cession of part of Czechoslovakia to Germany.
Mar. 10–16, 1939	The republic of Czechoslovakia was dissolved, becoming a German protectorate.
Aug. 23, 1939	Germany and Russia signed a nonaggression pact. This startling about-face cleared the way for Germany to attack Poland without fear of Russian intervention and thus, in a sense, set off World War II.
Sept. 1–3, 1939	Germany invaded Poland on Sept. 1, and Britain and France declared war on Germany on Sept. 3. Thus began World War II.
May–June 1940	The British were forced to retreat from France (through Dunkirk), and France signed an armistice with Germany on June 22.
July 1940– June 1941	The "Battle of Britain" was a prolonged air-sea attack on British cities, communications, and shipping until the German attack on Russia.
Sept. 2, 1940	The United States transferred 50 destroyers to Britain in exchange for naval bases.
Mar. 11, 1941	President Roosevelt signed the Lend-Lease Act.
June 22, 1941	Hitler's armies invaded Russia in what became the largest land battle in the history of warfare. The British Prime Minister, Winston Churchill, promised to assist Russia in every way possible.
Dec. 7, 1941	The Japanese bombed Pearl Harbor and thus brought the United States into the war.
May 3–8, 1942	In the Battle of the Coral Sea, a Japanese carrier force suffered such heavy losses that the Japanese plan to occupy Port Moresby on the southern coast of New Guinea was canceled.
June 4–7, 1942	A Japanese naval force attempting to capture Midway Island was heavily damaged and forced to withdraw.
Aug. 7, 1942	U.S. Marines began the long, bloody battle to take Guadalcanal in the Solomon Islands northeast of Australia.

Table 1-1—*Continued*

Date	Event
Nov. 8, 1942	An Anglo-American force under General Eisenhower landed in French North Africa. The British had been fighting in Libya and Egypt for some time.
July 10, 1943	The Allies landed in Sicily.
Sept. 3, 1943	Italy accepted an armistice, and the campaign against the Germans in Italy began.
Mar. 1944	General MacArthur was directed to prepare to invade the Philippines. His forces landed on Leyte in October.
Feb.–April 1944	U.S. forces attacked Iwo Jima on Feb. 19 and Okinawa on April 1.
June 6, 1944	The Allied invasion of France began in Normandy.
May 7, 1945	An instrument of unconditional surrender was signed by German representatives in Reims, France.
Aug. 6, 1945	The first atomic bomb was dropped on the Japanese city of Hiroshima.
Aug. 14, 1945	Japan accepted Allied terms of unconditional surrender.

had been pursued largely to provide basic knowledge of the higher radio frequencies, which would be of use for expanding telephone communications. In 1937, radar development seemed remote from the normal Bell effort, and a considerable amount of exploratory work would certainly have been required to demonstrate the technical feasibility of the system desired by the Navy. Thus, Bell Laboratories start on radar was a modest venture beginning with an agreement to conduct a year of exploratory work at AT&T expense. This led to a demonstration of an advanced-model radar in mid-1939 and to a contract for the design of a production version to be manufactured by Western Electric, as covered in the next chapter.

Meanwhile, the signs of an impending war became more and more evident, and the various laboratory areas began to explore other fields where their capabilities might be useful.

Experience in World War I[2] had shown the value of the Bell System's technical skills, and there was every indication that technology would be of even more significance in the future. When the National Defense Research Committee (NDRC) was established by executive order of President Franklin D. Roosevelt on June 27, 1940, the action had been anticipated by many persons, and the technical and manufacturing or-

[2] For an account of Bell System activity and communications development during World War I, see the first volume of this series; *The Early Years*, pp. 175–177, 368–385, 584–585, 845–846, and 935.

ganizations were prepared to join in the nationwide mobilization of science and industry for technical warfare, which was the broad objective of the National Defense Research Committee.[3]

The NDRC, which after a year came under the auspices of the newly formed Office of Scientific Research and Development (OSRD), became a remarkably effective organization in bringing together the scientists from industry, academic circles, and military organizations in the United States. It also provided effective and highly productive liaison with their counterparts in the Allied countries, particularly the United Kingdom. Members of the NDRC were appointed by the President, and the committee was well financed by funds placed at the President's disposal by Congress. It was empowered "to correlate governmental and civil research in fields of military importance outside of aeronautics." It was to "supplement, and not replace, activities of the military services," and to form a link between them and the National Academy of Sciences, leaning on the latter for broad scientific advice and guidance. It was completely free "to enlist the support of scientific and educational institutions" and "individual scientists and engineers, throughout the country."[4]

The Committee itself was to consist of not more than 12 members drawn from the Army, Navy, National Academy of Sciences, and other leading scientific bodies. The supporting staff, drawn from industry and the academic world, was organized into divisions having cognizance over various fields of technological warfare. The NDRC could contract for many kinds of scientific studies but was not authorized to build and operate its own laboratories. However, it could and did encourage academic institutions to establish laboratories that operated under contract with the NDRC. One example was the Radiation Laboratory of The Massachusetts Institute of Technology which, together with Bell Laboratories, designed essentially all United States radars used in the war.

A truly remarkable degree of cooperation was achieved between the military and civil R and D organizations, and in the latter, the industrial and academic scientists worked together as never before in applying their talents to the solution of problems—not only those at the highest theoretical levels but also those arising in application and production.

Much of the success of the NDRC was owing to its nonbureaucratic approach. There was little tendency toward preparation of long reports transmitted through "channels" before action could be taken. There was

---

[3] Frank B. Jewett, president of Bell Laboratories and of the National Academy of Sciences, was one of those consulted by Vannevar Bush in formulating the proposal for the NDRC. Jewett became chairman of the board of Bell Labs in 1940, a position he held until his retirement in 1944. He was president of the National Academy from 1939 until 1947 and served during the war as its representative on the NDRC.

[4] Bush, the first chairman of the NDRC and later director of the OSRD, thus described the function of NDRC; see James Phinney Baxter, 3rd, *Scientists Against Time* (Boston: Little, Brown, 1946), p. 15.

much direct contact between the individuals concerned with a project, regardless of the organization, civil or military, involved. Contracts were made directly with the appropriate military organizations by both industrial and NDRC-promoted laboratories with only enough oversight by the NDRC to assure that needed work was accomplished with little duplication of effort. Emphasis was placed on getting the job done, and this was achieved while preserving a remarkable degree of cooperation among research groups and maintaining a very high level of security.

IV. BELL LABORATORIES MOBILIZES FOR WAR

From the very beginning of the war, work in the Bell System (and indeed elsewhere) was characterized by a tremendous sense of urgency—of scientists and engineers working side by side around the clock to invent and design against time, of preproduction shops to produce preliminary models, of heroic efforts for mass production shops to produce early models to meet urgent needs, of enormous efforts for mass production in the factories of Western Electric (Fig. 1-1) and its many subcontractors, and of rapid conversion of Bell Laboratories research and engineering staff from peacetime activities to the application of its knowledge in developing new instrumentalities for warfare.

The rapid conversion from Bell System communications type work to military projects is well illustrated by Fig. 1-2. From a level of about 200 "equivalent members of technical staff"[5] in 1940, the number rose to well over 2,000 by 1943. There was, however, very little increase in total scientific and engineering staff. As one might expect, the research and development expenditures followed a similar pattern, as shown in Fig. 1-3. From the level of about 2.5 percent of the company budget in the year 1940, work on military projects rose to nearly 85 percent of budget at the peak.

Even these figures do not give the full measure of Bell Labs' war effort. Supporting the technical effort was a large staff of assistants carrying out the clerical, secretarial, purchasing, security, and numerous other support tasks. Since technical workers were in very short supply, their total number did not change greatly during World War II, but their effectiveness was greatly increased by the enlarged supporting staff, which resulted in an increase in total employees from 4,600 early in 1941 to about 8,000 in the peak war years. But this, too, tells only part of the story. Early in 1942, the normal 48-hour work week was increased by nearly 40 percent, and the actual hours worked often went far beyond, in some urgent cases reaching 80 or 90 hours. Holidays were reduced to one or two per year.

---

[5] An "equivalent member of technical staff" is a Bell Labs designation used to provide a measure of number of technical people used. A scientist or engineer is a full member of technical staff. Two supporting technicians are considered to be "equivalent to" one full member of technical staff.

(a)

(b)

(c)

Fig. 1-1.   Western Electric production facilities in 1945.   (a) Kearny, New Jersey. (b) Hawthorne Works in Chicago.   (c) Point Breeze Works in Baltimore, Maryland.

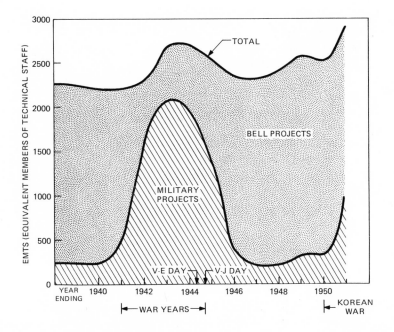

Fig. 1-2. Proportion of Bell Laboratories engineering staff assigned to military projects.

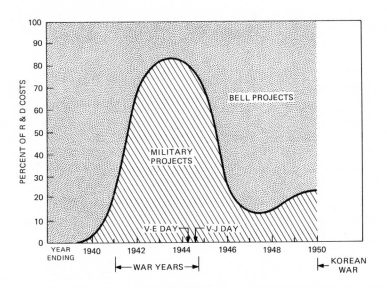

Fig. 1-3. Proportion of Bell Laboratories budget allocated to military projects.

The standard two-week vacation was retained for health reasons, but few realized the full allotment.

Of the technical staff not actively assigned to military effort, practically all were devoting their effort to the immense expansion in communications required to support the increased military and industrial mobilization. This was an unglamorous and consequently somewhat unpopular job, but those doing it were among the many unsung heroes of the war and should not go unmentioned. Fortunately, development of carrier systems during the depression years provided facilities for much of this expansion with only minor additions to plant and minimal use of critical materials. The capacity of main routes was often expanded manyfold by the addition of a small cable and sometimes with no additional use of copper at all. As the need for circuits increased and copper became in even shorter supply, electronics technology developed means for multiplying the available circuits by two through a frequency-translation and filtering process that divided a normal circuit of nominal 3-kHz bandwidth into two half-band circuits. This degraded quality of transmission somewhat, but such circuits were still usable and indeed preferable to the long delays which would have resulted from a lack of circuits. At the peak use of this device,[6] essentially all circuits over 1,000 miles in length were of the split-band type, and shorter ones were also used in critical situations.

Another facet of Bell Labs' effort may not adequately be covered by the expenditure and other data mentioned previously. Under normal conditions, the support of Bell Laboratories was divided between AT&T and Western Electric. Broadly speaking, AT&T paid for research, exploratory development, and other items likely to be of use to any part of the Bell System, the specific part being unpredictable in advance. Development for manufacture was paid for by Western Electric and recovered through the sale of products to its users. During the war years most Bell Labs military work was done under contract with Western Electric (on a cost-plus-fixed-fee basis),[7] with Bell Labs being a Western Electric subcontractor. Under this arrangement, Bell Labs' costs on a project were a part of the Western Electric contract cost. This was a fair way to handle a project for a military weapon, but AT&T was reluctant to have Western Electric accept a contract for a research project which might ultimately benefit the Bell System more than the military. For this reason, AT&T bore the cost of a number of exploratory jobs until such time as it became apparent that a contract would be appropriate because the specific work covered could be aimed at developing a useful and producible military device or system. Some of this reasoning was responsible for the AT&T

---

[6] This was known as an "EB Bank." Its conception has been attributed to C. W. Carter, who had the substantial assistance of K. G. Van Wynen. The latter liked to refer to it as the "amoeba," since it multiplied by division.

[7] All contracts were subject to renegotiation each year.

payment for early radar exploration and also for research on a digital type of communications system together with many other exploratory projects of a fundamental nature.

V. SCOPE OF THE WARTIME EFFORT

The Bell System contributions to the successes of World War II were as varied as they were massive. They ran the gamut from the deeply scientific at Bell Laboratories to expedited production of hundreds of millions of dollars worth of highly sophisticated electronic equipment by Western Electric; from research on materials for the atom bomb to training programs for the armed forces; from the development of radar for land, sea, and air to the sending of trained field engineers to every theater of war; from inventions conceived through necessity to the application of modern quality control methods in the manufacture of shell cases; from high-speed cameras capable of "stopping" a bullet in flight to hundreds of instruction manuals; from maintaining the nation's communications system in the face of shortages in men and material to producing special radio and wire-line communications systems for the front lines; from aircraft training simulators to proximity fuses for shells; from sonar systems and homing torpedoes to high-power loudspeakers for battle announcing aboard ship and battle direction on newly won beachheads; from aircraft- and blimp-mounted magnetic detection equipment for submarine location to the electronic computers for gunfire control; from the development of new magnetic materials to high-volume production of frequency stabilizing crystals; from the bazooka and control of rocket launchers to intercommunication systems for noisy aircraft; from electronic countermeasure equipment to highly complex secrecy systems for communication among the highest levels of the Allied governments.

Space limitations prevent the complete coverage of this varied list of activities. We are obliged to be selective and have limited this history to the coverage of a few of the activities which illustrate both the wide scope of the work and the engineering and scientific capabilities which fitted Bell Laboratories and its associated organizations for their extensive contributions to the war effort. Therefore, this volume covers only four areas of wartime effort which not only meet these criteria but also include projects which rank among those having the greatest impact on the prosecution of the war. Those chosen for a detailed account are radar in its various forms, electrical computers, communications (both radio and wire line), and acoustics in a wide variety of air- and water-transmitted applications. Much additional work has been documented elsewhere, and titles of these papers are included in the list of references.

The chapters on wartime applications of engineering and science are followed by coverage of some of the postwar projects carried out between 1945 and 1975, a period when defense of the country against submarines and atomic weapons was the prime concern of the country. Since the Bell System was very active in these fields, the later chapters of this volume illustrate the effort by covering work on the following: submarine-detection systems, systems for providing early warning of air attack, defensive systems for countering attack of aircraft and ballistic missiles, communications systems and networks for command and control, computers for military application, millimeter waves, and sophisticated radar modulation techniques.

VI. THE HUMAN SIDE

The main concern of this volume is with the design and production of military weapons and other systems used in warfare. This approach tends to emphasize hardware and to neglect the people who produced it and made it work. In many cases it is possible to mention by name a few of the people who participated, but it is hoped that the reader will appreciate that for each person named there were dozens more involved, working long hours, traveling all over the world, and often sharing the risks of those in active military service.

In addition to those engaged in design and production, there were two groups that deserve special note, since they played such a large part in making the development projects effective. These were the Western Electric Field Engineering Force (FEF) and the Bell Labs School for War Training.

The FEF was established first. It was obvious that the radar systems used very complicated gear and that if they were shipped to the field without special provision for training the operators and checking the equipment, the chances of long and successful use were nil. This was particularly true under the conditions of accelerated production necessary to make the systems available at the earliest possible moment, and with the need for frequent retrofitting to keep up with the rapidly advancing technology. With some of these ideas in mind, the Navy, in mid-1941, asked Western Electric if it would establish a field force to handle some of the technical problems that were bound to arise. Western Electric chose J. S. Ward to recruit, organize, and lead the FEF. He quickly gathered about a dozen engineers who started training in Bell Laboratories. In September 1941 some of these first FEFs were receiving final "hands-on" experience in testing the first Mark 3 radar aboard the cruiser U.S.S. *Philadelphia* on its way to Norfolk, Virginia. Working long hours, often with the simplest of tools (Fig. 1-4), these men tackled any problem which might arise with Bell equipment (or any other critical situation which might arise). In the first five days after the Japanese attack on December 7, one of the FEFs at Pearl Harbor spent 85 hours repairing damaged radars and making new installations.

This group, originally intended to number 20, grew to a force of 431 on

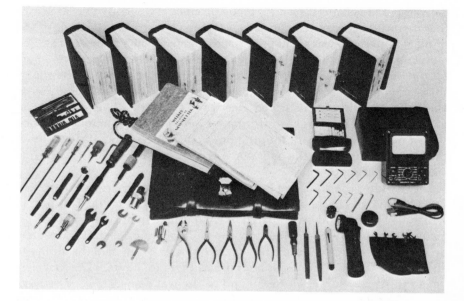

Fig. 1-4.   Typical Western Electric field engineer's tool kit.

V-J Day.   While Western Electric engineers formed the nucleus of the FEFs, the large number and the special skills required made it necessary in the long run for the FEF to recruit personnel from Bell System Operating Telephone Companies, universities, and broadcasting stations—indeed, from wherever men could be found who had both the proper technical background and a taste for adventure under dangerous circumstances. Three members of the group lost their lives in line of duty.

The original concept of the FEF called for a small force to assist in getting the radar project started in the field, but the organization soon expanded to include all Western Electric war products and all sorts of services. Stated briefly, the FEFs were a sort of "emergency squad" handling all kinds of jobs required to assure that Bell Laboratories designs and Western Electric products would give high-quality field performance.   In 1945, for example, their job was carried out at some 119 different places in the United States and at 80 locations overseas.   About 40 percent of the force received overseas assignments during some portion of 1945.   There is every reason to believe that without these men the complex electronic weapons used in World War II would have proved far less effective than they actually were.[8]

While the FEF could assure that the Bell System military equipment was

---

[8] In October 1943, the Office of Scientific Research and Development established an Office of Field Service similar to the FEF but with somewhat broader responsibilities.

delivered and installed as a high-grade product, it could give no assurance that it would be operated correctly. Operation was in the hands of the military, and there was small prospect that an adequate number of skilled men could be obtained through recruitment or selective service. Successful operation required the training of large numbers of military personnel in basic electronic techniques and the use of military equipment employing highly sophisticated electronic circuitry. The training had to be supported by a highly informative set of training manuals, which served not only as texts for training but as reference materials for solving problems arising when the operator was on his own far from the original source of instruction.

Shortly after the attack on Pearl Harbor, the armed services requested Bell Laboratories to set up a school called the School for War Training in which key men could be prepared to train others in military schools. A faculty was quickly assembled from the Bell Laboratories staff. Most had no prior experience with military electronics, but they had the ability to absorb new technical concepts and impart them to others. The first class began in April 1942. Before the end of the war some 125 courses were given to a total of over 4,000 students, who varied in background from radio repairmen fresh from their workbenches to graduate engineering officers with months of training at M.I.T. All Naval officers training for fire-control assignments attended the school, and a graduate of the school was required aboard each major combat vessel. At its maximum enrollment, the school, headed by R. K. Honaman as director, had a staff of about 75 instructors, mostly members of the Bell Laboratories technical staff or engineers lent by the various Operating Telephone Companies. These instructors were supported by a staff of clerks, guards, and laboratory technicians.

The school provided instruction on every major piece of equipment or system developed by the Bell System. For each equipment there was a special textbook. The development department had basic responsibility for the technical details of each book, but the school faculty often wrote the manuals and textbooks. To care for the rapidly expanding load of publications writing, editing, and preparation, an editorial department was established which worked closely with the training school and technical departments involved in book preparation and publication. In 1944, 366 separate instruction books and manuals were prepared, aggregating nearly 60,000 pages of text and 17,000 illustrations. In that year, Bell Laboratories became the country's largest publisher of new books. A few of the books are shown in Fig. 1-5.

The members of the training school staff and the book editors were truly among the unsung heroes of the war. They worked long hours in new fields. They trained thousands of people and anonymously wrote hundreds of books, yet they published no papers to give them personal fame.

Fig. 1-5.   Sample of instruction books and technical manuals produced by Bell Laboratories for the armed services.

The FEFs were also part of this large anonymous group, working as they did in remote parts of the world often in positions of great danger. For all these people the chief satisfaction was the knowledge that without them the sophisticated weapons produced for the Allied forces might well have ended as piles of deteriorating electronics that had mastered their users instead of being used to promote a successful conclusion to the war.

In retrospect, it is clear that much of the secret of the Allied success in applying electronics to weaponry lay in the cooperation among the organizations involved and the close liaison among all members of the production team from invention to installation and use of the finished products. It was a truly remarkable example of what could be accomplished by a team of highly dissimilar individuals working in concert. It was integration of effort at its best. While outstanding credit for this successful cooperation must go to the individuals involved, no small part is owing to the integrated organization that cultivated this approach as the basic way for solving technical problems.

Chapter 2

Radar

Radar systems, used for locating objects at a distance, played a most important part in many phases of World War II. In a sense it was a two-edged weapon. It served not only to enhance the effectiveness of major offensive weapons in the air, on the sea, and below its surface, but also to increase the capabilities of defensive weapons in the three media. To a considerable degree, World War II was a battle waged between scientists designing radar systems for these contending roles.

Development of this new instrumentality of warfare ranks among the very highest in its contributions to the Allied victory in World War II, and Bell Laboratories played a much larger role in the development of radar than any other industrial laboratory.

Prior to 1937, knowledge of radar was closely restricted to military organizations, but in that year the United States Navy asked the Bell System to provide assistance on radar development and production. Until that time, neither Bell Laboratories nor any other industrial laboratory had any direct knowledge or experience with radar. However, it was known to the military that Bell Labs had considerable experience with microwave transmission, antenna design, waveguides and other technology which the Naval Research Laboratory experts believed would be of value. This belief was well justified, since during the war years more than half of all radars used by the United States armed forces were designed by Bell Labs and produced by Western Electric, including nearly all of the fire control radar aboard naval seaborne and undersea vessels. Bell Laboratories not only contributed to all aspects of radar but also made major contributions to the fast-developing technology on which the radar developments were based.

I. BACKGROUND

Radar is an acronym for "radio detection and ranging."[1] As the origin of the word implies, radar is a radio system for locating objects in terms

---

[1] The acronym has been variously attributed to Commander Samuel M. Tucker, U.S.N., and to R. M. Page, of the Naval Research Laboratory. In any event, the credit goes to the U.S. Navy. *Radar* was made official for nonclassified use in a directive by the Office of Naval Operations dated November 18, 1940.

Principal authors: W. C. Tinus, W. H. C. Higgins, J. W. Emling, W. H. Doherty, and L. R. Walker

of both distance and direction from the radar equipment. It is unique in a number of ways. Although usually employed for detecting solid objects, it can be used for locating clouds, rain, or any perturbation associated with a change in the dielectric constant of the transmission medium. Unlike visual and aural detecting methods, it is effective far beyond the range of sight and sound, being operable day or night and through the densest smoke or fog. With these potentialities, it is obvious that radar was of enormous interest and value to all branches of the military, not only defensively (e.g., for preventing surprise attacks) but also offensively (e.g., for tracking enemy targets and even directing gunfire, bombs, and torpedoes toward their targets).

As with many devices, the invention of radar cannot be attributed to any one individual. It had its beginnings with the very first researches on radio, and over the years the concepts behind it grew as the radio art advanced. But in 1937, when the Navy first approached AT&T about a cooperative effort in the field, nothing about the concept of radar as a military instrumentality was known outside the government laboratories of a few major powers. A review of some of the background will give the reader a notion of the embryonic state of the art and of the many problems requiring solutions before radar could become an effective and manufacturable instrumentality.

Experimental radio began with the German physicist Heinrich Hertz in the years 1884–1888 (see the first volume of this history, pp. 349–368). He demonstrated that high-frequency electrical oscillations could produce electrical phenomena at a distance and also recognized that the effect was due to electromagnetic waves conforming to the laws of geometric optics. Hertz thus substantiated the predictions of the Scottish physicist James Clerk Maxwell, whose electromagnetic-wave equation had been published some 20 years earlier, in 1867.

Nikola Tesla is said to have predicted radar in 1899 and Christian Hiilsmeyer, a German engineer, was granted a British patent in 1904 on an apparatus using radio waves as a navigational aid to ships. Marconi also foresaw some of the potential of radio waves beyond communication and as early as 1922 strongly urged the use of short radio waves for detecting objects.[2]

But the principles on which radar is based can be clearly traced to the work of Hertz. He showed that an object "illuminated" by electromagnetic waves reflects a portion of the incident energy. Furthermore, he proved that radio waves travel at the constant speed of light. The invention of radar involved a specific application of these two facts. If one

---

[2] For the history of radar preceding Bell Labs' involvement, we are indebted in large part to L. S. Howeth, *History of Communications—Electronics in the United States Navy* (Washington, D.C.: Government Printing Office, 1963).

sends a very short pulse of radio energy toward a target, the returned echo can be used to determine its direction relative to the source. The time elapsing between transmission and arrival of the reflected pulse at the point of transmission is a measure of the distance traveled (i.e., twice the "range," or distance, between transmitter and target). The conversion of time intervals to physical distance was, of course, a simple matter since the speed of light was accurately known.[3]

The first use of the ranging principle appears to have been made by G. Breit and M. A. Tuve, of the Carnegie Institution, in collaboration with the Naval Research Laboratory, for measuring the height of the ionosphere. Their work, carried out in 1925, confirmed the Kennelly-Heaviside theory about the ionosphere (1902) and added another link in the chain of events leading to radar.

It was a logical and obvious step from the work of Breit and Tuve to the concept of radar for object location, but it is difficult to assign credit to an individual for taking that step because the potential value of radio location for military purposes was quickly recognized by many organizations. Quite independently, and almost simultaneously, exploratory work was undertaken by government laboratories in the United States, England, France, Germany and, to a lesser degree, in Japan—all, of course, in great secrecy. However, it was roughly ten years after the Breit-Tuve work before the technological developments required for making this seemingly obvious step were achieved. And much more sophisticated technology was required before the concept of radar was implemented as a practical adjunct to warfare.

It appears that the world's first radar equipment was designed and constructed by the Naval Research Laboratory in 1934, but with mediocre results. One year later, however, the Navy's pulse radar was demonstrated to high government officials and the Chief of the Bureau of Engineering directed that the project be given the highest possible priority. In that same year, the Naval Research Laboratory designed and developed a duplexer to permit the use of the same antenna for both transmission and reception. Credit for this early work on radar must go principally to Dr. R. M. Page and his associates at the Naval Research Laboratory.

The U.S. Signal Corps Laboratory was also active in the field, as were military organizations abroad, but until 1937 when the Navy first approached AT&T, nothing was known outside of government laboratories about this evolving technology.

At the beginning of the war, radar technology was at about the same level of development in Germany, England, and the United States, whereas that in Japan was much less advanced. As the war continued,

---

[3] In some cases the range computation was not quite as simple as indicated, because atmospheric conditions sometimes cause radio waves to bend in transit, but for small ranges the error is not large.

United States technology was improved at a much greater pace than that of the Axis powers.[4]

The United States supplied its armed forces with a tremendous volume of specialized equipment of ever-increasing effectiveness, and military personnel, in turn, rapidly mastered the new tools and modified strategy and tactics to use them to maximum advantage. One possible reason why the United States and its Allies advanced radar technology faster than the Axis powers is that radar in its earliest useful form was regarded as a defensive device—good only to give early warning of approaching aircraft with a rough indication of direction and range. Both Germany and Japan apparently had little interest in defensive developments, since they planned to fight a blitzkreig war. A little later, when radar had become a powerful aid to offensive military operations, they found themselves hopelessly behind.

But this is only a partial explanation of the Allies' ultimate superiority in radar. The United States concentrated its full effort in research, development, design, and production on means for waging war. Not only was the expenditure on radar multiplied 40-fold between 1940 and 1945, but the technical development and application were accomplished with great flexibility, which expanded its use and constantly took advantage of new developments through retrofitting.

Radar performed many functions. A first and continuing one was to give early warning of airborne and seaborne attackers. Its capabilities were increased so that it could track individual attackers to which defenders could be guided. The tracking capability was ultimately harnessed to gun directors, which automatically controlled artillery fire against targets in the air and on the sea at distances far beyond the capability of optical instruments. It was also coupled to aircraft bombsight equipment to give an accuracy at night that was comparable to daytime performance.

While radars came to have a wide variety of forms, all have common basic elements. These are:

1. A transmitter to generate high-power pulses of radio-frequency energy at hundreds or thousands of megahertz;

---

[4] The history of the development of radar components and systems in the different countries is a fascinating subject which cannot be covered here. Since this is a history of Bell System technology, we shall naturally emphasize Bell System radar development and manufacture. However, it is only proper to note that United States and British work in the field was well coordinated and new ideas, wherever created, were quickly shared with Allied specialists. Each developer and manufacturer was free to apply and improve on innovations made by another. As a consequence, it is often difficult to assign credit for initial concepts and practical applications of the literally hundreds of contributions in this field. Deserving of special mention, however, is the Radiation Laboratory at Massachusetts Institute of Technology, established in 1940 under an NDRC contract with M.I.T. This organization carried out a most important program of research and development work. The 28-volume Radiation Laboratory Series (McGraw-Hill, 1947–53) is a compendium of this organization's contributions.

Table 2-1.   Radar Frequency Bands

Band designation	Approximate Midband	
	Frequency (MHz)	Wavelength (cm)
P	300	100
L	1,000	30
S	3,000	10
X	10,000	3
K	20,000	1.5
Q	40,000	0.75

$$\lambda(\text{wavelength}) \text{ in cm} = \frac{30,000}{f(\text{frequency}) \text{ in MHz}}$$

2. An antenna system to accept the transmitter output, to direct it to "illuminate" the portion of space which is of interest, and to receive the resulting echoes, or backscattered energy, from objects in the illuminated space;

3. A receiver to detect and greatly amplify the returning signals; and

4. A video and display system to process the signals into the form desired and to present them to the operator, usually on an oscilloscope.

Thus, a radar gathers intelligence from its surroundings as distinguished from, say, radio broadcasting, which sends intelligence to its surroundings. It is not a single instrument but a system consisting of many pieces of equipment designed to work together so as to meet the requirements of the system's intended function.

The portion of the spectrum used for radar can be described in several ways, the length of the wave or its frequency being the main designations; but workers in the field often used letters to indicate the general range. Although wavelengths are of considerable significance in indicating radar performance, frequency designations will be used where practical, since this usage will be more consistent with other parts of this history.   Table 2-1 shows the relations between the various classifications.

The early work on radar employed transmitters and receivers operating in the vicinity of 200 megahertz (MHz) and using rather large antennas (about 20 feet square).   Radars useful for early warning resulted from that work.   However, it was clear to the Navy that much higher frequencies would be required to extend the potential of this new technology from early warning applications to the accuracies needed for control of gunfire, an important naval radar objective.[5]   Without higher frequencies it would

---

[5] Higher frequencies were called for because highly directional antennas, needed for accurate location of targets and for good resolution *between* targets, must have dimensions of the order of 50 to 100 times the length of the wave.   Moreover, while longer waves were effective for detection of airborne targets at fairly long ranges, they were at a disadvantage against the low-flying targets even at relatively short ranges.

not be possible to obtain antenna beamwidths narrow enough for this purpose using antenna structures of manageable size aboard ship. Yet components required for the higher frequencies were not available at that time.

With this need in mind, the Navy approached high officials of AT&T in 1937, as already noted, and asked if it might obtain the help of Bell Laboratories on a highly secret project of great importance to the nation. There followed a complete disclosure of all technical details of the radars made by the Naval Research Laboratory to Bell engineering people and Western Electric officials. Earlier that year the Navy also disclosed its radar work to the Army Signal Corps Laboratory, where work of a similar nature was being carried out.

It was not at all surprising that the Navy should seek help from Bell Labs. Its pioneering work dealing with directive antennas and waveguides was well known to the Navy, as was the continuing work on pushing the usable frequency spectrum ever higher in order to expand communications. At the time, a research project at the Holmdel Laboratory included work in the range of a few thousands of megahertz. The Navy also knew of Bell Labs' skills in the many other disciplines that would be essential for full realization of this new method of "seeing in the dark." And, of course, the Navy was well aware of the enormous capacity of Western Electric to manufacture such equipment on a large scale should the need arise—as it soon did.

The Navy request was given most careful consideration, although it was not apparent that anything approaching the Navy's objectives could be delivered within a reasonable interval. It was decided not to accept a Navy contract at the outset. However, because of the obvious importance of the matter to the national defense, AT&T authorized Bell Labs to explore possibilities for a year, promising to report back to the Navy on the results of this investigation.

Thus, in early 1938, a small group of highly skilled engineers was assigned to the Whippany Radio Laboratory location in New Jersey, about 30 miles west of New York City. Established in 1926 for the development of transatlantic and broadcast radio work, the location afforded ideal conditions for such an undertaking. The isolated rural setting met the requirements for absolute secrecy as well as the open terrain required for carrying out such work.

The Whippany group, under the leadership of W. C. Tinus, had to start from scratch, even designing and building their own instruments since none were commercially available for the frequency range to be explored. Transmitters, receivers, antennas, and cathode-ray indicators had to be devised. And finally a model had to be constructed with which to demonstrate what might be done.

This crude early model, operating at 700 MHz, was demonstrated to representatives of both the Army and Navy in July 1939. The site was a rented cottage on an 80-foot bluff overlooking New York Harbor at Atlantic Highlands, New Jersey. From this vantage point a continuous parade of shipping provided an unending stream of "targets."

This demonstration gave convincing proof that radar was practical at frequencies three or four times those used by the early equipment of the Naval Research Laboratory and resulted in a Navy contract with Western Electric for a production version to be developed by Bell Labs and manufactured by Western Electric. The first of these—known as CXAS in the experimental models and as FA or Mark 1 in production—was installed on the cruiser U.S.S. *Wichita* at the Brooklyn Navy Yard in June 1941. Several more installations were under way on ships of the fleet at Pearl Harbor when the Japanese made their attack on December 7, 1941.[6]

An event of the utmost significance for United States radar developments occurred at Whippany on October 6, 1940[7]: the demonstration of the newly developed British multicavity magnetron. Prior to that time, the high power that would be needed ultimately for radar transmitters was simply not attainable at high frequencies even with the best available research-type vacuum tubes. Thus, the early transmitters used in the Navy demonstration and in first production employed two "doorknob" tubes stressed to the utmost. These tubes, designed for continuous wave (CW) operation, were capable of about 20 watts continuous output at 700 MHz. In a circuit carefully designed to avoid external flash-over, it proved possible to get about 2 kilowatts (kW) of pulse power from this dual-tube transmitter—albeit with a pulsed plate voltage of about ten times the rated value and with a sacrifice of cathode life by overheating to supply large emission during the pulse. This dual-tube transmitter, together with a carefully designed receiver, antenna, and indicator, gave very useful performance.

But radar was revolutionized with the multicavity magnetron.[8] In the very first experiment at Whippany, using a magnetron brought into this country in the greatest secrecy by Dr. E. G. Bowen, pulse power in the vicinity of 10 kW was obtained at a frequency of 3,000 MHz. The excitement created by this event was electrifying. Whoever dreamed of seeing arcs drawn from a transmitter output at a wavelength as short as 10 centimeters! The impact on the future of Allied radars was evident.

This interchange of technology with the British had been made possible

---

[6] A Signal Corps early warning radar on the island had detected the approaching aircraft; however, the report from this "newfangled gadget" was simply too fantastic to be believed. The consequences made history.

[7] *Radar Systems and Components* by members of the Technical Staff, Bell Telephone Laboratories (New York: D. Van Nostrand, 1949), pp. 5, 56.

[8] Conceived by a group of British physicists headed by Prof. N. S. Oliphant of the University of Birmingham. For a more detailed account, see Section IV.

by the formation of the National Defense Research Committee (NDRC), as described previously. This organization quickly arranged for the exchange of technical information among the Allies; and the magnetron was one of the disclosures made by the first British technical team visiting this country.

Immediately after the test of October 6, Bell Labs' vacuum-tube experts, under the guidance of James B. Fisk, scaled the British magnetron to operate at 700 MHz to match the needs of the production radars already designed in all other respects for that frequency. Work was also started on other designs for systems yet to be conceived. Many important contributions to magnetron theory and design are discussed at greater length in Section IV of this chapter.

The activities of NDRC also brought into being the Radiation Laboratory at M.I.T., as pointed out above (Section I), under the direction of Lee A. DuBridge. Its purpose was the mobilization of scientists from the nation's universities in behalf of the defense effort on radar. Here again, the most complete interchange of information was established with industrial organizations engaged in the war effort. Close collaboration was maintained between Bell Labs and the Radiation Laboratory throughout the war. Much of the success of the Allies in World War II can be attributed to such fine cooperation, both within the United States and among the Allies.

II. TECHNOLOGY

Radar refers to no single instrument. Instead it is an assemblage of equipment designed to work together as a system to meet the desired overall objective. To a considerable extent the various types of radar in World War II used a common technology, but each system was designed specifically to meet the requirements of the application at hand. Thus, radars assumed a great variety of sizes and shapes. Some involved massive equipment for permanent installation on land or on a battleship; others were lightweight assemblages that could be backpacked up a mountain by the Marines. Still others were compact units fitted into the small spaces available on aircraft and submarines. Fig. 2-1 illustrates some varieties of radar equipment.

Basic to the radar project was the development of a whole new technology born just before World War II and rapidly advancing in a very few years as it was applied to more and more complex problems. The growth of this technology quite appropriately constitutes a major part of this chapter. During the war Bell Labs undertook about 100 major radar developments. Some 60 of these were carried through preparation of manufacturing information, produced in large quantities by Western Electric, and given wide use in combat. But even more important than the magnitude of this radar production was the scientific and engineering

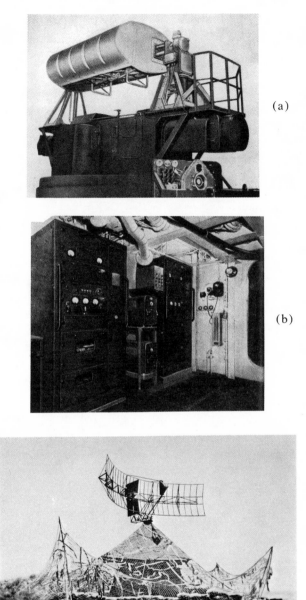

Fig. 2-1.   Radar Systems in use early in World War II.   (a) Fire control radar antenna.   (b) Range-measuring radars (Mark 3 and Mark 4 below-decks equipment) on USS *New Jersey*.   (c) Aircraft early warning radar (AN/TPS-1) on Okinawa.

contribution to the technology necessary for system implementation, as well as the rapidity with which the work was accomplished. This came about to a large extent because of the solid background of research on high-frequency circuitry, waveguides, and other pertinent technology carried out in the prewar years.

For convenience, the material in this section on technological innovation and application is organized into sections dealing with specific radar system components. The reader should be aware, however, that the success of the radar work was highly dependent on the close coordination of the effort on the various components so that the result was integrated systems rather than an assemblage of parts.

2.1 Radar Transmitter

A little work was done before the war on CW (continuous wave) types of radio object locators. This technique found application during and after the war in altimeters for aircraft. It was particularly suitable for this use wherein there was only one target—the earth below. For the more complex case of many targets, the pulse-echo method was far more suitable. All of the following discussion pertains to this method.

The earliest radar transmitters developed in the military laboratories just before the war, operating in the region of 100 to 200 MHz, used two or more triodes or tetrodes in a self-excited oscillator circuit. Bell Laboratories undertook further development of this system, designated SCR-268, for manufacture by Western Electric at Kearny, New Jersey. In an effort to get the maximum power output, one design employed a number of tubes in a ring circuit, the connecting bars between the tubes comprising the resonant circuit, as shown in Fig. 2-2. Such a circuit was several wavelengths in circumference and hence had many possible modes of oscillation. Nevertheless, by careful empirical design the tubes were made to "pull together," and a power output several times that of a simpler circuit with two tubes was obtained.

Bell Labs' first radar transmitter, shown in Fig. 2-3, designed as part of the CXAS radar system, also employed triodes, but at the much higher frequency of 700 MHz. No more than two could be made to behave properly. As mentioned earlier, the original tubes had been designed for a CW output of about 20 watts, but by overloading the filaments to get more electron emission and by modulating as described in the next section, a pulse power output of about 2 kW was obtained on a highly intermittent duty basis. A tunable Lecher-rod mechanical system permitted the transmitter to be adjusted in frequency over a range from 500 to 700 MHz.

Triodes of special design for intermittent duty were hurriedly developed and played a part during the war in relatively low-frequency radar transmitters, i.e., those operating at 200 MHz. As related in the preceding

Fig. 2-2.   SCR-268 radar transmitter developed by U.S. military research laboratories.

section and discussed more fully in Section IV, the opportunity for higher
frequencies came with the invention of the multicavity magnetron in
England in 1940.   The device, duplicated and improved at Bell Labs in a
matter of days, laid the first sound basis for practical airborne radars, which
required at least 3,000 MHz to obtain a usefully narrow beam with an
antenna small enough to mount on an airplane.   An enormous development followed at Bell Labs and later at the Radiation Laboratory, as power

Fig. 2-3.   CXAS radar transmitter developed by Bell Laboratories.

and frequency were pushed ever upward and refinements like tunability were added.   The magnetron was universally used in all radars during the war at 1,000 MHz and higher; some typical designs of it are illustrated in Fig. 2-4.

2.2 Radar Modulator, or Pulser

Some of the early transmitters developed in the military laboratories were "keyed," or made to produce short pulses of output in the simplest possible manner.   The circuit was proportioned to act as a blocking oscillator; when oscillation started, the grid capacitor rapidly charged to a high negative voltage and stopped the plate current in an interval of a few microseconds.   When the charge on the grid capacitor leaked off, in perhaps 1,000 microseconds, the cycle would repeat.   A small trigger pulse was introduced to get uniform firing.

In Bell Labs' first work at 700 MHz, it was immediately found that the little triodes could be pushed to much higher power output if they were relieved of all strain between the pulses.   This was accomplished by using a direct-coupled pulse amplifier effectively in series with the transmitter oscillator and the power supply.   Again no tubes suitable for this kind of duty were available, and the necessary current capability to provide the high-power pulse was therefore obtained by paralleling a number of available tubes.   The electron tube development department hurriedly

Fig. 2-4.   Several types of multicavity magnetron high-frequency, high-power generators.

improved the design for this intermittent high-current duty and modulators of this type were used in some radar systems throughout the war. A simplified diagram of such a modulator driving the original two-tube 700-MHz oscillator is shown in Fig. 2-5.   The capacitor at the output of the power supply was made large enough so that the voltage supplied during the pulse dropped only slightly.   Also, so that the rectangular shape of the pulse desired to minimize frequency change could be further preserved, the capacitance load on the modulator tubes was held to a minimum.   The RF chassis was air insulated from ground with a minimum solid-insulator support, and the filament power to the oscillator was supplied similarly by an air-insulated transformer.   The RF output was from a coupling loop that isolated it from high dc voltages.

The air-insulated filament transformer was later universally used with the cavity magnetrons, which were designed to have their anode at ground

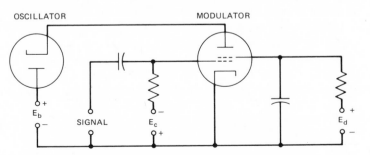

Fig. 2-5.   Simplified schematic of CXAS modulator.

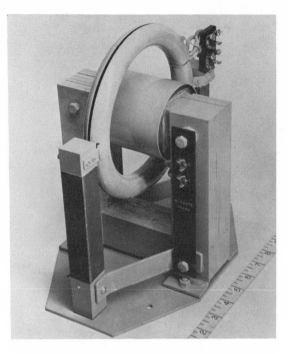

Fig. 2-6.   Air-insulated filament transformer.

potential.   A picture of an early model is shown in Fig. 2-6.   It was typical
of the many new devices and problems that arose and had to be quickly
solved as radio and communication engineers hurriedly transferred their
skills from the familiar world of low frequencies, low voltages, and steady
state to the new world of much higher frequencies, high voltages, and
transient waveforms.

Since the rapid development of airborne radar immediately followed
the introduction of the magnetron, much effort was applied to devise a
very light modulator, or pulser, for aircraft.   The most widely used was
called the line-type pulser.   In this scheme, the energy required for a
single pulse was stored in an artificial line—a network of coils and capacitors—and then dumped into the magnetron by a switch.   The requirements on the switch were severe.   It had to withstand very high
voltage between pulses as the network was being charged, and then had
to be able to pass very heavy current during the brief interval of the pulse.
For efficiency, it also required a low voltage across it during the current-
carrying interval.   The spark gap switch of the earliest days of radio
telegraphy was resurrected and served admirably in this role, both as a

9 The interesting story of the development of spark gap switches for radar is given in detail
in *Radar Systems and Components*, pp. 270–309.

(a)

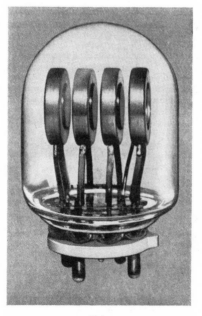

(b)

Fig. 2-7.   Two types of spark gap switches.   (a) Rotary
spark-gap modulator.   (b) Three-gap spark pulser tube.

rotary gap operating in air and as a fixed gap sealed in a gas-filled tube (see Fig. 2–7).[9]

Another, entirely different type of radar modulator was developed and was used on many shipboard and all submarine radars. It was called the "coil pulser" and depended for its switching action on the magnetic properties of a nonlinear coil, examples of which are pictured in Fig. 2-8a with the circuit and its characteristic effect shown in b, c, and d. Such coils, operating at low power levels, had been developed during the 1930s for use as harmonic generators in the telephone plant. One of these low-power coils was, in fact, used as the radar pulse generator in the first Navy radars. The remarkable development of similar coils to handle hundreds of kilowatts was a natural evolution at Bell Laboratories, where advanced magnetic materials had long been under development for various telephone applications. These modulators were particularly applicable to radars requiring very short pulses and needed virtually no maintenance.[10]

2.3 Antenna

The earliest radar systems used separate antennas for transmitting and receiving, which reduced to some extent the tremendous overload on the receiver during the transmitted pulse. From the start, however, Bell Labs was committed to a single antenna for transmitting and receiving to facilitate installation on shipboard. The first antenna for the CXAS experimental Navy radar employed a cylindrical parabolic reflector with a linear array of dipoles along the focal line, as shown in Fig. 2-9. The dipoles were connected together by a coaxial transmission-line harness containing impedance-matching sections to present a matched load to the single line going through one or more rotary joints to the radar unit. The transmitter and receiver were connected to this line by a duplexing technique described in the next section.

The antenna was 6 feet square—a dimension that had been targeted by the Navy as being practical for general use aboard ship. The beam width was about 12 degrees, but by means of a lobe-switching technique (described in Section 2.7 below) the angular position of a target tracked in this manner could be determined to about one-quarter degree. From this early start, antennas assumed many sizes and shapes to fit the various applications. Thus, for example, the antenna for the main battery on battleships that fired only on surface targets was only 3 feet high but 12 feet wide, as shown in Fig. 2-10. This gave a broader beam in elevation to prevent losing the target when the ship rolled and a narrower beam in azimuth for greater angle accuracy.

---

[10] The operation of coil pulsers is described in detail in "Coil Pulsers for Radar," in *Radar Systems and Components*, pp. 257–269.

(a)

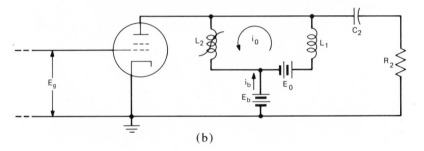

(b)

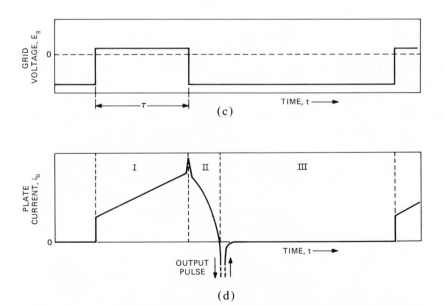

(c)

(d)

Fig. 2-8. Nonlinear coil and power pulsers used in radar transmitters. (a) Three nonlinear coils and their containers. (b) Simplified power pulser diagram; L2 is the nonlinear coil. (c) Rectangular wave of grid voltage impressed upon tetrode of (b). (d) Plate current wave (i) corresponding to time scale of (b).

Fig. 2-9.   Antenna for CXAS radar.

Fig. 2-10.   Mark 3 radar antenna on USS *New Jersey*.

Fig. 2-11.　An SE search-radar antenna.

At the higher frequencies that rapidly came into use, antennas were generally smaller and took on a wide variety of shapes. Search antennas for small ships were mounted in small cylindrical housings, as in Fig. 2-11, transparent to the radar beam. Antennas for submarines presented a very difficult mechanical design problem because they were mounted on a rotatable tube, as shown in Figs. 2-12 and 2-13, and had to withstand tremendous force in case of a crash dive at top speed. Moreover, the "feed" had to be capped with a thick dielectric window that would not only withstand the water pressure at great depths, but would reasonably terminate the waveguide even when submerged. In some cases—for example, the SH antenna for surface vessels shown in Fig. 2-14—it was desirable to mount much of the radar equipment close to the antenna to minimize transmission loss. Some Navy fire control antennas were designed to rapidly scan electronically without movement of the assembly as a whole. One type used in the Mark 8 fire control radar was the polyrod

Fig. 2-12.   SJ, ST, and SV radar antennas on a submarine.

Fig. 2-13.   SJ radar antenna used on a submarine.

Fig. 2-14.   Radar equipment mounted adjacent to SH antenna.

antenna shown in Fig. 2-15.   Each element of this array consisted of a fixed vertical array of three polyrods.   Fourteen of these elements were arranged in a horizontal pattern with a spacing of about two wavelengths between elements.   Energy was distributed to the system through rotary phase changers, which produced a beam that swept repeatedly from left to right across the 30-degree scanning sector.

Fig. 2-15.   Polyrod antenna used with Mark 8 fire control radar.

Fig. 2-16.   SCR-520 airborne radar antenna.

Airborne antennas usually consisted of sheet metal parabolas excited by a feed horn or dipole at the focus.   On large aircraft, they were usually mounted on the belly of the airframe in a transparent radome for protection from the elements.   A typical early design of this kind of antenna is shown in Fig. 2-16.   It was mounted on a two-axis mount and could be rotated through 360 degrees to scan the entire horizon.   Later designs were made more efficient by using a wide aperture horizontally to increase the horizontal resolution and a specially shaped surface in the vertical plane. This arrangement directed most of the energy horizontally toward the distant horizon and a lesser amount downward, where the distance required did not exceed the altitude of the aircraft.   Similar shaping of antenna fan beams was applied to ground-based antiaircraft search radars to illuminate more efficiently only the space in the vertical fan beam up to the maximum altitude aircraft could fly.

The mounting of radar antennas on the unstable platforms of ships and planes presented many complex problems caused by roll and pitch.   For the radar data to be useful in fire control, the effects of such motions had to be removed. In Bell Labs' first Navy radars, this was accomplished by using the existing servo systems, which, in Navy parlance, "levelled and cross-levelled" the older optical telescopes and optical range finders. In these radars, the antenna was provided with a two-axis mount atop the optical gun director housing, with which it turned in azimuth and thus provided the required three axes. Mechanical linkages were provided between the optical devices and the antenna mount to remove roll and pitch motions from the antenna itself. The basic data for controlling these servos came from the ship's stable vertical and gyro compasses.

In aircraft, it was usually not practical to use a three-axis mount for the antenna. However, it was necessary to remove yaw and roll, which tended to smear the radar picture on the oscilloscope. Yaw was corrected by a servo controlled by the heading gyro, and roll was controlled by the attitude gyro. In some cases, information from the radar was corrected by data processing techniques rather than by stabilizing the antenna itself. Thus, radar antenna mounts rapidly became a challenging object of study full of difficult mechanical and electrical problems.

2.4 Duplexing

In radio communication, a common antenna is frequently used for transmitting and receiving alternately, a mechanical switch providing the transfer. In radar, transmitting and receiving is also an alternating process, but the switching must be so rapid that electronic rather than mechanical means must be employed. In the first experimental radar, this was accomplished as follows: A mechanically adjustable length of coaxial line was used to connect the transmitter and the receiver to a common junction leading to the antenna. For a particular operating frequency, the lengths were adjusted so that during transmission the overloaded receiver appeared at the junction as a high impedance and absorbed little power, while during reception the transmitter appeared at the junction as a high impedance and absorbed little of the weak returning echoes. This operation depended on the fact that the transmitter impedance was very different with power on and off, and the receiver input (a "doorknob" vacuum tube) was a very low impedance under heavy overload.

With the introduction of the much-higher-power magnetron transmitters and with extremely delicate silicon crystal mixers as the only practical input stage of the high-frequency receivers, which were rapidly coming into use, much better protection of the receiver was required. The Navy laboratory in the United States and the British organizations had used crude gas-filled tubes to provide the switching function. Since this appeared to be the best approach, a Bell Labs team was assigned to develop improved transmit-receive (TR) tubes and to extend the technique to higher frequencies. There were many problems to be solved. It took a

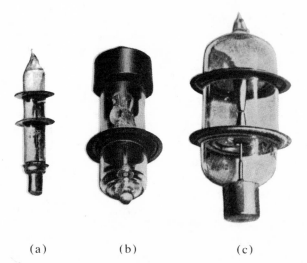

(a)   (b)   (c)

Fig. 2-17. Gas vacuum tubes used in radar transmission and receiving components. (a) 721A tube. (b)
1B23 tube. (c) 724B tube.

gas tube a small but finite time to ionize and become a low impedance.
During this time a "spike" might get through which could damage crystal
mixers. This problem was solved by adding an igniter or "keep-alive"
electrode to provide some ionization before the transmitter came on.
There were also problems in obtaining a rapid recovery to high impedance
after the transmitted pulse, which were solved by proper gas filling.

As radar moved up to 3,000, 10,000, and finally 24,000 MHz, the "TR
box" became a major area of developing radar technology. It was no
longer practical to use adjustable lengths of coaxial line to obtain the impedance transforming function. The gas tube became an integral part of
a high Q resonant cavity. Both the tube and the cavity had to be designed
with negligible or compensating temperature coefficients. Another gas
tube was added—dubbed the anti-transmit-receive (ATR) tube—to further
remove the effect of transmitter impedance. These precision assemblies
were designed to minimize or eliminate tedious adjustment during field
service.

Typical gas tubes for use in TR box assemblies are shown in Fig. 2-17.
These and other Bell Labs designs were made by Western Electric by the
hundreds of thousands, and they were used in nearly all United States
radars.

2.5 Radar Receiver

Since returning radar echoes are exceedingly weak, a very sensitive
receiver is required. Superheterodyne radio receivers of very high gain

Fig. 2-18.   Three generations of IF amplifier designs for military radar applications.

and stability had been used in communications long before the radar age. However, when the first Bell Labs radar receiver was built in 1938, it was immediately apparent that some new tricks had to be learned fast.   The first new problem encountered was that a radar receiver is inevitably severely overloaded during the transmitted pulse and is expected to be back in business with high sensitivity a very few microseconds later.   An ordinary intermediate-frequency (IF) amplifier, such as that used in radio communications receivers, would, after such an overload, be completely dead for many milliseconds.   The reason is, of course, that the capacitors in the isolation filters used to prevent feedback between stages, and therefore obtain stability, would charge up during the overload and would require a relatively long time to discharge.   It was apparent that the time constant of these isolation filters would have to be reduced by orders of magnitude while still maintaining the required stability.   This problem was solved by careful mechanical design with very short connections.

As the radar program rapidly accelerated during the following years, a great deal of effort was devoted to improving the IF amplifiers for use in radar systems.   Three successive generations are shown in Fig. 2-18. The one on the right in the figure is notable in that it weighed only 9 ounces, had 100-dB gain with a 2-MHz bandwidth, and was completely stable with no adjustments. The amplifiers shown in the figure and the vacuum tubes they used were developed at Bell Labs, each generation incorporating improvements as the state of the art advanced. Of particular importance was the low-noise 6AK5 tube used in the smallest amplifier. This tube was manufactured by the millions at Western Electric and several other manufacturers, and became standard in all American and British radars.

At radar frequencies there is no appreciable atmospheric static or man-made interference. Thus the noise generated in the front end of the receiver determines how weak a signal can be detected. In 1938, the best available tube for either a radio-frequency (RF) amplifier or a mixer as the first part of a 700-MHz receiver was a smaller version of the doorknob tube used in the transmitter. The first experimental system used one of these as an RF amplifier and another as the mixer. The noise figure of this combination was about 24 dB[11]—very bad by later standards. However, before the first Navy fire control radars went into production, a two-stage RF amplifier using the just-developed General Electric "Lighthouse" tube was designed, which reduced the noise figure to about 9 dB. The importance of this improvement can be appreciated by considering the basic radar range equations, which are discussed in some detail in Section 2.10 below. Briefly, these equations show that the range can be doubled by improving the receiver by 12 dB; to obtain an equivalent improvement in range by increasing transmitter power would require an increase by a factor of 16.

At frequencies of 1,000 MHz and higher the only device suitable for the mixer as the first element in a radar receiver was the silicon crystal with a "cat-whisker" contact—a throwback to the earliest days of radio, when such detectors were commonplace. These crystal mixers, or converters, had been used at the Holmdel Laboratory all during the 1930s in research on microwave communications, in which much effort had been expended on improving them. The noise figure was not too bad, but the mixers were very easily damaged by the overload from the transmitter. This is understandable, since the leakage power from the transmitter had to be dissipated at the tiny spot where the pointed cat-whisker touched the crystal. The mixers were also easily damaged by shock or vibration, which moved the point from the sensitive spot to which it had been adjusted.

With the advent of the magnetron, which solved the transmitter power problem at 3,000 MHz, a major development effort was started to improve

---

[11] The term *noise figure* is the ratio of the equivalent noise power at the input of the receiver to the theoretical noise power (Johnson noise) attributable to the input resistance of the receiver. It is given by the expression:

$$NF = \frac{output\ power}{gain} \Big/ KT\Delta f$$

where T is temperature in degrees Kelvin, Δf is the bandwidth of receiver, and K is Boltzmann's constant.

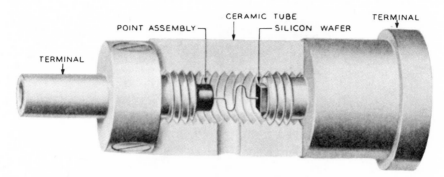

Fig. 2-19.   Silicon crystal rectifier for microwave radar receiver.

the crystal mixers in receivers.   The availability of the necessary talent in metallurgy, chemistry, and other fields made rapid progress possible. Improved silicon with proper surface treatment made it unnecessary to search for a sensitive spot; better structure, with a gel filling, greatly improved resistance to shock and the effects of humidity.   Better understanding of the material led to p- and n-type units—the beginnings of the semiconductor revolution that occurred after the war.   After the NDRC was set up there was intimate cooperation with the British and with the Radiation Lab at M.I.T.   Crystal-mixer units were standardized, as shown in Fig. 2-19, and made in very large quantities by Western Electric and others.   Thus, the critical "front-end" problem for radar receivers during the war was solved by the simultaneous development of the TR tubes, previously discussed, and more rugged crystal mixers.

Another essential part of a radar receiver is the beating oscillator.   It must provide a small amount of power which is offset from the transmitter frequency by the IF frequency.   Very fortunately for radar, the velocity-modulated, or klystron, type of tube had been invented shortly before the war.   This was fully capable of oscillating at frequencies up to 3,000 MHz and had been used at Holmdel as a low-power transmitter and in test equipment for microwave transmission research for several years.   A diligent, sometimes almost desperate, attempt had been made at Bell Labs during the first years of radar to push such tubes up to high power for use in microwave transmitters—a completely abortive effort since the highest pulse power obtained at 3,000 MHz was about 50 watts at the time the British magnetron arrived on the scene and produced 10 kW.   But, for the beating oscillator supply in radar receivers, they proved to be a very good answer.   A large effort was started in Bell Labs to improve the early types and to extend them to 10,000 MHz.   Eventually, near the end of the war, they reached 24,000 MHz.   An enormous development effort was involved as they were pushed upward in frequency and the refinements of electronic tuning were added.[12]   Suffice it to say here that by the end of

---

[12] *Radar Systems and Components*, pp. 578–581, 648–649.

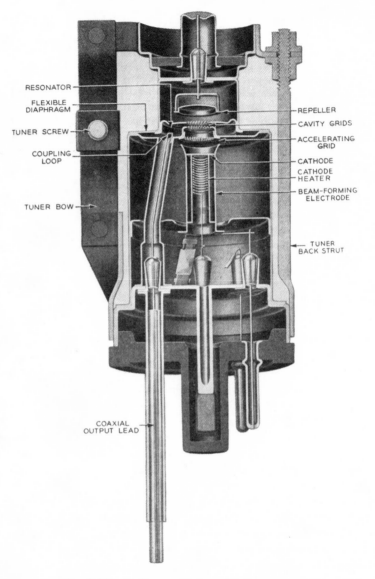

RESONATOR

FLEXIBLE
DIAPHRAGM

TUNER SCREW

COUPLING
LOOP

TUNER BOW

REPELLER

CAVITY GRIDS

ACCELERATING
GRID

CATHODE

CATHODE
HEATER

BEAM-FORMING
ELECTRODE

TUNER
BACK STRUT

COAXIAL
OUTPUT LEAD

Fig. 2-20.   Reflex oscillator with 3-cm range.

the war 11 general types (each usually including several varieties for
specific frequencies) were standardized by the United States and British
armed forces and produced in very large quantities by Western Electric
and others.   Nine of the 11 were designed by Bell Labs for production (one
is shown in Fig. 2-20) involving very tiny parts where millionths of an inch
were important.   Some were designed cooperatively with the Radiation
Lab at M.I.T. after it was set up to contribute to this important field.

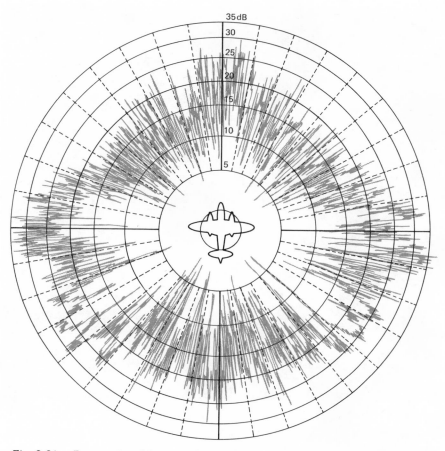

Fig. 2-21. Return signal from a B-26 aircraft at 10-cm wavelength as a function of azimuth angle. (From Ridenour 1947, p. 76.)

Thus, the most critical problems in pushing radar up to the microwave part of the spectrum were solved by the timely invention of the multicavity magnetron for the transmitter, the improved crystal detector, and the reflex klystron for the beating oscillator in the receiver.

One other point regarding early radar receivers should be mentioned here. Radar returning signals, like all other radio signals, fade up and down with time—often over a very large range. A radar target behaves much like a piece of tinsel illuminated by a flashlight. An aircraft, for example, scatters energy received in all directions, with the "graininess" of the scattered energy dependent on the wavelength of the incident energy. Fig. 2-21 shows the scattering pattern of a B-26. Since an aircraft continually changes slightly in aspect in relation to the radar beam, the received echo rapidly changes in strength over a very wide range.

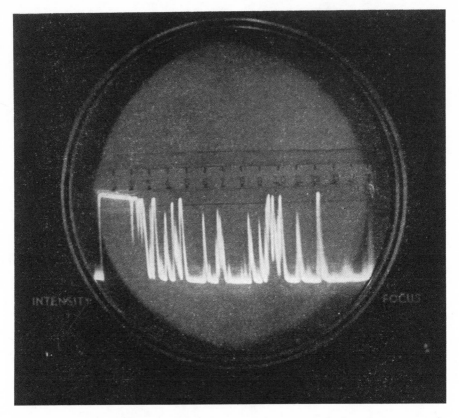

Fig. 2-22. Display of a cathode-ray oscilloscope supplied with a saw-tooth wave—known as an A-scope presentation. Range increases from left to right. (From Ridenour 1947, p. 165.)

The use of automatic gain control (AGC) in radio receivers to hold a received signal constant as it faded had been standard practice for years before the radar age. But radar was different. The many echoes received did not fade synchronously. What was required was means for holding constant the amplitude of the particular target being tracked by a fire control radar. This involved gating the particular echo being tracked and causing it alone to adjust the receiver gain. This type of AGC, operating on a signal that is present only during a tiny fraction of the total time, was first accomplished in the initial fire control radars for the U.S. Navy, which went into production in 1940. This problem is discussed further in Section 2.8 below.

2.6 Video and Indicator Systems

The output of the second detector of a radar receiver is a sequence of video pulses resulting from the outgoing transmitter pulse, followed by

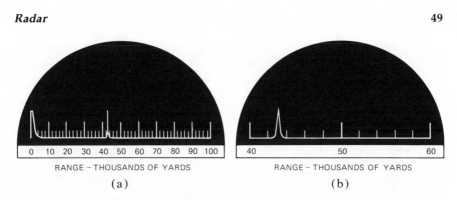

Fig. 2-23. Range marks displayed on CXAS radar A-scope. (a) Normal. (b) Expanded.

a train of pulses due to echoes from objects in the beam of the antenna. In the early radars, these signals were amplified and applied to the vertical deflection plates of a cathode-ray oscilloscope being supplied with a sawtooth wave that started synchronously with the outgoing transmitter pulse. Such a display became known as an "A-scope" and appears as shown in Fig. 2-22. A calibrated mask placed along the horizontal was used to estimate range. This arrangement had served fairly well in radars intended for early warning, in which accurate measurement of range was not required.

Since Bell Labs' first radar work was directed toward helping the Navy realize its ambition of making radar a fire control instrument, better range accuracy was essential. The first radar design of this type, manufactured and demonstrated to the Navy in 1940, incorporated electronic range marks displayed together with the radar signals as sharp vertical deflections on the A-scope, thus eliminating errors due to parallax, nonlinearity in the sweep, etc. The sweep circuits also provided for expanding any desired portion of the range scale for closer examination. This equipment probably was the first to use electronic range marks, shown in the scope display of Fig. 2-23.

The Navy Mark 3 and Mark 4 fire control radars which went into operational use in the fleet in 1941 for main batteries (against surface targets) and secondary batteries (against both aircraft and surface targets), respectively, used a more complex electronic range mark system, which is discussed in Section 2.7 below.

Many other types of radar indicators were devised to meet the needs of particular applications during 1941 and 1942. One indicator widely used in both ground- and air-based radars for search, early warning, and air navigation was the plan position indicator (PPI). In this, the range sweep on the oscilloscope is radial from the center of the tube, and the sweep is rotated synchronously with the turning of the antenna. The video signals are applied to the grid of the cathode-ray tube to modulate

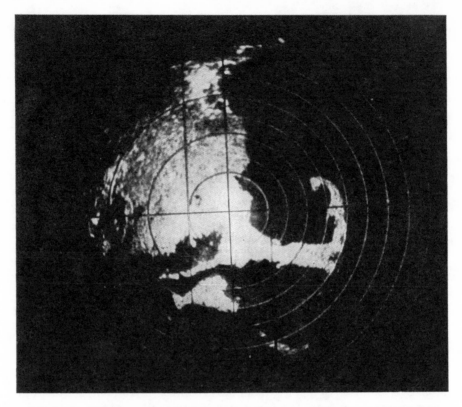

Fig. 2-24.   PPI scope display of Cape Cod area scanned by 3-cm airborne radar.
(From Ridenour 1947, p. 277.)

the brightness of the spot on the screen.   Thus, the tube presents a picture
of the surroundings as if they were illuminated by a powerful light at the
radar location and viewed from a point far above.   The clarity of such a
presentation is shown in Fig. 2-24, which makes it apparent that radar was
indeed a major blessing for air navigation.   In this picture, the radar data
have been arranged to portray a true maplike picture.   This involved
delaying the start of the sweep until the first echoes arrived from directly
below the aircraft (otherwise there would be an open circle—the altitude
circle—in the center) and making the sweep nonlinear in order to present
true ground range.

The origin of the PPI idea is in doubt, since it apparently came to the
fore almost simultaneously among early radar workers in several laboratories in the United States and England.   The credit for it is usually given
to R. M. Page of the Naval Research Laboratory.

Other types of indicators were devised.   One, called the "B-scope," was
a rectangular display with the range sweep vertical, the horizontal sweep
oscillating back and forth, or linearly from left to right as in the Navy Mark

8, in synchronism with the antenna beam, and the signals again applied to control the brightness of the display. It was widely used in air-to-surface bombing radars and was applied in Bell Laboratories designs for the SCR-517 and SCR-520 radars in 1941 and 1942.

Another widely used type of radar presentation was the C-scope, in which horizontal deflection was again azimuth, and vertical deflection was elevation; the signals were applied to brighten the spot. This presentation could only be used after a target had been selected from an A-scope or other presentation and was gated out for presentation on the C-scope. Otherwise, the noise from all ranges would pile up on the C-scope and seriously reduce performance. Radars for aircraft intercept were usually arranged so that the target could be selected and tracked in range on a B-type presentation and then closed upon with the C-type presentation. These presentation methods were applied in the design of the SCR-720 and APS-4 radars in 1942.

2.7 Measurement of Angles: the Field-of-View Problem

The angular resolving power of a radar is grossly inferior to that of the eye or an optical instrument. Although a radar beam can provide useful search or early warning information simply by scanning continuously around the horizon, it is necessary to use more sophisticated methods to obtain the angular accuracy of a small fraction of the beam width, which is required for fire control. The initial solution for this problem was called "lobe switching." It involved *electronically* causing the antenna beam to shift rapidly between two positions, each slightly displaced from the antenna mechanical axis, and synchronously causing the scope display to shift back and forth by a small amount. Thus two signals from a single target were seen side by side. They were of equal height only when the target was precisely on the antenna axis. This scheme capitalizes on the fact that the rate of change of signal with angle is zero on the nose of the lobe, but quite rapid on the sides. It also gives "direction of error," i.e., the operator knows which way to move his control to keep the two equal, and thus can furnish smooth, slowly changing target angle to the computer—an essential requirement for fire control. The process is illustrated in Fig. 2-25. The signals, shown side by side on a scope, would be of equal magnitude (as shown at the left in Fig. 2-25) only if the target was midway between the extreme positions of the lobes, as shown by target A in the figure. If the target, as shown by B, is at one side of the mid position, one lobe will give a much stronger signal, as shown by the right-hand display. This scheme was first applied by the Signal Corps Laboratory in the SCR-268, a 200-MHz radar developed in 1938 and put into production by Bell Labs and Western Electric in 1941. A picture of this equipment is shown in Fig. 2-26. It employed three antennas on a common mount—one for the transmitter, one for the elevation receiver, and one for the

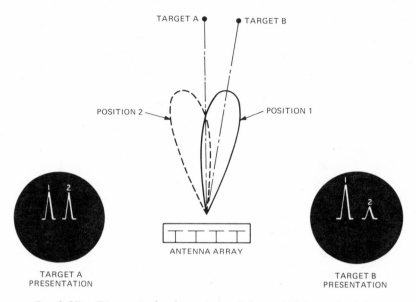

Fig. 2-25.   Diagram of radar antenna lobe-switching principle.

azimuth receiver.   At angles well above the horizon an accuracy of about
1 degree was obtained.   The SCR-268 radar was widely used throughout
the war for surveillance and for pointing searchlights but was hardly accurate enough for fire control.

Fig. 2-26.   The 200 MHz SCR-268 radar.

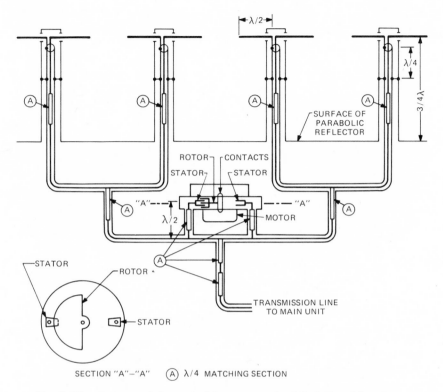

Fig. 2-27.   Antenna lobe-switching system for Mark 2 and 3 radars.

The challenge posed to technical people by the U.S. Navy in 1940 was to improve the accuracy of angle (and range, as discussed later) by a substantial factor, and to arrange the radar to fit the Navy's existing optical system and its associated data transmitting system so that the same operators could use both by simply moving their eyes from telescope to oscilloscope without hiatus in the smooth flow of data to the guns.   This had to be accomplished on a single antenna mechanically boresighted with the existing gyro-stabilized optics, and the development had to be carried out on a very short schedule.[13]   Figure 2-27 shows how lobe switching in azimuth was accomplished by a mechanical phase shifter in the antenna feed system for the Radar Mark 3, used against surface targets, and Fig. 2-28 shows how the same principle was extended to both azimuth and elevation in the Radar Mark 4, used against both surface and aircraft targets.   The Mark 4 was probably the first radar anywhere to obtain accurate information in all three coordinates with a single antenna.   Tests were carried out in 1943 on a destroyer firing against drones and towed sleeves

[13] How this was accomplished is discussed in detail in *Radar Systems and Components*, pp. 26–55.

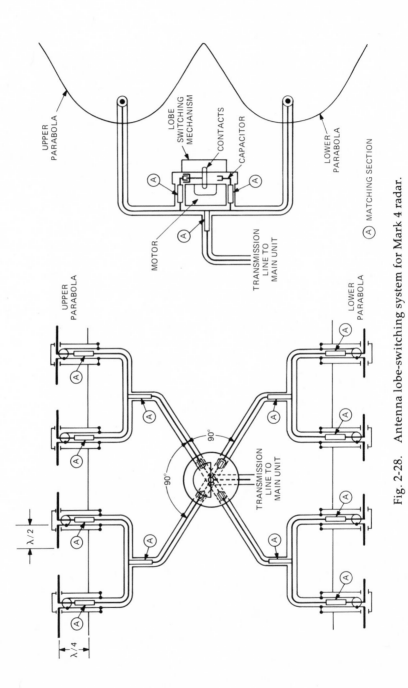

Fig. 2-28.   Antenna lobe-switching system for Mark 4 radar.

at Cape May, New Jersey. This was the first time complete radar information was used in firing against aircraft.

As radar frequencies moved up to 3,000 and 10,000 MHz, lobe switching was accomplished in different ways. In some antiaircraft systems using a parabolic dish reflector type of antenna, the dipole at the focal point was rotated to cause the beam to sweep in a conical fashion about the axis of the dish. This system caused the polarization of the signal to rotate also. In other systems the point feed was made to nutate in a circle, which maintained constant direction of polarization as the beam rotated. One Bell Labs aircraft radar accomplished the same result by leaving the feed fixed and rotating the dish, which was mounted slightly off axis. This was thought to be advantageous because some targets had different effective areas for different polarizations, and rotating polarization could introduce synchronous fading, which would then put a bias into the measurement.

One might suppose that to measure angles accurately the narrowest possible beam should be used. While this is generally true, problems arise. As with a high-power telescope, a narrow-beam radar has a small field of view. Before one can track a target one must acquire it, and a broad field of view is essential if this is to be done quickly. Many different ways to reconcile these conflicting requirements were implemented during the war and debate continued endlessly concerning their relative merits. Some arrangements involved separate surveillance radars which transmitted acquisition data in the form of rough azimuth and range to the fire control radars. This was not acceptable to many experienced military people, because the fire control radar was helpless if acquisition information was unavailable for some reason, e.g., because of battle damage. In other systems, the narrow-beam radar was switched to a different mode for scanning a substantial field of view before being used to track. Variations of this scheme were used in most aircraft radars and in the radars for the smaller automatic weapons on shipboard.

The first Bell Labs radars to be used in combat were the Navy's Mark 3 with a 6-degree beam for surface targets directing the main battery, and the Mark 4 with a 12-degree beam for aircraft targets directing the secondary battery. These systems were so successful in the initial clashes with the Japanese in the Pacific that the fire control officers involved were convinced the compromise between angle accuracy and field of view was about optimum. They therefore wanted no part of the later, more modern designs with narrower beams. The range operator could see all the targets in the general direction of the one being fired upon, and could switch to the next most threatening one in a very few seconds after the first had been hit (which he could observe on the radar). This scheme worked well against the tactics used by the Japanese in attacking a ship. The usual plan was to send in a group of planes almost simultaneously from about the same direction in an effort to overload both the fire control equipment and the guns on the ship in that quadrant.   In spite of such tactics the battleship *South Dakota* shot down an even 38 out of 38 attackers on October 16, 1942.   A score like this made it difficult to sell the people involved a better mousetrap as more modern radars were developed.   Although later designs were being installed on all new ships for several years, there were still over 300 Mark 3's and Mark 4's in the fleet on V-J Day.

The convenience of relatively broad beams for easy acquisition is accompanied by some limitations, which the enemy in World War II was quick to exploit.   The Japanese learned to hide their ships in bays and coves to take advantage of the limitation of our initial, relatively broad beamed radars for control of the ship's main battery.   In this case, the beam produced ground clutter over a wide angle, obscuring the return from the target.   Shortly after the magnetron made 3,000-MHz radar possible, Commander Samuel M. Tucker, of the Bureau of Ships, pointedly posed the problem to W. H. Doherty.   Doherty's recollection in his own words is interesting:

> Tucker's concept on the FH (later called Mark 8) was that we should use the narrow beam—2 degrees—that a 10-foot aperture at 10 cm would supposedly give us, and somehow cover a wider field at the same time (he suggested 30 degrees) so that other targets, as well as possibly shell splashes, could be observed in combat.   As well as I can remember, this was the first time anyone had proposed a track-while-scan operation.

> Feldman [Bell Labs' C. B. Feldman] and I pondered this for some weeks. He said a waveguide version of the MUSA[14] might be worked up for doing the scan as fast as I thought necessary without having to wigwag the antenna.   I was much concerned with the presentation problem, and it seemed to me that we couldn't use slow scans and smudgy long-persistence screens. From primitive television theory (and movie practice) we knew that 20 scans per second would be almost flickerless; so, for a weapon, as contrasted with entertainment, I decided we should go half that fast.   This meant that with a pulse rate of around 1,600 and scanning 30 degrees, we should get about 10 good hits on the target on each sweep, with some weaker trailing-off ones on each end.   The dots would be about $1/5$ degree apart.

> Over a period of a few weeks I made a lot of crude pencil attempts to try to depict what targets would look like, both with good signal-to-noise ratio and when submerged in noise.   Feldman (who knew a lot more about signal to noise than I) was very pessimistic: "No, Bill, you'll never do it." Tucker had said we had to try for $1/10$-degree accuracy.   I reasoned that by brightening one (range) sweep from a pip generator on the antenna phase shifters and using it as the centerline marker, a $1/5$-degree spacing of the dots should give me an accuracy of $1/10$ degree when viewed and averaged by the eye for a second or two.

The Mark 8 was implemented on the basis of Doherty's reasoning. The scan was produced by a tapered phase shift over 14 fixed elements in

---

[14] H. T. Friis and C. B. Feldman, "A Multiple Unit Steerable Antenna for Short-Wave Reception," *Bell System Technical J.* 16 (July 1937), pp. 337–419.

Fig. 2-29. Experimental "rocking horse" antenna—Mark 13 prototype.

a horizontal array. The shift was produced by high-speed rotating elements in round waveguide invented by A. G. Fox (U.S. Patent No. 2,438,119). The individual radiating elements were tapered polystyrene rods. The "polyrod," developed by Feldman and his colleagues, was an extremely rugged radiator that gave the blunt-nosed pattern associated with the end-fire radiators, plus freedom from side lobes as required by the element spacing of the array. The difficult mechanical design was carried out under A. K. Bohren. The assembly, necessarily heavy (as can be seen in Fig. 2-15), found wide use on battleships and cruisers and played a key role in many Pacific battles and in shore bombardment. The Navy credited it with an accuracy of 1 mil—$\frac{1}{17}$ of a degree.

A third-generation fire control radar for main batteries of ships followed the Mark 8. It was the Mark 13 at 10,000 MHz. At this shorter wavelength it was possible to obtain a 0.9-degree beam with an 8-foot snowshoe-shaped reflector, which was then wigwagged over a total angle of 10 degrees at 5 cycles (10 scans) per second by a very ingenious mechanical design conceived by H. T. Friis of the Holmdel Laboratory. The antenna, shown in Fig. 2-29, and dubbed the "rocking horse," was almost perfectly reaction-balanced to avoid vibration on the mount.

As indicated below in the discussion of microwave propagation (Section 2.10), when a radar beam is directed horizontally over a reflecting surface (e.g., the ocean), the beam pattern in elevation breaks up into a many-lobed

Fig. 2-30.   Mark 4 antenna (right) and Mark 22 antenna (left) mounted above gun director on shipboard.

interference pattern.   In other words, at low elevation angles the broad-beam radar sees both the real target and its image in the water.   As the signals fade, the elevation data wander up and down between the true and false targets.   Japanese flyers soon learned to come in very low.   The Navy's first reaction was to fire into the water in front of the target and depend on the splash to down the aircraft, and to use optical elevation angle data if possible.   Something had to be done quickly to improve the elevation accuracy at low angles of the Mark 4.

A solution which could be carried out quickly was proposed by Ralph Bown.   It involved adding a small 10,000-MHz radar as an auxiliary facility for the sole purpose of improving elevation data at low angles.   The RF unit from a current airborne system development was mounted on the Mark 4 antenna and connected to a scanning snowshoe antenna supported outboard on the Mark 4 antenna's elevation axle, as shown in Fig. 2-30. The snowshoe thus turned with the larger antenna in azimuth and elevation but had a separate drive which caused it to scan up and down a few

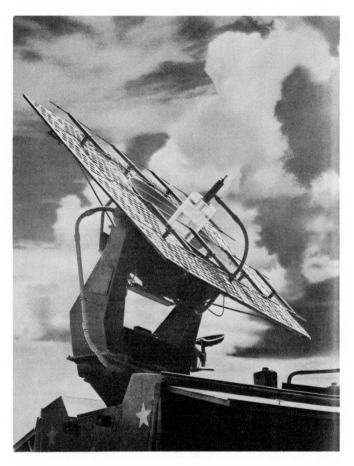

Fig. 2-31.   SCR-545 antiaircraft radar.

degrees, about twice per second, with respect to the larger antenna. An additional small intensity-modulated indicator was provided for the elevation operator. In it the operator could see the target and its image separately and could thus provide good data. This auxiliary system was called Mark 22. It was rushed through development and production and delivered to the fleet within ten months of being proposed. It was retrofitted on all Mark 4's and became an integral part of the second-generation Mark 12 Navy antiaircraft system.

Still other solutions were sought for the right compromise between angular tracking accuracy and field of view. A bull-by-the-horns solution was used by Bell Labs in the SCR-545, an antiaircraft radar for the Army. In this system, both a 200-MHz radar with a wide field of view and a precision-tracking 3,000-MHz radar were on the same mount with interleaved antennas, as shown in Fig. 2-31. The data from both were available to the operators. This radar was unique in that automatic tracking was provided in all three coordinates. It was the world's first radar with such capability. It served the Army well in the Anzio beachhead area and in the Pacific during the war. Its design was started under a Signal Corps contract late in 1941. Just one year later a complete prototype was towed to Camp Davis, North Carolina, for testing with 90-mm antiaircraft guns and the T-15 electronic gun computer, discussed in Chapter 3. By overlapping production with development, it was possible to deliver the first systems in time for the Anzio beachhead operation.

2.8 Range Measurement

In Section 2.6 above, on indicator systems for radars, mention was made of the stationary electronic range marks used on Bell Labs' first experimental radar. The production design required a much more sophisticated arrangement, since it was necessary to provide an accurate and continuously changing range signal to the gun computer.

The system developed to meet this requirement can be briefly described as follows: It was decided that the maximum range scale should be several times maximum gun range; hence, 100,000 yards was chosen. A radio wave goes out to this distance and back to the source in the time corresponding to one cycle of a 1.639-kHz oscillator. A master oscillator at this frequency drove the transmitter through a nonlinear coil pulser that caused the transmitter to fire at precisely the same point in each cycle. The master oscillator signal and its 18th harmonic (29.5 kHz) were separately put through two phase shifters which were geared together with precision gears in the ratio of 18 to 1. The output of the low-speed phase shifter produced a gate which selected a particular cycle of the 18th harmonic. This was the input to the high-speed phase shifter, which in turn could shift the phase of the range notch to be presented on the range oscilloscope. A diagram of this range-measuring system is shown in Fig.2-32.[15]

The phase shifter was a specially shaped variable capacitor which, in a suitable circuit, permitted continuously shifting phase through 360 degrees. It was the same as the shifter in a phase-measuring bridge that had been designed by L. A. Meacham for use in measurements on communications circuits. It had an accuracy of about 1 part in 300, but by the use of the two-speed scheme this improved to 1 part in 5,400 (300 × 18), which met the accuracy requirements of the early radar: 100,000 yards divided by 5,400, or about 18 yards.

The first Bell Labs airborne system used the range system described above, but a new problem arose when the airborne systems were soon

---

[15] A more complete description of the system is given in *Radar Systems and Components*, pp. 39–43.

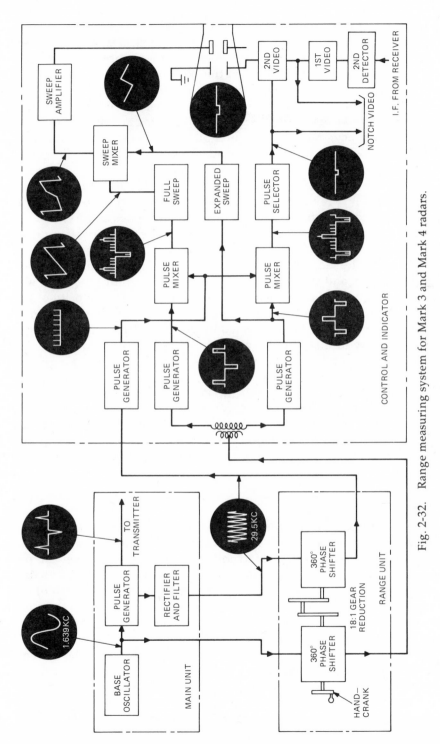

Fig. 2-32.   Range measuring system for Mark 3 and Mark 4 radars.

changed to use spark gap pulsers to reduce system weight. There is substantial jitter in the firing time of a spark gap, which precludes the use of a stable master oscillator as the range-measuring reference. This problem was quickly solved by S. C. Hight, of the Whippany Lab, who substituted for the master source a tuned circuit shock-excited directly from the spark gap and quenched at the end of each range-measuring interval. A little later Hight and Meacham collaborated in designing an improved system of higher accuracy, smaller and lighter but using the same principles. It was widely used on many different radar systems and became known as the Hight-Meacham range unit.

An entirely different type of range unit was also developed at Whippany by W. Shockley. It employed two piezoelectric crystals in a temperature-controlled column of liquid. One crystal was fixed at the end of the column and connected to launch a very short pulse of sonic waves down the column synchronously with the outgoing pulse from the radar transmitter. The second crystal was driven along the column by a precision lead screw and connected so as to receive the sonic pulse that was made to produce the range mark for the indicator. The velocity of the sound wave in the liquid was accurately known; hence, the position of the second crystal could be calibrated in terms of radar range. The ratio of this velocity to that of radio waves in space was of the order of 1 to 1,000,000, so the unit was of convenient size. The Shockley range unit was used in several Bell Labs submarine radars.

Shockley, along with J. Bardeen and W. H. Brattain, was later awarded the Nobel Prize in Physics for the invention of the transistor a few years after the war. He was typical of the many research scientists in Bell Labs who laid aside their fundamental work for the duration of the war and devoted themselves to helping with the pressing wartime engineering problems.

2.9 Radar Data Transmission

The data obtained from radar were used for much more than providing a simple display on a scope. The data gathered on range, azimuth, and elevation are often transmitted to additional points where they are put to use. For example, on shipboard, the radar data are combined with data from a gyro system that continuously measures the roll and pitch of the ship, and are further combined with data from a gyro compass that continuously determines true north. The corrected data are then fed to a computer that generates gun-pointing orders allowing for wind, air density, gun ballistics, etc. Different but in many ways similar systems are involved in airborne systems. Within the radar assembly itself, data transmission takes place, for example, between the antenna mount, range unit, and indicators in order to put the various electronic marks in the proper position on the scope.

In many radar systems of the war period, the data take-offs were designed to fit existing external facilities which had previously accepted data from optical sensors. In some all-new systems, Bell Labs pioneered in developing dc data transmission systems of very high accuracy. They employed specially shaped potentiometers of exquisite precision generating—for example, an output dc voltage representing the sine or cosine of the angles of the antenna mount. These dc voltages were used in military dc computer units, which are discussed in Chapter 3. This same chapter also deals at some length with Bell Labs' contributions to military computers and requires no detailed discussion here. However, for completeness brief mention should be made of a few of the approaches used in the early systems. The radars on shipboard for the big guns firing on surface targets and for the 5-inch heavy antiaircraft guns were teamed with the existing electromechanical computers that had been used with optical input data. Although these computers had not been designed particularly to capitalize on the precise range information the radars produced, the combination worked well and was kept throughout the war. But as radar was progressively extended to the smaller guns aboard ship, it usually became necessary to design new computer facilities, as part of the radar system, to generate the gun orders directly.

As radars were put into aircraft early in the war, an effort was made to use them with the existing optical bombsight and its associated mechanical computer. The objective was to take advantage of the fact that optical systems were already in large production and that many men were being trained in their use. This effort was less than completely successful, however, and a little later new, more suitable computer facilities were designed as integral parts of the bombing and gun control systems used in aircraft.

2.10 Microwave Propagation and System Design Equations

Harald T. Friis and his group at the Holmdel, N.J., Laboratory had been exploring the possible usefulness of microwaves for broadband communications throughout the 1930s. They had made a number of propagation tests by the laborious method of choosing a particular path, setting up attended equipment at both ends, and making measurements over a period of time. The basic phenomena up to about 3,000 MHz were at least partially understood by the time radar development began.

Shortly after the first experimental 700-MHz radar was operating at Whippany, a test site was rented at Atlantic Highlands, New Jersey, to explore in a more realistic way the Navy's interest in higher frequencies. The site selected was on a bluff about 80 feet high (representing a typical height above water for an installation on a Navy ship) and overlooked Sandy Hook and lower New York Bay. A constant stream of shipping entering and leaving New York harbor provided a variety of radar targets.

Fig. 2-33.   Bell Laboratories radar antenna test site in Atlantic Highlands, New Jersey.

When this first radar was turned on, the buildings of lower Manhattan, 20 miles to the north, were immediately apparent on the radar, as were the buildings and large gas tanks in Brooklyn and many so-called fixed targets in all directions where a line of sight was available.   The little ferry boat which plied between Staten Island and the nearby dock at Atlantic Highlands several times each day became a familiar and reliable test object. Thus, the radar provided a very convenient means of observing the anomalies of radio propagation over paths in all directions without having an attended station at the other end.   Many facts were quickly learned. The experimenters learned first that weather conditions substantially affect transmission.   When there was a light surface fog and temperature inversion, the radio waves were obviously refracted downward, and targets far beyond the optical horizon came up strong on the radar.   A principal target for these observations was the Fire Island Lightship some 40 miles away, which on normal days could not be seen at all.

As the radar development program at Bell Labs rapidly accelerated, many designs operating in different frequency bands were taken in their experimental form to the Atlantic Highlands laboratory for tests.   A photograph of the test deck at the laboratory is shown in Fig. 2-33.   At this site both the Army and the Navy witnessed the performance of Bell Labs' 700-MHz radar in 1939 and noted that in spite of its relatively low-power

2-kW transmitter, it outperformed their much-higher-power 200-MHz transmitters for surface targets. The reason for this deserves a word of explanation. When a radio beam having a single lobe in free space is directed along the horizontal over a highly reflecting surface (e.g., the ocean), it breaks up into an interference pattern of maxima and nulls in the vertical plane. The angle above the horizontal at which the first maximum appears depends solely upon the height of the antenna above the surface in wavelengths. Thus, the shorter waves at higher frequencies have a decided advantage for surface targets, which were the Navy's first concern in their effort to make radar a fire control instrument for battleships against surface targets.

Radar is inherently two-way radio. Thus, the radar transmitter "illuminates" a distant target. The target reflects or scatters the received energy more or less in all directions and in so doing becomes a second, reradiating transmitter. Thus, the radar signal has two spherical expansions during its round trip instead of the one expansion that occurs in radio communication.

As far as the author knows, the radar equation relating the above facts mathematically was first produced in this country by the Holmdel radio research group under Harald Friis at the request of the Whippany radar group. In its early form, it related the echo power received at the radar to the power transmitted, the effective area of the transmitting antenna, the effective area of the receiving antenna, the effective scattering area of the target, the wavelength, and the distance. The formula for P_R, the power received by an antenna after reflection, is:

$$P_R = K \frac{P_T A_T A_R A_S}{4\pi\lambda^2 d^4},$$

where

P_T = power radiated from the antenna,
A_T = effective area of transmitting antenna,
A_R = effective area of receiving antenna,
A_S = area of reflecting object at distance d,
λ = wavelength, and
K = factor >1, which allows for the fact that the average reradiation from the target to the receiving antenna is greater than if it were reradiated equally in all directions.

This equation merits careful scrutiny. At first glance it is observed that wavelength squared is in the denominator, which would seem to indicate that decreasing the length of the waves employed would increase the power of the echo returned to the receiver. However, the numerator contains two antenna areas, each of which involves the dimensions of wavelengths squared. Thus, one of these cancels the wavelength squared in the denominator. This leaves another wavelength squared in the numerator, which indicates, when all factors are considered, that the longer the wavelength used, the more echo power enters the receiver. These statements assume that the sensitivity of the receiver and the power transmitted are the same at any wavelength. They also assume that the effective area of the target is unchanged. In the early days of radar, these assumptions were far from true. Quite generally, the transmitter power available went down as the wavelength decreased and the sensitivity of the receiver decreased. The effective area of the target at different wavelengths was completely unknown until empirical data was accumulated over the next few years.

Later the radar equation was rearranged and put in the form of the maximum range which can be expected of a radar, assuming all other pertinent quantities are known.[16] Suppose the minimum power required for satisfactory detection, S_{min}, is known. The maximum range of detection, R_{max}, is

$$R_{max} = \sqrt[4]{\frac{P\sigma A^2 f^2}{4\pi S_{min}\lambda^2}},$$

where

P = peak pulse power (in watts),
λ = wavelength (in feet),
A = area of antenna aperture (in square feet),
σ = target cross section (in square feet), and
f = fraction denoting effective aperture of antenna.

The Radiation Laboratory at M.I.T. was dedicated from its inception in late 1940 to pushing microwave radar to the shortest possible wavelengths. In most applications, this proved to be a wise course, but in the enthusiastic pursuit of the original goal, it was found that the objective could be pushed too far. Frequencies eventually reached 24,000 MHz, where atmospheric attenuation made them wholly unsuitable for most of the wartime problems. Throughout the war there was intimate and constructive collaboration between Bell Labs and the Radiation Lab, although differing opinions and spirited debate often occurred. Although Bell Labs played a major part in the development of so-called microwave radar (2,000 MHz and higher), work was continued on lower-frequency radar when lower frequencies might provide a better solution to the problem at hand.

III. RADAR SYSTEMS

A number of the radars designed by Bell Laboratories and manufactured by Western Electric have already been mentioned in Section II in con-

---

[16] Louis N. Ridenour (ed.), *Radar System Engineering,* 1st ed., M.I.T. Radiation Laboratory Series, Vol. 1 (New York and London: McGraw-Hill, 1947), p. 22.

nection with the technological development which helped to bring them into existence. The present section briefly discusses the more important systems, which are grouped functionally and chronologically so that the reader will be able to obtain an overall view. The variety of radars was so great that all cannot be adequately covered here, but Table 2-2 lists all the radars worked on by Bell Labs for which major development (i.e., construction of the model) had been completed by the end of 1945. Omitted are a number of systems started before 1945 but completed later. Some of these will be mentioned in Part II of this volume, which covers the postwar years.

3.1 Shipboard Systems

The first radar systems Bell Labs developed were shipboard systems (some of the early Navy fire control radars are discussed above). The experimental CXAS was, of course, the precursor of all the early systems and this, in improved form with a magnetron, became the Mark 1, which was the first fire control radar in the United States fleet. While 10 of the Mark 1 systems were being produced, development began on the Mark 2, which was designed to meet shipboard conditions better and to integrate with existing optical fire control equipment. Before Mark 2 was completed, a higher-power transmitter tube—the magnetron—became available; on its addition to the system, the designation was changed to Mark 3. The latter system was used in heavy ships for controlling the main batteries, which were used for surface fire only. A further expansion of the system, designated Mark 4, provided a means for measuring target elevation as well as range and direction, and thus provided a capability for antiaircraft fire control. It was used with the 5-inch guns making up the secondary battery of heavy ships and the main battery of the lighter ships. The Mark 3 and 4, as well as their predecessors, operated at 700 MHz; both were in production before the Pearl Harbor attack. More than 900 were delivered in the next two years for installation in the fast-growing fleet. They gave the Navy a tremendous advantage over the Japanese in the many naval battles of that period.

When enemy air attacks in the Pacific showed that the accuracy of the Mark 4 system was not sufficient at low elevation angles to meet the Japanese low-altitude attack tactics, the Bown proposal described in Section 2.7 was adopted. This involved adding to the existing equipment a special elevation-measuring system operating in the X band (10,000 MHz). The design of the supplementary system, designated Mark 22, was rapidly undertaken by using a number of X-band subsystem components then being manufactured at Western Electric for an Air Force radar system. The Mark 22 proved highly successful in closing the gap in the Navy air defense in the Pacific. The combined antenna systems are shown in Fig. 2-30.

Table 2-2.   Radar Systems Designed by Bell Laboratories—1937–1945

Service and Function	Designation (Code No.)	Frequency Band	Development Initiated	Model Completed	WE Production*
SHIPBORNE					
Fire Control, Surface	R&D Models	200 MHz	1938–40	Jun 1939	...
	CXAS	L	Jan 1940	Feb 1941	...
	MK 1	L	Jul 1940	Jul 1941	1941
	MK 3	L	Dec 1940	Oct 1941	1941
	MK 2	L	Feb 1941	Jul 1941	...
	MK 8	S	Jul 1940	Oct 1942	1942
	MK 8, Mod 1, 2	S	Jan 1943	Nov 1943	1943
	MK 8, Mod 3	S	Feb 1944	Dec 1945	1945
	MK 13, Mod 1	X	Jul 1942	Oct 1944	1944–45
	MK 13, Mod 2	X	Nov 1944	(Feb 1947)	...
Fire Control, Antiaircraft	MK 4	L	Oct 1940	Sep 1941	1941
	MK 4 Auto	L	Nov 1941	Jul 1942	...
	MK 7	S	Aug 1941	Feb 1942	...
	MK 7, Mod 1	X	Jul 1942	Mar 1943	...
	MK 9	S	Oct 1941	Sep 1942	1942
	MK 10	S	Aug 1941	Nov 1942	1942
	MK 12	L	Apr 1942	Jul 1943	1943
	MK 12 Auto	L	Mar 1944	Feb 1945	...
	MK 19	S	Sep 1942	Sep 1943	1943
	MK 19, Mod 1	X	Jun 1943	Sep 1944	...
	MK 18	S	Mar 1943	Feb 1944	1944
	MK 25	X, K	Mar 1944	Aug 1945	...
	MK 34	X	Apr 1944	Feb 1945	...

Category	Model	Type			
	MK 34, Mod 1	X	Jul 1944	Oct 1945	. . .
	MK 34, Mod 3, 4	X	Aug 1944	Sep 1945	Postwar
	MK 34, Mod 2	X	Jul 1945	Postwar	Postwar
	MK 28	S	Nov 1943	Apr 1944	1944
	MK 28, Mod 2	S	Jul 1944	Postwar	Postwar
	MK 28, Mod 3	S	Nov 1944	Postwar	Postwar
	MK 22	X	Jun 1943	Dec 1943	1943
	MK 22, Mod 1	X	Jul 1945	Postwar	Postwar
	MK 25, Mod 2	X	Nov 1945	Postwar	Postwar
Search	SH	S	Jul 1940	Nov 1941	1941–43
	SLX	X	Sep 1941	Sep 1943	. . .
	SE	S	Apr 1942	Dec 1942	1942
	SL	S	Jun 1942	Dec 1942	1942
	SL-1	S	Aug 1943	Dec 1943	1943
	MK 27	S	Jul 1943	Feb 1944	1944
	MK 27, Mod 1	S	Jul 1944	Jan 1945	1945
SUBMARINE Surface Search & Torpedo Control	SJ	S	Jul 1940	Dec 1941	1942
	SJ-1	S	Nov 1942	Sep 1943	1943
	SS	X	Apr 1943	Jul 1944	1944
	ST	X	Feb 1944	Dec 1944	1944
Aircraft Warning	SV, SV-1	S	Feb 1944	Jan 1945	1944–45
GROUND BASED Search—Early Warning	SCR-268	P	Jul 1940	Jun 1941	1941
	SCR-668-T2	L	Sep 1942	Jun 1943	. . .
Searchlight Control	MK 20, Mod 0	L	Jul 1943	Jun 1944	1944
	MK 20, Mod 1	L	Oct 1943	Nov 1944	1944

Table 2-2—*Continued*

Service and Function	Designation (Code No.)	Frequency Band	Development Initiated	Model Completed	WE Production*
Search—Early Warning	SCR-602-T3	L	Jun 1942	Feb 1943	...
	AN/TPS-1	L	Mar 1943	Sep 1943	1943
	AN/TPS-1B	L	Oct 1943	Sep 1944	1944
Search—Ground Control Intercept	AN/CPS-5	L	Jan 1944	Nov 1945	1944-45
Gunfire Control—Surface	CXAS (Adaption)	L	Jul 1940	Jun 1941	...
	SCR-296	L	Nov 1941	May 1942	1942
	MK 16	L	Jul 1942	Sep 1943	1943
Gunfire Control—Mortar Locating	AN/TPQ-2	L	Dec 1944	May 1945	Postwar
Gunfire Control—Antiaircraft	SCR-545	P, S	Jan 1942	Jan 1943	1942
	SCR-547	S	Sep 1941	Sep 1942	1942
	T33 & M33	S, X	Dec 1944	Postwar	Postwar
AIRBORNE Aircraft Intercept	SCR-520-A	S	Mar 1941	Nov 1941	1941
	SCR-520	S	Apr 1942	Dec 1942	1942
	SCR-520-T3	S	Jul 1941	Mar 1943	...
	SCR-540	P	Apr 1941	Feb 1942	1942
	SCR-720-A	S	Apr 1942	Jul 1943	1943
	SCR-720-B	S	Jun 1942	Dec 1942	1942
	SCR-720-T2	X	Apr 1942	Feb 1944	...
	AN/APS-4	X	Jul 1942	Sep 1943	1943-44
	AN/APS-4A	X	Nov 1945	(Feb 1947)	Postwar

Category	Model				
Aircraft Gunlaying	SCR-523-T1	S	Apr 1941	May 1942	...
	SCR-523-T2	S	Feb 1941	Sep 1941	...
	SCR-523-T3	S	Apr 1941	Nov 1941	...
	AN/APG-1	S	Jan 1943	Jan 1944	1944–45
Aircraft Search	SCR-517-A	S	Oct 1941	Mar 1942	1942
	SCR-517-B	S	Oct 1941	Mar 1942	1942
	SCR-517-C	S	Jul 1942	Feb 1943	1943–45
	ASC	S	Jan 1942	Apr 1942	1942–44
	SCR-717-A	S	Apr 1942	Dec 1942	1943
	SCR-717-B	S	Apr 1942	Dec 1942	1943
	SCR-717-T3	X	Feb 1942	Jan 1943	...
	AN/APS-1A & 1B	X	Jul 1943	Apr 1944	1944–45
	AN/APS-1A & 1B	K	Jul 1943	Apr 1944	1944–45
	AN/APQ-34	K	Nov 1944	(Nov 1947)	Postwar
	AN/APS-23	X	Sep 1945	Postwar	Postwar
High-Altitude Bombing	SCR-519-T3	S	Sep 1940	Apr 1942	...
	SCR-519-T5	S	Jun 1942	Jul 1943	...
	MK 15	X	Jul 1942	Feb 1944	...
	AN/APQ-7 (Eagle)	X	Apr 1943	Jul 1944	1944–45
	AN/APQ-10	X	Feb 1943	May 1944	...
	AN/APQ-13	X	Jul 1943	Aug 1944	1944–45
	AN/APQ-16	X	Nov 1944	Postwar	...
	AN/APS-1K	K	Apr 1944	Jun 1945	1945
Low-Altitude Bombing	AN/APQ-5	X	Jul 1942	Jun 1943	1943
	AN/APQ-5A & 5B	X	Jul 1942	Jun 1943	1943–45
	MK 31	X	Jul 1943	Jun 1944	1944
Aircraft Missile Control	MK 15, Mod 2 (Bat)	S	Feb 1943	Mar 1944	1944–45
	MK 31, SWOD (MK 2)	S	Dec 1943	Dec 1944	Postwar

* Western Electric production, in many cases, was concurrent with Bell Labs model testing, and invariably started ahead of model completion.

Fig. 2-34.   Components of the Mark 8 fire control radar.

The second-generation radar for the main battery was the Mark 8, also previously mentioned.   The complete equipment is shown in Fig. 2-34. The antennas were mounted atop the two main battery gun directors, the

Fig. 2-35.   Mark 12 and Mark 22 radar antennas mounted on a Mark 37 director.

Fig. 2-36.   Mark 28 fire control radar on antiaircraft gun mount.

operator's units were located within the director alongside the corresponding optics, and the other units were below deck.   It was undoubtedly
the world's first "track-while-scan" radar—i.e., one that furnished precise
data on one target while it also kept a close eye on a wide field of view.   It
operated in S band (roughly 3,000 MHz) and served with spectacular
success in many Pacific battles.   It was followed by the Mark 13 operating
in X band (10,000 MHz) with a much lighter antenna that made it suitable
for wider application for the same function.   An important feature of this
type of radar with its "B" scope was the ability to see at one time the
splashes from all the shells and thus "spot" (in Naval gunnery parlance)
for the next salvo.

Figure 2-35 shows the Mark 12-22, which was the second-generation
radar for the secondary battery, replacing the Mark 4-22 shown in Fig. 2-30.

RADAR

SONAR

Fig. 2-37.   Example of number and placement of fire control radar antennas and sonar ranging equipment on large warship.

Fig. 2-38.   SL search radar antenna aboard a destroyer escort.

It was an extremely useful dual-purpose arrangement, providing accurate fire control data for use against both surface and aircraft targets.

As the more difficult problems of providing radar fire control for heavy machine guns in a practical manner were resolved, several Bell Labs designs for fire control of such guns were also put into production.   Typical of these was the Mark 28 shown in Fig. 2-36.

The proliferation of fire control radars—all designed by Bell Labs—on a typical heavy ship by 1944 is illustrated Fig. 2-37.

While Bell Labs and Western Electric did not develop heavy search radars for the Navy, they did design and produce a number of small search radars for use on landing barges and small vessels.   One of these was the SL shown in Fig. 2-38.

3.2 Submarine Radars

Bell Laboratories began to study radar for submarines in 1940.   It was obvious that the antenna would have to be small and not much above water; hence, the highest possible frequency would have to be used.   Early in 1941 the Navy outlined the urgent need for submarine radar to detect low-flying enemy planes, locate enemy ships, and provide fire control for torpedoes.   Thus began a program which resulted in Bell Labs and Western Electric designing and supplying all the Navy's submarine fire control radars throughout the war.

With the magnetron in hand for generating frequencies of 3,000 MHz or more, it appeared that a useful design was possible, but many difficult problems lay ahead, probably more mechanical than electrical. There was no appreciable design information available regarding the environment. There was a large submarine construction program under way with no room left for radar equipment. Where could it be squeezed in? How much vibration? How much shock would be felt on board if an enemy scored a near miss with a depth charge? How to get a waveguide and cable through the hull to the antenna? (An extra hull penetration in a submarine is not a simple matter.)

The mechanical design of submarine radars was worked out by A. K. Bohren's mechanical design group at Whippany after countless conferences with the Naval Research Laboratory and the appropriate Navy bureaus and yards. The first submarine radar, the SJ, is pictured in Fig. 2-39. It was the first microwave radar designed for submarines. In an improved model called the SJ-1, it was used throughout the war. It operated at S band (3,000 MHz) and was followed by the SS and SSa models, which operated in the 10,000-MHz region and included many new features. These radars were used primarily for surface search and torpedo fire control. They were tremendously successful in enabling our submarines to destroy enemy ships in night as well as day attacks. The first SJ was delivered by Western Electric in April 1942, and was followed by hundreds of this and later models, some for special purposes, as will be discussed below.

The Navy had equipped some of its submarines just before the war with 200-MHz air search radars (not produced by the Bell System) to give early warning of nearby enemy aircraft. It is fundamental that the transmitted radar pulse can be received at a far greater distance than that at which the much weaker echo from a target can be detected. Enemy patrol aircraft learned early in the war how to receive the 200-MHz pulses and thus to detect the presence of a United States sub and to home toward it before the sub had detected the aircraft. This situation resulted in a crash program at Bell Labs to produce an early warning microwave radar for subs which, for a time at least, the enemy could not monitor. The result was the SV and later the SV-1, which was in production about the end of 1944.

The story of the SV system is worth telling in some detail, since it illustrates some of the techniques frequently used in conducting crash programs. When the problem of Japanese detection of United States submarines from the 200-MHz radars became serious, the Navy asked Bell Laboratories if a higher-power, 3,000- to 3,500-MHz, aircraft search radar then in development could be expedited so that the first system would be available for installation in six months! The Whippany, New Jersey, Laboratory was assigned design responsibility and a group of people at West Street, New York City, previously working on commercial electro-mechanical switching problems under E. J. Kane, was recruited to do the

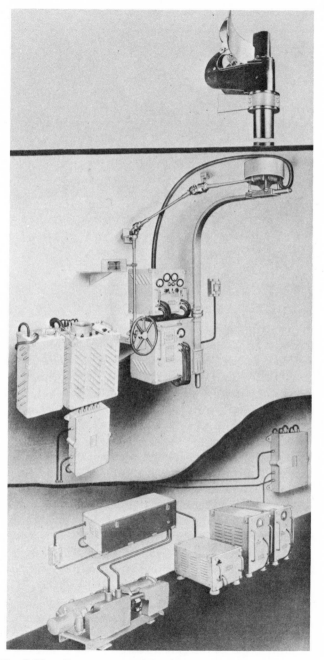

Fig. 2-39. Components of the SJ submarine radar system.

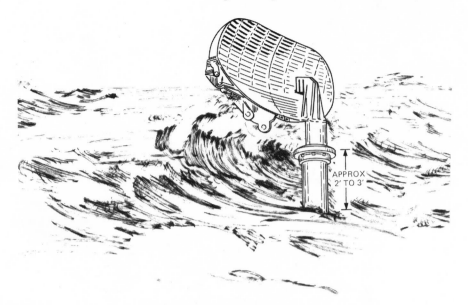

APPROX
2' TO 3'

Fig. 2-40.   SV submarine antenna in operating position.

engineering for manufacture.   To save tooling time, 30 initial units were
produced by a special laboratory model shop at Chambers Street,[17] New
York City, before Western Electric took over manufacture at a rented plant
in Passaic, New Jersey, and continued production without a break.

The large rotating microwave antenna had to be installed on a separate
mast to permit the aircraft search before a submarine surfaced.   Since Bell
Labs had no mechanical group available at the time, the machine shop of
General Mills, used in peacetime for food-packaging machinery, was asked
by Bell Labs for assistance in the design and manufacture of the periscope
rotating system.   The Holmdel, N. J., Laboratory under H. T. Friis solved
the critical antenna feedhorn problem.   With the high peak power of 500
kW, the waveguide system had to maintain a low standing-wave match
under all operating conditions.   This meant that the antenna feedhorn
impedance had to be matched to air, to water as the antenna broke through
the surface, and to part air and part water as waves broke over the surface.
It also had to withstand the high pressures and other requirements imposed by crash dives.   Engineers at Holmdel solved the problem with a
horn system that proved satisfactory.

In carrying out this crash job, the peacetime switching engineers were
converted almost overnight into microwave designers.   The first system
model tested on the roof of the Chambers Street building was shipped six

[17] The Bell Labs model shop at Chambers Street was used for other projects requiring expedited production of small-quantity items or high-priority system modifications.

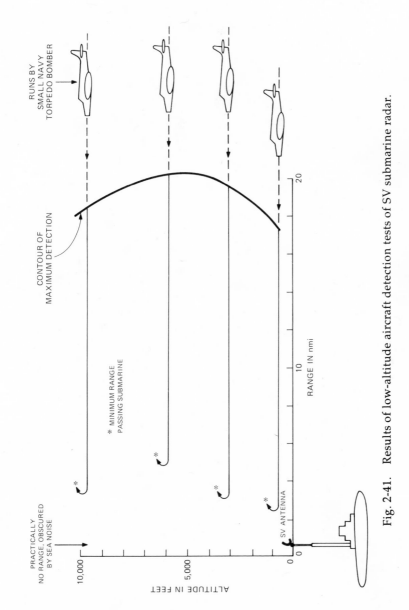

RUNS BY
SMALL NAVY
TORPEDO BOMBER

CONTOUR OF
MAXIMUM DETECTION

* MINIMUM RANGE
PASSING SUBMARINE

PRACTICALLY
NO RANGE, OBSCURED
BY SEA NOISE

SV ANTENNA

10,000

5,000

0

ALTITUDE IN FEET

0

10

20

RANGE IN nmi

Fig. 2-41.   Results of low-altitude aircraft detection tests of SV submarine radar.

Fig. 2-42.   SJ-1/Mark 27 submarine radar antenna.

months after the Navy's urgent request for it and installed by the Electric
Boat Company at New London, Connecticut, on the latest submarine for
testing off Long Island against United States aircraft.   With only the antenna breaking above the surface, as shown in Fig. 2-40, the Navy objectives for detecting any aircraft flying within 15 to 20 miles and up to 15,000
feet in altitude were met in these tests, as shown in Fig. 2-41.

The antenna of a submarine radar presented a substantial visual target
above water during use.   This was an important problem during the later
war years, and the Navy, in order to reduce target size, requested development of an accurate range-only radar that could be used with azimuth
data provided by the optical periscope.   A very small antenna on the re-
tractible periscope would provide the necessary information and yet ex-
pose to enemy observation only the very small periscope tube.   The difficult problem of getting a 10,000-MHz connection through the optical
tube was resolved by the Naval Research Laboratory working closely with
Bohren's group.   The result was the ST radar system produced in 1944 and
widely applied.

A closing word on the mechanical problems of submarine radar: the
exposed antennas had to be extremely rugged, not only because of crash
dives but also because they might strike floating debris in a battle area.
The design which Bohren's group produced is illustrated by the SJ-1
shown in Fig. 2-42.   The feedhorn was a massive pedestal rugged enough
to take any likely abuse.   The reflector was hinged and held in operating

Fig. 2-43.   ST and SJ-1 radar systems installed on forward bulkhead and left side of submarine control room.

position by a shear pin designed to take the calculable forces of a crash dive.   Thus, if debris were struck, it could fold back and not be permanently damaged; and at first opportunity thereafter the reflector could be erected, the shear pin could be replaced, and the radar would be back in operation.   This feature was completely successful and was used on all Bell Labs designs.

An example of the problem of squeezing radar equipment into the below-deck space is shown in Fig. 2-43.   Figure 2-12 shows the superstructure of a submarine with a full set of Bell Laboratories-Western Electric radars.

3.3 Ground-Based Radars

Radars operated from the ground found broad application by the Army ground forces, the Marines, and the Army Air Force in the protection of airfields and other fixed installations against enemy air attack.   They were also used extensively in the protection of newly won beachheads and permanent shore installations against attacks by ships and planes.

During the 1930s the Army Signal Corps carried out a pioneering development program on radar at its Fort Monmouth laboratories, and later at Fort Hancock, under the direction of Col. Roger B. Colton. By 1939 the Corps had completed two prototypes that performed usefully—one a heavy system operating at about 100 MHz and intended for permanent installation for early warning, and the other a mobile system operating at about 200 MHz and intended for both early warning and searchlight control. The transmitter of the latter employed a ring oscillator similar to that shown in Fig. 2-2.

Bell Laboratories was brought into contact with the Signal Corps work in 1938, and from that time there was a continuing interchange of information between the two groups. In mid-1939 when Bell Labs moved its 700-MHz equipment to Atlantic Highlands (near Fort Hancock) for field testing, Col. Colton and his aids were among the first visitors, and they continued to follow the work there.

In the spring of 1940, the Signal Corps asked Bell Labs and Western Electric to undertake the design-for-production and manufacture of the Signal Corps mobile radar system. The Corps wanted this system in quantity production at the earliest possible time. Therefore, a team of engineers and draftsmen was organized under the direction of R. E. Poole to carry out the production design task. The Signal Corps made space available for them at Fort Hancock so that they could work alongside the prototype being tested. As a result, improvements were made on the production drawings within hours after they were devised, and up-to-date equipment was rolling out of Western Electric factories in February 1941—less than eight months after the effort began. More than 1,000 units of this equipment, coded SCR-268 (Fig. 2-26), were delivered in the next two years. Since this radar was available well before the Pearl Harbor attack, it found very wide use in training many thousands of men, and was the only available ground radar system in most combat areas for the first year and a half after Pearl Harbor.

Combat experience with the SCR-268, which was heavy, soon indicated the urgent need for a very much lighter early warning radar for use in protecting newly won beachheads and airfields. The requirements arrived at after much discussion with the Marines and Air Force were indeed severe. The radar was to have at least twice the search range of the SCR-268 but one-tenth the weight, use a much smaller antenna, and be packaged in small units which could be hand-carried up a mountain if necessary—indeed a tall order. Fortunately, the rapid progress in two laboratory areas brought this undertaking within the realm of feasibility. The magnetron group under J. B. Fisk had developed an efficient and very-high-power tube at about 1200 MHz. The airborne radar group had made great strides in reducing the size and weight of modulators and power supplies. With these advances in technology, the job was undertaken, still more Bell System work was laid aside for the duration, and a new radar group was organized under the direction of R. W. Chesnut and A. D. Knowlton to carry out the design of what became the TPS-1 series of portable ground radars. Development began in July 1942 and production deliveries in mid-1943. This radar and later improved models rapidly became the favorite of the Marines and Air Forces; over 600 units were produced.

When the Marines assaulted Mt. Suribachi on Iwo Jima Island, they had several objectives. One was to wipe out the Japanese artillery which harassed their men below, another was to plant the flag to let their fellows know they had succeeded, and still another was to get a TPS-1 on the summit to give very early warning of the repeated attacks by enemy aircraft. The Marines used the radar for the same purposes at Okinawa and elsewhere. A picture of the TPS-1B at Okinawa is shown in Fig. 2-1c.

In late 1941, the Signal Corps worked out with Bell Labs a specification for a very sophisticated, mobile antiaircraft radar. It was to perform both the search and fire control functions for 90-mm and 120-mm gun batteries and was to be equipped with both synchro and dc potentiometer data outputs so that it could be used with several types of computers.[18] Further, each of the three operators (range, azimuth, and elevation) was to be provided, independently, with a switch to choose straight manual, aided manual, or fully automatic tracking, as the tactical situation might demand. Development began in December 1941, and a complete prototype was tested with a high degree of success at Camp Davis, North Carolina, in December 1942 with the Bell Labs T15 computer and live gun batteries. Production units of the radar, coded SCR-545, were delivered in 1943 and saw combat service in both the European and Pacific theaters. It was the first radar to track automatically in all three coordinates. A close-up of the dual-frequency antenna is shown in Fig. 2-31; the complete trailer-mounted system is shown in Fig. 2-44.

Two aspects of the SCR-545 are worth noting here. First, in early 1943 the prototype was set up at Fort Monmouth for demonstration to a large number of interested visitors. A test target airplane was available and the pilot was simply instructed to fly around the area. The operators locked the SCR-545 on the target and got out of the operator's cab. As visitors filed by all afternoon, the radar held on to the target continuously, although there was occasionally no line of sight as the target passed behind buildings or hills. This spectacular result was possible because, when the microwave signal faded, a relay automatically transferred the tracking circuits to a low-frequency search system, in which the longer waves could

---

[18] Chapter 3 deals with gun control computers.

Fig. 2-44.   Trailer-mounted SCR-545 radar.

still see the target by refraction around the obstacles.   Thus, the antenna
and range unit would stay on target, albeit a little sloppily, until the target
came back into view on the microwave system, when control would switch
back and tracking would immediately tighten up to fire control
quality.

The second event concerns the Allied invasion of Italy at the Anzio
beachhead in January 1944.   For the first few nights, the landing groups
took a severe pounding from the Luftwaffe, and their toehold was pre-
carious.   After the SCR-545 and associated guns and the Bell Labs M-9 gun
director were landed, the situation dramatically improved.   The hills
around the beachhead were soon littered with the wrecks of German
bombers.   The Germans were then goaded into using, and thereby revealing, a radar countermeasure that both they and the Allies had developed in great secrecy but had not—to the author's knowledge—used in
combat up to that time.   Called "Chaff," it consisted of thousands of foil
strips dropped from aircraft to clutter up the sky and make it more difficult
to track aircraft by radar.   The Chaff used by the Germans would probably
have caused considerable trouble for earlier radars, such as the SCR-268,
but it had no substantial effect on the SCR-545.

In tests at the Atlantic Highlands test site Bell Labs demonstrated to the
Army that 600-MHz radar could provide data having fire control accuracy
on surface targets well beyond maximum gun range.   Shortly afterwards,
the Army Coast Artillery recognized the enormous advantage radar could
give it in carrying out its responsibility.   At that time the coast defense

guns were directed by optical telescopes. The system depended on good visibility and widely spaced stations to get accurate range by triangulation. Radar, on the other hand, offered all-weather operation from a single station. Bell Labs and Western Electric were asked in the fall of 1941 to produce a modification of the Navy ship design that would be suitable for the coast defense function. The bulk of the equipment was similar to that used by the Navy, but the antenna was mounted on a high tower and disguised to look like a water tank. Deliveries of the system, which was coded the SCR-296, began in 1942. Over 200 units were produced. They were installed along the coasts of the United States, at the Canal Zone, in Iceland, and at other places where the Coast Artillery had defense responsibility. Although German pocket battleships and submarines were roaming the seas and there was much fear that critical coastal installations might be attacked, this system—as far as the author knows—never saw combat. The Army reported an unhappy incident off the mid-Atlantic coast. An SCR-296 was tracking a merchant ship, well beyond maximum gun range, when it saw a smaller signal near the ship, heard the SOS, and saw both signals shortly disappear. This was but one incident in a very serious situation in 1942, when "our Atlantic seaboard shipping was slaughtered at the rate of 75 ships per month by an operating group of approximately 38 submarines, which suffered casualties amounting to only 3 per month."[19] Bell Labs played a part in the solution of this problem—both with sonar development and with a crash shift in emphasis on airborne radar from aircraft interception (AI) to search radar, as described in the following section.

The Bell Labs-Western Electric team produced a number of other ground-based radars to meet military needs in various applications. One was a range-only set, at S band, using separate dishes for transmitting and receiving, mounted on an army sound locator pedestal where the antennas replaced the sound horns. This was the SCR-547, promptly dubbed "Mickey Mouse"* from its appearance, as shown in Fig. 2-45. Another was the Mark 20 lightweight searchlight control radar for the Marines, shown in Fig. 2-46. Still another was the Mark 16, an easily portable S-band fire control radar for the Marines.

Late in the war it was obvious that L band (approximately 1,000 MHz) was optimum for heavy early warning or search radars and that the 200-MHz sets still in production at General Electric and other manufacturers were becoming obsolete. Wanting to switch quickly to L band, the Army asked Bell Labs and Western Electric to supply General Electric with the frequency-sensitive parts to make this possible. These parts included the transmitter, receiver front end, and antenna. The result was the CPS-5, shown in Fig. 2-47, which set a pattern followed in the years after the war for this kind of service.

* Registered trademark of Walt Disney Productions.
[19] Howeth, pp. 471–472.

Fig. 2-45.   SCR-547 ground-based range radar.

Experience with fire control radars during the early years of the war demonstrated that an operator could often see gun shells in flight. If the field of view, the acquisition facilities, and the operator's dexterity were adequate, the radar could frequently lock onto the fast-moving target and

Fig. 2-46.   Mark 20 lightweight searchlight control radar.

Fig. 2-47.   AN/CPS-5 ground radar used for air base protection.

track it with precision for considerable distances.   Late in the war a serious problem was losses from enemy mortars which produced almost no flash or smoke and which could be moved before they were located and attacked.   The Army therefore asked Bell Labs to devise a small, easily portable radar to serve as a mortar locator.   The scheme developed was to produce two wide fan beams fixed at different angles above the horizon, as shown in the diagram of Fig. 2-48.   Each fan was to be produced by a needle beam oscillating back and forth so rapidly that a mortar shell could not pass through it without being hit by several radar pulses.   Thus, the radar measured two points on the shell's trajectory where the shell passed through the two fans.   Since mortar trajectories are well known, a built-in computer could provide the ground coordinates of the source almost instantly.   Thus, counter-fire could be directed toward it before the enemy's shells hit the ground.   An ingenious mechanical scanner-type antenna to produce the beams was invented by the Friis group at the Holmdel Lab.   Prototype equipments were rushed into production and 10 sets were delivered.   They were coded TPQ-2.

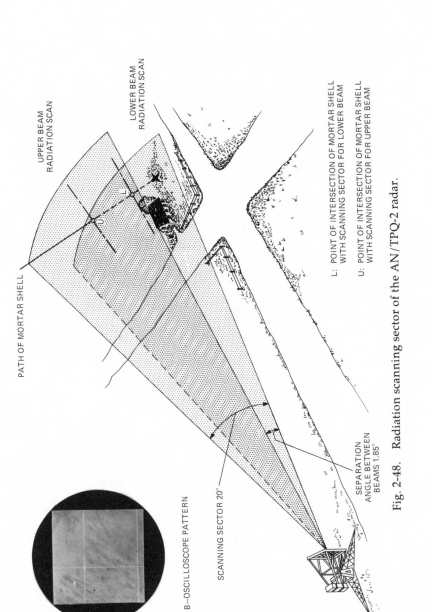

UPPER BEAM
RADIATION SCAN

LOWER BEAM
RADIATION SCAN

PATH OF MORTAR SHELL

L: POINT OF INTERSECTION OF MORTAR SHELL
   WITH SCANNING SECTOR FOR LOWER BEAM

U: POINT OF INTERSECTION OF MORTAR SHELL
   WITH SCANNING SECTOR FOR UPPER BEAM

B−OSCILLOSCOPE PATTERN

SCANNING SECTOR 20°

SEPARATION
ANGLE BETWEEN
BEAMS 1.85°

Fig. 2-48. Radiation scanning sector of the AN/TPQ-2 radar.

It is of interest to note that the SCR-545, described above, could readily acquire and track the German V-2 rocket.   At the height of the V-2 menace in the Netherlands, this and other antiaircraft radars and many antiaircraft guns were being mobilized by the American and British armies to try to control this problem, but the threat ended before preparations were complete.

3.4 Airborne Radar

3.4.1 Background

As described in previous sections, early Bell radar developments were concentrated on large equipment which could be accommodated in Navy ships and Army trucks or permanently located on land.   At the time, such equipment was the only kind possible with available technology, and fortunately it met the current urgent needs for early warning of air attacks, for target location, and for fire control of ordnance—particularly under conditions where optical methods were ineffective because of range in-accuracy or limited visibility.

However, the enormous bombing raids on Britain in 1940 and the growth of submarine attacks on shipping clearly demonstrated the need for airborne radar.   The most immediate need was for directing the fire of night fighters against enemy bombers.   Ground installations were ef-fective in directing fighters in the general direction of bombers, but at night the latter were practically invulnerable when the fighter was de-pendent on optical means for the final attack.   Thus, target location and fire control provided the first urgent needs for airborne radar, but its use was soon expanded to sea search for submarines[20] and to the control of bombing at night or through overcast.   There were other applications of airborne radar, but space limitations restrict this discussion largely to the mainstream of development.

Many problems required solution in adapting the principle of radar to the many special requirements of airborne use.   Two requirements were outstanding: (1) reduction in size and weight and (2) greatly improved resolution.   The latter was of particular importance for bombing, since a fine-grain display of terrain details was essential for accurate target location.

The key to meeting both of these requirements was the use of higher frequencies (shorter wavelengths), since this led to both smaller compo-nents and finer resolution.   Of particular significance was the potential

---

[20] Submarines of the time could remain practically invisible during much of the day (except for occasional periscope exposure), but were obliged to surface at night for battery charging, at which time they were highly vulnerable to airborne radar search systems.   Ultimately, sophisticated radar systems became available which could even locate exposed peri-scopes.

Table 2-3.   Magnetron Frequency Band Available 1940–1944

Desig-nation	Frequency Band (MHz)	Approx. Wavelength (cm)	Year Available
L	1,200–1,400	25	1940/41
S	2,600–3,500	10	1942
X	8,500–9,400	3	1943
K	13,000–16,000	1.5	1944

for antennas of reasonable size.   To provide good resolution, an antenna had to be many wavelengths in size and, unless it was kept small, was a difficult device to locate on a plane.   It is not surprising, therefore, that wavelengths that were as small as 1.25 cm became an objective for radar designers.

The British magnetron (see Section IV), was the essential element needed for airborne radar, since it generated high peak power at the required high frequencies.   But these requirements were not achieved at once.   Not only was it necessary to develop magnetrons of very small size and high precision, but it was required to have other matching circuitry and components based on previously little-known techniques.   Fortunately, the work carried out during the 1930s at the Holmdel Laboratory of Bell Labs, under the leadership of H. T. Friis and G. C. Southworth, on microwave components for future Bell System communications provided the waveguide, converter, diodes, and antenna technology for this microwave radar application.

It is probably fair to say that much of the history of airborne radar is the story of developing techniques for using waves of ever higher frequency. (See Table 2-3 for relation between frequency band designations and year available.)   This was ultimately pushed to 24,000 MHz, a frequency beyond the usable range since this so-called K_a band was found to be close to the absorption peak of water vapor, which limited transmission in the atmosphere to impractically short distances and forced a retreat to about 15,000 MHz (K band), at which transmission losses were manageable.

The radars discussed in this section are the airborne systems in which Bell Laboratories and Western Electric played a major role.   In all cases Western Electric was a principal manufacturer, but some systems were also produced by other suppliers.   In general, Bell Laboratories was responsible for overall system design and the preparation of manufacturing information.   However, subcontracting of both component design and manufacture was common.

Two important characteristics of much of the war effort were the extreme speed with which systems were produced and the widespread cooperative effort of technical designers and manufacturers.   The former was accomplished not only by extraordinary effort by the personnel, but also by overlap of design and manufacture and by the step-by-step conversion of an existing design to one achieving advanced objectives. These techniques resulted in occasional false starts, errors, and retrofitting. In peacetime such procedures would have been less satisfactory than a slower approach in which designs could have been carefully checked before being committed to manufacture, but in wartime it was necessary to adopt all measures that met the need for speed. The cooperation among diverse producers was also an essential element in the success of these radar systems. For example, at one time Bell Labs began work on a bombing radar, using elements of an earlier radar, while the components of the new higher-frequency system were still under development at the Radiation Laboratory. The whole, when completed, had to be fitted into the new B-29 bomber, which was less than one year from deployment in a military theater. This was a far cry from peacetime methods and required large amounts of manpower, and good will, to coordinate the work in the various organizations which were constantly bringing about technical changes. The process was not very efficient, but it worked and the schedule was met.

Hopefully, this background will give the reader a feeling for some of the special problems of airborne radar design and manufacture, and we can now proceed to the specifics of the more important systems in which the Bell Labs-Western Electric team played a major role. The sections which follow are not intended to cover comprehensively Bell System work on airborne radar nor do they treat any of the other systems developed that were successfully tested but not produced because of rapidly changing requirements and priorities as the war progressed on many fronts.

3.4.2 Early Bombing Radar: SCR-519

In Bell Laboratories, concern over the need for an airborne radar developed as early as 1940. As a consequence of the radar work started in 1938 at the request of the U.S. Navy, the Whippany laboratory had acquired a sound knowledge of the current radar technology and was developing ideas on how the existing problems could be solved and how the use of radar could be expanded to airborne applications as well as to shipboard applications.

Thus, it happened that in July 1940 experimental work was begun at Whippany to develop an RF power source that would operate at a short enough wavelength (about 10 cm) to obtain suitably narrow beams from the much smaller antennas required by aircraft. A two-cavity klystron capable of about 10-watt continuous-wave output was developed, whereupon effort was then applied to obtaining maximum peak power from this device for radar purposes. By September of that year, a contract was obtained to develop this device into an airborne bombing radar for the Army Air Corps.

Fig. 2-49.   Components of first airborne radar designed by Bell Labs—the SCR-519-T3 bombing radar.

By great good fortune, the award of this contract was made at nearly the same time that the first magnetron arrived from Britain. This model, designed for a wavelength of 10 cm, produced at least ten times the peak power expected from the klystron. Effort was immediately shifted to use of the magnetron power source, and resulted in construction of a bread-board model of an S-band (10-cm) radar, which was tested at the Atlantic Highlands site in December 1940 and successfully flown in a B-18 bomber in January 1941. The system employed a parabolic antenna that was manually scanned in azimuth for search. Mechanical lobe switching of the beam provided accurate angle information on a target by a pip-matching display. Work then began on a laboratory model and a delivery model, which was designated SCR-519-T3 (Fig. 2-49). Engineers termed this the BTO (bombing through overcast) radar. Flight tests of the labo-ratory model in April 1941 produced results exceeding the specification requirements. The radar was delivered to the Army Air Corps at Wright Field, Dayton, Ohio, in September 1941. Tests were then conducted during the next few months.

At the same time, work was in progress to provide an airborne version of the electronic analog computer first developed as the M-9 antiaircraft gunfire computer.[21] The airborne design of the computer was attached to the SCR-519 in December 1941. In January 1942 the model radar and

[21] See Chapter 3 for a discussion of fire control computers.

computer were installed in a B-18 twin-engine bomber from McDill Field, Florida. Tests were conducted during January, February, and March 1942 against a corner reflector target in the Gulf of Mexico. A circular error probability (CEP) of 17 mils in angle was achieved against this isolated target from an altitude of 10,000 feet.

Intensive effort for the next year was applied to a design for production of the SCR-519 at the Western Electric plant in Hawthorne, Illinois. However, production work was discontinued in 1943 when the emphasis of the Air Corps changed to the bombing of land targets. The S-band SCR-519 radar with its lobe-switching steering system was not suitable for resolving a complex of ground targets. The computer of the SCR-519 was then adapted for use with an X-band radar designated AN/APQ-10. Ten of these were built by Bell Laboratories and delivered for evaluation in 1944.

This development work at the Whippany laboratory was closely coordinated during the summer of 1941 with a new radar group that was set up at the facility on Varick Street, in New York City, to work on intercept radar, as related in following sections. The experience obtained through the development of the SCR-519 system at Whippany and the cooperation between the Whippany group and the new Varick Street organization on the interim SCR-540 intercept radar explains to a large extent why preliminary designs for transmitters, receivers, antennas, and indicator units were available by the fall of 1941, when as explained later, formal authorization was received for a completely new series of airborne systems, coded SCR-520/517, for intercept and sea-search applications.

3.4.3 Early Intercept Radar: SCR-540

Work on intercept radar began in May 1941 when the U.S. Army Signal Corps brought a British aircraft interception (AI) radar, AI Mark IV to Bell Laboratories for examination and testing. With this set, British defensive night fighters were able to detect and intercept German bombers and thereby greatly restrict the German forays. The Signal Corps asked Bell Laboratories' assistance in improving this earliest airborne radar and in developing an American version.

At that period of radar development a number of technical groups at the Whippany laboratory were already concentrating their full effort on new or improved radar components, innovative circuits, higher power, and other aspects of radar, as described earlier. Accordingly, this additional effort on the British intercept set was assigned to the television transmission group in New York City, which was experienced in cathode-ray tubes, video circuits, synchronizers, and amplifiers needed in radar, but which had no previous experience in this type of system. Starting with one or two people to flight test and study the British AI Mark IV, this source of technical manpower was to be used for a good share of the development effort on airborne search and bombing radar covered in the following paragraphs. Other groups, mainly at the Whippany laboratory, guided this work and also subsequently developed the small, lighter-weight radars which were built in large quantities for carrier-based airplanes.

The British AI Mark IV radar was tested at Bell Laboratories and flight-tested at the Army's Aircraft Radio Laboratory at Wright Field, Dayton, Ohio. It operated at about 100 MHz, using triode oscillators with a Lecher-wire tuning system. The antenna system consisted of four Yagi antennas, two mounted on each wing tip of the airplane. It employed two cathode-ray displays using 3-inch tubes, one for giving information on the vertical angle to the target and the other for indicating the azimuth relative to the interceptor. The vertical-angle display used a vertical and the other a horizontal base line. The antennas were commutated sequentially by a motor-driven device which also switched the cathode-ray display so that reflections from the target generated suitable pips, the pip from one antenna being on one side of the base line and the one from its complementary antenna being on the other. Basically it was a pip-matching scheme in which, by turning the airplane, one matched the two complementary return pips (received by the antennas on the wing tips) and thereby directed the aircraft into a collision course with the target. The position of the pips along the base line indicated the range to the target, and the ground reflection could be used to measure fighter altitude. The switching commutator resembled an automobile distributor in form and principle. The model equipment had been built by Kolster-Brandeis in London and appeared to contain many modules which had been taken off that company's TV production line.

The new recruits from the TV group were able to raise the operating frequency of the Mark IV to around 195 MHz, almost double that of the original design, and to improve the generally unreliable commutating switch. The British antenna system was retained in order to achieve production in the shortest possible time, but nearly all subsequent airborne radars used microwave frequencies and parabolic antennas to achieve sharper beams giving an order-of-magnitude improvement in system resolution.

A flight-test model was constructed and in September 1941 was installed in an A-20 airplane at Mitchell Field, Long Island, New York. It was necessary to fly at maximum altitude in order to attain a reasonable range for closing on the target,[22] but many flights, especially those at night when the target plane was not visible, proved the effectiveness of this relatively

---

[22] A basic fault of the Mark IV system was that there were strong ground reflections which could obliterate the target reflection if the range to the latter exceeded the fighter's elevation.

simple radar. The flight tests were completed on December 5, 1941, just before the attack on Pearl Harbor. The design, designated SCR-540, was quickly put into production at Western Electric. Several hundred were used in the Pacific and Mediterranean theaters during the early part of the war, as well as for training purposes later.

3.4.4 SCR-520 and SCR-517 Intercept and Sea Search Radars

Even before the flight tests of the British AI Mark IV in the United States and the design of the SCR-540 in mid-1941, steps had been taken to develop the more sophisticated SCR-520 radar for the new U.S. Army Air Corps "Black Widow" fighter. Operating at S band, this radar had a parabolic antenna that rapidly scanned mechanically in azimuth with a slow vertical scan. Position of the target with this radar was provided by a rectangular B-scope in which azimuth angle was the abscissa and range the ordinate. The target pip on the scope was then determined with reference to the azimuth center cross hair and an adjustable horizontal range marker. In addition a C-scope, in which elevation is displayed against azimuth, permitted the elevation of the gated range target to be determined. The technical experience gained from the development of previous radar systems made possible remarkably rapid development of the SCR-520. Although the project was not formally authorized until August 29, 1941, development flight tests were made later that year; and the first units of the SCR-520 were coming off the production line in May 1942. This equipment, shown in Fig. 2-50, used a number of newer components to improve performance, but it still weighed more than was desirable, except as an interim step, and did not have an adequate long range against bombers. However, it represented a large advance technically over the SCR-540 and proved to be an effective intercept radar for fighter aid.

Under contract to the Navy, an ASC system for sea search was under development using the S-band transmitter-receiver of the 520 radar and a modification of the 520 antenna. German submarines severely punished the United States merchant marine after Pearl Harbor, and by the spring of 1942, coastwise shipping losses were critical. Vital lend-lease shipments crossing the Atlantic, were under continual attack, and heavy losses were experienced. Such an alarming situation required urgent action. Earlier consideration of how best to aid in the response to the submarine menace had led to the design of an airborne radar antenna system rotating 360 degrees and coupled to a plan position indicator (PPI) that permitted a wide display of sea or land beneath the aircraft. Although models of the ASC radar were delivered to the Navy, the Army Air Corps took over the development for sea search and coded the unit 517-T4 (experimental, 5 models) and 517-B for production. Shortly thereafter a new modification was made to add beacon (airplane homing) circuits, and the modified system was coded 517-C. The SCR-517 system, compared with the

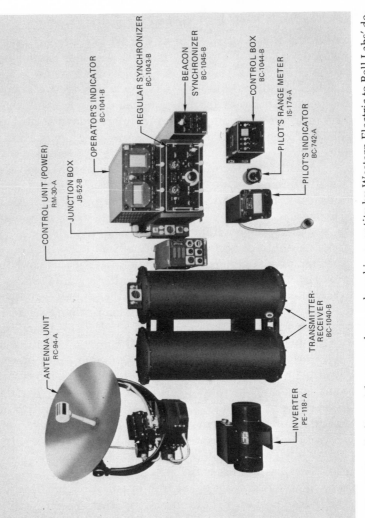

Fig. 2-50.   Earliest airborne radar produced in quantity by Western Electric to Bell Labs' design—the SCR-520-517.

SCR-520 intercept system, employed a relatively slow azimuth scan and employed a 7-inch PPI display.

The conversion of the early production SCR-520 radar components to the SCR-517-A for sea search was put on a crash basis to provide a new Air Force antisubmarine bomber command with very effective equipment to monitor and control large ocean areas. Bell Labs personnel were later gratified to hear that their radar equipment had played an important role in nearly eliminating the submarine menace along our coasts. For this important use, together with air intercept and some other services, over 2,000 of the SCR-520/517-B series of radars were produced and used effectively throughout World War II.

One of the other applications of the SCR-517-A system was for installation on Navy subchasers, where a B scan display (517-A and -C both had B scans only) was used in place of a PPI. But radar technology was developing rapidly. Even as the SCR-520/517 series was being designed and produced, better and more sophisticated systems were being devised. These are the subject of the next section.

3.4.5 SCR-720 and SCR-717: Small-Package Intercept and Sea-Search Radars

The 500 series of radars employed some large and relatively heavy units which had been developed on a crash basis to meet the paramount need for radars at the earliest possible time. The weight of these units limited the plane's performance, but it was mainly the size of the units (particularly the high-power RF units, modulators, and power supplies) that made it difficult to find any location for the equipment in an already crowded airplane. Thus, early in the war (while the 500 series was being produced), it was realized that the development of smaller and lighter component units was necessary, along with increased sophistication in circuitry and higher-power operation. The term *small-package* was used at that time to distinguish the desired units from the large-package units then available.

In July 1942, a Western Electric-Bell Labs letter noted that although there were orders for large-quantity production of SCR-517 and 520 radar equipment, there also were development contracts for small-package AI-10 and aircraft-to-surface-vessel (ASV-10) radars and the probability was that the large-package contracts would be renegotiated to cover the small-package equipments whenever the latter became available. It was evident that along with the imperative need for design and production of radars for the war then under way, a steady improvement program had to be carried on that would aid the users in their operations. (This continuing development also kept the United States ahead of its enemies in the ability to attack or bomb accurately without the likelihood of detection.) Accordingly, new small-package units with generally improved performance were developed from time to time. Originally these units, as well as the 520/517 series, operated in the S band. Hence, the new small units with improved performance were integrated into the 500 series whenever appropriate. Ultimately a complete small-package system became available and was coded in the 700 series. The gradual changeover is the reason why the records of that time do not indicate a particular period of changeover from the SCR-520/517 large-package series to the small-package SCR-720/717 series of advanced radars (Fig. 2-51). The continuing flow of new component units during 1942 and 1943 also made it possible to quickly engineer systems for special purposes, such as the AN/APQ radar bombsight and the AN/APG-1 gunlaying radar, discussed in later sections. By mid-1943 this development of new components, as well as the generation of innovative ideas, all of which were sought with wartime urgency, were at a peak and directed thinking to advanced systems using them.

It was universally agreed that still shorter wavelengths (and higher frequencies) would be necessary to achieve better resolution and even smaller packages. Their use later formed the basis for the development effort on one of the SCR-700 series of radars (SCR-717-T3), which operated in the X band (3 cm) instead of the S band (10 cm). The higher-frequency X-band components were integrated into earlier systems as they became available.[23] As an example of the overlapping progression of development, even as the S-band sets were being readied for production, work was authorized in early 1942 to put X-band (3-cm) components into one flyable model of the SCR-520-A radar. That model was coded SCR-520-T3 and delivered to Wright Field on January 26, 1943 for Army Air Force testing of the new components prior to production.

The SCR-720-T2 intercept radar, incorporating improved performance and the advanced features of the smaller, lighter, higher-power X-band transmitter, was produced in large quantities by Western Electric starting in June 1943. As an intercept radar, the parabolic antenna was scanned rapidly in azimuth and slowly in elevation. Improved B- and C-scope indicators were developed for angular and range target data. The SCR-720 basic system was made for both British and American use, and large numbers of 720-A, S-band sets were sent to the British. In the European theater the SCR-720 protected American and British lines, and the areas back of the lines, from night raids by German planes. It was the one night-fighter radar that was there in large numbers at the right time.

Like the 500 series, the 700 series was modified for various applications. The SCR-717-B antisubmarine search system, operating at S band, employed an antenna slewing through 360 degrees in azimuth with a slow

---

[23] This involved changing the transmitter-receiver modules and waveguide feeds in the original installations.

Fig. 2-51. SCR-720B airborne bombing radar.

vertical nod. An X-band version, the SCR-717-T3 search radar, with its narrower scanning beam, provided better resolution when operating over land. Some of the other applications of the 700 series components were those made in the AN/APQ-5 and AN/APQ-13, both X-band sets, which are covered in the following sections.

3.4.6 AN/APQ-5 Low-Altitude Bombsight

Some early work on the development of a bombing radar, the SCR-519, has been mentioned in a previous section (3.4.2), but the major Bell effort on bombsight systems was the outgrowth of the SCR-517 and 717 radars.

In July 1942, as the production SCR-517/520 radars were being modified for sea search, the possibility of using their basic system for bombsighting was being studied. The radars accurately gave the slant distance to the target, and this data, together with altitude above ground and flight speed, could be used to compute the ground range and bomb release point. These were not simple calculations, and since this was long before the days of miniature solid-state devices, the computer size and complexity threatened to become unreasonable. In this predicament the former "television people" proposed an ingenious idea in late 1942. If one bombs at low altitude, they pointed out, the ground range is almost the same as the slant range, in which case some computations become much simpler. Thus, a radar bombsight could be devised with operating characteristics similar to those of the Norden optical sight on which bomber crews had been trained.[24]

Low-altitude bombing (LAB) had the advantage of allowing bombing to be done at night or in overcast weather without much danger to the attacking bomber because it could not be seen by the enemy target. The Air Force wanted this system promptly because they had many trained bombardiers who could use it effectively against the enemy in the Pacific, whose "Tokyo Express" shipments to the expanding number of Japanese bases in the South Pacific needed our critical attention.

Some months and considerable cooperation among many technical groups were required to develop and construct a flight test model of what was then coded as the RC-217 auxiliary sighting unit. In the meantime small-package development had progressed rapidly and the components of the X-band and 700-series radars could be adopted for use with the bombsight.

A two-month test in Florida ending in April 1943 showed that the new equipment was as simple to operate as a Norden bombsight and produced high bombing accuracy. The Air Force requested the immediate outfitting

---

[24] While the concept was simple, many circuit developments were required to reduce it to practice. The U.S. patent covering the system, No. 2,733,436, was granted to S. Doba, Jr. and L. W. Morrison, Jr. It was filed March 21, 1944 and issued January 31, 1956.

Fig. 2-52.   AN/APQ-5 airborne low-altitude, radar bombsight (bombardier's position).

of a wing of B-24 bombers with this equipment.   Twenty preproduction models were quickly constructed for this purpose in the Bell Laboratories shops, but a further simplification was made combining three units into one control unit.   The equipment was now coded AN/APQ-5.   (See Fig. 2-52 for view of operator's controls.)

The wing of B-24s left Langley Field, Va., in great secrecy in late 1943 with a Bell Labs and a Western Electric engineer aboard, and flew to Guadalcanal, where they set up operations.   Within weeks the crews completed training and entered combat.   The Japanese were supplying their bases with convoys of ships escorted by destroyers and light cruisers, which usually passed through the Solomon Islands group at night.   The B-24 squadron with the AN/APQ-5 located several of these nocturnal parades and succeeded in destroying much shipping with very little damage to itself.   One report revealed that, during the four-month period from December 1943 to April 1944, this squadron sank 47 percent of the total tonnage destroyed by its Bomber Command and in doing so utilized only 1/5 of the planes, bombs, and personnel employed by that command in attacks against enemy shipping.   A heavily censored report of these operations was sent on January 12, 1944, in a congratulatory telegram by

General H. H. Arnold, Chief of Staff for the Air Force, to O. E. Buckley, President of Bell Labs:

> Directly as a result of the outstanding contribution made by your organization in the development of special electronic equipment and in the making of preproduction models thereof it has been possible for the Army Air Forces to take the offensive with telling effect against Japanese shipping in the South and Southwest Pacific areas at a much earlier date than would otherwise have been possible and under conditions which normally would have made such operations impossible.
>
> It is my great pleasure in behalf of the Army Air Forces to express our appreciation for this contribution and to congratulate you and your people on their achievement.[25]

A number of published articles described in detail the successful exploits again accomplished by cooperation.[26] Over 4,000 units of the AN/APQ-5 were produced.

3.4.7 AN/APQ-13 High-Altitude Radar Bombsight

Another application of the 700 series radar components was a source of inputs to systems used for high-altitude bombing. Two of these manufactured by Western Electric were the AN/APQ-13 and AN/APQ-7. Since these two systems differed rather markedly, they are described separately.

Bell Laboratories was the prime contractor for the AN/APQ-13, which was to be based on the SCR-717 X-band radar used in combination with the H2X bombing unit and computer being developed by the Radiation Laboratory. The need for it, and many of its development problems, arose from the introduction of the B-29 bomber. A crash program was set up by the Army Air Forces in February 1943 under a directive from General Arnold to take whatever necessary action to commit the B-29 airplane to combat without delay. Arnold pointed out that production experts had worked out a schedule which promised to deliver 150 B-29s during 1943. At this critical stage of the B-29 program, evidence was accumulating from the European theater that poor visibility made radar bombsight equipment a necessity, and it was anticipated that weather conditions would make all-visual bombing even more difficult over Japan. The decision was clear that the B-29s must be equipped with radar, particularly radar suitable for search and homing as well as high-altitude bombing. The AN/APQ-13 development grew out of this urgent requirement.

The technical and development problems for a system operating in a B-29 were many. The equipment was required to function properly at

---

[25] J. W. Rieke, "Low-Altitude Radar Bombsight," *Bell Laboratories Record* 25 (January 1947), p. 16.

[26] "Low Altitude, High Precision," *Radar Magazine* (April 1944), p. 17; and "Lab vs. Jap Shipping," (November 1944), p. 3.

altitudes to 30,000 feet, far above that of previous planes. Not only did this higher-altitude requirement mean increased problems due to voltage breakdown and corona, but it also meant operation at still colder temperatures ($-50°$C). Accurate ranging up to 300 miles (rather than about 100 miles) was now to be required because of the higher altitude. Also, more detail with more uniform illumination was desired in the scope presentation of the ground/sea area below the plane. Finally, scope presentation fixed with respect to the ground was desired so that yawing of the airplane would not blur the detailed presentation.

Development of the AN/APQ-13 radar system was begun in July 1943 with the imperative objective of matching the B-29 airplane schedule, which called for production by the end of the year. Such a schedule for the AN/APQ-13 could be contemplated only because the project came at a time when X-band radar components light enough and compact enough for airborne use and giving better target resolution were being developed at Bell Labs. Moreover, the Radiation Laboratory at M.I.T. was in the process of developing a radar bombing system known as H2X, which was expected to be put into production in the summer of 1943.

A tentative technical outline of the proposed system was issued in mid-August 1943. In September, an S-band SCR-717-B system was obtained from Western Electric, and an H2X range unit from the Radiation Laboratory. These units were modified to provide a laboratory model of the AN/APQ-13 operating at X band. New X-band RF components with an associated hard-tube modulator had been under development for another system and were immediately adapted for the AN/APQ-13.

In adapting the H2X range unit, schedules limited the modifications to those necessary for Western Electric manufacture and for the severe environmental conditions resulting from altitudes of 30,000 feet. The antenna design adapted from the H2X was previously used only at much lower altitudes and required substantial redesign for use in the B-29 at the high altitude. It was also necessary to develop several refinements, such as attitude stabilization of the PPI display and widening of the receiver bandwidth. These refinements in turn necessitated an extensive redesign of the indicators.

Three preproduction systems were made by the Bell Labs model shop and delivered by the end of October 1943. The last of the 35 preproduction systems was completed by the end of December 1943. The first two AN/APQ-13 production systems were shipped on January 31, 1944; and when the first B-29s took off for the CBI (China, Burma, India) theater in March 1944, every plane was equipped with the AN/APQ-13. By V-J Day in 1945, Western Electric had shipped 4,106 APQ-13 systems and 3,796 APQ-13A systems, the latter involving only simple modifications in the connecting interfaces. The locations of the components of the AN/APQ-13 in a B-29 bomber are shown in Fig. 2-53.

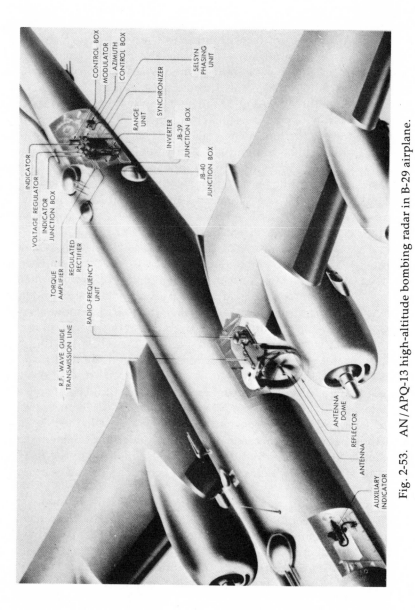

Fig. 2-53.   AN/APQ-13 high-altitude bombing radar in B-29 airplane.

The first strike of the 58th Wing, operating from the CBI theater, occurred on June 15, 1944. The first strike from the Marianas, by the 73rd Wing, occurred on, November 24, 1944. By V-J Day three more wings, the 313th, 314th, and 315th, the latter equipped with the higher-resolution APQ-7 (discussed in the next section), were in operation with a total of almost 1,000 B-29's. With the arrival of the 315th Wing on Guam in June 1945, the APQ-13 and APQ-7 stories coalesced, as far as the attack on Japan is concerned.

Some sense of the significance of Bell Labs' contribution in this area seems in order. No doubt there will never be complete agreement on the part played in the Japanese surrender by the B-29 attacks prior to the atom bomb. But that it was not small is evidenced by a statement made by Prince Konoye, who had been premier of Japan until mid-October 1941: "Fundamentally the thing that brought about the determination to make peace was the prolonged bombing by the B-29s." Radar bombing equipment was essential in two types of operation: (1) night incendiary area bombing, and (2) mine laying. The heavily destructive night incendiary attacks were almost totally radar-directed, but the less well-known mining operations were perhaps the finest technical accomplishment of the APQ-13. They warranted a message of congratulations from Admiral Chester W. Nimitz to the XXI Bomber Command about the "phenomenal success" of the tactics.

One important aspect of the APQ-13/APQ-7 program closely resembled Bell System peacetime development procedure. This was the participation of technical people from Bell Labs in the field under real-life operating conditions. Almost from the beginning of large-scale B-29 operations from the Marianas, this participation provided direct information on problems in equipment design. Moreover, the information flow from the designer to the user ensured that the latter was cognizant of design intent and system capabilities.

The relatively primitive nature of the original impact-predicting radar bombsight for the APQ-13, taken over from the H2X system, was recognized, and limitations in its accuracy were to be expected. Thus, the development of an improved bombing computer could be anticipated. Development of this device, originally coded the MX-344 and later the APA-44 ground position indicator, was begun at Bell Labs in August 1944. Among the improvements provided was the capability for accommodating offset between the target and some favorable radar sighting point. Other features incorporated in the design deserve mention. The first was that a large number of precision potentiometers were designed for quantity production. The second was that complicated gear systems were designed to properly relate the electrical quantities in performing the computing function and thereby minimize the skill required of the radar operator. At that time, a high-level War Department committee, called the Stratton

Committee, was set up to review the possibilities of high-accuracy, high-altitude bombing systems. It was decided that production should be based upon the use of an ac-type of analog computer[27] rather than the dc-type computer used on the H2X. The dc amplifiers required manual rebalancing at about 30-minute intervals. While the process could have been made automatic, as it was later done in ground systems, the weight and volume would have been increased for a computer already substantially heavier than the ac computing system. The use of ac computing systems for the first time in a bombing system provided significant advantages in stability of calibration. However, new filters and amplifiers had to be developed.

The schedule for the APA-44 was extraordinarily short. Manufacturing information was given to Western Electric on December 1, 1944, four months after work on the project was initiated. The first laboratory flight model was completed in mid-February 1945; the first flight tests, which led to the inclusion of a few minor improvements in the production models, were made on March 17, 1945. A preproduction lot of 50 APA-44's was made between mid-April and mid-June 1945. The first production equipment was delivered April 30, 1945; 503 systems were manufactured by the cessation of hostilities.

In summary, then, the outstanding feature of the APQ-13 development program was the necessity of assembling a number of developed but largely untried components that had to be fitted into an aircraft still under development. No time was allowed for mistakes. Not only did the production schedule keep pace with that of the B-29, but crews were trained and an operational system was tested in the field. As a refinement late in the production phase, a radically improved radar bombsight computer based on newly conceived principles, the APA-44, was developed and put into production.

3.4.8 AN/APQ-7 High-Resolution Bombing Radar

As mentioned previously, an X-band radar of the 700 series was also a source of input for the very-high-resolution AN/APQ-7 bombing radar, shown installed in Fig. 2-54. The latter's resolution, greatly improved in comparison with that of the APQ-13, was achieved by the use of an ingenious but complicated antenna system devised by the Radiation Laboratory. The system later used the AN/APA-44 computer.

Improved resolution became practical as higher-power transmitters and more sensitive receivers were adopted, thus making it possible to see small targets at long ranges and also to differentiate them from larger targets nearby.

The AN/APQ-7 was developed to provide the bombing precision needed to home in on a munitions factory or an oil tank surrounded by

---

[27] Early work on the ac computer was done by the Radiation Laboratory.

Fig. 2-54.   AN/APQ-7 high-resolution bombing radar.

nonmilitary construction—in Tokyo, for example.   This meant not only short wavelength (such as 3 cm, in the X band) but a very-large-aperture antenna in azimuth.   Compared with the parabolic dish antennas provided with all except the earliest airplane radars, the one used with the AN/APQ-7 was unique in concept.   The new antenna, devised by the Radiation Laboratory for express use with a bombing radar, was given the name "Eagle" to symbolize its detailed view from on high and the capability it provided for striking a particular small target once it had been identified.

The Eagle antenna in final design was essentially an adjustable waveguide 16½ feet long installed along the plane's wingspread, with 250 dipoles spaced at one-half wavelength intervals.   The dipoles were energized by coupling probes extending into the variable waveguide, each of which had to be separately adjusted during production.   Scanning was accomplished by varying the width of the waveguide along its entire length by means of a push-rod assembly that maintained precise parallelism of waveguide sidewalls throughout its length as the line was adjusted.   It fell to Bell Labs to engineer and design this tricky device into a usable and trouble-free entity for Western Electric production and aircraft tactical use.   The various manufacturing tolerances were in thousandths of an inch along the 16½ foot length.   It required the selection of the highest-grade tool manufacturer for its production, and Western Electric's best talent to set up the electrical production and inspection tests.   Some idea of the precision required during the construction and adjustment of the device was suggested by one of the participating engineers:

> In order to get this long waveguide antenna straight enough to meet the electrical requirements, it was necessary to hire men who had spent years sighting through and tweaking gun barrels straight, to do the same thing on our antennas.

The antennas were carefully mounted in their own wing-like enclosure and suspended under the fuselage of the plane.

The results were worth the great effort. The beamwidth (to half-power points) was reduced to 0.4 degree in azimuth as compared to 3.0 degrees for the standard AN/APQ-13 radar with its 29-inch-aperture parabolic antenna, at the same 3-cm transmitting wavelength. The improvement can be seen by comparing the resolution obtained with the AN/APQ-13, shown in Fig. 2-55a, with that obtained with the Eagle and shown in Fig. 2-55b.

A bombardier could now select his relatively small target from its surroundings. However, he still needed a precise computer to give him bombing accuracy comparable to the precision provided by the ingenious antenna and radar system. As indicated above, the H2X bombing system with its computer lacked sufficient accuracy to fully capitalize on the improved radar resolution. The development at Bell Labs of the AN/APA-44 improved bombing computer that was to replace the H2X was not at a stage where it would be available for use with the initial quantity of AN/APQ-7 radars. So again, as in the case of the APQ-5 (Section 3.4.6 above), the need was met with an interim bombing system that simplified computations with only slight loss of accuracy. This system was incorporated into two development models by May 1944, which made it possible for the Army Air Force to flight-test them in Florida. The tests proved so successful that added pressure was applied to Western Electric for an accelerated production program. Forty preproduction AN/APQ-7 sets were produced by Bell Labs by September 1944 to allow the earliest possible use in the China, Burma, India, and Japanese theaters, as mentioned in the preceding section on the APQ-13 equipment. Western Electric produced 344 more AN/APQ-7 systems by the end of 1944 and continued to make them (1,366 systems in all) until late 1945, when the new high-precision computer, the AN/APA-44, became available just before V-J Day.

3.4.9 AN/APG-1 Gun Director Radar

The account of the efforts by Bell Labs and Western Electric to aid in the prosecution of the war would not be complete without mentioning the AN/APG-1 airborne radar, although it did not see combat service. This radar required a large development effort but was produced in relatively small quantity.

The SCR-720 series was developed as night-fighter radar that would bring the pursuing plane so close to the enemy bomber that even on the

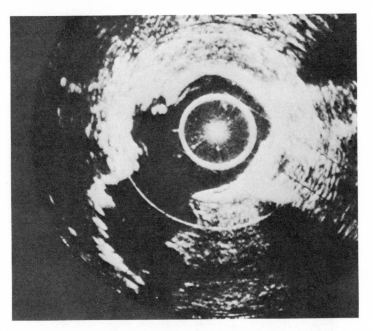

(a)

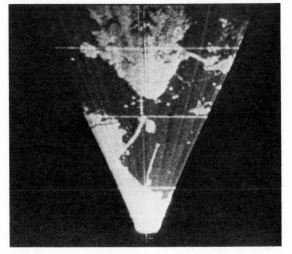

(b)

Fig. 2-55. Two radar scope displays showing difference in quality of resolution. (a) Resolution obtained with the AN/APQ-13 radar (3-degree beamwidth). (b) Improved resolution obtained with the AN/APQ-7 radar using the Eagle antenna (0.4-degree beamwidth) at same radio wavelength. (From *Radar Magazine* 1945, No. 10, p. 28.)

Fig. 2-56.   AN/APG-1 airborne gun-director radar.

darkest night the night-fighter pilot could see the bomber and attack it. However, if the enemy developed a good tail gun radar, it would be possible for the enemy to fire on and possibly destroy the SCR-720-equipped plane before it closed in. The AN/APG-1 (Fig. 2-56) used major components of the Western Electric SCR-720 system, together with the antenna, the handsight, the gyroscope, and a control unit from a General Electric system. Considerable additional development and design work then produced a radar system which, in addition to being able to locate an enemy bomber at a distance of about 10 miles, also incorporated an automatic airborne gun director that provided continuous range, azimuth, and elevation information on the target airplane. With this director, the night fighter was able to make a completely automatically controlled attack, beginning at the extreme range of his guns and continuing while it was at a safe distance from the tail gunner, rather than attacking only at point-blank range with the SCR-720 under visual firing control.

In Florida the Air Force spent much time testing this gunlaying radar system mounted in a P-61 fighter plane. Hits were scored in 40 percent of the rounds fired. This was stated to be an improvement of more than 1,000 percent over the best scores of a skilled manual gunner at the same ranges.

The AN/APG-1 was developed in 1943 and early 1944, and the total production of 200 units was completed in 1944. Since the Axis powers did not produce a good tail gun radar during the war, the SCR-720's did not become obsolete. In fact there was no pressing need for the APG-1. However, it was very essential insurance and pointed the way to the intercept radars of the postwar era.

3.4.10 AN/APS-4 Radar for Carrier-Based Airplanes

One of the systems different from those described so far was the AN/APS-4 radar (originally called the "ASH") for Navy carrier-based airplanes.

In April 1942, a Navy commander and two members of the Bell Labs technical staff discussed the need for a lightweight radar for carrier-based airplanes. By June, the design objectives had been established. The system was to combine into one radar the search and homing functions of the SCR-517/717 and the airplane intercept functions of the SCR-520/720. The new radar had to have almost the same operational figures of merit as the SCR-717 and SCR-720, but in addition to combining the two functions it had a total weight objective of 135 pounds. Since each SCR-717 or 720 weighed about 450 pounds, reduction in weight and size was of primary importance. And since space for radar in the small high-performance carrier-based airplane was extremely limited, it was decided to include as much as possible of the radar system in a bomblike enclosure under the airplane wing. This assembly had the advantages of easier servicing and installation, but it limited the antenna size and thereby, to some extent, the radar resolution. In addition, the aerodynamic drag on the airplane was affected. The final design employed a radome about 1½ feet in diameter and 5 feet long, shown in Fig. 2-57, to enclose everything except the operator's scope and control unit and some cabling.

Meeting the low-weight requirements while still maintaining high performance required a design attack on every unit and component. X-band frequency was essential to minimize the antenna size and component weights. Even the IF amplifier, which provided most of the receiver amplification, was completely redesigned to reduce its size and weight (from 32 to 10.5 ounces) and still maintain its full gain and improved bandwidth characteristics.

By March 1943, the first laboratory model was ready for tests by the Navy. It was estimated at that time that the first production system would weigh about 175 pounds—a great reduction from the weight of the 700

Fig. 2-57.   AN/APS-4 radar for carrier-based airplanes (housed in cylinder attached to underside of wing).

series but still 40 pounds over the objective.   The Navy was highly pleased by the performance and encouraged Bell Labs to greater speed.   In view of the urgency, the first production design was ready in July 1943.

As the first laboratory model was beginning to take shape in February 1943, Bell Labs started sending information to Western Electric on those items that seemed reasonably firm in design at that time and supplemented or modified that information in subsequent months.   This was a risky process for production people since there were inevitable changes in design resulting from continuing testing of the model, which affected plans for manufacture.   Another aid to speedy production of the first equipment was the Navy's request that design refinements be introduced while planning and production were proceeding.   Thus many small changes were introduced as the first production equipment was tested by both Bell Labs and the Navy.   A first pilot run of production equipment, totaling 39 systems, was completed in December 1943.   Navy tests of these units and continuing engineering made it possible to establish a design for full-scale production which included plans for further weight reduction. It is interesting to note that during this critical period in which performance was being balanced against weight and size, the Navy accepted the production AN/APS-4 system weighing 181 pounds because it provided performance considerably better than that prescribed by the initial requirements.   Production designs were continually improved as a result of combat use, which eventually reduced the weight of the system to about the desired 135 pounds while increasing operating reliability without loss in performance.

The Western Electric Hawthorne plant in 1944 produced some 6,686 AN/APS-4 systems in record time by increasing production facilities and subcontracting. Production continued until V-J Day, the 1945 total then being 8,398. As one Navy pilot pointed out, these systems were used throughout the Pacific area to

> ...perform the many jobs we [carrier-based pilots] are called upon to do. The jobs not only include searching out Japanese targets (ships as well as island installations), navigating in strange territory and homing to their airplane carrier, but also helping the pilots fly in, over, and around tropical rain squalls, and pointing out targets through overcast.

3.4.11 SWOD — the "Bat"

The increasing sophistication of airborne radars during the war years made it possible for Bell Labs to develop in 1943 a novel bomb termed Special Weapons Ordnance Device (SWOD) by the Navy. This was a glide bomb, not self-propelled, which contained a radar and associated control circuits to keep the bomb homed-in on a selected target until impact. This bomb was nicknamed the "Bat" because, like that mammal, it was able to guide itself, even in darkness or overcast, toward an enemy ship by means of its wings and control surfaces. It was launched from under the wing of its host airplane. The nose of the device contained an antenna and radar equipment, which, while the missile was attached to its launching plane, fed information to a cross-pointer meter and range indicator in the plane. When an enemy ship had been selected as the target, the Bat's radar system could be locked onto the target echo signal for homing and the missile could then be launched while the plane was still at a safe distance outside the range of the vessel's guns. The circuits for this device were similar to the homing systems of other airborne radars, but utilized many components especially designed to meet the particular electrical and physical requirements of this unit. Three hundred Bat devices were produced by Western Electric in 1944 and 2,800 in 1945, together with 82 control systems for the launching planes. Three Navy patrol squadrons equipped with the Bat systems saw successful action in the Pacific before the war ended.

IV. MAGNETRON RESEARCH AND DEVELOPMENT

No other technological advance was integrated into Allied military operations more thoroughly than radar. What transformed this concept from a hopeful idea to an operational tool was the British development of the microwave magnetron. It was the refinement, adaptation, and massive production of this device by United States governmental and industrial laboratories and manufacturers, under the constant spur of systems requirements, that brought about the amazing proliferation of radar applications.[28] Bell Laboratories and Western Electric played a major part in this effort from the beginning.[29] Because of the extreme urgency of military demands and the constant interchange of information with other laboratories, the normally separate activities of research, development, and large-scale production became thoroughly intermixed, each reacting continually on the other. The production of more than 100,000 magnetrons in Western Electric factories indicates how successful such a sustained group effort could be.

4.1 The British Breakthrough

In September 1940, when early warning radar was making its first decisive contribution in the Battle of Britain, a British mission led by Henry Tizard arrived in Washington, D.C. Its purpose was the exchange of scientific and technical information. As a sequel, on October 6 at the Bell Labs radio laboratory in Whippany, New Jersey, a British 10-cm magnetron invented by J. T. Randall and H. A. H. Boot, and brought by the Tizard mission, was tested for the first time in the United States. Its peak power output when operated at 10 kV with 1-microsecond pulses and a 1,000-cycle/second repetition rate was estimated to be about 10 kW. This had to be compared with the best results of about 2 kW at 40 cm which Whippany was getting from triode pairs being used in a fire control radar development. Since the prospect for appreciably improving the triodes was dubious, whereas the potentialities of the magnetron were largely unexplored, it was clear that there had been a major breakthrough. Unlike conventional vacuum tubes with their components exposed in a glass envelope, the new tube was an inscrutable copper cylinder with cathode leads and a coaxial line emerging from it. Since it was not expendable, X-ray photographs were used to explore the inside. With these photographs and a drawing of a different model, it was successfully reproduced and operated by early November 1940.

Considerable work had been done on magnetrons between the wars. The term broadly refers to any device with a cylindrical, but not necessarily circular, cathode and anode (which may consist of several segments) placed in a uniform magnetic field parallel to the cylinder generators. The electrons execute motions of considerable complexity in the crossed electric and magnetic fields. When coupled to resonant circuits, such arrangements can generate RF power in a variety of ways. In 1935 it was shown that one possible mode had the electrons circulating about the

---

[28] G. B. Collins (ed.), *Microwave Magnetrons,* M.I.T. Radiation Laboratory Series, vol. 6 (New York: McGraw-Hill, 1948). Discusses most of what was known about magnetrons until January 1946.

[29] Their contribution is set forth in J. B. Fisk, H. D. Hagstrum, and P. L. Hartman, "The Magnetron as a Generator of Centimeter Waves," *The Bell System Technical J.* 25 (April 1946), pp. 167–348, which was reprinted in *Radar Systems and Components,* pp. 56–237.

cathode so that on the average they kept in step with a rotating component of RF field on a multisegment anode connected to coupled resonators.

The British used this configuration in the following manner. In a copper block a central hole is surrounded by a set of equally spaced holes, and each of the latter is joined to the former by a radial slot. The slot, largely capacitive, and the hole, largely inductive, form a quarter-wave line with a voltage maximum at the central end of the slot. Magnetic flux linkage between neighboring holes couples the resonators together. The entire block is now a multisegment anode. The cathode, rather than being a simple filament, is an oxide-coated cylinder of appreciable size. Here necessity and good fortune met. The British had discovered empirically the factor which, above all others, made their magnetron a success. This was that, for the tube to operate efficiently, the cathode had an optimum dimension, relatively large; if this had not been the case, it would have been impossible to draw the requisite high currents. The RF power was taken out on a coaxial line fed by a loop in one of the holes, and the cathode was mounted on radial leads. Fragile glass and glass-to-metal seals supported these elements. In the 1940 form, these seals were distressingly breakable, dire need having left no time for mechanical refinement.

4.2 The Bell Labs and Western Electric Contribution

The first objectives of this urgent effort were to see whether a 40-cm magnetron could be built which would replace the inadequate triodes, and to get as much experience as possible with the 10-cm version. This involved observing the operating characteristics, changing the number of resonators, experimenting with the hole and slot dimensions, and varying the cathode size. The first project, carried out essentially by trial and error, resulted in a series of tubes (700 A-D) that gave 40-kW peak output power at an overall efficiency of 30 to 40 percent. These tubes were structurally very much like the 10-cm prototype but were modified to keep the weight down. Many initial production difficulties arose in outgassing the copper block, which weighed nearly 12 pounds, and the cathode with its 1.5-square-inch surface. By later standards, these tubes were rather primitive, but they were so far in advance of the triodes that they served immediate systems needs.

Throughout the war, magnetrons in the 20- to 40-cm range were designed and built only by Bell Laboratories and Western Electric. Figure 2-58(a) shows one of the later and most refined tubes, and Fig. 2-58(b) is a section of the same tube.

Field experience and laboratory experiment had early uncovered the distressing fact that the 10-cm tube, when pushed harder than normally, would skip abruptly to another frequency. A remarkable solution to this problem, devised in 1941 by J. T. Randall and J. Sayers of the University of Birmingham, had far-reaching consequences, some of which were not

(a)

(b)

Fig. 2-58. 5J26 tunable magnetron (600 kW, 1,220–1,350 MHz).
(a) Complete unit. (b) Sectional view.

foreseen.   They tied the alternate anode segments together with short
pieces of wire straps at each end of the block.   It was already known that
the efficient mode of operation was that in which alternate anode segments
were 180 degrees out of phase (π-mode), that the links would clearly not
upset this (except to add capacitance and increase the wavelengths), and
that any other mode would in some way be disturbed.   The effect of this
"strapping" was to widen the range of normal operation and to increase
its efficiency everywhere, which was a bonus.   The process of strapping
opened the way for real progress at 10 cm.   Strapping became standard

on all 10-cm tubes and on the later 3-cm tubes and was incorporated into improved long-wavelength tubes. As more experience was gathered, the wires were replaced by two concentric rings at each end; these were usually made of flat copper strips with feet brazed to alternate segments of the anode.

The reasons for the success of strapping began to emerge as more cold test data were taken on the resonant properties of the anode block and as some understanding of the electronic properties of the space charge cloud was gained. The primary function of strapping is to increase the mode separation between the π-mode and all the unwanted modes. Strapping does this by increasing the coupling between the resonators. When this was understood, the size of the straps could be used as a flexible tool for varying this coupling. The increase in observed efficiency was a happy accident. As a result of later, extensive studies on the properties of output circuits, it became possible to relate systematically the efficiency of RF power generation to the impedance seen at the slot openings. The effect of strapping, leaving the rest of the RF circuit untouched, was to lower this impedance, and this, for the original 10-cm tube, was in the direction of improving its efficiency.

With strapping, several tubes were now produced in the 10-cm band with routine outputs of 150 kW peak. These all saw extensive use and were produced in large quantities. The finished tubes came with a heavy glass boot over the cathode leads and had cooling fins brazed to the anode shell. As was the rule for all military applications, all magnetrons had to meet rigid specifications to ensure ruggedness and serviceability. At about this time, Western Electric had worked out a very successful method for anode fabrication. All the holes in the anode block were first drilled, and then a broach with radial spines was pulled through the center hole to cut all the slots simultaneously.

It is perhaps pertinent at this point to mention some of the general ideas about magnetron operation emerging at this time. One of the most useful of these was scaling. This rests simply upon the observation that if Maxwell's equations and the dynamic equations for the electrons are written down, it can be seen that their joint solutions will not be changed if all the variables in the problem—voltages, currents, magnetic fields, lengths, and frequencies—are mutually adjusted in the proper way. Practically, this means that if we have information about a magnetron at one wavelength, we can predict the behavior of a suitably scaled version at another wavelength. This principle was experimentally verified and became a key tool in designing for new wavelengths.

A rigorous theory of magnetron operation was then far too difficult to obtain. The intuitive concept that the electrons move around the cathode at an average velocity equal to that of a rotating RF field was, however, substantially confirmed by some British calculations. These showed that in a system of axes rotating with the RF electric field, the electrons are phase-focused into spokes of charge. These spokes are at rest in this system. The individual electrons execute more or less cycloidal paths within the spokes and gradually lose energy to the RF field as they go out to the anode. Some electrons whose initial phase is adverse gain energy and return to the cathode. (This process of back bombardment was a well-established experimental fact.) This picture makes it clear why the cathode can turn out to be so large: it is not the size of the cathode that counts, but largely its separation from the anode. There is, in fact, no reason why one should not have a magnetron with a linear cathode and anode. As will be seen later, this is the direction in which development moved empirically as shorter wavelengths made bigger relative cathode sizes important; in other words, the number of resonators was steadily increased.

Another area upon which light was being shed was that of getting the power out of the tube and of presenting the electron stream with the proper impedance. Also, at this point, the armed services were beginning to require a specified stability in frequency against definite changes in external load. The techniques of microwave measurement had become sufficiently routine to enable these questions to be examined on cold magnetron models. In the earliest tubes, all impedance matching had to be done outside the tube with consequent severe breakdown problems. It became necessary at higher power levels to do this within the vacuum. Thus, by hot measurements, one could determine what impedance the tube liked to see and then, by cold test, one could design an internal transformer to produce this, given a matched external line. To avoid current-carrying junctions between the output and the external line, coaxial choke joints were developed which simulated short circuits without contact. These features were incorporated with good results in a high-power 10-cm tube (720A-E), which gave 1,000-kW peak output, and also were incorporated in later tubes (5J23 and subsequent tubes) at longer wavelengths.

The progress at 10-cm now whetted the military appetite for the development of airborne radar systems, which called for smaller antennas and shorter wavelengths. The selected band was centered at 3.2 cm. Some work had already been done, both at Bell Laboratories and at the M.I.T. Radiation Laboratory, on magnetrons in this range, and an M.I.T. tube, the 2J21, had been put into production. It had a peak output of 15 kW. The rather inadequate performance of this tube stemmed mainly from the fact that it had been designed before the scaling principle had been fully established. When an 8-resonator 10-cm tube was scaled directly to 3 cm, a much more efficient tube resulted. However, the demands on the cathode were now very severe. By moving up to 12 resonators and strapping heavily to restore the separation of the modes, the problem became difficult rather than impossible to solve. The situation was sufficiently hopeful for a 3-cm program (725A) to be started with the support of resident visitors from M.I.T. and the Columbia University Radiation Laboratory. Because systems development with the 2J21 tube were already advanced, it was necessary that the new tube be a mechanical and electrical replacement for the old.

Improved techniques were not required for anode fabrication. By this time the anode was only 0.25 inch high, and the anode hole radius 0.102 inch. Anodes were now fabricated separately, carefully deburred, and examined before being brazed into a shell. The natural way to get power out of the tube should have been a waveguide output, since 3-cm external plumbing did not use coaxial line. The interchangeability requirement, however, precluded this. It was necessary to use a coaxial output fed by a loop over one of the holes, which was then matched into a small section of guide that was part of the tube. To obtain satisfactory impedance transformation was at first a very delicate problem, and the height of the loop over the block had to be held within ±0.001 inch. The severe demands on the cathode were met by a significant advance in its design. This was the use of fine nickel mesh welded to the nickel cathode sleeve; the mesh was then impregnated with the oxide coating. (The latter was then somewhat protected from back bombardment, and the mesh helped to dissipate the resultant heat.) In the 725A and its variants, as well as other 3-cm tubes, the heater was shut off after the tube started, since the necessary heat was supplied by back bombardment. The 725A produced 55 kW while meeting all the service requirements. It saw extensive combat use. Having been adapted also by the Raytheon Manufacturing Company for other methods of fabrication, its total production at Western Electric, Northern Electric, and Raytheon was over 300,000 units. A sectioned 725A is shown in Fig. 2-59.

The problem of making a magnetron tunable had arisen quite early. Such a tube promised great advantages, one of which was eliminating the need to stock a whole series of fixed-frequency tubes in a given band. Naturally, any method of making a given magnetron tunable still had to leave it interchangeable with its untuned predecessor. This problem was satisfactorily solved in the long-wavelength tubes. For example, in strapped tubes at such wavelength, it was possible to mount a "cookie-cutter" on a flexible diaphragm above the straps and to vary the separation between the cookie-cutter and the straps. This effectively changed the coupling produced by the straps and gave the required tuning range of a few percent. When the 725A became viable there was a demand for a tunable version. Tampering with the strap impedance was too finicky an operation at these wavelengths. A solution worked out at the Columbia Radiation Laboratory was adopted in the work on a tunable 725A tube, the 2J51. This involved using an array of pins mounted on a diaphragm; the pins could then be inserted into the resonator holes to a variable depth.

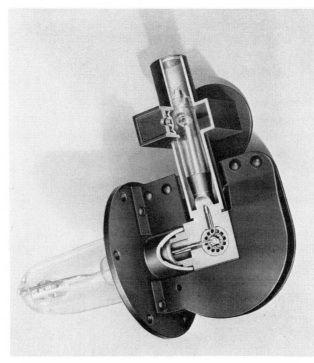

Fig. 2-59. 725A magnetron (55 kW, 9,375 MHz).

This gave rather smooth tuning over a ±7-percent range. The output circuit of the 725A was found to need relatively little adjustment to work over this range.

The 2J51 incorporated two new, associated features. It had an axially mounted cathode and its own magnets. The last feature is referred to as "packaging." The two ends of the tube now consisted of iron blocks of square cross-sections and two horseshoe magnets, suitably clad to prevent their being accidentally demagnetized, making contact with these blocks. The overall weight reduction was considerable. The technology of packaging the 2J51 was then used to produce packaged versions of the untuned 725A.

Progress in understanding the magnetron and in techniques of construction had now reached the point where it was always possible to visualize a much better tube than the one being developed. One of the few opportunities to develop a magnetron in a fairly uninhibited way came with the attempt to increase the power available at 3 cm. Two tubes, the 4J52 and 4J50, were envisaged: the first to operate at somewhat higher voltages than the 725A but to produce 100-kW peak output, the second to have the same structure but large magnets so that higher voltages could be used. About 250-kW peak output was expected. The project was again supported by resident collaborators who were from the M.I.T. Radiation Laboratory.

The number of oscillators was increased to 16, with some loss of mode separation, to ease the demands on the cathode. Also, a further advance in cathode design was of great significance. This entailed sintering fine nickel powder to the basic nickel sleeve to form a porous conducting matrix for holding the oxide coating. This cathode was remarkably effective, being able to operate satisfactorily with 5-microsecond pulses, which was a very severe test. It was supported axially by a heavy metal cone attached to a rugged glass sleeve and Kovar-to-glass seal.[30] Since this design was packaged, the structure had to be inserted through a hole in the pole piece. So that magnetic distortion would be avoided, the holes were partly restored by mounting annular rings of permendur, which is still magnetic at red heat, at each end of the cathode.

These were the first tubes built at Bell Laboratories with direct waveguide output. In these tubes a waveguide transition section was needed to transform from the resonant system to the standard 3-cm guide. This section could be brought down to the size of the tube by using a guide of H-shape cross section. The bar of the H was a slot cut in the anode block to the hole of one resonator. The posts of the H were formed by milling wider slots in the anode block, which was fabricated separately; the H was then formed when the pole pieces were put on at each end. The RF power found access to the external waveguide through a circular glass window in a Kovar cup isolated by choke joints. This whole section was designed for low reflection. The final tubes were very compact, rugged designs that easily met their performance goals. They remained in production well into the postwar period. Figures 2-60 and 2-61 show the 4J52 and 4J50 types.

Each time progress was made at one wavelength, the desirability of proceeding to a shorter wavelength was emphasized. The next step was to the band centered on 1.25 cm. Some exploratory work had been done at this wavelength in Bell Laboratories; but because of Bell Labs' commitment to the 3-cm development, the main responsibility for finding a viable 1-cm design was assigned to the Columbia Radiation Laboratory. The Columbia group found a very ingenious approach. After its feasibility had been demonstrated, the group joined with Bell Laboratories in its development. It was clear that making a strapped tube at 1-cm wavelength out of copper would be a very tricky undertaking, the size of the details and the mutual clearance having become so small. The Columbia Lab resolved this problem by finding a new resonant structure that eliminated strapping. This structure, known as the "rising sun," had simple wedge-shaped resonators, which were of two different, alternating

[30] Kovar is a registered trademark of Carpenter Technology Corp.

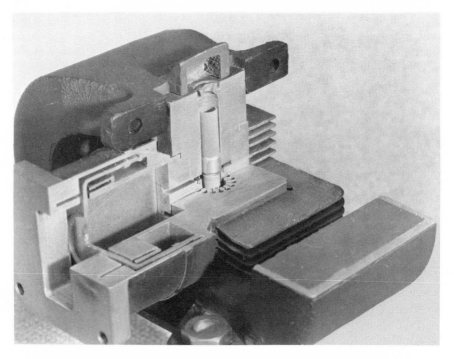

Fig. 2-60.   Sectional view of the 4J52 magnetron (100 kW, 9,375 MHz).

Fig. 2-61.   4J50 magnetron (280 kW, 9,375 MHz).

Fig. 2-62. Sectional view of the 3J21 magnetron (60 kW, 24,000 MHz).

lengths. The π-mode no longer had the lowest frequency but was situated in a large gap in the mode spectrum so that adequate mode separation was preserved. The version developed at Columbia had 18 resonators, this large number, as in the 3-cm development, being chosen to obtain as large a cathode as possible. There were some quirks associated with this structure. If one examined the RF electric field pattern in the anode-cathode region, one would see that it had a uniform tangential component. Such a field could interact strongly with the electron cloud at a certain magnetic field (essentially a cyclotron mode), and the normal operation of the tube would be badly affected. Fortunately, knowledge about the magnetron had now been advanced to the point where these facts could be understood and circumvented.

The cathode, which here had a diameter of only 0.096 inch, had to deliver about 50 amperes per square centimeter. The sintered cathode was again used, mounted axially for mechanical rigidity and precise assembly. Since there was no room for an adequate heater within the cathode, the latter was made of a solid nickel rod and heated from one end like a soldering iron. Such a small tube required that very close tolerances be maintained in fabricating the anode and the output circuit. Some of the sensitivity of the latter was decreased by incorporating what was essentially a stabilizing cavity in the waveguide output. The tube, designated

Fig. 2-63.   Anode structures of the principal magnetrons designed by Bell Laboratories at wavelengths from 40 to 1.25 cm.

as 3J21, was built in packaged form with magnets delivering 8,000 gauss and weighed $6\frac{1}{2}$ pounds in all.   A very satisfactory output peak of 60 kW was achieved.   A sectional view of the 3J21 is shown in Fig. 2-62.   Figure 2-63, which shows the anode structures of all the Bell Laboratories tubes from the original 40-cm tube down to the 1.25-cm, gives some idea of the range.

The foregoing account sketches the magnitude of the contribution to magnetron development and production made by Bell Laboratories and Western Electric.   They were the only producers responsible for pulsed tubes at all wavelengths from 40 cm to 1 cm, which came in all varieties, strapped and unstrapped, with tunable and fixed frequency, with coaxial and waveguide outputs, and packaged and otherwise.   In a situation where the primary objective was to assimilate new technical information, to use that in making a reliable manufacturable device in the minimum time, and to see it into production, their performance was outstanding. J. B. Fisk had the overall responsibility for the development of all types of magnetrons and was very directly involved with the day-to-day problems.   With skill and tact, he headed an unusually dedicated and cooperative team, each of whose members worked on a variety of tubes.   Three others in the group played major roles.   P. L. Hartman contributed greatly to the 40-cm and 10-cm tubes, H. D. Hagstrum to the 10-cm and 3-cm tubes, and A. T. Nordsieck to the 1-cm development.   Other vital contributors were V. L. Ronci and his associates, who were responsible for mechanical design and model building; L. A. Wooten and his group, who solved innumerable problems of cathode development; and P. P. Cioffi, who designed magnets for each of the tubes.

The multicavity magnetrons which have been described were remarkably successful devices.   But, as has been emphasized, they were produced to meet emergencies and restrictive service demands; as a result, many solutions to problems were compromises. In the postwar years, many of the resulting deficiencies became apparent in the face of new demands. In 1954, J. Feinstein and R. J. Collier introduced a major development in magnetron circuit design that greatly improved performance, frequency stability, and reliability. This is known as the coaxial cavity magnetron[31] or circular electric mode magnetron. The strapping feature of the old magnetrons was always an untidy scheme; it was rather irksome to build and to use it as a tuning element because of small clearances and because the presence of the straps gave rise to stray RF fields in the interaction space. To preserve the mode-separating function of the straps, the new scheme coupled the resonators tightly together at high-current rather than high-voltage points. Alternate resonators were coupled, by means of slots at the back, into a coaxial cavity surrounding the original anode block. The cavity was thus excited in the TE_{011} mode. Most of the stored energy of the tube now resided in this coaxial cavity. Frequency stabilization was greatly improved, and the tuning was very simply effected by changing the length of the cavity. The design thus represented a solid advance over the earlier forms in several ways with no attendant drawbacks. It has been implemented in a number of tubes used by the military services.

V. RADAR TEST EQUIPMENT

The radars of World War II were highly complex devices using precise components and circuitry based on new technology. There was little prior experience with this technology except in a few of the laboratories of the armed services, Bell Laboratories, and a small number of other organizations where limited work had been done in the microwave domain. A single radar might use as many as 50 to 250 vacuum tubes. Some handled very high transmitter power, others very low received RF inputs, and many operated at microwave frequencies far above the range normally used for radio communication. Radar designs and operation dealt with a wide variety of new technical fields, such as shaped pulses of microsecond duration, video data transmission, and computers of both the analog and digital type.

Unlike some electronic systems, the radar displays gave no inherent indication that warned the user of degraded performance. Therefore, it was obvious from the beginning that means had to be provided for testing radar operation and adjusting the equipment for optimum performance. This test gear had to meet many difficult requirements. It had to be usable by personnel with only a minimum of basic technical training and, in

[31] J. Feinstein and R. J. Collier, "The Circular Electric Mode Magnetron," in E. Okress (ed.), *Crossed-Field Microwave Devices*, 2 vols. (New York and London: Academic Press, 1961), vol. 2, pp. 123–134.

addition, had to provide accurate measurements over a range of environmental conditions covering extremes of temperature, humidity, and altitude. Often, it had to be small and lightweight and far more portable and rugged than normal commercial equipment.

It was evident that the provision of test gear would be a complex but highly necessary part of radar development. However, in the hectic days of 1940 and 1941 during the crash development of systems and their expedited production and field distribution, use got well ahead of the development of field-test equipment—even so far ahead of defining what was needed that many expedients were resorted to by the designers of early radar systems. Voltmeters, tube checkers, and portable oscilloscopes were available from prior communications experience and were furnished with the first systems. But radars performed many new functions and operated in new and much higher frequency bands for which nothing was available but unsuitable laboratory equipment. When commercial equipment was unavailable or could not be adapted to meet the testing requirements, the radar designers built equipment that would serve until standardized test gear could be produced.

The first radars were usually tuned for optimum performance by adjusting the transmitter and receiver to maximize the range of returning clutter or echoes from the surrounding landscape. This was not very satisfactory because the clutter varies with weather conditions. For a land-based radar, it was usually possible to find a hole in the ground clutter (a shadowed spot not illuminated by the transmitter) and erect on that spot a pole with a stable corner reflector to act as a reference target.

At sea this expedient could not be used. The sea clutter returning to a radar from various directions depends on the magnitude and direction of the wind, which are highly variable quantities. On a perfectly calm sea there is a residual clutter extending perhaps a thousand yards or so (more ahead and astern than abeam), which was correctly attributed to the outgoing pulse bouncing back and forth in the ship's rigging and superstructure until it died out. On such a calm day, a Western Electric field engineer at sea with one of the first Bell Labs-designed fire control radars made an interesting observation. He found that when the antenna was pointed in a particular direction, the clutter extended far beyond the normal range, and that this was true only when a particular deck hatch was open. The propped-up lid was reflecting the radar pulse "down the hatch," where it bounced around a large metal compartment feeding clutter back to the radar for a time corresponding to that of a range of many thousands of yards. It was probably the original echo box—an item later developed in small-size, high-Q form for the higher frequencies and widely used in testing radars.

Interesting as the early expedients were, they could not take the place of a well-designed series of equipment planned specifically for installing and maintaining radar systems. To meet this need, a group was formed under the direction of E. I. Green, and people with suitable qualifications were diverted from Bell System work to staff it. Their work was closely coordinated with that of groups in Bell Labs and the Radiation Laboratory that were designing radar systems in an effort to give the resulting test sets the widest possible application. The first Bell Labs designs were delivered from Western Electric production early in 1942, and more than a dozen of them were in production by the end of that year, mainly for application in L and S bands (100 to 3,000 MHz). Many more sets went into production in later years as the frequency range was extended and as radars became ever more complicated in their functions.

As the use of radar equipment expanded during the war, it became apparent that the large variety of required test gear would get out of hand unless it was minimized by designing radars to use, as far as practical, uniform measurement and adjustment procedures. The Bell Labs groups involved in radar and test set design, using systems engineering techniques, worked with many technical groups in the different military services in order to make each test set efficiently serve the maximum number of different radars. This coordination helped to make many of the later test sets usable on a number of radars.

In spite of this effort, the nature of radar required test sets serving special purposes, such as different signal generators for the L, S, X, and K bands, power meters for different frequency bands, frequency meters, range calibrators, phantom targets, echo boxes, oscillographs, dummy antennas, computer test sets, and standing wave detectors. Table 2-4 lists the sets designed and produced by Bell Labs and Western Electric through 1943, and some of the sets are illustrated in Fig. 2-64. Obviously, the histories of this large variety of equipment would be too long for presentation here. However, a few words concerning signal generators, a very basic category of radar test equipment, might exemplify the process of development that test sets went through as radars became more and more sophisticated during the war.

The signal generator of the IE30 test set, deliveries of which began in May 1942, produced pulsed RF signals in the 10-cm range using sine wave synchronization. A few months later the Army's IE57A (the Navy's LZ) test set was developed. It covered a broad frequency band of 20 percent in the vicinity of 10 cm and was designed to be triggered by the RF pulse from the radar instead of by a separate synchronizing connection. This set and a later, smaller version saw wide use with Army, Navy, and Marine Corps radars.

Delivery of another radar test set, the TS-35/AP, including a signal generator operating in the 3-cm band, began in the fall of 1943. It furnished either a train of pulses or a train of FM signals. It covered a 9-percent frequency band with no tuning adjustment except for the oscil-

Table 2-4.   Radar Test Equipment in Production or under
Development in 1943

Armed Service	Nomenclature	Type of Equipment
Already in Production in 1943		
Army	IE-30A	S-Band Radar Test Set
Army	BC-1077A	S-Band Pulsed Signal Generator
Navy	CW-60AAX	S-Band Pulsed Signal Generator
A/N	BC-1087X	Oscilloscope
Army	RC-124A	Test Antenna
Navy	CW-66ACX	Test Antenna
Army	BC-1167A	Video Probe Amplifier
Navy	CW-50ADB	Video Probe Amplifier
Army	I-203	S-Band Standard Power Meter
Navy	CW-60ABU	S-Band Standard Power Meter
Army	TS-6/AP	S-Band Frequency Meter
A/N	TS-89/AP	Video High Voltage Divider
Navy	LW	L-Band Radar Test Set
—	D-150337	Heterodyne Detector and Scope
—	D-150338	Pulsed Signal Generator and Scope
Production Started in 1943		
Army	BC-1277A	S-Band Signal Generator
Navy	CW-60ACA	S-Band Signal Generator
Army	BC-1287A	Oscilloscope
Navy	CW-60ACB	Oscilloscope
Army	RC-124A	Test Antenna
Navy	CW-60ACX	Test Antenna
Army	TS-19/APQ-5	Precision Range Calibrator for AN/APQ-5
Army	TS-5/AP	Range Calibrator for Search Radars
A/N	TS-34/AP	Oscilloscope
Army	TS-3/AP	S-Band Frequency and Power Measuring Set
Army	RF-4/AP	S-Band Wobble-Tuned Ring Box
A/N	CW-60ABM	S-Band Frequency Meter
A/N	TS-33/AP	X-Band Frequency Meter
A/N	TS-35/AP	X-Band Signal Generator
A/N	TS-36/AP	X-Band Power Meter
Navy	TS-45/APM-3	X-Band Radar Test Set
Navy	TS-45A/APM-3	X-Band Radar Test Set
Army	RF-3/AP	X-Band Wobble Tuned Ring Box

Table 2-4—*Continued*

Armed Service	Nomenclature	Type of Equipment
Under Development in 1943		
Army	TS-98/AP	Video Voltage Divider
A/N	TS-90/AP	Video Dummy Pulser Load
A/N	TS-102/AP	Video Precision Range Calibrator
Army	TS-158/AP	Computer Test Set
Navy	CW-49499	S-Band Coaxial-Waveguide Transformer Set
Navy	CW-49500	S-Band Coaxial-Waveguide Transformer Set
Army	TS-74/UPM	S-Band Dummy Antenna
Army	UG-78/AP	S-Band Tapered Adapter
Army	TS-61/AP	S-Band Ring Box Test Set
Army	TS-110/AP	S-Band Ring Box Test Set
Navy	CXGU	S-Band Ring Box Test Set
Navy	TS-46/AP	S-Band Frequency Meter
A/N	TS-108/AP	X-Band Dummy Antenna
A/N	X-66362-A	X-Band Directional Coupler
Army	X-66362-B	X-Band Directional Coupler
Army	TS-62/AP	X-Band Ring Box Test Set
Navy	X-63630-A	X-Band Ring Box Test Set
Army	TS-103/TPM-1	L-Band Signal Generator
A/N	TS-128/UP	L-Band Signal Generator
A/N	TS-104/TPM-1	L-Band Connector Box
A/N	TS-105/TPM-1	L-Band Dummy Antenna
A/N	TS-106/TPM-1	L-Band Line Monitor
A/N	TS-107/TPM-1	L-Band Frequency-Power Meter
A/N	TS-130-UP	L-Band Standing Wave Detector
Navy	TS-91-UP	L-Band Test Antenna
A/N	TS-91/AP	L-Band Ring Box Test Set
A/N	X-66162	L-Band Ring Box Test Set

lator. A later model covered a 12-percent band. Great progress was made in reducing the size and weight of test sets. The reduction in size can be seen in Fig. 2-65. As for weight, the IE 30 signal generator weighed 121 pounds; the IE-57, 74 pounds; and the TS-35 and TS-35A, about 30 pounds.

The magnitude of test set development during the war is indicated by the following data: Prior to 1944 Bell Labs had developed over 70 different radar test sets. During 1944, 43 new designs were developed and standardized. In 1945, 10 more designs were nearing completion by V-J

Fig. 2-64.   Representative types of test equipment developed for use with Bell Laboratories radars.

Day.   The reduction in the number of new designs introduced as the years passed was to a large extent an indication of the effectiveness of the coordinated effort to make each test set serve the maximum number of radars.

Test sets were produced by Western Electric at high rates: about 2,300 sets based on 15 Bell Labs designs were produced in 1943; about 36,000 sets based on 27 designs in 1944; and about 27,600 sets based on 19 designs (17 of which were new) in 1945.   Testing work grew throughout the war, at the end of which Western Electric was delivering 5,000 items a month for use on Allied radars throughout the world.

The design and production of radar test gear represented a very substantial Bell System effort superimposed on the rest of the radar devel-

(a)   (b)

Fig. 2-65.   Comparison of two signal generators designed by Bell Laboratories for military use.   (a) Model produced in 1942.   (b) Improved model produced in 1945.   Size and weight were significantly reduced.

opment and production programs. Furthermore, other Bell System war efforts, covered in later chapters, also required test set design and thus placed additional burdens on personnel skilled in the art of developing highly precise electronic measuring equipment. Considering all fields involved, including radar, some 200 different test sets were designed during the war; production of them totaled close to 80,000 units with an aggregate value of $48 million.

VI. SUMMARY

The realization of the hope of the military organizations that Bell System technical and manufacturing expertise would be of value in the development and production of radar systems exceeded all expectations. Even though the Bell System had no specific experience with radar before the Navy discussed their problems with AT&T in 1937, more than half of the radars used by the U.S. armed forces had been designed by Bell Labs and produced by Western Electric by the time World War II had ended.

A number of factors contributed to this commendable performance. First, it resulted in no small part from the skill, devotion, and hard work of the many individuals involved, only a few of whom have been mentioned in this chapter. But of equal importance were the skills possessed by the Bell System in the management of R and D and in the manufacture of complex and reliable electronic and mechanical equipment. These skills had been built up by over 50 years of experience with an integrated organization set up to promote the effective cooperation of technically oriented people in maximizing their capabilities in research, development, and production. This background had provided a highly knowledgeable, loyal, and flexible group of technicians who could quickly adapt to the new circumstances required by the war effort.

Also important was the wisdom of maintaining a high level of R and D effort during the prewar years in spite of an acute economic depression. During these years, much technical knowledge had been acquired that proved immediately applicable to radar—knowledge covering the fields of microwave transmission, the use of waveguides, the design of antennas, and the design and application of vacuum tubes.

The multitude of equipment designed and put to work for the military exemplifies the success of the radar program. What is not so obvious is the tremendous advance in technology that was made during the war years. With practically all scientific personnel mobilized for the war effort, no single organization can claim a monopoly of the advances made in technology. It was truly a cooperative effort of scientists working throughout the Allied nations. However, the Bell System can certainly look with pride upon its technical position, which allowed its early entry into the design and production of radar, and its many achievements in technology, which made it the major designer and producer of radar.

Chapter 3

Electrical Computers for Fire Control

Improved fire-control systems developed during World War II used computers to translate radar data on the existence and location of a target into gun orders designed to direct artillery shells to, and cause them to burst at, a point where the target and its hostile mission are most apt to be adversely affected. Bell Laboratories entered this field because a few members of its staff became interested in the problem of using radar data for gun control. These people had broad scientific backgrounds and broad familiarity with a wide range of telephone and electronics technology, although the extensive available experience with existing fire control systems was well beyond their knowledge or indeed that of Bell Laboratories. Their proposals evolved into a series of gun directors, developed by Bell Labs and manufactured by Western Electric, which were highly effective in controlling antiaircraft guns. These directors could be manufactured mainly by mass production methods, since they did not depend for their accuracy, as did previous directors, on a variety of high-precision mechanical components requiring many highly skilled mechanics for their production.

Bell Laboratories digital computers were used during World War II principally in the design and testing of electrical analog gun directors. These computers evolved from the pioneer work of George R. Stibitz (in the period from 1937 to 1940), who designed and put to work at Bell Laboratories the first electromechanical digital computer.

I. ELECTRICAL ANALOG COMPUTERS

As we have seen in the previous chapter, radar is basically a system for detecting and locating targets in the air, on the ground, or on the sea; airborne targets, because of their much greater speed and maneuverability, were by far the most important ones. It has many uses by itself, but its major military value depended on its integration with fire control equipment—that is, with devices using present position data to control the accurate aiming of suitable ordnance so that the projectiles will have maximum probability of seriously damaging the object under attack.

Principal authors: W. H. C. Higgins, B. D. Holbrook, and J. W. Emling.

Before the development of radar, the detection and location of targets to be countered by antiaircraft artillery required the use of optical tracking equipment. Basically, this equipment consisted of an optical range finder and a transit-type instrument to determine angles. The optical equipment was of very high quality, and when skillfully used under favorable conditions provided accurate information concerning the present position of the target. This information was fed into mechanical analog computing gear, which used it to predict the course of the target during the flight of the projectile and from this to determine the gun orders and the fuze setting to cause a shell burst at or very close to the target.

Unfortunately, favorable conditions for use of such equipment were not in fact very common. Dark of night, obscuring fog, broken field of view caused by storms, patchy clouds, or smoke of battle, and other effects all contributed to degrade more or less seriously the effectiveness of this system of fire control.

Effective radar equipment greatly altered the situation for the better: radar data could almost always be obtained, and unlike optical data, it was usually available continuously during action. In World War II, effective radar equipment could be manufactured and maintained with no more trouble than that needed for optical tracking equipment, though the manufacture of either type in wartime required many sacrifices in product lines less critical for national defense.

The mechanical analog computers, or directors, as many of them were designated, could often be modified to use radar rather than optical inputs, but they presented problems to the armed services for two reasons. In the first place some of them had been designed before the capabilities of World War II aircraft were foreseen and would require extensive redesign to be really useful. Secondly, and more importantly, these devices were built from a variety of very-high-precision mechanical components. Thus, their manufacture in the quantities needed for World War II would require more precision machine tools and more precision craftsmen to operate them than were apt to be available. And in this area there were no "less critical fields" whose needs could be sacrificed for the war effort.

At the beginning of the war it was evident that new computer techniques might also be required. The mechanical devices then available performed admirably but required precise machinery and highly skilled personnel for their construction, but neither appeared likely to be available in sufficient quantity to meet the contemplated large war program. As it turned out, the technology of telephone systems was in many respects just what was needed for the next generation of fire control systems.

1.1 The Dream

Usually the initial impetus for the application of new technology depends on someone familiar with the available tools recognizing a class of new problems that it might be very worthwhile solving. Frequently the discovery of the application comes about through a meeting between a man with a problem and a man with a possible solution to it; but in the case at hand, the meeting happened to be one between two states of consciousness of a single person. In the spring of 1940, a group at Bell Laboratories was developing an improved automatic level recorder. D. B. Parkinson, a young engineer unaware of the technology of fire control, was a member of the group. To quote Parkinson, the level recorder was

> . . . a sort of recording voltmeter. Applied voltage caused an inking pen to move across the width of a strip of paper, the paper being driven at uniform velocity along its length. It was basically a strip chart recorder, but the pen motion was not linear with applied voltage, but rather with the log of the voltage. The logarithmic function was obtained by using a wire-wound card of the proper shape as the control element of a small potentiometer associated with the pen drive. The pen and its linked potentiometer arm were driven continuously in such fashion that the voltage picked off the potentiometer card matched exactly the applied (and rapidly varying) voltage that was to be recorded.[1] The system was, for its day, very fast. The control potentiometer was approximately $1\frac{3}{4}$ inches in diameter and consisted of a distinctively shaped wire-wound card wrapped around a cylinder of black rubber. There was a very small and light contact arm. To all intents and purposes this small potentiometer could be said to control the motion of the pen.

> In the spring of 1940 everyone was of course much concerned by the rapid drive of the German Army through Holland, Belgium and France. It was much discussed and it preyed on everyone's mind—mine included. I had been working on the level recorder for several weeks when one night I had this most vivid and peculiar dream.[2]

> I found myself in a gun pit or revetment with an anti-aircraft gun crew. I don't know how I got there—I was just there. The men were Dutch or Belgian by their uniforms—the helmets were neither German, French nor English. There was a gun there which looked to me—I had never had any close association with anti-aircraft guns, but possessed some general information on artillery—like a 3". It was firing occasionally, and the impressive thing was that *every shot brought down an airplane*! After three or four shots one of the men in the crew smiled at me and beckoned me to come closer to the gun. When I drew near he pointed to the exposed end of the left trunnion. Mounted there was the control potentiometer of my level recorder! There was no mistaking it—it was the identical item.

---

[1] Previous level recorders had used, in place of the wire-wound cards, commutators with appropriate resistors between the bars to approximate the logarithmic function. The development of means for winding cards of suitable shape promised a useful improvement in the accuracy of measurements in telephone transmission.

[2] The evacuation of Dunkirk, under heavy continuous attack by Stuka bombers, extended from May 26 to June 4, 1940, and was extensively reported on American radio and in the press. The dream seems to have occurred over a weekend, but in the succeeding rush of events the date does not seem to have been recorded. The first sketch is dated June 18; this suggests that Parkinson's dream was inspired by the events of Dunkirk since June 2 was a Sunday.

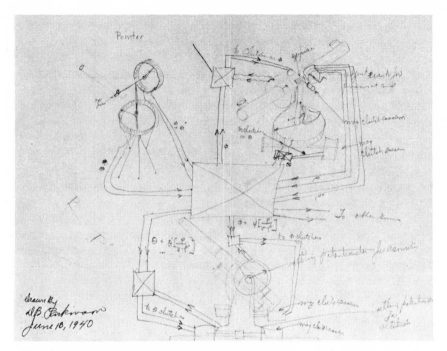

Fig. 3-1.   Early sketch depicting electrical control system for directing antiaircraft guns.

The whole scene then faded out, and some time later I woke up, still retaining a remarkably clear memory of the details.   It didn't take long to make the necessary translation—if the potentiometer could control the high-speed motion of a recording pen with great accuracy, why couldn't a suitably engineered device do the same thing for an anti-aircraft gun!

I discussed this with my friend and supervisor, Dr. C. A. Lovell, and we both pitched head over heels into a study of the possibilities.   The first written material on it was called "Electrical Mathematics"; this was a series of dissertations on how the tools we now imagined could be used to add, subtract, multiply, divide, integrate, differentiate, and make use of tabulated data—the very operations needed to make a gun director.[3]   We soon had to report to Dr. Lovell's supervisor, and to those above him, on what we were doing.   I made a hurried sketch of the proposal (signed and dated June 18, 1940) [shown in Fig. 3-1] to use in a meeting scheduled for this purpose.   On this sketch, altitude and azimuth were inadvertently interchanged, but it still served its purpose.[4]

---

[3] C. A. Lovell, D. B. Parkinson, and B. T. Weber; U.S. Patent No. 2,404,387; filed May 1, 1941; issued July 23, 1946.   See also C. A. Lovell, "Continuous Electrical Computation," *Bell Laboratories Record* 25 (March 1947), pp. 114–118.

[4] Account written by D. B. Parkinson on January 5, 1975, at the request of his son David.

1.2 Early Planning for an Antiaircraft Director

The salient features of this proposal were as follows:

1. Distance was to be represented in the machine by a scaled dc voltage. The primary measured quantity, converted to a voltage, was the range to the target's present position.

2. The target's azimuth and elevation angles were used to derive from the measured range the three Cartesian coordinates of present position. This required sinusoidal potentiometers and the provision of both positive and negative signal voltages of precisely equal magnitude.

3. Electrical differentiation of the dc voltages[5] representing present position gave the rectangular components of target speed. Multiplying these by the time of flight of the projectile and adding the results to the components of present position gave the future position of the target at the time a projectile, fired at the present instant, would arrive.

4. Given the future position, the firing tables for the gun, which were also stored on suitably shaped potentiometers, provided the time of flight required in step (3) above, the superelevation of the gun barrel needed because of the gravitational fall of the projectile, and other corrections requisite for accurate firing. With this information, the necessary gun orders and fuze setter orders could be derived. These could then be transmitted directly to the gun mount and fuze setter mechanism.[6]

Some of the "electro-mathematical systems" are shown in Fig. 3-2.

Neither Parkinson nor Lovell had any experience in fire control; they did not even know of the existence of mechanical gun directors. But it was clear to the management of Bell Laboratories that the importance of their proposal required that the Army be immediately apprised of it, and that development work be started at once. Lovell was therefore told to organize a task force, draft the needed expertise from other departments, and get on with the task.

Since Bell Laboratories was primarily in the communications business, it first notified the Army Signal Corps, which was in any event fully cognizant of radar development. The Corps, informed of the proposal before the end of June 1940, immediately recognized its importance and arranged a conference of ordnance and artillery officers and Bell Laboratories personnel to consider the matter. This turned out to be a very timely move, as Army Ordnance was greatly concerned about the avail-

---

[5] This was done by observing that the response of a suitable resistance-capacitance network measures the rate of change of the applied dc voltage.

[6] C. A. Lovell, D. B. Parkinson, K. D. Swartzel, and B. T. Weber; U.S. Patent No. 2,408,081; filed May 1, 1941; issued September 24, 1946.

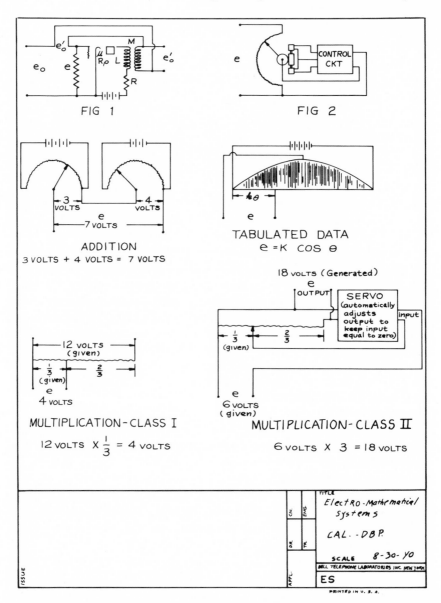

Fig. 3-2.   Examples of "electro-mathematical" systems utilized in electrical gun directors.

ability of mechanical directors in the event the United States was forced into the war.   The available mechanical directors were beautiful mechanisms, but there were not enough of them to go around, and unfortunately their procurement depended on making large numbers of a variety of high-precision mechanical components, such as angle resolvers, ball-

and-disc integrators, and highly accurate three-dimensional cams, all of which depended on the availability of precision-grade machine tools worked slowly and carefully by precision-grade mechanics. It was very clear that, in the event of war, precision-grade machine tools and people with the skills needed to use them effectively would be extremely scarce, and that in the circumstances the modification of directors to take care of improved projectiles or to utilize new sources of data (such as radars) would further constrict the bottleneck. Thus, Army Ordnance was already considering the possible use of electrical computing methods, even though such methods represented a radical departure from existing practice. The Bell Laboratories proposal offered a means of testing electrical methods, and at the same time envisioned a type of equipment that could be manufactured by people with skills very different from those required for the mechanical directors.

At about the same time (in the summer of 1940), the National Defense Research Committee was organized; Bell Laboratories therefore also brought the idea to the attention of the NDRC section (D-2) on fire control, which consulted the Coast Artillery Board on the subject. Bell Laboratories engineers presented a detailed description of the idea to the full membership of the NDRC fire control section in late October, and, on November 4, a conference with Army Ordnance, the Coast Artillery Board, and the NDRC agreed that development should be continued under NDRC funding, with the collaboration of Army Ordnance for such data and assistance as might be needed.

Just two days later a contract was awarded to Western Electric (which handled such contractual matters for Bell Laboratories), and an officer of the Fire Control Division of Frankford Arsenal was designated for liaison. This contract called for the development and construction of a model of the first electrical gun director, the T-10. This was to be designed as an antiaircraft director for use with a standard 90-mm gun and with the existing M-1 optical height finder or, alternatively, with radar range data. Fortunately, the basic system design of the new proposal and its assumption that the aircraft target would continue in nonaccelerated linear flight were substantially the same as the plan prediction method used in existing mechanical directors, although the means of implementation were radically different. Following a similar system plan would provide an opportunity for direct comparison of the performance of the two types.

1.3 Development of the T-10 Director

A development program begun at the end of 1940 had to allow for a number of things that could not then be foretold. In the first place, no one had yet shot down an aircraft target with a gun using radar data alone. Thus, it was necessary to provide capability for working with the existing M-1 optical height finder and its associated optical goniometric equipment, as well as with radar range and angular data. These circumstances put somewhat unusual requirements on the design of the input channels and the data-smoothing characteristics of the director; in addition, since the relative accuracy of angular and distance measurements from a radar might turn out to be quite different from those obtained from optical devices, it was necessary to provide a good deal of flexibility in the early design until more experience was acquired with the actual performance of tracking radars.

Another problem was posed by the time fuzes used to control the point in its trajectory at which the projectile would detonate. At the beginning of the war, the time fuze was the only mechanism for causing detonation close enough to the target to do any good, and throughout the war it was often the only practicable means. The fuze was essentially an alarm clock, or more precisely an interval timer, mounted in the nose of the shell, which exploded the shell after expiration of a time (measured from the instant of firing the gun) that had been set by a device called a fuze setter as it had been ordered by the director. The time fuze was in some cases a powder train, but more usually it was a rugged mechanical clock.

Unfortunately, while the other gun orders could be kept up to date until the gun was actually fired, the fuze setting had to be done before the shell could be loaded into the breech of the gun. Thus, the fuze-setting order had to be calculated on the basis of a prediction time that was increased by the "dead time," that is, the total time required to remove the shell from the fuze setter, insert it into the gun breech, close the breech, and fire the gun. While gun crews were of course trained to work to constant dead time, there was always some variation, particularly when the gun elevation was high. In addition, the fuze-setting order involved predicting farther ahead than the other gun orders, and even the best time fuzes were subject to some inaccuracies.

Meanwhile, the development work on this program proceeded under forced draft: Lovell's task force began working a full six-day week during the summer of 1940, and its membership increased steadily, partly to expedite the pace, but often to add people with the additional skills needed to solve unexpected but crucial problems as they turned up. Here only a few of the developments that turned out to be important can be cited—to indicate the range of talents that had to be provided.

As previously noted, the T-10 used dc voltages of both positive and negative polarity to represent the target's present and future positions, its velocity components, and the like. Since the signal voltages had to be accurate measures of distance, it was necessary that the amplifiers handling them should be highly accurate. Such amplifiers had been available for about a decade—in fact, ever since Harold S. Black[7] invented the feedback

---

[7] H. S. Black, "Stabilized Feedback Amplifiers," *Bell System Technical J.* 13 (January 1934), pp. 1–18.

amplifier and Hendrik W. Bode[8] provided mathematical methods of designing it to known tolerances. Before their day, the vacuum tube amplifier had gain, but that was about all you could guarantee about its performance. The amplifier's output was very like its input in form, but rarely exactly like it; the amplifier gain enlarged the output, which was usually about what the designer had in mind but which in practice varied from hour to hour and sometimes from minute to minute. After Black and Bode, the vacuum tube amplifier, when properly designed, became a high-precision instrument.

The amplifiers for fire control applications were usually designed to have very low input impedance; this permitted them to add or subtract signal voltages applied in parallel to the amplifier input, each through its own very-high-resistance path. If one of the inputs was derived from a linear potentiometer card, fed by a constant voltage, and subtracted from one or more inputs from other sources, the resulting voltage measured the discrepancy between the potentiometer setting and the value indicated by the other sources. The amplifier output could thus be used, by a servomechanism, to move the potentiometer brush until the difference became zero. By putting other suitable potentiometer cards on the same shaft, an exact copy of the source voltage, or other desired functions of it, could be continuously derived as required.

The design of suitable servomechanisms depended on the observation that a servomechanism is basically a feedback system. The fact that it may include a potentiometer card, an electric motor, and suitable gearing, in addition to vacuum tubes, is interesting in that it permits it to do things beyond the capacity of pure electronic equipment, but its design presents the same mathematical problem.[9]

By feeding a potentiometer with a voltage representing a quantity, A, and moving its brush to a shaft position, B, multiplication is achieved: for the output voltage at the brush is then $A \times B$, or (if the potentiometer is shaped to a nonlinear form) $A \times f(B)$.

In the present case, this required the development of operational amplifiers. These were feedback amplifiers built to handle dc signal voltages, which had very accurately controlled characteristics. The amplifiers could handle both positive and negative signal voltages, and could often provide both signs in the output. The design also had to minimize zero drift and provide means to adjust this as needed; this was often necessary when the machine was first turned on. These features required novel design of the feedback networks as well as the use of input stages with two triodes in a single envelope. The triodes were set up as a differential amplifier, with the signal applied to only one of the triodes. The other triode, which had

[8] Hendrik W. Bode, *Network Analysis and Feedback Amplifier Design* (New York: D. Van Nostrand, 1945).

[9] LeRoy A. MacColl, *Fundamental Theory of Servomechanisms* (New York: D. Van Nostrand, 1945).

the same temperature and other conditions, compensated for the varying ambient.

Thus, an important step in the development of these amplifiers was the procurement of suitable feedback, adding, and differentiating networks. These in turn required high accuracy and stability of the resistors and capacitors used in them. In both cases obtaining them presented problems for quite different reasons.

Suitable capacitors for differentiating the signal voltages were not easily found. The difficulty was that the solid-film dielectrics then used for precision capacitors for ac circuits unfortunately polarized when subjected to dc voltages, and thus retained a bound charge that vitiated the accurate differentiation of dc signals. Fortunately, members of the Chemical Research Department knew of a polyester film, just then becoming available, that could solve this problem because it was free of polarization effects and could be conveniently used in standard dry-electric capacitor manufacture. This material had been developed by Du Pont, which apparently hoped it would prove to be a suitable packaging material, competing, for example, with cellophane. Its manufacture for use as dielectric film was undertaken by Du Pont at the urging of the NDRC; under the name òf Mylar[10], it has since been widely used for this purpose, even when polarization is no problem. As it turned out, the utility of Mylar for packaging was very limited, since it is so tough that getting the package open might be very difficult.

The feedback and adding resistors were initially precision wire-wound resistors made of small-gauge alloy wire. This material was also essential to the manufacture of the numerous potentiometer cards required in the T-10 and similar directors. (It may be noted that a single large card might require as much as one-third of a mile of such wire.) Studies made during early planning of director development indicated that the country's facilities for drawing alloy resistance wire would have been just about adequate to meet the demand for wound resistors for directors of the type envisioned. Since similar wire was also crucial to the manufacture of potentiometers for the same directors as well as many other critical applications, it became essential to develop a suitable substitute requiring only noncritical materials.

The resistors developed for this purpose by the Transmission Apparatus Development Department[11] were deposited carbon resistors. These were similar to products available in Europe before the war, but were improved to obtain the new properties needed in this application. Deposited carbon resistors are made by laying down very thin films of pyrolytic carbon on suitable ceramic cores. This is done by carefully controlled decomposition

[10] Trademark of E. I. Du Pont de Nemours.
[11] See A. C. Pfister, "Precision Carbon Resistors," *Bell Laboratories Record*, 26 (October 1948), pp. 401–406.

of gaseous hydrocarbons at high temperatures. The process, as Pfister noted, is "like that by which the undesired carbon deposits in internal combustion engines are formed." [12]

Resistors with values up to tens of thousands of ohms could be produced by making uniform thin films on ceramic rods. Values into the megohms, needed for many purposes in the directors, were "obtained by grinding a helical groove through the carbon film making, in effect, a carbon ribbon wound around a ceramic core." [13] This process made it possible to increase the resistance by a factor of a thousand or more. Both the resistors and the capacitors had, of course, to be measured and padded out to precise values and then properly packaged to protect them from humidity and from differential temperature effects.[14]

The techniques of making the shaped potentiometers (Fig. 3-3) that were the heart of the director also posed many problems. The potentiometer of Parkinson's dream was less than 2 inches in diameter, but some potentiometers had to be ten times that size. Cutting the potentiometer cards to the requisite shapes was fairly easy; but it must be remembered that the functions represented by the voltages picked off the potentiometers had to represent not only sinusoids but also some fairly arbitrary-looking functions required to represent the ballistic properties of the gun, such as time of flight, superelevation, etc. Winding resistance wire to lie tight on a card so shaped, and at the same time to maintain accurately a constant pitch along the card, required both hard work and ingenuity. The winding machines that solved this problem were initially developed by Parkinson, but Muller and a number of others also contributed to their success.[15]

The characteristics of resistance wire also caused a great deal of difficulty. The diameter of such wire can be held to very close tolerances, but its specific resistivity along its length is subject to a good deal of variation, depending on the mechanical working to which it has been subjected. Since winding the wire on a nonuniform card necessarily works some parts of the wire more than others, it is difficult to make a potentiometer that will accurately deliver the desired function at its brush pick-off. In the initial model of the director (the T-10) accuracy was obtained by using only fully hard wire and winding it on the potentiometers with extreme care. This technique worked for the model, but something better was needed for manufacturing purposes.

[12] Ibid., 402.

[13] Ibid., 403.

[14] See E. C. Hagemann, "Precision Resistance Networks for Computer Circuits," *Bell Laboratories Record* 24 (December 1946), pp. 445–449.

[15] D. B. Parkinson; U.S. Patent No. 2,406,397; filed November 19, 1942; issued August 27, 1946. A. H. Muller; U.S. Patent No. 2,406,846; filed June 28, 1940; issued September 3, 1946.

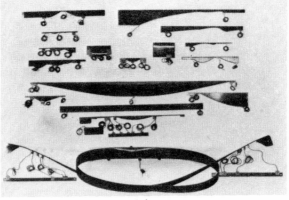

(a)

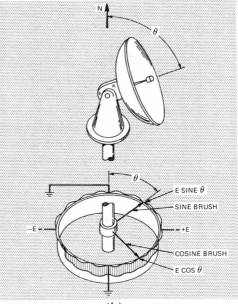

(b)

Fig. 3-3.   Potentiometers developed for use in gun directors.   (a) Typical styles and shapes of potentiometer cards.   (b) Use of potentiometer for generating sine and cosine functions.

An improved procedure was devised by J. J. Kuhn and his co-workers.[16] The cards were purposely made longer than the circumference of the sturdy drums provided for mounting them.   After each card had been wound with ordinary care, an operator used a Wheatstone bridge to locate

16 H. L. Coyne, S. S. Kuhn, and J. E. Ross; U.S. Patent No. 2,408,046; filed October 2, 1943; issued September 24, 1946.   See also D. G. Blattner, "Precision Potentiometers for Analog Computers," *Bell Laboratories Record* 32 (May 1954), pp. 171–177.

and mark distinctively the winding turns corresponding to specified fractions of the total resistance of the card. When this had been done, the potentiometer was held in a suitable fixture around, but not initially touching, the drum it was intended for. Another operator adjusted each marked turn to exact agreement with the corresponding angular mark on the mandrel and then used a permanent ring-and-wedge arrangement to clamp the two members mark by mark. This insured that the potentiometer voltage ratio and the angular position of the brush would agree at n positions around the drum. With suitable design of the process, this procedure made it possible to keep the maximum error effectively under control. It was used not only for the M-9 but also for all subsequent Bell Labs fire control developments.

Such a controlled method of mounting cards on drums did, in fact, do much more than take care of variations in the wire's specific resistivity. Once a good deal of careful setup engineering had been done, it was possible to manufacture precision potentiometers with relatively little dependence on highly skilled mechanics for making the individual parts. The potentiometer cards could be cut, and the drums made, to less exacting tolerances than were required for the final product. Winding the wire on the cards no longer had to be done with precise control of the winding tension. Though they had to be done with great care and under close supervision, marking potentiometer turns with a suitable bridge and the mark-to-mark matching of potentiometers to their drums were jobs that could be learned quickly by people who had little previous mechanical experience.

In addition to mechanical and materials problems such as these, there were design problems that required theoretical developments. The T-10 was the first fire control equipment for which the methods of network design theory were adapted to provide gun orders representing a least-squares fit to the less-than-perfect target position data provided by the radar or optical sources used to feed the director. Three different networks were provided, giving smoothing times of 5, 10, and 20 seconds, to be used as tactical conditions required. It was also necessary to provide for variations in ambient conditions, such as wind, temperature, and the like.

1.4 First Tests and Standardization: M-9 and Its Companions

Development and construction of the T-10 engineering model proceeded apace, and on December 1, 1941, it arrived at Fortress Monroe, Virginia, to be set up for firing tests. The first tracking of an aircraft target on December 4 revealed the need for further adjustments. Tests comparing the T-10 to mechanical computers were therefore delayed until December 15. In the meantime Pearl Harbor was bombed and the United States entered the war on December 7.

The performance of the T-10 in the early tests revealed that there were

Fig. 3-4.   Amplifier bay of the T-10 gun director computer.

still changes needed in data-smoothing methods and in correcting contact problems at the potentiometer brushes; even so, the results were quite comparable with those of the mechanical computers, which had been continuously refined for many years.   It was clear that the electrical director could be substantially improved and that it had notable advantages from the point of view of procurement.   As previously noted, much of the manufacturing could be done by people with quite different skills (requiring, on the whole, less training) from those involved in making mechanical directors.   And while some of the needed components, such as the potentiometers, had hardly been seen before, the amplifiers, networks, and the like were of types for which manufacturing methods were very well known.

It was therefore recommended on February 12, 1942, that the electrical director be made a standard of procurement to supplement the limited number of mechanical directors that could be obtained.   The T-10 (Figs. 3-4 and 3-5) accordingly became the prototype of a series of directors for use with various guns, including the British 4.5-inch antiaircraft gun.

Fig. 3-5.   Tracking unit of the T-10 gun director.

Production versions of United States directors, all derived from the original T-10, were known as the M-8, M-9, M-10, M-12, M-13, and M-14.   The British version, known as the T-24, was completed in prototype form in May 1942 and was tested in Wales and at Woodyates near Salisbury, England.   The report on the British tests noted that although complete data were not yet available, it appeared that "the over-all performance of the predictor system using the Bell Labs computer is better than any predicting equipment heretofore tested by the United Kingdom."

1.5 Defense Against the Buzz Bomb

The selection of the M-9 for standardization turned out to be a happy one.   With design improvements and production planning both well

Fig. 3-6.   Typical installation of the M-9 electrical gun director.   The tracking unit with its two operators is in the foreground.   Other units of the system are installed in the truck and on the antiaircraft gun mount.

under way, the first M-9 director was delivered on December 23, 1942.   It appeared in the field early in 1943 (Fig. 3-6) and did yeoman service on many fronts.   Its finest achievements, however, were in the so-called Second Battle of Britain.   In the one month of August 1944 nine out of ten German V-1 buzz bombs originally destined for London were shot down over the cliffs of Dover.   (The first V-1 was launched on June 12.)   In a single week in August, the Germans launched 91 V-1's from the Antwerp area, and heavy guns controlled by M-9's destroyed 89 of them.

The M-9 was an essential part of the spectacularly successful defense effort, but a great deal of credit must be given to other elements of the defense, notably the SCR-584 radar, the VT fuze, and the admirable 90-mm gun developed by Army Ordnance.   This winning combination was a fine example of the cooperative work of technical organizations from several fields working on military problems.

The radar story is covered in other chapters of this book.   The particular radar used in the Second Battle of Britain, the SCR-584, was a product of the Radiation Laboratory at M.I.T.   Fortunately, its designers had been so impressed by the T-10 director that they had equipped the SCR-584 with M-9 type potentiometers as part of its output facilities.   This made the interconnection of the SCR-584 and the M-9 director very simple and straightforward.

A second important member of the team was the VT fuze, also known as the influence fuze and the proximity fuze, which caused the shell to burst only when it came sufficiently close to the target.   The development of the VT fuze was far from an easy matter. The work was mainly done in research groups under the direction of M.A. Tuve of the Carnegie Institution of Washington, with the assistance of a number of other research organizations. Two methods were explored, one detecting the target optically, the other by radio waves. In both cases the fuze had to contain electronic elements—and during the war this meant vacuum tubes (VT). (The transistor was not invented until several years later.) Thus, special tubes of small size and capable of withstanding the enormous forces encountered during firing of the shell (several thousand times the force of gravity) had to be developed and manufactured in very large quantities. Bell Laboratories participated in development of both the optical and radio types of the fuze; the radio version proved in the end to be superior and was very widely used.

The VT fuze substantially improved the performance of heavy antiaircraft systems. The principal advantage was of course that it avoided the inaccuracies related to dead-time computation; thus any projectile whose trajectory brought it within influence radius of a target would burst within lethal radius, rather than too early or too late, as often happened with time fuzes. A less important, but hardly trivial, effect was that the VT-fuzed shells gave less advance notice to enemy aircraft that they were in dangerous territory. The use of VT fuzes required only the supply of alternate ammunition; even if the director computed fuze settings, there was no necessity to pass the shells through the fuze setter.

On the other hand, there were problems as well. A VT-fuzed shell would detonate on any other target within influence radius before or after passing the intended target. Since this circumstance applied to friendly aircraft, in some cases it was necessary to clear the range before using VT fuzes. And in any event VT-fuzed shells would detonate just before reaching the ground and give an excellent imitation of the effects of shrapnel. This characteristic severely restricted their use over friendly territory. Finally, letting highly classified VT-fuzed shells that had failed to burst—their operability never reached 100 percent during the war—fall on land, even though friendly, posed substantial security risks. For these reasons, there still remained a need for the use of time fuzes for antiaircraft purposes. In addition, time fuzes were needed for star shells, which illuminated battlefields.

In the defense against the V-1 bomb, tactics were an important consideration. By the second week of the attack, Allied tactics called for the deployment of the antiaircraft batteries on the channel coast or close to it. This made it possible to intercept most incoming buzz bombs before they were over land. There were several advantages to such a plan of interdiction. Early detection was easier to achieve over water; more of the bombs could be brought down over the channel, where they were relatively harmless, than on southern England; and the VT-fuzed projectiles that missed their targets would drop harmlessly into the channel. And finally, Allied aircraft attempting to bring down the targets that leaked through the antiaircraft barrier could do so in far greater safety than if they operated near the launching sites.

1.6 Alternative Choices in the Design of Antiaircraft Systems for Tactical Situations

While the M-9 turned out to be very successful in general use (and spectacularly effective in defense against the V-1), it represented only one of the many possible choices available for designing an antiaircraft system. Some of the technically practicable choices were dictated by the tactical situation to be dealt with. For example, the Army antiaircraft battery sits in a fixed location and on solid ground, and its primary concern is to protect important installations or cities, which are normally some distance behind the battery, against enemy bombers that do their best to sneak through between batteries. At the time the M-9 was developed, the enemy aircraft flew as high as possible, and were constrained by the characteristics of the available bombsights to fly unaccelerated courses for some time before reaching the bomb release point. At the other extreme, the antiaircraft equipment of a Navy ship has the primary duty of protecting the ship itself against enemy aircraft; it must therefore maintain continuous fire while the ship rolls and pitches in the sea and takes full advantage of the ability to change both course and speed as evasively as possible to avoid becoming a sitting duck for the attacking aircraft. As a result, those in charge of naval antiaircraft equipment are far more concerned than their Army counterparts with such targets as dive-bombers, which can be successful only if they twist and turn until the last possible instant. Most naval antiaircraft fire will be at close-in targets. Also, a ship can carry only a limited amount of ammunition and must expend it frugally, while an Army battery can usually be resupplied when necessary and can count on only occasional hits within the ranges at which it must usually work. Thus, in the case of the Navy, while some of the data in the fire control system must be in fixed coordinates, much of it must be in coordinates of the ship itself, derived from such sources as the ship's compass, speed indicator, and gyroscopic stable element.

Similarly, there were many alternatives in deriving target rates by differentiating present position data. Historically this was done, in manual or semimanual systems, by variants of the plotting board; in World War II, the German Navy obtained rates for its heavy antiaircraft batteries by automatically plotting the components of present target positions (in fixed coordinates) on three strip charts. In front of each strip chart sat a rating operator who continuously adjusted a goniometer to tangency with the plot; and these goniometer settings defined the target rates for prediction. This method, forming part of an otherwise highly mechanized process, provided excellent shooting accuracy, considering that it almost always had to depend on optical input data.

Some form of aided tracking was often used to assist operators following the target (usually in range, bearing, and elevation) by either radar or optical means in keeping their crosshairs or other indicators continuously on the target. When an unknown target is first picked up, each operator must maintain his aim by full use of his control, but each time he makes a correction, the adjustment affects not only the position of the crosshairs but also the pertinent rate setting. The U.S. Navy used a refined version of this method, in which the rates were for obvious reasons maintained in stable coordinates. This regenerative tracking provided rates that served at the same time to keep both the crosshairs and the gun's projectiles on target. In addition, in most tactical situations it permitted any useful knowledge of the characteristics of the target (its usual speed, for example) or target movement of immediate interest to the ship (its being clearly on a crossing course) to be preset into the rates to reduce the solution time.

1.7 Alternative Design for Army Use: the T-15 Director

At the time the T-10 contract was awarded, it was clear that many of these alternatives should be explored, and this process was immediately begun. The T-10 required conversion of range and angle data to Cartesian coordinates and subsequent reconversion to polar coordinates to obtain gun orders. This procedure permitted derivation of constant rates for a target in unaccelerated flight by the use of simple differentiation. Although Section D-2 of the NDRC gave full technical and financial support to the T-10 project, the section members believed that a somewhat different approach might lead to a more accurate system. They reasoned that "a preferable system of coordinates is one in which future position is obtained by adding components of 'lead' to values of the polar variables of present position, these having been subjected to no deteriorating process of resolution and synthesis." [17] They also felt that improvements might be made by a judicious mixture of electrical and mechanical components in place of the almost completely electrical solution used in the T-10. Further, the NDRC also envisioned the use of ac signal voltages instead of dc, which would reduce the problems of drift in the dc amplifiers (at this point it was not yet known if this might not be a major problem) and substantially reduce the size of the equipment and worries about possible maintenance problems of operational amplifiers and their power supplies. These views were shared by Warren Weaver of the Rockefeller Foundation, Thornton C. Fry of Bell Labs, and Samuel Caldwell of M.I.T.

On February 1, 1941, Bell Labs was asked to explore these ideas, and the

---

[17] Foreword to Final Report on Antiaircraft Director T-10 to the National Defense Research Committee, June 24, 1944.

work was first assigned to the Lovell group working on the T-10 project. It was soon found that it was impracticable to have one team working on two competing systems; the resulting distraction interfered with progress on both jobs. The new project, under the name T-15, was accordingly assigned to a separate group headed by Walter A. MacNair. An important member of this group was Hendrik W. Bode, who in the early 1930s had developed the mathematical basis for feedback amplifier design and subsequently applied it to the design of networks for improving the accuracy of predictions based on present position data more or less polluted by atmospheric or instrumental noise.

The T-15 carried out its calculations basically in polar coordinates, as obtained directly from radar or optical tracking equipment, rather than converting everything to Cartesian coordinates and then back, as in the T-10. The method was called "one-plus," since the computed prediction was only the increment, in polar coordinates, which had to be added to the observed present position to obtain the predicted position at the time the shell would burst. In 1941, it was expected that the "plus" would normally be much smaller than the "one"; by the end of the war, with much faster targets, which often had to be attacked close to the zenith, it was sometimes questionable whether this was an advantage or whether this was a detriment.

Target speed was determined in the T-15 by a memory-point method. In this method, a fixed point in the target flight was stored in memory (by freezing the brushes on one set of duplicate potentiometer cards following target position) when a designated operator pushed a button; in most cases, this would occur as soon as the target was well tracked. As the tracking of the target continued, both the distance and the time elapsed from the memory-point were measured; speed was then merely the distance divided by the time. For unaccelerated flight, the accuracy would improve with time because perturbations in the raw data would be smoothed; thus, the method gave a continuously variable smoothing time. This method required neither integration nor differentiation of target position data, and thus made perfectly straightforward the use of ac signals with the advantages noted previously. There was, of course, a minor disadvantage to the use of ac signals: without careful design it could cause discrepancies in the phase of signals due to distributed wiring capacitance. This was easily corrected at the cost of somewhat increased design effort. For targets in unaccelerated flight, this method had a number of possible advantages over the T-10 procedures; how important these would turn out to be could only be determined by trial.

On the basis of Bell Labs' proposed implementation of this approach, funds were made available for its development on November 10, 1941. The first model of the T-15 (Figs. 3-7 and 3-8) was completed in November 1942 and shipped to Camp Davis, North Carolina, for testing on December 4.

Fig. 3-7. Front view of T-15 gun director computer with covers removed.

Fig. 3-8. Typical potentiometer used in T-15 gun director.

Fig. 3-9. Main computing equipment of the T-15 gun director modified for curved-course prediction.

At that time, Bell Labs' SCR-545 radar was already being tested there along with the Radiation Lab's SCR-584.

The preliminary report of the Anti-Aircraft Artillery Board dated April 15, 1943, found the performance of the T-15 very satisfactory and somewhat more accurate than the T-10. The report noted that with the T-15 there was no need for zero setting of amplifiers and that the settling time (i.e., the time to smooth out the transient oscillations that arise when a new target is first tracked) was only about half that of the T-10. The Board recommended that for these and a number of less important reasons the T-15 be standardized in preference to the T-10 (actually in preference to the M-9, the production model of the T-10).

At that time, however, the M-9 was already in production, the first delivery having already been made on December 23, 1942. Development of a production model of the T-15 and the procurement of the necessary tooling could hardly have been accomplished before mid-1944. Although the proving ground tests favored the T-15, neither method of computation had been tested under battlefield conditions. But the possible advantages of the T-15 could hardly balance the immediate availability of the M-9.

Although the T-15 was not placed in production, the development was continued under the auspices of NDRC to investigate some further possibilities, mainly in connection with prediction of the future position of aircraft in curvilinear flight. Such prediction was conceived by Hendrik Bode and implemented by Walter MacNair's development team. (Some of the modified equipment is shown in Fig. 3-9.) A basic idea behind the proposal was that "there was no point in firing shells at places where the airplane could not possibly be; for that reason the design precluded firing at any point outside the range of maneuverability of the aircraft."

The work on curvilinear prediction progressed, but the project was soon superseded by research and development on antiaircraft guided missiles, work which was first begun under the direction of MacNair and Bode. The new undertaking profited from the experience gained in the study of curvilinear prediction. An interesting by-product of the curvilinear studies was the development of precise automatic plotting boards; later manufactured under Bell Labs patents, these were widely used in university and industrial laboratories for a great variety of engineering and scientific projects.

1.8 Fire Control for Coast Artillery

The results obtained with the M-9 director for antiaircraft fire control were so promising that the Coast Artillery Board requested development of similar gear for use with coast defense guns; the resulting equipment was known as the M-8 gun data computer.[18] Since the M-8 was designed to handle a radically different tactical problem from that of the M-9, its characteristics differed markedly from those of the M-9, although it employed the same electrical analog techniques.

The first major difference between the two was that while the M-9 dealt with high-speed, readily maneuverable targets moving freely in three-dimensional space, the Coast Artillery was concerned with low-speed targets of limited maneuverability confined to the surface of the water.

---

[18] H. G. Och, "Computer for Coastal Guns," *Bell Laboratories Record* 24 (May 1946), pp. 177–182. Note that the term *director* implies that the gear in question can actually see the target, optically or by radar, although it may also do computing. On the other hand, a device that reduces data obtained from remote observing equipment is usually called a computer.

And while the antiaircraft problem requires the computation of fuze-setting orders (though they may not always be used), coast defense guns use contact-fuzed projectiles. These are required for two reasons: (1) against armored ships, a delayed detonation is desirable because it permits penetration of the armor before the shell bursts; and (2) observation of where the shell bursts on the water around the target permits an observer to make accurate spotting corrections for the gun orders, which is quite impracticable in the three-dimensional situation. Thus in coast defense the basic problem is reduced from three dimensions to two dimensions, although correction for the earth's curvature is necessary, and the amount of computation is also further reduced by the use of contact-fuzed ammunition.

Another difference is that target position in coast defense is obtained by surveying techniques—that is, by reduction of angular data obtained optically from stations at the ends of a long base line accurately known in length and bearing. Before the day of the M-8, the data was plotted manually at fixed intervals (usually every 20 seconds); and from this plot, target course and speed, and in turn gun orders, were derived. The M-8 computer solved the requisite trigonometric equations directly and continuously and thus avoided errors introduced by manual interpolation between target observations. As a result, guns could be fired as soon as they were loaded and aimed.

While the coast defense problem addressed by the M-8 was thus a good deal simpler than that solved by the M-9, computation for the M-8 had to be made with greater accuracy, since the coast defense guns, ranging from 6 to 8 inches, were much larger than antiaircraft guns, the 90-mm being the Army's standard antiaircraft gun. Thus, the range of the coast defense gun was about two and one-half times that of the antiaircraft gun, and the projectile time of flight of the former was proportionally greater. In addition, in this matter of relative problems, a contact-fuzed projectile does no damage unless it actually hits the target, whereas time-fuzed or VT-fuzed shells can do great damage by exploding in the target's vicinity.

Basic elements of the M-8 computer, shown in Fig. 3-10, included a line balancing unit, which made corrections for differences in the characteristics of the transmission lines from the remote observation points, a triangle solver and a position generator to determine present position, and a predictor to provide aiming information for gun orders. The computer had to allow not only for the nonstandard conditions affecting the solution of the antiaircraft calculations, but also for several others, such as the height of the tide and the height of the gun above mean water level. A single computer controlled the two guns of a coast artillery battery but had to make separate calculations for each gun because the guns might have been far enough apart to require different firing data. For the large 6- and 8-inch coastal guns, the computer was located in a protected case-

Fig. 3-10.   M-8 gun data computer installed in trailer.   The position generator is at left, the triangle solver is adjacent and to its right, and the predictor unit is partly visible in the rear.

ment back of the gun positions.   For use with mobile 155-mm guns it was installed in trailers.

A number of M-8 gun data computers were manufactured and delivered to the Army.   In a comparison of the test performance of the computers and the actual experience with the manual plotting methods previously used, it was found that the computers made the work of the plotting crews much simpler, greatly reduced the error rate, and increased the accuracy and rate of fire.   The continuous flow of data from the M-8 enabled the guns to fire as soon as loaded, without waiting for the time-interval bell, and resulted in firing 30 percent more rounds in a given time and hence in more scored hits than was possible with the other method. In the tests of the M-8 gun data computers, enemy targets were never fired upon: there were none off the coast to fire at.

After the war, the technology developed for fire control, using the dc signal methods of the M-9 director and the M-8 computer, was applied, under the direction of Emory Lakatos, to the design of a very useful general-purpose analog computer (GPAC), nicknamed the "Gypsy," which was extensively used for over ten years for the solution of problems in many scientific and engineering areas. This was the basis for the development of the analog computer industry. The first Gypsy was built largely from unused components for M-8 computers left over from the wartime development.

1.9 Fire Control for Naval Dual-Purpose Guns

It will be recalled that the procurement problem for mechanical directors was an important factor in the Army's decision in 1940 to support development of the T-10 (later the M-9) director. The Navy had similar qualms about wartime procurement, particularly of the mechanical computer that was the heart of the fire control system for the dual-purpose 5-inch guns that served on destroyers and aircraft carriers both for heavy antiaircraft defense and as the main, or surface, battery, and on larger ships as the secondary battery. It was abundantly clear that a great many destroyers and carriers would have to be built, and the Navy had an excellent mechanical computer to control the 5-inch guns. The question was whether it would prove possible to speed up construction from the slow peacetime rate to meet the greatly accelerated deliveries needed to equip ships already on the ways or planned.

The Navy's problem lay in the very limited supply of the critical skills and facilities needed to make high-precision mechanisms in greatly increased quantities. In a number of respects, the Navy's problem was worse than the Army's. In the first place, the Navy computer had to do a great deal more computing than the Army's director, since it had to operate and provide continuous control of gunfire on a ship that was rolling, pitching, and maneuvering. And, in addition, the Navy computer was the core of the fire control system and had to work properly with a topside director having optical and radar target-tracking equipment, with the ship's compass and log, with the gun mounts, and with a gyroscopically stabilized element that told the fire control system all it needed to know about the tilt of the ship's deck. Finally, it was necessary to provide a number of methods of backup operation to keep the guns in operation, even though less effectively, if any other part of the fire control system should be shot away or rendered inoperative in battle. Thus, a computer for the Navy required far more equipment than an Army director.

Finally, the Navy's existing mechanical computer was built almost entirely of various aluminum alloys, carefully chosen and matched to ensure continued high-precision performance as the parts expanded and contracted over wide temperature ranges. But with the enormous growth of aircraft production, the continued availability of the requisite alloys was becoming doubtful, and a redesign of the computer to use other materials would be very time-consuming.

Accordingly, the Navy's Bureau of Ordnance and its supplier of mechanical computers began an extensive exploration of possible solutions to the problems of accelerated precision manufacture in wartime and of the supply of aluminum alloys. In addition, the Bureau of Ordnance, at about the time of the attack on Pearl Harbor, asked Bell Labs, using its new electrical techniques, to develop an alternative computer to be put into production if adequate supplies of the mechanical equipment could not be assured. Bell Labs assembled a team, under the direction of A. W. Horton, to develop the Mark 8 computer,[19] as the electrical analog model was called. The first meeting with the Bureau of Ordnance, to find out just what was wanted, was held early in January 1942. A proposal for this computer was sent to the Navy on February 24, 1942, a letter of intent was issued on April 4, 1942, and the development contract became effective on September 28, 1942. By the latter date, development was well under way.

The Navy's first requirement for the Mark 8 computer was, of course, the use of Bell Labs' electrical analog methods, permitting manufacture by people with very different skills from those needed for making precision mechanical equipment. The second was that the Mark 8 should be built without the use of aluminum. The third was that the Mark 8 computer should be functionally equivalent to, and even mount interchangeably with, the existing mechanical computer, the Mark 1. The first requirement had a corollary: that under the circumstances there was a good deal of urgency in developing the Mark 8. As a result, the design relied heavily on experience gained in the design of the M-9 and T-15 directors, and many of the circuit elements, such as amplifiers, were taken over directly with only minor changes in mechanical construction. The second requirement had only minor effects on the development of Mark 8. The third requirement naturally limited the extent to which radical changes and improvements could be incorporated in the design of the Mark 8; anything that required changes in any other element of the fire control system was not to be considered.

The need for the Mark 8 to mount interchangeably with the Mark 1 put very strict limits on the maximum size of the new computer, and determined that like the T-15 it would use ac signal voltages; the M-9 method,

---

[19] The Mark 8 should not be confused with the M-8 computer, which was concurrently being developed for use by the Coast Artillery. (see Section 1.8).

using dc signal voltages, would make the machine too bulky to be gotten into the plotting room at all.   Because the director and guns are mounted on a moving ship, the development of the geometry and method of solution was necessarily different from that used in land-based directors.   It was also different from that used in the Navy's Mark 1 computer.   In addition, the need to control the Navy's standard Mark 37 director dictated the need for accurate electrical integration; a new form of electrical integrator was therefore developed for this project.

The pace of development was somewhat reduced in the second half of 1943 when it became apparent that the Navy Bureau of Ordnance and its principal suppliers had solved the problems in producing complex, high-precision mechanical computers within a time frame close enough to that of mass production to meet the urgent schedules; even before this, furthermore, the supply of the necessary aluminum alloys had been assured.   The production problems had been solved by a great many ingenious innovations in manufacturing methods and by improvement in the rapid training of young men who had mechanical aptitude but little or no actual experience.   The training methods quickly made these beginners very skillful "single-operation men."   One of the rules of the training course was: "Never let them get the idea that working metal to tolerances of 1 or 2 ten-thousandths of an inch is at all difficult."   By the fall of 1943, the production of Mark 1 computers had risen from the peacetime rate of perhaps one per month to almost one per day.

With adequate production of the Mark 1 computer assured, the Navy no longer needed the Mark 8 as a backup, and production contracts for the Mark 8 were not considered.   The Navy felt that regardless of any tests on the Mark 8, the problems of introducing a new computer into the fleet would be too great in midwar.   These problems included the installation of new computers on ships urgently needed for service elsewhere, the provision of new classes of spare parts, and retraining personnel on the care, feeding, and maintenance of electrical computers.   The veto of the use of aluminum in the Mark 8 made it weigh about twice as much as the Mark 1, which was an additional drawback.   And it was felt that the performance of the Mark 1 mechanical computer was adequate for the purpose at hand.

The development model of the Mark 8 (Figs. 3-11 and 3-12) was delivered to the Naval Research Laboratory Annex at North Beach, Maryland, on February 15, 1944, whereupon extensive comparison tests of it and the Mark 1 were made, using both the Mark 37 director and the Bell Labs Mark 7 radar as tracking devices.   These tests were primarily photo-data runs, with actual aircraft (usually executing ordered maneuvers) as targets; firing tests were not practicable at North Beach.   These tests indicated that the two machines were comparable in the accuracy of the gun orders delivered, except in regions where mathematical approximations inherent in

Fig. 3-11.   Exterior view of Mark 8 computer.

the design of the Mark 1 somtimes resulted in substantial errors.   (The Mark 8 geometry was substantially free of such errors.)   It was also found that the Mark 8 reached solution much faster than the Mark 1.   Since one of the drawbacks observed in fleet experience with the Mark 1 was its sluggishness, it was decided to attempt to modify the Mark 1 in accordance with the principles of the Mark 8 to obtain a faster solution time.

After these and other tests at North Beach were completed, the Mark 8 was installed on the U.S.S. *Wyoming*, the Navy's seagoing school of antiaircraft gunnery and fire control.   Here it was used in actual firing tests against radio-controlled drones in experiments related to the new fire control problems that had arisen during the course of the war.   These included the testing of nonstandard methods of using fire control equipment, weapons, and tactics against targets simulating kamikaze and baka bomb attacks.   (The baka was a small-winged rocket airplane that

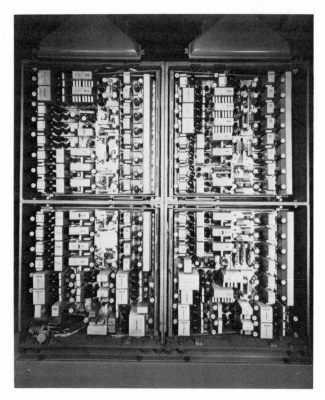

Fig. 3-12.   Rear view of Mark 8 computer with grilles removed.

carried a bomb and was released from a larger airplane.) Such experimentation gave the Navy experience in the maintenance of electrical fire control equipment under seagoing conditions.

1.10 Other Wartime Analog Computer Applications

Analog computers were also developed for use in aircraft for bombing and navigational computation. These computers used input data from either optical or radar sources having either actual target tracking or tracking of an offset aiming point. However, they came along too late in the war to see actual combat. The most sophisticated of these airborne bombing computers was the AN/APA-44, covered in Chapter 2, Section 3.4.7.

Quite a different application of the electrical analog computer was made in the operational flight trainers used in the training of pilots and navigators. In these the computer continuously solved the equations of aircraft motion on the basis of design parameters of the particular aircraft being simulated. Such a computer was built for an operational trainer simulating the PBM-3 that had the appearance and operating characteristics of the Navy's Martin Mariner patrol bomber (Fig. 3-13). Subsequently, similar equipment simulated the Grumman Hellcat fighter and the Consolidated Privateer patrol bomber.[20]

1.11 Postwar Military Applications of Electrical Analog Computers

The basic electrical analog technology developed by Bell Labs during the war for fire control purposes continued in use for 15 years or more and was used in two or three succeeding generations of fire control systems developed for the military services by Bell Labs and by other defense suppliers. Most applications were based on the dc-signal technology of the M-9 gun director and the M-8 gun data computer, but some used the ac-signal methods of the T-15 gun director. These methods were of course continuously improved to employ redesigned and modernized components and design techniques as needed to meet increasingly more stringent requirements.

The postwar Bell Labs systems making extensive use of such electrical analog technology include:

1. The M-33 antiaircraft fire control system[21]—a fully integrated system for acquisition, tracking, and control of land-based gunfire against aircraft.

2. The Nike-Ajax system[22]—developed for control of guided missiles as defense against the bombers of the immediate post-war period.

3. The Nike-Hercules system[23]—developed for control of longer-range and more powerful guided missiles as defense against greatly improved bomber types.

4. The Mark 65 project[24]—development of automatic target evaluation and weapon assignment systems for the U. S. Navy. This project also required provision of dc-signal analog computers for track-while-scan purposes.

II. DIGITAL COMPUTERS

2.1 From Dial Systems to Relay Digital Computers

Not all the computers developed by Bell Labs during the war years were of the analog type. A few were digital machines—early forerunners of today's high-speed electronic computers.

---

[20] R. O. Rippere, "An Electrical Computer for Flight Training," *Bell Laboratories Record* 25 (February 1947), pp. 78–81.

[21] Described in Chapter 7 of this volume.

[22] Ibid.

[23] Ibid.

[24] Described in Chapter 11 of this volume.

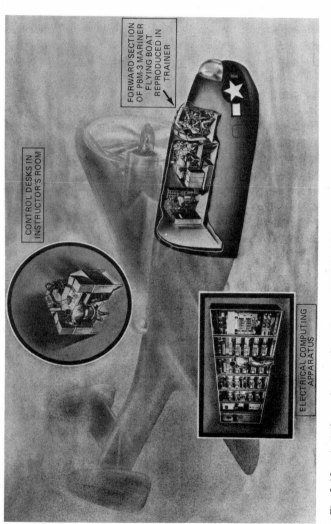

CONTROL DESKS IN INSTRUCTOR'S ROOM

FORWARD SECTION OF PBM-3 MARINER FLYING BOAT REPRODUCED IN TRAINER

ELECTRICAL COMPUTING APPARATUS

Fig. 3-13. Artist's rendering of mock-up of PBM-3 Mariner showing crew positions, instructor's and radio control positions, and electronic computing system.

Many of the basic concepts of electrical digital computers were first extensively employed and tested in Bell System dial telephone switching technology. While dial systems did not add or multiply, they performed many other operations needed in computation. In sophisticated dial systems the operations included the following:

1. Counting dial pulses to determine the next digit
2. Registering the dialed number
3. Translating one or more digits of a number into a different numbering system
4. Looking up tabulated routing information
5. Suspending the normal process of setting up a call and taking appropriate alternative action if the called line was busy or out of service or if the call could not be completed

At the time of World War II, almost all metropolitan dial offices used an assortment of relay circuits, of varied size and complexity, for detailed control of the numerical and logical operations necessary for call processing. Each type of circuit performed a specific task, and a circuit was normally used on a single call only for the time required to do its specific job and then released to serve other calls in turn.

Before 1937, the design of relay circuits was an art known only to a small circle of experts. But in that year Claude E. Shannon, who joined Bell Labs in 1941,[25] showed how Boolean algebra could be used as a powerful tool for the synthesis, analysis, and optimization of relay circuits. As a result, the design of relay circuits changed rapidly from being a somewhat esoteric art to being a science, and it became possible to teach it as an engineering discipline.

At about the same time, new circuit elements became available to the designer. These included bistable vacuum tube circuits and solid-state diodes; the latter led to new and useful gate configurations, such as the digital OR gate first described by A. W. Horton, Jr.,[26] and the AND gate of W. H. T. Holden.[27] The new digital devices, and the later development of the transistor, led to new developments in digital circuit design methods. These methods are now hard to recognize as being related to Boolean algebra but are nevertheless descended from one or more of its isomorphs, such as the calculus of propositions.

The technology of dial switching systems had by this time reached a point that made relay computers entirely practicable; indeed, many of the standard relay circuits of advanced dial systems needed only minor modifications to fit them in as subsystems of digital computers. At the same time, the load of routine computation involved in the design of wave

---

[25] Shannon had worked at Bell Labs in the summer of 1937 while a student at M.I.T.
[26] U.S. Patent No. 2,244,700; filed September 21, 1939; issued June 10, 1941.
[27] U.S. Patent No. 2,299,898; filed October 16, 1941; issued October 27, 1942.

filters, equalizers, and other transmission networks at Bell Labs was steadily becoming more burdensome. An important part of these computations involved multiplication and division of complex numbers, which were done on desk calculators—a time-consuming and tedious job, and hence prone to error. The departments concerned with this problem had been consulting with the mathematical research people off and on for a decade or more; while there had been some advances, there were no large improvements in computing techniques.

But in 1937 George R. Stibitz, of the mathematical research group, became interested in relay circuitry and quickly envisioned a possible solution: he sketched out the initial design of a relay computer specifically intended for doing arithmetic on complex numbers. Although the components available, mainly the relay and the teletypewriter, were relatively slow by today's standards, such a computer was much faster than the customary calculator and had the added virtue of flexibility.

The Complex Computer, as it was called, was designed and constructed during 1938 and 1939 under the direction of Samuel B. Williams, an engineer with long experience in the development of dial switching systems. Initially, it was designed to be merely a feasibility model. As a result, many features that would have appeared almost automatically in dial switching equipment were omitted, such as redundant numerical coding and provision of contact protection for the relays.

The Complex Computer was put into routine operation on January 8, 1940, in the old Bell Laboratories headquarters at 463 West Street in New York City. It had 450 relays and 10 crossbar switches, the latter being number registers. A unique and very modern feature was its remote stations, each with an input keyboard and a teletypewriter for output, at three locations, which were convenient to groups that were heavy users of the facility.

An event that foreshadowed the use of telephone lines for remote computer input occurred on September 11, 1940, in connection with presentation of a paper by Stibitz describing the computer before a meeting of the American Mathematical Society at Dartmouth College in Hanover, New Hampshire. A remote terminal at the lecture room in Hanover was connected via a slightly modified teletypewriter circuit to the computer at West Street in New York. After Stibitz had read his paper, those in attendance were invited to use the keyboard to give to the computer problems involving addition, subtraction, multiplication, or division of complex numbers; the answers were printed out on the teletypewriter in less than a minute. One of those who tried the facility was Dr. Norbert Wiener, who, characteristically, tried to stump the computer—without success. This was Wiener's first introduction to the computer concept.

As noted above, the Complex Computer, later renamed the Bell Model I, was built as a feasibility model. From the time it was placed in operation it was very heavily used. Normally a number of changes to improve its reliability and maintainability would have been made. Unfortunately, World War II broke out before this could be done. As the demands on the computer increased rapidly with the growth of military work at Bell Labs, maintenance became a problem. Finally, the deterioration resulting from the lack of contact protection required stripping most of the relay contacts off the springs and replacing them by new contact material. This work was carried out with tools developed by Western Electric to keep central offices with contact problems in service until the end of the war. The Complex Computer remained in continuous service at West Street until its retirement in 1949.

2.2 Wartime Relay Digital Computers

When the United States entered World War II, the digital techniques pioneered by Stibitz and Williams found their way into computers designed for military projects. These computers were intended to be special-purpose machines, but after the war, with some modifications based on experience, they proved very useful in other areas. As it happened, all three of the machines (known as Models II, III, and IV) were built for testing antiaircraft directors or for investigating other phases of fire control work. All the machines were programmable, with the program punched on paper tape, though the instruction complement was somewhat limited in view of the special-purpose classification. In addition, data input and output were handled almost entirely on punched tape. All three machines were also designed with standard dial system features needed for reliability and for ease of maintenance, such as redundant numerical coding and almost complete contact protection facilities.

The Model II machine was designed to handle a heavy load of highly routine computing that arose in the following way. The NDRC had developed equipment for dynamic testing of antiaircraft directors (including the Bell Labs-developed M-9 system). The equipment was driven by paper tape punched with digital information about the detailed behavior of a possible target; the tester in turn simulated corresponding input signals to the director so that its performance on that particular target could be observed. Making the tapes to drive the tester required a very large amount of interpolation from tabulated data. Therefore, the NDRC commissioned Bell Labs to design and build an all-relay digital computer called Relay Interpolator, with the program and input data on punched paper tape and the output available on teletypewriter or punched tape. The basic scheme was sketched by Stibitz, and the detailed design was carried out by E. G. Andrews and his group. This second machine was placed in service in the West Street laboratory in September 1943. This machine's arithmetic skills were limited in the main to addition, although it could multiply by a constant specified in the program. These capabilities sufficed, however, for the machine's normal work. Stibitz noted:

> It was exciting and a bit weird to watch this interpolator go about its work *sans* human boss: days, nights, Sundays and holidays. This was a year before [the Harvard] Mark I was formally demonstrated, and the use of teletype tapes and readers, under the control of an impersonal bank of relays, was new. At that time it seemed to us we had a highly intelligent machine—this first programmable computer. It could call for the next program step from one tape and the next data from another at exactly the right instant, and detect any extra holes worn in the tape by repeated runs. Those tapes took a pounding,[28] and things were not perfect in this imperfect world. Sometimes we would come in on a Monday morning expecting to find hundreds of feet of tape ready for the dynamic tester, only to find that sometime during the weekend a tape had worn or torn through, leaving the computer without instructions.[29]

The Model II computer had 440 relays and five pieces of teletypewriter equipment. It was built on two relay racks and contained six registers for storing numbers. Basically, it performed a linear iterative operation on numbers provided by the data tape. It could handle problems in harmonic analysis, solution of differential equations, and the like, but during the war it was kept too busy with routine interpolation and smoothing to do much else. Late in the war the Model II was moved to the Naval Research Laboratory, where it remained in service until 1961.

The Model III computer (see Fig. 3-14), a much larger and more powerful machine than the Model II, was also planned by Stibitz and developed for the NDRC by E. G. Andrews and his group to provide additional facilities for handling the enormous amount of computation required for fire control testing and development. It contained 1,400 relays mounted on five relay racks, provided ten number registers, and controlled seven pieces of teletypewriter equipment. Its checking facilities, based on redundant numerical coding, provided 100-percent self-checking of all operations. The machine stopped positively on any kind of single failure and on most combinations of two or more simultaneous failures. The standard teletypewriter readers were modified to move tapes in either direction and were controlled by "hunting" circuits that directed the forward or backward motion of the tapes to permit them to search for any address asked for by the master control. The searching operations proceeded independently of calculation; this arrangement greatly speeded up the work on many problems without requiring much internal storage, always a very expensive provision when relays were, of necessity, used for this purpose.

The Model III was completed in June 1944 and installed at Camp Davis,

---

[28] The program tape was looped, with the ends glued together, and ran repeatedly through the reader.

[29] George R. Stibitz, as told to Mrs. Evelyn Loveday, "The Relay Computers at Bell Labs (Part Two)," *Datamation* 13 (May 1967), pp. 45, 47.

(a)

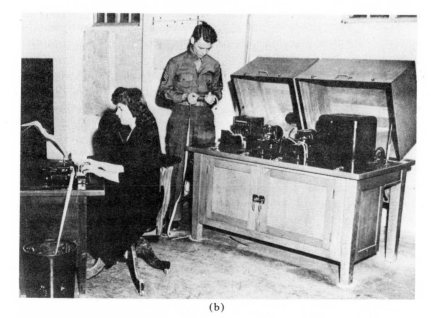

(b)

Fig. 3-14. Model III ballistic computer. (a) Equipment racks. (b) Paper-tape terminal.

North Carolina. Regularly running seven days and seven nights a week, it turned out as much work as could be done by 25 to 40 skilled operators using desk calculators. It was later moved to Fort Bliss, Texas, and modified to expand its facilities and usefulness; the alterations involved increasing the number of relays by 300 to 400, adding four more number registers, and making changes in its control arrangements. The Model III continued in use at Fort Bliss until 1958.

The Model IV computer, a slight modification of the Model III, was built for Naval Ordnance and installed at the Naval Research Laboratory in March 1945. It could handle trigonometric functions of negative as well as positive angles in problems relating to the control of guns on a rolling or pitching deck. This machine was known to the Navy as the Mark 22 computer and it continued in service until early 1961. Like the Model III, it was considerably reworked after the war to adapt it to handle problems other than those for which it was initially designed.

It is indicative of the reliability and the continuous-service capabilities of the wartime relay computers that all of them remained in service several years after commercial electronic computers of much greater speed were readily available.

2.3 Postwar Relay Digital Computers for the Military

After the war a much more powerful relay digital computer (Model V) was developed. This was a larger and much more capable machine than those built during the war, and was designed as a general-purpose digital computer, and thus was much more than an adjunct to investigations into fire control problems. Two units of the Model V were built; the first was delivered in 1946 to the National Advisory Committee on Aeronautics (NACA) Laboratory at Langley Field, Virginia, the other (in 1947) to the Army Ordnance Ballistic Research Laboratory at Aberdeen, Maryland.

The Model V could be equipped with up to six arithmetic units and ten problem positions. It used about 9,000 relays, and could handle up to 55 pieces of teletypewriter equipment (mainly tape readers). The machines actually delivered were somewhat more modestly equipped: each had two arithmetic units, and three or four problem positions. The design permitted arithmetic units to function continuously; problems were loaded onto idle problem positions, each of which had one tape reader for input data, up to five readers for programs (this permitted great flexibility in use of subroutines), and as many as six readers for tabular data. Heavily used tables (logarithmic and trigonometric) were permanently wired into the machine. When an arithmetic unit completed its assigned problem, it immediately picked up another from a new problem position.

The calculators of the Model V provided floating decimal point, multiplication by "short-cut addition," automatic round-off if desired, and extensive conditional transfer facilities. The Model V was normally worked around the clock, and when so used, handled about as much calculation as about 225 desk-calculator operators. In at least one week, one Model V operated for 167 out of a possible 168 hours, most of the time running completely unattended.

After the Model V machines were replaced by electronic computers at their original locations, one was sent to Fort Bliss, Texas, and was later given to New Mexico State University at Las Cruces, where it continued in use for educational and research purposes at least until 1964. The other machine, after use at the White Sands Proving Ground, was given to Texas Technological College in 1958. Unfortunately, on this trip it was severely damaged in transit and was of no further use except as a source of spare parts for the machine at Las Cruces.

The Mark 65 Project[30] also used relay computers of a much simpler character for switching data from search radars, after processing by analog track-while-scan computers, to directors, and for connecting directors tracking "hot" targets to gun mounts. This equipment used relays specially balanced to withstand the inevitable shocks to be expected on a warship.

III. SUMMARY

The technology of fire control was well advanced long before the entry of the United States into the war. It used optical means for locating targets and highly sophisticated mechanical analog computers to process the optical data for aiming ordnance. But optical location, because of atmospheric limitations, was a weak link in the system. Radar would obviously provide great improvement in target location if sufficient accuracy could be achieved. The possibility of obtaining improved target location was, indeed, a main objective of the early R and D work on radar initiated by the Navy, which led to the extensive and successful work in this field by Bell Laboratories and others already described.

Fortunately, and almost by chance, a few members of Bell Laboratories' staff, with no knowledge of ordnance or fire control, became interested in the problem of gun control by radar in 1940. They proposed using what was essentially an electrical form of analog computer. Their ideas proved so interesting to the military that a development contract was awarded Bell Laboratories early in November 1940. This led to the first electrical gun director, designated the T-10 and intended for control of 90-mm antiaircraft guns. Tests conducted in late 1941, just as the United States was entering the war, were so successful that in February 1942 the electrical director was adopted as standard military hardware.

The T-10 became the prototype of a series of M-9 directors for antiaircraft guns, which turned in impressive records against manned aircraft in many

---

[30] See Chapter 11.

areas. Guns controlled by such directors, using proximity-fuzed shells, played a major role in the 1944 defense of Britain against the buzz bomb. Deployed along the English Channel, they shot down 90 percent of the V-1's aimed at London and effectively pulled the teeth of Hitler's first "victory weapon."

Throughout the development of electrical directors, it was necessary to foresee, as far as possible, potential wartime difficulties involving scarce materials or manufacturing methods. In addition, the design of the T-10 involved making many choices between available alternatives. Since the electrical director was entirely new to the fire-control art, some of these choices had to be pretty arbitrary: there was as yet no experience on which to base rational decisions. As a result, the National Defense Research Committee and Bell Laboratories agreed that development would be desirable of a second type of director, intended for the same use but with major differences in methods of computation and determination of target rates, and using ac instead of dc signal voltages. Doing this would immediately broaden experience in this new art; and if difficulties arose when T-10 was tested, or in its manufacture or maintenance, this backup could be very valuable.

The Navy had before the war a good mechanical computer for antiaircraft fire control. Fortunately, this had been designed, at a time when optical input data was often spotty and sometimes quite erratic, to utilize continuous data in case it ever became available. Thus conversion to use of radar data required only a radar. But the necessarily greater complexity of the Navy's fire-control system made the procurement problem for mechanical computers even more critical than that facing the Army. The Navy thus also requested Bell Laboratories, about the time of Pearl Harbor, to develop an electrical computer as a possible replacement if procurement of its mechanical computers became difficult. Both the alternative Army director (the T-15) and the electrical computer for the Navy (the Mark 8) were completed, and on test proved somewhat better than their predecessors. But since the earlier machines were entirely adequate, and were by that time available in quantity, neither of these backup machines was put into production.

Thus Bell Laboratories, in addition to developing the directors of the T-10 family, which were manufactured in quantity and delivered yeoman service in many combat areas, also contributed heavily by developing two other computing systems of comparable complexity, both of which were deemed essential to provide backup production capability if it proved necessary. In neither case, as it turned out, was production needed; in both cases the experience gained proved very valuable in postwar fire-control development.

The basic technology of the electrical analog computer was also applied to the control of coast-defense artillery; a number of computers for this use were delivered to the Army. These performed very well under test; in service they had little to do, as there were no enemy targets to fire at.

The same basic methods were also applied to bombing and navigational computations in aircraft, and to simulators used in operational flight trainers for the schooling of aircraft pilots and navigators.

Not all Bell contributions to the computer art during World War II involved the use of analog techniques. In 1937 George R. Stibitz, a research mathematician at Bell Labs, conceived the idea of employing for purposes of computation the circuit elements regularly used for such things as counting, registration, and logical purposes in large dial central offices. The first Stibitz computer was built during 1938 and 1939, using only telephone relays and switches, which were the standard dial central office circuit elements at that time; a teletypewriter was used as the output device. This machine was designed to handle the multiplication and division of complex numbers, and it was placed in regular computer service at the beginning of 1940. It proved a great improvement over the desk calculators it replaced, although it was very slow compared to modern electronic computers. The design of this machine was carried out by people skilled in the telephone switching art; their only special training for computer work was a very short course (of one or two hours) in the details of binary arithmetic.

The techniques pioneered by Stibitz were used during the war in three special-purpose relay computers built for the extensive computations needed in connection with the testing of electrical fire-control computers and directors, and the investigation of proposed modifications of their design. All three of these built during World War II were delivered to Army or Navy service organizations concerned with fire-control problems. They all worked steadily, usually 24 hours per day, with only an occasional break for maintenance. They operated under control of programs punched on teletype tape, with their input data obtained from other teletype tape readers, and their output delivered either to tape punches or directly to a teletypewriter.

These computers were equipped with the standard features that extensive central-office experience had indicated were desirable for highly reliable performance. These included both equipment and systems features. One of the equipment features, for example, was the provision of extensive contact-protection facilities, which greatly decreased the incidence of sporadic misadventures. On the systems side, these machines used redundant binary coding of a type that permitted automatic error detection and resulted in stopping the machine and calling for maintenance when an error occurred.

All of these machines remained in service for 15 years or more, long after the problems for which they were specifically designed had been swept away by the advancing tide of guided missiles. And at least two of the machines were considerably reworked, long after their first youth, to extend their capabilities to classes of problems beyond the ken of their initial designers.

In the computer field the gun director was by far Bell Laboratories' greatest contribution to antiaircraft defense during World War II. It was an accurate and adaptable instrument, rugged and easy to maintain in the field. Its design made it manufacturable in quantity by mass production methods common to the telephone art, without requiring many highly skilled precision machinists. Perhaps the major significance of the story of the electrical director lay in the manner in which it was conceived. It arose, not from the experience of those skilled in the problems of ordnance, but rather through the efforts of people of solid scientific background, trained in applying scientific principles to the solution of problems requiring precision of thinking. These people had the imagination to suspect the existence of the fire control problem, and their background provided the tools needed for its solution. Having reached this point, they needed, in addition, access to experts in varied fields, ranging from mathematics to chemistry and to the engineering of new types of devices in forms that proved easily amenable to mass-production methods of manufacture. These people were fortunately already available on the staff of Bell Laboratories.

A great deal of credit is also due to those trained in ordnance for their perception of the value of electrical analog computers and for their immediate willingness to impart their knowledge to newcomers to their field. Indeed, the remarkable cooperation between concerned parties schooled in disparate disciplines, as well as the system for organizing liaison between scientists and military personnel, was essential to the results obtained in fire control in World War II. The spirit in which the joint commitment was carried out and the quick and effective interchange of ideas which it brought about contributed a great deal more to the American cause than the American public can perhaps ever realize.

Chapter 4

Acoustics

The application of acoustics to warfare was a logical role for the Bell System since much of telephony is based on this science. Some of the World War II applications, such as the design of special telephone instruments and high-power audio systems, were natural extensions of Bell's peacetime efforts. However, by far the greatest contribution was made in the area of undersea warfare, a field applying the basic principles of acoustics but reaching far beyond the familiar telephone experience. This work required the development of acoustic techniques in an unfamiliar and previously little explored medium. From this work there evolved means for locating submarines and homing torpedoes guided to their goal by sounds generated by their submarine targets, devices which played a major role in controlling the effectiveness of the previously almost invulnerable commerce-destroying tactics of the Germans.

I. INTRODUCTION

The Bell System was born of the insight into acoustics of Alexander Graham Bell, of whose telephone Lord Kelvin said, "Today I have seen that which yesterday I should have deemed impossible. Soon lovers will whisper their secrets over an electric wire." [1] With sound being the unalterable link at each end of the telephone system, it was necessary that extensive work be carried out on almost all phases of speech, hearing, and acoustics. This work in turn generated numerous by-products to the basic person-to-person voice communication, and the promotion of these gave broad acoustics training to many Bell Laboratories people. By 1940, there were probably as many highly trained people in acoustics research and electroacoustics development at Bell Laboratories as in the rest of the country.

---

[1] S. McMeen and K. B. Miller, eds., *Telephony* (Chicago: American Technical Society, 1923).

Principal author: C. F. Wiebusch

II. UNDERWATER APPLICATIONS

With this capability available it was only natural that the armed forces and the newly formed (June 27, 1940)[2] National Defense Research Committee (NDRC) would look to Bell Laboratories to take a leading role in acoustics-related developments for the anticipated war effort. Such developments took many forms: high-power sirens for air raid warning, underwater acoustic echo ranging (sound navigation and ranging, or sonar) for finding submerged submarines, sound locators to determine enemy gun positions, acoustically guided mines and torpedoes, battle-announcing systems delivering high levels of sound, helmet headsets, transmitters for use in oxygen masks, improved headset receivers, throat and lip microphones for noisy environments, and the very important measurement projects and standards. Under the skilled general guidance of H. Fletcher in research and W. H. Martin in development and design, much was accomplished in a very few years.

2.1 Underwater Acoustic Measurements

In a lecture in 1883, Lord Kelvin stated: "I often say that when you can measure what you are speaking about, and express it in numbers, you know something about it; when you cannot express it in numbers your knowledge is of a meagre and unsatisfactory kind." [3] This latter was the situation in underwater acoustics in 1940, and for this reason Bell Laboratories undertook exploratory work on underwater acoustic measurements. The work required an out-of-doors body of water, preferably one with a soft, low-reflectivity bottom, and Crystal Lake in Mountain Lakes, New Jersey, was selected. A group of engineers consisting of A. H. Inglis, F. F. Romanow, E. Hartmann and others was organized and a field laboratory was set up at the lake.[4] At this time there were no underwater transducer[5] standards for which the electrical-to-acoustical conversion characteristics could be determined by computation or simple air calibration techniques.

This work was called to the attention of the NDRC's Division 6, organized in 1941, whose main responsibility was the development of new and improved methods for detecting submerged submarines.[6] This division

---

[2] J. P. Baxter III, *Scientists Against Time*, Boston: Little, Brown, 1946, pp. 172–185.

[3] Sir William Thomson [Lord Kelvin], *Popular Lectures and Addresses: Constitution of Matter*, I, London: MacMillan, 1889.

[4] Letter from W. H. Martin to M. D. Fagen, January 20, 1974.

[5] In underwater acoustics, as in air transmission of sound, the term *transducer* is used to designate a converter between media by which sound waves are transmitted. The term *hydrophone* designates a transducer which converts acoustic waves in water to electric waves and is analogous to the microphone used for sound waves in air. The device corresponding to the telephone receiver or loudspeaker is usually referred to as a *projector*, which converts electric waves to acoustic waves in water. While these are the usual designations, almost all underwater transducers were reciprocal devices.

[6] Baxter, *Scientists Against Time*, p. 173.

recognized that one of the cornerstones of its program had to be the development of accurate methods for the measurement of sound in water, and in July 1941[7] it contracted with the Western Electric Company for the development of standard hydrophones, sound sources, and calibrating procedures. Under this contract Bell Laboratories expanded the testing laboratory at Crystal Lake and later established a second lab at Lake Gem Mary in Orlando, Florida. The latter is still in operation as a calibration station by the U.S. Navy. These stations covered the measurement range of frequencies from 2 Hz to 2.2 MHz, of ambient pressures to 300 psi, of temperatures from 35 to 100°F, and of acoustic powers to 1,500 watts.[8]

Suitable transducers were developed, and it then became possible by reciprocity calibration methods and by computations based on known constants to achieve a satisfactory degree of accuracy in measurements. While these new transducers were being used, it was found that the calibration of the previously accepted tourmaline crystal hydrophone standard was about 9 dB in error. It would be hard to overestimate the importance to all United States underwater acoustic projects of having accurate measuring tools. Theoretical studies began to have meaning, and specifications could be prepared with confidence and product-tested for compliance.

During this first year of United States involvement in World War II, the Navy asked the Western Electric Company to become a supplier of underwater sound gear. To prevent any appearance of conflict of interest, since equipment of other laboratories and suppliers would also need to be tested, Bell Laboratories suggested that the test stations have a different sponsor.[9] Therefore, in May 1942 the operation of the two test stations, together with most of the former Bell Labs personnel, was transferred to the Columbia University NDRC contract and became known as the Underwater Sound Reference Laboratories. At the end of the war, the Bell Labs people transferred back to their old departments. During the later years of World War II, Bell continued to work with the Reference Laboratories by developing new hydrophones and sound sources and by constructing instruments.

2.2 The Sounds of the Sea

A knowledge of the sounds in the sea is basic to the design and effective use of all underwater acoustical systems used in offensive and defensive warfare. Background noise, always present in the sea, is a limiting factor in devices (such as those described in the next section) used by submarine and surface ships in locating targets. This "ambient" noise comes from

[7] Ibid.

[8] "Basic Methods for the Calibration of Sonar Equipment," Summary Technical Report of Division 6, National Defense Research Committee 10, 1946 (Defense Documentation Center No. ATI 15826).

[9] Baxter, *Scientists Against Time*, p. 175, 176.

many sources and varies greatly with the sea conditions and aquatic life. Sounds produced by ships are also a significant factor in designing passive detection devices and acoustically controlled weapons. These sounds, too, are highly variable, depending on both the characteristics and speed of ships.

Before the standardization and calibration work noted in the preceding section, only makeshift means were available for determining these important data on underwater sound. Each design group had to supply its own information, since errors in calibration and differences in measuring techniques made it impractical to compare data obtained by different organizations. This resulted in much duplication of effort and considerable uncertainty about design parameters.

Once standardized measurement equipment and methods were available, it became possible to reduce these problems and to build up a bank of data on the sounds of the sea, based on the output of experimenters working in many parts of the country, which would be of use for many projects. Division 6 of NDRC assigned the responsibility for this project to V. O. Knudsen of the University of California, a member of the Division. Three members of Bell Labs (R. S. Alford, T. Dow, and J. W. Emling) were relieved of their regular duties and assigned to work with Knudsen to coordinate and systematize data on underwater sound collected by the various groups working in the field.

This group ultimately issued three reports covering ambient noise[10] and the sounds of submarines and surface vessels. Naturally this was a continuing, long-term job, since each set of new data, as it came along, added to the total understanding of the subject. But many projects could not wait for the comprehensive reports, and while these were in preparation the Bell Labs group kept in close contact with a large number of acoustical projects and served as an informal clearing house for furnishing available information to those needing it.

2.3 Sonar

Although originally intended to cover only underwater acoustic echo ranging (active devices), the usage of the word *sonar* has been extended to all underwater acoustic devices, including means for simply listening for ship sounds (passive devices), used for the detection and/or location of submarines, ships, or other noise-generating underwater objects. A number of Bell System people, including F. B. Jewett and O. E. Buckley, had worked on submarine detection in World War I and recognized that submarines were again going to be a major threat to the Allies. They

---

[10] While some of the material remained classified under national defense security regulations, the report on ambient noise was published in condensed form in a paper by V. O. Knudsen, R. S. Alford, and J. W. Emling, "Underwater Ambient Noise," *J. Marine Research* 7 (1948), pp. 410–429.

decided that with the acoustics background available at Bell Laboratories, work on submarine detection should be undertaken.

Echo ranging was not a new technique; it had been worked on for the Navy by the Submarine Signal Company between the two wars and was widely used on ships for depth sounding. Basically echo ranging depends on the transmission of a short pulse of sound into the water and the measurement of the time required for an echo to return from the bottom or from some object in the water, such as a submarine. The velocity of sound in the ocean ranges from about 4,700 to 5,000 feet per second, depending on water temperature, salinity, and depth. For most practical purposes, for calculating the distance to an object causing the echo, an average figure of 4,800 feet per second is used. For producing the sound pulse, an electrical pulse is fed into an electroacoustic transducer, which converts it into underwater sound just as a loudspeaker converts electrical energy to sound energy in air. The returning echo is converted back to an electrical pulse, either by the same transducer or by a separate one. To prevent the echo from the ocean bottom from overpowering and masking an echo from a submarine, the transducers are made directional. The directional characteristic of the receiving transducer permits learning the direction to the target. This direction, together with the distance found from the arrival time of the echo, gives the actual location of the target relative to the sonar.[11]

However, things are not as simple as they may seem. Sound transmission in all media follows the same fundamental physical laws; only the constants differ. Variation in density of the medium affects the velocity and causes bending of sound waves as do lenses with light waves. Since the density of water depends on temperature, salinity, and pressure, and since these vary with location and depth, it is easy to understand that sound seldom travels in a straight line except over short distances.

Salinity is almost constant except near the mouths of large rivers; depth needs little explanation since it is the depth at which the sound pulse is at any instant; but temperature is unpredictable, especially near the surface where the water is stirred up by waves. This upper, mixed water is called the surface layer—or more often just "the layer," as in the expression, "the submarine is hiding just below the layer." Sound therefore travels along curved paths and often creates shadow zones where little or no sound arrives. These basics were understood, but most of the practical details

---

[11] Readers will note the similarity between underwater echo ranging and radar. There were, however, important differences which greatly affected the design and application of the two techniques. Radio waves travel at the speed of light (186,000 miles per second). Hence, radar reflections return from a target in small fractions of a millisecond, and a rotating antenna can scan 360 degrees in a few minutes. By contrast, an echo from an underwater target only a mile away requires over 2 seconds to return, and the scanning process is much slower. The attenuation of acoustic waves in water confines the use of underwater devices to low frequencies, usually under 30 kHz, which require the use of longer pulses than are possible with radar, which uses frequencies many magnitudes greater.

had to be learned the hard way during the war. All these factors affect the sound power required, the directivity characteristics, and the display of the information in the echo.

The Navy had a supply source for some sonars, but wishing another source it asked Bell Laboratories to undertake the development of echo-ranging sonars for use on antisubmarine patrol ships only. But, since the equipment designed by A. C. Keller and his group proved highly successful, it was put on destroyers as well. During the war, four different sonar systems were designed and put into production by the Western Electric Company. The first of these, the QBF, went into production in May 1943. Using an array of Rochelle salt crystals in an improved dome with an acoustic screen to shield it from the ship's own propeller noise, the QBF was about half the size of units then in use by the Navy. Its improved noise characteristics permitted U.S. destroyers to use submarine detection equipment while operating at considerably higher speeds than before.

The second equipment, the QJA, which was designed in 1943 and went into production in 1944,[12] is described in more detail in the following discussion. In addition to sound listening and echo ranging, the QJA incorporated underwater telegraph communication. For listening, any 3-kHz band between 10 and 30 kHz could be shifted down to the audio range, and the trained listener could often determine whether the sound source was a submarine, a surface ship, or some form of marine life. If the submarine was making sufficient speed for the propeller to make noise, the listener could make a good estimate of the rpm of the propeller and hence of the submarine speed. This was called the "turn count." The receiving unit, consisting of an array of crystals, was directional, and the operator could swing the unit to point in any direction and therefore could find the direction from which the sound was loudest—in other words, obtain a bearing on the target.

If an enemy submarine were attempting to remain undetected, it would operate under ultraquiet "creep" conditions with the propellers turning so slowly as to make no audible noise and, as was found on a German submarine captured by the British in 1942, with the crew wearing crepe-rubber-soled shoes and using rubber-faced hammers for repair and maintenance work. For such quiet targets the echo-ranging mode of the destroyer's sonar had to be brought into play. In this mode, a short pulse—whose frequency could be selected within limits by the operator but which was usually about 25 kHz on the QJA—could be transmitted, and from the echo, the direction and range to the target could be obtained. Unfortunately, the echo tells very little of the true character of the echo source; whales, seamounts, submarines, and some other unknowns look

---

[12] A. C. Keller, "Submarine Detection by Sonar," *Bell Laboratories Record* 25 (February 1947); 55–60; *Trans. AIEE* 66 (1947): 1217–1230.

Fig. 4-1.   Indicator and control unit for QJA sonar.   (*Trans. AIEE,* 1947, p. 1225.)

much alike, and postanalysis has shown that only about 1 out of 13 of the supposed targets that were attacked was actually a submarine.   In spite of this high false target ratio, the QJA and other active sonars developed by other laboratories proved highly effective.

Operating as a telegraph, the QJA permitted the sending or receiving of messages through the water to and from other compatibly equipped ships or submarines.   Such ship-to-ship communication has the advantage that it is range limited to a few miles and cannot be intercepted at great ranges—as can radio.   It can take the place of the blinker light during times of low visibility.

The entire sonar set consists basically of two units: (1) the control unit containing the beam steering control, the electronics, and the display, all mounted topside on the ship; and (2) the dome containing the transducer, mounted at the bottom of the hull.   This dome could be retracted into the hull when not in use, or lowered into the water for a clear view in any horizontal direction.   The transducer unit could be rotated within the stainless steel dome by a handwheel at the control unit.

Figure 4-1 shows the indicator and control unit of the QJA.   As can be seen, the central part of the face has an outer circular scale calibrated for target range.   Inside this scale is a rotating disc equipped with a neon lamp. As the lamp crosses the zero line, the acoustic pulse is sent out and when an echo returns, the lamp flashes (shown as a spot on the right-hand side of the scale).   The next circular scale is fixed and graduated from 0 to 360 degrees, with 0 degree corresponding to the ship's bow. The circular dial inside this unit is a compass repeater connected to the ship's gyrocompass system, in which the zero is true north. The pointer shown repeats the transducer position relative to the ship. The lamp flash position then gives the range, and the pointer shows the bearing from which the echo came.

Prewar sonars had large magnetostriction transducers. The Naval Research Laboratory and other suppliers had developed sound projectors using Rochelle salt crystals for the active elements, and Bell Laboratories adopted this design for its first sonar, the QBF. Rochelle salt has several shortcomings in temperature range and in power-handling capacity. In prewar research, Bell Laboratories had experimented with about 150 synthetic crystals; and with this background, the ADP (ammonium dihydrogen phosphate)[13] crystals were selected and adapted to produce the first ADP sonar projector to be put in service. The efficiency of the ADP crystals was greatly increased when W. P. Mason developed a gold-plating process that improved the contact to the crystal surfaces.·

Because of the importance of the project, cooperative development work was carried on with the Brush Development Company, which had done most of the early work on ADP, and with the Naval Research Laboratory. Bell Laboratories set up a pilot plant for growing and processing ADP crystals; and in the latter half of 1943, Western Electric set up a large manufacturing area in its Hawthorne Works near Chicago that produced about one million ADP crystals during the war. These crystals were used in Western Electric sonars and in sonars built by other suppliers.

The transducer consists of an array of crystals, as shown in Fig. 4-2. The arrangement of these crystals is designed to give the desired directivity and the necessary power output. This new transducer was much more efficient than any previous Navy transducer and required only 150 watts for the same acoustic output. It also operated over the frequency range of 10 to 30 kHz instead of at a single frequency as in previous systems. This permitted the operator to shift frequency by changing the setting of a single dial instead of having to replace the entire transducer. These advantages were in addition to the reduced size, and since this same transducer was used for both receiving and listening, the wider frequency range gave improved performance here also.

Design models of new transducers were first tested at the Mountain Lakes or, later, the Orlando Sound Reference Laboratories; but then, for simulating field conditions and motion through the water, they were installed on the chartered cabin cruiser the *Elcovee*, shown in Fig. 4-3. With the new dome, designed in conjunction with the Navy's David Taylor Model Basin, the maximum destroyer operating speed for submarine de-

---

[13] W. P. Mason, *Electromechanical Transducers and Wave Filters*, D. Van Nostrand, 1948; W. P. Mason, "ADP and KDP Crystals," *Bell Laboratories Record* 24 (July 1946), pp. 257–260.

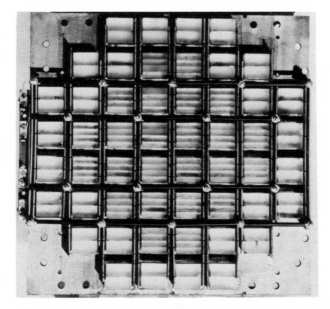

Fig. 4-2.   Crystal array of the sonar transducer using the ADP piezoelectric crystals.

tection was almost doubled.   The limiting factors for sonar operation are flow noise over the dome and the ship's own propeller noise.

It was not practical to test a product by putting each unit or an adequate number of product samples on a boat.   To permit production testing, Bell Laboratories developed for the Western Electric Company the underwater equivalent of an anechoic chamber, shown in Fig. 4-4.   This was generally referred to as the "artificial ocean."   The tank was lined with underwa-

Fig. 4-3.   The *Elcovee,* used as a floating test laboratory for studies of sonar systems.

Fig. 4-4.   Acoustic testing tank.   (*Trans. AIEE, 1947,* p. 1229.)

ter-sound-absorbing material and could be pressurized to simulate ocean
depths.   Good design, protection, and quality control gave the Navy the
kind of equipment that reflected credit on the Bell System.

2.4 Magnetic Detection of Submarines

Although magnetic detection of submarines may seem out of place in
a chapter on acoustics, it is closely intertwined with acoustic detection.
As mentioned earlier, a very serious problem with sonar search was the
13 to 1 false target ratio for echo ranging.   If the submarine was running
fast or was otherwise noisy, listening could often give a positive identification of the target, but a submarine in hiding is not likely to be so cooperative.

Alexander Graham Bell had an early interest in magnetic detection.

After President Garfield was shot on July 2, 1881, confirmation of the surgeon's estimate of the bullet's location became important. It was reported in *Frank Leslie's Illustrated Newspaper* of August 20, 1881:

> The most important event of the past week in the case of President Garfield was the location of the bullet in his body. The instrument used is called the induction-balance, and was invented by Professor Alexander Graham Bell. ... The decisive experiments were made on the morning of August 1st, being conducted by Professors Bell and Laintor in the presence of Drs. Agnew, Reyburn, Barnes, Bliss and Woodword. The machinery was placed in the library, the room adjoining the President's so that only the telephonic attachment and the bullet-seeker were visible in the patient's room as shown in our illustration [Fig. 4-5].[14]

Professor Bell's method was not a direct forerunner of the technique later used in submarine detection, except that his had a similar purpose (finding metal) and made use of magnetic effects. His was an "active" method in contrast to the one used in submarine detection, which could be classified as "passive" (although it does depend on relative motion of the detector and the target). This distinction is similar to that between active and passive sonar.

A submarine contains many hundreds of tons of iron and steel which distort the earth's magnetic field in its vicinity; in other words, it creates an anomaly in the field. Detectors for finding such anomalies have been christened with the acronym MAD, for *Magnetic Anomaly Detector*. The earth's magnetic field in middle latitudes is about 60,000 gamma (0.6 oersted), and a World War II submarine produced an anomaly of only about 1 gamma at 500 to 600 feet. This anomaly decreases inversely as the

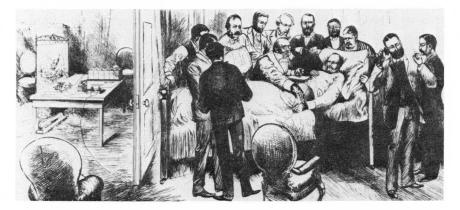

Fig. 4-5. Alexander Graham Bell's induction-balance being used on President James Garfield to determine location of assassin's bullet—July 2, 1881 (*Frank Leslie's Illustrated Newspaper*, August 20, 1881.)

[14] *Frank Leslie's Illustrated Newspaper*, August 20, 1881.

square of the distance. A magnetometer passed over the submarine at even the 500- to 600-foot range would have to detect a change of 1 in 60,000 in the magnetic field. In addition, the earth's magnetic field has small variations in time and space, giving rise to the familiar signal-to-noise problem. Although the predictably short ranges offered little hope for initially finding a submarine, the device could provide all-important "classification" information (that is, information needed to identify a target as a metallic object) after detection by sonar (or by sonobuoys which were developed in England and by the New London Underwater Sound Laboratory). MAD not only reduced attacks on false targets[15] but also improved attacks on real ones. This was an advantage which made the device attractive in spite of its short range, since, if a positive identification occurred, the target position was determined accurately enough to make depth charges effective.

Bell Labs' development of the MAD—under the direction of W. J. Shackelton, E. P. Felch, and W. J. Means—was carried out at the request of and in cooperation with the Naval Ordnance Laboratory. The NDRC had a parallel development, and there was a free interchange of information between NDRC and Bell Labs personnel. Both groups used at the heart of their detector the standard 4-79 molybdenum permalloy that had been developed many years earlier.[16,17]

The Bell Labs work resulted in the AN/ASQ-3 and the AN/ASQ-3A magnetic airborne submarine detectors, both of which were put into production by Western Electric in 1943. The two detectors were quite similar, but the 3A system was developed for applications at lower aircraft speeds and for applications requiring the measurement of very slowly varying field strengths, as in carrying out magnetic surveys.

The equipment of the AN/ASQ-3 consists of two major parts: (1) the magnetometer unit which can be mounted in a streamlined "bird" towed by the airplane or, for larger airplanes such as the PBY, it mounted in a plywood tail extension; and (2) the electronics, power supply, and control and display units which are distributed within the aircraft.

The detection unit within the bird consists of three inductors. Each consists of a core 1.5 inches long and 0.1 inch in diameter, rolled up in slightly more than one turn of 1-mil permalloy. This core, after annealing, was slipped over a glass tube and then inserted into a lucite spool carrying a single winding. If an alternating current is passed through the coil together with a superimposed steady magnetomotive force, the magnetic flux in the core will depend on the sum of the two. The rate of change

---

[15] Depth charge attacks on false targets were to be avoided because they not only wasted ammunititon but also churned up the water and made listening conditions poor, or even impossible, for some time afterward.

[16] Western Electric Co., *1944 Renegotiation*, pp. 84–85.

[17] E. P. Felch et al., "Air-borne Magnetometers for Search and Survey," *Trans. AIEE* 66 (1947), pp. 641–651.

of this flux will induce a back electromotive force in the coil which will be unsymmetrical and will contain both odd and even harmonics. The system described here used the second harmonic as a measure of the magnetic field strength, all other components being filtered out. A 1,000-Hz oscillator supplied the alternating driving magnetomotive force to the inductor, and the 2,000-Hz second harmonic of the back electromotive force was passed by a 2,000-Hz filter to the electronic detector. This second harmonic voltage can be calculated as a function of the alternating H_0 and the superimposed field. The value of the alternating force was adjusted to give the maximum sensitivity for the detection of small variations in the harmonic caused by anomalies in the field resulting from magnetic objects.

Such a single inductor responds only to the component of the magnetic field parallel to the axis of the core. Calculations showed that if such an inductor were moved over the earth, its orientation would have to be held constant to better than 0.001 degree to avoid masking a magnetic anomaly of one gamma. This is impractical, and as a result a modified approach was necessary.

The three inductors of the AN/ASQ-3 were mounted with their axes mutually perpendicular. The square root of the sum of the squares of the three outputs gave a measure of the total magnetic field independent of the orientation of the group as a whole, provided that the three units were truly perpendicular and closely matched in electromagnetic characteristics. These severe requirements could be relaxed to practical limits if the orientation of one of the inductors was held parallel to the earth's magnetic field to-within two degrees. This condition was satisfied if the other two inductors were within two degrees of being perpendicular to this field. The outputs of these two were used to operate a servo system to control the orientation of the inductor group.

The AN/ASQ-3A could measure the absolute magnitude of a magnetic field and not just the rate of change of the field, as did the AN/ASQ-3. This capability introduced the problems of direct current balancing, much as in dc amplifiers, thus complicating the adjusting problem for the operator. For submarine detection, the absolute magnitude of the field was not needed, but it was needed for magnetic mapping. The U.S. Geological Survey and the U.S. Coast and Geodetic Survey are using somewhat revised forms of these instruments for the mapping of natural resources, thus providing another instance of a useful byproduct of a wartime military development.

2.5 Acoustic Mines and Torpedoes

From the time of the development of the first self-propelled torpedo by Robert Whitehead in 1864 for the Austrian navy, much attention has been given to guiding these missiles. Until the start of World War II, the only practical method used a gyro for horizontal control and a pressure unit plus pendulum for vertical control Homing on the sounds of a target was much discussed from 1918 on, but the idea was always discarded as impractical because of the high noise level that was generated by the torpedo itself.

Following some torpedo self-noise measurements by the British, the U.S. Navy in the fall of 1941 requested the NDRC to set up a research and development program for a small, slow-speed, acoustically controlled, air-launched, antisubmarine torpedo.[18] The program was considered extremely urgent, since during the period from April to December 1941 U-boats were sinking an average of 175,000 tons of Allied shipping each month, and the prospects were that this incidence would increase—and it did.[19]

A first meeting of representatives of the Navy, NDRC, General Electric Company, Harvard University Underwater Sound Laboratory, and Bell Laboratories was held at Harvard on December 10, 1941. A second meeting was held at Bell Labs on December 24 to outline the general requirements and responsibilities. These tentative requirements were: electrical propulsion using a lead storage battery, a speed of 12 knots for 5 to 15 minutes, an explosive charge of 100 pounds, and acoustical directional control with a homing range as great as possible. The General Electric Company took responsibility for the design of the propulsion and steering motors; the Navy's David Taylor Model Basin was authorized to give any assistance it could; and both Harvard and Bell Labs were asked to attack the overall problem with independent lines of approach but on a cooperative and information-sharing basis.

Bell Labs started work immediately and submitted a formal proposal to V. W. Houston of the NDRC on January 8, 1942. Two departments were set up in the research area, one group under J. C. Steinberg to work on the ultrasonic range that depended on sound level discrimination between hydrophones of a pair, and the second group under R. L. Wegel to work at low frequencies, such as 250 Hz, and to use phase discrimination. Early in February, A. F. Bennett and C. F. Wiebusch were designated in the Apparatus Development Department to follow the work both at Bell Labs and at Harvard and, if there appeared to be good prospects for an effective torpedo, to make recommendations for development and then head the torpedo program.

Results at the higher frequencies at both of the laboratories soon appeared promising so that in view of the urgency, Bell Labs was authorized in a letter of May 15, 1942, from J. T. Tate of NDRC to R. L. Jones to

[18] *A Survey of Subsurface Warfare in WW II*, Summary Technical Report of Division 6, National Defense Research Committee (Defense Documentation Center No. AD221292).

[19] C. M. Sternkell and A. M. Thorndike, *Antisubmarine Warfare in World War II*, OEG Report No. 51, Office of C&O, Navy Department, 1946, (Defense Documentation Center No. AD221292).

start a development program aimed at design for production.[20,21] This torpedo project became by far the largest of all of the acoustic programs at Bell Labs during the war. At this time the project had the code name "Fido" but with the project now classified Top Secret, the name was considered revealing. Both for security reasons and because of the Navy's desire to get the work into the mine section instead of the torpedo section of the Navy Bureau of Ordnance, the new device was coded as Mine Mark 24.

The development of a device as complex as an acoustic torpedo, for which at that time little background information existed, required the bringing together of people with many differing skills. In addition, high security severely limited the possibility of farming out parts of the project which would be too revealing of the total project or its intended uses. The nerve center of the torpedo had to be electronic circuits, which in a manner to be described later, took the signals from hydrophones and other sensors and processed them in a way to control the motion of the torpedo. These circuits were designed under the direction of A. C. Dickieson and mounted on a circular panel to just fit the 19-inch diameter of the torpedo body. The overall design of the electrical system was carried out by K. M. Fetzer and his group. There were, of course, many mechanical and hydrodynamical problems that had to be solved, and groups under J. M. Hardesty and B. A. Merrick carried out this work and also provided the necessary manufacturing information to Western Electric.

While experimental work on self noise and guidance was going on, body mock-ups were made and taken to several airfields to check fitting and launching arrangements in the various types of aircraft used in antisubmarine missions. Fully weighted body models were made and fitted with simple steel-ball-plus-lead-plug accelerometers to measure the impact accelerations as the body hit the water after dropping. A thin plywood spoiler ring resembling an old-time cheese box was designed for the nose and plywood fins were added to the tail to assure smooth entry into the water. Figure 4-6 shows the outline of the agreed-upon body for the new mines without the spoiler ring and extra fins, these latter being shattered and thrown clear on impact.

In a clearing in the woods at the Murray Hill, N.J., location of Bell Labs a dropping tower with a heavy concrete base was built. The base had a steel-lined hemispherical receptacle into which lead plugs were fitted to give the mine, when dropped on the base, a deceleration of about twice that found in the field tests. This factor of two made up for the longer time duration of the deceleration in the water drop. For a cross-check, occasional drops with full, but not necessarily working, equipment were made

[20] Mine Mark 24 Experimental Model, Report to OSRD-NDRC Division 6, Section 6.1 sr-785-1327 (Defense Documentation Center No. ATI111035).

[21] M. B. Gardner, "Mine Mark 24: World War II Acoustic Torpedo," *J. Audio Engineering Society* 22 (October 1974), pp. 614–626.

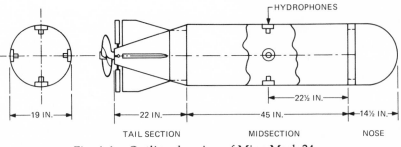

Fig. 4-6.   Outline drawing of Mine Mark 24.

from an airplane into water at speeds and heights in excess of the 125-knot 250-foot design values.   Except in the case of the battery, the sea drop results on damage correlated well with the laboratory drops, thus permitting the latter to be used almost exclusively in the development process.

Bell Laboratories gave a development contract, and later Western Electric gave a production contract, to the Electric Storage Battery Company for the lightweight, 48-volt, shock-resistant, lead-acid storage batteries.   These could not be made adequately shock resistant in themselves, and a shock pad had to be provided in the body of the mine at the forward end of the battery.   At a later time, when it became desirable to use higher-speed aircraft, drogues with release mechanisms were designed and supplied.

The early research models used a stock 16 × 16 propeller.   But since the acoustic homing range depended on the self-noise and since propulsion was one of the major sources of noise, a low-noise propeller was needed. Neither Bell Labs nor Harvard had any background in low-noise propeller design, so a Bell Labs mathematician and an engineer went to the David Taylor Model Basin to see their expert, Karl Schoenherr.   Hoping to get some advice, references, and perhaps even some help, the Bell Labs visitors discussed the problem for about 20 minutes while Schoenherr sketched freehand on a large piece of paper.   He then handed over the paper with the comment, "Here is your prop."   When they protested that this did not seem useful, he called a draftsman to scale off his sketch and make a dimensional drawing.   After lunch, Bell Labs had its design for a propeller with a 14 ¾-inch diameter and a 12-inch pitch.   This procedure was most unsatisfying from a scientific viewpoint, and work to improve on the design was undertaken at Harvard and later at Penn State, but it was 1950 before a better propeller for the purpose was made.[22]

---

[22] Measuring the noise produced by a propeller was not easy, since there was not sufficient space in the mine for the sound-measuring equipment then available.   Among other tests were some made jointly by Harvard and Bell Labs in a towing tank at the David Taylor Model Basin.   These tests showed an adequately low self-noise level even though the tile-lined tank was highly reflective and indicated much greater noise than would have been measured in the open sea.   Further tests in the tank showed that Dr. Schoenherr had designed a very good propeller indeed.   The noise remained satisfactorily low until cavitation occurred, and this did not take place until the body drag was increased to many times that which would be experienced under operating conditions.

One of the first things the development engineers wanted was to see existing torpedoes and get drawings; but with one excuse or another the Bureau of Ordnance kept putting this off, so it was necessary to go ahead from scratch—which was, of course, what the Navy wanted. The new body was designed of rolled, formed, and welded sections with wide tolerance joints sealed by O rings and held together by eight studs and nuts. The production facility for these, found by Western Electric and Bell Labs engineers, was a bathtub manufacturer whose most precise measuring instrument appeared to be a wooden yardstick. But with the aid of a few go–no go checking gauges and some engineering assistance, the company made and shipped the large number of interchangeable sections with few defects. When the new design of body was well along and some standard torpedoes were seen, the reason for the Navy's holding back was obvious: the standard bodies were carefully forged and lathe-turned with very precise ground-tapered joints between sections—manufacturing procedures which were not only very expensive but also required highly specialized equipment for production.

As pointed out in an NDRC report,[23] the main differences in the Bell Labs and Harvard research systems were the location and type of hydrophones. The method of operation was the same, although there were various circuit differences. The Bell Labs model used crystal hydrophones mounted in the cylindrical section of the body, whereas the Harvard model used magnetostriction hydrophones mounted in the nose section.

The functional diagram shown in Fig. 4–7 with minor modifications applied equally well to the Harvard and Bell Labs research models and the final design for production. Consider first the operation of the horizontal channel, as shown by the solid lines. The outputs of the two hydrophones were rapidly switched to the input of the high-gain amplifier, which had an associated slow, automatic volume control. This amplifier output was rectified and separated by an output switch synchronized with the input switch.

The ratio of the rectified signals was proportioned to the ratio of the hydrophone signals. This differential was combined with voltages from the zero adjustment and from a follow-up potentiometer indicating the position of the pair of rudders. The resultant voltage was amplified and operated the differential relay, which in turn caused the steering motor to shift the rudder position and its associated follow-up potentiometer. The motor would run until the voltage from the potentiometer just balanced the differential voltage from the hydrophones. With the rudders away from their neutral position, the mine would turn and, with proper polarity, would turn toward the source of the sound. The outputs from the two hydrophones then became more nearly equal, and thus there was less voltage from the follow-up potentiometer for a balance. The differ-

[23] *Survey of Subsurface Warfare.*

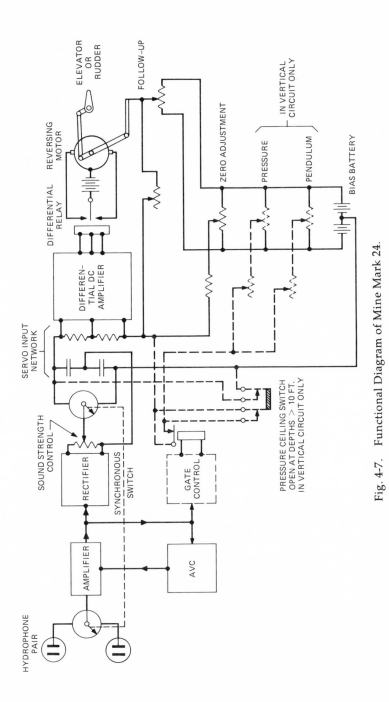

Fig. 4-7. Functional Diagram of Mine Mark 24.

ential relay then called on the steering motor to move the rudder toward its neutral position. This action was repeated until the mine was headed toward the sound source, which, in the case of a submarine target, was the propeller or some of the machinery in the stern.

The vertical control differed in that it was desired to have the mine run at a fixed predetermined depth, for instance 40 feet, until it picked up the sounds of a target and started homing on it. As shown by the combination of solid and dashed lines, this was accomplished by the addition of a pressure-operated and a pendulum-operated potentiometer. The pressure voltage told how far above or below the preset depth the mine was, and the pendulum voltage told how rapidly it was moving toward or away from this desired depth. Without both of these, the mine would oscillate too much in depth. This is equivalent to operating an automobile where the experienced driver reacts to both how far he is off the center of his lane and to what his heading is—in other words, anticipation. Much theoretical and experimental work was done to determine the best relationship between the rudder speed, the pendulum control, the pressure control, the sound strength control and the dynamic constants of the body. Early in the program, rate gyros were included in both the vertical and horizontal circuits, but it was later found that by proper adjustment of the other constants the gyros could be eliminated at a great saving in cost and especially trouble.

Tests indicated that there was little difference in performance with the hydrophones located in the forward end of the body section and with those located in the nose. Since the nose had to contain the explosive, which had to be loaded at an ammunition depot, having the hydrophones in the nose would have been most inconvenient. The NDRC agreed that the production design should have the body hydrophones, thus eliminating all need for electrical connections between the nose and the remainder of the mine. This permitted the explosive section to be handled completely independently and attached just before it was loaded into the aircraft.

Most of the research was done using Rochelle salt crystal hydrophones peaked at 16 kHz feeding through a 15- to 17-kHz filter; however, experiments indicated better signal-to-noise and therefore greater homing range at 24 kHz. The higher value was adopted for the production design. Figure 4-8 shows the 24-kHz Rochelle salt crystal hydrophone used in the mine. At a later time when ADP crystals became available, these were used, eliminating the storage temperature restrictions. Due to the hydrophone's inherent directional properties plus the shadowing by the mine body, single-lobe broad directivity patterns existed for each hydrophone with crossovers on the axis of the mine. It is on the forward crossover that the mine steers, but the maximum homing range is determined by the signal-to-noise on the peak of the hydrophone lobe. At

Fig. 4-8.   Rochelle salt crystal hydrophone.

these high frequencies most of the ambient noise in the ocean originates from white caps on the surface and is directed downward.   Additionally, noise from the mine machinery and propeller is reflected from the surface, the net result being greater vertical noise than horizontal.   In operation, it was desirable that the mine home from as large a range as possible, run at its preset depth until quite near the target, and then dive or rise directly to the target.   This plus the noise consideration led to a much lower vertical acoustic sensitivity and, in addition, to the use of the gate control shown in Fig. 4-7.   The control cut off the pressure and pendulum units when the vertical target noise became high enough for the final attack.

Measurements were made, mostly by the Underwater Sound Laboratory at New London, of the sound output of U.S. submarines under various operating conditions.   Relative to 0.0002 dyne per square centimeter, these measurements gave an average value, at 25 kHz, of 36 dB in a 1-cycle band with the submarine at a distance of 200 yards and running at 6 knots at periscope depth.   Combining this with self-noise, measurements predicted homing ranges of 500 to 1,000 yards.

A test station was set up at Solomon's Island on the Patuxent River (Maryland), which has deep water.   A rugged magnetostriction transducer to simulate the submarine sound was suspended from a float carrying the power supply for the transducer. This was used as a target for test runs. Using a special test head on the mine that could record time, rpm, acoustic levels and differentials, depth, rudder angle, elevator angle, pendulum angle, horizontal rate gyro, and vertical rate gyro, it was possible to reconstruct the running path and attack. Figure 4-9 is a plot of a typical run showing the attack plus three reattacks.

The magnetostriction sound source was surrounded by a 6-foot-diameter cage made of $\frac{3}{16}$-inch spring steel wire—to simplify the testing. The source was suspended as before but was also equipped with a small hydrophone with leads to a nearby boat. Success was judged by hits on the cage, which could be heard via the hydrophone. Since in actual use the mine, if not exploded, should sink, test heads were made which dropped a weight at the end of the run and thus permitted the mine to rise to the surface for recovery. Most tests were made by launching from a boat; however, drops from aircraft were also made. In a demonstration for the Navy at Key West, a submarine was equipped with a protective cage around her propellers and towed a marker buoy astern. Six mines had been loaded on planes, but after the first three hit the submarine repeatedly until they battered themselves to pieces, the captain in command called off further tests, swore everyone to secrecy, and advised them to stay out of submarines. Of course, these mines had only been loaded with plaster, not with explosives.

The Western Electric Company was given the sole contract for production, with the design essentially frozen by October 1942. Some of the features included in this design, as well as alternates that were considered, are shown in outline in Figure 4-10. The first production model was delivered to the Navy in March 1943 and 500 units had been delivered by May 1943. Successive lots for a total of over 8,000 were made, with the price of the last lot just over $1,800 each, which is a small fraction of the price of previous nonhoming torpedoes.

Traditionally the Navy insisted on having every torpedo proof-tested by being run on a range and then taken apart and refurbished. For the Mine Mark 24, it was possible to persuade the Bureau of Ordnance to accept normal Bell System sampling and quality control methods. The quality was such that few proof samples had to be run.

Well before the first production, a school was set up at the Murray Hill, N.J., location of Bell Labs by R. H. Galt for teams of one officer and five technicians. As soon as a lot of six or eight mines was ready for shipment from Kearny, N.J., one of the teams would travel, stay, and live with this lot until it reached its base in the United States or overseas. Because of security the mines were at all times kept hidden from view and were loaded into the airplane in a closed off area. The airplane crew was given no information about the weapon except instructions on how to drop it. This led to some queer results, as indicated by one pilot's report: "Saw

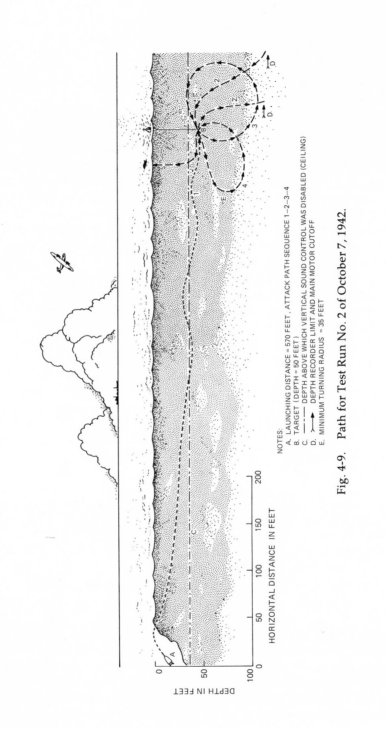

NOTES:
A. LAUNCHING DISTANCE = 570 FEET, ATTACK PATH SEQUENCE 1—2—3—4
B. TARGET (DEPTH = 50 FEET)
C. —————— DEPTH ABOVE WHICH VERTICAL SOUND CONTROL WAS DISABLED (CEILING)
D. ———→ DEPTH RECORDER LIMIT AND MAIN MOTOR CUTOFF
E. MINIMUM TURNING RADIUS = 35 FEET

Fig. 4-9.   Path for Test Run No. 2 of October 7, 1942.

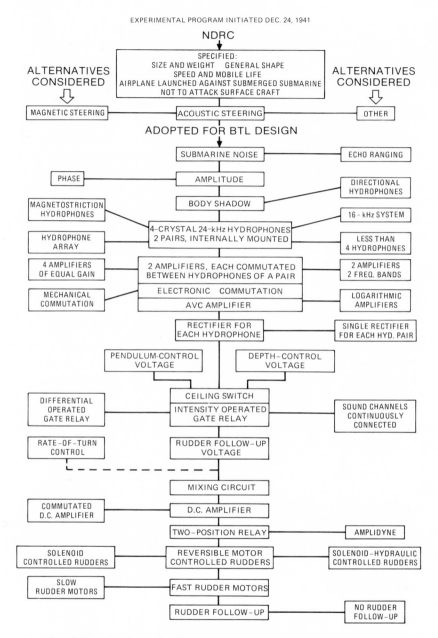

EXPERIMENTAL PROGRAM INITIATED DEC. 24, 1941

NDRC

SPECIFIED:
SIZE AND WEIGHT   GENERAL SHAPE
SPEED AND MOBILE LIFE
AIRPLANE LAUNCHED AGAINST SUBMERGED SUBMARINE
NOT TO ATTACK SURFACE CRAFT

ALTERNATIVES CONSIDERED

ALTERNATIVES CONSIDERED

MAGNETIC STEERING — ACOUSTIC STEERING — OTHER

ADOPTED FOR BTL DESIGN

SUBMARINE NOISE — ECHO RANGING

PHASE — AMPLITUDE — DIRECTIONAL HYDROPHONES

BODY SHADOW

MAGNETOSTRICTION HYDROPHONES — 16-kHz SYSTEM

4-CRYSTAL 24-kHz HYDROPHONES 2 PAIRS, INTERNALLY MOUNTED

HYDROPHONE ARRAY — LESS THAN 4 HYDROPHONES

4 AMPLIFIERS OF EQUAL GAIN — 2 AMPLIFIERS, EACH COMMUTATED BETWEEN HYDROPHONES OF A PAIR — 2 AMPLIFIERS 2 FREQ. BANDS

MECHANICAL COMMUTATION — ELECTRONIC   COMMUTATION — LOGARITHMIC AMPLIFIERS
AVC AMPLIFIER

RECTIFIER FOR EACH HYDROPHONE — SINGLE RECTIFIER FOR EACH HYD. PAIR

PENDULUM-CONTROL VOLTAGE — DEPTH-CONTROL VOLTAGE

CEILING SWITCH

DIFFERENTIAL OPERATED GATE RELAY — INTENSITY OPERATED GATE RELAY — SOUND CHANNELS CONTINUOUSLY CONNECTED

RATE-OF-TURN CONTROL — RUDDER FOLLOW-UP VOLTAGE

MIXING CIRCUIT

COMMUTATED D.C. AMPLIFIER — D.C. AMPLIFIER

TWO-POSITION RELAY — AMPLIDYNE

SOLENOID CONTROLLED RUDDERS — REVERSIBLE MOTOR CONTROLLED RUDDERS — SOLENOID-HYDRAULIC CONTROLLED RUDDERS

SLOW RUDDER MOTORS — FAST RUDDER MOTORS

RUDDER FOLLOW-UP — NO RUDDER FOLLOW-UP

Fig. 4-10.   Outline of features and alternatives for Mine Mark 24.

sub dive three miles off my starboard, dropped weapon and sank sub."
However, security also paid off.   Postwar interrogations showed that there
was only one unconfirmed report by a German spy who had seen some

of the activity at Solomon's through field glasses. Since the attacks were on a surprise basis with the submarine submerged when the weapon was dropped, no reports got back to Germany and the spy was not believed.

The mine was an important factor in breaking the back of the submarine menace. The Navy assessment toward the end of 1945 was that 340 mines were dropped by all Allied forces in 264 attacks. This resulted in 37 U-boats sunk and 18 seriously damaged. The highest period was July to December 1943 when 18 were sunk in 50 attacks. Excellent photographs were obtained of some of the sinkings. The submarine would broach, then head back down with her stern blown open. This all happened so quickly that the submarine had no chance to get off a radio message. The submarine simply failed to return home.

As the German U-boat activities were being brought under better control, U.S. submarines were becoming more active in the Pacific. As they worked closer to Japanese-held areas, they suffered from attacks by large numbers of sampans carrying depth charges and crude sonars. The size and shallow draft of the sampans prevented their being hit by regular torpedoes, and if our submarine surfaced to use her gun, she would be attacked by a lurking destroyer. The only hope was to sneak away. On November 22, 1943, the problem was outlined by the NDRC, and Bell Labs undertook to develop a small, silent, deep-launched torpedo. The resultant design was based on much of the work that had been done on the Mine Mark 24. This unit was coded the Mark 27-0 torpedo, and initial production by Western Electric began in February 1944. The unit was 7 feet long, 19 inches in diameter, and was powered by a storage battery. Unlike the Navy's regular torpedoes which were ejected from the torpedo tubes by high pressure air making a loud noise, the Mark 27 swam out slowly and quietly under its own power. It then rose to its nominal running depth of 40 feet before the acoustic circuits were enabled, after which it searched out its small target. It had a speed of only slightly over 12 knots, but this was sufficient to attack ships usually searching at 4 knots or less. Later, a Mark 27-1 was introduced that was slightly longer and had more power and higher speed. The torpedo had a "floor switch" that activated it only after it rose above a predetermined depth, to prevent its accidentally attacking the submarine below, and an impeller on the nose which required a fixed safe-run distance before the exploder was armed.

The first reported patrol use of these torpedoes was in October 1944. By the end of the war 106 had been fired: there were 33 hits and 24 sinkings. A number of submarine commanders reported that this torpedo, which had been nicknamed "Cutie," was the greatest morale builder on their boat. For the first time they had something with which to fight back.

The standard, full-size torpedoes were, and are now, driven by turbines or internal combustion engines. These could be heard at long distances and left a trail of bubbles that could be seen from a ship. For effectiveness, they depended on high speed and on being fired in salvos; however, a highly maneuverable ship, such as a destroyer, could often evade them. Their success against regular ships was attested by the U-boat sinking of 2,753 ships during the war.[24]

Although electric torpedoes had been worked on sporadically since 1915, it was not until a German electric torpedo was recovered intact that a real program was started in the United States. The Newport Torpedo Station of the Navy and the Westinghouse Electric Company copied this design and it was designated the Mark 18 torpedo. It ran more slowly and more quietly, it left no trail, and it was an effective weapon against the Japanese.

Both Bell Labs and the Harvard Underwater Sound Laboratory made self-noise measurements on the 29-knot Mark 18 torpedo and concluded that it was too noisy for direct acoustic control. It was decided, however, that if noisy gears could be eliminated and the maximum speed reduced, a useful weapon could be produced. With Westinghouse as prime contractor and Bell Labs responsible for torpedo control features and requirements, the 20-knot acoustic Mark 28 torpedo was designed.

While this development was going on, the Germans also developed a standard-size antiship torpedo that was submarine-launched, electrically propelled, and acoustic-homing. An early one hit a ship, penetrated the hull, but failed to explode. It was recovered and brought to Bell Labs for study. This event greatly accelerated development work on various kinds of decoys.

Instead of the contra-rotating propellers of the Mark 18, the Mark 28 had a single direct-drive propeller. It was launched in the standard way by a blast of air and ran on a gyro course and range as set from the conning tower. The acoustic channels were then enabled; however, the torpedo was expected to continue on its gyro course until loud enough signals from the target would switch off the gyro circuits and put the torpedo under acoustic control. If it failed to hit on the first attack, it would reattack repeatedly. Unfortunately there are many noise sources in the ocean, and almost invariably one of these would be loud enough to switch off the gyro even if not within acoustic range of the target. Since no combination of sensitivity settings overcame this problem, the only solution was for the submarine personnel to set the enabling distance to be within homing range of the target. But this distance was most often not known with sufficient accuracy.

The need was considered sufficiently great that the factory-produced torpedoes were being shipped to Pearl Harbor in the hope that a solution could be found to permit changes before loading them on submarines. Two engineers were quickly dispatched to Pearl Harbor to work on the

---

[24] Sternkell and Thorndike, *Antisubmarine Warfare.*

problem.   They found that it could be solved by keeping the gyros in operation for the full run of the torpedo.   The control voltage produced by the gyros overrode the unwanted ocean sounds which had been prematurely transferring the torpedo to acoustic control.   But when the torpedo came within effective range of the target, the continuous sound from the latter exceeded the gyro voltage and took control.[25]   Using Nimitz's high-security telephone circuit to Washington to talk to Bell Labs and Western Electric engineers,[26] it was agreed that three Western engineers, together with necessary parts, could be at Pearl Harbor by the following evening.   In the meantime the Bell Labs engineers there, with the help of the Navy officers on the job, were to select 25 enlisted men (the men had no experience with circuits or soldering) and also provide the necessary work area, tables, scopes, and other items.   Within ten hours of their arrival, the Western Electric engineers had selected 20 of the 25 men, set up a production line, and had started to deliver modified product.   The torpedoes were sent on to immediate patrol duty, but by this time Japanese ships to be sunk were becoming scarce and the torpedo, although successful, did not get extensive use.

The three weapons just described—the Mark 24, Mark 27, and Mark 28—were the only homing mines, or torpedoes, to reach the services during the war; however, other homing torpedoes were worked on by Harvard, General Electric Company, Brush Development Company, Bell Labs, and others.   An interesting one worked on at Bell Labs was the Mark 31 Mine.   This was an anchored antiship mine which on receipt of the proper target sounds would release its anchor and home on the target.   A surface ship generates a high-frequency sound modulated by the rotation of the blades of the propeller.   For large ships this modulating frequency is low, but for smaller ships not worth sinking it is high.   The mine could be set to pick the ship of interest, and it incorporated a counting mechanism so that it could let any desired number of ships pass before making an attack.   This mine was not put into production because the war situation had changed and we were no longer interested in mining.

As mentioned above, other homing torpedoes were worked on at Bell and other places.   In general, these depended on echo-ranging techniques.   In some cases, entirely new torpedo designs were considered, but Bell Labs limited itself to applying echo-ranging controls to the standard Mark 14 submarine-launched and the Mark 13 aircraft-launched torpedoes.   The major problems revolved around the high self-noise of these units.   These problems were gradually being overcome and although models performed satisfactorily, neither project reached the final development and design stage by the end of the war.   In August 1945, all tor-

---

[25] C. F. Wiebusch; U.S. Patent No. 3,003,449; filed June 22, 1945; issued October 10, 1961.

[26] See Chapter 5.

pedoes, mines, parts, tools, test equipment drawings, and technical information were inventoried, packed, and shipped to the Bureau of Ordnance. All the people who had been on these programs were reassigned to telephone work.

2.6 Seawater Batteries

While the development of batteries cannot strictly be classified with underwater acoustical devices, the development of the silver chloride seawater battery was a direct outgrowth of the work on acoustic mines and torpedoes and is appropriately discussed at this point. In the preceding section, the advantages of electric drive were noted as compared to the turbine and internal combustion engines used in most torpedoes. The noise was less and there was no trail of exhaust gases to warn of the torpedo's approach. However, using existing types of storage batteries or primary batteries, there was a great weight penalty. A torpedo is weight limited; the total weight can be only a little greater than the weight of the displaced water. For use in torpedoes as well as in other expendable devices—such as beacons, fuses, and sonobuoys—the use of storage batteries has, in addition to high weight per unit of energy, the disadvantage of requiring periodic recharging with accompanying generation of explosive hydrogen. Available primary cells had short shelf life, especially at high temperatures.

In a letter of June 26, 1942, R. M. Burns[27] wrote to the Bureau of Ships: "It is conceivable that a primary cell might be developed which on a weight basis would have from 50- to 100-fold the capacity of a storage cell. For marine uses, sea water suggests itself as a suitable electrolyte." The use of magnesium was suggested as an anode. The principal problem appeared to be the invention of a suitable nonpolarizable cathode.

Authorization was obtained which afforded the priorities for materials and outside shop and fabricating services. After much study and experimentation, it was decided that the most suitable cathode material was silver chloride in some form. With magnesium as an anode and seawater as an electrolyte, the useful chemical reaction involved is

$$Mg + 2AgCl \rightarrow MgCl_2 + 2Ag,$$

which gives an open circuit voltage of 1.55 volts at 20°C. In addition there is a secondary reaction

$$Mg + 2H_2O \rightarrow Mg(OH)_2 + H_2,$$

which occurs at a rate proportional to the primary reaction and results in the formation of insoluble products that must be removed.

A problem with silver chloride as a cathode was that it was a poor con-

[27] Letter from R. M. Burns, Bell Laboratories, to W. C. Wagner, Bureau of Ships, June 26, 1942.

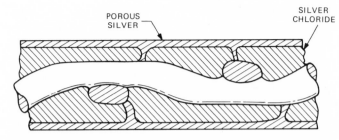

Fig. 4-11. Cross section of silver screen-type cathode. (Adapted from Haring, Patent 3,007,993.)

ductor and so inhibited any flow of current from the cell. Several means were invented for solving this problem, the one to be used depending on the operating life desired and, hence, the maximum current drain per unit area of electrodes. For instance, for a torpedo a life-to-voltage cutoff of 5 minutes might be wanted, whereas for a beacon a life of one or more days might be needed.

Historically, the first of these means and the one put into pilot production for such high-drain purposes as torpedoes used a silver screen as a base. A 40-mesh screen of 0.012-inch silver wire was anodized in an aqueous solution containing chloride ions until the wires were reduced to about half their initial diameters. The coated screen was then cathodized by reverse currents in a suitable electrolyte for a few seconds at a current density in excess of what the battery was expected to furnish. This produced silver filaments in pores of the silver chloride, which connected to the silver screen. On the outside, these filaments were spread out to cover part of the surface with porous silver by a further chemical treatment. The screen was then subjected to a pressure of about 8,000 pounds per square inch to form a compact electrode. A cross section of such an electrode is shown in Fig. 4-11.[28]

Figure 4-12 shows a stack of battery cells, each cell consisting of one of the above described cathodes separated from a magnesium anode on each side by insulating nylon rods about 0.02 inch in diameter. The anode, for which a common magnesium alloy containing 6.5 percent aluminum, 1 percent zinc, and 0.2 percent manganese was found to be good, was eaten away at the rate of about 0.001 inch for every 3-ampere-minutes per square inch. Mechanical considerations and current-carrying capacity dictated the use of 0.016-inch sheet. As shown, each cell had to be insulated from the next, since they were connected in series. Using thicknesses of 0.022

[28] H. E. Haring; U.S. Patent No. 2,988,587; filed March 29, 1945; issued June 13, 1966. D. T. Sharpe; U.S. Patent No. 3,005,864; filed March 29, 1945; issued October 24, 1961. H. E. Haring; U.S. Patent No. 3,007,993; filed March 29, 1945; issued November 7, 1961. R. L. Taylor, U.S. Patent No. 2,590,584; filed March 29, 1945; issued March 25, 1952. R. L. Taylor and H. E. Haring; U.S. Patent No. 2,622,272; filed May 14, 1947; issued December 23, 1952.

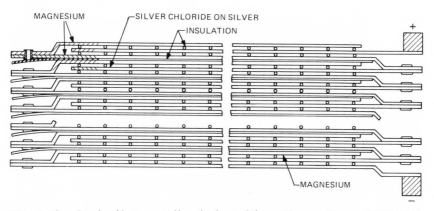

Fig. 4-12.   Stack of battery cells.   (Adapted from Sharpe, Patent 3,005,864.)

inch for the cathode, 0.016 inch for each of two anodes, 0.020 inch for the nylon spacers in two rows, and 0.003 inch for the cell insulator, the total thickness of a cell was less than 0.10 inch.   A battery built up of cells of this kind, each 8 × 10 inches, could supply 160 amperes at 1.1 volts per cell.

Cells or blocks of cells could be combined to give higher voltages and currents, but there was always a loss since the seawater electrolyte was common to all cells, although the path connecting the cells could be made long at a cost in size.   At the above high rate of discharge, 1 ampere per square inch on each side of the cathode, forced circulation was required to remove the secondary magnesium hydroxide mentioned earlier.   This flow could be parallel to the nylon rod separators and in a moving torpedo could be supplied by water scoops.   Figure 4-13 shows a battery mounted in a standard-size torpedo.   Water flow lines are indicated.

In order that the batteries could be stored indefinitely, they were sealed to prevent moisture from reaching the cells.   For torpedoes it was important that the battery come up to voltage quickly, which meant that the electrolyte had to fill the cells quickly.   Evacuating the battery solved this and had the further advantage that no tell-tale gases were exhausted.   A setup for studying this feature was installed at Murray Hill.   It consisted of a chamber having the size of a torpedo body containing the sealed-in battery and a glass viewing window; a seawater storage tank; and at the

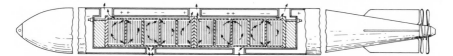

Fig. 4-13.   Battery mounted in standard-size torpedo.   (Redrawn from Sharpe, Patent 3,005,864.)

tail end a stack, 12 inches in diameter, reaching almost to the ceiling to absorb the water surge created as the valves were opened and the battery was connected. Incidentally, in laboratory experiments of this kind the silver could be recovered, whereas in regular use it was lost.

The experiment was demonstrated to a group from Washington, D.C. The three highest-ranking Naval officers were given the choice position at the viewing window. Although it had never happened before, this time a cascade of seawater erupted from the stack and completely soaked the three. Aside from dry clothing and a good lunch, the only solace that could be given them was that Naval officers confined to desk duty in Washington needed some contact with salt water.

The operating weight of the lead storage battery used for torpedoes was more than 15 pounds for each kilowatt delivered at a 4-minute rate. The seawater battery described above had a weight/power ratio of less than 4. This was, of course, far from the 50- to 100-fold improvement mentioned in R. M. Burns' letter, but it was great enough to make the torpedo a far more formidable weapon. During the period when the batteries were being built, research was directed toward further improvement. One outcome was "duplex" construction. An 8-kW sample of this indicated that whereas a 258-kW 4-minute battery of the screen type described above weighed 586 pounds, the equivalent duplex would weigh 475 pounds. The difference could be translated into greater endurance, more explosive or higher speed. Preoccupation with the manufacture and testing of the screen type and the end of the war terminated the work on the duplex.

It was decided that Western Electric should not attempt to go into the battery manufacturing business and the Edison G. E. Appliance Company (Hotpoint) was selected to be the manufacturer.[29] Bell Labs' responsibility extended through preproduction design and the exploration of feasible methods of manufacture. The resultant battery, coded as the Mark 4-Mod 0 Sea Water Battery, was first used in a new experimental Mark 26 torpedo.[30] Seawater batteries in torpedoes did not become operational before the end of the war; however, development of them outside Bell Labs continued and they are now in use.

In addition to the torpedo batteries discussed above, Bell Labs, during the period from January 1944 to September 1945, delivered about 80 seawater batteries of various types to other research and manufacturing facilities. These ranged from small long-life units to very-high-power units.[31] Bell Labs also provided consulting services to possible users and manufacturers when requested to do so by the NDRC and the Navy. The

---

[29] C. D. Hocker, internal Bell Labs memorandum, June 9, 1944.

[30] Battery section of Naval Ordnance Pamphlet on Mark 26 Torpedoes.

[31] Letter from W. H. Martin of Bell Labs to J. T. Tate of National Defense Research Committee, March 26, 1946.

success of these early developments has led to the use of seawater batteries to help solve a variety of military needs.   As the work was phased out at Bell, the United States government assigned continued development to the General Electric Company at Schenectady, and Bell Labs personnel collaborated with that company for some time afterwards.[32]

2.7 Practice Attack Meter

Prior to the development of the Mark 24 mine, the only weapons available to ships and aircraft for attacking submerged submarines were explosive charges dropped in the water in the vicinity of the submarine and set to explode at the estimated submarine depth.   The first of these devices had evolved during World War I.   It was the depth charge, consisting of a canister containing several hundred pounds of explosive, detonated by a pressure-actuated device set for the estimated submarine depth.   It was launched by rolling it from a rack in the stern area of an antisubmarine vessel.   In general, a 300-pound depth charge exploding within about 30 feet of a World War I submarine was lethal, but severe damage could still be caused at greater ranges.

In an attempt to improve on this performance, forward-thrown devices were developed during the early years of World War II.   They were developed by a number of laboratories, both in the United States and abroad, and were known under such names as Hedgehog, Weapon A, and the like. All such devices were intended for use by surface ships and were based on throwing a cluster of small charges, each of which would be lethal if it scored a direct hit.   Covering a large area with a single cluster greatly increased the chances of making a direct contact.

The Mark 24 mine provided a very effective airborne weapon against submarines, but throughout World War II, surface ships using depth charges and forward-thrown devices continued to be a large factor in antisubmarine warfare (ASW).   The latter weapons, while essential in attacking the submarine menace, were by their nature inaccurate, used largely in a "shotgun" approach and depended on highly skilled operators. In general, the only information available to the launching ship came from its sonar.   This imperfect information was the basis for calculating the submarine's course with proper lead so that the depth charges could be dropped at the right time to intercept or come close to the target both horizontally and vertically.

Rapid and successful training in dropping depth charges depended greatly on feedback to the operator on how close the charges came to the target so that he could learn to improve the estimates upon which the ship's course and the target release were based.   Practice against friendly submarines was unsatisfactory.   Real charges could not be used, and

[32] Letter from T. A. Durkin to C. F. Wiebusch, July 31, 1973.

dummies were of little value since their location relative to the submarine would be unknown, unless by rare good chance a direct hit was registered and its impact heard by submarine personnel.

To improve training, the Office of Scientific Research and Development (OSRD) asked Bell Labs to develop a Practice Attack Meter.[33] The meter required the use of a friendly submarine as a target and depth charges physically analogous to actual weapons but consisting of small, harmless charges set to explode 10 feet above the submarine depth to provide additional safety. The position of an explosion relative to the submarine was to be measured by acoustic means.

Early tests were made with charges composed of 20 grains of mercury fulminate. These proved to have a standard deviation in output of only 1.7 percent. However, a higher output seemed desirable for which mercury fulminate did not seem suitable; therefore, Hercules Powder Company developed a new unit. This was an assembly of an electric ignition fuse, a primer, and a charge of 1.35 grams of P.E.T.N., an explosive similar to tetryl. It did not prove possible to get a standard deviation less than 6.9 percent, but it was decided that this would be adequate.

The explosive unit was mounted on a small body designed to sink at the same 6 feet per second as a standard 300-pound depth charge. This body contained a bellows-operated switch to connect a flashlight battery to the electric ignition fuse. Since training tests were generally run with the submarine at a keel depth of 90 feet, the charges were set to go off at 40 feet to give the desired safety margin.

For locating the explosion, a single directional hydrophone was mounted above the bridge of the submarine and connected to recording equipment. The special hydrophone had two channels, each of which gave a cosine response pattern, the two channels being at right angles. From the relative output of the two channels the bearing of the source was obtained, and from the square root of the sum of the squares of the two outputs the range was obtained, provided the system and the charges were correctly calibrated. For checking the calibration, similar charges were mounted above the deck 50 feet from the hydrophone and were fired from within the submarine at the beginning of each day's run.

The hydrophone developed for this purpose consisted of a vertical square iron rod carrying a soft iron armature on each of its vertical faces. Coupled to each of the armatures by a compliance and mechanical resistance was an assembly composed of a magnet, a coil, and pole pieces. The square rod was fastened rigidly into a spherical aluminum shell, $2\frac{1}{16}$ inches in diameter, which was in turn covered by a rubber shell. This shell assembly was flexibly mounted to the hydrophone supporting

[33] "Practice Attack Meter," Report to Office of Scientific Research and Development, National Defense Research Committee Division 6, Section 6.1, March 25, 1943, Contract OEMsr-346.

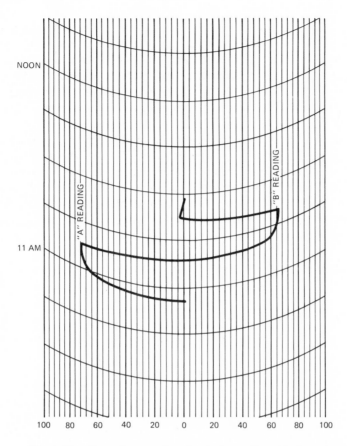

Fig. 4-14. Sample recorder chart of practice attack meter.

structure. Impinging sound waves vibrated the sphere, including the armatures, whereas the compliant coupling between the armatures and the magnet assemblies permitted the latter to remain essentially stationary above the resonant frequency of about 600 Hz. The relative motion of the armatures and magnet assemblies generated the output voltage.

In an underwater explosion, if the impulse is incident on one face of the hydrophone, the electrical output pulse will have one polarity; if it is incident on the opposite face, the output will have the opposite polarity. Suitable circuitry was provided to avoid 180-degree ambiguity in locating the explosion, and means were also provided to avoid spurious inputs due to echoes from the water surface or the submarine. The output of one channel was delayed 2 seconds relative to the other in order to distinguish the two inputs. Therefore, two pulses showed on the paper record, as indicated in Fig. 4-14; from their heights and their polarity the range and bearing could be calculated.

Included in the circuitry were fine gain controls to balance the two channels electrically, fine controls to adjust the calibration by using the charges fired from the submarine at the 50-foot distance, and finally a step control to select one of the three ranges. These were 50 to 250 feet, 100 to 500 feet, and 200 to 1000 feet. At low frequencies, the submarine generated considerable self-noise, and at high frequencies some high-power sonars on ship could trigger the circuits. To eliminate this, a 500- to 16,000-Hz band-pass filter was included in each hydrophone channel.

Many tests were run in the latter half of 1942, but these were all plagued by the lack of any other accurate reference means for determining the distance and bearing from the submarine to the explosion. The tests indicated a good consistency. They showed that the probable standard deviation of the bearing error was about 5 degrees and that of the range error about 8 percent. For the intended use this accuracy was good. The equipment served a much needed function in evaluating other equipment and in training personnel to use both depth charges and forward-thrown charges.

III. GROUND AND ABOVE-GROUND APPLICATIONS

As related in the volume of this history subtitled *The Early Years*, the first quarter of the twentieth century marked a period of great advances in electric circuit theory and the understanding of acoustics. The period beginning about 1920 was particularly fruitful in the application of theoretical methods in telephony. The study of acoustics had provided a basis for specifying design standards for telephone instruments and circuits, and the theoretical knowledge of mechanical and electrical systems (particularly the electric wave filter) provided means for designing transducers and circuitry to meet these standards.[34,35]

The 1920s was a period of rapid development in electrical circuit theory and especially electrical filter theory. Just as in the early days of simple electrical circuits, when much use was made of mechanical and hydraulic analogues, it was recognized that the new electrical techniques could be applied to vibrating mechanical systems. Calculations could be made by using mass, compliance and mechanical resistance as equivalent to inductance, capacitance, and electrical resistance. The same design charts could then be used for both the electrical and mechanical systems. Acoustical systems were treated in the same manner, recognizing that here mass and compliance are usually distributed. The conversion between electrical, mechanical, and acoustical power requires special treatment, but techniques for this were also developed during the period. Since most

[34] K. S. Johnson, *Transmission Circuits for Telephonic Communication: Methods of Analysis and Design* (Lancaster, Pa.: Western Electric Company, 1924; New York: Van Nostrand, 1927).

[35] W. H. Martin, "Seventy-Five Years of the Telephone: An Evolution in Technology," *Bell System Technical J.* 30 (April 1951), pp. 215–238.

of this work had been done at Bell Labs, the organization was well qualified to undertake the wartime acoustical projects covered by this chapter.
These included not only the underwater work covered in the preceding
section but also the special equipment, involving the air medium, covered
in this section and those following.

3.1 Telephone Instruments for Military Use

Prewar application of the techniques described above had provided the
Bell System with highly effective telephone instruments (transducers)
for commercial telephony, but as war approached it became evident that
quite different instruments would probably be needed for many wartime
applications. Most of the design of instruments for Bell System use was
the work of the organization headed by W. C. Jones. This highly capable
group undertook the design of new transducers, including most of the
basic work on underwater transducers already discussed.

Typical of the new telephone instruments required were those for use
in aircraft and the noisy mechanized forces.[36] From a technical standpoint
noise was the chief problem, whereas from the standpoint of mechanical
design extremes of temperature, humidity, and pressure—and in some
cases even submergence in salt water—had to be accommodated. When
Bell Labs undertook the development program, a goal was set to have a
minimum number of basic instrument designs that could then be adapted
to many military needs.

At the time of the Pearl Harbor attack, the armed services had available
a receiver with the frequency characteristic shown by curve 1 of Fig. 4-15.
This curve represents the acoustic output with the input turned as high
as could be tolerated by the listener. (As can be seen, frequencies near
1,000 Hz were at the pain level.) In some situations, even with ear pads,
tests showed noise levels at the ear as high as shown in the figure by curve
SS'. An oversimplified analysis that neglected the masking effect on a
frequency by other frequencies indicated that only a low effective amplitude of speech in the narrow band near 1000 Hz was available to
transmit information. This was adequate for code transmission but not
for voice. What was needed was a receiver with a nearly flat frequency
response over the voice range.

A receiver unit embodying these principles was designed by Bell Laboratories and was designated by the Joint Radio Board as an ANB (Army,
Navy, British) Standard. Its response is shown by curve 2 of Fig. 4-15.
This receiver unit, shown in Fig. 4-16, was equipped with a molded phe-
nol-plastic case having stepped contours to fit the various headbands of
the armed forces. The headset was used by ground forces and bomber

---

[36] J. R. Erickson, "Military Telephone Instruments," *Bell Laboratories Record* 23 (June 1945),
p. 193–199.

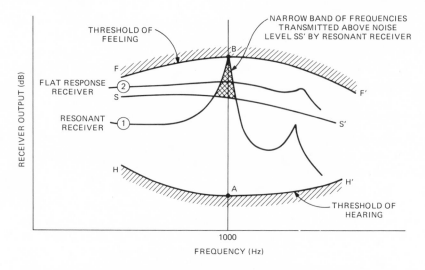

Fig. 4-15.   Characteristics of resonant and flat-response receiver plotted on the auditory sensation area.

Fig. 4-16.   Army, Navy, British standard headset designed by Bell Laboratories.

Fig. 4-17.   Throat microphone in use.

crews and wherever protective helmets were not required.   The same receiver could be placed in aviators' helmets.

For use under steel helmets a small headset was developed.   The receivers, only $7/8$ inch in diameter, were equipped with soft rubber ear plugs and had a flat response.   The wire headband could be bent to fit the user's head so as to not interfere with the helmet.

The pre-Pearl Harbor microphone situation was as inadequate as the receiver in the ensuing noisier environment.   Three types were developed to serve different needs: a throat microphone, a shielded microphone, and a lip microphone.   The throat microphone was a granular-carbon inertia device which responded to the vibrations of the throat but was relatively insensitive to sound waves such as noise.   As shown in Fig. 4-17, it consisted of two transmitter units worn high up the neck, each unit pressing against one side of the throat.   Chiefly the low frequencies of the speech sounds were transmitted through the tissues of the throat; the high-frequency sounds which were formed in the vocal and nasal passages were not included in the proper proportion.   Articulation was not good, but with practice, intelligibility became acceptable for combat use.

Fig. 4-18.   Aviator's oxygen mask and noise shield.

A more direct approach to improving the signal-to-noise ratio was made in the transmitter used in the aviator's oxygen mask, shown in Fig. 4-18. A good degree of noise exclusion was obtained, and at the same time the speech transmittal was highly intelligible because sounds from the nose and mouth reached the microphone.   The same microphone was used in a shield in place of the complete mask with similar results.   The unit made available for these purposes was standardized for the Army, Navy, and British and was supplied either as a granular-carbon or magnetic unit.

The third means of improving the signal-to-noise ratio was the pressure-differential, or lip, microphone, as shown in Fig. 4-19.   In this unit, the diaphragm was exposed on both sides, and the sound pressure from the distant noise sources reached both sides with about the same intensity and phase and therefore tended to cancel out.   If one talked very close to one side of the diaphragm, speech actuated the diaphragm principally from that one side, and hence the ratio of speech to noise transmitted was high.   The pressure differential microphone was equipped with a harness so that it could be worn on the lip, as shown, making the speech path to one side very short.   This lip microphone could be used with many of the

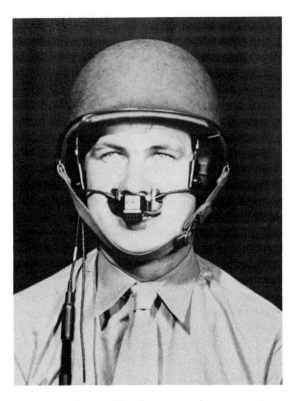

Fig. 4-19. Lip microphone.

devices provided by the military services and was standardized for Army and Navy use.

Another type of military telephone instrument was the sound-powered telephone. The sound-powered transmitter consisted of a diaphragm coupled to an armature that could move in a strong magnetic field. The change in magnetic field, resulting from the motion, generated the voice currents that were transmitted to the receiver. The receiver converted the currents into diaphragm vibrations and hence sound.

Since Bell's original telephone was a sound-powered instrument, it can be seen that the principle in the military instruments was not new. But the use of newer magnetic materials and the application of scientific design methods helped to make the new instruments adequately small and efficient. These telephones were used extensively for fire control on Pacific islands where communication distances were short and operation without the need for battery power was of great value, but their greatest use was on shipboard—not only for fire control but also for other applications— where they replaced the speaking tubes that formerly ran throughout the ship. The tubes prevented individual compartments from being effectively sealed against gas and water and, in addition, picked up noise where they passed through noisy locations. Sound-powered telephones were used extensively in portable field telephone sets, in which they eliminated the need for dry batteries, which gave poor performance in the Arctic cold and the tropical heat.

3.2 Gun Locator

An interesting acoustic development by F. K. Harvey and W. A. Munson was the GR-6 type of sound locator for the Signal Corps.[37] The function of the system was to locate the source of gun fire and especially mortar fire so that the Army could quickly retaliate. The system consisted of three or more microphones set up in a known configuration near the observer's post and connected by wire to terminal equipment at the post. Each microphone fed a transducer (recording head) which recorded sounds as a magnetic pattern on a loop of vicalloy tape (a metallic predecessor of the present-day oxide-coated tape). Associated with each tape loop was a movable reproduction head, the amplified output of which could be listened to by headphones or displayed on an oscillograph.

In use, the recorder was allowed to run, with the tapes synchronized, until the observer heard a shot or sound whose source he wished to locate, at which time he cut off the input to the recorder. With the reproducing channel on, the heads were shifted along the tapes until the operator determined either by headphones or oscillograph that the reproduced outputs were coincident. Since the tape speed was fixed, the relative head positions along the tape were a measure of the difference in travel time of the sound from the source to each of the microphones and could be read directly from scales associated with the heads. Since sound velocity is quite accurately related to air temperature, by observing this parameter one could convert the travel time differences into precise measures of differences in distance from each of the microphones to the source of sound. With a geometrical layout on a map one could then locate the source. In practice, these calculations and the layout were greatly simplified by the use of charts and plotting aids especially designed for the purpose.

Extensive tests of an experimental model by Bell Labs engineers in cooperation with military personnel in early 1944 determined the accuracy to be expected under various field conditions. These tests indicated that mortars at various ranges from 90 yards to 4,100 yards could be located in range within a standard deviation of about 2 percent and in bearing within a standard deviation of 1 degree. Large guns could be ranged to 9,500 yards, which appeared to be the limit of the equipment. Almost simul-

[37] F. K. Harvey, "Some Observations on the Operation of a Sound Locator of the GR-6 Type on Mortar and Other Gun Sounds," internal Bell Labs memorandum, June 29, 1944.

taneous firing from several positions and nearby noisy activity greatly reduced effectiveness and put a premium on highly trained observers.

The resulting GR-6 sound locator supplied to the military was manufactured by the General Instrument Company. The equipment was credited with forcing the enemy to put their mortars on wheels, with a consequent decrease in efficiency, which was caused by the time loss in frequent retargeting.

Bell System personnel also worked on gun locators in World War I that used much cruder equipment and provided much less precision than the World War II device. This is an interesting example of a more effective application of an earlier technique made possible by the great advance in technology between the wars.

IV. HIGH-POWER AUDITORY SYSTEMS

The knowledge and experience of Bell Labs in the field of high-power acoustic systems was also put to work on the design for a number of wartime applications.

4.1 Air-Raid Sirens

In 1938, a secret project called "Whistle" was started at Bell Labs' headquarters, 463 West Street, New York City. But *secret* was hardly the correct word, since everyone could hear an infernal noise coming up from a supposedly soundproof room in the basement. The purpose of "Whistle" was to create a highly efficient sound signal to be used for air-raid warning.

Acoustic sirens, which had been in use for many years, consisted essentially of a stationary disc or drum and a corresponding rotating disc or drum with matching holes in each. If air pressure was applied, puffs of air were emitted when the holes lined up, which created pressure pulses in the surrounding air and hence sound waves. At the time "Whistle" was started, there appeared to be no sirens with an efficiency greater than 1 or 2 percent.[38] Theoretical analysis by R. Clark Jones in terms of equivalent electrical circuits indicated that an efficiency in excess of 50 percent should be attainable, i.e., more than half of the mechanical power expended in compressing the air and rotating the disc should have been convertible to useful sound. Toward the end of 1941, when the need for an efficient air-raid warning system appeared urgent, the Office of Civilian Defense obtained a security release so that further development and testing could be carried out openly.

Theoretical considerations showed that the stator openings should be much narrower than the rotor openings so that for as much time as possible

---

[38] R. C. Jones, "A Fifty Horsepower Siren," *J. Acoustical Society of America* 18 (October 1946), pp. 371–387.

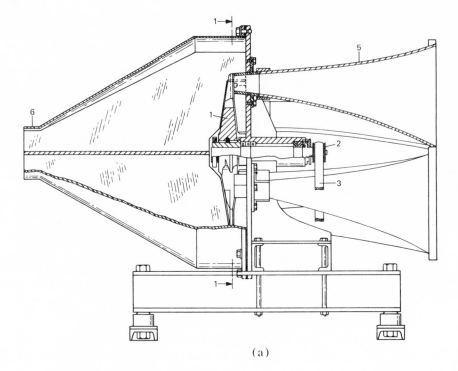

(a)

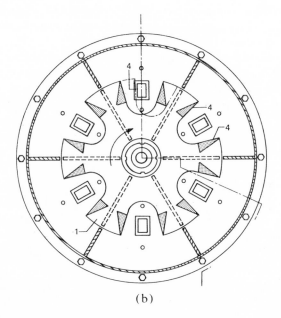

(b)

Fig. 4-20.   Acoustic siren.   (a) Side view.   (b) Sectional view.   (Adapted from O'Neill and Wente, Patent 2,354,684.)

Fig. 4-21.   View of siren mounted on truck.   The intake filter and compressor are shown on the right, the cone-shaped pressure chamber and exponential horns on the left.   (JASA, October 1946.)

the air passages would be either fully opened or fully closed.   (During the periods of partial opening, power was lost in air eddies.)   The next important finding was that there should be an acoustic match between each stator opening and the air outside and that this could be accomplished by making the stator opening the throat of an exponential horn.

Figures 4-20a and 4-20b are based on the patent drawings of the siren design.[39]   The rotor (no. 1) was driven by the pulley (no. 2) and belt (no. 3) and as it rotated, the openings (no. 4) covered and uncovered the rectangular throats of the exponential horns (no. 5).   A blower, not shown, supplied air at about 5 pounds per square inch through the opening (no. 6) to the plenum chamber, from which the air then flowed out of the horn throats when they were uncovered.   A completed unit mounted on a truck is shown in Fig. 4-21.   Also mounted on the truck is the 95-horsepower gasoline engine which drives the 10,000-rpm single-stage compressor through step-up gears.   Also included was a 20-horsepower engine to drive the rotor at 440 rpm.   The unit gave a sound output at 440 Hz with an approximately square waveform.

Acoustic measurements were made under the direction of F. K. Harvey on the western side of Barnegat Bay, N.J., far removed from any dwellings, in a location where there was a third of a mile of marsh and six miles of open water in front of the unit.   Such a remote location was needed for

[39] H. T. O'Neil, E. C. Wente, and R. C. Jones; U.S. Patent No. 2,354,684; filed August 20, 1942; issued August 1, 1944.

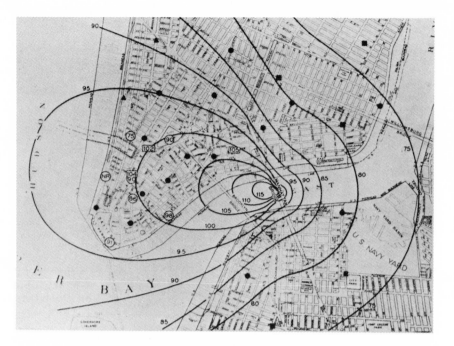

Fig. 4-22.   Map showing results of siren test in New York City, March 4, 1942.

extended testing, since even at two miles the sound pressure level was still 90 dB above 0.0002 dyne per square centimeter, which is about the upper limit of safety from ear damage during long-time exposure.   The horns of the model, the first used in this test, were made of plywood; after five minutes they had torn apart, the wood splintering because of the intense vibration due to the sound.   It was thus found necessary to make horns with two layers of sheet steel spot-welded together every inch.   The sound measurements showed an acoustic power output well in excess of 50 horsepower, which corresponded to an efficiency that was greater than 50 percent.

Because little information was available about the propagation of sound in cities, especially where there were tall buildings, it was decided to make some tests in New York City.   On March 4, 1942, the truck with the siren was placed near the center of the Manhattan Bridge with the horn pointed toward the financial district, as shown in Fig. 4-22.   The heavy lines show the free-field sound-pressure-level contours; the numbers in the rectangles show the measured levels on the roofs of tall buildings; the numbers in the circles show the levels in the street; the solid circles are police estimates of adequate signals; the solid squares indicate faint signals; and the solid triangles indicate places where no signals were heard.

Sirens based on the Bell Labs model were put into production by the Chrysler Corporation, which made some changes in design to improve construction and serviceability. These came to be called the "Chrysler-Bell Victory Sirens." About 20 were installed in New York, and a smaller 10-horsepower unit was also built.

4.2 Shipboard Battle-Announcing Systems

As early as the 1920s, Western Electric was supplying general-announcing systems to the Navy for paging on its ships.[40] The equipment for these was based mostly on standard telephone designs. During the thirties the Navy saw the possibility of expanded use and asked Bell Labs to design experimental equipment for tests. A major part of the design effort was to make noise surveys of ships and, on the basis of previous research by H. Fletcher and J. C. Steinberg, to estimate the best frequency response and compression characteristics for operating under these noise conditions. Much of this early work, aimed at determining the feasibility of producing intelligible speech under the existing severe noise conditions, was done by N. R. French. The theoretical work was followed by intelligibility tests conducted under simulated and working conditions to refine the requirements for the speech system. Included in these tests were studies to find the best "attention-getting" signals.

The field results of these tests were so successful that specifications for what were now called battle-announcing systems were prepared, and Bell Labs was asked to design systems to these specifications. The first systems built were put into service on battleships and carriers prior to Pearl Harbor, and were afterwards installed in ships of all sizes. The systems gave command a much more direct and speedy control of all operations on a ship.

Announcing equipment is divided into several interrelated subsystems, the most important of these being the commanding officer's system. Announcements on the latter are usually made from the point of ship control, such as the bridge, when a ship is under way or the control center during an action. As many as 200 loudspeakers might be distributed throughout the ship and might all be activated simultaneously for general instructions and battle progress reports or in such smaller groups as those in the engine room. Alarm signals are generated by electronic means and sent out over the loudspeakers.

Other subsystems permit the chief engineer to give instructions at machinery spaces, the gun turret officer to have two-way communication within his domain, and aviation control to provide instructions to personnel in the hangar and on the flight deck. This last requires very high

---

[40] L. B. Cooke, "The Voice of Ship Command," *Bell Laboratories Record* 23 (July 1945), pp. 241–245.

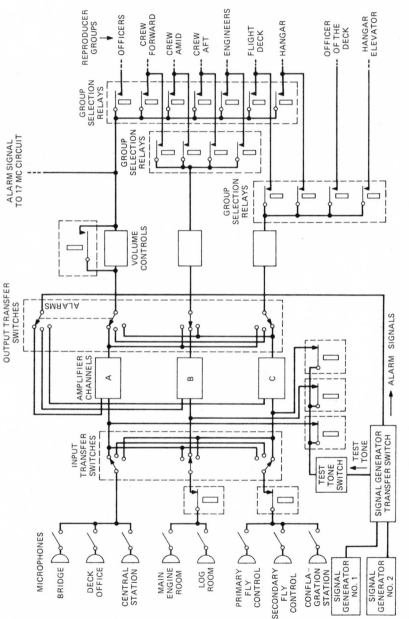

Fig. 4-23. Simplified schematic of announcing system.

sound power to override the high noise of aircraft engines located some distance from the loudspeakers.

The simplified schematic in Fig. 4-23 shows how the various microphone and loudspeaker locations could be connected in different ways. For a large aircraft carrier, the system consisted of two relay racks containing the switching and alarm signal generators and three amplifier racks. Each of the latter racks contained a high-gain 1,000-watt audio amplifier channel that consisted of one 40-watt and two 500-watt amplifiers.

The battle-announcing system for use on flight decks probably presented the most difficult design problems. From the acoustic standpoint, the major question was how to produce intelligible speech under noise conditions that were often near or above the threshold of feeling. Fortunately, analysis of the noise showed maximum levels at the low frequencies. Thus, by concentrating the speech energy at the upper frequencies, which carried much of the intelligibility, it was possible to obtain somewhat distorted, but quite understandable, speech without increasing the sound levels above the feeling threshold.[41] From the equipment standpoint, probably the most time-consuming and difficult part of the overall design was the development by H. F. Hopkins of the high-power loudspeakers for use on the flight decks. Several of these speakers are mounted on the island superstructure to cover the entire flight deck. Each of these is driven by one of the 500-watt amplifiers and permits "fly control" to give orders to pilots and deck crews while the airplane engines are warming up. Figure 4-24 illustrates some conditions to be met by these loudspeakers.

The first speakers developed consisted of a single, large moving coil driver feeding into an exponential horn. To reduce the length, it was folded down inside itself. Since the mouth of the horn had a rather large diameter, the higher frequencies dropped off rapidly away from the axis. A new design to eliminate this difficulty was then created. It was based on 16 separate, smaller exponential horns, each with its own moving coil driver. This approach had a further advantage: the failure of one or a few drivers did not put the speaker out of service. In the event of such failure, however, the input had to be reduced to prevent additional units from failing.

How effective the battle-announcing system proved to be was evidenced by the following telegram:

To the Men and Women of
Western Electric Company

One of our warships reports that her Battle Announcing System produced in your shops has rendered outstanding service during eighteen months of

---

[41] An important consequence of this innovation was that the power required by the amplifiers and loudspeakers could be substantially reduced.

almost continuous use under rigorous wartime conditions, including combat with the enemy. The report states "The reliability and effectiveness of this equipment was forcibly demonstrated during and after an extended period of battle, when many of the sound-powered telephone systems were severed and the automatic ship's service telephone was rendered inoperative, leaving the battle announcing system the only remaining method of disseminating information." From this it is clear that the quality you build into Western Electric communications equipment can be just as important to our fighting ships as the accuracy of their guns. You are to be commended for keeping quality and quantity of your production on a high level.

E. L. COCHRANE, Rear Admiral, USN,

Chief of the Bureau of Ships.

4.3 Sonic Broadcasting to Friend and Foe

With the background in the development of the high-power battle-announcing systems for aircraft carriers, it was natural that when the need developed for other high-power speaker systems, Bell Labs was asked to develop them.[42,43] From late 1943 through 1945, there was developed under the guidance of L. Vieth a series of systems related by technology if not by use. One of the first and one of the last of these, named "Polly," had the common objective of persuading the Japanese to surrender.

The first Polly was directed at the Japanese on Wotje from a twin-engine

Fig. 4-24. Personnel on flight deck of aircraft carrier are directed during emergency by commands from loudspeakers of battle-announcing system. Pictured above: a bomb carried by a Navy Avenger exploded as the airplane landed.

---

[42] L. Vieth, "Polly Gets the Japs," *Bell Laboratories Record* 24 (August 1946), pp. 305–307.
[43] Western Electric Co., *1944 Renegotiation*, p. 74.

Ventura PV1 flying at 2,700 feet, with a 15-minute broadcast of propaganda, music, and noise. Although Japanese were known to be on this by-passed atoll, no one was seen on this flight. On the second day small groups were seen, but on the third day the Japanese fired on and hit the plane; from then on the plane stayed above 5,000 feet. At this ceiling the system covered a speaking area on the ground of about three-quarters of a square mile. Its broadcasts of propaganda and surrender instructions over other Pacific islands resulted in the taking of many prisoners. However, the low altitude necessary to get a sufficiently loud sound level at the ground made the plane too vulnerable; and at Saipan, Iwo Jima, and Okinawa the plane was so badly battered it had to be abandoned, after first removing the Polly equipment. During these months of hard service there had not been a single equipment failure—not even a single tube was replaced.

The first Polly was a 500-watt system, but by 1945 the Navy wanted a new Polly that could be flown at 10,000 feet so that the plane would be out of machine gun range. On May 14, 1945, the Navy placed an order for three of the new systems, to be mounted in four-engine PB4Y-2's. Delivery was requested in 100 days, but design and manufacture were completed in only 84 days. Each system had four 500-watt amplifier channels feeding separate sections of the loudspeakers. Each of these sections consisted of a three-by-three assembly of nine horns, each horn powered by two driver units. A loudspeaker and its mounting in the airplane is shown in Fig. 4-25.

In October 1950, during the Korean conflict, Polly was remembered, and the services of one were requested. With utmost haste, sections of one system were found at West Coast bases, where they were being separately used in small planes to clear missile-firing test lanes at sea. Recombined and installed in an Air Force C-47 under the direction of a Bell Labs team, the system became the "U.N. Voice." The *New York Times* of October 26, 1950, gave the following account of one episode in the life of this equipment:

> WITH THE U.S. EIGHTH ARMY, Korea, Oct. 25—Two trucks loaded with North Korean soldiers were rolling toward the Manchurian border north of Anju when five United States planes came overhead. There was no rat-tat-tat of strafing guns and no bombs were dropped. The surprised Communists reached for their rifles as an unarmed C-47 came low and a Korean voice from the sky demanded their surrender, promising honorable treatment.
>
> Warning of annihilation from fighter craft if they refused to give up, the voice ordered the trucks to turn about. As the trucks began rolling back toward Anju, which was in American and British hands, the pilot observed other Korean soldiers filing from the hills and falling in behind the trucks. Soon a column of 300 to 500 Communist infantry was trudging behind the trucks.

(a)

(b)

Fig. 4-25.   Loudspeaker system mounted in PB4-Y aircraft. (a) Loudspeaker compartment. (b) Closeup view of
speakers.

Fig. 4-26.   Portable high-power public address system that permits the noise and confusion of an amphibious landing to be dominated by the directing voice of the beachmaster.

A sound system that was produced by the thousands was the Beachmaster, the Navy PAB-1 Public Address Set.[44]   This 250-watt system with its own gas-engine-driven generator was packaged in watertight buoyant cases so that, if required, it could be dumped overboard and floated ashore. There it was set up as pictured in Fig. 4-26 so that the beachmaster, acting as traffic controller and dispatcher, could direct a landing.   It was used at Iwo Jima and most of the Pacific landings after that.   A nearly identical equipment was the Ship Mounted Landing Craft Control Announcing System (Navy IC Circuit 6 MC).   Used along with the Beachmaster, it made possible two-way ship-to-shore speech communication.

The Beachmaster loudspeaker has a three-by-three assembly of horns, each with a single driver.   This unit extended the loudspeaker art by combining a weather-resistant plastic diaphragm with ribbon-type voice coil leads and blast screens for protection from heavy gun blasts.   The Beachmaster achieved distinction for its ruggedness and extraordinary service under combat conditions.   More than thirty years later, some of the systems are still operating.

The amplifiers had capability well beyond the 250- to 6,000-Hz range used for the voice commands.   Associated with loudspeakers suitable for

[44] L. Vieth, "Beachmaster Announcing Equipment," *Bell Laboratories Record* 24 (July 1946), pp. 261–263.

use at full power down to 100 Hz, the Beachmaster could serve as a sonic deception system and for this purpose was mounted on a half-track. Development for this use led to the production of a group of direct radiator speakers which later formed the basis of a line of 12-inch, 10-inch, and 8-inch speakers that became popular for studio monitors and high-fidelity equipment because of the quality known as "presence." [45,46]

Extensive measurements and tests at Pine Camp, New York, accumulated data on the relationship among acoustic transmission, terrain, and weather conditions that made it possible to predict proper sound-level settings for military use in sonic deception. Then a library of recordings of military equipment was gathered that could be used under many different environmental conditions. The successful use of sonic deception in Germany attested to the thoroughness with which the work had been done.[47,48]

For the acoustic deception operations in Europe the developments included four new lighter-weight systems code-named "Heaters." These were the AES 1, 2, 3, and 4 with ratings of 500 watts, 50-watts-wide range (AN/TIQ5), 250 watts, and 250-watts-wide range, respectively. The first company to go abroad (the 3132 Signal Co.) was equipped with these, and the second company (the 3133 Signal Co.) had tanks with dummy guns. Dummy tanks and other dummy military equipment were soon included in the expanding repertoire to add visual deception to the acoustic deception. A "stage" group consisting of a small number of special troops would move into an area occupied by our regular troops and would impersonate these while the regulars moved to a new location to mount an attack.

Practically every big military operation was helped by these deceptions. For the Rhine crossing, special recordings were made in Belgium. One first-person report[49] told how a special troop battalion, spread thinly near a small German town, simulated the 30th and 76th Divisions while these were able to cross at another location with a loss of only 30 lives.

Deceiving the enemy during landing operations was an important factor in the success of such operations. If the defenders could be made to believe that a landing would be made at a different place or that it was differently distributed, the defending forces would be weaker at the actual landing site. With this in mind, work under NDRC sponsorship was undertaken in the latter part of 1943 to develop a suitable deception device.

[45] Frank Nickel, "Quality Loudspeakers for Every Use," *Western Electric Oscillator* (July 1947), pp. 7–10,30.

[46] R. S. Lanier, "What Makes a Good Loudspeaker," *Western Electric Oscillator* (July 1947), pp. 11–13, 34.

[47] Memorandum from R. R. Galbreath to C. F. Wiebusch, August 17, 1973.

[48] *Worcester Daily Telegram*, October 4, 1945.

[49] Ibid.

The project, as well as the device that resulted, was called "Water Heat-er." [50]

A "Water Heater" consisted of a torpedo, 21 inches in diameter by 21 feet long, fired from a submarine. The torpedo contained the deception equipment. The body and propulsion system of the torpedo were sup-plied by General Electric, and the remainder by Bell Labs. On firing, the torpedo traveled on a gyrocourse to a preset distance of as much as several miles at a speed of 5 or 6 knots; at this time it ended up with its nose about 2 feet above the water and also dropped an anchor.

The exact time of occurrence of the deception could be set before firing for any time up to 12 hours. At the appointed time the top was opened and the loudspeaker was elevated six feet above the water and oriented by a magnetic compass to point in the desired direction. A sound program recorded on a magnetic wire was then reproduced over the 500-watt sound system. The program might consist of various tactical sounds for a total playing time of 30 minutes in one or more intervals. The Heater could be set to arm itself or set to destroy itself at the completion of the sound program.[51]

Field tests of the first model were made in the late spring of 1944, and a successful demonstration firing was made on July 14, 1944. Three sys-tems were completed, the last one being delivered in April 1945. By this time the war was so nearly over that Water Heater did not see service.

V. SUMMARY

As might be expected, the Bell System's knowledge of acoustic theory and application was the basis for a large amount of war effort involving two media, the air and the sea. The air is the acoustic medium used by telephony. To some extent, military applications for this medium were a modification or extension of techniques already used in developing telephone systems. However, military requirements were quite different from those of commercial systems, since the former called for operation under conditions of use, noise, and power output bearing little resem-blance to those of the ordinary telephone environment. Thus, military acoustical devices were not just copies or minor physical modifications of existing instruments but rather basically new designs. These were produced rapidly not only because of the researches into speech and hearing made in prior years but also because of the available broad un-derstanding of network theory and the use of electrical and mechanical analogs in designing acoustical devices. This knowledge, coupled with the manufacturing experience of Western Electric and a well established quality control system, made it possible to produce large quantities of

[50] L. W. Giles, Report on Contract OEMsr 908, April 30, 1945.

[51] L. W. Giles, ibid.

equipment with the rugged construction essential for military use. The devices ranged from the sensitive transducer required for speech transmission and gun location to equipment with enormously high power used for air raid warning over large areas and for announcing systems working in the high ambient noise of battle conditions.

The sea water medium was unfamiliar to Bell technicians. In fact, little work had been done in this field except that of a few workers in the military field who were keeping alive experimental work on submarine detection started late in World War I. While this included some useful ideas on how detection might be accomplished, there was a great lack of information on the basics of underwater acoustics, such as the characteristics of sound transmission through the sea, the nature and magnitude of the sounds, ambient and man-made, to be found in the sea, and means for accurately obtaining this information so essential to the design and application of acoustical devices. Bell Laboratories undertook the investigation of these matters and was largely responsible for establishing accurate measuring techniques and standardized means for calibrating hydrophones and codifying the sounds of the sea.

With this work as a cornerstone, Bell Labs accepted other projects in military acoustics. Chief among these were means for detecting submarines and the development of acoustic homing mines and torpedoes.

Several detection systems were developed, the most versatile being the QJA, which could be used for both passive (listening) and active (echoranging) detection and also for short-range underwater telegraph transmission. Along with the development of detection systems, new and greatly improved transducers were devised by using ADP crystals for converting between acoustic and electrical waves. To supplement the acoustic detectors and reduce ambiguity of the acoustic information, airborne magnetometers were devised which would detect the small distortion in the earth's magnetic field caused by a submerged submarine. A key element in magnetic detection was the use of 4-79 molybdenum permalloy developed by Bell Laboratories many years before the war. Bell Laboratories designed and Western Electric produced a number of the magnetic detection devices, and their use, either aboard or towed by an airplane in coordination with antisubmarine vessels, greatly increased the effectiveness of the latter.

The largest of all the acoustic projects carried out by Bell Labs was the development of the homing torpedo known as the Mark 24 mine. This device was carried by aircraft and dropped in the vicinity of an enemy submarine. Once in the water, the mine was electrically propelled toward the submarine under guidance of an acoustical system operated by the sounds produced by the submarine propulsion machinery. It carried a warhead which would explode with fatal effects on making contact with the submarine. Western Electric, the sole producer of the Mark 24, delivered the first production model in March 1943 and manufactured over 8,000 by the war's end. The mine was an important factor in breaking the back of the submarine menace. Some 55 submarines were put out of service by 264 attacks with Mark 24s—with no knowledge of the weapon responsible reaching the enemy.

The success of the Mark 24 led to Bell Labs' work on acoustic homing torpedoes. The most spectacularly successful torpedo was the Mark 27, used against small Japanese search ships, which were nearly invulnerable to conventional torpedoes because of their shallow draft. The 106 firings of Mark 27s during the war resulted in 33 hits and 24 sinkings.

An outgrowth of the work on acoustic mines and torpedoes was the development of a silver chloride seawater battery having about one quarter of the weight of an equivalent lead battery. The new battery made long-range, high-speed, electrically driven torpedoes practical. Although Bell Labs did most of the development work on these batteries, Western Electric did not manufacture them.

It is interesting to note that the largest part of the acoustic work done by Bell Laboratories was in areas in which the organization had little or no experience before the war. This serves as a reminder that successful development work in a complex field does not necessarily result from experience· instead, it is built on firm theoretical knowledge and a long background in research. In addition, a technical organization needs an adaptable group of techniques and also appropriate management techniques.

Chapter 5

Communications

As early as 1939 the Bell System began to make plans for the tremendous quantity and variety of communications that would be needed during a war. Both wire and radio systems for both voice and teletypewriter would be needed, and carrier systems would be called upon to save valuable copper. Among the more significant developments were the "spiral 4" cable and the integrated radio and wire system, widely used in military theaters of operation, and the AN/TRC-6 microwave system that drew heavily on prewar Bell Labs research and development. Mobile radio systems for tanks and aircraft were delivered to the armed forces in very large numbers. By war's end a global teletypewriter network had been built up that at one point kept General Dwight Eisenhower in Africa in communication with General Douglas MacArthur in Australia. The capabilities of this network were demonstrated in 1945 by a teletypewriter message sent around the world in 9 seconds.

An important adjunct to military communications were privacy systems, the most secure of which, the so-called Project X or "Green Hornet" system, was used at the highest levels of allied command. This was indicated later by a photograph showing that it was used in Churchill's underground headquarters in London.

As field-army communications grew in complexity as well as quantity, Bell System experience in systems engineering became ever more important. In one three-month period, Bell Labs people prepared and delivered to the Signal Corps 200 copies of a 350-page manual dealing with the engineering of military communications. This book was, at that time, the most comprehensive ever written on the subject.

I. INTRODUCTION

The previous chapters might seem to imply that during World War II the Bell System was involved in all forms of war effort except communications. That obviously was not so, since wartime tremendously increased the demand for all kinds of communication. Not only was the demand

---

Principal authors: F. J. Singer, R. L. Miller, J. W. Emling and J. G. Nordahl

for common carrier communications greatly enlarged to meet the logistical requirements of the military and its suppliers, but the mobilization and movement of manpower also increased the need for civilian communication. Additionally, the military had special communication needs to meet requirements very different from those of the common carrier network. These needs varied widely from simple modifications of existing systems and equipment to mobile radio systems for tanks and aircraft, sophisticated new techniques for secret telephony, and a global teletypewriter network providing rapid, reliable and secret communications between all echelons of the military forces.

These varied forms of communications are the subject of this chapter. As in the earlier chapters, emphasis is on the history of the scientific and engineering techniques that made the varied wartime communications possible. As a consequence, much of the text will be devoted to the development of systems aimed specifically at military needs, but first a few words are appropriate on the large part played by the research-based common carrier network built up by the Bell System and the connecting telephone companies during the roughly 60 years prior to World War II.

II. THE COMMON CARRIER NETWORK

The common carrier network, covering the continental United States and connected by radio to many foreign countries, formed the backbone of much wartime communication. It provided telephone and private-line telegraph communications linking the wartime suppliers of military equipment; it furnished communication between the vast pool of military personnel in the training camps and their friends and relatives at home; and it supplied most of the facilities for communications among military agencies within the United States and even to some countries abroad. Many of these needs could be met by the regular switched network, but in some cases minor modifications or additions were required for special military applications.

2.1 The Switched Network in Wartime

As early as 1939, the Bell System began to prepare for the communications emergency that might lie ahead. Telephone plant additions were launched to care for the expanded traffic that began with the declaration of war in Europe. The desultory activities of the first months of war gave time for preparing more specific plans. By June 1940, at the time of the Dunkirk evacuation, a series of high-level discussions between AT&T and government agencies was held to determine the best way for the Bell System to prepare for possible United States involvement in the war. Arrangements were made for liaison with the military; the Washington service representatives of the Bell System were put on a 24-hour schedule; and a permanent war office was established at AT&T headquarters in New York City, manned and equipped for instant action around the clock in meeting the emergency needs for both military and critical civilian service. Special security measures, established to guard against sabotage, were put into effect as needed.

All these measures involved normal Bell System activities, since it had long been experienced in handling emergencies of all sorts. The organization was accustomed to mobilizing specialized personnel from Bell companies throughout the country to meet unusual situations. Western Electric was normally prepared to provide and install large quantities of equipment to replace that destroyed in natural catastrophes. But none of these catastrophes had ever called for the quantities of new equipment required by the war. Throughout the war years, the ever-increasing demand for communications and the constantly changing requirements were to be the major problems in network construction and management. By 1942, the network was furnishing new and enlarged service at some 2,500 government ordnance plants in addition to countless privately owned plants. In the same year the headquarters service of the War Department was expanded to 15,000 dial telephones backed up by 300 supplementary operators.

Providing the telephones and switching systems was an enormous job, even though it was greatly facilitated by the long-established standardization of equipment and operating practices that made possible the gathering of installation and operating crews from all over the country. Probably an even greater job involved the supply of the outside plant transmission facilities. Many of the new military establishments were located in remote areas where telephone plant was hopelessly inadequate or nonexistent. This required much new construction, often on very short notice, making enormous demands on manpower and also on critical materials.

Of all the problems involved in supplying adequate network service, probably the greatest was that caused by the tremendous growth in long-distance traffic. Almost every phase of the war effort seemed to involve calls over long distances. During the two years 1940–1942, calls over the longer routes increased by an amount equal to peacetime growth of about 10 years. Supplying these needs by building new physical plant would have required enormous quantities of scarce materials. Fortunately, in the years prior to the war (many of them depression years) Bell Laboratories had made great advances in the development of carrier systems.[1] When the need for wartime long-distance service became critical, the Type C and J open-wire systems and the Type K cable systems were

---

[1] See the first volume in this series, Chapter 4, Section 4.2.5

ready for large-scale production. In 1939, four open-wire routes were in service west of Chicago. The quickest and simplest way to increase capacity was to add carrier facilities to these routes, since, where applicable, the C and J carrier systems increased capacity by a factor of about 8. These were added on the southern line to provide additional circuits to California with the least delay. Other routes could also have been converted, but in view of the vulnerability of open wire and the possibility (then still somewhat remote) of a war with Japan, it was decided to build a buried cable system through the central part of the country despite the large initial cost. Greatly affecting this decision was the availability of Type K carrier, which would provide circuits of highest quality over distances up to 3,000 miles. Of great importance was the fact that K carrier reduced the amount of critical copper required by a factor of about 10.

As the war progressed and traffic increased, carrier was added to more and more open-wire plant, and many existing cable routes were converted to Type K carrier. This system required two cables, and on heavy routes with multiple cables, conversion was relatively simple. Single-cable routes required the addition of a second cable, but this could be very small, since with carrier, adding a cable of only 30 pairs would increase the route capacity by over 300 circuits, an increase greater than would be obtained by adding two full-size cables for high-grade voice-frequency circuits. Even with the addition of all the plant permitted by available critical materials, there was still a shortage of circuits and the EB Bank[2] was devised and added to long-haul circuits where the need was the greatest. A rough idea of the enormous wartime growth can be gained from the fact that the number of circuit-miles of AT&T Long Lines circuits, which was 3.8 million at the end of 1939, increased to 9.7 million by the end of 1945. In the latter year, about 3.5 million circuit-miles were carried by EB Banks.

Except for the development of the EB Bank and some minor assistance in correcting problems arising from the massive growth of the new carrier systems, Bell Laboratories played only a small part in this expansion. Bell Labs' major work had been done much earlier in the research and development phases. The wartime expansion was largely a matter of engineering, which could be handled by experienced Operating Telephone Companies and by Western Electric as supplier and installer. The results demonstrated that the work was in good hands.

2.2 Extensions and Modifications of the Common Carrier Network

Communications for many military needs, particularly in matters of logistics and liaison with civilian organizations, differed little from the requirements of day-to-day civilian usage and were amply supplied by the common carrier network. But there were many occasions when the

---

[2] See Section IV, Chapter 1.

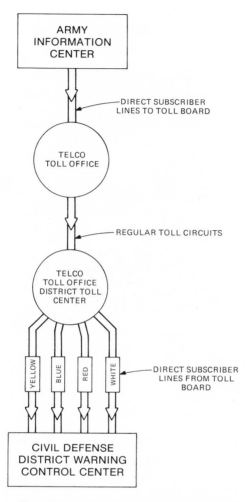

Fig. 5-1. Air-raid warning channels. Both the Army Information Center and the Civil Defense District Warning Center are directly connected to long-distance switchboards.

basic network could meet military requirements only with the aid of modifications or additions. Situations requiring such modifications covered a wide range, varying from the simple addition of portable equipment for communication to the staff of ships docked for repair to the installation of complex networks for disseminating air warning information and controlling civil defense activities (Figs. 5-1 through 5-3).

The warning and control systems were typical of much of the work conducted during the war years to expand the usefulness of telephone

Fig. 5-2. Warning receiving equipment.
The keys in the base of the telephone, and the
lamp caps of the visual signal, are colored
yellow, blue, red, and white. Each is connected to a separate line operated on order
from the Army Information Center.

systems originally designed for civilian use. The warning system developed was similar in many respects to that which had proved so valuable
during the Battle of Britain.[3] In the United States, a volunteer observer
corps, manned 24 hours a day, was set up with posts about every 15 miles
in the vulnerable areas. Sight or sound of a plane was promptly reported
by a "flash" telephone call reported by the nearest operator over commercial circuits to a regional "filter board" manned by the military. At
this point all reported observations were continuously plotted on a map
and the data evaluated to select bona fide data, which was then forwarded
by private-line telephone to an Army Information Center. Here reports
from various filter boards were consolidated and proper action was ordered, again by private-line telephone.

[3] In the early war years radar was in its developmental stages and in such short supply
and so badly needed for other purposes that much reliance in defending ground targets had
to be placed on suitably processed information obtained from visual and aural observations.
Winston Churchill in *Their Finest Hour* [(New York: Houghton Mifflin, 1949), vol. 2, *The
Second World War*], while giving radar due credit for early warning, points out that the Battle
of Britain was "fought mainly by eye and ear." Observers with field glasses and telephones
were the main source of information about raiders.

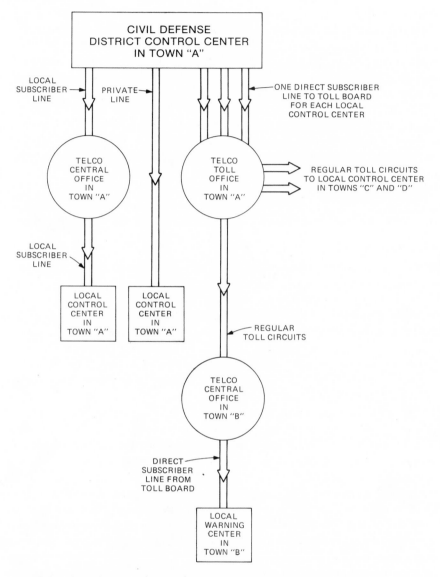

Fig. 5-3. Distribution of warnings. Shown are channels from a district control center to the control centers of several neighboring communities.

In addition to ordering military action, the Army Information Center also alerted the Civil Defense Air Raid Warning Centers. These, too, were manned by volunteers. Once again the telephone network was called into use, as shown in Fig. 5-1, to send color-coded signals (Fig. 5-2) to a district center, from which the information was further distributed, as shown in Fig. 5-3. The color-coded lights[4] were used when it was necessary to send full information to many locations simultaneously, but when only partial information was needed, telephones or limited-light signals were used. It is also interesting to note the combination of private-line and commercial circuits used in setting up this network, devised to meet the military requirements at minimum cost.

Except for a small amount of work by Bell Laboratories in designing special signal stations and circuitry for multipling lines, most of the networks for the air warning and Civil Defense networks were designed by the Operating Telephone Companies (including the AT&T Long Lines Department) with arrangements of facilities similar to, and often part of, the common carrier network.

III. THE GLOBAL MILITARY COMMUNICATION NETWORK

3.1 Introduction

It was apparent that the common carrier network could form the basis for much of the wartime communications needs within the continental United States. But it was also obvious that a much more extensive, and possibly different, network would be required to meet the needs of the military services if the United States was to become involved in a global war. Such a network would not only have to cover a vastly greater area, but it would also have to interconnect many military levels, meet special requirements for secrecy, and provide for construction and operation under conditions of great stress.

The rapid occupation of Western Europe by German armies after September 1, 1939 had a profound effect on the military policy of the United States. All services took steps to prepare for possible United States involvement. The Army Signal Corps was assigned responsibility for determining the composition of a communications network capable of accommodating the needs of not only the military, but also the War and State Departments in case the United States became engaged in the war.

At the outset, the Signal Corps recognized that its task would require the knowledge of experts in network planning and operations. Accordingly, the War Department arranged with the Bell System for Bell Laboratories to work with the Signal Corps in drawing up a network plan. This arrangement provided a reservoir of knowledge on all facets of communication technology that could be brought to bear on solving the complex system problem.

The following historical résumé covers the evolution of the global military network from the time of its conception in 1939 until the end of

---

[4] Yellow—Air raid is possible. Blue—Air raid is probable. Enemy planes approaching. Red—Air raid is imminent. Attack may occur in short time, say, 5 minutes. Sound public alarm. White—All clear.

World War II in 1945. It highlights the operational features of the network, technical advances required to meet operational requirements, and the way the network was used to handle telephonic and telegraphic communications among the various echelons of military command throughout the world.

3.2 Military Communications Materiel Before World War II

Pre-war, the communications facilities of the Navy included high-power radiotelegraph installations on the east and west coasts of the United States, sound-powered telephone networks for internal communication on ships, and radiotelephone and radiotelegraph sets on ships and naval aircraft for communication between ships, aircraft, and shore stations.

Army cars, trucks, tanks, and aircraft were equipped with radio for telephonic communication over moderate distances. Telephone sets, telegraph sets, field wire, power plants, and other products were supplied to provide communication with infantry and artillery command during tactical operations.

Thus the kinds and types of pre-war communications materiel available to the armed forces were mainly for coordinating tactical operations. In most instances they were suitable for telephone and manual telegraph communications over moderate distances within areas of operation but lacked many features necessary for communications over long distances, particularly on a switched network basis.

3.3 Factors Bearing on the Choice of Facilities and End Instruments

3.3.1 Wire Versus Radio

The network plan envisioned that radio instruments and systems would generally be better adapted to rapid installation than corresponding wire-line systems and would therefore be preferable as the primary communication means in fluid combat areas. Radio communication was considered essential for tactical control of highly mobile elements such as aircraft, armored units, and amphibious vehicles. Radio was also considered to be by far the most attractive medium for communication over large bodies of water such as oceans, over territory controlled by hostile forces, and over terrain where construction of wire lines would be impractical.

The network plan envisioned use of low- and medium-band radio systems for transmission over polar regions within the limits of their capability and use of high-frequency systems for most long-haul overseas communication. The very-high-frequency band was considered desirable for short-haul line-of-sight transmission within a theater of operations.

Wire facilities were considered to be more suitable than radio for handling the bulk of ground communications, particularly between permanent, semipermanent, or temporarily established locations in zones of interior and in theaters of operations. They were also considered suitable for use by forward observers and in fire control networks, especially where security was important. The available commercial wire-line networks in the United States and in certain parts of continental Europe were, of course, considered preferable means of handling communications traffic within noncombat areas.

The effective ranges of radio communication were known to be less predictable than those of wire lines. It was well known that high-frequency radio is subject to variations owing to changes in ionospheric conditions. Although very-high-frequency radio transmission is relatively free of these variations, reliable transmission was limited to line-of-sight distances between repeater points.

3.3.2 *Telephony versus Telegraphy*

The recognized advantage of the telephone is that it affords immediate personal communication between individuals. It provides a superior means of developing ideas or coping with special circumstances in a speedy manner. Its main disadvantages are its inability to record a conversation (unless a voice recorder is used), its potential for abuse by long-winded conversationalists, and its vulnerability to interception by electronic means or because of nonobservance of security regulations. Telegraphy was considered to be best suited to one-way messages or orders requiring little explanation. Handling most of the normal business by telegraph left the telephone circuits free for their principal purpose, i.e., exchange and explanation of ideas.

The architecture of the network plan took account of the fact that a telephone channel can transmit information faster than a single telegraph channel of the usual type. A fast talker without much training can read ordinary material at the rate of 150 to 250 words per minute, which can be understood over a good telephone circuit. With International Morse Code, most military telegraph operators could consistently handle up to about 15 words per minute, although highly skilled manual operators could reach 40 words per minute for short periods. Operators of direct-keyboard teletypewriters usually sent at a normal speed of about 25 to 30 words per minute, but when sending from previously prepared tape the standard speed of 60 words per minute was obtainable, provided the transmission medium was capable of handling teletypewriter messages at such a rate.

At the time the network plan was being formulated it was well known from Bell System experience that the traffic-carrying capacity of a high-grade wire-line telephone circuit could be increased for teletypewriter use. By applying six two-way channels of carrier telegraph to a two-wire telephone circuit, the information-carrying capacity of the two-wire telephone circuit for teletypewriter use could be increased to 360 words per minute in each direction. Similarly, by applying two-way channels of telegraph to each four-wire telephone circuit, the traffic capacity of the complete circuit could be increased to 720 words per minute in each direction.

3.3.3 Traffic, Compatibility, Reliability, and Security Problems

All the above factors had an important bearing on the choice of transmission media and related terminal facilities comprising the links within the fixed and semipermanent portions of the contemplated global network. It was considered essential that the transmission trunks used to interconnect higher-echelon communications centers both within the United States and overseas be capable of handling the vast amount of traffic needed to coordinate diplomatic, strategic, logistic, and tactical operations. It was proposed that alternate routes be provided for the long-distance portions of the network to ensure continuity of service between the higher-echelon communications centers during periods of failure of one route because of sabotage or for other reasons.

Teletypewriters had decided advantages over manual telegraph because they could be used by operators with little training and were known to have capabilities for providing superb security in the form of ciphered messages. There was no simple means then available for enciphering speech currents to the extent necessary to guarantee secrecy.[5]

The high-frequency radiotelephone and radiotelegraph facilities and submarine cables to overseas points in use prior to World War II were known to have inherent limitations that precluded their use in handling ciphered teletypewriter traffic:

1. The radiotelephone systems were suitable for voice transmission (except during severe conditions of fading within the sky transmission paths) but, as will be explained later, even moderate amounts of fading required the application of a sophisticated mode of modulation for digital-type telegraph signals to make them suitable for transmission of ciphered teletypewriter messages.
2. The radiotelegraph systems used by the Navy, RCA, Press Wireless, and others employed the CW, or open-and-close, method of keying the high-frequency signals emitted by the transmitter.[6]
3. The array of submarine telegraph cables extending from shore points of the United States and Canada to points in Europe and Africa and across the Pacific were limited in traffic-carrying capacity because of their inherent low-speed signaling capabilities.

---

[5] Means were developed later and are described in Section IV of this chapter.
[6] See Section 3.5.1 below for information on the techniques used to make these types of systems capable of handling ciphered teletypewriter communications.

3.3.4 End-Link Communication Arteries Operations

It was recognized that the stringent traffic and reliability requirements within the fixed plant portion of the global network could not be met by the end-link media that would be used to handle communications, mostly tactical in nature, between front-line troops and their command headquarters. The information-carrying capacity of the wire-line and radio media to be used in such end-link areas, while important, was not considered to be the governing parameter in choosing the modes of communication. The choice between radio and wire-line media would be governed by the degree of fluidity of a changing situation. The ranges of voice and telegraph transmission would be limited in any case by the compromises considered necessary to permit use of compact and light-weight instruments and transmission terminal equipment. For example, seven-strand field wire had a talking range without repeaters of about 10 miles, whereas its range for telegraphy was severalfold greater. Similarly, about 25 times as much power was required to transmit speech over a noisy radio circuit as was required to transmit telegraph signals by the conventional CW method.

Although teletypewriters had the advantages noted previously, their use with field wire and noisy radio facilities within forward areas was limited because of size, weight, and inability to "exercise judgment" in interpreting mutilated signals sent over poor-quality transmission media.

3.4 Impact of the Pearl Harbor Attack

After the Pearl Harbor attack, an estimate of the military situation by the Joint Chiefs of Staff of the War Department led to the decision that deployment of naval forces in the Pacific should of necessity be limited to reconnaissance and to supply and support of military forces at outposts in Hawaii, Guam, and the Philippines. Because of this decision, it was possible during 1942–1943 to mount an all-out effort in the Atlantic area of operations to supply Great Britain with war and other materiel needed in its defense and to assemble troops and materiel in Great Britain and North Africa to prepare for the unprecedented amphibious operations on the coasts of North Africa and Europe.

After the Pearl Harbor attack the reaction of the Army Signal Corps was profound and immediate. The Corps immediately put to use the findings of the network study so that it could determine the composition of a projected intercontinental military communication network—a network that could handle telephone and teletypewriter traffic between communications centers within the United States and with those that might be established overseas. The study was also used to determine the variety of communications materiel that would be needed by mobile ground and air forces in fluid areas of operations.

A service contract was made with the Bell System to cover expansion and use of its wire-line network to form the North American portion of the projected global military network. Contracts were also made with Western Electric and the Teletype Corporation for transmission system terminal equipment and telephone and teletypewriter apparatus needed to extend the network to foreign locations. The Signal Corps also contracted with other qualified manufacturers for communications materiel to be used by the ground and the air forces in the projected theaters of operations.

3.5 Composition of the World War II Global Military Network

The Bell System wire-line network met all traffic, compatibility, reliability, and security requirements for voice and teletypewriter communications that would flow between various governmental communications centers within the continental United States and into Canada. Consequently, the Bell System became the prime service organization for supply and maintenance of the voice and teletypewriter networks within the United States that were used by the War Department and other agencies of the government during World War II.

Immediately after Pearl Harbor, the Signal Corps had an urgent need to establish a global transmission network extending communications beyond North America to Great Britain, and later into other areas within the European and Pacific theaters of operations. Western Electric was selected as the prime contractor for development, manufacture, and supply of transmission equipment and systems required to interconnect the projected signal centers outside North America with each other and with the American network. Western Electric was also designated as a leading supplier of the telephone sets and related apparatus that would be needed to equip the various projected communications centers for voice communication. The Teletype Corporation was chosen as the prime supplier of teletypewriter apparatus.

Under terms of the initial supply contract between Western Electric and the Signal Corps (and other engineering agencies, principally the Navy Bureau of Ships), the systems approach was effectively applied with a minimum of formality. The engineering agencies specified the physical, operational, and environmental requirements, Bell Laboratories incorporated these requirements into the technical design of each product, and Western Electric used the design information provided by Bell Laboratories to prepare for and carry out all operations related to manufacture and supply. For teletypewriter apparatus, the Teletype Corporation and Bell Laboratories coordinated their technical operations to ensure that products were suitably designed to meet environmental requirements within the military network and allowed users to conveniently perform on-line and off-line operations, including ciphering.

3.5.1 Ciphered Teletypewriter Communications

Means for completely secure encipherment of teletypewriter messages were devised by G. S. Vernam of AT&T during the later years of World War I. In view of the other advantages of teletypewriters, it was logical that the engineers from Bell Labs and the Teletype Corporation working on the network plan should advocate the use of enciphered teletypewriter messages in handling all critical military and diplomatic communications. With the close cooperation of the Signal Corps and other agencies of government, modernized teletypewriter enciphering and deciphering arrangements were quickly developed, not only for off-line use in preparing a message for transmission, but also for direct on-line use. With the new equipment, messages could be typed in the clear and automatically enciphered by the associated on-line gear, the entire process thus providing practically the same ease and speed as the preparation of plain text messages. The Signal Corps started to use the new techniques soon after Pearl Harbor, and the Navy followed suit.

Figure 5-4 shows the elementary principles of enciphering and deciphering a standard five-unit teletypewriter code. Each character in the

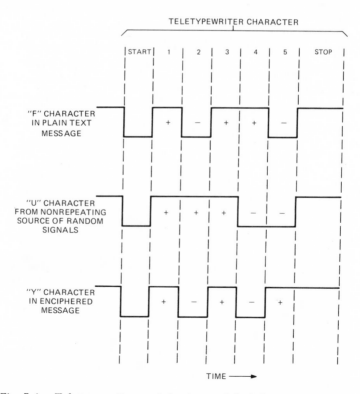

Fig. 5-4.   Teletypewriter enciphering and deciphering principles.

(a)

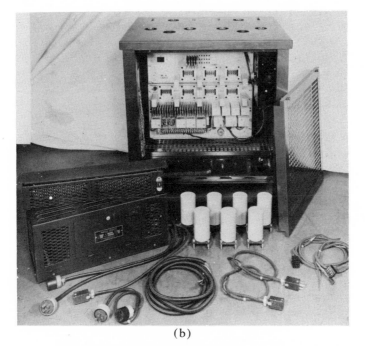

(b)

Fig. 5-5.   Cipher station arrangement.

message, such as F, is synchronously combined with another character, such as U, supplied from a nonrepeating random key source of teletypewriter signals available at each end of the link. The signals are combined in an algebraic circuit in which like signals produce a mark ($+$) and unlike signals a space ($-$). This electrical combination produces a resultant character Y, which is transmitted to the distant station where it is combined with the U supplied locally at the receiving station to give the original F. The same circuitry accomplishes the deciphering, as can be seen by reading upward from the bottom of the figure. Various methods of teletypewriter enciphering and deciphering came into use, depending upon the degrees of secrecy desired, but the nonrepeating key principle was the one used when the greatest secrecy was imperative. Figure 5-5 shows a teletypewriter with cipher equipment, including the table that housed the 131B2 subscriber set, the front view of which is shown in the lower portion of the figure.

3.5.2 The Long-Haul Multichannel Radio System: DBR (Double Band Radio)

Immediately after Pearl Harbor, the Army established a communications center in London. Direct trunks consisting of wire-line and radio links in tandem were set up to handle the plain-text voice and encrypted telegraph communications that began to flow between the London and Washington communications centers.

Initially, the conventional single-channel radiotelegraph systems available at the time were put to use to transmit encrypted messages in International Morse Code by keying the radio transmitter either manually or automatically. With this method, the sending key controlled the output of the radio transmitter. When the key was closed, energy at a particular radio frequency was transmitted; when the key was open, the transmitter was cut off. Either the listener would read the interrupted tone signals as dots or dashes, or these were automatically recorded on a tape.

There was an urgent need for a long-haul radio system that could handle several enciphered teletypewriter messages simultaneously. Bell Laboratories therefore developed a highly satisfactory long-haul multichannel teletypewriter system that made use of available single-sideband, twin-channel radiotelephone and carrier telegraph equipment, together with additional components needed to make the system suitable for reception of teletypewriter signals. The radio transmitters and receivers used in the system were the suppressed-carrier single-sideband types that had been in use for several years in Bell System overseas service arranged for transmission of two voice channels (or equivalent carrier telegraph). The multichannel telegraph equipment was an adaptation of the type used extensively in Bell System carrier telegraph wire networks.

As noted previously, the use of unmodified carrier telegraph systems designed for the stable wire medium was unsuitable for teletypewriter service over high-frequency radio because of the fading and selective distortion caused by the constantly varying ionospheric transmission path. Several means were used to adapt the standard carrier telegraph systems for this unstable medium. One was a change in modulation method, from amplitude modulation to frequency-shift keying. In the latter technique, the carrier signal was not turned on and off to designate mark and space. Instead, a signal of constant amplitude was transmitted, and two different frequencies were used to designate mark and space, the shift between them being controlled by the normal on-off telegraph signal. This system, combined with a limiter at the receiving end, provided a signal with much less ambiguity between mark and space when transmitted over a radio path with rapidly varying loss.

Frequency-shift modulation by itself was not sufficient for highly reliable transmission, since selective fading could cause the path loss over narrow frequency bands to exceed the operating range of the system. Frequency diversity was employed to minimize this problem—i.e., each telegraph channel used two sets of frequencies located in different parts of the voice frequency band (constituting a radio channel). In this way there was a strong probability that one set of telegraph signals would be received, even if the other was obliterated by fading. The penalty for obtaining this transmission reliability was, of course, the use of double the number of telegraph channels; only six could be transmitted over a voice channel instead of the 12 possible without frequency diversity. Thus, the twin-channel radio system could transmit six teletypewriter channels with one voice channel (or two voice channels if no telegraph was employed).

The first of these systems was provided a few weeks after it was requested, and it successfully operated between Washington and London using one sideband of the existing radiotelephone system to provide three simultaneous teletypewriter circuits in each direction. The capacity was later doubled. The Army operated a number of these multichannel transoceanic links for the duration of the war in a highly successful manner between such points as Washington and London and San Francisco and Australia. The Navy also obtained a number of these systems for use over their main global communications routes, such as between Washington and Honolulu.

A common military application of the system included six teletypewriter channels applied to one of the sidebands of the twin-channel radiotelephone system with the other sideband available for telephone. When used in this manner, the system had a teletypewriter traffic-carrying capacity of about 5,000 100-word messages per day in each direction.

The additional equipment for achieving high-frequency radio transmission was rather complicated. Figures 5-6 and 5-7 and the remaining

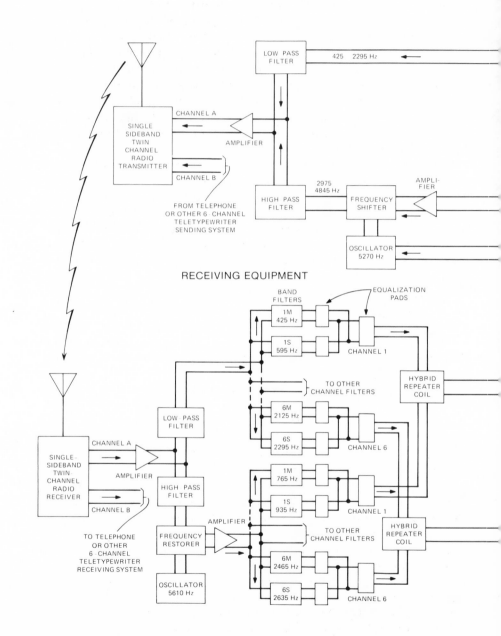

Fig. 5-6. Multichannel radio teletypewriter system or single-sideband twin-channel radiotelephone system.

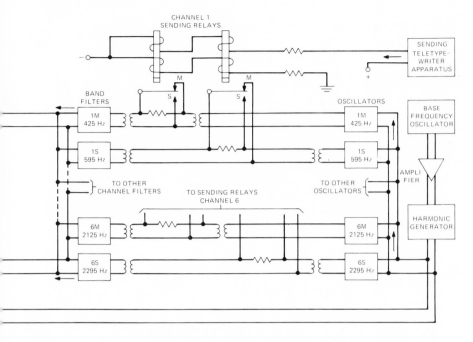

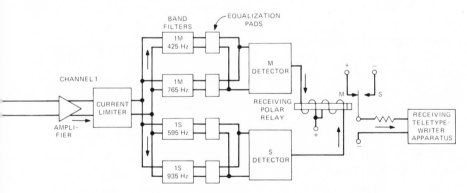

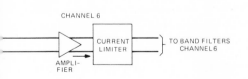

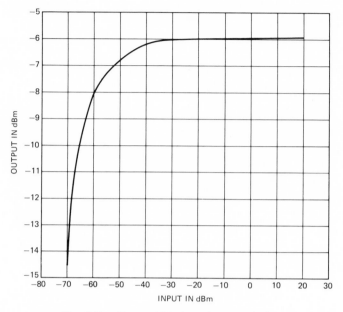

Fig. 5-7.   Current limiter characteristic.

portion of this section have been included for readers interested in details.

At the sending terminal, the two-tone carrier frequencies of each of the six teletypewriter channels (425 to 595 Hz for Channel 1) were modulated by a frequency shifter, and the resultant frequencies (4,845 Hz and 4,675 Hz for Channel 1) were combined with the lower unmodulated band of frequencies and impressed on one of the channels of the radiotelephone transmitter.

At the receiving end, the upper band of teletypewriter channel frequencies was separated from the lower band by filters. The higher band was then passed through a frequency restorer. The individual frequencies of each of the six teletypewriter channels were separated from those of other channels by means of bandpass filters and then combined in a common limiter and marking and spacing detector circuits.

The means used to provide for frequency diversity operation, which reduces errors under fading conditions, may be clarified by tracing the paths of teletypewriter Channel 1 through Fig. 5-6. The Channel 1 marking frequency (425 Hz) and spacing frequency (595 Hz) pass from the sending circuits into a three-branch network. Half the energy goes through the upper branch and a low-pass filter to the radio transmitter. The other half goes through the lower branch to the input of an amplifier and then enters the channel shifter for modulation by a frequency of 5,270 Hz. The modulation products (5,270 − 425 = 4,845 Hz, and 5,270 − 595 = 4,675 Hz) pass through the high-pass filter to the radio transmitter.

Table 5-1. Teletypewriter Channel Frequencies (Hz)

Channel	Within the Radio Sideband	Into the Channel Detectors
1M	425; 4845	425; 765
1S	595; 4695	595; 935
2M	765; 4505	765; 1105
2S	935; 4335	935; 1275
3M	1105; 4165	1105; 1445
3S	1275; 3995	1275; 1615
4M	1445; 3825	1445; 1785
4S	1615; 3655	1615; 1955
5M	1785; 3485	1785; 2125
5S	1955; 3315	1955; 2295
6M	2125; 3145	2125; 2465
6S	2295; 2975	2265; 2635

At the receiving end, the 425- and 595-Hz signals pass through the low-pass filter to the regular two-tone receiving equipment of Channel 1. The 4,845- or 4,675-Hz signals pass through the high-pass filter to the frequency restorer, where they are modulated by a frequency of 5,610 Hz forming, among other modulating products, frequencies of $5{,}610 - 4{,}845 = 765$ Hz or $5{,}610 - 4{,}675 = 935$ Hz. The output is amplified and the 765- or 935-Hz signals are separated from those of other channels by two auxiliary diversity filters. The outputs of the Channel 1 auxiliary diversity filters are combined with the outputs of the Channel 1 auxiliary filters in a hybrid coil. After amplification, the combined signals enter the limiter. At the output of the limiter they are separated by four filters. The filters corresponding to the two marking frequencies are connected to the marking detector, and those corresponding to the spacing frequencies to the spacing detector.

The diversity frequencies for all channels were made 340 Hz above their corresponding normal frequencies. For example, the normal Channel 1 marking frequency is shown to have been 425 Hz, whereas that from the auxiliary filter of Channel 1 was 765 Hz. If they were both 425 Hz, their phases would vary due to radio fading, sometimes reinforcing and sometimes neutralizing. By making the two frequencies different, the effects of this variation were minimized. Table 5-1 lists the audio frequencies of the various teletypewriter channels. Figure 5-7 shows the characteristics of the current limiter used in each teletypewriter receiving channel.

3.5.3 The Long-Haul Single-Channel Radio Teletype System: AN/FGC-1

The long-haul multichannel radio system described in the previous section, with a trunking capacity for either two speech channels or up to

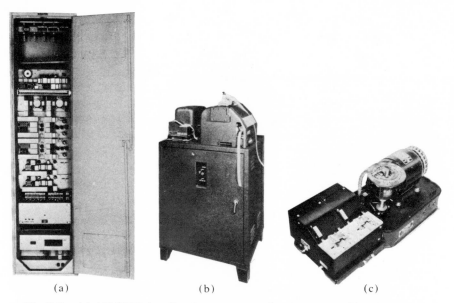

Fig. 5-8.   (a) AN/FGC-1 radioteletype terminal equipment.   (b) Teletypewriter subscriber set 132A2.   (c) Transmitter-distributor XD91.

twelve teletypewriter circuits, was rather ponderous.   Its assembly included a high-power, fixed-plant type of radio transmitter and associated receiver, with very large rhombic transmitting and receiving antennas. The large-size antennas and the bulk and weight of the radio and carrier telegraph equipment restricted its installation to points in North America and corresponding points in zones of interior within the European and Pacific areas of operations.

A less cumbersome radio system was urgently needed in zones of interior and in semipermanent areas within theaters of operations to provide reliable transmission of ciphered teletypewriter communications.   The developing military situation indicated that the system must have physical characteristics that would enable it to be readily transported, installed, and placed in service wherever needed.

These requirements were met by adapting an existing single-channel radiotelegraph system to provide frequency shift keying (with an 850-Hz difference between mark and space) and the use of space diversity to counteract the effects of selective fading.   By limiting the system to a single teletypewriter channel, the size and weight of the radio equipment were greatly reduced and antennas were simplified.   However, limiting the transmitters to one channel (to reduce size and weight) had the disadvantage of requiring two receivers and antennas to obtain diversity. When these were located an appropriate distance apart, there was good probability that deep fading would not occur simultaneously at both locations. Thus the same objective as frequency diversity would be attained with less frequency space and power.

Early in 1942, the Army Signal Corps contracted with Western Electric for the development and production of the carrier telegraph portion of such a system. The system became known as the AN/FGC-1 radio teletypewriter terminal equipment. Figure 5-8a shows a front view of the equipment. The assembly was made as compact, self-sufficient, and rugged as practicable to permit shipment by either airplane or ship to overseas locations. The total weight was about 635 pounds when crated for shipment. Other details which may be of interest to some readers are covered by Figs. 5-9 and 5-10.

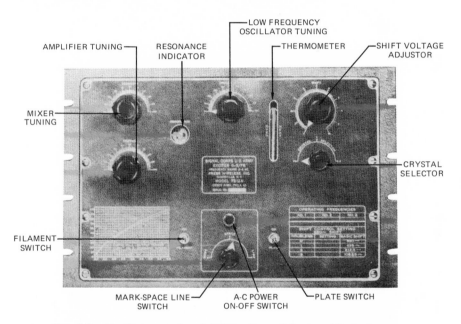

Fig. 5-9. Oscillator exciter 0-5/ER—Press Wireless FS12A keyer.

Figure 5-10 schematically illustrates the makeup of the system and the way it transmitted ciphered teletypewriter messages from origin to destination. The AN/FGC-1 radio teletypewriter terminal equipment was designed to be used for simultaneous transmission of messages in either direction, but when it was used in that manner it was necessary to install a radio transmitter bay and two radio receivers at each terminal of the long-haul radio link.

Conventional radiotelegraph transmitters were available for use with the AN/FGC-1. However, the method of keying each transmitter had to

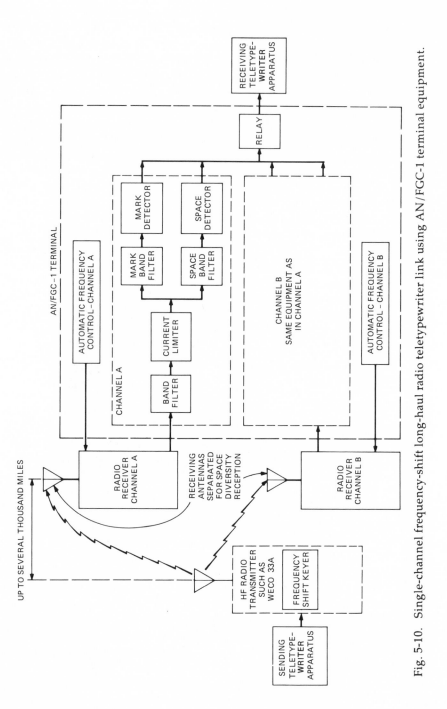

Fig. 5-10. Single-channel frequency-shift long-haul radio teletypewriter link using AN/FGC-1 terminal equipment.

be changed from the open-and-close (CW) method to the frequency shift (FS) method. The exciter unit shown in Fig. 5-9 provided the FS method, among other features.

In effect, the exciter unit was a substitute for the first oscillator unit in the radio transmitter. It consisted of a crystal-controlled oscillator having a frequency differing from the radio frequency by about 200 kHz and a stable 200-kHz oscillator whose tuned circuit frequency could be shifted by ±425 Hz. The radio-frequency oscillator was modulated by the 200 kHz + 425 Hz and 200 kHz − 425 Hz in response to teletypewriter marking and spacing signals, respectively. All of the modulation products, except the sum of the crystal oscillator frequency and of the 200 kHz ± 425 Hz oscillator, were filtered out, and the remaining radio-frequency signal with minor sidebands was fed into the first amplifier stage of the radio transmitter.

As shown in Fig. 5-10, the system included two radio receivers having separate antennas located several wavelengths apart so that fading over the sky paths would seldom cause the loss of signals in both simultaneously. This space diversity feature added stability to the transmission circuit. An interconnection between the detectors within the AN/FGC-1 radio teletypewriter terminal enabled output from the channel having the better signal-to-noise ratio to be used and thus effected a further increase in stability.

Each radio receiver converted the incoming radio-frequency signals to two audio frequencies, 2,125 and 2,975 Hz, for marking and spacing, respectively. The input filter within the AN/FGC-1 equipment (1,600–3,500-Hz passband) excluded noise frequencies outside the working band and passed the marking and spacing frequencies into a fast-operating wide-range limiter which prevented the currents from exceeding a prescribed maximum value. The limiter largely eliminated the effects of amplitude variations (fading), which were prevalent in the long-distance high-frequency radio paths. The marking and spacing frequencies from the limiter were then passed through filters into a double detector. The marking filter passed the band from about 1,700 to 2,500 Hz and the spacing filter from about 2,600 to 3,400 Hz. The outputs of the two space-diversity channels were combined in the receiving relay on a dc basis to avoid distortion from variable phase differences between the tones of the two channels.

During all development phases of the AN/FGC-1 program, engineers of the Signal Corps and Bell Laboratories maintained day-to-day communications to ensure maximum progress. As soon as the electrical and operational requirements of the exciter unit were established, the Signal Corps contracted with the Press Wireless Company for development and production of this unit. The 0-5/FR exciter unit shown in Fig. 5-9 became the standard Signal Corps product for use with the AN/FGC-1.

3.5.4 *Later Designs of Long-Haul Radio Teletypewriter Equipment and Apparatus*

During 1943–1944 both the Army and Navy required new development work in the rapidly growing field of long-distance radio teletypewriter communications. Emphasis was placed on lightweight, compact portable equipment, and apparatus having capabilities comparable to those of the AN/FGC-1 carrier teletypewriter system and its associated radio equipment.

The Navy became interested in providing for ciphered radioteletype communications from shore points to both large and small ships and between ships. Requirements for such service were more severe than for land-based equipment. Compact and lightweight equipment was required because of the shortage of shipboard space. In addition, the antennas presented serious problems. They had to be designed to minimize shock effects from gunfire and had to be located so as to maintain an unobstructed path for planes taking off and landing.

The equipment developed by Bell Laboratories for the Navy included a frequency shift keyer, coded FSA, and a converter unit, coded FRF. The former came into use as a means for keying Navy radio transmitters on ships; the latter, together with a pair of radio receivers, provided means for receiving the keyed high-frequency teletypewriter signals sent from a distant ship or shore point.

3.5.4.1 *The Navy Frequency Shift Keyer—FSA.*
The Navy FSA keyer was designed to operate on the same principle as the 0-5/FR exciter unit. Like the 0-5/FR unit, the FSA keyer could operate over a radio-frequency range from 2 to 27 MHz. It contained a highly stabilized keying network and other electrical components held to very close tolerances to meet Navy electrical, mechanical, shock, and vibration requirements. The degree of stabilization was such that variations in emitted radio-frequency pulses were held to a few Hz per million to permit the Navy to obtain better use of the congested frequency spectrum. There was a substantial reduction in interference between radio teletypewriter channels, which permitted the Navy to obtain more channels by providing stable radio receivers on ships and at shore installations.

Figure 5-11 is a photograph of the front view of the FSA keyer chassis. It was mounted either in a mobile cabinet for use at shore stations or in a shock-resisting cabinet for installation on ships. Six cable assemblies were provided for connecting the keyer to the radio transmitter, the power service, and other units.

Bell Laboratories completed design of the FSA keyer during 1944. It was successfully tested by the Navy on shipboard under typical conditions. During 1945–1946, Western Electric supplied the Navy with more than 700 of these keyers.

Fig. 5-11.   Model FSA keyer chassis.

3.5.4.2 *The Navy Converter Unit — FRF.* The Navy FRF converter unit provided all the essential electrical and operational functions contained in the AN/FGC-1 radio teletypewriter terminal equipment.   The photograph in Fig. 5-12 shows the relatively small size of the FRF unit when it is compared with the AN/FGC-1 equipment, being approximately one-third the size and weighing only about 150 pounds.

After successful operational tests of the unit by the Navy, Western Electric was given a contract to make about 400 converters, which were supplied during 1945 and 1946.   After V-J Day, the Navy continued to equip its ships with these units and with teletypewriters.

3.5.4.3 *Army Mobile Radio Teletypewriter Equipment — TRA-7.* During 1944, the Army Signal Corps gave a design and supply contract to Western Electric for a particular version of the AN/FGC-1 radio teletypewriter equipment for use with the mobile SCR-399 radio set.   The compelling reason for the contract was the recognized need for transmitting ciphered messages of a high security nature. Radio channels were needed to couple temporary communications centers in rear areas of fluid battlefronts with established higher-echelon signal centers within theaters of operations.

The SCR-399 set provided a radio link between communications centers up to about 100 miles for either voice or manual telegraph communications.   It could operate either in a stationary position or in motion as part of a military convoy.   It included a radio transmitter, coded BC-610, two radio receivers, each coded BC-342, other adjunct equipment and appa-

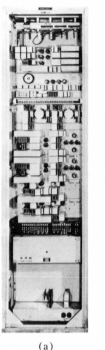

(b)

(a)

Fig. 5-12. (a) AN/FGC-1 radio teletypewriter terminal designed during 1942.
(b) Navy converter unit designed during
1944.

ratus, a power supply, and transmitting and receiving antennas. It operated over a radio path within the medium- and high-frequency spectrums from 1.0 to 18 MHz.

Figure 5-13 shows the association of the various units comprising the
SCR-399 set and AN/TRA-7 radio teletypewriter equipment when set up
at a temporary but stationary signal center.

The initial production of AN/TRA-7 radio teletypewriter equipment
was delivered to the Signal Corps during early 1945. Although the end
of the war in Europe in early May 1945 precluded more than limited use
in that theater, the equipment was used in the Pacific area prior to and after
V-J Day to provide additional long-haul radio links in the global wire-line
and radio teletypewriter networks.

3.5.5 Systems for Connecting Long-Haul Radio Teletypewriter Communication Centers — UF, UG, and UH Equipment

As the war intensified, the multichannel radio teletypewriter (DBR)
system and the Army AN/FGC-1 single-channel radio teletypewriter
system, along with an alternative system designed for specific use by the

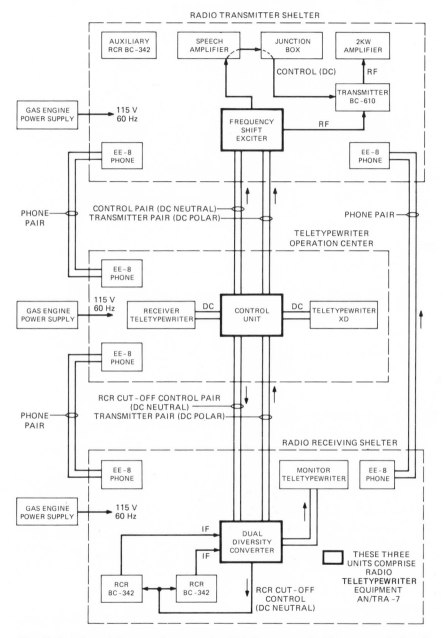

Fig. 5-13. Signal Corps radio set AN/MRC-2 composed of frequency shift radio equipment (coded radio teletypewriter equipment AN/TRA-7) with teletypewriter apparatus and radio set SCR-399-A.

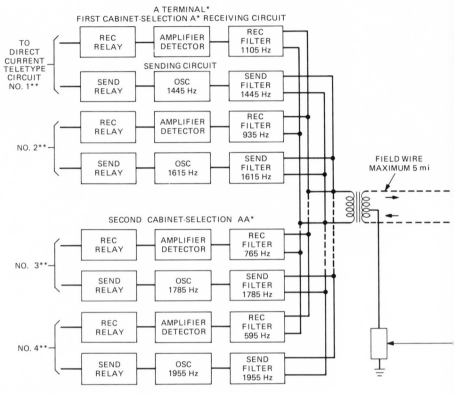

*SWITCHES IN THE CABINET PERMIT SELECTION A, AA, B OR BB WHICH DETERMINES THE
SENDING AND RECEIVING AUDIO FREQUENCIES AT TERMINAL A.
THESE FREQUENCIES ARE AS SHOWN; AT TERMINAL B THEY ARE THE CONVERSE.

** A SERVICE SWITCH IN EACH CIRCUIT PROVIDES OTHER SERVICE OPTIONS INCLUDING
A DIRECT CONNECTION TO A HF RADIO TRANSMITTER OR TO A LONG-HAUL HF RADIO RECEIVER.

(a)

Fig. 5-14.   Model UF carrier control system for U.S. Navy.   (a) System schematic.
(b) Two Model UG line terminal units.   (c) One Model UH radio line terminal
unit.

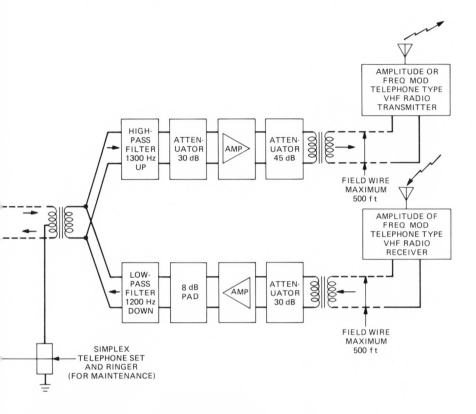

AMPLITUDE OR FREQ MOD TELEPHONE TYPE VHF RADIO TRANSMITTER

HIGH-PASS FILTER 1300 Hz UP

ATTEN-UATOR 30 dB

AMP

ATTEN-UATOR 45 dB

FIELD WIRE MAXIMUM 500 ft

AMPLITUDE OF FREQ MOD TELEPHONE TYPE VHF RADIO RECEIVER

LOW-PASS FILTER 1200 Hz DOWN

8 dB PAD

AMP

ATTEN-UATOR 30 dB

FIELD WIRE MAXIMUM 500 ft

SIMPLEX TELEPHONE SET AND RINGER (FOR MAINTENANCE)

(b)

(c)

Navy, coded AN/FGC-1A, came into extensive use as long-haul transmission links within the expanding intercontinental teletypewriter network. The use of these radio links to transmit teletypewriter messages of the same form that was used on wire-line circuits within the United States and abroad gave the global network a flexibility and security not attainable by other means. The radio links and inland wire circuits were associated with each other in ways providing speedy means for handling the growing amounts of traffic between teletypewriter communication centers within various interconnected inland points on different continents. The transportability and ease of installation of the AN/FGC-1 and AN/FGC-1A systems allowed increased traffic-carrying capacity of a particular transmission link and also alternative geographic routes between points of termination to ensure continuity of service.

The U.S. military forces established communications centers on Hawaii and progressively on other occupied islands of the Pacific as soon as the military situation permitted. It was essential to provide the command headquarters in these various areas of operation with teletypewriter communication links to higher echelons of command within the global network and with naval fleets in the Pacific. Some of the message centers were remote from the station containing the gateway terminals of the long-haul radio teletypewriter circuits. Either wire-line or radio systems interconnected the message center with the terminal station.

Most of the wire-line circuits on the occupied islands were known to be semipermanent and vulnerable to sabotage or natural failure. Consequently, during 1942 the Navy contracted with Western Electric for Bell Laboratories to design a short-haul radio teletypewriter system as an alternative interconnecting link. The system, coded Model UF, was a portable multichannel radio teletypewriter system capable of transmitting several teletypewriter messages simultaneously over a VHF (140- to 160-MHz) short-haul radio path up to almost 40 miles.

The Model UF system consisted of two classes of physical components: a Model UG line terminal equipment, which contained carrier telegraph equipments, and a Model UH radio line terminal equipment, which contained units for connecting the UG terminal to the VHF radio link. Figure 5-14 shows two Model UG equipments and one Model UH equipment. It also indicates how they were interconnected to provide four teletypewriter circuits over a two-wire line between a communications center and a radio line terminal.

Each circuit of the UG terminal used two different carrier frequencies, one for sending and the other for receiving. Switches in each of the two UG cabinets provided means for associating cabinets 1 and 2 in the proper manner to provide the A and AA terminal arrangements shown in the diagram of Fig. 5-14. At the other end of the radio link the switches in the UG cabinets were arranged to set up the B and BB frequency configurations which were the converse of those in the A and in the AA configurations.

If more than four and up to eight teletypewriter circuits were required over the VHF radio link, this number could be provided by using four UG cabinets at each communication center. For this service option, a four-wire circuit rather than a two-wire circuit was used to interconnect the UG and UH terminals, and the switches in the UG and UH terminals were set in the proper operating position to provide for eight circuits. Table 5-2 shows the manner in which the eight-circuit service was provided in the UG cabinets.

The UF system provided up to eight two-way teletypewriter circuits over a VHF radio link for distances up to 40 miles. If the military forces preferred to use wire lines rather than radio as the interconnecting transmission link, the circuits of the Model UB terminals were connected directly to the wire lines and the Model UH terminals were not used. The UG equipment was capable of operating over wire lines having an attenuation between terminals A and B up to 25 dB.

During 1943–1945, about 100 systems were placed in service throughout the world. Their performance was found to be most satisfactory by the Army, Navy, and Marine Corps.

3.5.6 Wire-Line Carrier Telephone and Telegraph Systems in Noncombat Zones and Rear Areas of Combat Zones

In North America and within noncombat zones of occupied overseas territory, wire lines were obviously the preferred means of interconnecting the various military communications centers. Compared to radio, the wire-line networks in such protected zones made it difficult for the enemy to intercept either telephone or telegraph communications. Hence, the telephone and telegraph traffic that flowed over the wire-line network could be mostly in plain text, though ciphered telegraph messages could be used when security was of prime importance. Also, analyses showed that the volume of telephone and telegraph traffic would be so great that it would be necessary to provide carrier-derived telephone and telegraph circuits of the types used in the Bell System network for application to wire-line circuits in occupied overseas territories.

3.5.6.1 Packaged Equipment for Signal Corps Fixed Plant Applications. To meet the immediate demand for carrier-derived facilities for use with open-wire lines in overseas areas, the Signal Corps in 1941 asked Western Electric to modify its commercial designs of carrier equipment to adapt them for military use in occupied overseas territories. The modified designs were furnished as packaged equipment in which the various groups of equipment normally used together were assembled and completely wired as a unit at the factory. By laying out the proper unit packages in

Table 5-2.   Eight-Circuit Service UG Terminals

Terminal Location	Send Channel Switch Position	Telegraph Circuit No. in Cabinet	Frequencies (Hz)	
			Sending	Receiving
A	A	1	1,445	1,105
		2	1,615	935
	AA	1	1,785	765
		2	1,955	595
	B	1	1,105	1,445
		2	935	1,615
	BB	1	765	1,785
		2	595	1,955
B	B	1	1,105	1,445
		2	935	1,615
	BB	1	765	1,785
		2	595	1,955
	A	1	1,445	1,105
		2	1,615	935
	AA	1	1,785	765
		2	1,955	595

desired combinations, all the desired communication circuits could be quickly set up.   The various conditions were anticipated as much as possible, and provision was made to enable the packaged equipment to meet a variety of local conditions.   For example, apparatus and wiring were "tropicalized" to make them suitable for use in tropical environments.

The packaged carrier equipment included all the elements needed to construct a complete long-distance telephone or telegraph multicircuit transmission link; these included voice-frequency repeaters, one- and three-channel carrier telephone systems, six- and twelve-channel voice-frequency carrier telegraph systems, dc telegraph systems, signaling equipment, testboards, etc.   Figure 5-15 shows an assembly of a typical configuration of one packaged terminal.

Western Electric delivered the first lot of packaged equipment to the Signal Corps during early 1942 and large quantities of it during the remainder of the war.   The equipment was used extensively to increase the traffic-carrying capacity of rehabilitated open-wire lines or of newly constructed lines in Africa, Europe, Australia, New Guinea, and other areas.   It proved to be of particular importance both in Africa and Australia, where communications over distances approaching 2,000 miles were required.   The equipment provided telephone and telegraph service comparable to that provided over long-distance routes within the Bell System network.

A very important project was providing communications facilities along the Alcan Highway between Edmonton, Canada, and Fairbanks, Alaska,

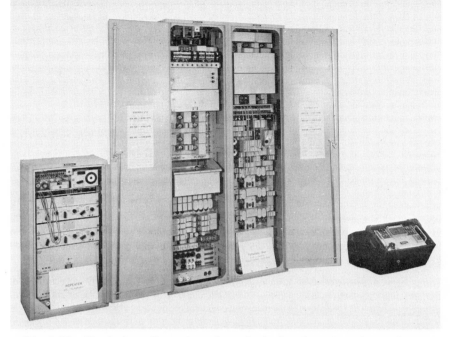

Fig. 5-15.   Typical configuration of terminal of packaged carrier equipment.

a distance of about 2,000 miles.   Western Electric cooperated with the Army Signal Corps in engineering, manufacturing, and installing carrier systems of the packaged type, which were applied to a new open-wire line constructed by the Army.   Due to the unusual nature of the project, certain special features were required and new equipment, when necessary, was designed by Bell Laboratories.   The circuits at Edmonton were connected over Canadian lines to the Bell System network to provide telephone and telegraph services from Fairbanks, Alaska, to Washington, D.C., a distance of almost 7,000 miles.

3.5.6.2 The Spiral-Four Cable Carrier System.   About mid-1941 the Signal Corps asked Bell Laboratories and Western Electric for advice on the development of a carrier system, using a field cable that could be plowed underground, and associated carrier and terminal equipment, for providing multicircuit transmission links between communications centers of Army groups, corps, and divisions within rear areas of combat zones.   Communication distances of at least 100 miles and up to 400 miles were desired.   Open-wire lines and the fixed plant packaged equipment were considered capable of meeting the requirements for traffic density and quality of transmission, but the construction of open-wire lines often could not proceed as rapidly as the troops advanced.   The conferences led to the development of an appropriate type of cable and carrier equipment to provide three telephone and four telegraph circuits over one cable.

By mid-1942, models of the carrier equipment and several hundred miles of the new type of cable, designated "spiral-four," were delivered to the Signal Corps for testing. During the last quarter of 1942 considerable quantities of cable and equipment were shipped to Africa and used in the campaign there during early 1943.

The spiral-four cable consisted of four rubber-insulated conductors in a spiraled square configuration with the diagonal conductors forming the pairs.[7] It was wrapped with a conductive paper foil and covered with a steel braid and a tough synthetic rubber jacket. The cable was slightly over $\frac{3}{8}$ inch in diameter and was shipped on reels, each containing a $\frac{1}{4}$ mile length. Each end of a cable was equipped with connectors so that successive lengths could be joined quickly. A small loading coil was contained in each connecting plug to reduce attenuation.

The spiral-four cable could be laid on the ground, attached to poles or trees, or buried in the ground. Burying the cable was considered highly advantageous where the terrain permitted. A plow was developed which could be drawn by an Army truck and which laid the cable in the ground at depths of a foot or more.

The equipment for the spiral-four carrier system, while using previously established frequency-division carrier techniques, was completely new, having been specifically designed to meet Signal Corps requirements. Basically, it was a physical four-wire system using the two pairs of the quad for the two directions of transmission. It consisted of four circuits of telephone bandwidth, any one of which could be used for transmitting four telegraph circuits, and it was usually used as a three-telephone, four-telegraph system. One of the basic circuits was transmitted in voice-frequency band and the remaining three at carrier frequencies, the top frequency of the system being 12 kHz. This arrangement provided telephone channels with an upper frequency limit of about 2,800 Hz. Without repeaters the communication range was about 40 miles, but with repeaters a range of 200 or more miles was achieved.

The equipment consisted of a carrier terminal, a telegraph terminal, signaling equipment, and an associated power supply at each end of the cable, with carrier repeaters (each with power supply) at about 25-mile intervals along the cable. Each equipment assembly was arranged so that the several assemblies comprising a system terminal or repeater could be connected and quickly placed in operation.

Figure 5-16 shows schematically the system configurations for a spiral-four cable with and without intermediate repeaters. Included are the CF-1-A telephone terminals and, for the repeated line, CF-3-A repeaters.

---

[7] This configuration was also known as a "Star Quad." In the spiral-four cable, the phantom circuit formed by the two pairs was not used.

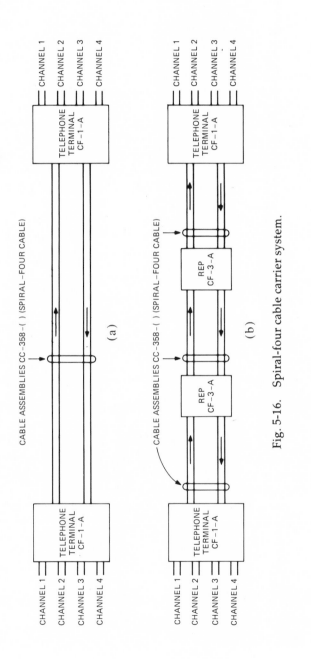

Fig. 5-16. Spiral-four cable carrier system.

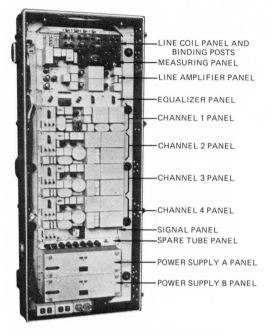

Fig. 5-17.   Telephone terminal CF-1-A.

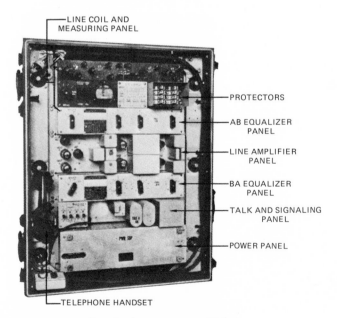

Fig. 5-18.   Repeater CF-3-A.

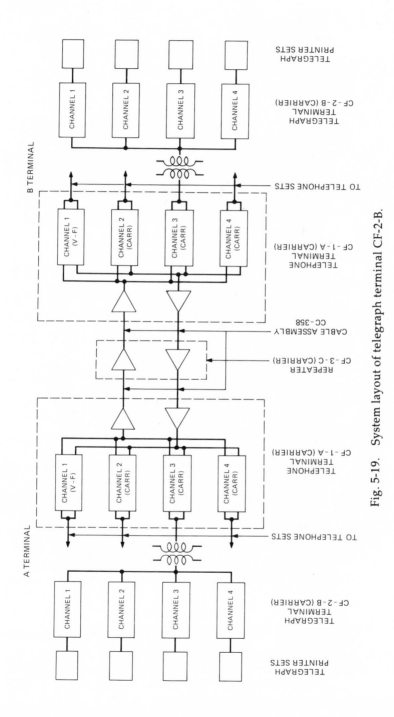

Fig. 5-19.   System layout of telegraph terminal CF-2-B.

Figure 5-17 shows a front view of telephone terminal CF-1-A, and Fig. 5-18 the front view of repeater CF-3-A.

Figure 5-19 shows schematically the connection of one of the carrier telephone circuits of the spiral-four system with a CF-2-B telegraph terminal to provide four carrier telegraph circuits over the selected carrier telephone circuit. Figure 5-20 shows the front view of the telegraph terminal.

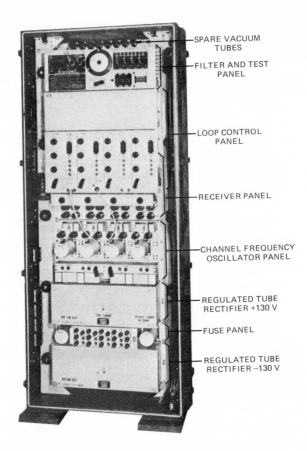

Fig. 5-20. Front view of telegraph terminal CF-2-B (carrier).

Figure 5-21(a) shows a typical spiral-four terminal arrangement as it was set up for service, including military telephone and telegraph switchboards, teletypewriters, and auxiliary equipment. Figure 5-21(b) illustrates the complicated spiral-four cable layout used at a large field headquarters in the European theater.

3.5.7 Front-Line Communications

Communications systems in and near battle areas were not strictly a part of the global system, since they were usually concerned with small geographical areas. They were, however, an essential part of the communications task, since they provided information to the higher echelons on the status of the front-line activities and furnished the means for conveying orders for front-line action.

Since World War II was fought under highly mobile conditions, much of the front-line communications were supplied by the radio systems described later in this chapter. However, wire communication still played an important part. In areas where troops advanced rapidly and extremely reliable contact with headquarters was required, the spiral-four carrier system was often installed soon after the troops arrived. Under difficult conditions, insulated field-wire pairs were the main link with troop activities. This rather primitive facility was suspended from trees or laid on the ground, as shown in Figs. 5-22 and 5-23. But this medium could be put in place only at a slow pace. Its many disadvantages led to a search for means more in keeping with the then new, technologically oriented war.

Early in World War II a suggestion was made in the National Defense Research Committee (NDRC) that it might be possible for espionage purposes to use aircraft for dropping sensitive microphones, attached to fine wires, behind enemy lines. Bell Laboratories undertook development work for the NDRC air-laid wire in 1942, making theoretical and laboratory studies on the uncoiling of lightweight wire at high speeds. A number of types of coils were produced which later found application in the laying of wire by ground vehicles, ski troopers, and bazookas. Although only very limited flight tests were conducted, the results of this early work looked promising, and the Army gave wide distribution to the related NDRC report. Even though several other methods were later investigated, the criss-cross type of coils developed in the early studies and shown in Fig. 5-24 formed the basis for the system adopted by the Army Air Force.

The NDRC report eventually reached the China-Burma-India theater, where conventional methods for providing communications were often inadequate. Radio transmission was not always reliable in the steaming jungles and over the rugged mountains; enemy radio direction finders were active; and shelling and bombing were often the fate of newly discovered radio posts. Army Air Force authorities in the CBI theater, eager for air-laid wire, cabled a request in January 1944 that development work be continued.

Shortly thereafter the Air Technical Service Command asked Bell Laboratories to resume work on air-laid wire on a rush basis. Standard Army field wire and a flying speed of 150 miles per hour were specified,

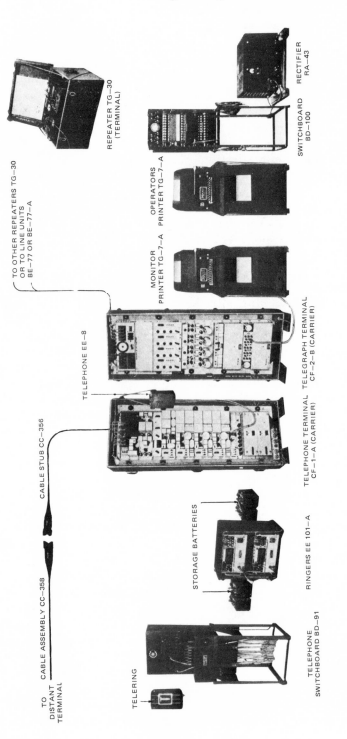

REPEATER TG—30
(TERMINAL)

RECTIFIER
RA—43

SWITCHBOARD
BD—100

TO OTHER REPEATERS TG—30
OR TO LINE UNITS
BE—77 OR BE—77—A

OPERATORS
PRINTER TG—7—A

MONITOR
PRINTER TG—7—A

TELEPHONE EE—8

TELEGRAPH TERMINAL
CF—2—B (CARRIER)

TELEPHONE TERMINAL
CF—1—A (CARRIER)

CABLE STUB CC—356

STORAGE BATTERIES

RINGERS EE 101—A

CABLE ASSEMBLY CC—358

TO
DISTANT
TERMINAL

TELERING

TELEPHONE
SWITCHBOARD BD—91

Fig. 5-21(a).   Typical spiral-four terminal installation.

Fig. 5-21(b). Special frame for supporting and routing cables of a spiral four carrier telephone network.

and the maximum length of wire to be laid in a single flight was set at 15 miles. It was agreed that after preliminary laboratory studies the Army Air Force would furnish a C-47 transport plane for flight tests to be made at the Army Air Base at Fort Dix, New Jersey.

The results of the early flight tests were inconclusive, and it soon became evident that a more comprehensive project was needed to include studies of a variety of wire types and additional packing and payout methods. An outdoor laboratory was then set up at Murray Hill, New Jersey; it included a 40-foot tower, near the top of which experimental packs of wire were placed. In a building several hundred feet away, a motor-driven drum drew wire from the packs at speeds up to 200 miles per hour. At this laboratory, the performance of various types of coils and packs was investigated with the aid of high-speed cameras and electrical devices.

Flight testing was also speeded up by establishing a field laboratory in a building provided by the Air Technical Service Command at Fort Dix Air Base and by the assignment of a flight testing team. Over 200 test flights were made in which the performance of the various types of coils

Fig. 5-22.   Telephone wire laid through dense tropic jungle on Bougainville
in the Solomon Islands.   Trees serve the moment's need as telephone poles.

Fig. 5-23.   In the early stages of the bloody struggle for Iwo Jima, a shallow
foxhole gives scant shelter to the communicator calling for artillery support, while
at the right, telephone wire is carried forward under fire.

(a)

(b)

Fig. 5-24. (a) Field wire was wound by a special machine into criss-cross coils so that it could be payed out rapidly and smoothly from an airplane in flight. (b) Ball of lacing twine.

(a)

(b)

Fig. 5-25.   Airplane wire-laying system made it possible to quickly
lay a wire communication system over difficult terrain—in this case,
jungle.   (a) and (b) Reels of field wire being loaded in Army cargo
plane.

Fig. 5-25(c).   Field wire being laid by airplane.

and packs as well as the intercoil splicing methods were thoroughly studied.

In July 1944, test samples were obtained of a newly developed field wire insulated with polyethylene, which appeared to have many advantages. Success was realized in 1-mile flights of this wire wound in criss-cross coils. Gradually, the number of successful runs increased, and the test lengths increased from 1 mile to 2 miles, then to 4 and 6.   Finally a 15-mile run, the specified maximum, was made over the flat but wooded terrain at Fort Dix.   As a final check of the system over heavily wooded and mountainous terrain, a demonstration flight was made over the Great Smoky Mountains. Here ground elevations along the course varied from 1,500 to over 5,000 feet.   Some of the spans of wire from crest to crest of the ridges were over one-half mile long.

After the Great Smoky Mountains tests, further work was done to adapt the criss-cross coil system to other types of field wire.   As finally turned over to the Army Air Force, the system could be used with C-47 cargo planes to lay either the new plastic-insulated wire referred to above or the heavier standard field wires used by the armies of the United States and Great Britain.   Though the system could be used at speeds of 150 miles per hour with the plastic-insulated wire, it was recommended that speeds be limited to 100 miles per hour with the heavier wires.

In the standardized system, two wires twisted together were wound on a specially designed machine into "criss-cross," or "universal," coils similar in form to the balls of lacing twine used by telephone installers. Each coil contained 1 or 2 miles of wire, depending upon the wire type. These coils had advantages over the ordinary layer-by-layer winding in that, when removed from the winding form, they were self-supporting and easy to handle. The various layers were also locked in such a manner that it was impossible to start two layers at the same time during payout, and the centrifugal forces on payout were less than with simple layer winding. Each coil was encased in a square wooden box with a hole in each side about one-half the outside diameter of the coil. The coil itself was unwound from the inside as with self-supporting balls of string.

When a mission was to be flown, the required number of boxes were loaded into a C-47 plane (Fig. 5-25(a)), lined up in sequence from the open doorway to the forward end of the cargo space, and secured to the floor. The outside end of each coil was carefully spliced to the inside end of the following coil. The inside end of the first coil was led outside the plane through a pipe about 6 inches in diameter (Fig. 5-25(b)) and brought back into the cargo space, where it was attached to a parachute and a suitable weight. After taking off, the pilot flew over the starting point of the line, which was identified by landmarks or panels on the ground, and a member of the crew threw out the parachute (Fig. 5-25(c)). As the wire left the pipe at speeds up to 250 feet per second, it settled to the ground with the parachute. Eventually the other end of the wire pulled free of the plane and was picked up by the second ground party. Rugged terrain required more slack, which was obtained by flying higher, since at the higher altitudes the weight of the wire in the air caused it to pay out at a rate somewhat faster than the speed of the plane.

On March 15, 1945, at the Fort Dix Air Base, the Army Air Force and Bell Laboratories gave the first public demonstration of the wire-laying system for the nationwide radio audience of "March of Time." Details of the system were disclosed to the press on March 21 during a tour of inspection of the wire-laying apparatus at Fort Dix.

The system did not arrive in time for extensive use in the Pacific theaters before the end of the war. However, it is believed that adaptations of it were used in Europe at river crossings during the Allied advance.

3.6 The Role of the Teletypewriter Network

During the early part of the war, when Bell Laboratories undertook the job of providing arrangements for operating teletypewriters over radio links for the Army and Navy, there was uncertainty whether or not successful systems could be devised. Other persons had worked in this field with little success. Bell Laboratories engineers, however, had the benefit of many years of experience with electronics and with teletypewriters and radiotelephone systems. The need for delivering signals which had little distortion after passing through the radio transmission medium, and for

Table 5-3.   Some Types of Teletype Equipment Produced in 1943 and 1944

Equipment	1943 Quantity	1944 Quantity
DC Telegraph Repeater		
TG 29	0	2
TG 30	30	3,512
TG 31	0	1,318
Package, X61824A (2 repeaters)	247	1,637
Package, X66031 (regenerative)	0	126
Miscellaneous	428	144
VF Carrier Telegraph System Terminal		
Spiral-Four CF-2-B (4 channels)	957	2,817
Package X61822A (6 channels each)	226	512
Miscellaneous	17	22
Frequency-Shift Receiving Equipment		
AN/FGC/1 (X-61789-A) (Army)	368	863
Teletypewriter Cipher Subset	1,280	4,117
Frequency-Shift System (Navy)	0	10
Multichannel Tone Link Model UF (Navy)	0	151
Switchboard SB-6	0	1,373
Teletypewriter Equipment		
XD-91/GL-2 Channel Transmitter Distributor	1	159
61TWX Converter Unit	3,013	377
TG-7 Teletypewriter Set	10,623	16,521
TG-26 and TG-27 Set	13	3,284
ME-7 Maintenance Parts Kit	347	0
Model 15 Teletypewriter	1,404	5,382
Model 19 Teletypewriter	430	4,465
51 Converter	3,631	4,454
55 Computer	2,262	2,240
ME-80 Maintenance Kit	0	2,100
ME-86 Maintenance Kit	0	177
ME-90 Maintenance Kit	0	292
TS-2/TG Test Set	0	282

studying and analyzing transmission data to determine the causes of distortion when it occurred, had been driven home to them.   Their systems engineering and development activities and the development activities of the Teletype Corporation, started during 1941, thereafter embraced many forms of teletypewriter apparatus, including enciphering and deciphering devices to provide secrecy, and also the planning for and development of both wire-line and radio transmission systems, some of which have been described.

Practically all the equipment making up the teletypewriter network was produced by Western Electric and Teletype Corporation.   A partial list of items produced during 1943 and 1944 is given in Table 5-3.

The total amount of telegraph equipment and teletypewriter apparatus delivered to the armed forces during 1943 was worth $31,730,000; that delivered during 1944 was worth $70,185,000.

Teletypewriter communication centers were interconnected to form overall Army and Navy global communication networks, partly shown in Fig. 5-26. In most cases the transmission links provided for teletypewriter traffic simultaneously in both directions at either 60 or 100 words per minute, the latter speed being used where traffic demanded it. A few of the links, shown by heavy lines, were operated on a multichannel basis over the single-sideband radiotelephone system and permitted two, three, four, or even six teletypewriter messages to be transmitted simultaneously in each direction at the rate of 60 words per minute. The quality of the service was such that traffic was permitted to flow at a uniform rate, hour after hour. Alternative routes were provided to ensure the reliability of communications.

Exemplifying the geographical dispersion of a local teletypewriter network, Fig. 5-27 shows the manner of interconnecting teletypewriter communication centers (designated signal centers on the figure) within the European theater of operations. Most of the interconnections used wire lines. The shorter ones were operated on a dc telegraph basis, usually using TG-30 (or X-61824-A) duplex repeaters.[8] The other interconnections used either packaged or CF-2 type carrier telegraph equipment to provide the transmission links. Either spiral-four cable or rehabilitated wire lines were used as the transmission media. The radio link between England and the United States was provided by the twin single-sideband multichannel system; other radio teletypewriter links used the AN/FGC-1 system.

The armed forces and State Department from time to time expressed their appreciation of the value of the teletypewriter network in handling the vast amount of distant telecommunications required to coordinate strategic, logistical, tactical, and diplomatic operations during the war. In 1943 a radio teletypewriter network had been installed on short notice to keep Washington in constant touch with the conferences at Casablanca, Cairo, and Teheran. Also, by means of the Algiers-Washington and San Francisco-Australia radio teletypewriter network connected from Washington to San Francisco by Bell System land lines, General Eisenhower in Africa was in direct, secret communication with General MacArthur in Australia.

The reliance placed on the then fully developed capabilities of the global teletypewriter network by the military and diplomatic leaders of the United States and its Allies was expressed by President Roosevelt in his speech to Congress on March 1, 1945, regarding the Yalta conference:

---

[8] These and other equipment units not described in the above subsections are described in *War Department Technical Manual TM 11-486*, April 25, 1945.

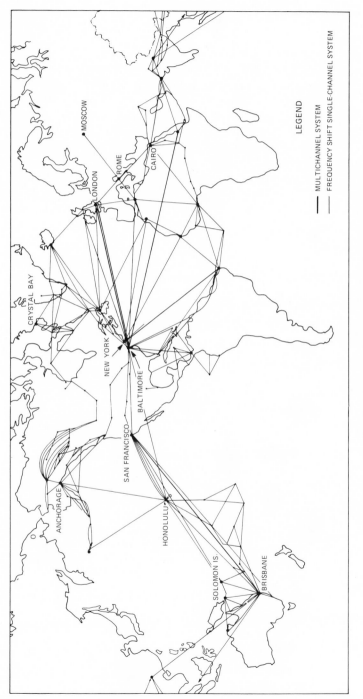

Fig. 5-26. Long-haul military radio teletypewriter circuits in 1944.

LEGEND

—— MULTICHANNEL SYSTEM

—— FREQUENCY SHIFT SINGLE-CHANNEL SYSTEM

MOSCOW

LONDON

ROME

CAIRO

CRYSTAL BAY

NEW YORK

BALTIMORE

SAN FRANCISCO

ANCHORAGE

HONOLULU

SOLOMON IS.

BRISBANE

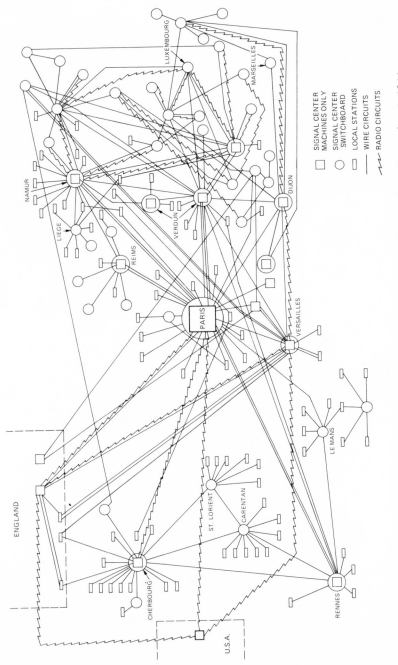

Fig. 5-27.   Fixed plant teletypewriter network—European theater of operations, December 1, 1944.

Far away as I was, I was kept constantly informed of affairs in the United States. The modern miracle of rapid communication has made this world very small; and we must always bear that in mind, when we think or speak of international relations. I received a steady stream of messages from Washington, and except where radio silence was necessary for security purposes, I could continuously send messages any place in the world. And of course, in a global emergency we could even have risked breaking the security rule.

And the *New York Times* stated on March 30, 1945:

When the Big Three Conference opened in Yalta early last month, President Roosevelt and the American delegation found at their disposal radio facilities for keeping in touch with every major Allied headquarters in Europe and the Pacific as well as affairs at home.

Although President Roosevelt did not specifically state so in his speech to Congress, the communications were largely by teletypewriter. Messages having the highest degree of security were transmitted between headquarters locations and displayed in plain text on screens located in each headquarters for visual reception by the conferees involved.

Immediately after V-E Day the Army Signal Corps demonstrated the speed capabilities of the global radioteletypewriter network. When a teletypewriter message originating at the Pentagon was sent around the world, its reception on another teletypewriter, also located in the Pentagon, began after an elapsed time of only one second. This event was reported in *Telecommunications Reports,* Washington, D.C., on May 3, 1945:

A new record for round-the-world radio transmission was claimed by the U.S. Army Signal Corps after it had sent a nine-word radioteletypewriter message around the globe in $9\frac{1}{2}$ seconds.

In a test, staged April 28, to demonstrate the flexibility of Army Communications Service's world-girdling system, the message was transmitted from Washington through automatic relay stations at San Francisco, Manila, New Delhi and Asmara, then back to Washington. Regenerative repeaters were used at the relay points.

Actually, the transmission was almost instantaneous. Exactly one second after the perforated tape containing the message began moving through the teletypewriter transmitter, a nearby receiving machine started printing the message at the end of its round-the-world journey. The one second represented the time lag in the electrical transmission, the other $8\frac{1}{2}$ seconds the time mechanically required to send the message.

3.7 Fixed Plant Telephone Networks: The Backbone Facilities

As indicated above, the global military network handled both telephone and telegraph communications. For security reasons, however, telegraphy and particularly the teletypewriter mode were used for practically all intercontinental communications and those between shore points and fleets at sea. Within North America and in various overseas theaters of operations, where existing or rehabilitated wire-line circuits could be used, voice

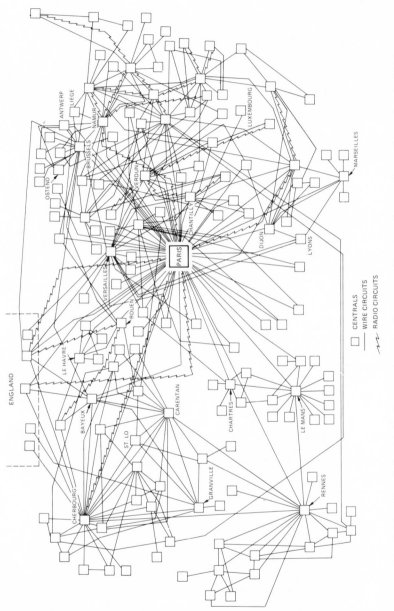

Fig. 5-28.   Fixed plant telephone network—European theater of operations, December 1, 1944.

Table 5-4. Western Electric Equipment for Military
Telephone Networks, 1943–1944

Equipment	Quantities	
	1943	1944
Spiral-Four Equipment		
CF-1 Terminal	1,042	2,611
CF-3 Repeater	1,898	1,049
CF-4 Converter	0	148
CF-5 Repeater	0	118
CF-7 Hybrid Unit	0	1,000
EE-101A Ringer	2,177	3,735
Packaged Equipment		
C Carrier System Terminal	120	388
H Carrier System Terminal	0	187
Telephone Repeater	450	3,500
Voice-Frequency Ringer	750	4,800
Commercial Carrier System	114	171
Commercial Telephone Repeater	394	487
Operations Center AN/TTQ-1	98	242
Service-Observing Cabinet and Equipment	7	718
Switchboard (approx. no. of connected lines)		
Tactical Type (for use in fluid areas)	130,000	180,000
Commercial Type	110,000	60,000
Instruction Type	75,000	0
Field Wire (miles)		
W-110-B	15,910	0
W-143	126	15,788
Spiral-Four Cable (miles)	27,705	24,658
Loading Coil for Spiral-Four Cable made by other manufacturers	315,000	554,000
Other loading coil	154,000	141,000
Rubber-covered wire (miles)	11,837	5,776
Lead-covered cable (millions conductor-feet)	7,824	5,383
Total price (of above)	$71,000,000	$87,700,000

communication made up about two-thirds of all traffic, the remainder being either manual telegraph or teletypewriter. There was also a small amount of transmission by facsimile reproduction of aerial photographs taken during reconnaissance missions on battlefronts and over enemy territory. The communications within each theater of operations, largely tactical and logistical in nature, were the means for coordinating the control by various echelons of command within the theater over mobile forces in the battle areas.

The scope and complexity of an installed fixed-plant telephone network, such as that in the European theater of operations, are illustrated in Fig. 5-28. Each communication center, or central, was interconnected by a wire-line circuit with one or more other centers, with radio used as an alternative means in a few cases. The network also provided alternative wire routes between a number of the higher-echelon centers to insure continuity of service.

Established "central" offices at or near the various fixed-plant military communications centers were similar to those in the Bell System. Each installation contained a manual switchboard and in some cases dial equipment, a distributing frame to provide a flexible means of connecting the station lines and interoffice trunk terminations into the switchboard, terminal equipment for the various wire lines (and radio if provided) required for interconnection to other central offices and to temporary communications centers of mobile troops in fluid battle areas, testing arrangements, and miscellaneous central office equipment, such as a service-observing board and power supply.

During the war, Western Electric and its subcontractors were by far the leading suppliers of all fixed-plant equipment shipped overseas for use in constructing the networks for the theaters of operations. Table 5-4, listing the equipment delivered to the armed forces during 1943 and 1944, emphasizes the size of the manufacturing task and the operating system.

3.8 Communications Systems Engineering

Systems engineering embraces the entire communications job. It assures that each overall objective is accurately known, keeps abreast of changing conditions and new requirements, looks for shortcomings and missing links, devises better ways to accomplish particular functions, appraises new ideas, and guides the general course of the development and employment of communications facilities. This broad approach was particularly important in dealing with complex communications systems, such as those required for the global military network.

As was pointed out in Section 3.1, during 1939 the War Department arranged with the Bell System for groups of engineers from Bell Laboratories to work with the Signal Corps in framing a network plan. Highlights from the information derived in this analytical work are covered in Sections 3.3.1 to 3.3.4. The information was used by the Signal Corps and other engineering agencies of the War Department in arranging for development and procurement from many manufacturers of the vast amounts of communications materiel needed by the Army, Navy and their respective arms during the war.

It is implicit in the systems engineering approach that those who plan and operate a complex network must also know how to use the tools at their disposal effectively and economically. It was no easy matter to teach the appropriate techniques to the communications people in the armed forces, who were drawn from all walks of life and quickly given responsibilities vital to huge military operations without the years of experience required for such personnel in peacetime. To assist in this difficult job, Bell Laboratories was assigned several systems engineering projects during the war.

3.8.1 Project C-79

During January 1943 Brig. Gen. Gordon Saville, of the Army Air Force, invited Division 13 of the NDRC to a discussion of the tactical Air Force communications situation. In this discussion, at which the Air Force and Signal Corps were represented, the NDRC group expressed the opinion that the difficulties in training personnel were less in the use of specific items of equipment than with complex communication systems. General Saville asked what the NDRC might do to help solve the systems problem. This led to the establishment of a Systems Committee within the NDRC to guide the project, designated C-79, and the award of a contract (OEMsr-1018), which became effective February 16, 1943, to Bell Laboratories to conduct laboratory and field work and to submit suitable recommendations.

The first assignment was to improve the communications system for the tactical Air Warning Service. Equipment for systems of the recommended type was procured by the Signal Corps for the Air Force. The second assignment concerned the complete tactical Air Force communications system. It led to the recommendation that each tactical Air Force should have its own special requirements, which would have to be considered individually, and that the best solution would be to provide sufficiently complete and basic systems engineering information so that communications officers in the field could adapt and integrate available equipment into a satisfactorily working system. Such information was provided in three extensive reports, which were used effectively in solving Air Force communications problems in every theater of operations.

Under Project C-79, a wide variety of other problems, several of which related to radar, were solved by Bell Laboratories. The solutions were reduced to practice in terms simple enough to be used by field officers. Bell Laboratories first investigated the adaptation of available radio sets in the 30- to 40-MHz band as a stopgap measure for providing air warning service and later their use in the VHF band. This work included theoretical research and field tests of (a) propagation of radio waves over many types of terrain and (b) the best locations for antennas operating in the VHF range. Simple charts were prepared for use by Signal Corps officers to enable them to predict radio performance over various paths. The performance of lightweight types of VHF antenna was determined and new types were developed, some of which could be improvised from materials available in theaters of combat. Bell Laboratories sought out and assisted other concerns to build a lightweight, 50-foot antenna mast that could be carried and rapidly erected by two men. Information on the antennas was provided to the Air Force and Signal Corps. New remote control features were designed so that a connection could be extended by wire from a radio set to a communications center or other post several miles away.

Frequently, a large number of military radio sets were required to operate close together without mutual interference. Tests of several typical radio sets were made to determine their production or reception of unwanted frequencies. To minimize interference, modifications were recommended to the Signal Corps. Mathematical analysis led to predictions of groups of preferred frequency assignments, later confirmed by Signal Corps field tests. Tables of these assumptions, issued to officers in theaters of operation, took the guesswork out of certain interference problems.

Reports from the Southwest Pacific theater indicated that even at frequencies as low as 2 MHz the transmission range through a jungle was extremely short because of excessive losses in tree foliage if radio waves followed the surface of the earth. As a solution, Bell Laboratories recommended sky wave transmission, demonstrated to Signal Corps personnel by a quantitative test in a secure jungle. It showed that the use of simple, properly chosen antennas was equivalent to increasing transmitter power several hundred times. Bell Labs also devised and furnished the Signal Corps with methods for adapting such antennas for use with tactical radio sets.

3.8.2 Communications Engineering Manuals for Staff Officers

Project C-79 focused attention on the systems approach to military communications problems and emphasized its importance to those responsible for Army communications. Maj. Gen. Roger B. Colton was instrumental in initiating a project, involving the Signal Corps and Bell Laboratories, for providing systems engineering information on a broad scale in the form of Army technical manuals directed, not to the soldier who had to operate a specific piece of equipment, but to the officer who had to plan the system and procure all components many months ahead of time, and to the staff officers who were responsible for establishing, extending, and rearranging various communications systems in the theater of operations.

The first general conference among Signal Corps and Bell Laboratories personnel to discuss objectives was held on January 4, 1944. The preparation of two companion technical manuals was recommended, one to tell what equipment was available and the other to set forth the engineering principles governing the establishment of various kinds of integrated systems. The need for this vast amount of information was acute because the largest military operation of all time, the Allied invasion of Western Europe, was imminent. The date of March 1, less than two months away, was set as the deadline for delivery of the engineering book.

No document existed that furnished a pattern for either technical manual. Bell Laboratories was, of course, very familiar with all products made for the Army by Western Electric, but there were many products furnished by other manufacturers, especially for radio, with which Bell Laboratories at that time had had little or no concern.

About 35 top specialists covering the entire military communications field—telephone, telegraph facsimile, wire, radio, development and operation—were marshaled and set to work, gathering information from innumerable sources and preparing the text. False starts were inevitable because a new rationale for presenting information of such breadth, succinctly and with reasonable uniformity, had to be developed. Every Signal Corps officer with experience in the Mediterranean and Pacific theaters who could possibly be reached was interviewed. Some of the information needed was not available anywhere and had to be developed quickly by computations or laboratory tests. To save time, it was decided to issue a preliminary edition in which the two manuals, equipment and engineering, were combined.

On March 15, 1944, Bell Labs delivered to the Signal Corps 200 printed and bound copies of a 350-page manual more comprehensive than any book ever written on the subject of electrical communications. The books were flown to various military headquarters all over the world. This first edition of the combined manuals was designated *Technical Manual 11-486*.

The following is a sample of many highly favorable comments received from operating theaters:

United States Army Forces Central Pacific Area Office of the
Commanding General APO 958

TM11-486 is an excellent volume which has already proved of considerable value for planning purposes and also contains a wealth of technical information not readily obtainable in such handy form elsewhere, which is of great help. The consensus of opinion of engineering and planning personnel of this office is that the book represents a big step forward in providing information to major headquarters located at remote points and that it should not only be continued but expanded wherever possible.

Bell Laboratories immediately started to prepare a more finished product, separating the material into two books as was originally planned. Comments on the preliminary version and many reports from the theaters were examined. A painstaking job of gathering information on all available communications systems equipments was also undertaken.

Bell Laboratories delivered copies of the *Electrical Communication Systems Equipment* manual to the Signal Corps during the fall of 1944. It was approved for publication and wide distribution throughout the War Department by General G. C. Marshall, Chief of Staff, on October 2, 1944.[9]

[9] The 518-page published document was designated TM 11-487.

Meanwhile, a number of intensive studies of engineering problems related to military communications systems were continued with the objective of making the engineering manual as useful as possible on vital engineering problems that confronted field officers in operating theaters. A. B. Clark, a vice president of Bell Labs, with another Bell Labs representative and an executive from RCA, made an extensive tour of the Mediterranean theater under the auspices of the Secretary of War for a firsthand appraisal of military communications. They interviewed experienced men of all ranks, examined plans, saw the equipment in service, and even conducted trials on the spot. They then proceeded to the United Kingdom and gave valuable engineering assistance during the weeks culminating in the Normandy invasion.

Additional information was obtained from the reports of Western Electric field service engineers who played a large part in establishing backbone communications during the advance across France. Many of the problems encountered by these men were referred to Bell Laboratories for advice. Further extensive discussions were held with officers newly arrived from the war theaters, who were keenly aware of the problems being faced.

Copies of the manual, entitled *Electrical Communication Systems Engineering,* were delivered to the Signal Corps during the spring of 1945. It was approved for publication by General Marshall, Chief of Staff, on April 25, 1945.[10] The first edition, consisting of 9,300 copies, became available on May 8, 1945. Two hundred copies were dispatched by air to various overseas headquarters.

Maj. Gen. H. C. Ingles, the Chief Signal Officer, sent the following letter to President C. G. Stoll, of Western Electric, regarding the engineering manual:

ARMY SERVICE FORCES
OFFICE OF THE CHIEF SIGNAL OFFICER
WASHINGTON

10 May 1945

Dear Mr. Stoll:

I am in receipt of Technical Manual, TM 11-486, "Electrical Communication Systems Engineering." Your organization did a very splendid job on this Manual. It is the best book of its kind that I have ever seen and it will be of very great usefulness in the Army.

We appreciate very much the great amount of work that your people have put out in producing this book.

With best personal regards,

Sincerely

H. C. INGLES
Major General

[10] The 610-page published document was designated TM 11-486.

3.9 Summary

Beginning in 1940 the Army Signal Corps recognized the importance, urgency, and complications involved in planning for a worldwide military communications network. Systems engineering experts at Bell Laboratories provided the Signal Corps with an analysis of the factors bearing on the choice of communications facilities and the network configuration required for a rapid and reliable global communications system. Using this information as a base as soon as the United States became engaged in the war, the Signal Corps and other engineering agencies of the War Department mounted a succession of development and procurement programs with manufacturers of communications products for all the wireline, radio equipment, and communications center materials needed. Western Electric supplied practically all the transmission equipment and a large part of the other facilities used in the fixed plant communications centers in the various theaters of operations.

During 1944 Bell Laboratories undertook preparation of electrical communication system manuals for use by staff officers in the theaters of operations. War Department technical manuals 11-486 and 11-487 were the ultimate result. These manuals are invaluable references for those interested in the many communication products used within the fixed plant networks and by mobile ground troops in fluid battlefronts. The manuals contain an inventory of products and engineering information concerning them.

IV. SECURE SPEECH TRANSMISSION

The global communication system just described was noteworthy not only for providing military communications among all areas in a worldwide war but also for the provision of encoded teletypewriter communication that was completely secure against enemy decoding so long as a random, continuously changing code key was employed. Unfortunately, the benefits of speech transmission could not be obtained where complete secrecy was required. Wire transmission was reasonably secure because of the difficulty of interception by the enemy; but until the work covered in this section was accomplished, the encoding of radio speech transmission was primitive and interception was easy. At best, privacy was provided against the casual listener, but until about 1942–1943 a determined listener with the proper equipment could decode the radio speech systems used in a short time, often in a matter of minutes. Thus, until that time secrecy of communication was unavailable for radio circuits except for teletypewriter messages.

4.1 Historical Background

In the summer and fall of 1940, the crucial Battle of Britain was in its early stages. During this period the United States government and other people responsible for communications became increasingly concerned about the degree of privacy offered by different communication systems. For one thing, highly placed government officials, both American and British, were wont to use the transatlantic radiotelephone for highly classified discussions on the assumption that the A-3[11] telephone privacy was better than it really was. While the A-3 system was excellent against normal forms of eavesdropping, it was still possible for an expert with sophisticated techniques to undo the scrambling.

One group primarily concerned with this problem was the division of the NDRC charged with military communications problems. O. E. Buckley, who became president of Bell Labs in 1940, was a member of this group, with R. K. Potter (later a full-fledged member) as his alternate. Potter was given the job of contacting military and other people concerned with communications security. As a result of this investigation, he concluded that there were two distinct areas of considerable military interest and need. These two areas were (1) short-term mobile privacy systems for low-echelon use, and (2) long-term, high-echelon secrecy systems, both suitable for telephone circuits. Buckley strongly favored undertaking work in both areas at Bell Laboratories; consequently, proposals that were later accepted were made to NDRC.

The two projects were to be kept quite separate, but both were coordinated by Potter. The first was assigned to a group under Walter Koenig, Jr., work being initiated in early October 1940. It was aimed primarily at the evaluation of short-term privacy schemes, though it necessarily included the development of "cracking" procedures. The history of this project is given in the next section.

The second project, concerned with long-term telephone security, was given more extensive consideration. Buckley suggested that the code name Project X be given to it. It was decided that two rather large groups be assigned to the work, one to carry out the basic research and the other to handle the practical problems of implementing design, construction, and introduction to the military. The further history of this project is covered later in Section 4.3 below.

4.2 Bell Work on Privacy Systems

As discussed in the first volume, work on short-term privacy systems had been started about 1920 when the use of radiotelephone communication was under early consideration. The A-3 system, used on later overseas systems, was moderately easy to break but provided enough security for most commercial purposes, particularly when combined with private codes that were frequently used in critical business conversations. With the outbreak of war, the whole project required reconsideration.

---

[11] See pp. 420–421 of the first volume in this series.

Fig. 5-29. Visible speech appears as a traveling pattern of light and shade. The patterns are the visual counterpart of the audible variations in intensity (brightness of the light) and frequency (height above the baseline of the pattern).

An important factor was the speech-pattern recording device developed by R. K. Potter and his associates,[12] also known as the sound spectrograph. This device could record portions of speech on a chart with time as the abscissa, frequency as the ordinate, and intensity indicating amplitude (Fig. 5-29). If speech had been previously recorded on a phonograph record, successive samples could be analyzed by the sound spectrograph and pieced together to provide a sample of this so-called visible speech as long as desired. The visible records of the various speech sounds differed somewhat with the speaker, but the speech patterns, particularly the vowel sounds, were highly distinctive and could be read by sight by a trained observer. What was even more significant, a trained observer could usually detect the type of process used to make encoded speech unintelligible. This knowledge greatly expedited the construction of equipment that would crack the code employed.

Many privacy systems had been invented before the war. A patent search was made in March 1941 by E. W. Adams and it disclosed a large number of possible techniques, but test and analysis showed that most of them had no practical value. Only three of the many ways to manipulate speech were explored extensively. These were rearrangement of frequencies, rearrangement of time order, and noise masking.

4.2.1 Frequency Rearrangement

Frequency rearrangement is the scheme used on commercial transoceanic radiotelephony discussed in Volume I. The simplest scheme was speech inversion,[13] invented by L. M. Clement of Western Electric and first used on the Catalina circuit in 1922. The inverted speech was un-

---

[12] R. K. Potter; U.S. Patent No. 2,403,997; filed April 14, 1942; issued July 16, 1946; and U.S. Patent No. 2,416,346; filed April 14, 1942; issued February 25, 1947.

[13] L. M. Clement; U.S. Patent No. 1,603,582; filed May 3, 1921; issued October 19, 1926. See also H. Van der Bijl; U.S. Patent No. 1,502,889; filed January 8, 1918; issued July 29, 1924.

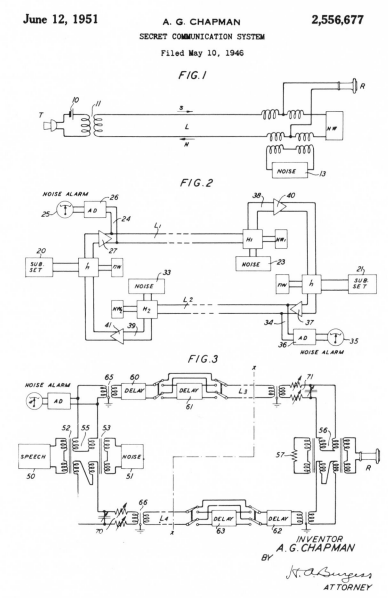

June 12, 1951   A. G. CHAPMAN   2,556,677
                          SECRET COMMUNICATION SYSTEM
                              Filed May 10, 1946

FIG.1

FIG.2

FIG.3

INVENTOR
A.G.CHAPMAN
BY

ATTORNEY

Fig. 5-30.   Scheme devised by A. G. Chapman for adding noise to
speech and subtracting the identical noise at receiving end.

intelligible to the average listener, but it was soon found that a device for
reinversion was easily constructed and that some experienced observers
could even learn to interpret the inverted speech.   The next step, for which
L. Espenschied[14] was responsible, was to split the speech into a number

[14] L. Espenschied; U.S. Patent No. 1,546,439; filed January 8, 1920; issued July 21, 1925.

of bands and manipulate them separately. Improvements by A. C. Dickieson turned the split-band technique into a workable device that allowed the interchange of bands, which were individually used either rightside-up or inverted. With a four-band system nearly 800 combinations were possible, but tests showed that only about 8 were truly unintelligible. The A-3 system that grew out of this work employed five bands but used only 6 of the 3,600 possible combinations.

With the proper equipment the particular combination used by the A-3 could readily be detected and decoding devices could then be built. In fact, it was possible to obtain fairly intelligible speech by using a narrowband superheterodyne receiver to select one of the middle bands of the clear speech and manipulate the encoded band into its correct, uninverted position in the spectrum. This led to schemes[15,16] for coding systems which were frequently switched in synchronism at the ends of the circuit. This improved the privacy and was used to some extent; but, given a little time, the voice spectrograph provided means for analyzing the scheme used on a particular call, and once this was accomplished, equipment for decoding was easily constructed.

4.2.2 Time Rearrangement

As early as 1930, schemes were proposed[17,18] and tested for rearranging the order of small time samples of speech. Later the basic scheme was improved by using synchronous switching of time intervals selected on a random basis. Limited tests did not succeed in cracking this arrangement, although further work with word patterns probably would have succeeded. For short-term privacy, time rearrangement might well have been useful, but it was not pursued further, since the equipment was too bulky for most mobile use and there was an inherent delay in speech transmission that was annoying to the users.

4.2.3 Noise Addition

Over the years several schemes had been proposed[19,20,21] for adding noise to the speech and subtracting the identical noise at the receiving end. This was essentially an impossible task when the transmission medium

[15] L. Espenschied and G. D. Gillett; U.S. Patent No. 1,709,901; filed October 8, 1925; issued April 23, 1929.

[16] A. C. Dickieson; U.S. Patent No. 2,132,205; filed June 23, 1937; issued October 4, 1938.

[17] R. V. L. Hartley; U.S. Patent No. 1,605,023; filed May 19, 1921; issued November 2, 1926.

[18] D. Mitchell and S. B. Wright; U.S. Patent No. 1,981,114; filed March 3, 1933; issued November 20, 1934.

[19] J. Mills; U.S. Patent No. 1,480,217; filed December 29, 1916; issued January 8, 1924.

[20] A. G. Chapman; U.S. Patent No. 2,556,677; filed May 10, 1946; issued June 12, 1951.

[21] J. W. Emling and D. Mitchell, "The Effects of Time Delay and Echoes on Telephone Conversations," *Bell System Technical J.*, 42 (November 1963), pp. 2869–2891.

was as variable as radio. However, during the war years a practical scheme for doing this over short land lines[22] was devised and used for some important short-range wire lines. The method is illustrated by Fig. 5-30. The speech is sent through unchanged on the loop, but noise about 15 dB stronger than the speech is put into the loop through the other side of a receiving hybrid coil. The noise is then, in effect, balanced out by the listener by the extremely good balance between the line and the network. Four-wire circuits independently treated gave two-way transmission. An interesting feature of this system was that tampering with the line, even by means of a high impedance tap or other means for providing noise for subtraction, would disturb the sensitive line balance and give warning to the users.

4.2.4 Overview of Work on Privacy Systems

The Bell System devoted a considerable amount of effort to the search for speech privacy systems which would provide short-term protection against enemy interception. Means were found for providing protection for some limited applications and against casual listeners, but the work received little direct military application. Indirectly, however, the concomitant work on cracking coded speech was very valuable, permitting Bell Labs to determine the nature of encoding systems used by the enemy and to rapidly devise means for deciphering coding systems believed to be of value in protecting radio transmission. Perhaps its greatest value was that it showed that all attempts to manipulate speech sounds in a complex manner had little value except to demonstrate the indestructibility of speech and the need for a completely new approach if truly secret speech transmission were to be developed.

4.3 Project X – A True Secrecy System for Speech

4.3.1 Introduction

One of the more closely guarded projects in World War II, and for years thereafter, was known simply as "Project X." It concerned the origination and development of a completely secret speech enciphering and transmission system, which by its nature could not possibly be deciphered by other than its intended receiver. To the people who worked on it, it was known as the "X System." To the people in the Signal Corps who handled the system, it was most generally known as "Sigsaly" or "Ciphony I," and to the people in the telephone and radio transmission centers who handled its inviolate trunk circuits and were curious about its function, it was nicknamed the "Green Hornet" because the audible control tones were similar to the signature theme of a well-known radio program.

---

[22] A. G. Chapman, as in note 20.

Table 5-5.   Patents Related to Project X Research

U.S. Patent No.	Inventor	Filing Date	Issue Date
3,024,321	K. H. Davis, A. C. Norwine	12/29/44	3/ 6/62
3,076,146	M. E. Mohr	12/27/45	1/29/63
3,188,390	M. E. Mohr	12/20/43	6/ 8/65
3,193,626	H. L. Barney	12/29/44	7/ 6/65
3,340,361	R. K. Potter	7/ 9/45	9/ 5/67
3,373,245	N. D. Newby, H. E. Vaughan	8/27/42	3/12/68
3,394,314	L. G. Schimpf	7/17/43	7/23/68
3,405,362	R. H. Badgley, L. G. Schimpf	12/20/43	10/ 8/68
3,470,323	H. W. Dudley	6/30/44	9/30/69
3,967,066	R. C. Mathes	9/24/41	6/29/76
3,967,067	R. K. Potter	9/24/4	6/29/76
3,985,958	H. W. Dudley	12/18/41	10/12/76
3,897,591	A. A. Lundstrom, L. G. Schimpf	8/27/42	7/29/75
3,912,868	R. H. Badgley, R. L. Miller	7/17/43	10/14/75
3,937,888	O. Myers	7/17/43	2/10/75
3,991,273	R. C. Mathes	10/ 4/43	11/ 9/76
3,979,558	E. Peterson	6/30/44	9/ 7/76
3,976,839	R. L. Miller	6/30/44	8/24/76
3,965,296	R. L. Miller	6/30/44	6/22/76
3,887,772	R. L. Miller	6/30/44	6/ 3/75
3,891,799	A. E. Melhose	9/27/44	6/24/75
3,893,326	D. K. Gannett	9/27/44	9/28/76
3,968,454	A. J. Busch	9/27/44	7/ 6/76
3,944,744	D. K. Gannett	5/10/45	3/16/76
3,944,745	D. K. Gannett	5/10/45	3/16/76
3,953,677	D. K. Gannett	5/10/45	4/27/76
3,953,678	D. K. Gannett	5/10/45	4/27/76
3,924,074	E. Peterson	5/19/45	12/ 2/75
3,983,327	D. K. Gannett, A. C. Norwine	7/ 9/45	9/28/76
3,934,078	D. K. Gannett	5/ 1/46	1/20/76
3,965,297	D. K. Gannett	5/ 1/46	6/22/76
3,924,075	D. K. Gannett	3/20/47	12/ 2/75

While the project was important as the initial development of a completely secret speech transmission system, historically it was also important as the pioneering digital speech transmission system employing a form of pulse code modulation.   It was one of the starting points of the digital transmission age that followed.   Although it remained for years as an unmentionable system, many knowledgeable people in Bell Laboratories became acquainted with its operating principles either through working on the project or being consulted about some aspect of it.   In spite of this widespread knowledge, very effective security was maintained for many years.   A list of patents related to this project is given in Table 5-5.[23]

[23] For reasons of secrecy the basic patents and all details were withheld until 1975.

As noted previously, it was decided initially to assign two large groups to this project, one to carry on basic research and the other to handle the practical problems of design, instruction, and introduction to use. The Transmission Research group under R. C. Mathes was assigned the research task, one reason being that it included work on the vocoder under E. Peterson and H. W. Dudley,[24] inventor in the early 1930s of the vocoder. From the outset the vocoder was a logical candidate for consideration as a practical means of enabling the encipherment of speech signals, its virtues being that it offered a theoretical 10:1 frequency compression ratio for speech transmission and, secondly, that the control signals were in the telegraph range.[25]   An important prior example of a perfect ciphering arrangement was the telegraph system invented by G. S. Vernam during World War I (discussed in Section 3.5.1 above). It seemed likely that the vocoder might lead to an equally effective scheme for encoding speech.

The systems, as finally used during World War II, were not small. A terminal occupied over 30 of the standard 7-foot relay rack mounting bays, required about 30 kW of power to operate, and needed complete air conditioning in the large room housing it. Members working on the job occasionally remarked about the terrible conversion ratio—30 kW of power for 1 milliwatt (mW) of poor-quality speech.

However, the system worked. One can look back on it with a certain amount of pride, since today's equivalent of about 1,500 bits per second was transmitted and maintained in complete synchronism over the fading of the transatlantic shortwave radio with only occasional errors. The system would become inoperative about the same time the normal commercial transatlantic radiotelephone would become unusable. Transpacific links were apparently somewhat better than the transatlantic. Operators of the system have stated that connections were actually tested successfully that went across the Atlantic and the continental United States and thence across the Pacific to Australia, although it is not known that any official conversations were ever carried over such a path.

The remainder of the war period was spent in developing a second system, which was called "Junior X," or AN/GSQ3. It occupied only six 5-foot bays and could be placed in a movable van but was not completed in time to see active service.

4.3.2 Invention

During the first two or three months following the inception of the project in October 1940, a large part of the thinking and experimentation reflected earlier thinking on speech privacy. There was no lack of ideas. A search by the Patent Department at the time uncovered about 80 patents.

---

[24] H. W. Dudley; U.S. Patent No. 2,151,091; filed October 30, 1935; issued March 21, 1939.

[25] A more complete description of the vocoder is given in Section 4.3.2.

But all of these methods invariably had one fault in common: they were just complex ways of transmitting speech that a person could undo with the necessary equipment and enough time. These were privacy, not secrecy, systems. In a secrecy system it is assumed that an eavesdropper having the same equipment as the intended receiver cannot determine the message unless he knows the coding sequence.

The vocoder, a frequency compression device for the transmission of speech, was a logical prospect for investigation and study, since the process of the vocoder resulted in a privacy system. The basic premise of a vocoder is that the information carried by a speech wave varies at relatively slow rates. These rates depend on how fast a person moves his lips and tongue (i.e., on vocal tract configuration). This motion modulates the sounds emanating from the person's mouth. The simplified functional schematic shown in Fig. 5-31 illustrates the operation of the vocoder. The frequency spectrum of a speech wave is first divided into ten nearly equal bands in the range of 150 Hz to 2,950 Hz. The amplitude of the speech signal in each band is obtained by means of a linear rectifier and smoothed by a low-pass filter, which limits the variations to less than 25 Hz. In an auxiliary process it is necessary to determine whether the sound is voiced (vowel or consonant sounds, such as *o, v,* or *z*) or unvoiced (such as the sibilant sounds of *s* or *sh*). If the sound is voiced, it is necessary to measure the pitch, or fundamental frequency. This information also varies at slow rates and can be limited by a 25-Hz low-pass filter.

After transmission of the 11 low-frequency channels to a receiving terminal, the speech can be reconstructed. This is done by first generating a source of harmonics of the fundamental frequency if the sound is voiced or by using a white noise source if the sound is unvoiced. These energy sources are appropriately switched into a set of bandpass filters similar to those used in the analysis. The output of each filter is then amplitude-modulated under control of the corresponding spectrum signal from the transmitting end. The modulated outputs of the 10 channels are then combined to give a reconstructed speech signal.

The spectrum control signals resulting from this spectrum analysis are at syllabic rates (below 25 Hz) or in the telegraph range (and unintelligible). Early proposals were pointed toward permuting the 11 control channels, but it was soon realized that this was closely analogous to the A-3 split-band privacy system.

In early January 1941, both R. C. Mathes and R. K. Potter discussed the adding of random noise signals in the syllabic range to the control signals of the vocoder, with the thought of using the same noise signals in opposite polarity to remove the masking at the receiving end. But it became clear that unless a large ratio of noise to signal were used the presence of speech signals would be apparent, and that if large amounts were used it would be at least difficult, and probably impossible, to balance out.

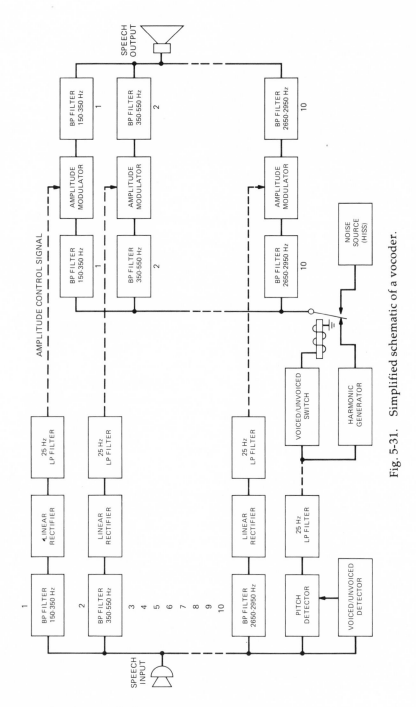

Fig. 5-31. Simplified schematic of a vocoder.

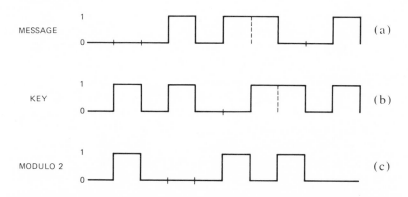

Fig. 5-32. Diagram of the addition of message and key signals by the Vernam method.

At this point, a letter was received from W. G. Radley, of the British Post Office, requesting design information[26] on the vocoder and hinting that it was to be used in a secrecy system. This acted as a stimulus to the brainstorming that was going on at Bell Labs. Incidentally, the information that was sent to the British was sunk by submarine attack and had to be forwarded a second time.

As mentioned above, the outstanding example of a perfect ciphering system was the Vernam system[27] used on telegraph signals. It involved the addition of a random or nonrepeating set of on-off telegraph signals to the message signals by a process now called Modulo 2 addition, or, more commonly, "half-adding." The Vernam process as used with teletypewriters is illustrated in Fig. 5-4. To readers trained in logic, Fig. 5-32 may provide an explanation in more familiar terms. In this diagram the on-off (0, 1) values of a possible telegraph message and a key are shown in lines (a) and (b). The Modulo 2 addition of the two signals is shown in (c). It will be noted that if the sum of the message and the key do not exceed 1, the sum of the two values is obtained. If the sum is equal to 2 (M = 1 and K = 1), a 0 is substituted. This means that if the message value is 0, either 0 or 1 can result, depending on the key value; likewise, if the message is 1, then 1 or 0 can result. Hence, if the key has a random occurrence of values, it will result in a transmitted message that is also random and cannot be undone unless a copy of the key tape is available. With this tape at hand, the key signals can be added to the transmitted signal to provide the original message. The feeling that this same sort of process was necessary in communicating speech was a constant nagging thought with people who were working on the problem.

[26] O. O. Gruenz, "The Construction Information on the Rebuilt 10 Channel Vocoder," internal Bell Labs memorandum, February 24, 1941.
[27] G. S. Vernam; U.S. Patent No. 1,310,719; filed September 13, 1918; issued July 22, 1919.

Finally, in late February, the first real breakthrough resulted from a proposal by R. K. Potter[28] that the individual vocoder channels be treated as on-off channels by the use of a relay with a suitably adjusted bias. This solved the problem of adding the key, as in the Vernam approach, but experiments in the vocoder by O. O. Gruenz soon indicated that the quality and intelligibility of vocoder speech was badly mutilated. The next obvious step was to use two relays adjusted to different values in each channel to improve the quality; while there was some improvement with this move, it was becoming apparent that quite a number of step values were needed to get the quality that might be acceptable. This approach will be recognized as the process now known as quantization—i.e., representing a continuously variable signal by means of a series of steps which approximate the continuous function. It is interesting to note that up to the point of using two or more steps per channel, the rationale called for treating the on-off pattern of the 10 vocoder channels as a telegraph character. The addition of the N-level dimension in each channel shook the thinking loose from this mooring.

The need for multiple levels in the vocoder channels led directly to considering the use of a similar multilevel key signal. However, the problem of how to combine the stepped key and message signals to achieve a result similar to the Vernam process became a puzzle. A clue to how this should be accomplished came from a discussion on May 27, 1941, between R. K. Potter and H. Nyquist, who came to the conclusion that the sum of the key and message should "fall as points on a circle." In other words, if the sum became larger than the maximum level, the value should reenter as in following points around a circle; hence the term "reentry," which was to be used as a descriptive term for this critical process. In today's logic language it would be termed modulo N addition. Mathematically, it is relatively simple to describe the process, even though it was not easy to think of it in the first place. If we let M be an integer value of the message $(0,1,2, \ldots , n)$, K the value of the key, and C the maximum number of levels of either $(n + 1)$, then the reentered value R is

$$R = M + K \qquad (M + K \leq C) \qquad (1)$$

$$R = M + K - C \qquad (M + K > C) \qquad (2)$$

Decoding at the far end is accomplished by subtracting a duplicate of the key from the reentered value. The message number is given directly if the result is positive, but with a negative result it is necessary to add $n + 1$ to give the message number. One possible way to visualize the process is in terms of a clock face with successive positions $0,1, \ldots , n$ with the speech levels (and the added code levels) stepping the hand by

---

[28] R. K. Potter; U.S. Patent No. 3,967,067; filed September 24, 1941; issued June 29, 1976.

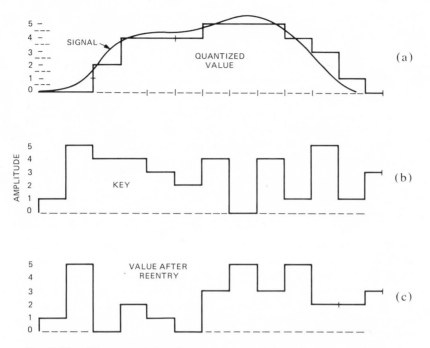

Fig. 5-33.   Diagram of signal quantizing and the subsequent addition of key by the reentry process.

amounts corresponding to the quantized signal and key levels.   Thus, when the signal and key are added, the sum is indicated directly if it is equal to or less than n.   If it is greater than n, the hand continues on a second round and points to a reentered number equal to the sum less $n + 1$.

An illustration of the reentry process is shown in Fig. 5-33.   Here the original analog signal is quantized by the stepper to the closest of the six available levels, as shown by (a).   The key (b) consists of a random series of the same possible quantized values.   The reentered values, as given by equations (1) or (2), are shown in (c).   It will be observed that if the sum exceeds 5, then the reentered value will always fall in the range of 0 to 5; likewise, any particular value of a signal, when reentered, can also result in any one of the six values, depending on the key value.   Thus, just as in the Vernam approach, a random series in the key will result in an equally random series in the transmitted message, although not the same one.   At a meeting in R. C. Mathes' office in the afternoon of the discussion between Potter and Nyquist, the thoughts on reentry jelled into a definite circuit proposal,[29] and the general building blocks of the overall system started

[29] R. C. Mathes; U.S. Patent No. 3,991,273; filed October 4, 1943; issued November 9, 1976.

to fall into place. A decision was made forthwith to proceed with the system's implementation.

While progress thus far represented a major breakthrough, the work and the inventing were far from over. In the end some 30 patent applications were filed. Thus, the final system represented the contributions of many minds. At this point, though, there were many aspects to be considered in addition to quantizing and reentry. Some of the main ones were the parameters of the vocoder, the mode of transmission to be used, synchronization, and production of the key.

About quantizing, one of the first problems to be solved was how many levels were needed for the vocoder. A quantizer, probably the first in existence, was constructed by M. E. Mohr; with it, any number of levels up to ten could be tried, and numerous tests could be carried out with the vocoder. Toward the end of the tests the use of nonlinear steps (instantaneous companding) was tried to obtain an improvement. Just who made this suggestion was never recorded. How many steps or quantized levels were needed turned out to be a compromise between an increase in the quality of the vocoder and a decrease in margins for the transmission of the stepped levels by FSK (frequency-shift keying) over such a circuit as transatlantic radio. The value that was finally settled on was six levels, which was somewhat over the knee of the curve in improving the quality of the vocoder and a reasonable possibility in transmission. In the end this turned out to be an excellent selection and was never changed. The basic design for the stepper and reentry circuits was carried out primarily by A. A. Lundstrom and L. G. Schimpf.[30] The design made use of a suggestion by H. W. Dudley[31] on how to simplify the originally proposed method of carrying out the reentry process.

A problem developed, however, in the transmission of the pitch signal of the vocoder, which turned out to be much more susceptible to the quantizing effect. Experiments soon indicated that it was going to need some 30 or more steps. The thought of using five channels to transmit this signal was not easy to accept. Shortly thereafter, a suggestion was made by R. H. Badgley and R. L. Miller[32] to use a technique which was likened to a vernier. The pitch signal would first be quantized to the nearest of the six levels, and then this value would be subtracted from the original signal. The remainder was then coded again to six levels.

An illustration of this process is given in Fig. 5-34. First a sample of the original pitch signal is taken. This acts to operate the main stepper.

---

[30] A. A. Lundstrom and L. G. Schimpf; U.S. Patent No. 3,897,591; filed August 27, 1942; issued July 29, 1975.

[31] H. W. Dudley; U.S. Patent No. 3,985,958; filed December 18, 1941; issued October 12, 1976.

[32] R. H. Badgley and R. L. Miller; U.S. Patent No. 3,912,868; filed July 7, 1943; issued October 14, 1975.

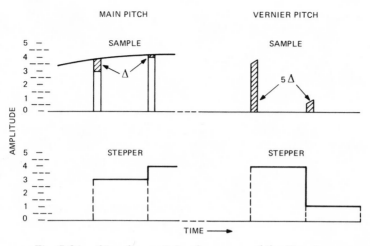

Fig. 5-34. Signal quantizing by means of the Vernier process.

The quantized value of the stepper, subtracted from the original pitch signal, will leave a small residual value Δ. The maximum possible value of Δ will be one-fifth of the total input range of the stepper; hence, after being multiplied by 5, this signal can be used to operate the same type of stepper as was used for the main operation. When the reverse process is carried out at the receiving terminal, the value of the vernier stepper must be divided by five before addition to the main value.

The vernier process in effect gave N^2 or 36 levels with two channels. It was soon realized that this was a very general process. Different numbers of channels and steps could be used to obtain many combinations (M^{ary} coding). Binary coding was one of the possible combinations to be considered, but at that time it was just another possible combination that did not lead in the right direction for the problem at hand.

A more important consideration was the fact that the desirable sampling rate of the vocoder channels was 50 Hz or a 20-millisecond (ms) sampling interval. Since it was known that the path delay differences causing selective fading on the transatlantic radio could be of the order of 2 to 3 ms, it was imperative that the sample interval be kept much longer; hence the six-level arrangement with a 20-ms sampling appeared to be about the best solution. Rather interestingly, this direct approach to multiple levels closely resembles the present practice in data sets, which convert to either four- or eight-level signals with longer sample intervals to obtain optimum transmission.

4.3.3 Transmission

The problem of transmitting a stepped or amplitude-quantized wave with multiple levels was a new situation. There was, of course, considerable experience with two-level telegraph signals. It soon became apparent that the use of amplitude modulation was not going to be possible on the transatlantic radio in the face of selective fades that could at times be as much as 20 dB. A six-level signal meant that amplitudes must be reproduced within about ±10 percent (1 dB). FSK (frequency-shift keying) had been used successfully with two-level telegraph signals and a similar scheme appeared to be the best solution for transmitting the X System signals. However, the job was much more complicated. For telegraph signals only two frequency positions were required to represent the two-state on-off signal. The X System used 6 frequency positions in each of 12 channels to represent all the information required for each speech sample.

Fortunately, sets of filters were available that could save much design time. Critical designs were required in both the frequency-shift oscillators and the limiter-detectors to obtain the required accuracy, stability, and freedom from transients at the pulse transition points. The oscillators were designed by M. E. Mohr around the use of a saturated-core inductor. L. G. Schimpf was mainly responsible for the limiter-detection circuit[33] for the receiving terminal.

For the first time the problem of the design of the filter system to give an optimum sampling of multilevel pulsed signals was encountered. This is the familiar "opening-of-the-eye" [34] problem in today's data systems. W. R. Bennett,[35] in an extension of H. Nyquist's telegraph theory, produced an excellent, as well as timely, solution to this difficult problem.

4.3.4 System Outline

A general outline of the system as it evolved is shown by Fig. 5-35. Actually, this is a functional schematic of the transmitting terminal; however, as will be explained later, the receiving terminal is surprisingly similar in structure. The slowly varying dc signals from the vocoder analyzer spectrum and pitch channels are applied to the message steppers, where they are periodically sampled as outlined in the processes of Figs. 5-33 and 5-34. The key steppers are quite similar but are operated directly by filtered signals from a phonograph record.

After the reentry process (Fig. 5-33), another stepper is used to regenerate the quantized signals. These signals are then used for controlling the FSK transmitting units (frequency modulation oscillators). The signals

---

[33] L. G. Schimpf, "A Regulated Limiter for Use in the X System," internal Bell Labs memorandum, September 30, 1942.

[34] This refers to the visual representation on a cathode ray tube display of the signal-to-noise margin of a data signal after modulation. A high quality signal has the appearance of an open eye. Distortion and other impairments tend to close the eye.

[35] W. R. Bennett, "Low Pass Filter Design for FM Detector Output of System," internal Bell Labs memorandum, March 3, 1942.

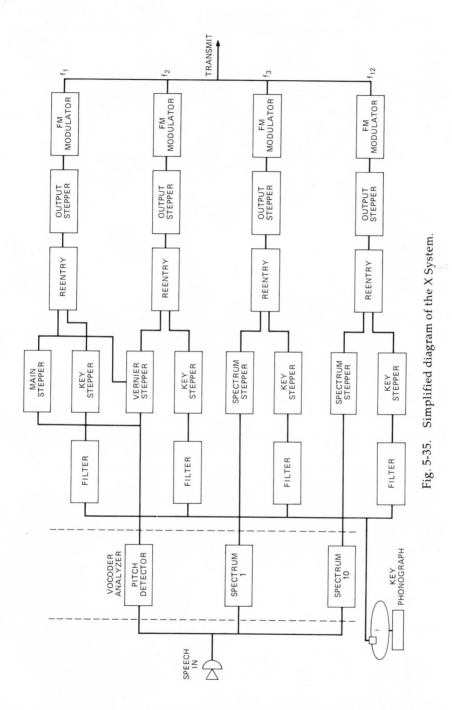

Fig. 5-35. Simplified diagram of the X System.

from these units are combined and transmitted to the receiving terminal. At the receiving terminal the quantized signals are reconstructed by frequency modulation detectors. From this point on the signals can be operated on in almost exactly the same manner as they are for the vocoder signals in the transmission terminal. By placing a simple inversion in the output signals of the fm detectors, the same reentry process will remove the key. The signals from the output steppers are then passed on to the vocoder synthesizer inputs.

4.3.5 Key Production and Synchronization

While the concept of having a key with six levels strictly random in nature was simple in itself, the actual implementation of this was one of the most difficult tasks in the development of the X System. Needless to say, from a security standpoint it was also the most sensitive. One of the well known requirements of a random step key for the Vernam system, which applied equally well to the X System, was not only that it be completely random but also that it never be repeated. Another problem, which might look prohibitive even to today's data transmission engineers, was the requirement that the systems be synchronized and maintained in synchronization over a 9,000-mile link, including shortwave radio, for hours at a time. Thanks to the way the parameters were chosen, this turned out not to be too difficult.

After much consideration it was decided to record the key on high-quality phonograph records. As might be imagined, the success of this approach hinged on carrying out a precision recording and reproducing process. Very precisely driven turntables were used for making the records as well as the reproduction at the terminals. Since only two records were ever made before a master was destroyed, even the very unlikely breaching of the elaborate distribution arrangement would probably not have been very useful. Early work on the key system was done by H. E. Vaughan[36] and N. D. Newby. Much of the responsibility for the final system rested with A. C. Norwine[37] and K. H. Davis. A great deal of credit for the mechanical design of the precision recording and reproducing equipment was due W. A. Marrison and I. E. Cole.

Although it occurred later, in the development phase, the design of a "mechanical" key source by A. J. Busch, O. Myers,[38] and A. E. Joel, Jr., rightly belongs under the heading of invention. This device, which made use of many relays, was affectionately called the "threshing machine" because of the noise it made in operation. Its theoretical security was not

---

[36] N. D. Newby and H. E. Vaughan; U.S. Patent No. 3,373,245; filed August 27, 1942; issued March 12, 1968.

[37] A. C. Norwine, "Noise Sampling Means for Vocoder Key Producer," internal Bell Labs memorandum, June 4, 1942.

[38] O. Myers; U.S. Patent No. 3,937,888; filed July 17, 1943; issued February 10, 1976. A. J. Busch; U.S. Patent No. 3,968,454; filed September 27, 1944; issued July 6, 1976.

absolute like the records; so it was never used for high-priority calls. But it was very useful for lineup and testing procedures, which made it possible to avoid using the precious records.

Although the synchronization of the systems initially looked like a formidable job, it was finally solved by the use of very precise frequency standards at each terminal. Because of the long message sample intervals (20-ms), once the system had been started in synchronization it would run for several hours without drifting out appreciably, and long-term drifting could be easily corrected. Short-term variations on even the longest links were never large enough to give trouble. Although links might fail for considerable periods, the system would still operate when transmission was restored.

An automatic frequency corrector designed by H. L. Barney made it possible to correct for frequency shifts which might occur in carrier or radio systems. In particular, this capability made it feasible to operate over long land links without upsetting the FSK transmission system.

4.3.6 Vocoder

Research and development on the vocoder had been carried out since about 1936 under H. W. Dudley. Thus it was much better developed than other parts of the system, which, for the most part, were quite new. Nevertheless, considerable effort was continuously applied to improve the quality and reliability of the vocoder. One of the main problems involved the derivation of reliable pitch signals from a wide range of talkers. Much credit is due R. R. Riesz for his work in this area throughout the war.

4.3.7 Experimental Model

A group under A. B. Clark was given the task of implementing design and construction of the vocoder. In the early stages of the project only a few members of the group were active, notably R. K. Potter, D. K. Gannett, and H. Nyquist. After several months of investigating and inventing, it became apparent that a workable system using the vocoder was feasible. For the first time digital coding of speech signals was utilized to accomplish the kind of task they were working on.

By late 1941 tentative designs and breadboard testing had been carried out for nearly all the system components without encountering any insurmountable snags. At this point it was decided to build a prototype model. To do this, the remainder of the Circuit Research group under A. M. Curtis was assigned to the job. A few had already been working on individual parts—e.g., I. E. Cole on phonograph turntables and H. E. Vaughan on the key. Besides making a complete working system, it was also desirable to have a complete set of working drawings so that the manufacturing process could be started if this step was decided upon.

A. E. Melhose did much of the coordination work in building the model as well as in developing the drawings. As the parts were finished, the system was assembled on the twelfth floor of the Graybar-Varick building in New York City.

The X System was made up of 12 parallel channels (10 spectrum, 2 pitch), which were nearly duplicates of each other except for their frequency position in the FSK arrangement. In March 1942 one complete channel of the experimental model became available for making fairly successful tests on an artificial fader simulating the fading of the transatlantic shortwave radio. In April a complete set of drawings was sent to J. L. Dow of the Switching Development group to arrange for manufacture. E. W. Olcott was to be in charge of the follow-up of manufacture.

The experimental model was completed in the latter part of August and was quickly tested for operation and stability. By November it was being tested over the transatlantic radio[39] with a synthetic set of signals from a signal generator that had been previously sent to England. As refinements of the system became available, they were continuously being tested and substituted in the experimental model to keep it up to date. This process was continued until mid-1943 when the manufactured systems were being installed in the field. So long as the experimental model was being updated, it served as demonstration equipment for training Signal Corps personnel.

4.3.8 Development and Manufacture

By August 1942 the research prototype model was completed. Enough experience had been obtained with the individual parts of the system to have confidence that the complete system would be successful. Up to this point Bell Laboratories had carried out the work on its own initiative, although NDRC and the Signal Corps were aware of the work and interested in the program. As early as February 3, 1941, General Mauborgne, Chief Signal Officer, had called attention in a radio talk to the problem of maintaining secrecy on the telephone in military service. Shortly thereafter (April 23), Potter made a trip to Washington to brief him on the possibilities as Bell Labs saw them. At about the time of the completion of the experimental system, the Signal Corps decided to sponsor the building of several terminals.

To carry out this expanded project, the effort was considerably reorganized and expanded in September 1942. P. W. Blye was appointed project engineer and given overall responsibility for coordinating the engineering and manufacture of the final system. He brought with him a large group from Transmission Engineering to aid in the process. The

[39] W. R. Bennett, "Transmission Over Fading Medium," internal Bell Labs memorandum, November 1, 1943.

work of the research group on the experimental model, which had been going on in several groups of the Circuit Research Department, was pulled together under D. K. Gannett. E. W. Olcott and C. R. Gray would direct the actual manufacture at Western Electric.

The first main effort was to go over the drawings of the experimental model to convert them into manufacturing drawings suitable for use by Western Electric. Emphasis was placed on substituting readily available standard components wherever feasible. The use of standard Western Electric amplifiers for gain was one important substitution, since many of the operations were carried out in the audio range. While this change added to the size of the overall system, it aided considerably in reducing the time for manufacturing. One Transmission Engineering group under D. Mitchell carried out this conversion process for the message coding equipment as well as arranging for the manufacture of the key records. Another group, under J. M. Barstow, carried out the same process with the vocoder system.

By the end of September the flood of orders for component parts had started. Arrangements had been made for Western Electric to manufacture the system at the vacuum tube plant on Hudson Street, New York City, a convenient location with respect to West Street and the Graybar-Varick building. A substantial number of manufactured system items were being obtained from Western Electric by January 1943. As items were finished and preliminary testing was completed, the parts were taken to Room L30 at West Street, originally the sound movie laboratory, and assembled as a system. The first system was completed by April 1; shortly thereafter, a second system was also assembled in the same area, the first system serving as a test vehicle to aid in checking out the second. By the end of April 1943, some two months prior to the invasion of Italy, several terminals were completed and installed in Washington, London, and North Africa.

This process was to be repeated over and over again as additional systems were made ready. Each would be assembled as a complete system, checked, disassembled by bays, and sent out to where it was to be installed. The shipping and installation of the finished systems for the European theater were carried out during June and July 1943. A system was installed in Washington, D.C., almost simultaneously with the assembly of the first system in Room L30. Other terminals were later installed in Paris, Hawaii, Australia, and the Philippines. Thus in the short span of about seven months a large and complex communication system, much of whose circuitry was completely new, was engineered, manufactured, and installed. It was a good example of Bell Labs' ability to bring to bear its varied talents and skills on a complex problem—which was demonstrated a number of times during the war.

To have trained people capable of handling these complex systems, Bell

Labs started a school for Signal Corps personnel about the same time manufacturing of the system began at Western Electric. Though isolated, this was actually part of the Bell Labs School for War Training administered by R. K. Honaman.[40] R. N. Hunter originally headed up the school for the X System. The Signal Corps set up what became known as the 805th Signal Service Company to handle the system. This company was a rather unusual one in that it contained almost as many officers as it did enlisted men, and nearly all the enlisted men were technical sergeants. Practically all the personnel had previously worked in the Bell System. They were not informed of what they were to be working on until their first briefing at Bell Laboratories. Only enough specialists to handle a few systems were trained at first. After being indoctrinated in the principles and circuits of the system, they were trained first on the experimental system and finally on the actual system. In the end they were usually involved in the testing and dismantling of the particular system they were to work with in the field. In all, 186 Signal Corps personnel were trained.

To ensure that the systems would function in the field, a team of two or three Bell Labs engineers accompanied each system to help in putting it into operation. The teams were often composed of one engineer from the Research area who knew the circuit operation intimately and others from the transmission and switching engineering groups who had been closely associated with the system as it was being put together. The manufacture and installation of the systems continued until about the middle of 1944.

4.3.9 Junior X System — AN/GSQ3

The size of the X System was not an accomplishment to be very happy about. Its use was feasible in a headquarters type of situation but not very practical in tactical situations. A number of possibilities for reducing its size had suggested themselves as the project progressed, but time was always the controlling factor. In the spring of 1943, as the assembly of the first manufactured X System was nearing completion, the pressures on the work of the Research group diminished considerably. At this point the Research people made a serious effort to see just how much the size could be reduced.

A step in this direction had already been made in a study[41] undertaken with the experimental system to reevaluate the effects of the number of quantized levels and of the number of vocoder channels on overall speech intelligibility. R. R. Riesz and O. O. Gruenz of the Research Department,

---

[40] See Section VI, Chapter 1.

[41] D. K. Gannett and R. L. Miller, "The Effect on Intelligibility of Reducing the Number of Channels and Steps and Increasing the Sampling Interval," internal Bell Labs memorandum, April 17, 1944.

working in cooperation with R. C. Edson and J. M. Barstow of the Transmission Engineering group, examined the basic vocoder system both with respect to an optimization of the number of channels to be used and with respect to the circuit design.

It was obvious from the start that a considerable saving in size could be obtained if specific circuit designs were optimized, rather than using existing amplifiers, power supplies, frequency standards, etc. Under pressure of the war, many vacuum tube types had also been reduced to miniature size. Basic redesigns of the FSK oscillators by M. E. Mohr[42] and the detectors by L. G. Schimpf[43] substantially reduced the size of these, especially with the miniature tubes. A proposal by R. L. Miller[44] to carry out the quantizing and coding operation in a single multiplexed arrangement, parallel to serial conversion, reduced the number of coders-decoders by a factor of 12. A more sophisticated form of the mechanical key was converted to an essentially all-electronic system, following suggestions of D. K. Gannett, A. E. Melhose, and M. E. Mohr.

The work on the basic design of the vocoder indicated that the number of spectrum channels could be reduced to eight without greatly affecting quality and intelligibility. This allowed a realignment and widening of the FSK channels and produced a corresponding improvement in transmission margins.

An outline of the much simplified system is shown in Fig. 5-36. With a serial sampling of the various vocoder channels, a common higher-speed quantizer and reentry system could carry out the necessary logic functions. By keeping the time between samples of a given channel to the 20 milliseconds used in the senior X System, an equivalent operation was obtained. With a holding, or clamp, arrangement at the output distributor, the signal operating the FSK transmitting oscillators was also kept at the 20-ms width necessary for overriding fading. This technique kept the synchronization problem the same, since the sampling of the transmitted signals was the critical process.

The design engineering and manufacturing procedures for the Junior X, or the AN/GSQ3 system (as it was later coded by the Signal Corps), followed a pattern similar to that of the Senior X System. In general, the same people followed up and worked on the same aspect of the system they had worked on before. The design and construction of the experimental prototype in the Research group occupied about a year.

In the fall of 1944, the Signal Corps contracted for a number of the systems. These were also built under the overall supervision of P. W. Blye,

[42] M. E. Mohr, "The Multivibrator as a Frequency Modulator," internal Bell Labs memorandum, April 17, 1944.

[43] L. G. Schimpf, "An Audio Frequency FM Demodulator," internal Bell Labs memorandum, April 17, 1944.

[44] R. L. Miller; U.S. Patent No. 3,965,296; filed June 30, 1944; issued June 22, 1976.

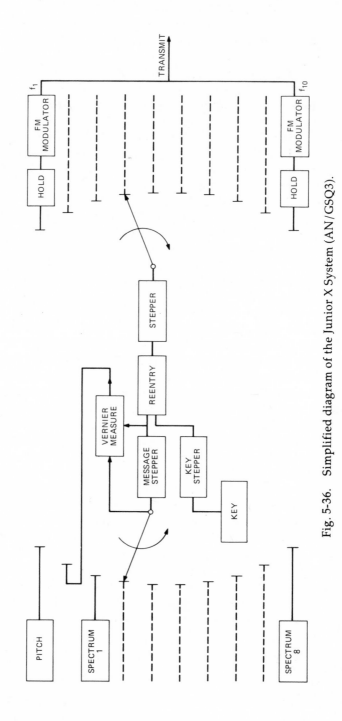

Fig. 5-36.   Simplified diagram of the Junior X System (AN/GSQ3).

with J. M. Barstow having the major responsibility. The system as finally constructed occupied only six 5-foot bays and could be placed in a trailer van. The systems were delivered in March 1946, too late for use in the war.

4.3.10 Application

As might be expected from the nature of the X System, not much is known about experience with it in the field, although numerous stories drifted back with returning technicians. A general staff officer was reported to have said that it was very valuable during preparations for the invasion of the Philippines.

A terminal intended fcr use in the Philippine invasion was unloaded in the surf at Port Moresby in New Guinea. The salt water bath did not help some of its sensitive electronic circuits, designed for air-conditioned surroundings. However, the equipment was cleaned in record time and put into service on a barge. The detachment of the 805th Company in charge received a citation for its efforts from General MacArthur. Bell Labs also received a War Department Citation for the development of the X System.

Even though it was one of the most sophisticated pieces of cloak-and-dagger equipment developed during World War II, stories concerning the X System seem to have been either very dull or infrequent. An investigation team touring Germany after the war apparently uncovered an intercept station that had recorded reams of the signals but had come to the conclusion that they were the output of a complicated telegraph system. This lack of knowledge even of the system's objective probably accounts for the lack of stories.

One of the big thrills for workers on the X System came from a picture and article in *Life* magazine describing Winston Churchill's underground headquarters in London. Plainly visible was the telephone set especially designed for use with the X System vocoder. The handset had a distinctive ball-shaped transmitter which had been adapted from the Western Electric "8 Ball" high-quality microphone.

4.3.11 Coding

As we have seen, the early phases of brainstorming and inventing for the X System in 1941 were, because of its hush-hush nature, largely confined to people in the higher echelons of Bell Laboratories and to a few restricted groups, mainly in the Research Department. As the processes of keying, quantizing, and coding of the signal evolved, considerable interest and enthusiasm developed among these people. It was a new area to think about, creating considerable discussion and speculation about its many facets. The ability to regenerate the quantized signal in the face of noise, along with the different possible combinations of quantization, raised some intriguing questions.   The relation of the signal-to-noise ratio to the probability of reproducing the signal was brought into sharp focus.

R. V. L. Hartley and H. Nyquist, major consultants at Bell Laboratories, were especially interested in the project.   Hartley in particular found the possibilities interesting because they were related to some of his previous pronouncements on the transmission of information.   He wrote a memorandum[45] philosophizing on the various processes in the system. M. E. Mohr, one of the more mathematically inclined researchers, had reached a tentative conclusion that a "tertiary," or three-level, system would probably be most efficient for general coding.

It was not until about the middle of 1943 that Bell Labs people became aware of the use of binary coding as already proposed by Alec H. Reeves, of The International Telephone and Telegraph Co.   Reeves had filed for a French patent in 1938, but his U.S. patent[46] had not been issued until late 1942.   In describing his invention, Reeves later wrote, "Having had it patented, for understandable reasons I then let the invention slip from my mind until the end of the war.   It was in the United States during World War II that the next step in PCM's progress was made, by the Bell Telephone Laboratories." [47]   Reeves was referring in particular to work carried out by H. S. Black and W. M. Goodall during and after 1943 (a part of the work being for the U.S. government) and described after the war by the first technical publications on PCM.[48,49]   Others who contributed to this phase of work on PCM were F. B. Llewellyn, C. E. Shannon, and J. O. Edson.

This emphasis on binary PCM, which was mainly pointed toward wideband circuits, did make the personnel working on the X System take another serious look at the coding arrangement to be sure that something had not been overlooked.   H. L. Barney[50] carried out a series of extensive tests with various possible combinations but came to the conclusion that for the situation it faced, the multilevel arrangement used was better. After the press of war work subsided, several people working on the X System or its fringes contributed to the further development of PCM, notably W. R. Bennett, E. Peterson, and L. A. Meacham.

It remained for C. E. Shannon to put together a complete theory of in-

[45] R. V. L. Hartley, "A Quantitative Measure of Amount and Quality of Information," internal Bell Labs memorandum, March 10, 1941.

[46] A. H. Reeves; U.S. Patent No. 2,272,070; February 3, 1942.

[47] A. H. Reeves, "The Past, Present, and Future of PCM," *IEEE Spectrum* 2 (May 1965), pp. 58–63.

[48] H. S. Black and J. O. Edson, "Pulse Code Modulation," *Trans. AIEE* 66 (1947), pp. 895–899.

[49] W. M. Goodall, "Telephony by Pulse Code Modulation," *Bell System Technical J.* 26 (July 1947), pp. 395–409.

[50] H. L. Barney, "Narrow Band Frequency Shift Transmission Using 2, 4, and 8 Valued Signals," internal Bell Labs memorandum, July 24, 1945.

formation. Shannon returned to Bell Labs in 1941 from M.I.T. and Princeton, where he had specialized in the application of Boolean algebra to switching. He had also become quite interested in cryptanalysis as a hobby. Although quite new in the company, his talents were well recognized and he served actively on some committees dealing with different aspects of cryptanalysis. He also became familiar with the X System, having been asked to take a close look at the reentry process to be sure that something had not been overlooked in the presumption that it was unbreakable. It is quite apparent that his work on cryptography and information theory was intimately tied up together, judging from his papers, "Communication Theory of Secrecy Systems" [51] and "A Mathematical Theory of Communication." [52] The former article was first issued as an internal memorandum in 1945, although it was not cleared for publication until 1949.

V. MOBILE RADIO SYSTEMS

So far in this chapter we have dealt mostly with backbone communications systems—those serving the daily business and logistical needs of the public and the military, which provided the vast network required for the new type of twentieth-century warfare. But in World War II there was also a great need for tactical communications, consisting mostly of radio. Tactical systems reaching out to the lowest military echelons are the subject of this section.

Since World War II was an extremely mobile war, the United States forces used vehicles of all kinds: tanks, personnel carriers, ships, and aircraft, to "press here" or "deploy there." There was little of the foot-slogging infantry or the trenches of World War I. There was, on the other hand, a great need for the coordination and control of the numerous enclaves of mobile troops in enemy territory. Reliable radio communication to and from these entities, and between them and an advancing headquarters, was an absolute requirement for air, land, and sea forces.

Bell Labs' deep involvement in airplane and mobile radiotelephone systems and equipment just prior to World War II provided a wealth of experience which the military sought when it suddenly faced the difficult task of outfitting the armed forces on a crash basis. Bell Labs' technical capabilities and Western Electric's large-scale manufacturing expertise combined to make a most effective team in this situation. In the first years of the war, this team was pressed to the utmost by the military need for new devices as well as for greater quantities of the old. As the war progressed, the technical requirements and military uses became more sta-

[51] C. E. Shannon, "Communication Theory of Secrecy Systems," *Bell System Technical J.* 28 (October 1949), pp. 656–715.
[52] C. E. Shannon, "Mathematical Theory of Communication," *Bell System Technical J.*, 27 (July 1948), pp. 379–423 (October 1948), pp. 623–656.

bilized, and it was then possible for development groups to bring out new and advanced designs for military equipment.

5.1 Bell Labs' Background in Mobile Radio

Prior to World War II Bell Labs had developed radio equipment for commercial aviation—transmitters, receivers, ancillary power, and control units—that was used extensively. Bell Labs was also developing radio equipment and systems for police use and other mobile ground uses. As part of this program, the merits of narrowband frequency modulation (FM) versus amplitude modulation (AM) were being actively investigated; thus, a choice could be quickly made when a decision was needed for military equipment. In addition, Bell Labs engineers were directly involved in the design of commercial radio communication systems just before World War II and thus gained the needed technical background in radio and electronics. But military equipment had to function in a much more severe environment (involving, for example, higher and lower temperatures, high humidity, and rough usage) than commercial equipment and was used differently.

Bell Labs learned much about military requirements, as well as how to work cooperatively with military personnel, during the development of radiotelephone and radiotelegraph equipment for Navy airplanes during the mid-1930s. Through Western Electric, it won competitive bids in those years for the GN, GO, and GP Navy aircraft radio transmitters and for the RAM, the radio receiver associated with the GN transmitter to form a system. Each of the transmitters delivered over 100 watts of radio-frequency power to the airplane antenna, over a wide frequency range, at what was then considered the high stability and settability requirements needed for radiotelegraph operation.

These developments gave mechanical design engineers at Bell Labs special training in military finishes, materials, strength-versus-weight considerations, and human factors. Since a number of other companies also obtained separate contracts for development of the same equipment, the Navy had an opportunity to compare the performance and reliability of the various designs. At the outbreak of World War II, the Navy requested additional quantities of GP-1 radio transmitters because "the WECo. GP-1 had proven to be the best of all of this type of equipment from all sources." However, it was not possible for Western Electric to accept that assignment because of the urgent commitments described below.

On the whole, then, the various commercial and military radiotelephone developments within Bell Labs prior to World War II provided a broad, directly usable technical background that could be applied immediately to the needs of an expanded military situation.

Fig. 5-37.   SCR-508 radio set, known as the Tank set.   Rugged and reliable, it was used in almost all ground mobile services by all military agencies.

5.2 Major Wartime Radio Equipment

A year before the United States found itself in World War II, groups in Bell Labs were dedicated to the design of two major classes of radiotelephone equipment for the military, which were subsequently built and used in large quantities and had a very important part in the successful prosecution of the war.   These were the Tank sets for use in all types of land and water vehicles and the ARC sets for use in Navy and Army Air Corps aircraft.

The Tank set was so called because it was designed initially for use in the left sponson of a light tank, which was considered by the Army Signal Corps to be the tightest space situation among any of the set's uses.   It was coded variously as the SCR-508, 528, and 538 radio sets for Armored Force use (Fig. 5-37).   A later series, coded as the SCR-608, 628, and 638 radio sets, was almost exactly the same as the SCR-508, except that the SCR-608 operated in the slightly higher frequency range used by the Field Artillery. All these sets, widely used in many battle situations, received the following commendation from the Signal Corps: "Their outstanding transmission performance and their rugged and trouble-free operation have extended their field of use to include applications not originally contemplated, such as use   by the Amphibious Forces (Navy/Army) in landing operations." [53]

The ARC, or aircraft radio communication, sets started as the SCR-183 and SCR-274 radio sets.   These had been developed by another company for the Signal Corps, but the company had only limited manufacturing and production-engineering capabilities, insufficient for a full-scale war. Bell Labs' improvement and subsequent major development of these sets

[53] Report of the Armored Force Board on Tests Conducted March 25–28, 1941, transmitted to Bell Laboratories.

for much higher frequencies with narrower bandwidths and crystal control broadened their capabilities and use so much that they became the basic radio equipments for military aircraft throughout the war.

Some details of the earliest design decisions on both the Tank and the ARC sets—including the development processes and engineering problems faced during manufacture and use—may give the reader an insight into the sense of urgency existing throughout the war and the ability of Bell Labs to draw on the varied, uncommon talents of its personnel to solve many kinds of problems.

5.2.1 Tank Sets — SCR-508, 528, 538[54]

The first formal discussion with the Signal Corps Electronics Laboratory (SCEL) on the Tank Set was held on September 4, 1940, to review the scope of the project and the problems presented in papers previously sent to Bell Labs covering the "military characteristics" (general technical requirements) of the "Signal Corps Type III Radio Set for the Cavalry." This conference discussed the following: space available for radio equipment in a light tank, the need for easy and fast installation and removal, the advantages of being able to instantly select any one of ten preset frequencies from among an available 100 quartz-crystal-controlled channels, operation in the 20- to 28-MHz frequency band (allocated to the Armored Force), the need for simple one-knob control of the transmitter and the receiver, use of a fishpole antenna not to exceed 15 feet in length, a power source of either 12 or 24 volts dc, voice communication only (i.e., not telegraph), and a flashing lamp to indicate when a signal was being received. SCEL also put an upper limit of 10 minutes on the time taken by a mechanic to change each preset frequency. Its representatives also noted the need for special microphones, earphones for use under crash helmets worn by crewmen, and filters in power and other leads to reduce ignition and other interference.

All this was a big order. Engineers were sent to the Aberdeen Proving Ground to look at combat cars and tanks and to check on space for radio sets and on operating conditions. Other engineers examined circuits and components. While ideas were being considered, Bell Labs asked the Signal Corps to install a Western Electric commercial amplitude-modulated 27A radio transmitter and a 29A radio receiver in an armored car so that the engineers could see their performance and reliability under military conditions. At a conference with SCEL on September 20, 1940, not quite three weeks after the first conference, it was reported that the commercial equipment did not have adequate range owing to receiver characteristics and that the cables frequently broke a few inches from the plugs. The

---

[54] The SCR-600 series, used by the Field Artillery, was so similar to this series that it need not be discussed here.

military people who were present educated the nonmilitary people on tank brigade tactics and their use of radio. The conclusion was inescapable: commercial equipment could not be modified to do the job. It would be necessary to design specifically for the intended application.

5.2.2 Development

Bell Labs' experience with amplitude modulation, crystal-controlled frequencies, and components near the desired frequency band was readily transferable to the new set. Development work was initially concentrated on the physical design, especially the use of push-button tuners, like those in today's car radios, for quickly changing channels, and on the breakdown of the system into its major units. In the meantime the Signal Corps, too, was studying the problems, so that by the next conference, on October 15, 1940, when a wooden mock-up of the complete amplitude-modulated tank radio set was exhibited, basic decisions were reached quickly on size, finish, power supply, antenna, number of channels, push-button mechanism, receiver and transmitter controls, and meters. The Signal Corps estimated that it might ultimately need radio sets for 50,000 tanks and vehicles. For such a large quantity of equipment, it was imperative that the designs be simple, efficient, and manufacturable by many suppliers, with assurance of reliable performance. An initial order for 2,000 sets was proposed to establish design and manufacturing information. However, the Signal Corps required delivery of three operating model equipments by January 15, 1941, only three months from the date of the conference. At this time the Allies were being pushed back in Europe, and convoys were often decimated by U-boats. Generally, however, Americans did not think it probable that the United States would, within a year, be directly involved in a world war. The military people thought differently and clearly conveyed their conviction and sense of urgency by requesting the extremely short delivery schedule for models. Designs were completed and the production of parts was expedited, but the long-range problems were not ignored. For example, correspondence between Bell Labs and Western Electric in this period noted the dependence of the design on quantity manufacture of low-cost quartz crystals and suggested the appointment of a cooperative design group on this subject.

Meanwhile, both Bell Labs and the Signal Corps were examining further the question of AM versus FM. The theory and preliminary tests indicated that narrowband FM, as required by the channel bandwith specified by the military, was not significantly better in signal-to-noise ratio than AM at the low signal levels which occurred over long transmission distances. In view of the short schedules and other problems, something new like FM seemed of doubtful value when the circuits and components of AM were well understood. However, it was decided in an early December 1940 conference with the Signal Corps that this matter be thoroughly reviewed before the overall design was irrevocably fixed. This was to be accomplished by building three FM sets for direct A-B tests against the AM sets. The Signal Corps also asked that the sets be competitively tested against FM equipment from other manufacturers. This decision came as an additional blow to mechanical engineers and shop people who were already overloaded by the short schedule for three AM sets. It required the assignment of a new group of electrical engineers who were familiar with FM and would probably mean complete chassis redesigns and new fabrication within the sizes already settled upon for each major unit.

From earlier R and D effort, considerable experience had been acquired at Bell Labs in FM technology. The knowledge was promptly and effectively applied. Narrowband FM (small frequency swing from the carrier frequency) had to be used in order to stay within the Army-specified 100-kHz channel assignments. The narrow bands were required by the need for as many channels as possible to accommodate large numbers of vehicles using these sets in close proximity. The AM superheterodyne receiver with its variable-frequency beating oscillator, then under design and fabrication, could be readily modified for FM by putting an FM discriminator in place of the AM detector, modifying the squelch circuit, and making other relatively smaller changes.

But the transmitter needed an entirely new design. A new circuit for simply producing phase modulation (similar to FM) had just been invented[55] in Bell Laboratories. It used a low-frequency oscillator operating into a nonlinear coil, a rectifier, and frequency multipliers, and it did away with the high-power audio-frequency amplitude-modulating circuits. Altogether it was a less demanding circuit. The problem was to engineer and produce it in large quantities. First, the tricky nonlinear coil, which had to operate magnetic materials at RF and had other magnetic requirements, demanded very careful production controls. Second, the circuit required a new and unproven low-frequency (300- to 450-kHz), quartz crystal that was rugged and small in size and had a zero temperature coefficient.

Naturally, there were some serious doubts about adopting such a new and untried system for use on a very large scale. However, with dedication and many hours of concentrated effort, and with highest priorities, experienced teams produced both the AM and the FM sets, including control boxes, interphone amplifiers, and mounting bases, as well as the receivers and transmitters. Delivery was made not quite by January 15, 1941, but soon enough after that date to allow SCEL field testing and review at Ft. Monmouth to be completed by the end of February.

System simplicity as well as the results of comparative field tests in

---

[55] L. R. Wrathall; U.S. Patent No. 2,311,796; filed August 27, 1940; issued February 23, 1943. Also see L. R. Wrathall, "Performance of a Magnetic Phase Modulation Transmitter," internal Bell Labs memorandum, May 1, 1940.

Signal Corps vehicles made FM the choice over AM. Immediately, the FM equipment was shipped to Ft. Benning, Georgia, where it was put into tanks and other Armored Force vehicles for direct comparison with equipment from two other companies. Bell Labs people were allowed to briefly instruct master sergeants in the adjustment and use of the equipment; from there on the process was exclusively a military operation with military personnel serving as operators and users. The report on the tests showed that the Bell Labs-Western Electric sets were better than others in distance of transmission and reception, ease of setup and use, and convenience of installation. The report, dated March 28, 1941, noted that FM proved better than AM and that the "SCR-508-T2 (FM) performance and flexibility establishes a standard of military radio communication which is without precedence and which will materially raise combat effectiveness of all armored force elements to a significant extent." [56]

During all the foregoing studies and development work, many people were involved throughout the organization in the thousands of design decisions on component parts, most of which had to be specially made. A new circuit is useless without proper components.

From Ft. Benning the FM tank set was sent by a special railroad boxcar directly to the Western Electric Hawthorne Works, which had by then been designated as the manufacturing location. It was thus possible for Western Electric manufacturing engineers to plan for the subcontracting and for the production while Bell Labs was completing the manufacturing information.

In short, it required just seven months to initiate a new development, develop basic and then detailed requirements, construct final models, get them tested and approved, and put these into the production process.

5.2.3 Production

The radio set sent from Ft. Benning was viewed by two very interested groups at the Hawthorne manufacturing plant in a suburb of Chicago. One was composed of the Western Electric manufacturing-engineering and production specialists who could now see and study the actual equipment they were expected to produce; the other group was the Bell Labs "cage" group.

The cage group was so named because it had been set up earlier as an on-site representative of the Bell Labs Whippany design groups to deal with design and production problems relating to radar at Hawthorne. Since this group and its highly classified information and drawings had to be separated from the large unclassified shop areas, a wire fence reaching to the ceiling had been thrown up around their area. The cage

---

[56] "Service Test of Radio Set SCR-508-T2," Report of Signal Corps Laboratory on Tests Conducted March 25–28, 1941.

group was staffed by experienced Bell Labs engineers and key draftsmen from Whippany and New York, supplemented with selected Western Electric people. They took care of the day-to-day problems, such as tolerances of the many mechanical and electrical parts which had to fit together, substitution of materials, flaws in design, and so forth; and they were invaluable in the contacts with the large number of parts suppliers both within and outside the Bell System.

In a few months almost every midwestern company that had ever made radio, electronic, or electrical equipment was tooled up and producing parts for the Tank set. A jukebox manufacturer was making the interphone amplifier unit; a broadcast receiver manufacturer was producing the pushbutton tuner for both the receiver and the transmitter; special power relays were made by new companies leasing old facilities; and audio transformers came from three old-line component companies. Throughout, Western Electric did the tasks for which it was best equipped, such as punching and bending the heavy mounting bases, as well as assembling, testing, and quality-inspecting the overall product. In all of this hectic but organized confusion the experienced cage group solved critical problems that daily occurred because of the fast pace of new production from new suppliers.

When the problems were basic ones, the cage group called upon the development group at Bell Labs headquarters. One such difficulty arose when the major units of the radio set made by different manufacturers did not properly plug into the mounting base. The development engineers were called in to completely review the plug and assembly tolerances; they proposed a set of assembly jigs for each manufacturer which thereafter eliminated the problem. Partway through production, Ft. Benning reported that antenna metering thermocouples were being burnt out. A colonel had insisted that his battalions were not going to use that long fishpole antenna, no matter what. He insisted on a short antenna that had very little RF resistance and therefore produced a high antenna current. This was quickly corrected by the development people, but some 1,000 sets piled up in the production department before all official approvals could be gotten to the Signal Corps inspectors on site. At one time some 3,000 radio sets were held up for low power output caused by use of a power amplifier tube from a new supplier. Serious production problems like these appeared regularly. When a basic change in specification or design was involved, the development engineer flew to Chicago and remained there until production was running smoothly again. Here the Signal Corps' faith in Bell System capabilities and their assistance were always helpful in clearing up difficulties. Both parties held to high standards of quality performance and were especially cooperative when particular situations demanded such effort.

One of the most serious and potentially catastrophic predicaments ap-

Fig. 5-38. FT-241A crystal unit that accurately controlled the Tank set transmitter frequency.

peared early in the production process. The new CT/DT-cut quartz crystals could not be produced in sufficient quantity; rejections were high. A team of engineers and scientists selected from research, development, and systems departments was sent from New York to Hawthorne; and after a week or so of preliminary investigation, they began a major revision in certain production processes to automate as much as possible in order to improve reproducibility and reliability. This team looked into and modified a number of manufacturing steps, but probably their most ingenious improvement had to do with the soldering of the crystal leads to the center of each silvered face of the crystal. The amount of solder used not only affected the mechanical strength of the union but also affected the crystal frequency. The team developed a device that punched just the right amount of solder from a thin sheet, put the small disc of it in the center of the crystal face together with the lead wire, and then used a timed hot air blast to do the soldering neatly and uniformly. As the result of such methods and subsequent shop experience, the FT-241A quartz crystal (Fig. 5-38) used in the transmitter of radio set SCR-508 was made and sold to the Signal Corps for a price of less than $1.00 per unit near the end of the war. Almost 10 million of these FT-241A quartz crystal units were made, not only for the tank set but also for instruments and for other radio sets. The efficient crystal design reduced the amount of imported quartz needed, and the efficient production reduced the price.

With the same sense of urgency and cooperation which helped to develop the tank set in record time, the Bell Labs cage group working with the experienced and knowledgeable Western Electric production teams produced the first ten production-made sets by the time of the Pearl Harbor attack. During the war, as the sets proved their reliability in combat, they were specified for more and more uses. As quantities rose production problems and costs dropped, and Bell Labs was able to turn back some of the production engineering funds that had been allocated. In all, over 100,000 tank set transmitters and a greater number of receivers were produced during the war.

5.2.4 Later Radio Sets for the Signal Corps

By mid-1943 production problems on the tank sets were almost entirely in the hands of the cage group at Hawthorne. It was therefore possible to assign engineers at Bell Labs in New York to the development of an entirely new radio set meeting Signal Corps military characteristics derived from two years of war experience and from speculation about the future. The product was to be a standardized series of sets for ground and vehicular assignments, meant to be carried and used by a soldier in action or installed in a vehicle. Throughout its development the set was referred to as the G/V (ground/vehicular) set, although it was assigned radio set codes of AN/GRC-3 through -11. The ground-use requirement demanded that the sets use little power, be light in weight, and be waterproof (*waterproof* soon meant "floatable"). To ease the production and later logistical problems, the Signal Corps required that the set use a crystal-saver circuit, which not only used few crystals but also included them in the unit. The frequency bands, number of channels, width of the channels, and frequency swing were the same as those specified for the SCR-508 (Armored Force) and SCR-608 (Field Artillery), so that the new sets could gradually replace the old.

The development engineers came up with a new technique[57] for achieving suitable accuracy in setting the frequency to any of 120 channels with few quartz crystals and at the same time adjusting the antenna circuit for each transmitter operation. For minimizing weight and power drain, some circuits were used both in transmitting and receiving, an arrangement that soon came to be known as a transceiver. Realizing that only relatively small amounts of power are available to the ground user (generally from dry batteries), the engineers abandoned the electrical switching of frequency in favor of direct physical control by the operator. This led to optimization of the overall design; that is, more duties were required of mechanical devices than was normal in the usual equipment. The heart of the transceiver was a two-shaft multigear train device that performed all switching and rotating functions needed to provide a "tens" channel control knob on one shaft and a "units" channel control knob on a second shaft. In addition to the transceiver, which was the major unit, there were

[57] J. B. Harley and J. G. Nordahl; U.S. Patent No. 2,539,537; filed April 29, 1949; issued January 30, 1951.

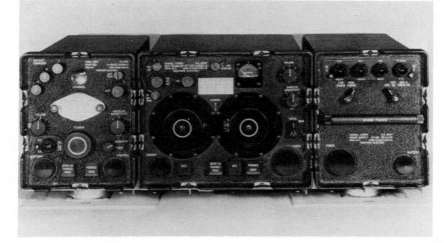

Fig. 5-39.   AN/GRC-3 through -11 radio sets developed to replace the Tank set.

separate auxiliary receivers having accurate dial and detent tuning mechanisms, various vibrator power units, control boxes, mountings, and other ancillary items allowing complete flexibility in assignment and use. A view of the three major units of the G/V radio set is shown in Fig. 5-39. Just as World War II was ending, Bell Labs delivered three complete model sets to the Signal Corps, and then turned its attention to commercial projects.

5.2.5 Aircraft Radio Sets – SCR-274 and AN/ARC 1, 4, 5, 12, 19

In August 1940 the Signal Corps approached Western Electric and Bell Labs with a request to manufacture an aircraft command radio set very similar to the SCR-183, which had been developed by a small radio company that did not have the capabilities for large-scale production.   The new set was subsequently coded the SCR-274 aircraft radio equipment (Fig. 5-40).   A first contract for 1,500 sets was awarded to the original developer, but the sets were produced entirely by Bell Labs and Western Electric, except for mounting racks and hardware; this was viewed as an effective means for Bell Labs and Western Electric to ease into the problems encountered in quantity production.   Subsequent contracts for the radio sets were awarded directly to Western Electric, which made them in shops at Kearny, New Jersey.

This arrangement was the initial step in what turned out to be a continuing involvement in the development and improvement of military aircraft radio sets throughout the war.   The radio set consisted of three radio receiver units covering 190 to 550 kHz, 3 to 6 MHz, and 6 to 9.1 MHz, three radio transmitter units together with modulator units covering 4

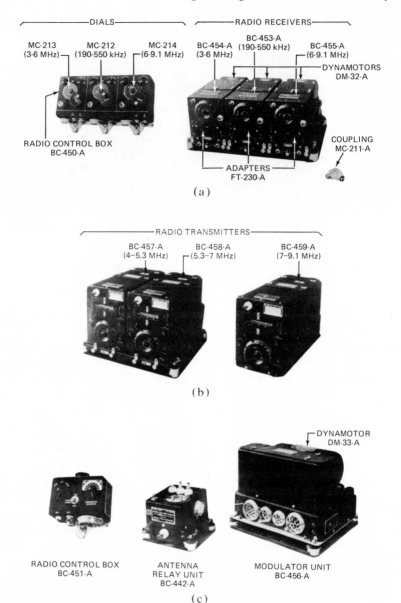

Fig. 5-40. SCR-274N radio set—first of the series of military aircraft radio communication equipment developed during the war.

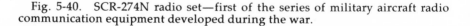

to 5.3 MHz, 5.3 to 7.0 MHz, and 7.0 to 9.1 MHz, remote control boxes, and ancillary items. The receiver and transmitter units were plug-in items so that airplane equipment could be tailored for a variety of objectives. The sets were powered from the 28-volt dc airplane source, with high

voltage supplied by dynamotors. Amplitude modulation was used for all bands.

The problems of using someone else's drawings in manufacture showed up quickly. Tolerances and materials were not as perfectly specified as they should be for assembly-line production. This lack was immediately responsible in the first few production sets for a serious difficulty with frequency drift as the sets warmed up. The transmitter oscillator frequency was determined by a high-quality variable air capacitor and a carefully designed inductor. It was necessary to make incremental changes in the capacitor to counteract small changes in the inductor as the temperature of the transmitter changed with use or ambient conditions. Compensation had to be effective over the entire tuning range, which made the design difficult and the testing program tedious. The many and varied factors that affected this balancing of component characteristics had to be studied in time-consuming detail, and a number of specifications and drawings had to be improved before smooth large-scale manufacture was possible.

There also were, of course, the normal production problems of supply, new components and critical materials, and small improvements throughout production. A contract renegotiation report for 1944 noted that over 163,000 SCR-274 receivers, transmitters, and modulators were delivered by the end of 1944, together with numerous control boxes, mounting racks, and spare parts. These sets provided most of the Air Force aircraft communications during the early stages of the war, and throughout the war they continued to provide the reliable longer-range circuits for communication between an airplane and its base.

However, there was a very great need for short-range airplane-to-airplane communication whereby a group aircraft commander could talk with or direct the planes in his flight without revealing to the enemy that he was on his way. Just as in the case of the tank set and ground communications, here, too, the experience of Bell Labs and Western Electric in the radio communication field provided a prompt answer for urgent military needs. Before the war Bell Labs had designed a number of types of radio equipment for airline use. One of these was the 233A radio set for Pan American Airways, which could operate on four preset frequencies in a small band near 140 MHz. This gave line-of-sight communication for airplane-to-ground communication at airports without skip-distance effects or over-the-horizon interference at distant airports. Vacuum tube and circuit performance at these "high" frequencies in the prewar period left much to be desired, but for the particular military and Pan American needs the 233A radio set was quite adequate. The military version of this set was coded AN/ARC-4 radio set. Some 18,300 sets were produced for the Navy.

The success of the 233A/ARC-4 led to the start in 1942 of development

(a)

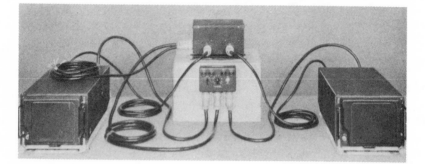

(b)

(c)

Fig. 5-41. (a) AN/ARC-1 radio set developed to provide high-frequency line-of-sight communication. (b) AN/ARC-18 airborne automatic radio relay unit for communication between aircraft carrier and its airplanes. (c) Airplane equipped with AN/ARC-18 acting as automatic relay station between carrier and distant airplane.

for the Navy of a completely new set that could operate on any one of ten preset frequencies in a 100- to 156-MHz band plus a fixed monitor or guard channel. This unit was later coded as the AN/ARC-1 radio set (Fig. 5-41a). Of 71,000 sets ordered, about 40,000 were delivered—a little more than half by Western Electric and a little less than half by Westinghouse, which was the second source for this equipment in each of the major production contracts.

The 233A development experience as well as Bell Labs' continuing state-of-the-art development in what at that time was a difficult frequency range (100 MHz and higher) provided a good basis for the development of the ARC-1 radio set for the Navy. Nevertheless, there were innumerable problems to solve. One of the major studies was directed toward improvement of the signal-to-noise ratio (or the noise figure) at low received RF signal levels. Great care in the choice of components and circuits produced small improvements, but it was not until Bell Labs developed the 6AK5 vacuum tube that signal-to-noise performance reached a level that could be termed very good. The 6AK5 tube had a greatly superior figure of merit over the miniature tubes previously available. As a consequence, radio receiver performance improved dramatically.

A major problem throughout the development and early production of the ARC-1 radio set was the need for high receiver and transmitter performance in small volume and weight. To achieve these objectives, the main unit was designed as a transceiver in which the receiver local oscillator was quartz-crystal-controlled. A submultiple of the receiver local oscillator frequency was supplied to the transmitter, where it was mixed with the output of another crystal-controlled fixed frequency oscillator operating at a submultiple of the receiver intermediate frequency. A modulation product was selected, multiplied, and amplified to produce the transmitted frequency at the required output power level. Amplitude modulation of the output stage was employed.

The heart of the receiver was a seven-gang variable air dielectric capacitor built in two side-by-side sections, which were ganged together through antibacklash gears and upon which were mounted all the RF circuit inductors, trimmers, and vacuum tube sockets. The capacitor was coupled to one of three tuning devices driven by a common motor operated from the 28-volt dc supply in the aircraft. The other two tuning devices were coupled, one to the transmitter roller coil shaft and one to the combined tuning and loading circuit of the antenna. Each of the three tuning devices could be preset accurately to any 10 frequencies in the 100- to 156-MHz band.

A great deal of attention had to be given to the receiver circuits in order to achieve stable high gain and high selectivity in a very small space. Additionally, very careful design was necessary in the balanced modulator employed in the transmitter to produce the transmitter carrier frequency from the receiver crystal control source. Without precise balance of the modulator circuits and a high degree of selectivity in following circuits, transmission of unwanted, spurious radiation would have resulted.

After the initial design and model construction, a thorough engineering

Fig. 5-42. AN/ARC-12 radio set developed for aircraft use. The set operated in the 225- to 350-MHz frequency band to provide more secure communication channels.

review brought about redesign effort in such equipment or functions as the drive-motor brake mechanism, bearings, ceramic roller coil forms, tuning-capacitor rotor ground contacts, improved shielding, added filtering, and removal of an unnecessary stage in the modulator. The changes were incorporated in a system recoded AN/ARC-1A.

With the changes developed after initial model construction and after tests of initial production models, greatly improved performance resulted from the equipment manufactured during 1944. For several years after the war many commercial airlines used the ARC-1A units for air-to-ground VHF voice communication.

The ARC-1 and ARC-1A were used extensively and very effectively in many carrier-based aircraft during the war in the Pacific. The distances flown were sometimes beyond the line-of-sight range of the ARC-1A, so a radio relay set, the AN/ARC-18 (Fig. 5-41b), was devised, consisting of two ARC-1 sets in series and a transmit/receive switching unit, all mounted in an airplane positioned to act as a relay station (Fig. 5-41c). This broadened the usefulness as well as the range of these sets. Development was also pursued to increase the operating frequency to 225–350 MHz (AN/ARC-12 radio set shown in Fig. 5-42) and 225–400 MHz (AN/ARC-19 radio set shown in Fig. 5-43). Eleven hundred ARC-12 radio sets were produced by Western Electric.

Just as the Navy was able to quickly outfit its aircraft with the necessary line-of-sight VHF communications equipment by adapting the 233A radio set while development of a new set was under way, the Signal Corps, acting for the Air Force, was able to achieve similar goals. Just before Pearl Harbor day, it requested the development of radio equipment that would add a line-of-sight VHF capability to the high-frequency, long-range

CONTROL UNIT
C-266 (XN-2)/ARC-19

CONTROL UNIT
C-267 (XN-2)/ARC-19

CONTROL UNIT
C-268 (XN-2)/ARC-19

Fig. 5-43. AN/ARC-19 radio set—similar to the ARC-12 set but covered a wider frequency band.

Fig. 5-44. SCR-274/ARC-5 radio set which added line-of-sight capability to the standard SCR-274 multiband equipment.

SCR-274 system developed earlier. This new VHF equipment (Fig. 5-44), coded the AN/ARC-5 radio set, orginally specified operation on preset frequencies in three VHF frequency bands. This arrangement was modified during development to correspond with state-of-the-art progress in obtaining improved performance from receiver and transmitter vacuum tubes and circuits at these very high frequencies. The development was eventually expanded to provide operation over the full 100- to 150-MHz band. The improved equipment included a narrow receiver bandwidth (which would reduce interference and increase the number of usable channels), remote selection of 10 channels, and quartz crystal frequency control for both the receiver and transmitter. Over 35,000 of these radio sets were built and delivered from 1943 through V-J Day in 1945.

5.2.6 Other Radio Equipment

The tank and the Field Artillery radio sets, together with the various Signal Corps and Navy aircraft radio sets, were major contributions to military communications during World War II. However, other Bell Labs-designed radio equipment also played vital, if not so dramatic, roles.

One of these was the runway localizer receiver. Before the war Bell Labs had developed, and Western Electric had produced, a small radio receiver for Pan American Airways and other airline customers that operated at a VHF frequency to localize an approaching airplane with respect to the landing strip. These sets were found to be of such inestimable help at military airfields, especially during bad weather, that tens of thousands of the small RC-103 runway localizer receivers were ordered and used throughout the wide-ranging air warfare.

A marker-beacon receiver and a glide-path receiver had also been developed along with the localizer receiver to form the airplane complement of an instrument landing system. (Companies other than Western Electric developed the ground equipment.) Accordingly, quantities of the marker-beacon and the glide-path receivers were also produced for military use, although not in such large numbers as the localizer receiver.

Another significant development for the Navy was the ZBX and later the ZB3 homing receivers, designed to permit carrier-based aircraft pilots to find their home base as both aircraft and surface vessel maneuvered. The transmitter aboard the carrier radiated a signal from a rotating antenna at about 250 MHz. As the antenna was rotated through 360 degrees, tone modulation on the radio carrier was keyed in Morse code letters (A, B, C, etc.) around the points of the compass. By this means, each pilot would hear the code letter for his direction with respect to the aircraft carrier. At other times he would receive no signal. Knowing that, for example, the letter *P* was southeast, a pilot could fly in a northwest direction, keep on the *P* code and reach the carrier. If a change in carrier location required a corresponding change from the northwest path, the pilot would receive a different code that would tell him to make a course correction. This system was very effective. The use of UHF at that time provided secure transmission because the frequency band was not then used by the Japanese. Security could be further enhanced by periodic changes of the direction codes.

The ZBX receiver used several UHF-type tubes commonly known as acorn tubes. Thousands of the ZB-type receivers were manufactured during World War II. Many pilots assigned to the Pacific theater owed their safe return to their carrier bases to the homing receiver.

Other Bell Labs radio designs that were helpful during the war were the 33A and 34A radio transmitters previously developed for Bell System mobile radio and for use in airline ground radio. These amplitude-modulated radio transmitters operated over a 3- to 13-MHz band and delivered an RF carrier power of 350 watts. The Signal Corps found a number of these sets useful in a variety of ground radio systems.

The radio telephone equipment described in this chapter, as well as equipment supplied by other organizations, required microphones and headsets in much greater numbers than the large quantities of radio sets.[58] Literally hundreds of thousands of T-17 hand-held microphones, T-30 throat microphones, and under-helmet headsets were developed by Bell Labs and built by Western Electric. Quartz crystals were another component required in extraordinary numbers. The large number of FT/241A crystal units needed for the tank sets has already been mentioned. In addition, other quartz crystals were also developed and produced in large quantities (millions) for other equipment, such as the CR-1A crystal in the 5- to 10-MHz band of the ARC-1 radio sets, and for equipment manufactured by other companies.

Every section of Bell Labs was useful to the military departments during the war. However, all the aircraft and tank radio sets covered in this section were developed and engineered through production by a group of engineers, technicians, and draftsmen in the Graybar-Varick building on Varick Street in New York City throughout the war. In addition to developing all design aspects of the new sets, they also took care of the more mundane jobs—recommending and testing substitutes for critical materials and components, clearing up shop troubles, and writing specifications and instruction books.

VI. MULTICHANNEL MICROWAVE RADIO RELAY SYSTEM— AN/TRC-6

While the mobile radio equipment described above made up the major part of the tactical communication systems designed and built during the war, a far different ground-based field system deserves mention. This

---

[58] See also Section 3.1, Chapter 4.

was the AN/TRC-6 radio set developed at the Signal Corps' request to provide a multichannel trunk-line type of communication to and from Army field headquarters.   This set was so new in concept at the time that the development personnel for the RF portions were selected from the Radio Research departments at West Street and the Holmdel and Deal locations.   The multiplexing equipment was developed by engineers selected from the Transmission Department at West and at Varick Streets.

The design of this set owed much to prewar Bell Labs research and development in microwave and carrier telephone.   As a result of this prewar work, Bell System management was well aware of the postwar possibilities for commercial application of microwave relay systems.   For this reason, AT&T continued to sponsor Bell Labs' fundamental research on aspects of microwave systems that might later have commercial value.   Specific designs aimed at trial systems meeting military requirements were covered in the usual manner by contract between the Signal Corps and Western Electric.

As it turned out, later commercial relay systems operated on quite different modulation principles, but the success of the Army system stimulated considerable interest in radio relay as a commercial communication medium both within and outside the Bell System.   A number of system elements based on the Bell Labs fundamental research were incorporated in a number of the commercial systems.

The AN/TRC-6 was an eight-channel, time-division, microwave radio-telephone system using pulse position modulation, which could be used for carrier telegraph and other signals as well as telephone.   It operated on frequencies in the region of 5,000 MHz and was intended as a radio relay system on trunk routes requiring several speech channels for the use of a field army.   It was capable of high-grade two-way communication over continental distances.   The equipment, shown in Fig. 5-45, could be transported by truck and be set up and put into operation within a few hours.

Though each link was limited essentially to line-of-sight operation up to a maximum of about 100 miles,[59] links could be placed in tandem to cover much greater distances.   The system used 50-foot guyed aluminum towers, which supported antennas with 5-foot parabolic reflectors.   The transmitters and receivers were of small size and were mounted directly behind the antennas.   The transmitters produced a few watts of power using reflex klystrons.   In an immediately subsequent part of the development, the radio equipment was placed on the ground and used only a single antenna, which was directed at a plane reflector at the top of a tower. With this arrangement, waveguide filters were used to separate the transmitting band from the receiving band of frequencies.   Because of the high directivities, the small transmitting power used, and the type of modulation, several pieces of equipment could be operated in reasonable

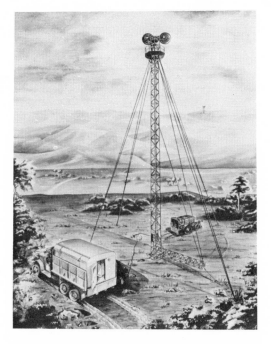

Fig. 5-45. AN/TRC-6 radio set—first micro-wave multichannel communication equip-ment.

proximity. In addition to the radio equipment, there was multiplexing equipment housed in a truck.

Perhaps the most important feature of the equipment was the use of pulse modulation. In the unmodulated condition, the transmissions consisted of a 4-microsecond pulse for synchronizing, followed by eight 1-microsecond pulses, one for each of the eight channels. This sequence was called a frame. The voice modulation of each channel varied the timing of the pulse of that channel so that it came earlier or later in time than with no modulation, depending linearly upon the amplitude and phase of the voice at the instant when the pulse was generated.

This equipment operated on the principle that if two or more samples of the amplitude of a speech wave were taken per cycle of the highest speech frequency, the whole speech wave could be reproduced from these samples. Eight thousand samples per second were taken from each of the eight channels, which required an equal number of frames per second to be transmitted. The equipment operated on a stop-start basis from the synchronizing pulses, which initiate the opening of each of the eight gates

[59] This was the maximum capability of the equipment, assuming adequate earth clearance was available. Over flat terrain, the nominal distance between 50-foot towers was limited by earth clearance to 25 to 30 miles.

in succession to separate the channels. The receiving multiplex equipment converted the pulse position or time modulation into pulse length modulation by initiating a new pulse that started when the received pulse arrived and continued to the end of the time allotted to that channel. The pulse length modulation was then converted into speech by passing it through a low-pass filter. As with subsequent pulse systems, slicers were used that made the equipment operate on only the center 5 percent of the amplitude of the received pulse, which thus greatly reduced the effects of noise and interference.

Since little information was available on the performance that could be expected from microwave equipment of this sort, the four development models delivered in November 1943 were subjected to extensive field tests jointly with the Signal Corps. Two-way voice transmission over radio links totaling 1,600 miles and one-way tests over 3,200 miles were successfully conducted. To do this, ten radio sets were set up to form five two-way eight-channel systems, each operating simultaneously over the same 40-mile air path. The five links and eight channels could then be connected in tandem to make a 1,600-mile two-way circuit or a 3,200 mile one-way circuit.

One of the tests was to set up and operate the equipment between Catalina Island and the California mainland. The effects of interference between the direct wave and the reflected wave from the ocean were found to be very detrimental. The system of vertical space diversity afterwards used extensively on microwave circuits was devised at this time. In this system, one antenna was placed above another in such a position that if the direct and reflected waves directly opposed each other at one antenna, they would add in phase at the other antenna. The receivers that were used with these antennas were then connected for diversity reception in the usual manner. So far as is known, this was the first use of this diversity system.

A total of 8 preproduction models and 84 production equipments performed significant service in both the European and Pacific theaters of World War II. As the Allied armies moved forward on a broad front in the last stages of the European hostilities (in December 1944 and later), the U.S. Army used the AN/TRC-6 equipment extensively, particularly in the Rhine Valley, as the major communication trunk to and from headquarters. As late as 1950 an AN/TRC-6 link was used between General MacArthur's headquarters in the Dai Ichi Building in Tokyo and the high-frequency transoceanic radio stations some miles away as insurance against the loss of wire lines by storm or sabotage.

Chapter 6

Overview of the War Years

The total wartime effort grew out of the individual efforts of a large group of dedicated and talented people. In addition, management practices of promotion from within meant that at Bell Laboratories there existed an extensive network of diversified capabilities made up of people with knowledge of one another's abilities. As a result, transitions from peacetime to wartime projects could be effected rapidly. Moreover, there existed a broad base of knowledge of acoustics and electrical communications that was extremely valuable in the fields of radar and underwater sound as well as in systems more nearly related to the conventional peacetime communication systems.

This base of knowledge extended to a deep understanding of materials, which led to important contributions in the production of synthetic rubber after supplies of natural rubber were cut off by the war. Other materials-related projects resulted in the delivery during the war of up to 25 million quartz-crystal units per year for armed forces equipment, and the solution of a difficult barrier-diffusion problem that allowed the separation of the U_{235} isotope needed for the atom bomb. In another development, a Bell Laboratories employee with an interest in rocketry did work that led to the invention of the bazooka, a rocket-propelled missile.

I. THE PEOPLE AND THE JOB

It is only fitting to begin with the people who created the technology and combined its products into highly complex and successful systems. Those who participated in the Bell System effort undoubtedly recall World War II with varied emotions. To some it was a period of exciting and rapid advance in communications technology, which was largely an extension of achievements in the prewar years. Technical developments, related in other volumes of this history, had by the late thirties led to a common carrier network covering the country, which was gradually being extended abroad by overseas radio. For many who had been working in this field, the war meant a rapid extension of communications (largely by telegraph) on a global basis, meeting not only the day-to-day requirements of business

---

Principal authors: J. W. Emling and F. J. Biondi

but also the special needs of rapid and secret communication characteristic of military operations. Others adapted their knowledge and experience with radio, based on limited commercial applications, to meet the much greater field of use brought about by highly mobile warfare.

Somewhat farther removed from the prewar effort was the application of work in the microwave field, which was still in the research phase before the war. It was groundwork in this field that played a large part in the pulse modulation systems first used in the war years and in the extensive work on radar. Many a research scientist whose prior interest in wave propagation, diodes, waveguides, and pulse modulation techniques had been largely an academic search for fundamental knowledge found himself a practicing technologist helping to design complex systems in which he had little previous concern. To many scientists, such an excursion into areas of application was a new and fascinating experience, in some cases leading to a permanent change in technical interest and in all cases providing a greatly expanded understanding of the relation between theory and practice.

Still other areas of the wartime effort had a basic connection with prewar communications experience but developed along lines only remotely connected with the background of the people involved. Examples were radar (with its associated fire control systems) and underwater acoustics. In both instances the initial effort began with small groups having a related background of experience, but the war effort grew so fast and so broadly that the projects were soon staffed by technicians who had not even a remote previous connection with them. Designers of telephone switching and transmission systems soon found themselves transformed into developers of microwave systems and radar equipment. They became the inventors of computing devices for fire control and worked in new areas of acoustics where little was previously known about propagation characteristics or other fundamentals. Here the success achieved was attributable not only to the high quality of the technical personnel and their sound training in fundamentals but also to their eagerness to accept the challenge of new fields. Many of these people must still recall the thrill that came from the challenge and the satisfaction in demonstrating an ability to achieve and even exceed the goals confronting them. To some, the tasks presented not only an intellectual challenge but also a physical and psychological challenge as their technical missions put them in submarines and aircraft in war zones in the far corners of the world. Many a "desk engineer" must recall with satisfaction his response to the emergencies met in line of duty in a field so far from that anticipated when he first began Bell System employment.

The new experiences and the excitement of advancing much needed technology undoubtedly played a large part in the success of the Bell Labs-Western Electric war effort. But not all jobs were glamorous and exciting. Many must have seemed pedestrian and frustrating to jobholders working far from the scene of war on highly essential work under intense pressure, often with low priorities for needed materials.

Regardless of the job, one characteristic of the worker stands out clearly: the spirit of dedication. The devotion to the job and the willingness to work countless hours to achieve success exceeded all other motivations except possibly the universal belief that no matter how difficult the goal, a way would be found to achieve it. It was a period of unfailing confidence in the power of technology and the capability of the practitioner. Perhaps this is only another way of saying that wartime morale was at a high peak. But in looking back, this statement seems too simple to do justice to the participants, even though some of this wartime spirit was a carry-over of organizational morale and the faith in cooperation that was an accepted work pattern in the Bell System long before World War II.

II. MANAGEMENT TECHNIQUES

Everyone on the technical team faced problems in adapting to wartime conditions, which involved not only tasks in unfamiliar fields but also unusually long hours and heavy pressure for the rapid achievement of results. An initial major problem was the transition of Bell Labs from communications systems to related but quite different and unfamiliar fields. This transition required an orderly termination of communications projects, as logical stopping points were reached, and the reorganization of the people into new groups best suited to the military projects taking shape. While most of the technologists had broad, solidly based backgrounds, it was still necessary to make certain that each new organization was best suited to its job and was staffed with capable people so that the transition could be made with minimum lost time.

Fortunately, it had been the custom of Bell Labs to give responsibility to all levels of the organization and to promote from the ranks. Consequently, each level was, through long association, familiar with the background and capabilities of a large number of people. When organizational changes were required, the period for "getting acquainted" at Bell Labs was short in comparison with the time required to develop such rapport in other companies.

The transition problems were also reduced by an early start at Bell Labs. For a number of years Bell Labs had handled communications-related projects for the military and had kept the latter well informed on R and D that might be of value. Cooperation with the U.S. Navy was particularly close, and as early as 1937 the Navy approached Bell Labs with a radar research proposal. Beginning about the same time, groups from the Signal Corps and the academic community were brought to Bell Labs at Holmdel, New Jersey, for briefings on microwave and other advanced research work being conducted there. Bell System management correctly foresaw the possibility of United States entry into the war and, in light of its previous experience, realized that this would require an intensive mobilization of technologists.[1] This early perception not only gave management time for an orderly transition but also stimulated Frank B. Jewett, President of Bell Labs, and other high-level management personnel to promote the activities of their professional colleagues, as in the formation of the National Defense Research Committee (NDRC), needed to mobilize scientific and technical skills in wartime.

The Bell Labs policy of promotion from the ranks also helped with another management problem. This was the necessity for achieving interchange of ideas and information between groups working under conditions of great secrecy. Bell Labs had long before discovered the value of encouraging free interchange on scientific matters, both within and outside the organization. Technical memoranda were widely distributed within Bell Labs, and papers on technical subjects were frequently presented before professional societies. *The Bell System Technical Journal* and the *Bell Laboratories Record* were founded in 1922 and 1925, respectively, to make information about new technology freely available to all.[2] Wartime conditions, of course, limited information to those with a "need to know," a situation which naturally encouraged duplication of effort. Fortunately, however, duplication could often be avoided in Bell Labs, since the broad knowledge of the organization by top-level managers frequently enabled them to tap existing sources of information for immediate use instead of setting up new projects that would only repeat previous efforts. The need for high-level technical direction and coordination of classified projects that proved so helpful in Bell Labs undoubtedly played a significant part in establishing the NDRC in 1940.

Other factors also helped Bell Labs management in the effective and rapid transition to war work. In early 1939 AT&T saw the signs of approaching war in Europe and recognized the inevitable demands that would be made on communications and all kinds of technology, particularly if the United States became involved. The Bell System was highly experienced in meeting emergency situations, and AT&T encouraged both Bell Labs and Western Electric to plan ahead for such contingencies. The close teamwork which had long tied the Bell operating companies, R and D, and production into one integrated system greatly facilitated the flow of information required for such planning; hence when complete mobi-

---

[1] At the time of the Pearl Harbor attack, about 30 percent of Bell Labs activity was devoted to defense activities.

[2] These publications were not confined to presenting developments within Bell Labs. The classic papers by K. K. Darrow on "Some Contemporary Advances in Physics," prepared largely to interpret subatomic research in terms useful to the communications engineer, were published in the *Bell System Technical Journal* between 1923 and 1939 and became one of the most popular features of that journal among readers outside the Bell System.

lization for war came, the Bell System was ready to meet not only the many military demands for additional communications facilities but also the need for the design and production of combat materiel based on high-level technology. The design and production of materiel were greatly promoted by the years of close cooperation between Bell Labs and Western Electric. The formation during the war of the Western Electric Field Engineering Force and the Bell Labs "cage groups" in Western Electric factories further promoted this cooperation and established patterns that evolved further in the postwar years.

III. INFLUENCE OF PRIOR RESEARCH AND DEVELOPMENT

A capable and enthusiastic group of employees, together with an imaginative management experienced in R and D techniques, was undoubtedly important in achieving success in the multitude of military projects undertaken by Bell Labs. Fully as important was the long-existing practice of preparing for the future through fundamental research, which provided the basic knowledge for undertaking technical projects. Such research was conducted whenever it seemed likely that it might ultimately be of use in communication or related projects. Often it was years before a commercial Bell System application became economically practical. Sometimes the research proved to be of little value to the Bell System but was of inestimable value to others in the scientific community.[3]

By the late 1930s Bell Labs had developed a broad base of knowledge in communications and was launched on many research projects of great promise. All this was put to work and expanded wherever it appeared to benefit the war effort. In acoustics, for example, much of the work on shipboard announcing systems and other applications in high ambient noise areas was based on the knowledge of speech and hearing acquired years earlier by Harvey Fletcher, J. C. Steinberg, and others. Similarly, the analytic methods used in designing loudspeakers and telephone instruments were put to work in designing and calibrating underwater transducers.

The work on radar and microwave transmission serves as a more detailed example of the research pattern and the manner in which it provides a basis for many lines of development. Bell research on radio began well before the 1920s and provided much of the fundamental knowledge later put to use in building overseas systems and early mobile equipment. By 1932 the research on ultrashortwaves was showing promise for radio application of many kinds, ranging from land-based radio relay systems to

---

[3] For example, K. G. Jansky, in his studies of radio propagation, discovered the basis for radio astronomy. His propagation work was continued and proved of great value to the Bell System and other organizations, but he did not continue his work on radio astronomy after it became apparent that it was not likely to be of use to the Bell System. Jansky's work was later applied by astronomers and became a very useful tool in their field.

mobile and broadcast systems. As a consequence, a "case"[4] was established to cover such work. By 1934 a radio link was established between Green Harbor and Provincetown, Massachusetts, and was used to study propagation and the special techniques required for handling very high frequencies. Two years later considerable progress had been made in understanding propagation, and the construction of amplifiers had developed to the point where a model of a 150-MHz repeater could be constructed and used experimentally. By 1938 the workable frequency of amplifiers had been extended to 1,000 MHz, and frequency modulation had been explored. By 1940 propagation of frequencies up to 6,000 MHz and the use of horn antennas were part of the study plan.

Also in the early 1930s, a research case (i.e., one paid for by AT&T) had been set up to study ultra-high-frequency transmission by waveguide. Initially, this was broadly exploratory, but before long investigations were being made of waveguide filters, horn antennas, waveguide transmission to elevated antennas, etc., all matters of interest in microwave radio communication. To some extent the work on the two cases had begun to merge and, though practical application to relay communications was some years away, much basic work had been done that could support the military radar and radio projects, which were beginning to occupy so much Bell Labs manpower. Undoubtedly the foresight which initiated the ultra-shortwave research in 1932 and its subsequent yearly funding was, five to eight years later, beginning to pay off handsomely in a communication-related field not dreamed of when the case was originated.

IV. CHEMISTRY AND MATERIALS RESEARCH

The long history of Bell Labs research in chemistry and materials science, going back to before World War I, proved of inestimable value to the nation as it faced the second World War. The sustained programs of work in magnetic materials, dielectrics, and piezoelectric crystals made it possible, as the needs arose, for Bell Labs to make significant contributions, many of them critical.

A national crisis arose when the war in the Pacific put an end to the supply of natural rubber from southeast Asia. Though the United States rubber companies had been experimenting with synthetic substitutes, there was no adequate replacement. Bell Laboratories, through the work of W. O. Baker, C. S. Fuller, and J. H. Heiss made essential contributions

---

[4] In Bell System parlance a case is an authorization for funding work in a specific area to be paid for by either of the two Bell Labs owners, AT&T or Western Electric. The former owner pays for research and fundamental development; the latter for specific systems development. Cases are commonly authorized for a year, the amount of funding being based on a review of prior work and proposals for the forthcoming year. The research work done under the cases discussed here was paid for by AT&T, although much of it ultimately led to military development. Expense resulting from work on specific military projects was charged to cases covered by military contracts.

in characterization and control of new compounds which proved to be highly successful.[5] The Bell Labs work was part of a program of the United States Office of Rubber Reserve, in which a number of industrial and university laboratories took part.

In the years before World War II, chemists at Bell Labs had been studying the relation of mechanical strength to molecular structure in polymers, a class of substances which includes synthetic plastics and synthetic rubber. Fundamental investigations by Fuller, Baker, and N. R. Pape had shown that crystallinity was an important contributor to strength of the material. From this and other basic discoveries, much was learned about the intimate details of polymer molecular structure.

In the case of synthetic rubber, Baker and his associates developed ways of compounding butadiene and styrene, the key ingredients, so that a uniform, reproducible, superior product could be manufactured. They advanced new theories of chemical combination and developed methods of measurement and control of processing. The program for the Office of Rubber Reserve, in which chemists of Bell Labs were central, produced the first GR-S (Government Rubber-Styrene) in December 1943, just 16 months after the initiation of the project. By 1945, annual production of GR-S exceeded 700,000 tons. The achievement was vital to the successful prosecution of the war effort, and the science and technology that came from it formed the basis of the subsequent synthetic rubber industry.

Important Bell Labs contributions were made in the supply of many other strategic materials and new materials for electronic devices. Quartz crystals and techniques for large-scale production were jointly developed and perfected by the Bell Labs/Western Electric organizations, who produced the major portion of the nation's output. Manufacture of quartz crystal units jumped from a few thousand per year in the late 1930s to over 25 million during the peak war years. Low-loss steatites, a superior insulation for high-power vacuum tubes, were produced as a replacement for an unavailable natural product (Italian lavite). Thermistors made of semiconducting oxides were developed in Bell Labs, and the knowledge was made available to outside manufacturers to meet military needs in microwave instrumentation. Deposited carbon resistors of very high precision and matched temperature coefficient were developed for use in gun directors and radar bombsights. The silvered mica capacitor was another contribution from Bell Labs and Western Electric—an innovation in improved stability, precision of initial adjustment, and low temperature coefficient. Out of the basic chemistry research came impregnants and stabilizers which gave rise to greatly improved paper-dielectric capacitors used in large quantities in military electronics.

The foregoing are a few examples of how scientific discoveries and

---

[5] A more complete account of this work appears in the third volume of the *History*.

technological innovations in the field of chemistry and materials were directly applied to the nation's defense in the World War II years. In the following chapters more will be said about postwar applications of these and other materials and devices in the continuing support of our defense effort.

V. SOME ATYPICAL PROJECTS

Only a few of the major Bell wartime projects have been discussed in this history. These are good examples, but there were many similar projects, the treatment of which has been precluded by lack of space. In addition, a number of projects in which Bell System personnel were involved did not follow the usual pattern. Two of these projects will serve as illustrations.

One of the cases of far-reaching importance was the work of C. N. Hickman, who, in 1918 and 1919, before joining Bell Labs, had worked with Professor Robert H. Goddard, the early American advocate of rocket missiles. Although Hickman's work at Bell Labs had no connection with rockets, he had never lost his interest in those devices. On June 20, 1940, he wrote a memorandum to Dr. Jewett pointing out the many potential benefits of these devices and suggesting that the NDRC initiate work on rocketry.[6] The military was, on the whole, unenthusiastic about low-velocity, inaccurate weapons, but the Navy saw some possibilities in a jet-accelerated armor-piercing bomb and suggested that the NDRC investigate the possibilities. As a result, by the end of July, Hickman's work at Bell Labs was temporarily halted and he found himself the head of Section H (for Hickman) of Division A of the NDRC. The large field of research and development that opened up in this area is beyond the scope of this history, but one of the devices that played a large part in land warfare was the bazooka. This grew out of work by the U.S. Army Ordnance Department to develop an armor-piercing projectile that could be fired by an infantryman from a hand-held launcher. A successful projectile based on the well-known "Munroe effect" was devised.[7] Even though a high velocity was not required by this device, the launching problem was not easily solved until Captain (later Colonel) L. A. Skinner, working with Hickman, designed a small rocket propellant and a simple, recoilless tube launcher that was light in weight and protected the user from blast. The "bazooka" was thus born; for the first time the foot soldier could fight back against the tank. Later Section H was responsible for developing an even more accurate and safer "super-bazooka" as well as

---

[6] See John E. Burchard (ed.), *Rockets, Guns and Targets* (Boston: Little, Brown, 1948), pp. 17–18.

[7] According to the Munroe effect, discovered by C. E. Munroe in 1888, a shaped charge of explosive that presents a concave surface against a metal will do more damage than a flat charge.

many other applications of rocketry. Hickman's hobby, which caused him to write to Jewett in 1940, had borne good fruit.[8]

Another somewhat atypical project was related to the development of the atomic bomb and grew out of the close connection between Bell Labs researchers and the academic community. The history of the interaction of Bell Labs—first with Columbia University, then with the Office of Scientific Research and Development (OSRD), and later with the Strategic Alloy Materials Lab (SAM) of the Manhattan District Project (MDP), which was later absorbed by the Atomic Energy Commission (AEC) and succeeded by the Energy Research Development Administration (ERDA) and now by the U.S. Department of Energy (DOE)—was recorded in volumes written while the history was fresh, in the late 1940s, and was then placed under security regulations, not to be released until some future date when such release would not be harmful to the national interest. Similarly, all patent disclosures of substance were classified under security regulations. Therefore, much of what follows was pieced together from material published in a number of publicly available histories of the Manhattan Project.

The earliest involvement of Bell Labs personnel was that of Harvey Fletcher, then Director of Physical Research, as a member of the Reference Committee. This committee was organized in the spring of 1940 by the National Research Council, the operating arm of the National Academy of Sciences, to voluntarily reduce the publication of papers, in particular on uranium fission, in accordance with a policy applicable to all fields of science with possible military interest.

A second involvement was that of Frank B. Jewett, who was President of Bell Labs until October 1940 and also President of the National Academy of Sciences. In his NAS role, Jewett appointed a Reviewing Committee in the spring of 1941 to evaluate the importance of the uranium problem and to recommend to the government the level of expenditure at which this problem should be investigated. B. Gherardi was a member of this committee, but he was unable to serve because of illness. By June 1941 O. E. Buckley, then Bell Labs president, was also added as a member. These individuals were senior members of the science community; their involvement reflected the high esteem in which members of Bell Labs management were held by their peers and the U.S. government.

As often happens, the Bell Labs experimental work with the Manhattan Project began in an oblique way. At the time, early 1939, William

---

[8] This is not the only case where scientific interest far beyond his normal activities led a Bell Labs employee to a highly valuable discovery. R. R. Williams, who later became Chemical Director of Bell Labs, had become interested in Vitamin B1 in the early thirties. Working with associates at Bell Labs and Columbia University, he developed an improved process for isolating the vitamin that several years later led him to a process for its synthesis, an achievement that won for him the Elliot Creson Medal. His work in this field was carried out apart from his research activities at Bell Labs, except for the encouragement and stimulation he received from his colleagues and Bell management.

Shockley and Foster Nix were studying order-disorder phenomena in certain alloys; and at nearby Columbia University, where many Bell Labs staff members were pursuing graduate degrees under Bell Labs sponsorship, a fertile team of physicists—including E. Fermi, J. R. Dunning, and G. B. Pegram—was involved in experiments with neutron collisions with the nuclei of large unstable atoms. In the Columbia Chemistry Department, H. C. Urey had concentrated deuterium.

Shockley and Nix visited Columbia to seek advice in the use of neutrons in their order-disorder studies. At that time, 1939, they learned of the early experiments of the bombardment of U_{235} with neutrons and the subsequent fission and of the proposal in the Columbia community to devise methods to enrich the presence of U_{235} in a mixture of U_{235} and U_{238}. (U_{235} occurs at a level of 0.7 percent in natural uranium.) H. C. Urey was given this responsibility by the Uranium Committee, now working through OSRD. Urey was working with J. R. Dunning and others on methods of devising porous barriers that could be used as gaseous diffusion barriers to concentrate U_{235} in its gaseous form as the hexafluoride. Through Nix's interaction, Bell Labs was encouraged to seek an OSRD contract to study the use of pressed powdered metals to produce such barriers, first in disc and later in sheet form. At that time, early 1942, Nix formed a small group, including Donald MacNair, George Clement, and Elmer C. Larsen. Later in 1942 Frank J. Biondi joined the group.

Early approaches failed to produce useful material, according to physical tests of strength, porosity, and the ability to efficiently separate mixtures of He and CO_2 used at Bell Labs as a test mixture to avoid having to work with the radioactive uranium hexafluoride mix of isotopes.

While these experiments were being conducted at Bell Labs with a small group, which at its maximum had three members of technical staff and eight aides and assistants, extensive efforts involving many hundreds of scientists and engineers were under way at Columbia University, the M. W. Kellogg Company (and later, its subsidiary, the Kellex Corporation), the Houdaille-Hershey Corporation, and elsewhere in attempts to produce porous barrier materials by a variety of methods.

By the summer of 1942 the engineering functions of the Planning Board of the Uranium Committee became the now famous Manhattan District. And at Bell Labs, by mid-1943, Foster Nix left and was succeeded by A. H. White. E. C. Tolman joined the program and E. C. Larsen left to join the chemistry group at Murray Hill. Among others involved were H. E. Kern, E. J. Becker, H. Sutcliffe, A. H. Williams, A. C. Korn, T. C. Lew, and N. J. Ross.

The Bell Labs program had, by 1944, evolved a process whose product was characterized by a separation factor higher than that for materials of competing processes and at reasonable rates of flow, together with good mechanical properties and resistance to corrosion of the process gas.

Samples of the Bell Labs material were being checked weekly by a test lab at Columbia and at the Kellex Corporation. The process was due primarily to F. J. Biondi, with contributions in the later stages of development from E. C. Tolman.

By 1944 it became evident that it was time to transfer the effort of the group at Bell Labs to organizations with facilities of the type needed to make larger quantities of the barrier. None of the Western Electric factories had facilities of the proper kind, because they were crowded and hard pushed in their own war efforts.

Part of the program was taken to the Bakelite Division of the Union Carbide Corporation in Bound Brook, New Jersey, and other parts to the Linde Division of Union Carbide at Tonawanda, New York. F. J. Biondi and E. C. Tolman went to the Strategic Alloy Materials (SAM) Lab at Columbia to transfer Bell Labs technology to that organization. As the competing processes were shown to be less satisfactory, the Bell Labs process was adopted by the SAM Lab and became the process by which the barriers used in the gaseous diffusion plant, K25, at Oak Ridge, Tennessee, were eventually fabricated.

While the barrier production effort was going on at West Street, the New York City location of Bell Labs, a group supervised by G. T. Kohman, including N. B. Hannay, J. J. Fry, E. C. Larsen, W. E. Campbell, H. A. Sauer and K. H. Storks, was examining barrier materials for their ability to withstand the corrosive nature of hexafluoride-type process gases, especially in the presence of small leaks, without substantially altering the porosity or the separation efficiency. The results of this work were fed back to the barrier development group at West Street and helped convince the committee that chose the final barrier-making process of the good performance of the Bell Labs barrier.

After a series of small-scale trials and with the knowledge that the Bell Labs process was producing barrier material, the Bell Labs personnel were withdrawn from the project early in 1945 and were transferred to other, more conventional Bell Labs activities. More than 36 years later, the Bell Labs method is still the process chosen for fabricating the long-life, reliable barrier material not only in the Oak Ridge plant but also in the Paducah, Kentucky, and Portsmouth, Ohio, plants.

It was by this indirect route that a communications-oriented research organization played a part in the production of the atomic bomb. It illustrates not only the versatility of the communications R and D staff but the unpredictable benefits that so often result from the pursuit of fundamental research.

As one reviews the preceding sections, it seems rather obvious that man, management, and organization all played important roles in Bell Labs' war effort. These factors were noted in some comments by F. B. Jewett, on the Bell System philosophy of research, expressed rather informally in an internal letter written in 1942. Very much condensed, Jewett's conclusions, based on 40 years of Bell System experience, were as follows:

1. In the long run the greatest benefits to the Bell System result from the successful conduct of fundamental work; but, of necessity, our work must run the gamut from fundamental investigation to emergency work of a current nature.
2. The effectiveness of an R and D organization depends upon continuity of teamwork by a carefully selected group of skilled and trained scientists and engineers who have worked together continuously without being subjected to violent swings in personnel.
3. The real power of an R and D organization is grounded on the ability of people and their training, not on the particular skills that have been acquired in the course of that training. Such a group, accustomed to working as a stable team, will be understanding and flexible enough to adapt to changing programs required by the current demands of business or such emergency situations as war.

Throughout the war years as much long-range, fundamental work as practical was continued, but with goals adapted to the new circumstances. The reaction of Bell Labs personnel fully justified Jewett's expectations.

VI. THE END AND A BEGINNING

By late 1944 and early 1945 it was apparent that the end of the war could not be far off. While the precise dates could not be predicted, it was obvious that major military projects begun after 1944 would have little chance of affecting the war's outcome. As a consequence, Bell Labs' military effort was concentrated on completing projects nearing fruition or obviously useful in the immediate postwar years. Gradually, personnel became available for an orderly return to peacetime effort so that the long-deferred development and growth of the Bell System could continue. A few of the more urgent development projects that had been stopped upon the approach of war were restarted and gradually expanded as more manpower became available.

Everyone, in all walks of life, looked forward to V Day. Bell System personnel could look back on a period of great activity and the weariness accumulating in four or more years of work without letup. It would be a great relief to look forward to the activities of peacetime, but a perceptive individual could not help knowing that there would be no return to the life of the late 1930s.

Five years of communications shortages had to be overcome as soon as possible. The Bell System faced an enormous problem. Because of shortages in materials and manpower, wartime expansion had been limited to military necessities. None of the previously planned expansion and replacement of outside plant or switching systems had been possible.

New stations and services had been deferred and temporary expedients had been resorted to in place of needed replacement. All this is a story in itself, beyond the scope of this volume, but it is pertinent in showing that the pressures on all parts of the Bell System (Operating Telephone Companies, Bell Labs, and Western Electric) were enormous and remained so long after the war's end. When the war ended, some 2 million applicants were waiting for service. By 1951, 10 million new main-station telephones had been added to the system, but material shortages and the Korean crisis had by then prevented the complete fulfillment of service requests.

Meeting the pent-up demands for service after five years of shortages was only part of the problem. In addition, five years of rapidly growing technology had to be put to work; reducing costs, upgrading existing service, and supplying new services and systems were jobs immediately facing Bell Labs. The wartime pressures had been reduced, but it was easy to see that technological growth had speeded up the pace of life and that there would be little letup in the demands for communications R and D. Finally, the realist could see that the unconditional surrender of the enemy would not mean the end of growth in military technology and that there were still military areas where Bell Laboratories might be called upon to play a part.

The story of the continuing contributions of Bell System engineering and science in service to the nation in the postwar years (1945–1975) will be covered in the remainder of this volume. Subsequent volumes will resume the analysis of Bell System applications—those occurring after the first 50 years of telephony. Those volumes will include the important prewar contributions that laid the groundwork for Bell Labs contributions in the military field and for the application of rapidly expanding technology after the war.

Part II

Post-World War II—1945 to 1975

Introduction

THE PHASE-DOWN PERIOD

With the surrender of Japan in August 1945, World War II ended. Bell Laboratories' most important task in reducing its major R and D effort was to reassign personnel as quickly as possible to Bell System projects. With approximately 75 percent of the technical personnel working on military programs during the war, Bell Labs work for the Bell System had been limited to the engineering necessary to keep the nationwide and overseas communication network operating reliably. Now it was necessary to move rapidly into short- and long-range development projects dropped at the start of the war, such as nationwide dialing, broadband transmission for television, and basic research work such as that which led to the invention of the transistor. Fortunately, most of the organizational structure had been retained throughout the war.

A second part of the transition was the release of temporary employees. Personnel with relevant radio background and experience had been recruited from Bell System Operating Companies, Western Electric and, to a lesser extent, from outside fields such as broadcasting. These people augmented Bell Labs' technical staff and made important contributions to the war effort. With the war over, their companies were anxious to have them return to peacetime jobs. A small number of these temporary employees who had shown strong interest in, and adaptability for, R and D work were recruited as permanent employees with the consent of their previous employers.

The Whippany, N.J., Laboratory, entirely devoted to military work during the war, became the principal location for military work in the postwar years as a number of projects were transferred to it from other locations. However, many other locations continued military work in important support roles. A number of engineers, who had transferred to Whippany from Bell System departments before the war build-up, had become interested in the diversity of technical work offered by these projects and asked to remain at the Whippany location. In most cases these requests were honored with the consent of their original departments. The Whippany Laboratory also experienced a shift of some of its personnel back to the development of commercial products, particularly radio broadcasting equipment, carried on prior to World War II under the leadership of W. H. Doherty, the inventor of the Doherty high-efficiency amplifier for powerful AM broadcast transmitters (U.S. Patent No.

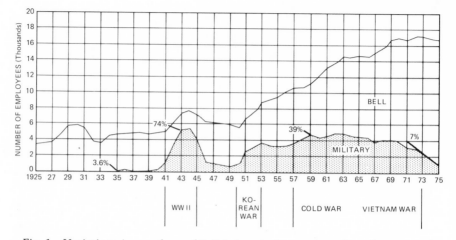

Fig. 1. Variations in numbers of Bell Laboratories personnel working on military programs.

2,210,028, filed April 1, 1936, issued August 6, 1940). Under the same leadership after World War II, Bell Laboratories developed and Western Electric manufactured an entire new line of FM broadcasting equipment and carried on laboratory development of a broadband television transmitter for the UHF band. Western Electric continued to manufacture broadcast transmitters until about 1950, when it was decided to concentrate production facilities on meeting the heavy postwar demand for telephones. Just prior to the Korean War, Bell Labs personnel were reassigned to military programs needing additional help.

During this period the military effort at Bell Labs, relative to total employees, declined from the peak of about 75 percent mentioned earlier to about 12 percent by 1950, as shown in Fig. 1. With the Korean War, the cold war, and the Vietnam War, the Department of Defense and the military services asked Bell Labs and Western Electric to take on major new programs that increased the Bell Labs R and D effort about 40 percent by 1960, as shown in the same illustration. Twenty-five years later, in 1975, the military effort had again dropped back to about 7 percent.

POSTWAR MILITARY PROGRAMS

At the end of World War II the military services, faced with large cutbacks in funding, had to make hard choices concerning which programs to cancel and which to continue. At Bell Labs a number of R and D projects that were already under way prior to the end of World War II were authorized for completion of development and manufacture. These were primarily short-term projects. In addition, long-range study and development efforts were requested that might lead to major improvements in the country's defense capabilities.

A number of radar developments started toward the end of World War II were based on fundamental developments carried on throughout the war. In the case of Navy fire control radars, laboratory work focused on complete automatic tracking with servo mounts exploiting the basic principles of negative feedback to obtain substantial improvements in accuracy with automatic angle tracking. These features were applied to a Navy Mark 25 fire control radar in the early stages of development at the end of the war. The Navy authorized continued development and manufacture. This is an example of a short-range postwar program in which the Navy wished to take advantage of many years of basic development during World War II to modernize its smaller postwar fleet with the most advanced equipment.

Another example of a relatively short-range program was an antiaircraft fire control system for the Army. Under the pressure of war needs, radars, computers, and command and control equipment were developed separately. A sound, system approach called for a fully integrated system in which all elements, except for the guns, would be developed as a unit. Such a system, known as T33 and later coded M33, was under way at Bell Labs at the end of the war. The Army requested that the development and manufacture of the system be continued to modernize its field army and continental air defense.

Bell Labs management was receptive to long-range military programs that would be challenging to the technical staff and that could become major steps forward in our country's defense. A number of projects requested of Bell Labs were turned down because they involved current technology that could be handled by any one of a number of other companies. Two examples of long-range programs undertaken for post-World War II development were a guided missile program for air defense, started under Army and Air Force authorization, and an automatic target evaluator and weapon assignment program for Navy ships. Both programs, starting with system studies followed by R and D laboratory and field tests, were well-matched to the broad-spectrum expertise of Bell Labs scientists and engineers. Furthermore, the armed services were enthusiastic to have Bell Labs start such programs and were prepared to fund the work adequately. With concern for future defense needs, Bell Labs felt that by allocating some of its resources to such long-range military programs it could most effectively serve the nation.

Division of Military Effort

In taking on new postwar military programs, the Bell Labs management tried to maintain a reasonable balance of available resources between the Army, Air Force, and Navy programs. A balance was not always possible, however, when international incidents required expedited development of a particular weapon. This occurred in 1950 at the time of the Korean

War when the government came to Western Electric and Bell Labs and asked for an intensified effort on the development and manufacture of the Nike missile air defense system. On other systems, such as the anti-ballistic missile (ABM) programs, the size of the development effort would have meant dropping all other military programs and expanding the size of Bell Laboratories if most of the development was to be carried out within Bell Labs. Rather than follow these unattractive options, Bell Labs sub-contracted major hardware developments on the ABM programs, retaining for itself overall system responsibility and specific developments for which it felt it was uniquely qualified.

Outline of Military and Other Government Programs

Some 30 years of specific system developments carried out by Western Electric and Bell Laboratories for the military services are covered in the following chapters on air defense, underwater systems, radar, tactical and strategic defense systems, and command and control. A chapter on communications describes the developments, installations, and operating services provided for the special needs of the military and other government agencies, including the Federal Aviation Agency and the National Aeronautics and Space Administration (NASA). Bell Laboratories broad system studies and exploratory programs for the military, such as advanced computer technology, radar-circuit innovations, millimeter-wave applications, and the like are covered in the chapter on military systems engineering and research. The final chapter on special projects highlights a number of important special assignments, projects, and developments carried out by Western Electric and Bell Labs for various government agencies under high priority. The general public is not fully aware of the responsibilities assumed by the Bell System in these assignments. The purpose of the chapter is to provide the background and objectives and to describe the manner in which Western Electric and Bell Labs have carried out the work. Important examples are the management support to the Sandia Corporation and the Bellcomm contributions to NASA.

Chapter 7

Air Defense

In the 30 years following World War II, Bell Laboratories and Western Electric played a principal role in the country's air defense. A major share of Bell Labs' military R and D effort was therefore devoted to this aspect of defense. The period 1945–1975 experienced a drastic change in offensive air-threat capability starting with high-speed, high-altitude bombers and later including intermediate- and intercontinental-range ballistic missiles (IRBMs and ICBMs) sometimes referred to collectively as the "ultimate threat." These threats were further complicated by nuclear warheads, the tactics of saturation multiple attacks, decoys, and rapid advances in the technology of electronic countermeasures. Part of the air defense program was the evolution of the United States weapons systems necessary to meet the step-by-step increase in offensive capability. Each of the system challenges required basic system studies, research, exploratory development, and laboratory testing that tapped the wide range of scientific and engineering talents at Bell Laboratories. When the government asked for early deployment of a weapons system, as it did during the Korean War, the full resources of Western Electric were applied to manufacture, quality control, field installation, training, and continued field engineering to assure high reliability and performance. The combined expertise of Bell Labs and Western Electric was also necessary in major R and D defense programs, such as the Antiballistic Missile (ABM) program, in which tests had to be carried out 8,000 miles from home base. In the ABM program, Bell Laboratories was responsible for system engineering, overall system development, and test planning, whereas Western Electric assumed full responsibility for transportation, equipment engineering, and installation and maintenance of the system elements. Early warning of approaching air threats was an important element in the country's overall defense and Western Electric and Bell Labs played important roles in developing and installing key early warning systems during the mid-1950s. These systems had to be installed in the arctic under the most difficult weather and logistic conditions. After a trial installation of one system element, the Air Force selected Western Electric and Bell Labs to be responsible for the complete system. Important parts of the remote warning systems were the innovative communications systems developed to meet rigid reliability requirements.

Principal author: C. A. Warren

I. AIR DEFENSE WEAPONS SYSTEMS

1.1 The T33/M33 Antiaircraft Fire Control System

The system approach to air defense weapons systems that formed the basis of Bell Laboratories' R and D work in the postwar years actually started in 1944—a year before the end of World War II. In 1944 the Army asked Bell Labs to undertake a study that would be the basis for the development of a fully integrated radar/computer antiaircraft fire control system. As a result of this study, which included a visit to the European theater of operations in the summer of 1944, development of an integrated fire control system, which was designated T33 and later coded M33, was begun in 1945. Earlier fire control systems were a collection of individual equipment elements gathered together from various sources and organized into working units by the military user.

The study had indicated that the new system should include a medium-range search radar and display facilities integrated with the control of a separate target-tracking radar to facilitate pickup of a designated target by the narrow-beam tracking system. Facilities were to be provided for manual, aided-manual, and automatic tracking of the target. An optical system was to be provided for orientation purposes and for target-tracking under conditions of adequate visibility. The computer, similar in principle to the M-9, was to include a number of improvements in ballistic design, setting of ballistic controls, and simplification of operating adjustments. Tactical control facilities were to enable the tactical control officer to monitor the complete engagement and to control the battery with visual and audible signals rather than over voice telephone links. The control officer was also to have automatic plotting boards for displaying present and predicted target positions in both horizontal and vertical planes. This new system was to include special facilities for the conduct of preparatory fire. The system, except for the acquisition antenna mount, was to be housed in a full trailer constructed of lightweight material to make it feasible for air transport. The system was designed to permit operation by as small a crew as possible. The trailer was to be heated and ventilated for the comfort of personnel and for optimum system operation. The new system was designed to make extensive use of plug-in components in order to facilitate maintenance and to reduce downtime.

The M33 system fulfilled the study objective of being complete except for the guns. It consisted of a specially designed van-type trailer for the radar and a flatbed trailer for transporting the acquisition antenna and a 400-Hz 35 kVA prime power generator unit. The tracking antenna was mounted on top of the radar trailer (shown in Fig. 7-1). A second van-type

Fig. 7-1.   Tracking antenna of the M33 fire control system mounted atop radar van.

Fig. 7-2.   Acquisition antenna of the M33 fire control system.

Fig. 7-3.   Typical tactical emplacement of the M33 fire control system.

trailer, similar to the radar trailer, housed the acquisition antennas during transport, spare parts, and test equipment. The acquisition antenna assembly (Fig. 7-2) sat on a demountable pedestal separate from the radar trailer. A typical tactical emplacement of the radar and antiaircraft guns is illustrated in Fig. 7-3.

Fig. 7-4 shows a layout of the components of the radar trailer. The tactical control console, in the center, is further illustrated in Fig. 7-5. It contains a control panel for directing the operation of the system and battery, the acquisition radar PPI (plan position indicator) and B-scope displays, and the computer control panel. In front of the console are the three plotting boards to display present and predicted positions of the target in the horizontal and vertical planes. To the left of the console is the computer cabinet. It contains power supplies, the major portion of the computing system, and the servos used to store the ballistic information and to provide coordinate conversion facilities and multiplying elements for the computing system. At the front end of the trailer (far right in Fig. 7-4) are mounted the radar power units and some of the radar components. This cabinet also contains the trailer's heating and ventilating unit. Facing it is the tracking console manned by the three tracking radar operators (Fig. 7-6). This console contains, in addition to the tracking radar scopes, a duplicate of the tactical control officer's acquisition display. Just above it (Fig. 7-7) are the eyepieces for the azimuth and elevation trackers for optical tracking. Another eyepiece is available for the use of the tactical control

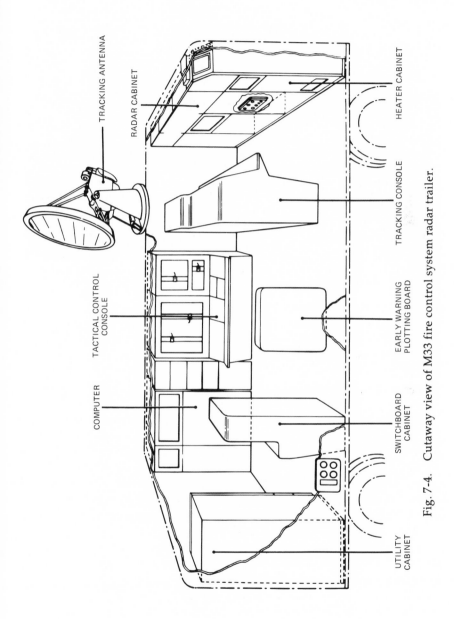

Fig. 7-4. Cutaway view of M33 fire control system radar trailer.

Fig. 7-5.   Tactical control console for plotting boards of the M33 fire control system.

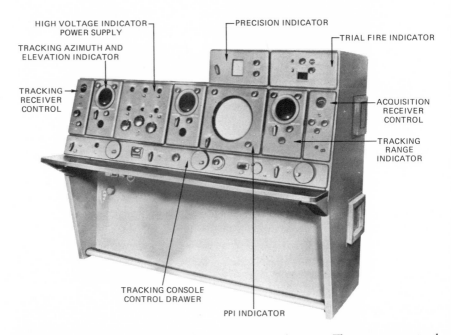

HIGH VOLTAGE INDICATOR
POWER SUPPLY

PRECISION INDICATOR

TRACKING AZIMUTH AND
ELEVATION INDICATOR

TRIAL FIRE INDICATOR

TRACKING
RECEIVER
CONTROL

ACQUISITION
RECEIVER
CONTROL

TRACKING
RANGE
INDICATOR

TRACKING CONSOLE
CONTROL DRAWER

PPI INDICATOR

Fig. 7-6.   Tracking console of the M33 fire control system. Three operators track azimuth, range, and elevation of target prior to automatic lock-on tracking.

Fig. 7-7. Optical sights for azimuth and elevation tracking operators on the tracking console of the M33 fire control system.

officer. The tracking antenna components (Fig. 7-8) are mounted on the roof during operation and stowed on a rack in the center of the trailer during travel. A small cord-type telephone switchboard and manual plotting board for external target data are included in the trailer. The normal operating crew for this system consisted of five people: three tracking operators, one acquisition operator, and the tactical control officer.

In a typical tactical situation (Fig. 7-3) the system operates as follows. The operating crew on duty performs certain routine operations more or less continuously to be ready for an engagement. The operation of the two radars is checked at intervals; the acquisition set may actually be in continuous operation. The ballistic controls on the computer are positioned to reflect the current meteorological conditions. At the guns, the power controls are checked periodically and, of course, the ammunition is kept ready. Target information derived from long-range early warning radars is fed continuously to the trailer from an antiaircraft artillery operations

Fig. 7-8.   Tracking antenna of the M33 fire control
system in operating position. Offset feedhorn was
rotated for conical lobing.

center and is manually plotted on an early warning plotting board
mounted in the trailer behind the tactical control officer. As a target of
potential interest comes within range of the acquisition radar, it is identified on the acquisition PPI. Two controllable electronic markers, a range
circle and an azimuth line, which are provided on this PPI, are positioned
on the target echo, or blip, by the acquisition operator. At an appropriate
time, the tactical control officer designates the target to the radar operators.
The system is so designed that upon designation the track radar can immediately be slewed to the range and azimuth of the electronic markers.
For this operation, the azimuth and range operators continue to follow
the target in range and azimuth on their acquisition displays, using a track
radar position marker. During this time the elevation operator searches
the track system in elevation until he sees the target echo on his A-scope.
The other two operators then turn their attention to their A-scopes, gate
the target, and switch to automatic tracking. The computer operator now
comes into the picture. When the track radar locks onto the target, dc
voltage data representing target X, Y, and H positions feed into the computer. After a few seconds the computer has measured the components

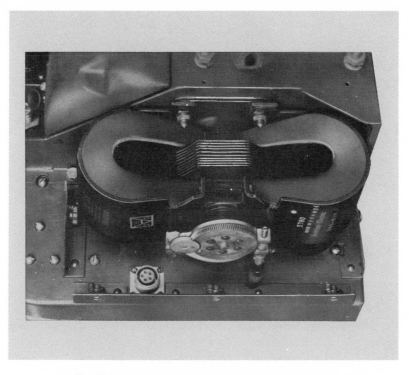

Fig. 7-9.   X-band magnetron (type 5780) used in the M33 fire control system.

of the target's velocity and has developed the gun pointing data. Thereafter it transmits up-to-date information continuously to the guns. The plotting boards are now operated to display present and predicted target data for the use of the tactical control officer. When the target is within range, or in accordance with standard operating instructions, the tactical control officer transmits a fire command to the guns, which fire at the rate of some 20 to 25 rounds per gun per minute until a cease-fire is ordered. Once identified on the PPI, the target can be acquired in about 10 to 15 seconds; the computer output is available 4 seconds later, and in another second or two the guns can fire.

Two of the significant technical developments in this system were the magnetrons for the acquisition and tracking radar transmitters. These were considered high power at that time and were tunable over a 12-percent band. The associated receivers had automatic frequency control so that the radar frequency could be changed to avoid interference or jamming during search and track. The two magnetrons were the 5780 (for X-band) and the 5795 (for S-band), shown in Figs. 7-9 and 7-10, respectively. The

Fig. 7-10.   S-band magnetron (type 5795) used
in the M33 fire control system.

5780 delivered a 250-kilowatt (kW) peak with a 0.25-microsecond (μs) pulse width. The 5795 generated a 1-megawatt (MW) peak with a 1.3-μs pulse width.

The tracking radar antenna used a broadband waveguide phase-advance lens fed with an offset rotating feedhorn for conical lobing (Fig. 7-8). The final acquisition antenna was a pillbox reflector type that produced a narrow beam in azimuth and either a pencil or cosecant squared beam in elevation. It was enclosed in a radome, as shown by Fig. 7-2.

The acquisition radar used in system serial numbers 1 through 131 utilized a metal-plate lens-type antenna mounted in the same way as the final acquisition antenna shown in Fig. 7-2. The lens-type was replaced by the reflector-type after field experience had indicated marginal range performance under certain tactical conditions. The earlier lens-type antenna is shown in Fig. 7-11.

Fig. 7-12 is a view of the dc amplifier, many of which were used in the computer. This component is illustrative of the plug-in concept used throughout the M33. The amplifier used a specially designed twin triode having high stability and extremely low grid current.

Two pilot models of the M33 system were built in the period 1948–1950, during which time a production contract was awarded to Western Electric. The second model was delivered to the Army for tests at the Aberdeen Proving Ground in the spring of 1950. The first production system was delivered in the summer of 1950, only a few months after delivery of the pilot model. This kind of scheduling was possible because of the close liaison between Western Electric and Bell Labs; Western Electric personnel had been stationed at Whippany throughout the development period. The production run of the M33 system, consisting of 645 units in all, was continuous—first at Burlington, North Carolina, then at Western Electric's Fullerton Avenue plant in Chicago, and then at Burlington again.

Fig. 7-11. Lens type of acquisition antenna used in early M33 fire control systems. Antenna was replaced by pillbox-reflector type shown in Fig. 7-2.

Fig. 7-12. DC amplifier—a plug-in component—used in large quantities in the M33 fire control system.

The systems were deployed in the continental United States (CONUS) and supported by Western Electric Field Engineering Force personnel. At the request of the Army, Western Electric established depot repair centers for rehabilitation of major system components. Some systems were sent to South Korea late in the Korean War, and some to Turkey.

The tests of the pilot model at the Aberdeen Proving Ground were made principally to evaluate the major components of the system. The computer was exercised and checked for accuracy, and the radar range performance and tracking accuracies were evaluated. Early production systems underwent similar testing at Fort Bliss, Texas, culminating in gun firings at towed targets. This testing established the effectiveness of the system, i.e., that it would fulfill its mission requirements. After the systems were deployed with 90- or 120-millimeter guns, the antiaircraft artillery batteries participated in an annual service practice at Rehoboth Beach, Delaware, or White Sands Proving Grounds, firing at targets towed by aircraft. The crews were scored on accuracy, which reflected their ability to properly align the equipment and use correct operating procedures.

1.2 Nike R and D

Project Nike, named after the winged goddess of victory in Greek mythology, came into being in February 1945 when the U.S. Army Ordnance Corps and the Air Force asked Bell Laboratories to explore the possibilities of a new antiaircraft defense system to combat future enemy bombers invading friendly territory at such high speeds and high altitudes that conventional artillery could not effectively cope with them. This study resulted in a verbal report in May 1945 followed in July 1945 by a written document called the AAGM Report ("A Study of an Antiaircraft Guided Missile System"). This far-sighted proposal represented the results of five months of very intensive study by a small, closely knit group of scientists and engineers, which included W. A. McNair, H. W. Bode, G. N. Thayer, J. W. Tukey, and B. D. Holbrook. It was vitally important to ensure the development of a new weapon so expeditiously that it could be tactically available by the time any enemy might conceivably have high-speed, high-altitude bombers in tactical operation. Therefore, the study group postulated that the defense equipment should be derived, as far as possible, from devices, methods, and techniques well known and understood. Furthermore, the group argued, its development should not await the results of research projects that were still in a stage of uncertain success, such as those on ramjet engines, radically new fuels, and drastically new guidance or homing techniques. Another axiom of the system design philosophy was that the expendable projectile should be as simple and inexpensive as possible and thus leave the more complex and more expensive equipment on the ground, where it would have the benefit of routine maintenance and least severe environment. This aspect of the design philosophy was maintained through some 30 years of Bell Laboratories work on air defense systems.

The AAGM Report was considered a classic in its thoroughness because of its insight and scope covering a wide spectrum of disciplines from propulsion and guidance to prospective aerodynamics and because of the small amount of time (five months) required to complete such an in-depth study that formed a solid conceptual basis for the five years of R and D work that followed. The specific recommendations of the proposal were: (1) a supersonic rocket missile should be vertically launched under the thrust of a solid-fuel booster, which would be dropped on completion of its function; (2) then, self-propelled by a liquid-fuel motor, the missile should be guided to a predicted intercept point in space and detonated by remote control commands; and (3) these commands should be transmitted by radio signals at a time determined by a ground-based computer associated with radar that would track both the target and missile in flight.

Immediately after the verbal presentation of the AAGM Report in May 1945, the Army Ordnance Corps, with the agreement of the Air Force, assumed full responsibility for Project Nike and charged Western Electric and Bell Laboratories with full responsibility for its development. Bell Laboratories realized that while its engineering staff comprised outstanding experts in the fields of radio, radar, communications, mathematics, computers, and servo systems, the job would profit from entrusting certain tasks outside these areas, notably those concerning projectiles and their propulsion, to specialists with previous experience in these branches of technology. The integration of the individual efforts into a smoothly functioning organization would remain the responsibility of Western Electric and Bell Labs, the prime contractor. The Douglas Aircraft Company (and later the McDonnell Douglas Astronautics Corporation), which had already been active in the missile field during World War II, was selected as the major subcontractor on the design of the missile, booster, and launcher. The relationship with Douglas grew into an essentially full partnership lasting for the next 30 years of work in the nation's air defense. With regard to this team effort, the late Army General H. N. Toftoy, when acting as chairman for a classified presentation before the Institute of Aeronautical Sciences commented, "It is interesting to note that the success of the project under these conditions was made possible by the rapid communications and transportation provided by the peacetime products of these two concerns—the telephone and the airplane."

Authority to proceed was conveyed by Contract W-30-069-ORD-3182 between the Army Ordnance Corps and Western Electric. This contract called for Bell Labs to conduct the R and D necessary to produce an antiaircraft guided missile system for demonstration and test purposes. The step of engineering the weapon for mass production and tactical deployment was left until favorable experience had been acquired in the R and D test program.

The original, unsophisticated estimate in 1945 of the time needed to take the R and D program up to the point of system demonstration was four years. Actually, the entire R and D program through system test and demonstration required six and three-quarter years, until April 1952. The major steps in the R and D of the project up to the start of the system tests are shown in Fig. 7-13.

The major elements of the Nike System were a radar to track the target, a radar for tracking and communicating with the Nike missile, and the ground guidance computer for developing guidance commands to bring about interception of the target by the missile and for issuing a warhead burst command at the time of closest approach. The search acquisition radar required to complete the system was already under development as part of the M33 antiaircraft system.

Some of the principal innovations in the development of these Nike subsystems merit brief discussion at this point. One of the major projects was the development of tracking radar with a degree of accuracy never before attained. In the fall of 1945 a searching study of echo fluctuation measurements on airplanes in flight led to the conclusion that conical lobing methods would be inadequate to yield the smoothness and accuracy of data required for the Nike system. Rapid echo amplitude variations of 20 to 30 decibels (dB) had been measured. Hence, a more accurate radar in which a complete angle measurement is made every pulse, called monopulse, would have to be developed specifically to meet the Nike requirement of a one-half-mil standard deviation of angular difference between the line of sight to target and the missile. Furthermore, the smoothness of output had to be such that target acceleration maneuvers could be promptly detected and countered without long delays needed to smooth rough data. With the monopulse type of radar, no angular perturbations are caused by any rapid pulse-to-pulse fading.

Another important radar feature responded to the need for obtaining high transmitter power, with a wide range of tunability, to obtain the maximum protection against jamming. The tube department therefore developed two tunable magnetrons for the Nike (and M33) track and search radars—one a 250-kW X-band magnetron, the other a 1,000-kW S-band magnetron. J. P. Molnar was responsible for the successful development of these advanced magnetrons, tunable over a 12-percent band.

Both target and missile-tracking radars were identical, except that the missile track radar was equipped for tracking an X-band beacon in the missile. This radar sent pulse commands with a specific missile address that triggered the beacon, provided pitch and yaw guidance orders, and issued the burst command.

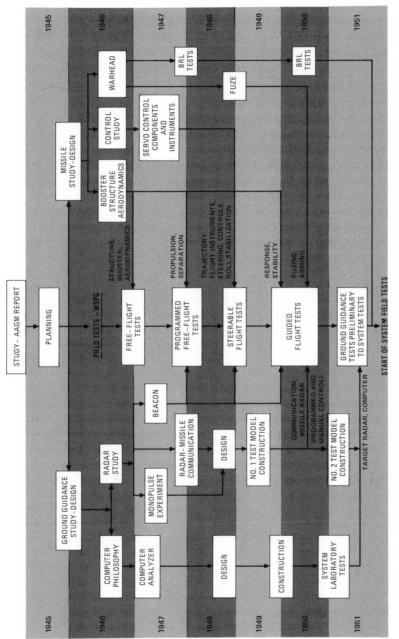

Fig. 7-13.   Synopsis of major steps of Nike development.

In a system like Nike, the characteristics of the guidance computer were of critical importance during the last few seconds before intercept. It was realized that one of the terminal accuracy problems centered on the possibility of filtering out the tracking noise without unduly delaying the recognition of true target maneuver. (One of the advantages of a command guidance missile is that it will match any maneuver by the target to avoid close intercept. In contrast, the gun antiaircraft system has no means of changing the course of the projectile once it has been fired from the ground.) Consequently, early in 1946 a computer-analyzer was built in order to analyze the end game, or final stage of flight. This apparatus solved the guidance equations in two dimensions so that, with its aid, lateral miss could be studied under wide variations in the steering order equations, the noise level, the smoothing and stability parameters, and the magnitude, nature, and timing of target evasive maneuvers. Over 7,000 runs, comprising nearly 700 distinct situations, were made and analyzed. From these runs emerged optimum smoothing, prediction, and order-shaping techniques, in addition to a large body of knowledge concerning the effects of various kinds of target maneuvers. The final circuits of the Nike computer were based on these simulations. The actual construction of the computer was started in 1948, after accuracy studies showed that error sources in the analog components selected, such as electrical computing potentiometers and dc amplifiers, would not lead to significant degradation of Nike system performance.

Although the principal design of the Nike missile was carried out by Douglas, Bell Laboratories provided all the missile's electronic guidance equipment and other critical components as well as circuits for the missile's hydraulic servo control system. A critical component developed by Bell Labs was the Nike hydraulic control valve, made after a survey of the state of the art. The valve, shown in Fig. 7-14, had a sliding plunger grooved to open and close a four-way array of ports in the valve body. The plunger ends protruded beyond the valve body into a pair of opposing solenoids that were driven by a push-pull dc amplifier. Zero signal caused current to flow in the two solenoids, which permitted a mechanical spring to center the valve and stop the oil flow. A plus signal caused current to increase in one end and decrease in the other, which pulled the plunger and allowed high pressure oil to flow to one side of an actuator piston. A negative signal gave the opposite effect. With only 0.4 watt of electrical power available, the valve controlled 0.75 horsepower of hydraulic power, which amounted to a 30-dB gain for a single-stage mechanical amplifier. Although many variations of this type of valve are available today, pioneering effort was required to meet the Nike missile control requirements.

Bell Laboratories also accepted the initial responsibility for the circuit design of the complex missile control system with its many feedback paths.

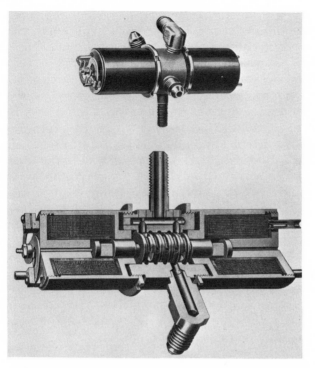

Fig. 7-14. First Nike missile hydraulic control valves designed by Bell Laboratories. Actual size was $3\frac{1}{2}$ inches long.

E. L. Norton was heavily involved in solving the most difficult equalization circuits. To test the servos before they were used in flight, simulators, as shown in Figs. 7-15a and 7-15b, were devised for artificially creating the predicted situation for the servo systems. On the simulators, the nature of the aerodynamic coupling between control surfaces and sensing elements could be varied, and the behavior of control loops containing nonlinear components could be studied with greater precision. Douglas sent personnel to Bell Labs to become experienced in the design of such complex control systems so that the final design responsibility could later be transferred to them.

An important element of the Nike R and D program was the system tester equipment, which simulated the entire Nike system and permitted many runs under many variations in input conditions. A diagram of the final system tester is shown in Fig. 7-16, and a photographic view in Fig. 7-17. Original plans called for the system components to consist of the computer, missile gyros and accelerometers, missile steering control, and roll-stabilizing fin drive servos. The remainder of the equipment and functions were to be provided by means of dc analog computer techniques, with which Bell Laboratories had considerable experience. The final version closely followed the originally conceived plan, the main exception being the simplified electronic missile simulator shown in Fig. 7-16 instead of the original electromechanical missile simulator.

The system tester was put to much valuable use in support of the Nike project. In the summer of 1951, when the system tester was used to test the Nike computer prior to shipment to White Sands, an error in the computer was uncovered that would have prevented a successful firing against a ground target, which had been planned for the first test. Later, in 1953, a complete evaluation of the Nike system was made with the entire system tester to duplicate the White Sands Missile Range (WSMR) system test field firings. After a close comparison of system tester results with field results had been made, the system tester was then used for the major purpose intended for it, namely, the exploration of Nike system effectiveness at the outer limits of target range, altitude, speed, aspect, and maneuverability. Such tests could not possibly have been accomplished by actual field firings because of the lack of suitable targets and the prohibitively large number of test missiles required to obtain statistical answers for the various combinations of pertinent parameters. Many thousands of runs in the system tester were necessary to fully establish the Nike capability under wide variations of target conditions.

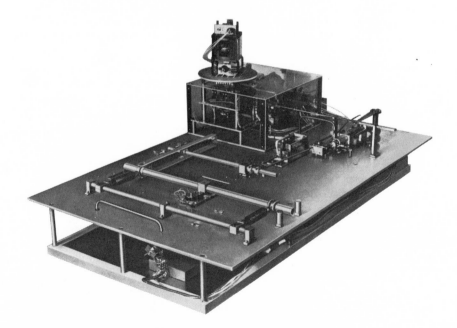

Fig. 7-15(a). Laboratory model of Nike missile roll simulator.

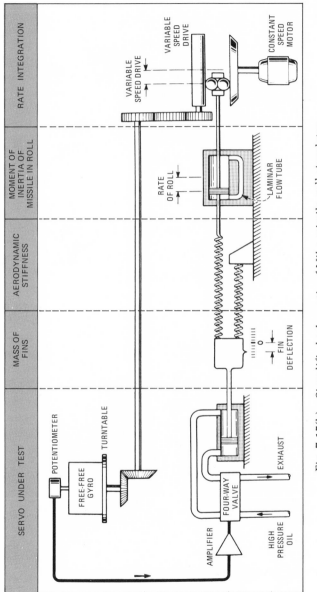

Fig. 7-15(b). Simplified schematic of Nike missile roll simulator.

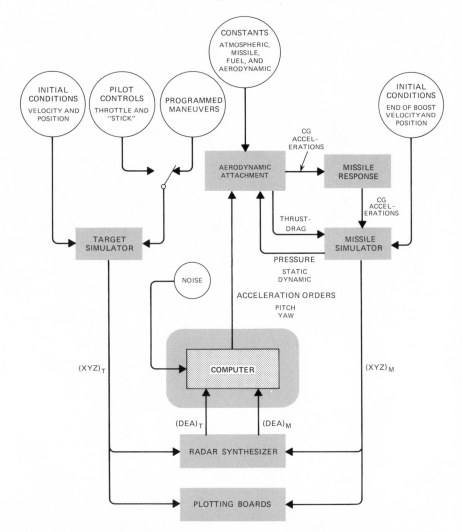

Fig. 7-16.   Diagram of the final version of missile simulator used to test Nike system.

During the period 1946–1951, the major elements of Nike underwent tests at WSMR. Starting with the most rudimentary initial firings of a booster, with a ballasted wooden dummy simulating the missile, the missile test firings progressed in well-planned, step-by-step development leading to controlled missile flights. The missiles were instrumented in an effort to gain as much quantitative information on performance as possible from each flight. The R and D philosophy was governed by a decision that missiles were never to be fired as mere test vehicles but only as steps in the evolution of the eventual weapon. Bell Labs engineers

Fig. 7-17.   Nike system-tester laboratory.

working with Douglas engineers played key roles in analyzing the results of each missile firing and in planning each phase of testing at periodic meetings. By the summer of 1951 some 80 Nike firings had taken place, and the missile was declared ready for overall system tests in the fall of 1951.

Parallel with the missile development was the development of the Nike monopulse radar, which began to take shape in 1948. The proposal for two antennas 12 feet apart on a common rotating platform had been abandoned in favor of two identical radar mounts, missile and target-tracker, sited 50 to 100 feet apart. One of the difficult requirements faced with a monopulse radar was maintaining relative phase shift within close tolerance in three intermediate frequency (IF) channels. This required not only minimum phase shift in the three pre- and main IF amplifiers but, in addition, automatic control of the respective gains within 5 dB of each other with an input level change of over 70 dB. After thorough testing at Whippany, the missile-tracking portion of the Nike radar was sent to WSMR by air and truck in November 1949. In the series of missile tests that followed, the radar tracked successfully all missiles from before firing, through boost and separation, and in most cases to impact. This was a major advance in the test program because missiles could now be controlled from the ground through the X-band radar link, and the point of impact in the White Sands desert could be accurately established for recovery. Early reflection tracking of aircraft also established the radar's performance as a target-tracking radar. By early 1951, as a result of three years of test experience, improvements and refinements in the radar design made it ready for the overall Nike system tests. By this time, a second radar for target

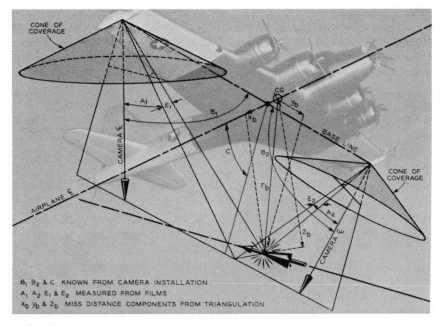

Fig. 7-18.   Geometry of ITOR (intercept target-borne optical recorder) camera triangulation from drone aircraft.

tracking, constructed at the Whippany Laboratory, was shipped to WSMR for the system test. During the joint tests of both radars, a very accurate method of boresighting the radars was developed that used a small X-band RF test source mounted on top of a 60-foot pole, along with optical targets, some 600 feet in front of the radars. With this equipment and with optical telescopes on the radar mount, a special technique of "dumping" the antenna to eliminate the effects of any ground reflections was developed to make possible boresighting the radar electrical axis to the optical telescope with an accuracy of 0.05 mil. From this calibration, optical telescopes were used as the reference in boresighting both radars with respect to each other for the system test. Accurate radar boresighting was critical to intercept accuracy, and the procedure developed for it at WSMR was carried over to the Nike tactical deployment.

The Nike computer was developed at Whippany independently of the field testing of missile and radar, since it was not required until the start of system tests. Prior to its shipment to WSMR, the computer was put through qualitative testing in the Nike system tester laboratory as a Nike system component. A second computer, to be retained in the system tests for the simulation testing, replaced the first model.

The R and D system tests were an unqualified success. They demonstrated that the Nike system, with a command guidance missile system, was a major advance in bomber defense. The first test was a most cautious

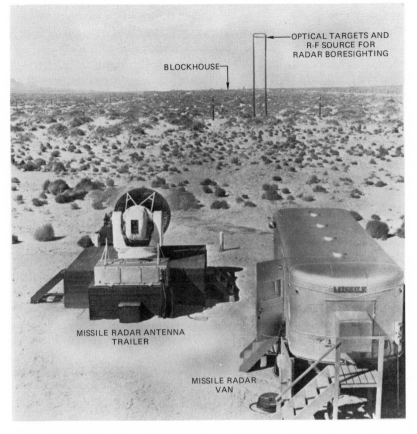

BLOCKHOUSE

OPTICAL TARGETS AND
R-F SOURCE FOR
RADAR BORESIGHTING

MISSILE RADAR ANTENNA
TRAILER

MISSILE RADAR
VAN

Fig. 7-19.   Missile radar seen from C Station, White Sands Missile Range.

procedure in which the target-computer-missile control loop was closed for the first time toward a fixed ground target located by topographical survey. Round 67 was fired on November 15, 1951, and was followed by another round on December 18, 1951. Both of these came within 50 feet of the ground target, which was located about 18 miles from the radars at C Station, WSMR. The necessity for testing the Nike system against aircraft was recognized at the beginning of the project. The chance of an incapacitating hit, however, even without a warhead in the missile, was considered too great a risk to consider firing at manned aircraft. Hence, unmanned, remotely controlled drones had to be used despite their cost, complications, and operational limitations. Also, at that time no aircraft was available that would meet the Nike target specification of a bomber flying 600 mph at an altitude of 60,000 feet, and capable of 3-g evasive maneuvers at 40,000 feet. Practical considerations dictated the selection

Fig. 7-20.   Microwave apparatus and telescopic camera on target radar.

of the QB-17G drone (a modification of the Flying Fortress bomber). The drone was equipped so that under ground control it could execute a 2-g evasive maneuver timed to occur about 5 seconds before expected intercept—a time of maximum stress to system performance. Two camera systems were developed to score the actual intercept miss distance. Douglas developed innovative airborne intercept instrumentation called the Intercept Target-borne Optical Recorder (ITOR) (Fig. 7-18), composed of clusters of wide angle cameras mounted in wing pod. The Army developed a ground scoring camera system called the Intercept Ground-stationed Optical Recorder (IGOR) and installed this equipment at WSMR for the Nike tests. Views of the Nike equipment for the start of the system tests are shown in Figs. 7-19 through 7-22.

Some 20 system test missiles were fired at QB-17G drones during the period between November 27, 1951, and April 24, 1952. The very first round fired at the drone was an impressive and unqualified success: radars, computers, and missiles worked perfectly. The drone came in at 33,000 feet at 350 mph, and the token flash detonation, representing warhead burst at intercept, came well within what would have been lethal proximity for the warhead. The closest approach of missile and aircraft was 16 feet. Some of the close intercepts are shown in Figs. 7-23a and 7-23b. In Fig. 7-23b, the token flash is shown directly in front of the plane; after the flash, the missile drilled through the entire length of the aircraft. Fol-

(a)

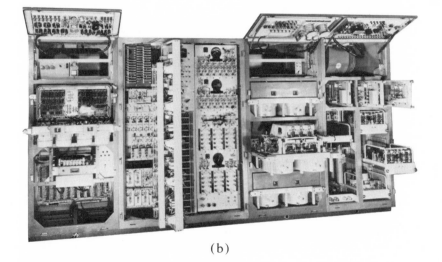

(b)

Fig. 7-21. Nike R and D computer. (a) Normal operating condition. (b) Panels open for access.

lowing these tests of the system without warheads, a full-scale demonstration of the complete, Nike system was conducted with a series of five live warhead rounds fired during April 1952 in the presence of a large number of senior generals of both the Army and Air Force. The spectacular results of two of these firings are shown in Fig. 7-24a,b. From these impressive demonstrations, it became clear to all the witnesses that a highly effective missile defense against any bomber of the future had been developed.

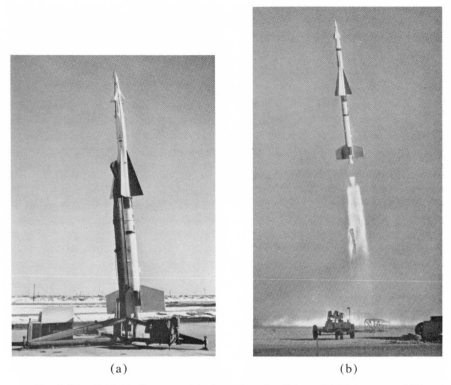

(a)   (b)

Fig. 7-22.   (a) Missile erected in launcher for firing. (b) Firing round 75.

1.3 Tactical Nike System — Nike-Ajax

About a year before the effectiveness of the complete R and D Nike system was demonstrated at WSMR, the Korean War had started (in June 1950); the United States no longer had a monopoly of the nuclear weapon. (The first atomic explosion in the Soviet Union reportedly occurred in September 1949.) With concern for defense against high-altitude bombers, the Department of Defense and the Army asked Western Electric and Bell Labs to produce as soon as possible a tactical version of the Nike system, called Nike I and later Nike-Ajax. President Truman appointed K. T. Keller, chairman of the board of Chrysler, to become the full-time missile chief. Keller asked Western Electric to take all steps necessary to produce the new Nike air defense weapon for the Army as soon as possible.

The Bell System responded with a fully integrated team effort that made it possible to complete a production design and first production system from Western Electric and missiles from Douglas in 1953—two years after the authorization of production. Full advantage was taken of the M33 design, operating concept, and trailer packaging arrangement in the tactical Nike-Ajax to meet the tight development and manufacturing

Fig. 7-23.   IGOR photographs of firings with dummy warhead. (a) Round 75.
(b) Round 83.

schedule. Throughout Bell Labs, departments engaged in Bell System work were recruited to expedite the conversion of R and D designs to Army tactical designs. The Western Electric North Carolina Works used advance information from Bell Labs engineers to build the first units within the shortest possible time. In the end, Western Electric produced 358 ground batteries and delivered 14,000 missile control and guidance units to Douglas for assembly in a similar number of Nike-Ajax missiles.

The Nike-Ajax batteries were deployed throughout the country, including Hawaii and Alaska, in defense of major cities and defense estab-

Fig. 7-24.   IGOR photographs of firings with live warhead. (a) Round 90.
(b) Round 92.

lishments. In addition, they were deployed in European and other
countries sharing common defense interests with the United States. The
mobile nature of the system permitted its initial testing with assigned
personnel against small drone targets at the Red Canyon Range in New
Mexico. Each year after being deployed, the battery and its crew were returned to this range for a similar evaluation of performance. A key cadre
of experienced Western Electric and Douglas field engineers was made
available to the Army for service in this country and overseas to make sure

that ground equipment and missiles were kept ready at full capability. Bell Labs and Western Electric also developed training material, with Western Electric conducting training classes for the Army.

1.4 Terrier

In 1951 the Navy Bureau of Ordnance asked Western Electric and Bell Laboratories to develop a fire control system for a mobile land-based surface-to-air guided missile system for the Marine Corps. Two other major elements of the Marine Corps system were the missile and missile launchers. At that time the Navy was well along in the development of a shipboard guided missile system called the Terrier System. This system was being developed under the guidance of the Applied Physics Laboratory at The Johns Hopkins University. Logistic considerations led the Navy to require the Marine Corps to use the same missile as that fired by the Terrier System. The third major element, the launchers, were developed under a Bureau of Ordnance contract by the W. L. Maxson Company of New York City.

The requirements for the system, and of course for the fire control system, were that it be capable of being deployed and ready to fire within 48 hours of its arrival at an action station, that the fire rate average eight missiles per minute with a peak capability of eight missiles in salvo at a $2\frac{1}{2}$ second separation between launches. This meant that eight missiles could be riding the tracking radar beam simultaneously. The Terrier System employed the beam-riding principle for guidance rather than the command guidance principle used in the Nike System. Once the missile was inserted into the guidance beam tracking the target, circuitry aboard the missile detected departures from the center of the radar beam and generated steering orders to direct the missile back to beam center, where it rode the beam to target impact. The fire control system to be developed by Bell Laboratories was to acquire, evaluate, and identify targets, then to direct the missile launchers in order to effect a successful insertion of the missile into the tracking beam, and, finally, to provide information to the missile during flight to correct steering orders for the differences in the coordinate systems used by the missile and the radar.

Development work was started on the Terrier guided missile fire control system, AN/MSG3, in 1951. The system comprised four major elements: the tracking and guidance radar, the acquisition radar, the fire control computer, and the capture radar. The same antenna system was used to transmit the tracking and guidance beams, which, therefore, although differing slightly in frequency, had the same geometric patterns. By using the same antenna system, coincidence of the beams was guaranteed. Launcher geometry and missile characteristics were such that it was not possible to steer the missile to beam center at launch and stay within the confines of the narrow guidance beam; hence, the capture transmitter was needed. This transmitted a broad beam collimated with the tracking and guidance beams but offset from them at beam centers by approximately 4 feet. This beam was sufficiently wide to allow capture of the missile at launch. Once the missile settled down in the center of the capture beam, control was transferred to the guidance beam. One of the control computer's functions was to aim the launchers so that the angle of entry of the missile into the capture beam allowed missile capture within the confines of the beam.

A prototype of the entire Terrier surface-to-air missile system was assembled at the Whippany Laboratory in the latter half of 1953. Since the launchers arrived late in the year, the launcher compatibility testing and tracking tests were performed during the winter months and through the spring of 1954. In the early summer of 1954 the prototype was shipped to the China Lake Naval Air Station in the Mojave Desert, Inyokern, California, for a live firing test. The first missile was fired in the late fall of that year, and testing of the prototype model continued on into the summer of 1955. The first of the production systems was sent to the air station in the early summer of 1955 for field exercises. In the first exercise it was deployed and readied for action, and the missile was fired at a drone target within the 48-hour design limit, successfully intercepting the target. In fact, tests with the prototype as well as the production systems verified that the Marine Corps had a viable fire control system for their Terrier missile.

Ten systems of the original design were produced by Western Electric in the period 1954–1955. Thirteen Model II equipments were produced, five being totally new construction and eight conversions from the first design. The manufacture of Model II took place in 1959–1960.

1.5 Nike-Hercules

With the introduction of the command guidance Nike-Ajax system, the Army asked Bell Laboratories in 1953 to continue to study possible improvements in the system so that its effectiveness might be increased against all types of future bomber attack strategies. An important area of concern was the threat that closely spaced bombers could degrade the ground target angle accuracy and present high-traffic levels which could saturate the Nike-Ajax system. As a result of this study, the Army asked Bell Labs to work with Douglas in exploring the possibility of adding a larger missile to the Nike-Ajax system that would be capable of carrying a nuclear warhead and extending the range of the system from 25 to 50 miles. (As it turned out later, the missile developed had a range of 100 miles, and improvements in ground equipment alone actually increased the system range from 25 to 100 miles.) The kill radius of such a warhead would force any enemy to space its attackers to avoid multiple losses. The resulting system change in Nike-Ajax, initially called Nike-B and later

Nike-Hercules, was made so that the ground system could fire both Nike-Ajax missiles and the larger, longer-range Nike-Hercules missiles from the same battery.

The design target chosen for Nike-Hercules was a formation of B-47 size bombers having a speed of Mach 1. Tests made later with the radar showed that the system was very effective against a much smaller and much faster target, such as a B-58. The Nike-Hercules system was designed for CONUS and field operation in three different modes: surface-to-air, low-altitude, and surface-to-surface. The principal mode of operation was surface-to-air. In this mode the system would intercept aircraft or other targets approaching from any direction from very low to very high altitudes. Because of the system's great accuracy and the lethality of the nuclear weapon carried by the Nike-Hercules missile, a 100-percent probability that the missile would destroy the enemy's bomb at the maximum intercept range was possible.

The acquisition radar for the Nike-Hercules system was a modified version of that used in Nike-Ajax, the antenna of which looked much like the M33 antenna shown in Fig. 7-2. One of the principal changes was the introduction of a traveling-wave-tube RF amplifier that provided a low-noise-figure receiver giving greater range performance than the Nike-Ajax receiver. The target track radar was also modified to give much longer range performance, obtained in part through the use of a larger and more efficient antenna like the Cassegrainian parabolic reflector. The antenna in its radome is shown in Fig. 7-25. The missile track radar was similarly modified so that both track radars would remain interchangeable. A pulse position code for communication between the missile track radar and the Hercules missile was added to provide reliable communication with the Hercules missile at the farthest limit of its range.

The Nike-Hercules missile design benefited from the many years of Nike-Ajax development and the firing experience of the Bell Labs and Douglas people. Bell Labs retained control of the electronic guidance unit with its stable reference platform, while Douglas was responsible for the rest of the missile. The size of the Nike-Hercules missile was determined by the size and weight of the nuclear warhead it carried. The cruciform-dart configuration of the missile, shown in Fig. 7-26 provided the desired aerodynamic stability and maneuverability at all altitudes. Low aerodynamic drag characteristics assured superior missile performance for a given amount of engine thrust. Tail control permitted the use of the same set of control surfaces for both steering and roll control. A solid-fuel rocket motor assured high thrust independent of altitude. The booster consisted of four booster units of the Nike-Ajax missile in a cluster. The Nike-Hercules system permitted the missile-borne equipment to be relatively simple and, unlike the vacuum-tube design of Nike-Ajax, used all solid-state components except in the beacon transmitter. Three basic launching complexes

Fig. 7-25.   Target tracking radar supplies precise target
position information to the computer.

were designed for the Hercules missile: a mobile field installation launcher
capable of accommodating either Nike-Hercules or Nike-Ajax missiles,
a semipermanent subsurface launcher raised by elevator from a below-
ground magazine, and a semipermanent cellular design. The latter is
shown in Fig. 7-27 with the missile partially erected. Fig. 7-28 illustrates
the mobility of the equipment.

In 1956 Bell Laboratories was asked to study possible post-1960 threats
and to determine what improvements could be made in the Nike-Hercules
system to meet these threats. The anticipated threats were indicated as
increased electronic countermeasures, high-performance targets, and
combinations of both. Typical targets expected after 1960 were Mach-2,
medium-size bombers operating at altitudes up to 70,000 feet and small
air-supported missiles and rockets operating at velocities of Mach 3 and
altitudes up to 100,000 feet. Sophisticated electronic jammers capable of
high-level barrage-noise jamming were included in the conditions
postulated.

Addressing these threats, Bell Laboratories designers capitalized on the
inherent growth potential of Nike-Hercules to develop the Improved
Nike-Hercules system. In their view, it was imperative that an acquisition
radar have sufficient power to detect small radar targets at long ranges and
to provide simultaneous coverage of all altitudes. The designers established the requirements for such a radar operating in the L-band called

Fig. 7-26. Seconds after launching, Nike-Hercules missile accelerates to supersonic speeds.

"high-power acquisition radar" (HIPAR), and Bell Labs and Western Electric chose General Electric to develop and manufacture it. Fig. 7-29 shows the HIPAR antenna with its superimposed geodesic radome. The rationale of electronic jamming called for the use of antijamming circuit improvements and exploitation of the logistical aspect by the use of multifrequency bands. The rationale was implemented by having HIPAR operate in a new frequency band different from that of the Hercules acquisition radar and by Bell Labs' developing a new "range-only" radar operating in the very high frequency K band. In addition, the Hercules target track radar was improved to provide advanced performance capabilities against small targets and to increase the X-band power level that a jamming aircraft must produce to interfere with system operation. An improved Hercules site is shown in Fig. 7-30.

During 1960 and 1961 extensive evaluation tests of the Improved

Fig. 7-27. Nike-Hercules missile being erected into firing position from underground cell.

Nike-Hercules prototype system were performed at the Missile Range near White Sands, N.M. Achievement of several milestones in the art of missile defense highlighted the evaluation program. The "kill" of the Corporal ballistic missile in June 1960 marked the first intercept of a ballistic missile in this performance class. Later in 1960, four equally historic intercepts were achieved against "enemy" Hercules missiles, the highest-performance targets then available. Another capability of the improved system, the ability to detect and track targets in severe electronic countermeasure (ECM) environments, was demonstrated with equal success. Of the 19 evaluation firings, 16 were fully successful and 2 were qualified successes (qualified because intercept was precluded by target malfunction).

Fig. 7-28. Nike-Hercules was highly mobile—its transporters were able to travel even where no roads existed.

Fig. 7-29.   Antenna of the high-power acquisition radar (HIPAR) used in the Improved Nike-Hercules system. Shown is a composite photograph of antenna and geodesic dome in which it is housed.

The success of the overall Nike-Hercules program is illustrated by the 393 Nike-Hercules ground systems produced by Western Electric at its North Carolina Works and the more than 9,000 guidance units for the Douglas Hercules missile. (A smaller number of ground systems were

Fig. 7-30.   Artist's rendering of a hypothetical Nike-Hercules air defense site.

modified for the Improved Nike-Hercules System.) As indicated earlier, the system was tested at White Sands with a wide range of threat possibilities, including the interception of the supersonic Hercules missile. Although the Nike-Hercules system has been recently phased out of most continental United States air defense areas, a large number of the Hercules batteries were still operational in North Atlantic Treaty Organization (NATO) and other overseas countries in the mid-1970s.

1.6 Antiballistic Missile Program

The ABM research and development program carried out over the 20-year period 1955–1975 by Bell Laboratories and Western Electric was the largest and most extensive program in depth and breadth of technology carried out by the Bell System for the military services. The program started in February 1955 when Army Ordnance asked Bell Laboratories to start an 18-month study of a new, forward-looking air defense system with which to defend the zone of the interior against future target threats in the period 1960–1970. At that time a small group of military systems development engineers at the Whippany, New Jersey laboratory had been working with a team from Douglas on a study of a single-stage, solid-propellant missile for possible air defense. The team was immediately directed to this broad 18-month system study.

Initial thinking placed primary emphasis on being able to cope with the super air-breathing-type target, while keeping in mind ballistic targets and the desire to provide defense against the extremely difficult ICBM with a reasonable extension of current radar and missile technology. In other words, the system that would be designated as Nike II was to be considered not a solution to the ICBM defense program, but rather a step toward its ultimate solution. However, discussions with the Army and the Department of Defense in June 1955 brought to light increasing concern over the possibility of an early ICBM threat. Bell Laboratories was therefore asked to place primary emphasis in this area.

The major developments in the 20-year evolution of ABM defense are covered in the following sections, which trace the history of the step-by-step advance in technology that kept the United States well in the forefront of ABM defense and led eventually to the SALT I agreement with the Soviet Union in 1972. A complete history of the ABM program at Bell Labs is covered in detail in three publications.[1]

From the initial Nike-Zeus system, which extended earlier air defense technology (designed for protection against the bomber) to meet the ex-

---

[1] Bell Laboratories, *ABM Research and Development, Project History,* October 1975, for U.S. Army Ballistic Missile Defense Systems Command; Bell Laboratories, *ABM Research and Development at Bell Laboratories, Kwajalein Field Station,* October 1975, for U.S. Army Ballistic Missile Defense Systems Command; Clifford A. Warren, "Ballistic Missile Defense Testing in the Pacific: 1960–1976," *Bell Laboratories Record* 54 (September 1976), pp. 203–207.

treme ICBM threat of very high speed and small radar size, to the more advanced systems designed later to afford protection against highly sophisticated threats, a large number of truly innovative developments were required. These began with the Zeus system, whose acquisition radar with Luneberg lens and three-dimensional automatic detection and tracking, together with a high-performance missile combining aerodynamic and jet control, made possible the first successful intercept of an ICBM in 1962 at Kwajalein, after earlier testing at Ascension Island in the South Atlantic, the White Sands Missile Range, and Point Mugu, California.

With the decision in 1963 not to deploy the Nike-Zeus System, a period of more than four years followed, from January 1963 to September 1967, in which major steps forward were made to develop an ABM defense system (referred to as Nike-X) to counter the increasing complexity of the ICBM threat. An exhaustive program of reentry research was carried out with the Zeus radars used at the three test sites as sensors for data gathering. Electronic phased-array radars, which, in contrast to the Zeus mechanically steered radars, had inertialess antenna beams, were developed for multifunction applications in the MAR (Multifunction Array Radar) I, MAR II, and MSR (Missile Site Radar) Subsystems. These radars were the major step required to meet the high traffic threat.

A superaccelerating missile called Sprint was developed to permit delayed, low-altitude discrimination for close-in terminal defense. This missile represented another major step in technology, since it required high-impulse, short-burning motors, and the ability to tolerate skin temperatures about three times those of the Zeus missile. The requirements for data processing meant yet another major advance in computing technology to meet the need for high-speed calculations (up to 30 million per second), multiprocessor organization, and an order-of-magnitude improvement in reliability of the basic logic circuits. Closely related to these advances in hardware technology and work on discrimination was a continuing systems engineering activity to determine the optimum subsystem arrangements and deployments to meet various defense objectives of the Army and the Department of Defense.

The new technologies and systems approaches carried out in the Nike-X period between 1963 and 1967 were devised "on the shoulders" of the R and D ABM advances made during the development of the Nike-Zeus System. When the Secretary of Defense made the decision in September 1967 to deploy an ABM system called Sentinel, its major elements were available from Nike-X development, except for the perimeter acquisition radar (PAR), which was then under study. Later, in March 1969, when this deployment was changed to provide Minuteman defense under the Safeguard program, these same elements—then under test at WSMR and Meck Island—again met the defense requirements.

A major contribution of the R and D program in the last seven years was the successful development of one of the most complicated real-time software systems ever conceived. Critics of ABM defense in the late 1960s viewed the software as being too complex to provide the reliability needed. However, the high reliability achieved with the tactical system at the Grand Forks (North Dakota) site 24 hours a day, 7 days a week, was a convincing answer to such critics. Furthermore, the software R and D effort on Safeguard produced a solid background of experience and knowledge that would be helpful in building new defense systems in the future.

Another major contribution of the ABM R and D effort, extending from the first installation of a Zeus track radar on Ascension Island in 1958 to completion of the effort in January 1976, was support of offensive weapons programs. During this period, hundreds of data packages (trajectory information, radar cross-sections, scintillation characteristics, etc.) obtained from reentry missions were supplied to the Air Force and other Department of Defense (DOD) agencies as a byproduct of having the most versatile and accurate radars available at the test ranges. For example, during the last three years of operation of the MSR Subsystem on Meck Island, some sixty data packages were supplied to other agencies concerned with offensive technology. Thus, the ABM program not only advanced its own defense technology, but made important contributions to offensive technology as well.

Each of the developments throughout the 20-year history of ABM activity contributed valuable experience and brought new insights to the challenge of meeting an increasingly sophisticated threat.

1.6.1 Nike II Study[2]

The relatively small study team available in February 1955 to carry out the Nike II work was actually a well-coordinated task group of Bell Laboratories and Douglas Aircraft people who met at regular intervals to review completed tasks and outline future objectives. C. A. Warren and J. W. Schaefer coordinated the overall systems work supported by the Bell Laboratories Mathematical Research Department, whose efforts were coordinated by D. P. Ling and R. C. Prim. At Douglas Aircraft, J. L. Bromberg was responsible for project coordination, supported by R. L. Johnson, M. Hunter, N. Weiler, and J. Tschirgi.

Initially, the objective was to explore the possibility of a common antiaircraft defense system to cover all future high-altitude threats without substantially compromising the overall defense. It was felt that any antiaircraft defense designed for the extreme ICBM targets would overlap a system capable of handling the future air-breathing high-performance

---

[2] Sections 1.6.1 through 1.6.5, with some modifications, are taken from the Bell Laboratories report *ABM Research and Development at Bell Laboratories, Project History* (October 1975) for U.S. Army Ballistic Missile Defense Systems Command.

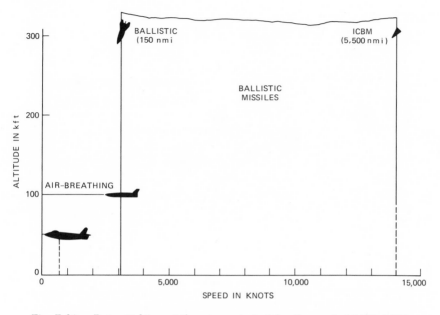

Fig. 7-31. Potential target threats projected for the period 1960–1970.

targets. Consequently, by adding certain specialized elements of one to the other, there was the attractive possibility of having an antiaircraft system capable of attacking any future air target.

The spectrum of possible future target threats in the period 1960–1970 considered for the Army study is shown in Fig. 7-31. It covered a wide area of performance capability from the maximum speed of the air-breathing ramjet to ICBM speed of 24,000 feet per second (ft/s), and at altitudes far beyond 100,000 feet. For the ballistic targets, the short-range, 150-mile, 5000-ft/s rocket of the V2-type set the lower boundary.

The authorized funding for the 18-month study effort was to include exploratory hardware development in those areas of radar and missile technology that could be defined as critical to successful development of a Nike II system.

1.6.1.1 ABM Defense Requirements. The first full status report on the Nike II system study was presented to Army Ordnance at Redstone Arsenal on December 2, 1955, about 7 months after the beginning of the study. It is interesting to note here how many solutions proposed in this preliminary report, after only one-third of the study was completed, remain basic even today to any ICBM defense. Some highlights presented at this status review follow.

To handle the full range of threat, a common data-gathering system was proposed. The system would use a defensive missile with interchangeable

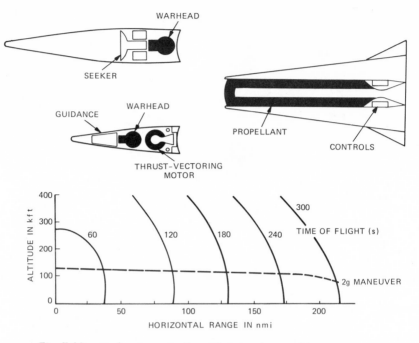

Fig. 7-32.   Defensive missile with interchangeable noses.

noses as shown in Fig. 7-32. One nose, for use in long-range intercepts of the future air-breathing targets, would contain an active seeker. The second nose would have no seeker but would contain a jet-control mechanism to provide maneuverability at altitudes above 120,000 feet. This nose would be used when engaging ballistic targets.

In World War II air defense objectives, a 10- to 15-percent attrition rate was acceptable. But the nuclear warhead threat for Nike II required defense levels of 95- to 100-percent attrition against a tough-to-kill reentry target. Studies showed that using a 50-kiloton nuclear warhead in the defensive missile required relatively small miss distances to kill the enemy warhead. But the use of a high-yield warhead did not relax the need for a guidance system with great accuracy.

One of the first questions in the initial study concerned the point in the offensive missile's trajectory where intercept should take place. Consideration was given to making the intercept near the middle of the trajectory. However, not only would this necessitate a defensive missile as formidable as the offensive weapon, but it would also require gathering information on the offensive missile almost at its point of launch. With the obvious advantage of choice of launch time belonging to the offense, it did not appear feasible or economical to attempt mid-course intercepts. Consequently, Bell Labs proposed that the intercepts be much closer to the point of impact. (See Fig. 7-33 for the ICBM trajectory.)

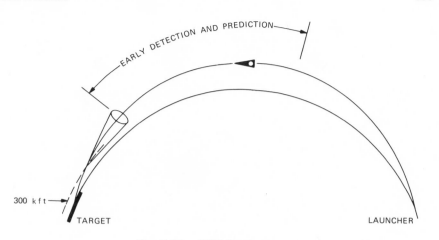

Fig. 7-33. ICBM trajectory.

Further studies indicated that the most attractive guidance method was a command system based on extension of the Nike-Ajax and -Hercules Systems. The use of homing seemed precluded by the extremely high closing rate of over 5 miles per second, necessitating homing ranges that did not appear attainable on so small a target as a ballistic reentry body (only one one-thousandth the radar size of an aircraft). The terminal nature of the defense also made command guidance feasible and attractive.

Ballistic missiles entering the atmosphere would suffer deceleration of up to 100 g's at altitudes dependent on the shape of the reentry nose. A comparison of ballistic target characteristics is given in Fig. 7-34. The guidance problem and related missile maneuverability requirements could be eased, as was proposed by the Bell Laboratories Mathematical Research Department, through the use of analytical prediction of ICBM deceleration well in advance of the actual high-g deceleration.

An extensive communications network, data processing, computation, and tactical control would be necessary to the functioning of the ABM defense system. Local radars in the vicinity of the defended area and forward radars for initial detection would require integration with an extensive network of communications. The importance and complexity of fast response were strongly emphasized with speeds so high and reaction times so short that all operations would have to be automatic with only the power of veto exercised by man. Dependence on a 10- to 15-minute early warning could be relatively loose and flexible, but once a target was acquired, all system elements would have to function as an integrated whole to successfully meet mission objectives.

A major concern pointed out in the first full status report was the problem of separating radar decoys from warheads. Chaff or balloon decoys having high drag-to-mass ratios would be held back by the atmosphere and separated, but rods or jacks cut to the defensive radar frequency

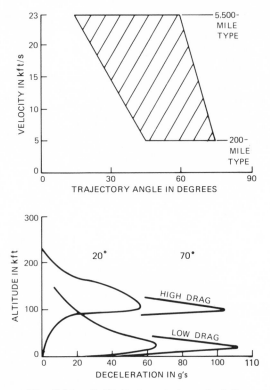

Fig. 7-34.   Ballistic target characteristics.

might be made to have approximately the same drag-to-mass ratio as the warheads. Rate of arrival of ICBMs over a target area and unresolved decoys could present high traffic levels requiring a target tracking and guidance system capable of engaging up to 20 targets per minute.

On December 28, 1955, Lt. Gen. J. M. Gavin, Army Deputy Chief of Staff for Research and Development, visited Whippany for a review of all the Nike programs. A somewhat shortened version of the Nike II status report was presented. General Gavin was impressed with the study to date and gave it top priority, particularly for defense capability against ICBMs. F. R. Lack, Vice President of Western Electric, and J. B. Fisk, then Bell Laboratories Executive Vice President, W. C. Tinus, R. R. Hough, L. W. Morrison, and C. A. Warren were among those present at this meeting.

1.6.1.2 Additional Defense Considerations.   On January 4, 1956, a similar Nike II briefing was given by R. R. Hough of Bell Laboratories to the Army Policy Council. At this briefing Hough responded to an Army request for information concerning what could be done to provide an interim solution to the intermediate- and long-range ballistic missile de-

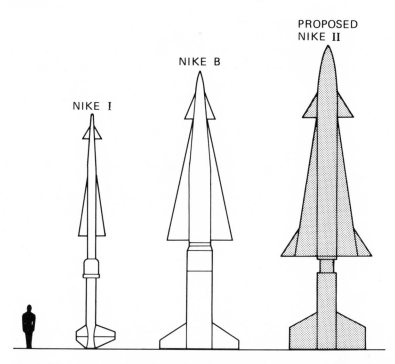

Fig. 7-35.   Comparative sizes of early antiballistic missiles (ABMs).

fense problem. It was pointed out that regardless of the approach taken, information gathering was the difficult part of the problem. Furthermore, a high level of defense was essential and a marginal interim capability might not be worth extensive effort. Also, any interim solution should be directed along lines that would lead to the final solution.

A long-range, high-data-rate acquisition radar was essential to any ballistic missile defense solution. If development could start immediately on this critical element, an interim ICBM defense might be possible with a Nike B missile and system. Hough reported that Bell Laboratories was currently studying the problem of ICBM interim capability with Nike B and would report back to the Army within the next two months on this defense possibility. A comparison of early ABM sizes is given above in Fig. 7-35.

Since the Air Force was also interested in ABM defense, in the fall of 1955 it issued a technical request to industry for a 12-month ABM defense study. In this period the roles and mission of the Army were defined as "terminal" defense and those of the Air Force as "area" defense. Since the ABM concept covered both roles,[3] Bell Laboratories recognized that any

---

[3] Area defense involved the long-range acquisition radars tied together by a communications network, while terminal defense involved the missiles, local tracking radars, and computers.

successful ABM system would have to combine area and terminal defense within one integrated systems approach. Bell Labs therefore bid on the Air Force's 12-month study with the proviso that the additional effort for the Air Force would be concentrated on the forward acquisition radars (FARs) and the communications network. However, the results of the complete ABM study would be made available to both the Army and the Air Force.

An Air Force contract with Western Electric was authorized on November 15, 1955, and was directed specifically to anti-ICBM (AICBM) defense only. Two other defense contractors were selected for this Air Force study.

As the Nike II study and the complementary Air Force study proceeded through the first six months of 1956, Bell Laboratories and Douglas were requested to make a number of presentations not only to the Army and Air Force but also to a number of high-level DOD and special defense panels as well. These briefings included:

Nike II and the Study of Early Solution to ICBM Defense	Briefing for Dr. C. C. Furnas, Assistant Secretary of Defense Research and Development, March 30, 1956
Air Force AICBM Weapon Study First Status Report	Air Force Scientific Advisory Board, May 2, 1956
Nike II	Presentation before Dr. Murphree's Antimissile DOD Defense Committee, September 17, 1956

1.6.1.3 Proposed ABM System. The defense problem and the early system proposed as a solution against future threats, including the ICBM, presented to the Assistant Secretary of Defense for R and D on March 30, 1956, involved a number of significant features. The defensive missile with the interchangeable noses for the air threat (seeker) or the ICBM threat (Fig. 7-33) (thrust-vectoring motor for outside atmosphere) was proposed. Early acquisition of the ICBMs would be obtained by a series of forward acquisition radars with fan beams well north of the defended areas, as shown in Fig. 7-36. The overall system is illustrated in Fig. 7-37. The local high-data-rate acquisition radar shown pictorially in Fig. 7-38 was based on the principle of the Luneberg lens antenna (Fig. 7-39). The possible characteristics of this radar are given in Table 7-1.

During the period of the Nike II and Air Force AICBM study, many scientists in the various government agencies and in universities believed it impossible to intercept a target going 24,000 ft/s, comparing the feat to "hitting a bullet with a bullet." An analog simulation room used in testing the Nike-Ajax and -Hercules systems at Bell Laboratories in Whippany was modified to handle ICBM intercepts. Some 50,000 intercept runs under

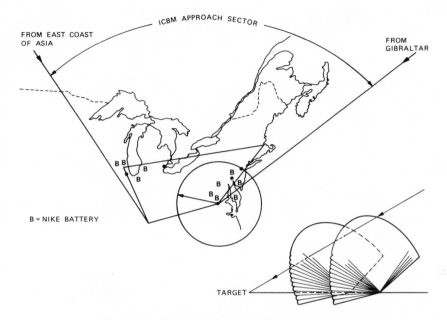

Fig. 7-36. Deployment for ICBM defense.

varying threat parameters and intercept altitudes convincingly demonstrated that ICBMs could be accurately intercepted when the guidance was
properly scaled to the high-speed target. Furthermore, the use of analytical
prediction in these simulations showed that the 60-g slowdown of the
ICBM could be adequately handled by a defensive missile of much lower

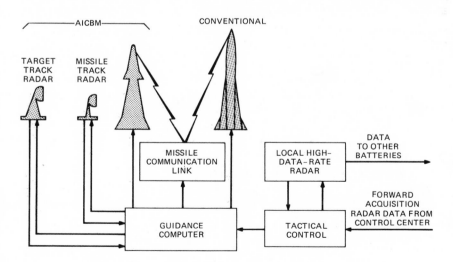

Fig. 7-37. Antiballistic missile (ABM) battery.

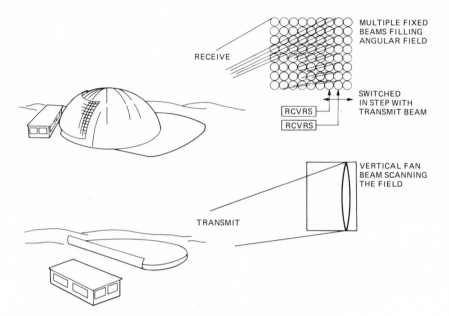

Fig. 7-38.   Anti-ICBM acquisition radar.

steering capability than the ICBM. Following a series of visits to Bell Laboratories by DOD and military groups to witness these simulations, the question of being able to accurately intercept an ICBM was no longer seriously challenged, although full-scale intercepts of actual ICBM targets

Table 7-1. Characteristics of the AICBM Local Acquisition Radar

Coverage	120° azimuth × 60° elevation
Data interval	1 s
Repetition rate	120 pps
Radio frequency	500 MHz
Power	
Peak	5,000 kW
Average	300 kW (each of two)
Transmit antenna	
Aperture	2 ft × 120 ft
Beam	60° × 1°
Gain	27 dB
Receive antenna	
Aperture	120-ft diameter
Beam	1° × 1°
Gain	43 dB
Range of ICBM	600 nmi

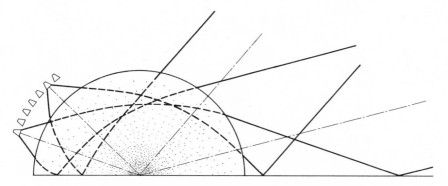

Fig. 7-39. Luneberg lens antenna.

were not confirmed until 6 years later when tests were conducted at Kwajalein Island in the Pacific.

1.6.2 Results of Nike II Study

In October 1956 the results of the 18-month Nike II study were presented in the Pentagon to Lt. Gen. J. M. Gavin and the Army General Staff. The final written report was published the following spring. The report included both defense against air-breathing targets with a seeker-nose missile and defense against ICBMs with a separable thrust-vectoring nose for intercepts outside the atmosphere. In the report, the Luneberg lens type of acquisition radar was fully refined and proposed for two applications. It would be used for both the forward acquisition coverage called FAR and for a high-data-rate (2 seconds) local acquisition radar (LAR) within the defended area to provide hemispheric coverage and multi-tracking of 50 to 100 targets. The plan of integration is shown in Fig. 7-40. Artist's views of the acquisition radars proposed are shown in Figs. 7-41 and 7-42, and the weapon battery is shown in Fig. 7-43. The precision target track radar (TTR) is shown in Fig. 7-44. The ICBM defensive missile shown in Fig. 7-45 would carry a 400-pound nuclear warhead and provide 10-g maneuverability at 100,000 feet. The thrust-vectoring nose would be required for end-game steering at altitudes above 80,000 feet.

In late 1956 a report on the same system was given to the Air Force upon completion of the year's study. As mentioned earlier, the additional effort for the Air Force was applied to studies of the forward data gathering and on the communications network required for connection to local defense elements.

In reporting on an ABM communications system the studies for both the Air Force and the Army made the following recommendations:

1. The system should be completely automatic with all elements electronic and capable of operating at high speed. A communications message-

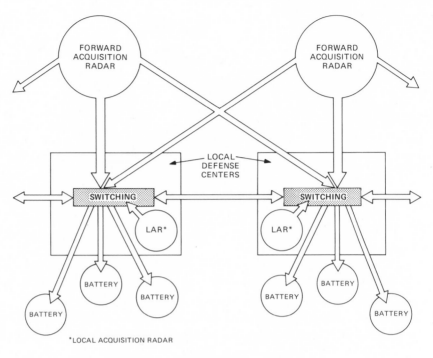

Fig. 7-40.   Nike II plan for integration.

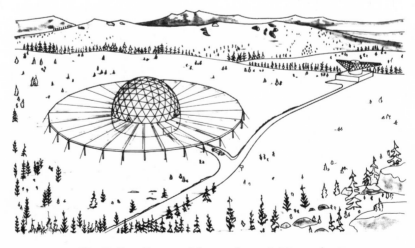

Fig. 7-41.   Proposed forward acquisition radar.

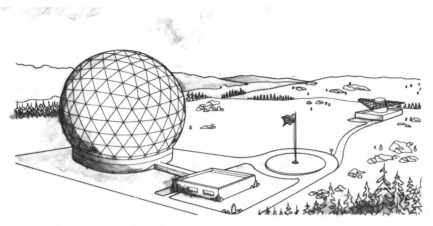

Fig. 7-42. Proposed local acquisition radar.

numbering plan should be used, based on the destination of the data (from FAR to specific battery).

2. The system should use intermediate switching to reduce the number of channels required for a full Continental United States (CONUS) defense network.

3. Multialternate routing should be used to provide reliability.

4. Error checking should be incorporated in the system to ensure accuracy in transmission.

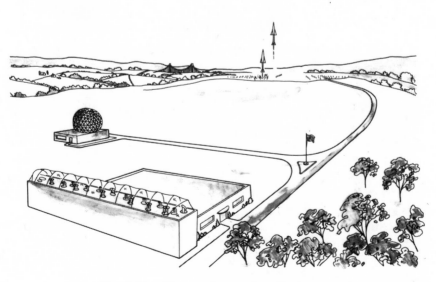

Fig. 7-43.   Weapon battery installation.

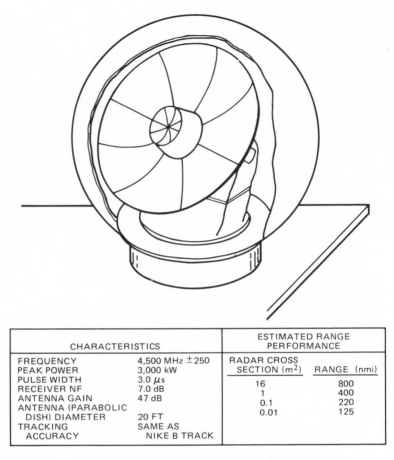

CHARACTERISTICS		ESTIMATED RANGE PERFORMANCE	
FREQUENCY	4,500 MHz ±250	RADAR CROSS SECTION (m²)	RANGE (nmi)
PEAK POWER	3,000 kW		
PULSE WIDTH	3.0 µs	16	800
RECEIVER NF	7.0 dB	1	400
ANTENNA GAIN	47 dB	0.1	220
ANTENNA (PARABOLIC		0.01	125
DISH) DIAMETER	20 FT		
TRACKING	SAME AS		
ACCURACY	NIKE B TRACK		

Fig. 7-44.   Long-range target track radar.

5. Each message should be acknowledged to increase reliability.

6. Voice-bandwidth channels should be used universally. (A proposed communication route was presented for the defense of the northeastern United States.)

As part of the final, March 1957 report, a complete development test plan for the proposed system was included. It covered a 6-year period from initial development to system demonstration tests against real ICBM targets at a remote testing range.

During the period of these studies, there was intense rivalry between the Army and the Air Force for the mission of ICBM defense. The work at Bell Laboratories resulted in one system concept, while the additional Air Force effort afforded an opportunity to study the overall communications network, including problems of data processing and data trans-

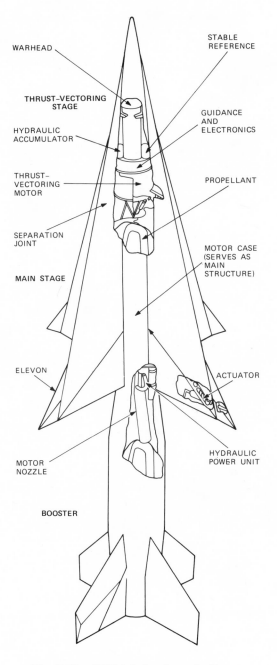

WARHEAD

STABLE
REFERENCE

**THRUST-VECTORING
STAGE**

GUIDANCE
AND
ELECTRONICS

HYDRAULIC
ACCUMULATOR

THRUST-
VECTORING
MOTOR

PROPELLANT

SEPARATION
JOINT

MOTOR CASE
(SERVES AS
MAIN
STRUCTURE)

MAIN STAGE

ELEVON

ACTUATOR

MOTOR
NOZZLE

HYDRAULIC
POWER UNIT

BOOSTER

Fig. 7-45.   ICBM defensive missile.

mission. General Hertford of the Army had no objection to include appropriate parts of the results of the Nike II study in the report to the Air Force. In presentations to top DOD and special antimissile committees, the same Bell Laboratories and Douglas systems concept was presented by both the Army and the Air Force. (The roles of these services were subsequently redefined to give responsibility for the AICBM effort to the Army.)

1.6.3 Nike-Zeus

In February 1957 the Army awarded Western Electric and Bell Laboratories prime contractor systems responsibility for development of an AICBM defense system and changed its name from Nike II to Nike-Zeus. With the growing concern for the ICBM threat, Bell Laboratories was asked by DOD and the Army to concentrate solely on the ICBM defensive missile and hence to terminate work on the seeker nose for air-breathing targets. The level of research and development effort for the first year included subcontract work by Douglas on the missile, RCA on the transmitter, and Goodyear Aircraft Company on the antenna structure. Changes were made in certain elements of the Nike-Zeus System from that described in the March 1957 report during the early development phase.

One of the major research and development problems mentioned in the AICBM reports to the Army and Air Force was the task of separating the reentry body from the various decoys and junk that might accompany it. Consequently, research and systems work continued on this high-priority problem as development work on the overall system was initiated. The TTRs in the proposed Nike-Zeus System would have to see all the objects in a cloud assigned to them by the acquisition radar and track one of the objects (preferably one near the center of the cloud). At the same time, the radar would have to systematically examine all received signals of objects in the cloud at a high data rate to permit discrimination analysis of the radar return signals. The implementation for scanning would be such that once the reentry body was identified, precise automatic position and velocity tracking of the target would have to be established in a few seconds by the TTR.

Note that at this particular time radar measurements of incoming ICBMs were not available, since the first successful ICBMs were not flown until 1959–1960. Consequently, such discrimination possibilities as scintillation, radar size, and slowdown were proposed among other methods whose success might depend on the ability of the TTRs to obtain the high data rate mentioned. Thus, three methods were considered to increase the angular field of radar coverage for examining an incoming cloud: (1) scanning the TTR beam, (2) increasing the TTR beamwidth, and (3) providing additional receiver beams in the same TTR focusing structure. The first method was dropped, because the intermittent data would seriously limit radar data rate and would present a problem in tracking one of the objects while the cloud was being scanned. The second method was not practical because of the serious loss in radar range and accuracy. The third method was then proposed as a modification to the TTR, the result being named the "fly's eye" antenna.

The principle of the fly's eye antenna is shown in Fig. 7-46 where an array of antenna feedhorns is clustered about the monopulse horns, which would be used for accurately tracking the target after discrimination. The center monopulse horns would transmit and receive in the conventional manner. The cluster of horns located on the main reflector would act as range-only receivers and provide a field of view of about $4\frac{1}{2}$ by $4\frac{1}{2}$ degrees, as shown in Figs. 7-47 and 7-48. A separate transmitting antenna slaved to the large TTR mount would provide the illumination for the range-only receivers. So that the losses caused by the hole in the main reflector would be avoided, a grating of vertical wires would be stretched across the horn openings, and the secondary reflector would be designed to shift the polarization from horizontal to vertical.

With these changes, and with pulse-collapsing chirp techniques for fine-range resolution together with multiple range-tracking circuits, high-data-rate signature outputs on objects in a cloud would be provided for radar signature and aerodynamic discrimination. The discrimination circuits would accept the individual gated signals from the multiple

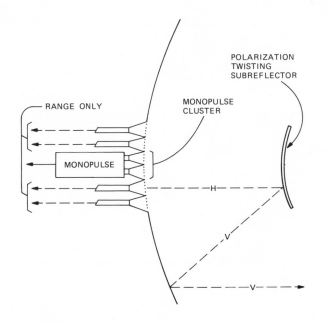

Fig. 7-46.   Fly's eye antenna.

range-tracking equipment and perform tests based on differences in amplitude, frequency spectrum, radar frequency sensitivity, ionization, aerodynamic-slowdown characteristics, etc.

On further study of various threat possibilities, the fly's eye TTR concept had the major drawback of a multifunction requirement in a mechanical dish-type radar. Where more than one reentry vehicle (RV) was in a cloud of objects, the discrimination function would have to be terminated once the first RV was acquired and precision-tracked for intercept. Furthermore, off-angle data on objects would not be sufficiently accurate for fast acquisition of an RV once it was selected for intercept. The decision was therefore made to have a completely separate discrimination radar (DR) and to time-share the TTRs to provide precision track of designated targets 6 to 10 seconds before intercept.

The DR became the Zeus system's instrument to select attacking warheads from debris and accompanying decoys. In performing the discrimination functions, the DR would examine a threatening cloud of objects designated by the acquisition radar. Radar returns would be processed by an associated DR data processor. The unique feature of this radar was a Cassegrainian-type antenna with a movable subreflector that permitted the radar to continuously widen its antenna beam and maintain cloud coverage as the range decreased. The radar could also provide angle information on all objects off the beam so that defensive missiles being

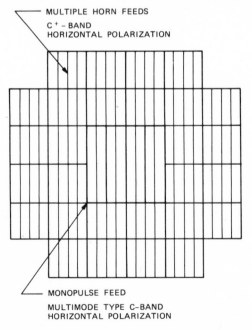

Fig. 7-47. Fly's eye antenna feedhorn structure.

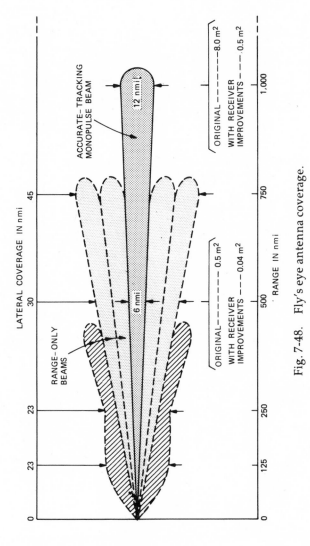

Fig. 7-48. Fly's eye antenna coverage.

launched could use this data. Prior to intercept, the data could be transferred to a precision TTR for automatic acquisition of the designated target.
The radar was to be designed for operation in the L-band with a 40-MW

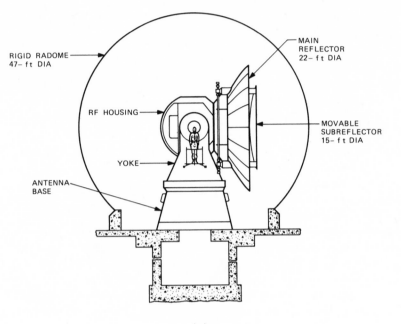

(a)

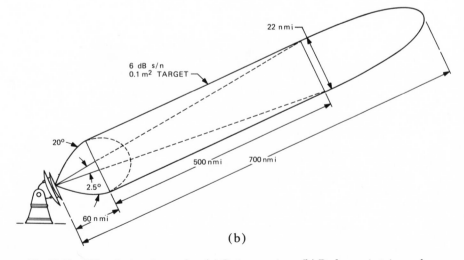

(b)

Fig. 7-49.   Discrimination radar. (a) Cutaway view. (b) Radar maintains volume
coverage by varying beamwidth.

peak power transmitter and a low-noise maser RF amplifier in the receiver. The beamwidth was to be continuously variable from 2 to 20 degrees. A cutaway view of the DR antenna together with its range and angle coverage is shown in Fig. 7-49.

The characteristics of the DR returns would be compared with radar characteristics of the reentry body stored in the DR data processor. Velocity data obtained by tracking individual objects would also be used by the data processor to measure the slowdown and determine the ballistic coefficient of the objects. Requirements were established for range-tracking up to 100 tracks with three-coordinate data on 10 tracks.

Later system studies of threat scenarios indicated a need for 3 DRs, 6 TTRs, and 12 missile track radars (MTRs) in a firing battery.

1.6.3.1 Acquisition Radar.

The ZEUS System Study Report included a forward acquisition radar (FAR) and a local acquisition radar (LAR) near the firing battery. Further system studies, however, raised serious questions about the defense of the FARs. Systems people took the position that if the few FARs were integrated and were important elements of the ICBM defense, then each should be defended n times as well as any of the single batteries associated with it (n being the number of batteries integrated with a single FAR). With the FARs located primarily in Canada, doubts were raised about just how essential the FAR installations were to the defense. As a result of the studies, the FARs were eliminated and all search and acquisition functions were assigned to the LARs at each battery. The LAR design, however, was changed from a spherical design to that of a hemispherical Luneberg lens, as proposed for the FAR, since the hemispherical lens could be made less sensitive to nuclear weapon overpressure effects.

In establishing the 500-megahertz (MHz) frequency of the Zeus acquisition radar (ZAR) during the 18-month study, all important radar parameters known at that time and their sensitivity to frequency were taken into account. However, the effect from nuclear burst at very high altitude was not yet known. The existence of a threat from this quarter was later shown theoretically and was partially verified by the high-altitude nuclear test program at Johnston Island.

It became clear through further study that radar-signal attenuation due to the effects of nuclear burst is reduced by the square of the radar frequency. This new factor was taken into account in balancing the optimum frequency of the ZAR. The tactical design chosen was modified for 1,000 MHz, although all prototype radars under way for White Sands Missile Range and Kwajalein were left in the 450-MHz range. While a tactical design radar was never constructed at 1,000 MHz, design effort and manufacturing plans for the Luneberg lens dielectric material, receivers, and transmitters were changed to the higher frequency.

1.6.3.2 Zeus Missile.   The missile design proposed in the 18-month study was to have a jethead-type nose for ballistic missile defense and an active-seeker nose for future air threats. With the new emphasis concentrated on ballistic defense, the seeker development was dropped, as mentioned earlier. The antimissile missile originally proposed had the aerodynamic control system packaged around the second-stage nozzle for controlling elevons on the main fins. This system was entirely separate from the control system for the jetavator motor in the nose section. It soon became apparent that substantial simplification could be achieved by changing to forward aerodynamic canard control combined with thrust-vectoring control. With such a change, two control systems would be reduced to one, and all electronic controls would be in the nose section. This was a major simplification.

This change, however, required that thrust control be obtained by exhausting the thrust motor's hot gases through the aerodynamic control fins. Although the change greatly simplified the electronics and hydraulic control system, the problem was transferred to the mechanical designers who had to design 180-degree reversal exhaust systems, through the fins, capable of withstanding extreme temperatures for the 12-second operation of the thrust motor. Many failures occurred during the step-by-step solution to this problem, which involved complex surfaces of tungsten and carbon materials. In the end, a highly reliable system was achieved, but not without some despairing moments for Douglas engineers.

1.6.3.3 Further Meetings on Nike-Zeus System.   A complete summary of all the presentations made to high-level personnel in the government during the development years of Nike-Zeus would fill many pages. A few of the presentations in 1959 were:

1. A Nike-Zeus meeting at Bell Laboratories, Whippany, in March 1959, attended by the following:
   W. A. Holaday, DOD Missile Director
   Dr. H. Skifter, DOD
   Maj. Gen. D. E. Beach, Dept. of Army
   Maj. Gen. W. W. Dick, Dept. of Army
   Brig. Gen. A. J. Pierce, North American Air Defense Command (NORAD).
   Representatives from AT&T, Western Electric, Bell Laboratories, and Douglas.

2. Briefing for Dr. Herbert York and his DOD staff on April 15, 1959, in Washington, D. C., covering possible degradation of system capabilities in the presence of various countermeasures.

3. Similar meeting with staff of presidential advisor Dr. James Killian on April 24, 1959, in Washington.

4. Army Policy Committee briefing by Army and Bell Laboratories representatives on May 6, 1959, in the Pentagon.

5. Briefing for Lt. Gen. C. E. Hart, Commander-in-Chief of the Army Air Defense Command (ARADCOM), on May 19, 1959; and for Gen. E. E. Partridge, Commander-in-Chief of NORAD, and Air Marshal Sleman, Deputy Commander of NORAD, on May 20, 1959.

1.6.3.4 Field Testing the Nike-Zeus System. Suitable locations for field-testing the high-performance subsystems of Zeus and for testing the overall Nike-Zeus system represented major new challenges to DOD, the Army Missile Command, and the system prime contractor. Some of the reasons for choosing test locations throw light on the magnitude of the R and D tasks.

Early testing of the Zeus missile in the fall of 1959 was necessary to establish the extent of the aerodynamic heating problem in such a high-velocity missile. White Sands Missile Range was selected for these critical tests, in which a modified Hercules missile radar was used for tracking. However, the test flights had to be limited to aerodynamic control below 100,000 feet to keep within the 100-mile limit of the range. Of particular concern was the very long carry range of heavy missile parts in case of missile failure during testing outside the atmosphere with the jethead thrust control.

Many presentations were made to top DOD R and D officials by the Army and Bell Laboratories showing the very low probability of any missile parts landing in a populated area. Some consideration was given to clearing a 25-mile extension of the range, but even this would not permit full altitude testing of the missile. A decision was therefore made to provide a second missile test site at the Naval Test Range at Point Mugu, California. A Zeus missile track radar, a guidance computer, launching equipment, etc., had to be installed at Point Mugu to permit testing the Zeus missile at high altitude outside the atmosphere. As it developed, Point Mugu proved to be a poor missile test site for Zeus because of the severe range-safety restrictions imposed by the Navy, which resulted in fail-safe delays of only a fraction of a second. This led to a number of good missiles being destroyed early in flight without obtaining any useful data.

R and D and continued field testing for ICBM defense were given top priority in August 1957, when the USSR announced that it had successfully tested an ICBM shortly after placing Sputnik I into orbit. It became increasingly important to ready the Zeus system for tracking incoming United States ICBMs as soon as they became operational in the Atlantic Test Range. We had to learn if we could successfully track a reentry body through slowdown and, in addition, what discrimination possibilities might be realized. These were questions critical to the success of the Zeus system. Top priority was given to the installation of a Zeus target track radar (TTR) on Ascension Island, the target area planned for ICBM launches from Cape Canaveral, Florida. At Whippany, a similar TTR installation was built simultaneously to provide a local prototype for correcting design problems.

In addition, a full-scale program was begun at White Sands Missile Range. This involved Zeus missile firings and the installation of major components of the Zeus system—the large spherical acquisition radar, the associated missile and track radars, and the ground guidance computer—to prove in the designs.

Still to be found, though, was a location where the entire Nike-Zeus system could be installed and eventually tested against real offensive targets. In January 1958 Bell Laboratories, Western Electric, and Army planners began shopping for a suitable location. Attention shifted to the Pacific area since Atlantic islands were not under United States control. Planners pored over maps and studied data about and photographs of a dozen Pacific islands and atolls. As the study progressed, Kwajalein Atoll in the Marshall Islands began to look more and more attractive, for a number of reasons.

Kwajalein was not owned by the United States, but it had been under American stewardship continuously since 1944. Kwajalein was once an active Navy base but appeared headed for phaseout, since it was on caretaker status. Although it was remote, it was still within a day's flying time of Hawaii; Johnston Island, another possible test site, lay almost directly en route between them. Most desirable of all, however, were Kwajalein's existing facilities and its geographic location. Kwajalein already had an airstrip, a harbor, housing areas, schools, a hospital, merchandising facilities, and more. In addition, Kwajalein was roughly 4,800 miles from the West Coast, a range nearly ideal for testing Nike-Zeus against ICBM targets of opportunity to be launched from Vandenberg Air Force Base in southern California.

On February 12, 1959, on recommendation of the Army Rocket and Guided Missile Agency (ARGMA), supported by Bell Laboratories and Western Electric, DOD approved a test program for Nike-Zeus with Kwajalein as the down-range test site. The sponsoring Army organization would become a tenant on the naval base. Plans called for a Kwajalein–Johnston Island testing complex, with Jupiter intermediate-range ballistic missiles (IRBMs) being fired from Johnston Island toward Kwajalein. A year later, however, Herbert York (then Assistant Secretary of Defense for R and D) ruled that only Air Force Atlas ICBMs launched from Vandenberg would be used as target vehicles for Nike-Zeus. Thus work on Johnston Island was halted. With the beginning of operations at Kwajalein, and for a number of years thereafter until Ascension Island— the South Atlantic test site—closed, the Nike-Zeus system development and test activities were 12,000 miles apart on opposite sides of the globe.

With selection of Kwajalein, project managers, anxious to inspect the new site, chartered a Pan American DC-7, which touched down on Kwajalein on August 4, 1959. The 41 passengers aboard represented various Army agencies, Bell Laboratories, Western Electric, and Douglas, and other subcontractors.

The initial work at Kwajalein was done by the Army Corps of Engineers and their subcontractor, the Pacific Martin Zachry Company, which was responsible for the Nike-Zeus technical building and launch facilities. They were followed later by Western Electric equipment engineers and installers responsible for the Nike-Zeus installation. On October 1, 1960, Bell Laboratories announced the establishment of the Kwajalein Field Station. Four days later R. W. Benfer arrived at the new Station as its first director.

1.6.3.5 Highlights of Nike-Zeus R and D Test Results

Early Firings

The Nike-Zeus System test program planned by Bell Labs required the solution of numerous problems before successful intercepts of ICBM targets could be accomplished. The Zeus missile, operating in the lower-altitude region with a peak velocity three times that of Nike-Hercules, presented aerodynamic heating problems even greater than an ICBM reentry body. During the 18-month initial study and exploratory development effort, Douglas aerodynamic engineers carried out wind tunnel tests at high-supersonic velocities and heat-tested various ablative coatings, such as Teflon[4] and fiberglass, as protective materials for the missile structure. However, the extent of the problem was not fully appreciated until the early Zeus missiles were flown at the White Sands Missile Range.

Catastrophic failure of these early flights occurred within a few seconds of the missiles' reaching peak velocities, and ground cameras recorded what appeared to be a fire aboard each missile prior to its failure. A hydraulic oil fire was suspected, and steps were taken to provide heat shields around the hydraulic power system for future missile flights. However, after these changes, fire was still observed in the nose section and missile failure occurred as before. It was not until missile pieces were recovered from the desert range and partly reassembled that the real problem was discovered.

It was clear from examination of the four control fins that their large-diameter hardened-steel shafts had been sliced off by aerodynamic heating, which resulted in loss of control and missile destruction. On the basis of aerodynamic wind-tunnel data, the control fins had been purposely

---

[4] Trademark of E. I. du Pont de Nemours.

Table 7-2. Summary of Early Zeus Firings

	No. Test	Failures	Partial Success	Full Success	Total
			Development Firings		
WSMR Point Mugu Kwajalein	—	15	7	34	56
	—	5	4	10	19
	—	2	1	1	4
				Total	79
			Missile Performance in System Tests		
WSMR Kwajalein	2	3	0	11	16
	5	12	7	28	52
				Total	68
				Total firings	147

shaped to have wide separation from the missile skin. After returning to the wind tunnel with much finer measurements of pressures under the fin surface, the engineers discovered high pressure points that resulted in concentrated heat levels. In the redesign, they provided a Teflon ramp under the control fin to give close spacing. In addition, they provided circular traps to protect the control shaft, much as a radar engineer would design protection for the ball bearings in a shaft from RF power. With these changes, the major aerodynamic problem was solved, which opened the way to successful Zeus missile firings. This ramp design and close spacing for the control fins were adopted by the Martin designers of the Sprint missile some six years later. As a result, even though Sprint's velocity was higher than Zeus' at lower altitudes, with much greater aerodynamic heating, the same basic design was successful in protecting its control fins.

The other major step forward in missile design was providing aerodynamic and thrust control with the same control fins. The problem of handling the hot gases of the third-stage motor through a manifold system into the control fins was solved by extensive ground testing with many configurations of tungsten and carbon materials. As a result, relatively few failures of the jet control system occurred in early flights at high altitudes from the Point Mugu range.

One important lesson learned from the Zeus development firings, and reaffirmed years later with Sprint, was that there is no substitute for missile testing over a ground range where the pieces can be recovered and the cause of failure found. This is especially true in a situation where the state of missile art is being advanced significantly and where there is a limit to the number of missile-borne sensors that are capable of detecting the cause of failures. A summary of the early Zeus missile firings is given in Table 7-2.

TTR at Ascension and Whippany

The first attempt of the TTR at Ascension Island to track an ICBM (a Titan) fired from Cape Canaveral took place on March 29, 1961. This attempt failed because the TTR computer did not properly translate trajectory data from Cape Canaveral to position the antenna needle beam. However, on May 28, 1961, an ICBM from Cape Canaveral was tracked along its trajectory down the Atlantic Missile Range. These initial tracking tests were not perfect, but for the first time they did permit analysis of target characteristics, and they measured our ability to track such high-speed targets.

Concurrently, a similar TTR at Bell Laboratories, Whippany, New Jersey, was used to investigate the early automatic tracking problems. On May 6, 1961, the Whippany TTR successfully tracked the Echo satellite at distances up to 1,400 miles. Later in the year, four ICBMs (two Atlases and two Titans) were successfully tracked by the Ascension TTR with continuous tracks of as much as 100 seconds. In the last tracking, the Atlas had a nose cone designed for Nike-Zeus tests at Kwajalein. The nose cone had the same radar cross section as a regular Atlas nose, but it also had special shaping to reduce the plasma-sheath effect (ionic layer) on radio signal propagation. This was required for a radio-doppler miss-distance indicator to be used later in system tests at Kwajalein.

White Sands Missile Range Tests

Initial operation of the Zeus acquisition radar (ZAR) as a system was accomplished at WSMR in June 1961. Typical targets were automatically acquired and tracked in three dimensions. The targets included balloons, aircraft, parachutes deployed from Highball missiles, and Hercules missiles. The three-dimensional tracks were transferred to battery control, where they were automatically acquired by the TTR subsystem.

These tests were historic in that the ZAR was the first track-while-scan radar system to successfully cover the entire hemisphere surrounding a radar position, detect the objects in that space, remember their past positions, and predict where the objects would next be located in three dimensions—all automatically, beginning with initial detection. Even today, considering the advances with phased-array radar systems, the ZAR represents the most efficient wired-logic system for detection, report sorting, track initiation, and track processing ever developed. Its stacked-array receivers on three rotating arms also provided the highest data rate (two seconds for full hemispheric coverage) yet achieved, which is not matched even by today's phased-array systems.

The TTR radar at WSMR was made operational without difficulty on the basis of previous testing with a similar design at Whippany and Ascension. The other major subsystem was the battery control building, which contained two missile track radars, the target intercept computer, and data communication equipment. The Zeus missile had been under development at WSMR for the previous two years with modified Hercules equipment used for ground guidance.

All elements of Nike-Zeus were checked out and system demonstrations begun in November 1961. On December 14, 1961, a major ABM system milepost was passed with the successful interception by a Zeus missile of a Nike-Hercules target missile. The miss-distance was less than 100 feet. A second Zeus system test against a Hercules missile was carried out in March 1962, with a miss distance of 45 feet. Major attention then shifted to the forthcoming system tests at Kwajalein against ICBM targets.

Nike-Zeus System Tests at Kwajalein

The entire Nike-Zeus system, consisting of the hemispheric ZAR, two target track radars (TTRs), one discrimination radar (DR), three missile track radars (MTRs), and battery control equipment with target intercept computer and four Zeus launch cells, was installed on Kwajalein and was

Fig. 7-50.   Nike-Zeus system installation at Kwajalein—viewed in the direction of the lagoon.

Table 7-3. Summary of Live-Target System Tests

Mission Number	Date	Target	Remarks
K1	6-26-62	Atlas D	Failure
K2	7-19-62	Atlas D	Partly successful
K6	12-12-62	Atlas D	Successful (first missile in salvo)
K7	12-22-62	Atlas D	Successful (first missile in salvo)
K8	2-13-63	Atlas D	Partly successful
K10	2-28-63	Atlas D	Partly successful
K17	3-30-63	Titan I	Successful
K21	4-13-63	Titan I	Successful
K15	6-12-63	Atlas D	Successful
K23	7-4-63	Atlas E	Successful
K26	8-15-63	Titan I	Successful
K28	8-24-63	Atlas E	Successful
K24	11-14-63	Titan I	Successful

ready for the first test of intercepting an ICBM on June 26, 1962. The photographs in Figs. 7-50 and 7-51 show this installation.

In the first attempt (probably in the world) to intercept an ICBM fired 4,500 miles down range from Vandenburg Air Force Base, the acquisition radar started tracking the tank at 446 nautical miles and immediately

Fig. 7-51.   Nike-Zeus system installation at Kwajalein, aerial view.

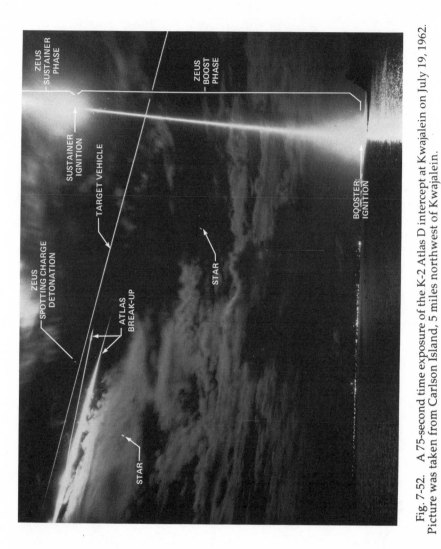

Fig. 7-52.   A 75-second time exposure of the K-2 Atlas D intercept at Kwajalein on July 19, 1962. Picture was taken from Carlson Island, 5 miles northwest of Kwajalein.

Fig. 7-53. View of the August 15, 1963, K-26 Titan I intercept test at Kwajalein. The Zeus thrust-vector motor trail and spotting detonation (arrow) mark the successful intercept.

transferred the track to the TTR. The TTR transferred from the tank to the nose cone (RV) at 131 nautical miles. When the tank began to break up, a clutter mode of operation was initiated in which any significant departure of the RV from a predicted trajectory would indicate that debris had taken over the tracking gate. The radar would then use extrapolated data to "coast" the range gate so as to reacquire the RV after it passed through the tank clutter. Unfortunately, in this first test the clutter mode did not properly indicate when tracking of the RV was lost. However, because of malfunction, the Zeus missile would not have achieved intercept.

Although this first system test was a failure, it did emphasize the need for sound logic and reliable circuitry to properly track RVs through severe tank clutter. This early lesson carried through to the 1975 tactical Safeguard system tests at Meck Island, where tracking through clutter was satisfactorily demonstrated under even more stringent conditions.

The first partly successful intercept of an Atlas D ICBM occurred on July 19, 1962, with the Zeus missile coming within 2 kilometers of the target vehicle at intercept. The large miss distance resulted from the Zeus missile losing hydraulic power owing to excessive roll during the last 10 seconds

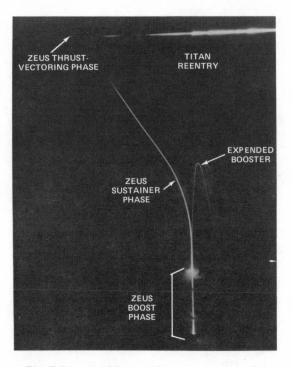

Fig. 7-54. A 120-second time exposure of the March 30, 1963, K-17 Titan I intercept test at Kwajalein. This was the first intercept test to be conducted against a target vehicle boosted by a Titan I.

before intercept. The second ICBM intercept—this one wholly success-ful—took place on December 12, 1962, with a miss distance well within acceptable limits. A two-missile salvo was planned for the first time with this test, but the second missile failed because of an instrument failure.

Another two-missile salvo intercept of an ICBM was attempted on De-cember 22, 1962. In this test, the first missile missed the target by 200 meters at a range of 55 nautical miles. Again, dual interception did not occur because of a failure with the second missile.

A summary of the live-intercept system tests of Zeus extending through November 1963 is given in Table 7-3. Of 13 system tests, 9 were successful, 3 were partly successful, and only the first failed. Photographs of some of these intercepts are shown in Figs. 7-52 through 7-55.

With completion of these live-target system tests and the decision not to deploy the Nike-Zeus system, no further live ICBM target tests were carried out. However, further tests under the satellite test program and system tests against taped live targets or simulated ICBMs continued at Kwajalein for another year and a half until June 1965.

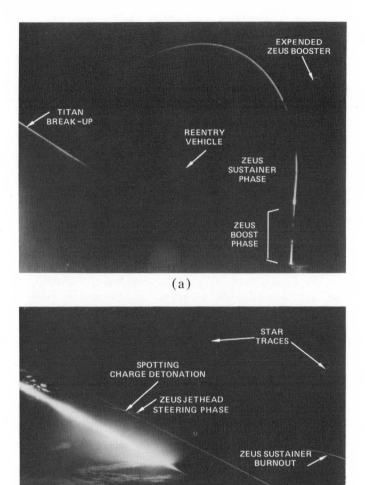

Fig. 7-55. Two 120-second time exposures of intercept test K-21 conducted April 13, 1963. (a) Overall view of test taken from Enubuj (Carlson) Island. (b) View showing successful intercept (spotting charge detonation) taken from Ennylabegan (Carlos) Island.

Miss-Distance Indicator for Zeus Tests

Miss distance between target and defensive missile at the instant of commanded warhead burst is the principal measure of performance of an AICBM system. To avoid suspicion of any self-generated miss distance within the Zeus system, considerable effort was directed at finding an independent miss-distance recorder for the Zeus system tests at Kwajalein. One method pursued involved a radioactive source in the ICBM nose cone and a detection system in the Zeus missile. This work was carried out starting in April 1961 on subcontract with the Giannini Control Corporation. However, a simpler radio-doppler miss-distance indicator (MDI) was adopted after its successful development by the Physical Science Laboratory (PSL) of New Mexico State University.

Well in advance of the Zeus system tests in 1960, PSL was given a contract to adapt a Navy AN/US Q-11 radio-doppler miss-distance measuring set to the environment of Highball and Speedball test-rocket targets being developed for Zeus tests, and to extend this adaptation to the ICBM target environment. The success of this system was dependent on tests carried out in December 1961 in the Atlantic Missile Range, which proved that signals from a UHF radio transmitter in a reentering ICBM nose cone could penetrate the surrounding plasma sheath. The planned miss-distance instrumentation required such a transmitter in the ICBM and a compatible receiver in the Zeus missile. The resultant shape of the doppler signal telemetered to ground during intercept, when correlated with the burst-command time, provided an independent measurement of miss distance. This system, made ready for the Zeus system tests at Kwajalein for live ICBM targets, provided quite accurate measurements matching reasonably well the self-generated miss-distance numbers within the Zeus equipment.

1.6.3.6 Satellite Test Program.   The Secretary of Defense requested the Army in early 1962 to prepare the Zeus system on Kwajalein to intercept and destroy satellites. Bell Laboratories advised the Army that the Zeus System could be readied for a satellite intercept demonstration at Kwajalein by May 1963.

Toward this goal, the first DM-15B series Zeus missile, modified for satellite intercept tests, was fired at White Sands Missile Range on December 17, 1962. The missile successfully intercepted a designated stationary space point at an altitude of 100 nautical miles. It reached the highest altitude of any missile launched at White Sands to that date. The DM-15S series was modified for this high-altitude, long-range application to include a two-stage (instead of a single-stage) hydraulic pumping unit, a high-performance polybutadiene acrylic acid (PBAA) booster propellant, and a 5-minute (instead of the normal 2-minute) battery capability. A second DM-15S series missile was fired at WSMR on February 15, 1963. In this flight, intercept of the space point occurred at an altitude of 151 nautical miles.

The first successful satellite intercept test and demonstration against a real target occurred on May 24, 1963, at Kwajalein. The target was a special Agena D stage of the Air Force 162A series. This target was instrumented with the Nike-Zeus single-path doppler miss-distance measuring equipment discussed earlier and a Luneberg lens for radar augmentation. The TTR first acquired the satellite at long range, and the missile was launched after a period of precision tracking. A close intercept was achieved, well within what was expected to be the lethal range of the Zeus nuclear warhead.

From this time through 1964, satellite intercept missiles were maintained at Kwajalein with one always checked out and in a state of readiness. Arrangements were made by the Army to make a Zeus nuclear warhead available if called upon for a real satellite mission. (Army personnel on Kwajalein would be responsible for launching the missile in a real defensive operation.) Bell Laboratories and Douglas personnel went through many test runs to minimize the time required to launch such a missile. In addition, successful test intercepts were carried out against simulated satellites and booster space targets in 1964 as part of the training of Kwajalein test personnel. Fortunately, intercept and destruction of an enemy satellite were never ordered. After 1964 the test personnel were relieved of this "ready" requirement and were once more able to concentrate fully on the normal R and D test program.

1.6.3.7 Discrimination and Supporting Research. As the Zeus R and D program moved forward, a continuing and expanded effort was carried out on the major problem of discrimination. For the purpose of supplementing its own internal effort, Bell Laboratories established subcontracts with Cornell Aeronautical Laboratories (now Calspan Corporation) and Avco Everett Research Laboratories. The principal types of discrimination under investigation in the early 1960s were aerodynamic slowdown, scintillation, polarization, frequency diversity, short pulse, and infrared/optical effects. Other supporting research was concerned with blast tests to determine the hardness of Zeus ground facilities, atmospheric effects of nuclear bursts, plasma studies of reentry bodies, and warhead requirements.

The Avco Everett investigation concentrated on infrared, visual, and ultraviolet reentry effects and was carried out with the aid of the Nike-Zeus TTR on Ascension Island. Phase I, which began in early 1961, determined discrimination criteria with simple instrumentation in a DC-6 aircraft operating out of Ascension. Optical/infrared data, particularly on wake spectra, were obtained on 14 of 17 ICBMs fired toward Ascension Island in 1961. Phase II started in early 1962, with more sophisticated instrumentation in the aircraft and on the ground. This permitted target designation between the TTR and the optical tracker in the aircraft so that the same object tracked by the TTR could be correlated with optical/infrared data. A Hercules missile track radar installed on Ascension Island tracked the beacon in a new WV-2 aircraft equipped with a stable reference platform. Positional data on incoming objects could then be transmitted in both directions between aircraft and TTR. Later on, the same aircraft was used at Kwajalein to obtain additional data.

Table 7-4. Major Nike-Zeus Subcontractors

Company	Location	Area of Activity
Goodyear Aircraft Corp.	Akron, Ohio	ZAR receiving and transmitting antennas
		DR antenna mount and MTR reflector
Armstrong Cork Co.	Lancaster, Pa.	ZAR lens media
Dow Chemical Co.	Midland, Mich.	
Continental Electronics Mfg. Co.	Dallas, Tex.	ZAR transmitter
Texas Instruments, Inc.	Dallas, Tex.	Tactical displays
Sperry Gyroscope Co.	Great Neck, N.Y.	DR and TTR transmitters
Vickers, Inc.	Waterbury, Conn.	DR and TTR antenna hydraulic drives
Narmco Mfg. Co.	La Mesa, Cal.	DR and TTR antenna reflectors
Continental Can Co.	Chicago, Ill.	TTR antenna mount
Allis Chalmers	Akron, Ohio	Steel weldments for TTR antenna mount
Steel Products Engineering Co.	Springfield, Ohio	MTR antenna mount
Sperry Rand Univac	St. Paul, Minn.	Target intercept computer
Douglas Aircraft Co.	Santa Monica, Cal.	Missile, launcher, and missile handling equipment
Thiokol Chemical Co.	Huntsville, Ala.	Booster and sustainer
AIResearch Mfg. Co.	Beverly Hills, Cal.	Missile hydraulic power unit
Epsco West	Anaheim, Cal.	Test equipment
Stromberg-Carlson	Rochester, N.Y.	Test equipment
Lear Inc.	Grand Rapids, Mich.	Stable platform
Burns and Roe, Inc.	New York, N.Y.	Architectural engineering for the R and D program
New Mexico State University	University Park, N.M.	Test targets
Airborne Instruments Laboratories	Mineola, N.Y.	ZAR antenna measurements
Cornell Aeronautical Laboratories	Buffalo, N.Y.	Decoy discrimination studies
Avco Everett Research Laboratory	Everett, Mass.	Infrared decoy discrimination studies
Varian Associates	Palo Alto, Calif.	High-power klystrons for ZAR transmitter

Although useful optical/infrared data were obtained in these tests, no solid discrimination criteria were uncovered to warrant adding optical airborne trackers to the Zeus system. Furthermore, in attempting to correlate radar and airborne optical data, these tests forcefully demonstrated the practical problems of trying to incorporate such an airborne platform into a tactical system.

In 1961 Bell Laboratories analyzed the effects of plasma on radar observation. It was hoped that the plasma (ionic layer) sheath caused by aerodynamic heating might provide additional means of discrimination against decoys. Other work at Bell Laboratories at this time showed that extremely short pulses could determine the length of a target and thus provide a possible discriminant.

Major effort at Cornell Laboratories in 1961 and 1962 was directed at testing various radar signatures in the laboratory. These signatures included scintillation, polarization, and frequency diversity. Both Bell Laboratories and Cornell examined methods of incorporating a number of radar signatures into a combined "likelihood" number that would reveal whether a given object was a warhead, since no one signature had proved powerful enough to do this by itself. Other work at Cornell Laboratories, in cooperation with the Ballistic Research Laboratory, involved a study of Atlas booster fragmentation with high-speed cameras.

The discrimination studies and supporting research carried out during this period of the early 1960s provided the basis for continued effort in the years ahead. The lessons learned from the Zeus program proved valuable in the ongoing R and D work for future ABM systems.

1.6.3.8 Zeus R and D Team. The Zeus R and D program was a team effort directed by Bell Laboratories with 24 major subcontractors and 89 other subcontractors located in many areas of the country. There were also hundreds of additional suppliers who provided components directly for Western Electric and Bell Laboratories or their subcontractors. In addition to having overall system responsibility, Bell Laboratories designed many of the major system elements. The Western Electric Company in North Carolina manufactured the R and D models of system elements designed by Bell Laboratories and installed, tested, and operated the R and D models at all test sites.

Douglas Aircraft Company was responsible for the design and development of the missile (less the Bell Laboratories guidance unit), launcher, and associated ground handling equipment. The major subcontractors and their areas of activity are listed in Table 7-4.

1.6.3.9 Zeus Multifunction Array Radar — MAR-I. In 1960 Bell Laboratories conducted fundamental investigations of phase-controlled scanning antenna arrays for possible application to the Zeus system. The potential advantages of radars using such antennas, envisioned at that time, were: (1) increased blast resistance capability, (2) greater power-handling capability, (3) flexibility of beam adjustment, and (4) capability of combining several functions in one radar.

Arrays with their inertialess beams would provide greater capability against the high-traffic-level threat. This consideration became one of the principal technical reasons advanced in 1963 for not proceeding with tactical deployment of the original Nike-Zeus System. There were, of course, many other reasons apart from strictly technical considerations in 1962–1964 for not deploying an ABM system.

In these forward-looking studies supported by the Zeus program, phased-array scanning was analyzed with respect to such factors as (1) element pattern directivity, (2) array pattern deterioration with scanning, (3) pointing-accuracy degradation with scan angle, and (4) frequency. The major steps involved in an engagement from acquisition of the target through intercept were quantitatively evaluated in terms of phased-array radar characteristics and the necessary data processing.

On November 18, 1960 at Redstone Arsenal, Bell Laboratories representatives gave a presentation to ARGMA on the subject of phased arrays in a terminal defense. The purpose of the meeting was to report on the study to date and to provide the basis for a proposal to do exploratory phased-array work.

Authorization to proceed with the design of a prototype model of a phased array, based on the Bell Laboratories study, was granted in June 1961. Western Electric had the prime contract and Bell Laboratories was responsible for supervising the design. Sylvania was selected as the major subcontractor for detailed design of the prototype model and fabrication of the model to be installed at WSMR. Sperry Rand UNIVAC was given the responsibility for a phase II digital computer as well as the programming for the prototype radar. Bell Laboratories was also responsible for major system elements, including the large number of solid-state RF amplifiers.

Originally, the prototype radar was named the Zeus multifunction array radar (ZMAR). Although not part of the Zeus System at that time, it was considered an exploratory effort that might be phased into the Zeus system in the future. Later, the radar was referred to as MAR-I. The basic concept involved using four installations to provide 360 degrees in azimuth; however, only one hardened installation was installed at WSMR for evaluation. Ground breaking for the MAR-I technical facility took place at WSMR in March 1963. Construction of the facility was the responsibility of the Army Corps of Engineers and their contractors. An aerial view of the installation is shown in Fig. 7-56.

One of the important lessons learned from the hardware installation and test of the MAR-I radar sensor was the need to thoroughly test in the

Fig. 7-56.   Aerial view of MAR-I at White Sands Missile Range.

laboratory all the elements duplicated in large numbers in an array radar. Design faults resulting in poor reliability were uncovered in such elements as the traveling-wave tube (TWT) and its associated filament transformer. Correcting these required an expensive redesign and replacement program because of the large number of elements involved. Because of this experience, designers of the later phased-array radars, MSR and PAR, were required to run exhaustive laboratory performance and reliability tests on elements that were to be duplicated thousands of times in the radar.

The testing of the MAR-I at WSMR demonstrated the feasibility of using a phased-array radar for a multiplicity of simultaneous functions and verified the analytical predictability of array performance in a multifunction role. Among the important test results were the following:

1. Extensive external antenna pattern measurements of single beams and multiple-beam clusters closely matched both the internal antenna pattern measurements (using the element alignment network) and the patterns calculated from basic phase and amplitude data of the individual receive and transmit antenna elements.

2. The stability and repeatability of these antenna patterns over extended time periods.

3. The ability to form and steer various search, track, and discrimination beam clusters with desired precision.

4. The dynamic tracking accuracy of airborne and ballistic targets and satellites.

5. Absolute tracking accuracy from precision tracking of solar microwave radiation.

The system demonstrated the inherent broad frequency-bandwidth capability of arrays using time-delay steering in both the transmit and receive modes. It demonstrated the ability of microsecond switching in time and the use of multiple frequencies for separation of simultaneous radar functions using various beam-cluster arrangements. An important demonstration was the use of a centralized digital computer to control all radar functions and to execute large-scale real-time data processing. This included generation and execution of all the beam forming and tracking functions, full automatic system control with provision for manual intervention, search detection and verification, precision tracking in range and angle, fault monitoring, display, and numerous other simultaneous and sequential system operations. In general, these tests verified on a full-scale basis the satisfactory performance of a multifunction array radar in a real target environment.

1.6.4 Nike-X R and D System

On January 5, 1963, the Secretary of Defense called for the priority development of an ABM defense system incorporating the most advanced components and techniques available. This new system was temporarily designated Nike-X, pending selection of a more appropriate name. The Army project manager of Nike-Zeus was assigned the task of implementing the new program. Bell Laboratories, as the system's development director on behalf of Western Electric, the prime contractor, was called upon to redefine the system by taking full advantage of the latest technical state of the art, but to have due regard for the economic restraints of production costs and the time restraints of deployment schedules.

1.6.4.1 System Objectives. In carrying out this system responsibility, Bell Laboratories was to conduct studies and R and D work directed toward including in the antimissile defense system the high-performance Sprint-type missile and a phased-array radar. The R and D field tests at Kwajalein, WSMR, and Ascension, previously described, were to continue essentially as planned to provide fundamental information needed for the new system. The technical reasons for continuing development at this time, rather than deployment, involved a concern that by the early 1970s the USSR could develop the ability to mount a high-traffic threat with decoys and chaff that could only be discriminated endoatmospherically. However, there were many sensitive political reasons for the decision not to deploy the Nike-Zeus system in 1963. Among these were (1) the high cost of a complete defense for the country, (2) the destabilizing effect of ABM defense, and (3) defense system coverage for only principal cities and industrial regions, which left major areas of the country undefended.

The basic plans for phased-array radar tests at WSMR to prove whether a single radar could perform acquisition, discrimination, and tracking of targets and defensive missiles were well developed in 1963. Furthermore, an advanced ABM study group at Bell Laboratories had shown the advantages of a high-acceleration, short-range Sprint-type missile to defend a limited area when discrimination of the RV was delayed until it reached low altitude. Actually, by 1963, the basic concept of the Nike-X system was well established at Bell Laboratories. Its objective was the terminal defense of the larger United States cities against the sophisticated USSR attack postulated for the mid-1970s.

Already being studied for Nike-X was a much more powerful multifunction array radar than the MAR-I planned for WSMR tests. This radar, referred to as MAR-II, was assigned the role of search, track, and discrimination and was considered the centerpiece for city defense. A second smaller radar, called the missile site radar, or MSR, was proposed for multiple tracking of defensive missiles and short-range target tracking. Later on, as a result of further study involving the economics of ABM defense for smaller cities, the role of the MSR was increased to include search, acquisition, and tracking of incoming targets, which thus provided autonomous operation for the defense of smaller cities. The long-range Nike-Zeus missile was carried over to the Nike-X system concept[5] to supplement the short-range Sprint missile.

1.6.4.2 Sprint Missile Development. On October 1, 1962, three contractors were given study contracts by Bell Laboratories for the proposed new Sprint-type missile. When their proposals arrived on February 1, 1963, seven technical subcommittees composed of representatives from Bell Laboratories, Western Electric, and the Army Missile Command were appointed to examine the proposals and select the successful contractor for Sprint development. On March 18, 1963, the Army announced the selection of Martin Marietta as the development contractor for the Sprint missile. Development work was to be carried out in the Martin Marietta plant at Orlando, Florida; initial testing of the missile would be done at WSMR and subsequent system firings would take place at Kwajalein.

What followed through the next twelve years was the successful development and test firing of a missile that was surely most challenging in light of the state of the art in missile technology in the early 1960s. The Sprint missile, with its acceleration to high velocity within the dense atmosphere at low altitudes, produced such high aerodynamic heating that its skin surface could be cooled with an oxyacetylene torch! The Martin

[5] Principal features of the Nike-X system concept were summarized in a paper, "Nike-X, Design Approach and Preliminary Description," which was presented at the Anti-Missile Research and Advisory Council (AMRAC) Symposium, April 15, 1963, in Monterey, California.

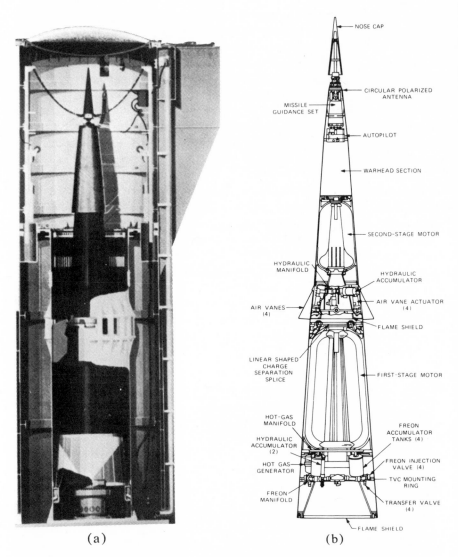

Fig. 7-57.   Sprint missile. (a) In underground launch cell. (b) Cutaway view.

and Bell Laboratories engineers lived through several years of unrelieved agony in overcoming the many problems of the early flight program. In the end, however, these problems were overcome and a highly reliable Sprint missile was ready for the Safeguard System tests at Kwajalein.

The Sprint missile, shown in Fig. 7-57, was deployed in an environmentally controlled, vertical launch station. When the launch signal was given, the launch station cover was opened by explosive charges, the launch-eject generator was fired, and the missile was expelled from its launch station by a gas-powered piston. The first stage ignited as the missile cleared the launch station and, as it burned, provided a very high acceleration resulting in high velocity at burnout. The first-stage separation was accomplished by skin-cutting ordnance activated by ground command. After drag forces had pushed the burned-out first stage away, the second stage was ignited by a preset signal or ground command, depending on the intercept point. The Sprint missile represented a major advance in missile technology in being able to accelerate to extreme velocities and maneuver within the lower atmosphere.

1.6.4.3 Missile Site Radar (MSR). Various configurations and parameters for the MSR were studied at Bell Laboratories. The agreed-upon concept was an S-band, phased-array radar with a single transmitter or receiver time-sharing a single phase-controlled antenna face. The ability to change the direction of the beam very rapidly was established as a requirement to provide high traffic-handling capability. After competitive proposals were received from seven companies, the Raytheon Company was awarded a contract for development in December 1963. The initial Phase I effort combined engineering personnel from Bell Laboratories and Raytheon to define the MSR in detail and to highlight areas requiring

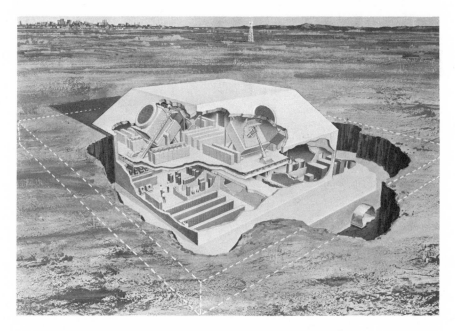

Fig. 7-58. Proposed tactical missile site radar.

Fig. 7-59.   Prototype missile site radar on Meck Island (Kwajalein Atoll).

maximum effort to meet development schedules. Varian Associates was selected to supply the high-power transmitter output tubes.

In early 1965 a decision was made to provide the MSR with its own data processing and command and control equipment to permit autonomous operation for the defense of small cities. Higher performance requirements were therefore established for the MSR to carry out search, acquisition, and longer-range target tracking. The major change was a fivefold increase in average transmitter power. These changes were formulated with Raytheon in June 1965. Once this was done, the schedule for power-on of a two-face MSR (the tactical version would have up to four faces) on Meck Island in the Kwajalein Atoll was set for May 1968. An artist's view of the proposed tactical installation is shown in Fig. 7-58.

When installed, the MSR operated at a higher average power than any existing radar in its frequency band. With the aid of its associated missile

Fig. 7-60.   Tactical missile site radar in North Dakota.

site data processor, completely autonomous operation was provided for the initial processing of multiple target data, tracking the defensive Sprint and Spartan missiles, and command-guiding the defensive missiles to intercept the targets. A high degree of redundancy made the radar a very powerful precision sensor capable of continuous use without shutdown. Fig. 7-59 shows a prototype of the MSR installed on Meck Island, Kwajalein Atoll, and Fig. 7-60 the tactical MSR deployed in North Dakota.

The digital beam-forming and steering logic for the MSR was the responsibility of Raytheon. However, in the interest of standardization, the same kind of hardware designed for the Bell Laboratories data processing equipment was supplied by Western Electric to meet Raytheon's logic requirements.

1.6.4.4 Multifunction Array Radar — MAR-II. The L-band MAR-II of the Nike-X system was specially designed for long-range search and acquisition and high-data-rate coverage for discrimination. Plans were made for installing a prototype model on Kwajalein (see artist's view in Fig. 7-61), while the MSR was to be located on Meck Island some 25 miles away. The high-power requirements for MAR (100-MW peak and 2- and 3-MW average per transmitter face) dictated separate transmitter and receiver array faces. Two transmitter and receiver array faces were planned to provide 180-degree coverage. From the start, two possible implementations of receiver beam-steering configurations were analyzed in scale

Fig. 7-61.   Multifunction array radar—MAR-II—planned for Kwajalein.

laboratory tests to determine which method would provide the optimum performance consistent with high reliability and lower cost. One method involved time delay—actually phase delay, a board-steered system (BSS)—and the other was a modulation scan array radar (MOSAR) technique developed by General Electric, Syracuse, New York, as part of an R and D contract with Bell Laboratories.

Raytheon was awarded the contract for the development of the high-power transmitter. A key requirement of the transmitter was the need for a long-life, broadband TWT used in large quantities to meet the high-power requirements. A team of tube engineers from Bell Laboratories' Murray Hill Laboratory with experience in building long-life TWT gun structures joined the Raytheon tube engineers in the development of the TWT to achieve a goal of 50,000 hours of life. Although the L-band TWT was not deployed, because of the later cancellation of the MAR-II, Raytheon later scaled the tube down to the PAR UHF band and supplied it to General Electric. Deployed in the PAR today, the tube gives promise of a life of 50,000 hours or more.

One of the features planned for the MAR-II was the ability to form multiple, independent beams for search and, simultaneously, to form separate clusters directed to different incoming clouds for discrimination. The transmitter beam width would be adjusted to match the receiver beam-cluster size.

The plans for time-delay steering, the BSS, employed phase delay in contrast to the MAR-I real-time delay steering. The BSS was compared with the MOSAR system from General Electric, which resulted in a recommendation to the Army Nike-X Project Office in March 1967 to drop further development of MOSAR and use the BSS for MAR-II. The final decision was based on the straightforward approach of BSS and a real concern about the complexity and cost of a full implementation of MOSAR.

Because of the high-power requirements and complexity, the MAR-II system costs were so high that even the deployment of an R and D prototype on Kwajalein had to be delayed and finally scaled down in January 1968. The scaled-down model, referred to as TACMAR, was to initially leave out some of the transmitter and receiver modules, though these could be added later. However, by this time the original requirements for ABM defense had changed, as discussed below, and a less expensive perimeter acquisition radar (PAR) was substituted for MAR/TACMAR in tactical deployment plans. In May 1968 the TACMAR prototype objectives for the installation on Kwajalein were changed from those of a tactical design to those of an R and D field-site radar referred to as CAMAR (and later Guardian) to provide basic field data on discrimination. However, the project, which was then supported by the Advanced Ballistic Missile Defense Agency (ABMDA), was cancelled in August 1969 because of a cutback in funding.

1.6.4.5 Data Processing System. Early in 1963 studies were in progress on the requirements for the Nike-X data processing system. What was clear from the start was the need for high-speed calculations (up to 30 million per second) that could be provided in modular equipment giving stepped capability for future growth. Equally important was the need for equipment having reliability better by an order of magnitude than any commercial computer then available or planned. In reviewing the status of computing equipment designs with manufacturers, it became clear that the Nike-X data processing requirements dictated a challenging new design approach.

Bell Laboratories enlisted the help of UNIVAC and formed a joint team with some of its personnel in the spring of 1963 to establish design requirements and specifications for the Nike-X data processing system. Studies were made in the areas of basic hardware and logic, computer organization, switching and control, displays, recording, programming, and fault location. Out of these studies came the decision that performance capability in a stepped-module structure and high system reliability could be met only by a multiprocessor design. Also, the basic logic integrated-circuit package had to meet a reliability goal of eight fits (failure in time) in one billion hours. The Bell Laboratories device group accepted the challenge of providing the integrated circuit to meet this reliability.

Many experts during the late 1960s, including a special committee of the National Academy of Science, reported to the Army that in their opinion a multiprocessor could not be made to meet the expected calculations per second—millions of instructions per second (MIPS)—predicted by Bell Laboratories. In final test measurements on Safeguard, MIPS were plotted versus processors in parallel. The curve was essentially linear through eight processors and met or exceeded the performance predicted early in the design. The integrated-circuit package developed for Nike-X, which was manufactured by Western Electric and three subcontractors for the Safeguard program, had, by 1975, accumulated many millions of device hours and showed reliability results approaching the eight-fit goal.

1.6.4.6 Reentry Measurements Program. In the earlier discussion of discrimination, reference was made to the initial studies and laboratory work that included initial radar and optical observations at Ascension Island during the early Zeus program. By 1962 the Zeus radar sensors were deployed and operational at Ascension, WSMR, and Kwajalein; and an organized reentry measurements program (referred to as RMP A, B, and C) was established as part of Nike-X R and D in the period from 1962 to 1970. The objectives of the program were to develop general discriminants for conical reentry vehicles based on radar-observable characteristics as

Fig. 7-62.   Target track radar (TTR 4) antenna. Forty-foot reflector and subreflector being readied for use in reentry measurements program.

a function of vehicle size, shape, and ablative material. Optical and infrared sensors were also provided as part of these measurements.

Starting in 1963, the measurements program at WSMR included the use of the Zeus elements ZAR, TTR, and DR, as well as an infrared radiometer installed on a Hercules mount. By June 1964 the WSMR was taking data on the first successful Athena test missile fired from Utah into WSMR. The major portion of the RMP tests consisted of full-scale reentry flights, principally into the Kwajalein Test Range. Special unique targets were provided by the Nike-X program; other targets were furnished by the Air Force, Advanced Ballistic Reentry Systems (ABRES), Strategic Air Command (SAC) Evaluation Missions, and the Navy Polaris program.

The Nike sensors, TTR and DR, went through major modifications at the end of the Zeus system tests at Kwajalein to adapt them to the sensor data-gathering requirements of RMP. For example, TTR No. 4 was changed from a 22- to a 40-foot antenna dish (Fig. 7-62) and a wideband 60-MHz coherent system. In addition, an X-band receiver system was added to provide telemetry reception from Nike-X supported RVs equipped with special on-board instrumentation. Similarly, the DR at Kwajalein was modified to include a coherent signal processing system (CSPS), as well as wideband recording equipment.

In January, 1964 a reentry physics panel was organized at Bell Laboratories with specialists in electromagnetic theory, plasma physics, gas chemistry, aerodynamics, and hydrodynamic stability. This group would help guide the reentry field measurements program and would represent Bell Laboratories in contacts with outside organizations having related interests.

1.6.4.7 Nth-Country Threat.
In February 1965, at the request of the Army, an intensive investigation was started on possible modifications of the Nike-X system and its hardware concept to reflect the heightened national concern about the "Nth country" threat. Special emphasis was to be given to the evaluation of alternate techniques for achieving effective high-altitude defense against relatively unsophisticated attacks with deployment growth to meet sophisticated threats. In particular, other options were to be considered leading to a less costly MAR-II. As part of this system study, the usefulness of VHF radars as supplementary sensors for acquisition, discrimination, or designation in defense against light, unsophisticated attacks was investigated. Included in this study was the blackout problem in the VHF band.

On April 23, 1965, the major conclusions of this study were orally presented to Dr. Harold Brown, Assistant Secretary of Defense for R and D. A variety of radar design approaches was summarized in terms of performance, cost, and growth potential. The radars proposed were a MINI-MAR—a lower-cost, reduced-performance array radar with potential for growth to a full-size MAR, supplemented by a comparison radar at VHF for long-range detection of sneak attacks that could be met by the Zeus missile. The MSR was the choice for missile guidance, although lower-cost S-band missile tracking radars could be used. For close-in defense, Sprint and MSR remained the choices. In May 1965, following this presentation, Bell Laboratories was authorized to revise the Nike-X System requirements to include certain modifications aimed at providing a more cost-effective defense against a possible Nth-country threat, in addition to the more sophisticated Soviet-type threats on which past Nike-X design had been based. This was in line with Secretary of Defense McNamara's rising concern early in 1965 over the nation's vulnerability to the kind of attack that some less advanced country might launch. For this reason, it was urgent to determine whether Nike-X was the most cost-effective way to provide an early defense against such a threat or whether there were less expensive ways.

As a result of these studies, the Nike-X concept was expanded to provide capability for a broad general defense of the whole continental United

States against the full threat spectrum. This change was made possible by increased confidence that large nuclear warheads borne by two or more modified Zeus missiles (altered for greater payload and range) in a barrage mode could provide large-volume kill capability—leading to the possibility of an umbrella coverage of the entire country. (Only as threat sophistication increased to extremely hard, or radiation-resistant, warheads and RVs, would the short-range terminal defense be required.) As visualized at that time by the Director of Defense Research and Engineering (DDR&E), the VHF radar would be a straightforward development, essentially off the shelf. Thus the actual development effort would not have to begin until production was authorized.

In October 1965, in response to a request from the DDR&E, a quick examination of minimum Nike-X hardware was made to assess the defense capability against simple first-generation Nth-country ICBMs. The hardware consisted of 4 VHF radars and 12 MSR sites, with 20 modified Zeus missiles at each site. Although good coverage against this particular threat was demonstrated in principle, the many limitations of such a defense concept were pointed out.

In November 1965 a new study of active defense for hardened sites was initiated by the DDR&E. Three teams—one each from Air Force, Advanced Research Projects Agency, and Nike-X Project—were to study the capability of defense systems to meet the threats and defense objectives defined by the DDR&E. It is sufficient to note here that while studies were being made concerning light area defense against Nth-country threat, Bell Laboratories was being asked to carry out studies of high-traffic terminal defense of United States offensive weapons. It was during the latter studies that the concept of pitch-and-catch for the missile-launch phase was seriously considered. Up to this time in all Nike system developments, being completely locked onto the missile prior to launch was considered an inviolate requirement. However, with the MSR inertialess tracking beam, it was found that Sprint could be acquired after launch with separations of as much as 20 nautical miles.

Since a suitable missile element was needed for the barrage-type defense against the Nth-country threat, authorization was received in January 1966 to start development work at Douglas on a modified Zeus DM-15C missile for this role. The missile payload would be increased to 2,900 pounds for the high-yield nuclear warhead, which necessitated larger first- and second-stage motors. The decision was made to use the modified DM-15C booster design for both the 5-second first stage and the 19-second second stage. The new three-stage Zeus missile was expected to have a peak velocity of 9,000 ft/s and a range of about 300 nautical miles. The first firing was scheduled for Kwajalein Island in March 1968.

As mentioned earlier, a VHF radar was being studied as a complementary long-range search and acquisition radar for defense against the Nth country threat. In December 1966 General Electric, Syracuse, New York, was selected to start Phase I study on this radar under contract to Bell Laboratories. Called the perimeter acquisition radar (PAR), this new equipment presented the General Electric and Bell Laboratories team with the initial, important system consideration of deciding on the operating frequency, VHF or UHF. A schedule for completing design definition by July 1, 1967, was established.

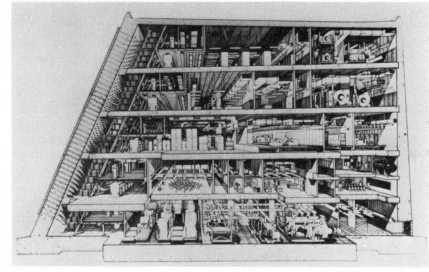

(a)

(b)

Fig. 7-63. (a) Cutaway view of perimeter acquisition radar (PAR) building. (b) PAR site in North Dakota.

An important consideration in this study was whether a UHF design matching the VHF performance could be realized without a substantial increase in cost. Cost comparisons were made for a UHF radar that matched the VHF performance, 3 dB down and 6 dB down. Bell Laboratories had agreed with the conclusion of a study made by the Institute of Defense Analysis in the summer of 1966 that the radar blackout from offensive and defensive warhead burst would seriously degrade a VHF radar; thus UHF was recommended. By April 1967 Bell Laboratories and General Electric completed a cost comparison of VHF and UHF for presentation to the Army and DOD. The decision was made to proceed with the planning for a PAR operating at UHF but arranged so that initial deployment would be 6 dB down to minimize initial cost. However, the design should permit later growth to 0-dB performance for smaller future targets.

The PAR was capable of automatic acquisition and tracking at long range of a large number of ballistic missiles over a 120-degree azimuth and 90-degree elevation. The radar system was designed to perform its mission in an environment containing false targets (aircraft, satellites, aurora, and meteors) and directly exposed to the effects of nuclear weapons. The radar was housed in a 120-foot-high, hardened, reinforced-concrete building that provided protection against nuclear thermal radiation and electromagnetic pulse (EMP) effects. A view of the PAR installed at Grand Forks, North Dakota, together with a cutaway cross section, is shown in Figs. 7-63a and 7-63b.

I-67 Studies Leading to Sentinel System

In December 1966 the Nike-X Project Office of the Army Materiel Command and DOD asked Western Electric and Bell Laboratories to study a deployment model for Nike-X designed to combine area defense with hardsite defense capabilities. This model, approved by DOD for production planning purposes, was officially designated as Plan I-67 Area/Hardsite Defense. The major objectives of the deployment were defense against a deliberate industrial/urban attack by the Chinese People's Republic (CPR) (a countervalue attack) and defense against a deliberate high-level ICBM attack from the USSR aimed at United States strategic forces (a counterforce attack). In making this request, Secretary of Defense McNamara invited top executives of the Bell System to Washington on December 9, 1966, to ask their support and experience in finding ways to minimize the cost of an ABM deployment while providing a system of high reliability. This meeting was followed by another on December 13, 1966, involving executives of Western Electric and Bell Laboratories and John S. Foster, Deputy Director for Research and Engineering, with his staff in the Pentagon, together with members of the Army staff. The meeting again emphasized that cost should be a most important parameter in the I-67 study.

As a result of the request, Bell Laboratories and Western Electric initiated a six-month study on January 16, 1967, to evaluate the I-67 plan. The most important aspect of the study was to optimize system elements with the objective of selecting the option with the greatest cost-effectiveness. A three-month status report on the study was presented by Bell Laboratories to Gen. I. Drewry and Gen. A. W. Betts on March 2, 1967, and again on March 4, 1967, to John S. Foster. A status report at the end of the study was presented to Secretary of Defense McNamara on July 5, 1967, at the Pentagon. Bell Laboratories made the primary presentation, while the Army presented possible growth options for the I-67 deployment model. Secretary McNamara was pleased with results of the study but asked for further investigation of questions dealing with growth aspects of the CPR threat and corresponding growth of the I-67 deployment model. A total report of the study was issued on July 5, 1967.

The results of the study were strongly influenced by three conditions: (1) the specific design threat, (2) a total investment cost not exceeding 5 billion dollars, and (3) an initial operational capability (IOC) within 54 months of a deployment decision, all of which limited the choice of equipment to Nike-X elements. The recommended deployment consisted of 6 PARs, one of which would be in Alaska; 17 MSRs, including one in Alaska and one on Hawaii; 480 Spartan interceptors (Spartan being the new name for a modified Zeus DM-15C with a large payload); and 455 Sprint interceptors, of which 325 would be for the defense of Minuteman sites. Other studies, directed by the Secretary of Defense, were carried out by the Office of the Director of Defense Research and Engineering (ODDR&E) and the Nike-X Project Office with threats and constraints changed from the Bell Laboratories study.

On August 1–2, 1967, at Los Angeles, D. P. Ling of Bell Laboratories made a presentation on the I-67 deployment to the Defense Science Board of DOD.

On September 18, 1967, Secretary of Defense McNamara announced that production and deployment of a "light defense" Nike-X system would begin before the end of 1967. The light-defense deployment was to include PAR, MSR, Sprint, and Spartan. This modified system, derived from the I-67 study, was limited in its initial role to a complete area defense against a CPR industrial/urban attack on CONUS, with a growth option for defense of certain U.S. ICBM bases against a USSR attack. With this decision, plans were set for completing the deferred development effort required to support the I-67 deployment. This development work included design and manufacture of the PAR prototype, tactical test equipment, a tactical software control center, tactical ground support equipment for Sprint and Spartan, and design documentation.

On November 1, 1967, the Department of Defense announced the locations of the first ten Sentinel sites, which included Boston, Chicago, and

Grand Forks, North Dakota. The initial Sentinel deployment was to consist of 6 PARs, 17 MSRs, 480 Spartans, and 220 Sprints. This deployment could later be expanded to provide both Minuteman defense (by the addition of 208 Sprints) and modification of the hardware and software located near the Minuteman bases.

1.6.5 Safeguard System

Construction contracts were awarded by the Army Corps of Engineers, and construction was started on the first Sentinel site (PAR) at Boston late in 1968. Strong opposition developed however, over the construction of such sites and against the deployment of missiles with nuclear warheads for ABM defense. The old demand faced with earlier Nike deployments was now made to a much greater extent; the opposition insisted, "Put it in someone else's backyard." In view of this strong reaction, the acquisition and construction of other sites were suspended on February 6, 1969, pending a review of the Sentinel system by President Nixon. On March 14, 1969, President Nixon announced that the Sentinel system would be "substantially modified" in the form of a new deployment called Safeguard, with the following new defense objectives:

1. First priority would be protection of our land-based retaliatory forces against a direct attack by the USSR, with the complement of equipment modified in accordance with this initial objective.

2. A growth option to provide defense of the United States against the kind of attack the CPR would likely be capable of launching within the decade.

3. Protection against the possibility of accidental attacks from any source.

The Safeguard deployment plan reduced the number of sites to 12, as shown in Fig. 7-64, and deleted most of the sites in large cities. The initial deployment was to proceed in two phases, the first to protect part of the Minuteman force and the second to complete the coverage of Minuteman sites and cope with more sophisticated threats.

Between the start of Safeguard in March 1969 and the signing of the Strategic Arms Limitation Treaty (SALT I) with the USSR in May 1972, the authorized deployment went through a series of changes. In 1970 approval was given to start work on two Phase I sites, one near Grand Forks AFB, North Dakota, and one near Malmstrom AFB, Montana. Advanced preparation of five additional sites (Phase II) was also authorized; this was later reduced to advanced preparation at only two of these sites, for a total of four sites. The four-site plan was the one authorized through most of this period until the signing of the SALT I agreement.

The SALT I agreement permitted the deployment of one ABM defense

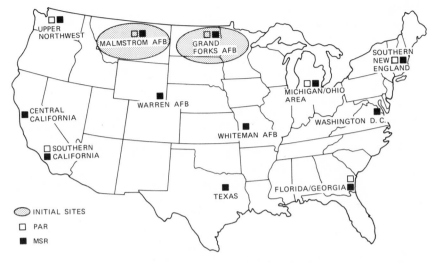

Fig. 7-64.   Safeguard deployment plan, March 1969.

Fig. 7-65.   Sprint cell with missile site radar building in background at Tactical Missile Direction Center in North Dakota.

site for offensive forces and one for the National Command Authority around Washington, D.C. With this agreement, the Minuteman site at Malmstrom AFB in Montana, then under full construction, had to be terminated, which left only the site near Grand Forks. Later the government decided not to proceed with the Safeguard defense of Washington, D.C.

In accordance with the terms of SALT I in May 1972 and the subsequent Congressional decision not to authorize the deployment around Washington, D.C., the Safeguard system consisted of the PAR and a Missile Direction Center (MDC), which included the MSR and local and remote missile launch farms in the Grand Forks, North Dakota, area. The system was under control of the Ballistic Missile Defense Center (BMDC) in Colorado. Under the SALT I agreement, only 100 defensive missiles were permitted. Both Spartan and Sprint missiles were collocated with the MDC, while additional Sprint missiles were located at four remote missile farms. A view of the tactical installation of the Missile Direction Center is shown in Fig. 7-65.

Fortunately, the changes in deployment objectives in going from Sentinel to Safeguard did not require major changes in the test plans for Meck Island. Most important still was the proving in of the prototype MSR with its associated software as an operational phased-array radar. Continued development firings were also required for the Sprint and Spartan missiles. Finally, to integrate these elements, a full series of system tests was carried out to progressively stress system capability against live ICBM and IRBM targets. Software packages, which were built up in complexity to match the system test objectives (called the M-test series) were introduced until the final software package (the part to be tested through live ICBM tracking or intercepts) matched the tactical software installed in the Grand Forks tactical system. The field testing at Meck complemented the more exhaustive testing of Safeguard software at the Bell Laboratories Tactical Software Control Site (TSCS) in Madison, New Jersey. Here, threat inputs were introduced to match the design threat levels not attainable in field testing. Actual tracking data from the Meck tests were used in forming the test input tapes for the TSCS evaluations.

During the Sentinel and early Safeguard period, much thought was given to the installation of a PAR prototype on Kwajalein or Meck. Time schedules (with PAR development awaiting a production decision) and costs dictated that the PAR prototype should be evaluated at the first tactical site and then turned over for tactical use after completion of R and D tests. Technically, a much more complete evaluation of the system could have been achieved with an installation on Kwajalein. However, it was also technically true that better evaluation of the PAR from a radar standpoint could be obtained from an installation further north in the hemisphere, where aurora effects, ground clutter with abnormal propagation, and low-angle atmospheric tracking errors could be determined. In discussions with the Army and DOD, it was agreed that simulation of PAR outputs for the Kwajalein system tests would be acceptable, although a larger deployment of Safeguard would certainly have dictated a PAR installation on Kwajalein later in the program.

Some of the key dates in the Kwajalein and Meck testing were as follows:

Mar. 2, 1968—First Spartan development firing at Kwajalein.

May 18, 1968—Power-on for the Meck MSR.

Oct. 8, 1968—First software data transfer, on satellite data link between Whippany and Meck.

Apr. 18, 1969—Demonstration of multiprocessor system at Whippany Safeguard Data Processing Laboratory in support of Meck tests.

Dec. 11, 1969—First MSR track of ICBM.

Apr. 14, 1970—Start of M-1 test series at Meck.

Aug. 28, 1970—First successful intercept of ICBM with Spartan.

Fig. 7-66. Aerial view of Meck test system during a Sprint salvo test.

Fig. 7-67.   Combined Bell Labs-Army systems operations room on Meck Island during a system-test mission.

Dec. 23, 1970—First live target intercept by Sprint.

Jan. 11, 1971—First Spartan salvo.

Mar. 17, 1971—First Sprint salvo.

Aug. 27, 1971—First M-2 mission.

Mar. 16, 1972—First remote launch of Sprint from Illeginni (about 20 miles from Meck) to test toss-and-catch.

May 1973—Delivery of Revision 19 of software to Meck for final M-2 series tests.

Aug. 1974—Final M-2 system tests.

Apr. 1975—Firing of final warhead and production missiles from Meck—2 Spartans and 1 Sprint.

From 1971 to mid-1975, the Sentinel and Safeguard systems were subjected to a series of tests, each posing increasingly difficult target conditions. The success achieved in the system tests was indicated by the fact that there were only 8 failures in 65 system test missions. Of the 8 failures, 7 were failures of the Sprint or Spartan defense missiles and the other was a failure of data processing hardware. An aerial view of the Meck test system is shown in Fig. 7-66 during a Sprint salvo system test. Fig. 7-67 is a view of the control room during a test mission.

The TSCS test facility at Bell Laboratories in Madison, New Jersey, contained the full PAR and MDC data processing equipment and all portions of the analog hardware that interfaced with the missiles and radars at the site. This facility accurately reproduced the software in its tactical operational environment and was indispensable in developing software relatively free of errors when introduced at the site. A system exerciser for tests at TSCS and at the site provided the means of introducing sufficient traffic capability and related attack parameters to test the tactical hardware and software at the required Safeguard design threat level. These evaluation tests, carried out during 1974 and until April 1975 at the TSCS, supplemented by the M-2 live-target tests at Meck, provided full verification that the Safeguard system deployed at Grand Forks met its performance requirements.

The equipment readiness data (ERD) for the Grand Forks site were ready several days before October 1, 1974, the scheduled date set almost four years earlier. Initial operational capability (IOC) was achieved shortly after the scheduled date of April 1, 1975, with operational missiles installed in their cells and full system operation under way, 24 hours a day and 7 days a week.

1.6.6 Summary of ABM Program

The major development milestones in the 20-year evolution of ABM defense, beginning with the early studies in March 1955 and leading to the installation of a tactical Safeguard system near Grand Forks, North Dakota, are shown in Fig. 7-68. These developments trace the history of the step-by-step advance in technology that kept the United States well in the forefront of ABM defense and led eventually to the SALT I agreement with the USSR. One of the challenging phases of the program was the extensive test program that required four test sites, two of which, Ascension and Kwajalein, were on opposite sides of the world. To carry out field test operations on Kwajalein Atoll 8,000 miles from home base required a fully integrated team effort. Bell Laboratories was responsible for system engineering, overall system development, and test planning; Western Electric had full responsibility for transportation, equipment engineering, and installation and maintenance of the system elements.

The Ballistic Missile Defense Test Program at Kwajalein drew to a close in January 1976. In the 16 years of field operation on Kwajalein, the Bell System used its wide range of expertise to maximum advantage. The research departments at Bell Labs supported the development groups in the design of the hardware and software systems and in the design and planning of the entire test program. The full range of Western Electric experience in manufacturing and quality control, technical building construction, equipment engineering and installation, and transportation was essential to the success of such a large research and development program and in deployment of the tactical site at Grand Forks.

The success achieved in the testing of the Sentinel and Safeguard systems at Kwajalein was unprecedented, considering the complexity of the

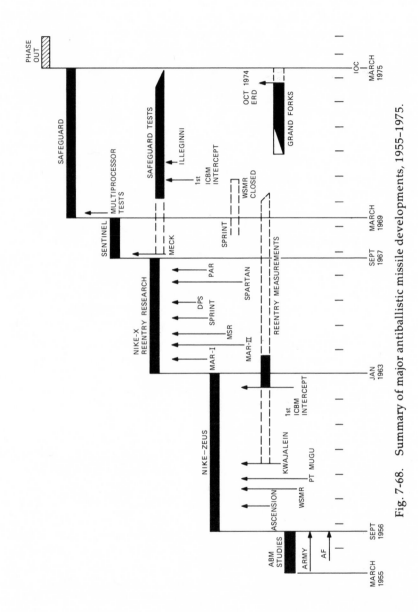

Fig. 7-68.   Summary of major antiballistic missile developments, 1955–1975.

system and the testing instrumentations. In 65 system test missions, there were only 8 failures—7 of these were failures of the Sprint or Spartan missiles, then still under development.

What factors contributed to the success of the Kwajalein operation? A primary one was the rotation of key systems hardware and software designers to the field site on two-year assignments. This not only helped keep the field test site up-to-date on current system design, but also provided valuable field experience for the designers—experience they applied to ballistic missile development when they returned to their laboratories. Second, by keeping the system parameters fixed during a given series of field tests, it was possible to produce proven and reliable equipment and software in the specified time. And finally, the repetitive simulated testing carried out prior to each live test mission ensured high reliability.

Similarly, the performance of the tactical Safeguard system installed at Grand Forks showed amazing reliability for such a complex system. Starting in April 1975 when the system became operational and continuing through November 1975, the system was in service 7 days a week and 24 hours a day, except for short periods of planned shutdown for modifications in capability. During this period the system was under Army control with routine maintenance carried out by Western Electric personnel. The system availability figure for this period was over 99.5 percent, which was determined by simulated inputs to test the operational capability.

II. EARLY WARNING FOR AIR DEFENSE

2.1 Early Studies and Tests

One of the largest undertakings in the postwar period was the development and installation of a complex generally referred to as the Far North Communication and Detection System. Rapid expansion of an aircraft detection network was deemed necessary for the national security in the post–World War II period. Bell Labs was responsible for the design and engineering of the basic system which, in the mid-1970s, stretched halfway around the world.

The idea of the warning line in what became the Distant Early Warning (DEW) Line detection system was conceived by a summer study group, which met in 1952 at the Lincoln Laboratory, M.I.T., to consider the problem of the evaluation and further development of air defense in North America. Bell Telephone Laboratories was a member of the study group.

As the first step in carrying out the recommendations of this group, Western Electric was asked in December 1952 to undertake the construction of a trial segment of the line along the northern coast of Alaska. This experimental line was to be used for a field trial of detection and communication systems under Arctic conditions.

Bell Laboratories was asked to plan the electronics system and to arrange a series of important tests—tests designed to demonstrate the technical feasibility of a detection line in the far north. Laboratories groups therefore procured special communications equipment, modified available search radars to add automatic alerting features, and planned extensive tests and test instructions. Special "fence" type equipment was also procured. This consisted of automatic units for detecting aircraft in the areas that would otherwise be unprotected gaps between the main and auxiliary radar stations.

2.2 The DEW Line

In general, the tests successfully demonstrated that a simplified, largely automatic system could be operated by a limited number of well-trained technicians, despite rigorous climatic conditions and difficult supply routes. The Air Force concluded, therefore, that a DEW Line extending completely across the Arctic from eastern Canada to western Alaska was practicable. Late in 1954 the Air Force asked Western Electric to undertake project responsibility for the overall deployment, which would involve the most difficult logistic and environmental conditions. The project drew upon the full spectrum of expertise in Western Electric and Bell Labs. Bell Labs planned the network, designed a large portion of the equipment, and acted as consultant to Western Electric. Western Electric, augmented by personnel from Bell Operating Telephone Companies, drew upon its wide experience with large Bell System projects to plan in detail the procurement, shipment, and equipment engineering for installations in the Arctic.

An important part of the project was selecting the route—a tremendous undertaking. Individual sites were chosen, and the stations were laid out according to criteria specified by Bell Laboratories. These criteria, besides the usual requirements for radars and communications, included many others imposed by the nature of operations in the far north: for example, the need for fresh water, access to the sea, and surfaces suitable for air strips.

In designing the detection and communication system, Bell Laboratories engineers drew upon recent advances in the art and upon their experience with the experimental network. The basic plan called for 58 stations, including auxiliary stations with automatic search radars about 100 miles apart and intermediate stations employing a doppler radar detection system as "gap-fillers" between the auxiliary stations. The detection information was passed laterally along the line via UHF "beyond-the-horizon" circuits (see below, Section 2.3) to the main stations, which were installed about 500 miles apart and equipped with all the facilities of auxiliary stations. The main stations also provided communications via

Fig. 7-69.   Back-to-back "pillbox" antennas of the automatic search radar. A geodesic radome 70 feet in diameter houses the antenna under arctic conditions.

VHF transmission to the mid-Canada line (a second tier of detection stations).

In addition to these basic systems for detection and communication, each location had fixed-station mobile-radio equipment for communication with vehicles and with intermediate sites: ground-to-air communication equipment in HF, VHF, and UHF bands; low-frequency beacons; and HF radio equipment for emergency use.

Some of the electronic items were standard commercial or military units purchased by Western Electric or supplied by the government. Other equipment, however, had to be developed—for example, the detection units, lateral communications equipment, the control consoles for the stations, and also special test gear. For these, Bell Laboratories monitored the design and production or, in some cases, actually designed the equipment.

Equipment developed by other organizations had to operate reliably for long periods under Arctic conditions. Antennas and other exposed equipment were designed for temperatures ranging from −65 to +65 degrees F, and for wind velocities up to 150 miles per hour. The exposed equipment was able to operate under conditions of snow, rain, or salt-laden air and could function with heavy coatings of ice or snow. The indoor equipment, however, was not subjected to conditions significantly more rigorous than those normally expected for indoor, ground-based electronic systems. Indoor designs emphasized automatic operation, trouble-free

(a)

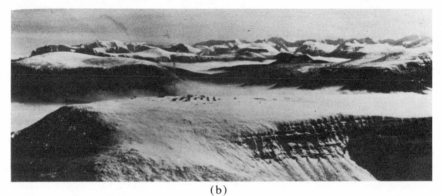

(b)

Fig. 7-70.   DEW Line station on Baffin Island, Canada, at the eastern end of the line. (a) Crisscrossed plastic dome protects the search radar antenna from winds that whip across the tundra at speeds up to 130 miles per hour. (b) Towering mountains, plunging fjords, and jagged terrain forced builders to bring in the first construction equipment by helicopter.

performance, accessibility of components for maintenance, and ease of operation.

The automatic search radar was a dual system with two antennas operating back to back, each normally supplementing the other and, together, called a "pillbox" antenna. During maintenance or emergency periods, either antenna could be arranged mechanically to provide coverage while the other half of the system was out of operation. The antenna unit, shown in the photograph in Fig. 7-69, was a scaled-up version of an earlier Bell Laboratories design used in another system. The radar proper was an extensive redesign of the system used on the Alaskan experimental line, which, though a good system, was designed for portability and was therefore not ideally suited for permanent installation.

The fence detection system, as mentioned earlier, filled the gaps between the larger radar stations. The parameters of this system were de-

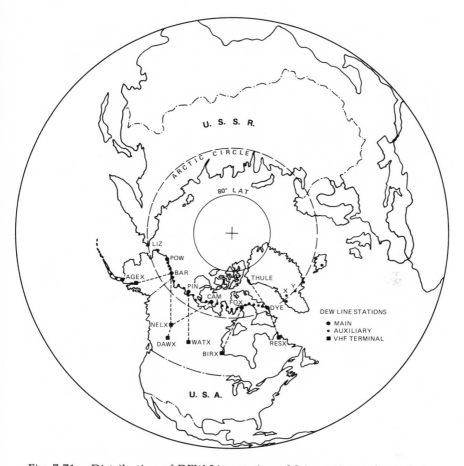

Fig. 7-71. Distribution of DEW Line stations. Main stations—located along the 70-degree parallel 300 to 500 miles apart—communicated with auxiliary and automatic stations via a multichannel, tropospheric, over-the-horizon system. Links from main stations to Colorado Springs Headquarters were via ionospheric scatter radio and land-line.

veloped after Bell Labs engineers had carefully analyzed the problems encountered on the experimental line. Particular emphasis was placed on reliability and freedom from false alarms in the automatic alerting features of this system.

The original DEW Line extended from Cape Lisburne in western Alaska to Cape Dyer on Baffin Island in eastern Canada, roughly along the 70-degree parallel—about 3 degrees above the Arctic Circle (Fig. 7-70a). The aerial view of the station at Cape Dyer, in Fig. 7-70b, shows the forbidding conditions under which many deployments were carried out. The system was connected to the Alaskan Aircraft Control and Warning System—a group of radar warning stations which provide air defense for Alaska itself and early warning for the United States and Canada. The map in Fig. 7-71 shows the position of the DEW Line and its communications terminals.

The objective of the warning system was to reliably detect winged aircraft flying anywhere from a few feet above the surface to high altitudes. Having detected such targets, the system then reported the tracks accurately and promptly to air defense headquarters in this country and in Canada.

2.3 Links with Global Communications Network

A most important part of all air defense projects, in addition to the radar sensors, was the rapid expansion of the global communications network necessary for national security in the post–World War II period. Bell Laboratories was responsible for the design and engineering of the basic systems which, in the mid-1970s, stretched halfway around the world. These systems are discussed further in Chapter 12, which deals with communications. Among the major communications systems, in addition to the DEW Line, were Polevault and White Alice.

Early in the ICBM era, in February 1958, Bell Laboratories was given engineering responsibility for the far-flung communications system linking the radars of the Ballistic Missile Early Warning System (BMEWS) with the North American Air Defense (NORAD) System headquarters at Colorado Springs, Colorado. This work involved exploration in a new mode of radio propagation to cover great distances over rugged and barren terrain with minimum installation costs. This mode, radio propagation through tropospheric scatter, was first investigated by Bell Laboratories in the late 1940s. It employed radio frequencies in the VHF, UHF, and SHF spectra propagated far beyond the horizon, thus greatly reducing the number of stations required.

Knowing of Bell Labs' work in tropospheric scatter propagation[6] and needing a reliable communications system for the widespread stations on the northern perimeter of the North American continent, the Air Force, in 1953, contracted with Western Electric for two studies on radio propagation. One study was carried out along the northern coast of Alaska and Canada in connection with the trial stations of the DEW Line. The second study, with the assistance of Bell Telephone Company of Canada, was carried out from October 1953 to October 1954 along the eastern coast of Newfoundland. The object of both studies was to determine the effects of weather, terrain, and radio frequency on tropospheric scatter propagation and thus find out whether it would be suitable for reliable com-

---

[6] See, for example, reports on Bell Labs' experimental studies referenced in a survey of the international literature in François Du Castel, *Tropospheric Radiowave Propagation beyond the Horizon* (Oxford: Pergamon, 1966), p. 14; and the reference to the experiments at the Whippany laboratory of Bell Labs by a group under the direction of Kenneth Bullington in *Bell Laboratories Record* 35 (October 1957), p. 430.

munications. The results of the two studies, as well as those of propagation studies made by Lincoln Laboratories and also by the National Bureau of Standards, indicated that beyond-the-horizon radio systems were practicable.

The satisfactory findings led to a crash program to build a communications system along the coasts of Labrador and Newfoundland that would link early-warning radar stations with Continental Command centers. This program, called Polevault, was initiated in 1954 and completed a year later. It showed that reliable voice and digital communications were possible with tropo-scatter and, in a comparison with the existing microwave systems, demonstrated vast reduction was possible in the cost of construction and maintenance for the new radio system.[7] Polevault became an important link in the global communications network of the Department of Defense.

III. SUMMARY

For over 30 years after World War II, Western Electric and Bell Labs had the responsibility for the development, manufacture, and installation of major air defense weapons systems and early warning radar systems for the defense of the continental United States and for the field army. At the end of World War II Bell Labs looked at air defense as a total system concept rather than as loosely linked individual units. This view led to the development of a fully integrated system for air defense, which included target acquisition and tracking, computation, command and control, and communication. The system, named T33/M33, was complete except for the guns provided by the Army. Production of it was started in 1950; 645 units were manufactured in the next several years at Western Electric plants in Chicago and North Carolina.

By 1945 it was clear that guns would soon become obsolete as a defense against the maneuverable, high-altitude bombers then on the drawing boards. The Army and Air Force therefore asked Bell Labs in 1945 to study the possibility of using guided missiles for air defense. A study completed in six months showed that a command guidance system with the critical radars and computers on the ground appeared the most feasible and promising goal. With the Army designated as the defense agency, Bell Labs was authorized to start research and development on the system, and Douglas Aircraft was enlisted as a partner-subcontractor to help develop the missile. Six years later the system, named Nike, was successfully demonstrated at the White Sands Proving Ground against manuevering bomber targets. With the outbreak of the Korean War, development and production of a tactical system named Nike I and later Nike-Ajax were

---

[7] H. N. Misenheimer, "Over-the-Horizon" Radio Tests, *Bell Laboratories Record* 24 (February 1956), pp. 41–45.

authorized in 1951, before the demonstration of the final R and D system. Two years later the first production system was delivered by Western Electric and Douglas Aircraft. In the end, Western Electric and Douglas produced 358 ground batteries and 14,000 Nike-Ajax missiles for the Army.

In 1953 the Army asked Bell Labs to continue study of the Nike system for possible improvements against future bomber attack strategies, particularly closely spaced bombers that might tend to saturate the Nike-Ajax system and also degrade radar tracking accuracy. Working with Douglas, Bell Labs proposed the addition to the system of a larger missile that could carry a nuclear warhead and would extend the system's range from 25 to 100 miles. Development of the new missile, named Hercules, was authorized, and the Nike system with this new missile was called the Nike-Hercules system. Modifications were also made in the range performance of the Nike ground radars to capitalize on the longer intercept range of the Hercules missile.

In 1956 Bell Labs was again asked to look at further improvements in Nike-Hercules to meet future threats, such as sophisticated electronic jammers, Mach-2 medium-size bombers operating at altitudes up to 70,000 feet, and air-supported missiles and rockets operating at Mach 3 and up to 100,000 feet. Modifications and additions were made to the Nike-Hercules System to meet these possible threats. Hence this altered system was called the Improved Nike-Hercules System. The success of the overall Nike-Hercules program is indicated by the 393 Nike-Hercules ground systems produced by Western Electric and the more than 9,000 Hercules missiles built by Douglas.

In February 1955 the Army asked Bell Laboratories to carry out a study looking to a prospective air defense system that would provide defense against threats, including ICBMs, in the period 1960–1970. From this initial study, an ABM research and development program was carried out over the next twenty years by the Bell Laboratories and Western Electric team. This turned out to be the largest and most technologically complex project mounted by the Bell System for the armed forces. The help of many key subcontractors, including Douglas (and its successor, McDonnell Douglas), was enlisted over these years. The first ABM system developed, Nike-Zeus, was demonstrated at Kwajalein with the successful intercept in 1962 of an ICBM fired from Vandenberg Air Force Base in California. A number of successful ICBM intercepts followed, including the successful intercept of United States satellites. The Department of Defense decided not to deploy Nike-Zeus and asked Bell Labs to continue its R and D responsibility and to seek significant advances in ballistic missile defense technology that would counterbalance the increasing sophistication of the ICBM threat. For over four years, from 1963 to 1967, work continued on new advanced subsystems, including multifunction electronic phased array radars, a superaccelerating missile called Sprint, and an exhaustive test on reentry effects. The new R and D system that encompassed all this was referred to as Nike-X.

In September 1967 the Secretary of Defense made the decision to deploy a limited ABM defense system for the United States using elements developed as part of the Nike-X R and D system. This system was called Sentinel. But it was modified two years later, in March 1969, to put first priority on the defense of the Minuteman missile silos, at which time the system name was changed to Safeguard.

The first tactical Safeguard site, at Grand Forks, North Dakota, was successfully tested and turned over to the Army for military operation on April 1, 1975. In the meantime, a SALT I agreement had been negotiated with the USSR in May 1972 that limited both countries to two ABM sites with only 100 defensive missiles. The further deployment of Safeguard was stopped, but it was clear that successful R and D testing at Kwajalein against ICBMs and IRBMs with the Safeguard system elements played a key role in bringing the Soviet government to agreement on SALT I. Another major contribution of the ABM R and D effort was the support it gave to the offensive weapons programs of the United States. During the years of R and D operations at Kwajalein, Bell Labs turned over hundreds of data packages obtained from reentry missions to the Air Force and other DOD agencies.

Another large undertaking in the postwar period was the development and installation by Western Electric and Bell Labs of a complex generally referred to as the Far North Communication and Detection System. The idea of the warning line in what became the Distant Early Warning (DEW) Line detection system, was conceived by a summer study group which met in 1952 at the Lincoln Laboratory, M.I.T. Bell Labs was a member of the group. In December 1952 Western Electric was asked to undertake the construction of a trial segment of the line along the northern coast of Alaska. Bell Labs was asked to plan the electronics system, including communications, search radars, and automatic alerting features. Western Electric had to contend with the most difficult logistical and environmental conditions in building the line between Cape Lisburne in western Alaska to Cape Dyer on Baffin Island roughly along the 70-degree parallel—about 3 degrees above the Arctic Circle. Today the basic system stretches halfway around the world. Similarly, early in the ICBM era, Bell Laboratories had engineering responsibility for the far-flung communications system linking the Ballistic Missile Early Warning System (BMEWS) radars to the continental command headquarters.

Chapter 8

Underwater Systems

At the end of World War II, knowledge of the acoustic environment in the oceans was inadequate. Beginning in 1950, the Navy called on Bell Laboratories and Western Electric to conduct research and to design and develop oceanographic facilities. It was recognized that it would be economically advantageous to collect as much of the needed information as possible without sending ships to sea. Oceanographic data could be collected and analyzed by the use of fixed underwater receivers connected to shore-based data-processing facilities by means of multi-channel transmission systems. The Bell System was recognized to be uniquely qualified to conduct such a program because of its long and successful experience in acoustics research, signal and data processing, and engineering of underwater cable communication systems. Many significant contributions were made in the spectrum analysis of ocean sounds—the background noise against which any attempt to identify submarines or other objects of interest must be made. As a by-product of this work, the Bell Laboratories/Western Electric systems were able to record and analyze unusual sounds from sources as many as 100 miles distant that were shown to be of biological origin. As a peripheral development, a system was devised through underwater acoustics research for locating the point of impact when a missile falls into the ocean.

I. INTRODUCTION

During World War II, the U. S. Navy's efforts to cope with submarine attacks against Allied shipping were frequently frustrated, in spite of significant wartime advances in sonar technology. As the war at sea progressed, it came to be appreciated that poorly understood ocean-acoustic phenomena limited sonar performance more than the state of the art in equipment development. This was reinforced at the end of the war by the discovery that the German Navy had better acoustic information about important regions of the Atlantic and Pacific oceans than did the United States.

As a result of World War II experience, the U. S. Navy was determined never again to lag other nations in its understanding of ocean acoustics.

Principal authors: R. R. Galbreath and R. A. Walker.

Accordingly, following the war, with the support of the Committee on Undersea Warfare of the National Research Council, the Navy undertook expanded oceanographic surveys. These were designed (1) to collect extensive experimental information about sound propagation in the oceans of the world and (2) to make comprehensive measurements of the many factors which affect it.

As the oceanographic surveys progressed, it became evident that there would be important economic advantages to collecting as much of the needed information as possible without sending ships to sea. Ships are expensive to operate and their use is weather dependent. The Navy saw the advantage of collecting much acoustic and supporting data with fixed underwater receivers connected to data-processing facilities on shore by multichannel transmission systems. Gradually, shore-based oceanographic research stations, which were known as U. S. Naval Facilities, were established.

Bell Laboratories and Western Electric were given an opportunity to play a role in the development of these facilities. Because of commercial experience in acoustics research, signal and data processing, and engineering of underwater cable systems, the Bell System was perceived to offer a unique combination of needed skills. Therefore, Bell Laboratories was awarded a research contract by the Office of Naval Research in December 1950. Under this contract, effort was dedicated to demonstration of technical utility and feasibility. Concept validation proceeded swiftly and was supported by trial installations in Sandy Hook Bay and on the continental slope off Eleuthera Island in the Bahamas, at a site occupied for acoustic experiments by Maurice Ewing and J. L. Worzel of Columbia University in 1944 and 1945.

A new laboratory, under the direction of Charles F. Wiebusch, was formed at Bell Labs to assume responsibility for continuation of the work. Navy manager for the effort was Commander J. P. Kelly, U.S.N. An organization comparable in size to that at Bell Labs was established at Western Electric to assume field engineering and contract management responsibilities. During the ensuing years, Bell Laboratories' involvement grew gradually to division strength. The Ocean Systems Division consisted of four laboratories between 1971 and 1974.

The character of the underwater systems work grew to cover a broad technical spectrum, including basic and applied research, systems planning and engineering, hardware and software development, and design engineering. Research efforts were concentrated principally in the areas of ocean acoustics and signal processing. Hardware development was focused on underwater receivers, underwater transmission technology, and shore-based data and signal-processing equipment. Software development grew in the 1970s, concentrated on computer automation of many data processing functions accomplished by hardware in earlier shore processing equipment. Up to 1975 there had been essentially four design phases in underwater hardware development, with corresponding cycles in the development of shore processing equipment.

II. PRINCIPAL FEATURES OF THE NAVAL FACILITIES

The Navy's approach to an improved understanding of ocean acoustics has been twofold. It has involved (1) direct experimental observation of acoustic phenomena and (2) the collection of data on environmental oceanographic factors such as temperature and salinity, for example, which are known to affect sound propagation. As a consequence of the Navy's interest in experimental observation, many of the underwater sensors deployed at sea have been hydrophones, which transform underwater sounds into electrical signals for transmission to shore facilities. Other sensors have been temperature- and current-measuring devices.

The early hydrophone installations were barely deployed at sea when it became clear that the underwater environment was anything but the "silent world" some people had believed it to be. Throughout the more than ten frequency octaves in which measurements have been made, the ocean has been found to be resounding with an endless symphony of fascinating sounds, both natural and man-made. The study of these sounds has constituted a major component of the Navy's ocean surveys because sonar detections must be made against their background interference. These studies have shown that the sound sources include, but are not limited to, rain beating on the ocean surface, wind blowing across it, underwater seismic activity, thunder from atmospheric storms, waves breaking on the surface, seismic prospecting, marine oil drilling, ships, and countless marine animals.

Since occasional references have been and will be made to signal processing, some explanation of the term *signal* is called for. At various times during Navy studies, attention has focused on different specific ocean sounds as being of special interest. Such sounds, by definition, have been inevitably regarded as signals. All other sounds have been considered noise to the extent that they have interfered with, or masked, the sounds of interest. Signal processing is that procedure by which the total collection of sounds is treated in such a way as to selectively accentuate the presence of, and the unique characteristics of, whatever sounds are the focus of attention.

One of the most powerful processing techniques for diagnosing complex signals, such as those which represent the total energy of the large variety of ocean sounds, is spectrum analysis. This process examines the relative amounts of energy in a large number of narrow, contiguous frequency bands across that portion of the frequency spectrum in which the contributing sounds contain detectable amounts of energy. Spectrum analysis is one of the techniques implemented on shore at the oceanographic stations to study ocean sounds.

The myriad sources of ocean sounds heard at hydrophone sites are scattered widely, and often nonuniformly, in azimuth. For studying the spatial distribution of ambient energy, some of the hydrophones are grouped into arrays. The resulting directionality and array gain enable acousticians to study sound transmission over specific, isolated paths. The outputs of array hydrophones are delayed and summed in beam-forming equipment located at the shore-based facilities.

The outputs of underwater sensors are carried to shore by underwater cables laid along the ocean floor. The cable transmission systems used have been based in the main on Bell System commercial technology, which has spared the Navy development expense. The needs of the Bell System and the Navy for increased bandwidth have closely paralleled each other. Early transmission systems employed multipair cable technology, whereas later installations utilized frequency-modulated carrier technology, with repeatered coaxial cable serving as the transmission medium. Navy installations have differed from commercial ones in one very significant way. Commercial systems are accessible at each end of the cable; the Navy cables at only one end. In the latter, it is not possible to control precisely the levels at which sensor outputs are launched onto the cable, which results in more demanding dynamic range requirements.

Although the need for the use of ships has been substantially reduced because of the reliance on shore-based facilities, the sensors at sea are initially implanted by ships. Because it is efficient to install transmission cable leading to shore immediately after sensor emplacement, cable layers have been used for both sensor and transmission-link implantation. Electromagnetic navigational aids have been used in the process, occasionally supplemented with bottom-mounted acoustic transponders. Because of the expense of such installations, underwater hardware development has required high reliability and long service life. In fact, twenty-year design life as a system goal has been exceeded.

Ships have also played a second important role. Naturally occurring sounds have not always sufficed in studying ocean acoustic phenomena. It has sometimes been necessary to introduce sounds of known characteristics and source levels at certain locations in the ocean. Calibrated sound sources, or projectors, have occasionally been employed. These have been towed by ship through areas in which sensors are located to make quantitative measurements of transmission loss or to study regions of anomalously intense or faint insonification.

Explosive charges are also very effective broadband sources of underwater sound. Their use has been complementary to the employment of ship-towed projectors. It has been possible to survey certain areas with great rapidity by dropping explosive charges from aircraft. The charges are preset to explode at designated depths.   They have the advantage of being operable at much greater depths than most available projectors.

These are the principal features and uses of the Navy oceanographic stations.   The remainder of this chapter is devoted to the identification of the major technical contributions made by Bell Labs to the design, creation, and use of the facilities.   Contributions to ocean-acoustics and signal processing research are examined first.   Then attention shifts to the development of underwater and shore-based hardware.   Finally, brief mention is made of two peripheral contributions that grew out of the technology developed.

III. RESEARCH CONTRIBUTIONS

3.1 Sound Transmission

Experience in World War II led to the observation that the field of sound from a point source was characterized by adjacent regions of markedly different degrees of insonification.   Even at comparatively short ranges from wartime sonars, shadow zones were encountered where no echoes could be received.   It was gradually suspected that refraction plays a major role in ocean sound propagation and that refractive effects principally arise from the nonuniform heating of ocean waters.   By 1941, preliminary thermal measurements by the Woods Hole Oceanographic Institution (WHOI) had confirmed the occurrence of such conditions.   In fact, by that time WHOI oceanographers had discovered the main thermocline of deep ocean waters in the temperate latitudes.   Nonuniform thermal structures were also found in the shallow waters over the continental shelves.   The acoustic implications of the main thermocline were quickly hypothesized by Maurice Ewing and others, who predicted the phenomenon of deep-ocean sound channeling and confirmed it experimentally at Eleuthera in 1944 and 1945.[1]

The speed of sound varies with depth as shown in Fig. 8-1a.[2]   This gives rise to alternate upward and downward refraction of deep-ocean transmission paths, depicted in Fig. 8-1b.   Some paths can cycle to substantial range without interacting with the bottom and thereby experience no bottom-loss attenuation.   Some of the oceanographic station hydrophones have been positioned on continental slopes to study such propagation paths.

Deep-ocean sound propagation is characterized by numerous interference phenomena because of its multipath character.   Fig. 8-2 depicts several transmission paths from a single source.   At certain points in the insonified field, adjacent paths converge and thus create caustic surfaces

[1] M. Ewing and J. L. Worzel, "Long-Range Sound Transmission," Part 3 of *Propagation of Sound in the Ocean*, Memoir 27, New York; The Geological Society of America, October 15, 1948 (reprinted 1963).
[2] D. C. Stickler, "Ocean Acoustics," *Bell Laboratories Record* 47 (April 1969) pp. 113–119.

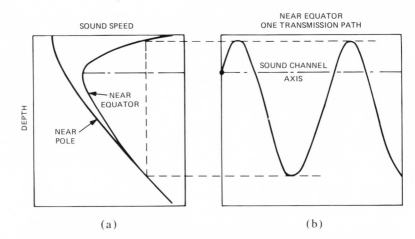

Fig. 8-1. Deep-ocean sound propagation. (a) Velocity profiles of deep ocean sound channel at polar and equatorial latitudes. (b) Transmission paths are bent toward regions of lower sound speed.

along boundaries of the resulting convergence zones. Field intensities are unusually high in such regions but with modulations due to interference effects. Shadow zones are often formed adjacent to convergence zones.

The formation of shadow zones and caustic surfaces can be portrayed qualitatively with ray diagrams like those of Fig. 8-2. Ray-tracing techniques have been highly developed in the ocean acoustics community, Bell Labs being a prominent contributor. In 1970, Bell Labs extended the value of ray tracing to the quantitative prediction of field intensities within convergence zones through the application of wave solutions. Comparison of such predictions with data is shown in Fig. 8-3. Field intensities in convergence zones are often 15 decibels (dB) greater than those in neighboring regions, and accurate predictions about the former are an important confirmation of the theoretician's insight.

The existence of sound channeling in isothermal surface ducts was experienced, albeit not well understood, in World War II. Postwar acoustics studies have attempted to refine the prediction of field intensities in such ducts. In 1973, Bell Labs investigators published their work on a virtual mode theory,[3] in which a normal-mode description was applied to energy trapped in surface ducts. It was shown that under velocity-gradient conditions often encountered, trapped energy predominates over nontrapped energy to ranges sufficiently great to be of practical importance in acoustic surveys.

---

[3] F. M. Labianca, "Normal Modes, Virtual Modes and Alternative Representations in the Theory of Surface Duct Sound Propagation," *J. Acoustical Society of America* 53 (April 1973), pp. 1137–1147.

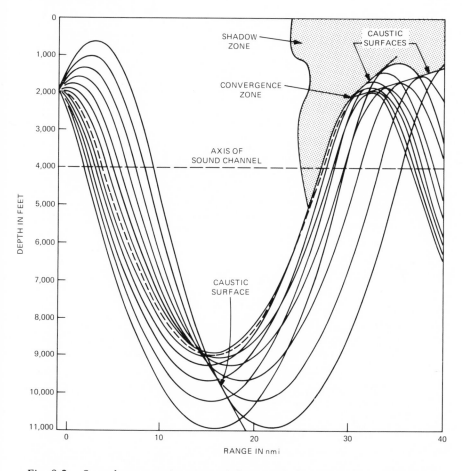

Fig. 8-2.   Sound rays moving around the sound-channel axis are periodically concentrated into high-intensity regions on caustic surfaces (a caustic is a locus of focal points, as in the case of a spherical mirror).   The convergence zones in the Atlantic Ocean (the caustic surfaces near the surface) are about 35 miles apart.

3.2 Ambient Sea Sounds

The general spectral distribution of the total energy of ambient ocean sounds was established by early measurements at Eleuthera in 1951.   The data are reproduced in Fig. 8-4.   In the literature, the total collection of all sounds is frequently referred to as ambient noise.   With appropriate filtering, it is often possible to measure the separate contribution of a single sound source to the total energy of all the sounds.   Bell Labs has played a key role in the study of ambient sounds because, among other reasons, transmission system hardware and shore-processing equipment must be designed to accommodate the spectral distribution of the total energy received.

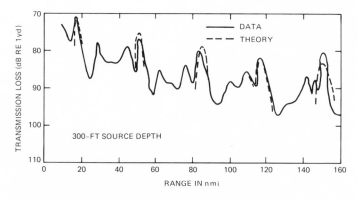

Fig. 8-3. Comparison of measured propagation losses in convergence zones with predictions of theory.

Variations of the ambient energy of all sounds with frequency, time, and geographic location have been studied. Principal findings from such measurements, to which Bell Labs has made substantial contributions, are:

1. Different sources of sound dominate the energy contributed to different frequency bands. Situations change with time, too. At frequencies used for World War II sonar, sounds made by snapping shrimp sometimes drown out all other sounds. Lower in frequency, capillary waves generated on the surface by wind some-

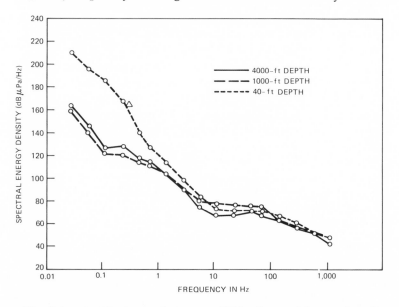

Fig. 8-4. Ambient sound energy off Eleuthera. Mean values for period July 11 to August 18, 1951; sea states 1–2.

times dominate the ambient energy, while at other times in the same frequency band rain beating on the surface predominates.

2. At lower frequencies, it is more likely that sources at a great distance contribute the bulk of the total energy received and that sounds generated by ocean shipping tend to dominate. Perhaps this is understandable, since about 2,500 ships, each over 1,000 gross tons, are at sea in the Pacific Ocean at any one time.

3. Under those circumstances, and at frequencies for which distant sources dominate, it should perhaps be expected that the total energy observed would depend on the quality of long-range transmission to the receiving site. At sites where acoustic transmission is characterized by relatively low losses, high ambient sound levels might be expected; and conversely, for high-loss transmission, low ambient sound levels might be expected. This, in fact, is observed when the contributions of distant sources dominate the sound field.

4. Total ambient sound levels show substantial variations in time and with receiver location. At those frequencies for which distant sources usually contribute most of the energy, seasonal changes in the short-time mean energy of the total sound field at a given location have been observed to range up to 12 dB, which is more than a tenfold variation in the amount of energy received.

As noted above, World War II sonars occasionally encountered conditions where sounds from marine animals limited sonar performance. The postwar surveys have discovered important sounds of biological origin at frequencies well below those used by World War II sonar. Several fascinating sounds have been discovered by Bell Labs investigators; one is detectable at ranges on the order of a hundred miles.[4] The investigators' suspicion that the latter might originate with certain species of whales was confirmed in 1963 by bioacousticians from the Woods Hole Oceanographic Institution, who observed experimental correlation between the sounds and those of finback whales.[5]

Sound transmission considerations lead one to expect that ambient energy at high frequencies might tend to arrive from an apparent source almost directly above a deep-bottomed hydrophone, while at lower frequencies energy might arrive almost horizontally. Bell Labs measurements reported in 1964[6] confirm such expectations, provided that,

[4] R. A. Walker, "Some Intense, Low-Frequency, Underwater Sounds of Wide Geographic Distribution, Apparently of Biological Origin," *J. Acoustical Society of America* 35 (November 1963) pp. 1816–1824.

[5] W. E. Schevill, W. A. Watkins, and R. H. Backus, "The 20-Cycle Signals and Balaenoptera (Fin Whales)," *Marine Bio-Acoustics—Proceedings of a Symposium at Bimini, Bahamas, April 1963* (New York: Pergamon Press, 1964).

[6] G. R. Fox, "Ambient-Noise Directivity Measurements," *J. Acoustical Society of America* 36 (August 1964), pp. 1537–1540.

for the high-frequency measurements, at least moderate sea states prevail above the hydrophone site. A Bell Labs theoretical model that assumed a uniform distribution of surface sound generators successfully predicted the results of such measurements.[7]

3.3 Signal Processing

The reason why spectrum analysis is such a powerful technique for the study of large collections of different sounds is that the sounds from one specific source or one type of source usually have quite unique spectral characteristics. Spectrum analyzer outputs contrived to display frequency content as a function of time in visual form enable the experimenter to readily identify "signatures" that signify the presence of each contributor to a large collection of sounds. Fig. 8-5 displays an example of such outputs. Of special interest in this figure are the parabolic patterns that result from multipath interference of energy radiated by a broadband source passing near the sensing hydrophone at constant speed. The graphic portrayal of information in this figure capitalizes on the observer's visual acuity, as well as other powers of discernment, to recognize such patterns, a capability sometimes referred to in the literature as that of "visual integration." The value of such displays first became apparent to R. K. Potter, G. A. Kopp, and H. C. Green, of Bell Labs. Their studies of "visible speech," published in 1947,[8] set the stage for some of the applications described here.

Certain Navy needs made it desirable to analyze ocean sounds continuously. To do this required spectral scanning at speeds greater than real time because multiple scans for all frequency components had to be accomplished without loss of information. The basic technique for achieving this analysis was invented by L. A. Meacham in 1951.[9] Recirculating memory was an integral feature of the spectrum analyzers that were developed. The first experimental equipment used unique magnetic tape machines in which slowly moving conventional tape passed over an input recording head and then over a high-speed rotating spool containing a pair of pickup heads. Input data were thus retained long enough to permit scanning of all data in the frequency domain, the sweeping being done at a rate compatible with the response time of a fixed-frequency analyzing filter. While these machines could be created quickly and served to validate signal-processing concepts, the tape and mechanisms presented maintenance problems.

[7] R. J. Talham, "Ambient-Sea-Noise Model," *J. Acoustical Society of America* 36 (August 1964), pp. 1541–1544.

[8] R. K. Potter, G. A. Kopp, and H. C. Green, *Visible Speech*, New York: D. Van Nostrand, 1947.

[9] L. A. Meacham; U.S. Patent No. 3,021,478, "Wave Analysis and Representation"; filed November 21, 1951; issued February 13, 1962.

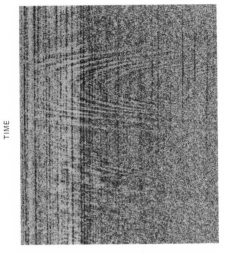

TIME

FREQUENCY

Fig. 8-5. Spectrum analyzer display portraying energy content as a function of frequency and time. Darker regions represent more energetic signal components.

A principle similar to that in Meacham's technique is used in the unique bifacial recorder-multiplier designed for maintenance-free service. In this, a rigid magnetic ribbon about 5 inches in diameter is slowly rotated, first past an erase head and then past a recording head placed on the outside of a short cylinder formed by the ribbon. Pickup heads are rotated at high speed on the inside of the cylindrical ribbon.

This equipment was the first known application of magnetic recording on one side of a medium with pickup on the opposite side. It was made possible by the development of a way to fabricate the magnetic ribbon by deposition as an overhang from the periphery of a disc. The minute clearances between heads and the rotating magnetic medium require extraordinary oil seals to prevent oil from causing drag on the rotating parts.

The ratio of the speed of the ribbon past a pickup head to the speed past the recording head is the multiplication factor of a frequency multiplier. The bandwidth of the fixed-frequency spectrum analyzer filter divided by this multiplier yields the analyzing bandwidth at the input baseband frequency. A low-speed limitation because of pickup sensitivity and a high-speed limitation because of material strength determine the greatest multiplication factor achievable with this type of device. To narrow the baseband analyzing bandwidth, one must achieve higher multiplication without disturbing the fixed-filter bandwidth and the sweep rate. For

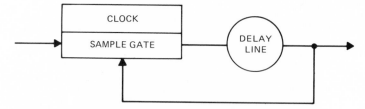

Fig. 8-6. Simplified diagram of the DELTIC processor.

a second-generation analyzer, a solution was found in using a solid-state recirculating memory known as the delay line-time compressor (DELTIC).

The principle of the DELTIC was proposed by V. C. Anderson,[10] of the University of California Marine Physical Laboratory of the Scripps Institution of Oceanography. Bell Labs developed a solid-state dual-channel DELTIC, which is a 1-bit digital memory that fulfills the same function as the recorder-multiplier just described. As shown in Fig. 8-6, the input signal to the DELTIC is first sampled. When the steady state is reached, the delay line contains a parade of sample digits (ones or zeros) whose spacing is determined by the clock. These digits, which are viewed at the output terminals, are recirculated, and in each round trip the oldest digit is replaced by a new sample. The product of clock frequency and delay-line length is the multiplication factor. To provide increased frequency resolution, one can achieve an n-fold increase in resolution by gating in a new sample only every nth round trip.

Even while a new spectrum analyzer, the digital spectrum analyzer (DSA), was being developed as a major advance, its departures from ideal were being assessed as a guide to future work. One-bit hard-clipping and the sampling operation were shown by comprehensive studies to degrade performance under some of the energy-distribution conditions encountered.[11-14] Additional degradation occurs if the input spectral energy is badly misequalized at the analyzer input. Delta modulation, now used in many DELTICs, alleviates that problem.

As mentioned earlier, analyzer outputs are often portrayed as displays of frequency versus time. These are generated with a fine stylus that marks electrosensitive paper as it sweeps the frequency axis while the

[10] V. C. Anderson; U.S. Patent No. 2,958,039, "Delay Line Time Compressor"; filed May 18, 1956; issued October 25, 1960.

[11] R. M. Lauver, "A Z Transfer Function and Output Spectrum for a Deltic," internal Bell Labs memorandum, September 14, 1962.

[12] R. A. Smith, "A Note on the Frequency Domain Behavior of a Deltic," internal Bell Labs memorandum, September 15, 1964.

[13] E. L. Kaplan, "Signal-Detection Studies, With Applications," *Bell System Technical J.* 34 (March 1955), pp. 403–437.

[14] H. T. Balch et al., "Estimation of the Mean of a Stationary Random Process by Periodic Sampling," *Bell System Technical J.* 45 (May–June 1966), pp. 733–741.

paper is advanced along the time axis. The first paper used was adapted from facsimile recorders and responded to variations in applied current. In later developments a paper was formulated and controlled to meet reproducibility requirements far more severe for this application than for facsimile. The light gray paper is blackened, as in halftone printing, by the application of stylus voltage. Between extremes of about 70 and 500 volts (depending on stylus speed and driving circuit), the probability of arcing, and consequent marking, increases nonlinearly within a range of about 7 dB. Marking by-products include solids and gases. For controlling these, vacuum equipment has been introduced—to keep solid particles out of mechanisms and to confine annoying fumes.

In addition to spectrum analysis, correlation techniques[15] have also been introduced for certain acoustic studies. These techniques consist of comparing complex waveforms received by two widely separated hydrophones. When the two signals received are added with an appropriate time delay for one with respect to the other, the time-averaged sum is maximized and a sensitive measure of the direction of the source is provided. Adequate directional information about signal sources is often thereby obtained with only two hydrophones rather than with an array of many.

Correlation methods are particularly well suited to broadband sources. The two hydrophones must be spaced closely enough so that received wavefronts are essentially coherent across their aperture. Correlator outputs can be processed to produce a visual display of source direction, or bearing, as a function of time. One such display is shown in Fig. 8-7. Two prominent sound sources exhibit bearing changes as a function of time. The trace on the left is made by a source radiating energy across a broader band of frequencies than that on the right.

Signal-processing developments in the mid-1970s have exploited the Cooley-Tukey fast Fourier transform (FFT) algorithm.[16] This algorithm provides great flexibility in selecting frequency resolution and analyzing bandwidth in the generation of power spectrum estimates.

IV. DEVELOPMENT CONTRIBUTIONS

In the material just discussed on signal-processing research, the reader probably noted certain implementation details that might have been classified more properly as development contributions. They were included only to provide continuity in the description of Bell Labs' signal-processing work. The material that follows summarizes the development contributions of Bell Laboratories on (1) acoustic arrays, (2) underwater

---

[15] H. B. Andrew; U.S. Patent No. 3,145,341; filed January 3, 1961; issued August 18, 1964.

[16] J. W. Cooley and J. W. Tukey, "An Algorithm for the Machine Calculation of Complex Fourier Series," *Mathematics of Computation* 19 (April 1965), p. 297.

LEFT-HAND ⌐
    TRACE   RIGHT-HAND TRACE

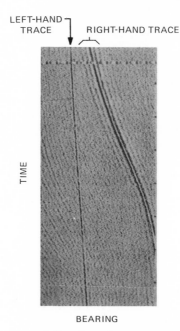

BEARING

Fig. 8-7. Correlator display.
The dark portions represent high
correlation.

transmission systems, (3) sea installation, (4) beamforming, and
(5) projectors.

4.1 Acoustic Arrays

Bell Labs pioneered in the design and operation of one of the first successful deep-water hydrophone arrays. That array consisted of a single
row of hydrophones embedded in a flexible cable structure lying con-
formally on the ocean bottom. It was necessary to set the array on a flat
segment of the bottom in order to achieve its intended performance
characteristics. The array was designed to be a simple in-line extension
of the transmission cable to which it was attached in order to facilitate
installation.

The hydrophones on the first array Bell Labs developed were uniformly
spaced. But this spacing optimized array performance for only a limited
band of frequencies. Later designs incorporated nonuniform spacing,
shading techniques, and departures from the straight-line configuration.
The principal objectives of such design modifications were to increase
bandwidth and to resolve the front-to-back ambiguities intrinsic in linear
designs.

A major improvement, completed in 1973, was the introduction of broadband arrays following studies going back over 20 years. Broadband designs included enough hydrophones in the physical array to provide spacings suitable for subarrays with different design-center frequencies. For achieving only one broadband output per beam from the whole array, signals from individual hydrophone channels were shaded, or weighted, by passing them through filters so that, in a given frequency region, contributions were summed from the hydrophones forming the appropriate subarray. The combined beam patterns extended the usefulness of the array over a wider frequency range, as shown in Fig. 8-8. In addition to providing broadband effective array gain, this type of array holds the beamwidth almost constant with frequency.

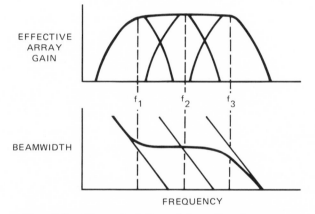

Fig. 8-8. Characteristics of broadband array compounded from three subarrays.

The broadband array concept relies on the performance of weighting filters. Their cutoff characteristics are critical to the achievement of desired performance in the transition regions. Low-pass (LP), high-pass (HP), bandpass (BP), and all-pass (AP) filters are required for designated channels. To preserve array performance, especially in the subarray transition regions, each filter is required to have the same delay, as well as linear phase, for all frequencies even beyond the 3-dB passbands.

Bell Labs designed, computer-simulated, fabricated, and field-tested filter systems. These systems had 60 channels, were multiplexed by time division, were programmable, and had built-in error-detection and automatic-substitution features. By adding or subtracting the responses of Thiran-type digital low-pass filters to or from the characteristics of all-pass delay networks, over 4,000 unique LP, HP, BP, and AP configurations were independently realizable for each channel.

4.2 Underwater Transmission Systems

As noted earlier, underwater hardware development through 1975 had cycled through four distinct generations. These closely followed corresponding evolutions in Bell System transoceanic communications technology. The four generations are categorized in what follows as (1) multipair, (2) multipair with hydrophone amplifier, (3) SB carrier, and (4) SD carrier. The order in which these are described is chronological.

4.2.1 Multipair

In this hardware generation, baseband transmission took place over balanced pairs. The array was formed as a flexible, wet-core "stub." Hydrophones were embedded in the cable where rubber core material had been cut out or removed. The electrical conductors ran outside the hydrophones and core, jute filler being used to maintain a uniformly thick conductor layer.

Passage of the array stub over shipboard sheaves under tension during installation put bending forces on the rigid hydrophones. The stub design was a compromise between softness of the embedment, which would protect hydrophones and conductors from those bending forces, and stiffness of the whole structure, which would protect cable terminations at the ends of the hydrophone cases. Careful selection of the lay angles of conductors and armor wires was an important ingredient in achieving that compromise.

The cable included electrical pairs that transmitted the outputs of thermal sensors and other oceanographic instruments. The hydrophone was the Bell Labs-designed moving-coil type, with its compliance developed by oil fill. It had a cylindrical housing made of red brass for corrosion resistance. A rubber covering bonded to the red-brass housing formed a diaphragm on one end, which allowed for expansion and contraction of the oil with temperature and pressure changes and admitted the acoustic signals.

Loading coils were used where necessary to preserve the design bandwidth of long cables. They had rigid steel housings, which provided strength against crushing. They were enclosed in oil-filled polyethylene bottles, which were splice-molded to the polyethylene insulation of the conductors to provide a water seal.

4.2.2 Multipair With Hydrophone Amplifier

The use of an amplifier with each hydrophone tripled the maximum loaded cable length that could be used for a given design bandwidth. This design marked the first underwater use of production solid-state circuitry.

4.2.3 SB Carrier

The introduction of a carrier system in the third generation of development again tripled the maximum possible cable length, while reducing the cost per mile and tripling the bandwidth. Undersea multiplexing and shore demultiplexing were connected by the Bell System SB transmission system[17] of cable and repeaters. Multiplexers using solid-state devices were embedded in an extension of the flexible hydrophone-array stub. Solid-state devices of high reliability included an alloy-junction germanium transistor having the lowest low-frequency noise level known. Multiplexer rigid housings were similar to the type developed for the loading coils in the multipair system. A suppressed-carrier scheme was used in which the receiver was arranged not only to work with sideband components extending into the vicinity of the carrier but also to eliminate the channel-to-channel phase ambiguity in what was previously the state of the art.[18]

4.2.4 SD Carrier

The SD submarine cable system, also a double-sideband carrier system, further extended maximum channel capacity and cable length. It used the same cable as the Bell System SD system.[19] New unidirectional repeaters employed solid-state devices based on technology developed for the Bell SF system.[20] The SD multiplexer had four channels in a housing similar to the housing developed for SD and SF repeaters. These housings were inserted in series with the array stub, which was similar to that used previously.

Multiplexer features included the first high-reliability underwater use of integrated thin films on substrates of improved properties and large size. Signal limiting was employed to control trunk repeater behavior during overload and to prevent overloaded channels from interfering with signals from other channels in the trunk repeaters. A hitherto uninvestigated transistor noise phenomenon—random sudden shifts in noise level—was identified in this development. This was studied as a potential threat to reliability. The shifts were related to power aging, and transistors that exhibited this behavior were screened from use in the underwater hardware.

New seals based on the Bridgman principle were developed to provide more penetrations per seal in a smaller space, to improve coaxial transmission through a seal, and to work at a greater water depth. Like their

[17] E. T. Mottram et al., "Transatlantic Telephone Cable System—Planning and Overall Performance," *Bell System Technical J.* 36 (January 1957), pp. 7–27.

[18] T. W. Eddy; U.S. Patent No. 3,391,341, filed September 23, 1965; issued July 2, 1968.

[19] R. D. Ehrbar et al., "The SD Submarine Cable System," *Bell System Technical J.* 43 (July 1964), Part 1, pp. 1155–1184.

[20] S. T. Brewer et al., "SF Submarine Cable System," *Bell System Technical J.* 49 (May–June 1970), pp. 601–798.

predecessors in SD and SF systems, each of these had primary and secondary sealing mechanisms involving the deformation of polyethylene. Instrumentation was developed that measured a diffusion rate of as little as 10^{-10} cubic centimeters per second (cm^3/s) through the polyethylene of seals during hydrostatic pressure testing. This made possible relatively rapid evaluation of various design features. A limiting value of 60-percent relative humidity in a housing after 20 years corresponds to a diffusion rate of 1.7×10^{-7} cm^3/s for each of seven seals. Achieved diffusion rates were two orders of magnitude less than this. The instrumentation developed facilitated the study of moisture transfer in a multiplexer during fabrication as components give up their moisture in the pumping operations.

The SD hydrophone balanced out signals generated by longitudinal vibrational modes of the cable itself by having two moving-coil motor elements. The pistons of the elements were actuated together by acoustic pressures transmitted through rubber windows in the hydrophone cylinder walls. The cylinder shell was made of beryllium-copper to provide increased resistance to bending of an assembly that was longer than its red-brass predecessor. A rubber diaphragm in one end provided for expansion and contraction of the oil filling. Being unique as a pressure-release material, silicone oil was used in spite of its tendency to stress-crack polyethylene. Polyethylene of high molecular weight was used. It was stress-relieved after shaping.

In the SD design, extreme care had been exercised to prevent electrical system noises from adding appreciably to the electrical signals originating at the oceanographic sensors. One example of a potential electrical noise source in the 6-kilovolt (kV) SD system is corona. Here *corona* means the rearrangement (or pulse-transfer) of minute amounts of energy—far below the levels usually associated with energy-robbing, carbonizing, glow-producing corona. Each component, each subassembly, and each assembly fabricated for later incorporation in transmission cables of various configurations must meet requirements that limit interference and spurious noise. Both in the laboratory and in the assembly shop, test equipment senses transfers of as little as 10 picocoulombs (pC) and counts the frequency of occurrence of the pulses as materials undergo changes in the state of relaxation or contamination. Control of corona has meant not so much the application of novel rules, but rather the dogged adherence to extremely stringent design and assembly procedures.

A significant difference between SD and the usual communications transmission system is that SD was designed to accept inputs distributed virtually anywhere along its length. This innovation provided versatility but required close attention to signal insertion levels and introduced intermodulation requirements. It also created a whole set of hardware design and installation problems.

Investigation of technical strategies to effect economic savings in cable transmission led to the invention of phase-locked quadrature modulation.[21] This technique doubled the number of channels that can be transmitted on a carrier system of given bandwidth. Although, as of 1976, it had not been incorporated into SD designs, initial laboratory tests simulating the fine-grain (in terms of frequency) irregularities of a long ocean cable suggested that the technique was technically and economically feasible for the future.

4.3 Sea Installation

For versatility, underwater sensors and transmission system components are designed to withstand the pressures of deep ocean-floor environments. Their housings, in particular, are massive. In the course of deep-water installation, the weight of such hardware in suspension before it reaches the bottom, two to three miles below, becomes enormous. During installation, static tensions in cables are often measured in many thousands, and sometimes tens of thousands, of pounds. The housings must be designed to support such tensions, in addition to being able to resist great pressure. In moderately heavy weather, cable ship handling is very difficult when precise positioning of hardware on the sea floor is required, and dynamic tensions often substantially exceed the static component attributable to the suspended weight alone.

Cable routes to shore must be carefully selected. A major objective is to avoid post-installation damage to the cable from underwater rock slides, turbidity currents, seismic activity, and bottom-trawling fishing operations. Since the commercial development of Bell System cable plows,[22] some cables have benefited from being buried. When repeatered cable is used, it is important to survey the ambient temperatures on the ocean bottom along the cable route in order to match repeater gains to cable losses, which are temperature dependent.

Since the design of underwater hardware is strongly influenced by the ruggedness required during installation, array and transmission-system design, installation procedures, and the design of ship machinery for cable laying are interdependent. Hardware trials have involved vessels and also mock-ups at the Bell Labs Chester Laboratory, where a testing facility of unusual size and strength was created for exercising and testing the hardware. With each new design, array hardware has grown larger and heavier and has therefore placed additional demands upon ship machinery and cable-handling equipment.

Instrumentation is incorporated into arrays to measure tension, depth, and tilt. This enables the cable ship to monitor and control the placement

[21] J. F. Lynch; U.S. Patent No. 3,391,339; filed November 6, 1964; issued July 2, 1968.
[22] H. A. Baxter and R. E. Mueser, "The Development of Ocean-Cable Plows," *IEEE Trans. Communication Technology* COM-19, Part II (December 1971), pp. 1233–1241.

of the array during installation. Other instrumentation measures shipboard cable tension and rate of payout. All readouts are continually available to the cable officer, along with the ship's track as it develops, so that placement of the array within a few feet of a desired location is not an uncommon feat. Accurate determination of the ship's position requires the extension of navigational techniques. Acoustic transponder beacons have been developed by subcontract for use as references.

A major contribution to the improvement of cable-handling machinery was the self-fleeting cable drum, proposed in 1967.[23] When being deployed, cable is typically restrained or lifted by a combination of two devices. One is the cable drum and the other is a linear double-caterpillar drawoff-drawback machine or some means of applying holdback tension, which can adjust its opening to changes in cable size. Between this machine and the overboarding sheave, the cable makes several turns around the cable drum to multiply the holding force by a factor depending on the number of turns and the friction developed between cable and drum. In old designs, cable was kept from piling up against a flange on one side of the drum by the use of a fleeting knife which forced the cable to slip laterally to make room for oncoming cable. But this method could cause overlapping of turns on the drum if it was used with an SD system, in which large electronic housings were employed. The self-fleeting drum not only prevents such rollover but also makes it possible to lay systems that have large changes in cable diameter and equipment size, which could not be handled by earlier technology. It permits the deployment of any sequence of grapnel rope, large array structure, and different housings and trunk cable.

On the self-fleeting drum, shown in Fig. 8–9, about two-thirds of the spool surface is made up of lateral, endless conveyor belts that move in synchronism with the drum rotation (one foot per turn). Cable is led on at a fixed point and is advanced across the drum in turns spaced to accept the largest-diameter electronic housings without interference between turns. Except for stretching, the cable remains in position on the conveyors for the duration of its contact with the drum. The machine achieves a force multiplication factor greater than that achieved with old designs because the cable is in static contact with the moving conveyor tracks, which can be fitted with high-friction surfaces.

4.4 Beamforming

To derive directional information about ambient sound fields, it is necessary to combine individual hydrophone outputs in beamforming equipment. Essentially, such equipment inserts into hydrophone outputs electrical delays that are equal to the acoustic delays with which wave-

[23] Royal T. Hawley, "Ocean Cable Laying," *Oceanology International* 5 (November 1970), pp. 18–21.

Fig. 8-9. Self-fleeting cable drum on foredeck of cable ship. Four turns of array cable are transported laterally across circumferential face of drum. Conveyor speeds are adjusted to space turns far enough apart to prevent repeater housing—shown just coming off drum—from touching adjacent turns when on the drum.

fronts reach individual hydrophones when arriving from discrete, oblique directions across the aperture of the array. For a given set of electrical delays, the summed hydrophone outputs are maximized, and the array response is correspondingly sensitized to the acoustic energy arriving from a single direction. Beamforming equipment has utilized a succession of delay technologies.

The electrical delay lines (EDL) first used consisted of low-pass sections. Signals from hydrophone amplifiers entered the delay lines through pads. Pads and amplifiers placed periodically in the delay lines gave all channels unity gain. The same pads and the very low output impedance of the hydrophone amplifiers served to isolate the various hydrophone amplifier loads. One of the first experimental EDL beamformers was steered by a commutator; another used relays. Early models used one delay line for each of many beams so that all beam outputs were available continuously. For a typical EDL system, about 600 electron tubes were used in beam-formers—an unprecedented number for one function. At a time when many electronic systems operated at thousands to tens of thousands of tube hours per replacement, the first Bell Labs equipment gave 170,000 tube hours per replacement, and beamformers later gave over 2 million tube hours per replacement. Besides having an ideal environment, being land-based and free from serious vibration and shock, these components achieved high reliability mostly because of the rigorous adherence to known principles. All designs assumed the component characteristics that were predicted to exist after a 20-year life. Feedback was of course used extensively. Heat, the principal cause of deterioration, was controlled by design, as, for example, in the electron tubes, which were operated for the most part at reduced voltage but with a 1-percent tolerance. The introduction of solid-state circuits in later designs further increased circuit reliability.

Fear that EDL reliability would be difficult to realize was one reason why a new design, the magnetic delay line (MDL), was developed. Other reasons, which became controlling, were the cost of providing EDL components with the tolerances required, floor space, granularity of delay, and high-frequency phase-linearity limitations. The MDL had a drum on which magnetic tracks were laid down, one for each beam. Delay (which was dependent on drum speed) was proportional to the distance from the output pickup head to the recording head connected to a given hydrophone. One triumph of production engineering was the control of dimensional tolerances during fabrication of the magnetic tracks.

Under development in 1976 was a new digital beamformer, known as a computer organized partial sum (COPS) beamformer. It economized on storage by keeping partial sums of digital samples in memory until contributions from each hydrophone were included. At less cost than its predecessors, this all-digital beamformer offered easier beam selection and provided high reliability by self-checking and automatic circuit substitution.

4.5 Projectors

The use of ship-towable projectors to introduce sounds of known intensity and frequency at known locations was alluded to earlier. Since the early 1950s,[24] Bell Labs has developed about a dozen different designs, varying in frequency, power, and depth of operation. While several have been capable of operating over as much as an octave, most have been resonant at a single frequency, with Q's of 10 to 30. About a dozen and a half projector types are described in surveys of the art. All of the Bell Labs units have been of the moving-coil type, with radiation from a diaphragm or a piston.

The moving-coil device, one of the few types well suited to low frequencies where low stiffness is essential, was a natural extension of the telephone art and the devices that were pioneered at Bell Labs for the high quality audio entertainment field. Resonance frequency was controlled by diaphragm stiffness or by tuning bars or springs that supported the piston. Typical projectors were somewhat over a foot in diameter and

---

[24] E. E. Mott; U.S. Patent No. 2,977,573; filed December 30, 1952; issued March 28, 1961.

several feet long and were enclosed in tow bodies with an overall weight of several hundred pounds in water. Acoustic power output ranged from a few watts at low frequencies to as much as 100 watts at high frequencies, with efficiencies of 0.5 to 30 percent.

Underwater projector development has been curtailed since the mid-1960s. To a great extent, transmission research during the decade 1966–1976 was supported by the use of explosive charges at the expense of some spectral detail. Inasmuch as explosions are broadband sources, they can be used for simultaneous measurements at many frequencies.

V. TWO PERIPHERAL CONTRIBUTIONS

Technology developed for implementation of the oceanographic stations found application in several peripheral programs. Two deserve mention here:

1. The development of underwater acoustic systems on the Atlantic and Pacific missile ranges to support targeting tests. (These systems determined the geographical coordinates of points of impact of test missiles with the ocean surface. They are designated missile impact location systems, or MILS.)

2. Bell Labs' contribution to the Navy's PARKA experiments.

5.1 MILS

The ocean missile ranges have been established for full-flight testing of long-range ICBM (intercontinental ballistic missile) and SLBM (submarine-launched ballistic missile) vehicles. Studies of targeting accuracy are an important component of such tests. Since a missile impact on the ocean surface generates energetic sounds, accurate targeting data can be gained by acoustic data processing that derives from sound arrival times at scattered hydrophones the geographical position at which such sounds originate. Underwater acoustic velocities of about one mile per second provide localization accuracies measured in a few tens of feet with appropriate positioning of bottomed hydrophones.

Starting development in February 1956, Bell Labs and Western Electric engineered and installed underwater hardware on both the Atlantic and Pacific missile ranges.[25] Two types of installation were implemented. One, designed to yield the most accurate targeting data, depended on the use of a distributed field of bottomed hydrophones within direct-path range (about 18 miles in water 3 miles deep) of expected impact points. The other gave less accurate positioning information over much larger areas. It employed hydrophones distributed around the perimeters of

[25] H. H. Baker, "Missile Impact Locating System," *Bell Laboratories Record* 39 (June 1961), pp. 195–200.

major ocean basins, and used sounds generated by explosive charges that were released from nose cones on impact with the surface. These charges were preset to detonate at the depth of the axis of the deep-ocean sound channel.

Hydrophones for the latter type of installation were suspended at axis depth above the bottom by submerged floats. Two hardware features of these suspensions were the submerged buoys and the articulated anchors, which were integral with the transmission cable carrying hydrophone signals to shore.

For each type of installation, the geographical locations of the impacts were derived by hyperbolic positioning techniques using acoustic arrival-time differences at the receivers as input data. The less accurate, broad-ocean-area networks yielded position accuracies on the order of a mile.

5.2 PARKA

During the period from 1968 to 1970, the Navy conducted comprehensive, long-range sound propagation experiments along carefully selected deep-ocean tracks. The experiments were designated PARKA I and PARKA II. Unprecedented in scope, this program marshalled a concentrated effort to establish relationships between fine-grain environmental descriptors and certain features of sound propagation not previously examined in such detail. The program was directed by the Navy's Maury Center for Ocean Science and was implemented by 14 participating organizations. R. H. Nichols of Bell Labs was appointed chief scientist for both PARKA I and PARKA II. In addition, in PARKA II Bell Labs conducted the bulk of the data analysis and interpretation, and generated reports covering the acoustic results and their comparison with predictions provided by the Navy's Fleet Numerical Weather Center. The acoustic and oceanographic data banks provided by the PARKA experiments have been extensively used to test recent theoretical models of sound propagation.

Chapter 9

Radar

Since many World War II radar projects had potential for further development, Bell Laboratories and Western Electric were involved after the war in a variety of radar systems for aircraft, shipboard, and submarine use. These systems performed important bombing, navigation, and gun-directing functions and represent significant advances in the radar art. At the same time, however, interest shifted toward broad, challenging programs in which radar was developed as an integral part of major defense systems, and straightforward radar developments were subsequently phased out of the Bell Laboratories/Western Electric defense activities.

I. AIRBORNE RADARS

After World War II, Bell Laboratories contributions to airborne radar systems for the United States Army Air Force—and for its successor in September 1947, the United States Air Force—were a continuation of the work undertaken just before and during the war. As described in Chapter 2 in the discussion of World War II airborne radar, development began in 1945 on a new computer (designed for alternating current) known as the AN/APA-44, or ground-position indicator, i.e. referring to the point on the ground directly below the airplane. One of its applications was to achieve higher resolution with a 1.25-cm wavelength K-band radar than that of the 3.2-cm X-band radar. The K-band radar, coded AN/APS-22, with further improvements in performance, was ready for testing with the AN/APA-44 computer in August 1945. The military B-17 airplane in which the system was to be flight tested was scheduled to arrive at Newark Airport on August 25, 1945, but V-J Day occurred before the airplane arrived, and the program was cancelled in the general wave of government contract cancellations.

After a brief interval, however, the AN/APA-44 computer contract was reinstated. In the meantime, it was found that the 1.25-cm K-band radar wavelength fell almost squarely on the water vapor absorption line in the

Principal authors: C. A. Warren, R. C. Newhouse, and L. W. Morrison atmosphere, with the result that the range of a K-band radar was very severely reduced compared to that of an X-band radar.   As a result, the production contract on the APS-22 radar was cancelled and the prototypes were reduced to a limited number for testing only.   Negotiations were therefore begun in late 1945 to substitute an X-band radar, designated the AN/APS-23.   This radar, with the AN/APA-44 computer, was coded the AN/APQ-24 bombing system.

In the meantime, the AN/APA-44 computer was lent for use with the APQ-7 (Eagle) system discussed in Chapter 2.   This improved computer, coded AN/APQ-16, was first flight-tested on December 16, 1945.   Flight tests continued at a slow pace throughout 1946 until the No. 2 engine of the B-29 test aircraft blew off, damaging the Eagle antenna.   Following repair of the bomber, flight testing began again in July 1947.

Although the 1.8-cm Kμ-band AN/APS-22 was not to go into production, flight testing with the APA-44 computer began in December 1946 in a B-17G airplane.   Testing was carried out in two phases.   In the first phase, Bell Labs investigated the performance of the APA computer; the second phase was conducted by the Air Force in order to evaluate operating results.

Ten test flights totaling 26 hours were made from Boca Raton, Florida, in January and February 1947 for system shakedown and operator training. Four flights with 46 bomb drops were made in February, and then, after a number of gyro and other airplane difficulties were corrected in March and April, final evaluation was begun.   Based on 12 bombing flights and two navigational flights, final evaluation was completed by June.   The equipment, known as AN/APQ-34 (the combined AN/APS-22 radar and AN/APA-44 computer), was turned over to the Air Force on June 3, 1947. A summary of the performance characteristics, which surpassed design objectives, follows: On straight approach, probable angle errors were

23 mils at 20,000-foot altitude.
23 mils at 10,000-foot altitude.
100 feet at 1,500-foot altitude.

On evasive approach with banks of 30° and turns of 20° to 40°, probable angle errors were:

21 mils at 10,000-foot altitude.

Maintenance during the period was very low, and all indications pointed to a thoroughly stable system.   The equipment was then turned over to the Air Materiel Command for continued testing.

As noted before, negotiations on the AN/APS-23 X-band radar, which was to replace the AN/APS-22 in an AN/APQ-24 bombing system, started before V-J Day with a design conference in May 1945 at the Whippany, New Jersey, location.   When the proposal was submitted to the Army Air Force on December 7, 1945, it covered two developmental models.   This

Fig. 9-1. Component parts of the AN/APS-23 X-band radar (at right) and computer assemblies that make up the AN/APA-44 ground position indicator (at left).

system was planned for installation in five Air Force bombers, the B-50, B-36, B-35, B-45, and B-47.

A combination of the AN/APS-23 radar and the Sperry AN/APA-59 computer, which was designated the AN/APW-31 radar bombing system, was also contracted for by the Army Air Force. An interconnection equipment conference on this system was held in December 1946.

The first AN/APS-23 radar was available in April 1947 and was accepted by the Air Force. A B-29 airplane left Boca Raton for Newark, New Jersey on June 13, 1947. The radar was installed and the airplane was ready to depart for Boca Raton on July 1; but the aircraft developed equipment problems on July 3, indefinitely delaying flight tests of the AN/APQ-24 bombing system. As a result, the radar was removed and shipped to Sperry Gyroscope, Great Neck, Long Island, for installation and test with the AN/APA-59 computer. The first flight operations occurred there on January 31, 1948, and were successfully concluded February 20, 1948.

As a result of these successful tests of the AN/APS-23 radar, it was decided that it would not be necessary to conduct additional flight tests of the radar with the AN/APA-44 computer, since the computer had already been thoroughly tested as part of the AN/APQ-34. Elimination of the flight tests was approved June 1, 1948.

Extensive design tests were conducted, both before and after the flight tests. These included vibration and shock, radio interference, and servo amplifier performance tests, which were completed in May 1948. With testing completed, two AN/APS-23 radar sets were delivered to the Air Force: one on April 15, 1947 with a 46-inch-wide antenna and one on June 25, 1948 with a 60-inch-wide antenna.

The component parts of the AN/APS-23 are shown in the right-hand portion of Fig. 9-1. On the left are shown the assemblies that make up an AN/APA-44 computer. The combination constitutes the AN/APQ-24 bombing system.

Fractionalization of the system in a multiplicity of boxes made it possible to install it in many types of airplanes, though installation w s often very crowded and messy, as evidenced by the combination facing the bombardier in the B-50 airplane shown in Fig. 9-2. This approach also aided maintenance by allowing the easy substitution of units for diagnostic purposes.

Production of an initial lot of 264 AN/APS-23 radar sets began at Western Electric in North Carolina in 1949 and continued through successively larger lots until 1956. The peak production years were 1951 through 1953. A total of 2,500 radars and 1,500 AN/APA-44 computers were manufactured. The radars were also used with the Sperry AN/APA-59 computer, which accounts for the larger number.

Bell Laboratories had a number of engineers who spent essentially full time visiting the various Air Force Strategic Air Command (SAC) bases

Fig. 9-2. AN/APQ-24 bombing system at bombardier position in B-50 aircraft.

to help them with installation, operation, and maintenance of the radar and computer systems. Early in the program, most systems went into B-50 aircraft and then later into B-36 aircraft.

Bell Labs engineers became trusted advisers of Air Force General Curtis Le May and subordinate commanders of SAC and were given complete access to the results achieved in SAC bombing competitions. There was an excellent match between the circular error probability of the bombing system and the lethal radius of the atom bombs which SAC carried; thus, SAC constituted a really effective overall weapons system. Its great effectiveness and its world-wide mobility provided such a strong deterrent that it never had to be used in the period of international tensions between the Korean and Indo-China wars.

This effectiveness was not achieved without constant and sustained effort. In addition to the production of new sets, Western Electric, assisted by Bell Laboratories, conducted recycling programs in which sets were returned to the factory for repair, modification, and modernization. Field complaints were promptly investigated, and fixes were designed to solve equipment problems encountered in the field.

One of the biggest problems was the relative unreliability and short life of the JAN (joint Army-Navy specification) type of vacuum tubes which had to be used in the radar sets. Often a specific type of tube was made by a dozen different manufacturers, and some characteristics that were important in the bombing system were not controlled by the specifications. This was particularly true of the magnetron transmitter tubes. While the components of the radar could be changed to work with the tubes of any

Fig. 9-3.   Mockup of nose section of B-66A aircraft with canopy removed.

one of the several manufacturers, it was never possible to get a circuit that would work with all.   Thus, necessity for tube selection was always an operating problem.

By early 1950, it seemed desirable to repackage the AN/APQ-24 bombing system to simplify it and make it more compact, and to include optical sighting provisions.   This work was authorized in April 1950.   As work progressed, it became apparent to both the Air Force and Bell Labs that to meet desirable objectives, it would be necessary to design a completely new bombing system, including automatic navigation equipment.   Therefore, a new program for the development of such a system, identified as Radar Bomb Directing Set AN/ASB-3, was started in 1951.   Before completion, it was redesignated Bombing and Navigation System, Optical and Radar, Type K-5.   The first salable model was delivered to Wright Field in September 1952, where it was installed and tested in a B-50 bomber.   Two additional models were delivered—the last in February 1953.

In the meantime, the Air Force had decided to have the K-5 modified to fit a specific bomber, the B-66A, and thus provide a good integrated design where all the equipment would be correctly positioned for the convenience of the operator and for easier maintenance.   This had never really been possible with the original AN/APQ-24, since it was designed and packaged for universal use in many different types of aircraft.

A one-sixth scale mockup of the nose section of the B-66A airplane was made at Bell Labs, Whippany, New Jersey.   Figure 9-3 shows a view of the mockup with the canopy removed, including the location of the radar equipment in the nose section, the pilot's compartment, the operator's compartment, and equipment accessible through removable side panels.   Figure 9-4 shows all of the units of the K-5 system.   The optics and cath-

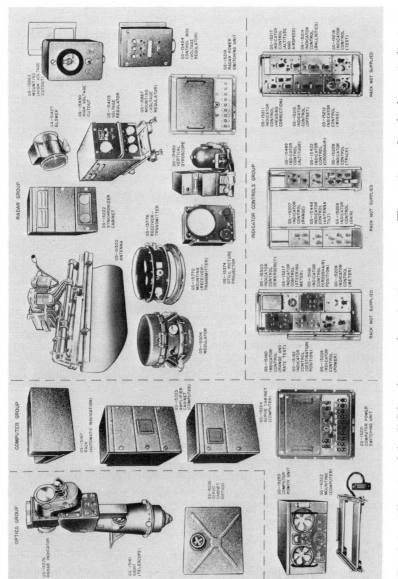

Fig. 9-4. All units of the K-5 bombing and navigation system. The optics and cathode-ray indicator are combined in one unit (upper left).

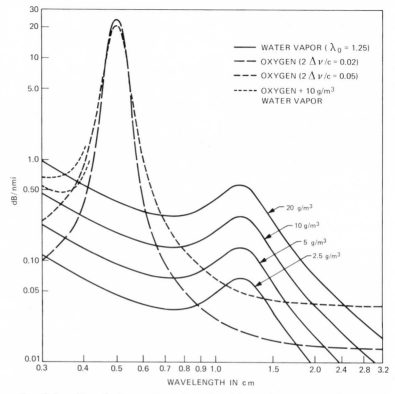

Fig. 9-5.   Signal attenuation at sea level by water vapor and oxygen. Characteristics were charted during study of possible compromise wavelength. (Redrawn from M.I.T. Radiation Laboratory drawing no. X6101-I, Report 41—December 14, 1944.)

ode-ray indicator were combined in one unit (upper left).   The first unit was ready April 12, 1954 for delivery three months ahead of schedule to Douglas Aircraft for installation in the first B-66B aircraft.   Western Electric produced 65 of these systems in the next two years.

As stated at the beginning of this chapter, bombing systems proceeded from the 10-cm wavelength band to the 3.2-cm band, and then to the 1.25-cm band in the search for higher resolution of targets.   It was necessary to abandon the 1.25-cm band because of atmospheric water-vapor attenuation, which could be as much as 1 dB per nautical mile (nmi) to the target greater than at the 3.2-cm band.   Thus, for a target 50 nmi away, the round-trip attenuation could be as much as 50 dB greater, which would have required impracticable amounts of transmitter power at 1.25 cm (K-band) to achieve comparable performance.

The possibility of a compromise wavelength somewhere in between seemed worth investigation (see Fig. 9-5).   For instance, the loss in dB/nmi is only one-fifth as great at 1.8 cm as at 1.25 cm, or, in other words, for a target 50 nmi away, the loss should not be more than 10 dB worse than at X-band (3.2 cm).

This was promising enough for Bell Labs to be authorized in 1948 to develop parts operating in the Kμ band (centered at 1.8 cm) to be substituted for the X-band parts in the AN/APS-23 radar. Five sets of parts were delivered to the Air Materiel Command. In 1953, the MA-1 Radar Modification program was authorized. A complete Kμ-band radar was developed and five models were delivered to the Air Force. Apparently, the higher resolution obtained was not enough to offset the poorer range performance. In any event, no production contract materialized.

The operating frequency of the AN/APS-23 radar was determined by the magnetron transmitter. All magnetrons whose frequencies fell within the 9,320- to 9,430-MHz band were accepted by the Air Materiel Command. However, as countermeasures improved, it became increasingly desirable to have the frequency under control of the radar operator and to have the radar capable of operating over a much wider band.

Thus, conversion of the AN/APS-23 radar to wideband, 8,600- to 9,600-MHz operation was undertaken by Western Electric with Bell Labs assistance in February 1955. This involved the manufacture of a conversion kit (designed by the Philco Corporation) which, when substituted in the radar, changed it to the AN/APS-64 radar. Later, complete AN/APS-64 radars were manufactured by Western Electric.

Since the Air Force disliked sole-source procurements, manufacture of the AN/APS-23 radar was divided between Philco and the Motorola Corporation in addition to Western Electric. This caused some extremely difficult problems, since fixes for field failures, change orders, refurbishing of equipment, and product improvement had to be done with full interchangeability of the various suppliers' units. The Air Force tried to help by arranging frequent conferences but finally found itself in an impossible situation.

To resolve the situation, the Air Force asked Bell Labs in August 1956 to assume full systems responsibility for the AN/APS-23A, AN/APS-64, and 64A radar sets. The contract required Bell Labs to:

1. Advise the Air Force of requirements for new equipment or modifications to improve the reliability, maintainability, and usefulness of the radar sets.

2. Review the engineering changes of associated contractors to ensure system coordination with other equipment.

3. Assist the Air Force to plan objectives and to monitor specific flight tests and field evaluations as required.

4. Participate in radar coordination meetings.

5. Review requirements for support test equipment and recommend modifications to existing equipment.

6. Furnish necessary engineering information and requirements to Wright Air Development Center, Air Materiel Command, and participating contractors as required to maintain engineering liaison.

7. Evaluate the effectiveness of the radar systems and associated equipment in aircraft, and provide recommendations to improve performance.

8. Investigate system efficiency.

9. Submit to the Air Force every 90 days a progress report of the various phases.

This contract gave authority to Bell Labs to do what it previously had attempted to do by persuasion. The contract was terminated in mid-1958 and constituted Bell Labs' last contribution to airborne bombing systems in the post-World War II years.

II. NAVY SHIPBOARD RADARS

2.1 Mark 25 Radar

Fully automatic radar tracking of aircraft targets was under development at Bell Laboratories in the early years of World War II, and the work was concerned with radar systems of both the land-based and shipboard types. The purpose of one research and development system, known as Mark 7, was to explore the highest performance capabilities possible in an automatic tracking radar. The fundamentals of feedback applied to automatic systems were evaluated as well as the importance of low antenna inertia and minimum or no backlash in the antenna drive systems. The optimum method of scanning the antenna beam for maximum accuracy was also part of the experimental Mark 7 evaluation. This experimental work, supported by the Navy, made it possible to start development near the end of World War II of an advanced fully operational complex for the Navy, known as Mark 37. Mark 37 was a complete gunfire control system of which the Mark 25 radar was the key element. This system provided an antiaircraft defense essentially free of manual input once the target was acquired.

Initial R and D work on the Mark 25, Mod 0, radar started in March 1944. The radar was a two-frequency system using X-band for a 7-degree vertical, 15-degree horizontal scan and, after target acquisition, transforming to K-band for tracking with a 0.9-degree antenna beamwidth. The resolution of the system was sufficient for an R and D model at Bell Labs Whippany, New Jersey, to resolve the landing lights at the nearby Morristown airport when test aircraft were being tracked while landing. This R and D model did not go into production because there was a desire to have all controls for the radar below deck and have the fire-control director unmanned.

A modified design, designated the Mark 25, Mod 1, retained the same two-frequency system, but further R and D work showed that the desire for all controls below deck resulted in great complexity for the remote controls. Further development work was stopped, and work was directed to a simpler design designated Mark 25, Mod 2.

Mark 25, Mod 2 was defined in March 1945. The radar operated at a single X-band frequency with 50 kW of power. The antenna had three modes: (1) circular scan around the horizon for picking up island shorelines and directing gunfire at ground targets, (2) spiral scan for aircraft acquisition, and (3) conical scan for tracking. The radar provided complete automatic tracking in angle and range on the designated aircraft target out to a range of 50,000 yards. A final model was tested at the Naval Research Laboratory Test Site, North Beach, Maryland, in May 1947 against test aircraft targets and met all Naval Research Laboratory requirements. Production was authorized, and Western Electric manufactured for the Navy over 400 Mark 25, Mod 2, systems.

The Navy asked Bell Laboratories to continue R and D on further improvements in the Mark 25 to meet future threats from high-performance jet aircraft, since the system had become a key element in the air defense of the fleet. From this work, a modified version, designated Mark 25, Mod 3, was developed. The transmitter magnetron power was increased from 50 kW to 250 kW, with remote-control frequency change within the X-band. Amplifiers were installed below deck in this model, with only the indicator tube in the lightly manned director. The upgraded radar had outstanding performance out to 150,000 yards range and could track the ship's shells as they left the guns, which served to check the ship's firing accuracy. The principal task, of course, was accurate automatic tracking of high-performance, present and future attack aircraft. Modification kits were provided to convert Mod 2 systems to the improved Mod 3 design. By early 1952, all of the Mod 2 radars were converted to the Mod 3 configuration and many are still operational in the fleet today.

2.2 Mark 17 Radar

By the end of World War II, the Navy had equipped many of the 40 mm and 3-inch, 50-caliber antiaircraft guns with Mark 16 radar. These X-band radars were part of a Mark 63 gunfire control system which used the so-called Handle Bar Director operated by a single man. The radar was used primarily when the optical system of the director was obstructed by clouds or darkness.

Postwar development of electronic weapons-direction systems created the need to update the designation capability of this radar. The Mark 16 was modified to permit the director to accept and display electronic designation information from the Combat Information Center on the ship and to add features that simplified mode selection, allowing quick changes to be made from search to acquisition and track. This permitted designation and search of the fire control system beyond the visual range and gave the ability to track at ranges comparable to the maximum useful range of the weapon system. The modified equipment was designated the Mark 17 radar and new production was designated SPG-34.

A later major update of the system was designated AN/SPG-50. In this design, the latest electronic techniques were used to miniaturize the electronics and to introduce improvements. A total repackaging concept was also introduced to reduce size, weight, and improve maintenance accessibility. A total of 196 systems were ordered, and first delivery was in February 1956.

III. SUBMARINE RADARS DEVELOPED AFTER WORLD WAR II

As described in detail in Chapter 2, all the radars operating on U.S. submarines at the end of World War II were developed by Bell Laboratories and manufactured by Western Electric. The original SJ S-band radar installed early in the war for surface search and torpedo control was followed later by the ST periscope-antenna X-band radar, the SS X-band surface search and torpedo control radar, and the SV S-band aircraft search radar with its antenna on a retractable periscope tube. In the Pacific theater of the war, millions of tons of enemy ships were sunk at night through the use of these radars.

At the end of the war, the Navy was anxious that the same Bell Laboratories R and D team continue to work on these radars to make improvements based on operational experience in the war and on projected future requirements. These changes were concerned with the SS and SV radar systems then being installed in the submarine fleet and with new productions of these systems. Other experimental R and D work was begun to evaluate possible new operational roles for the submarine force. A summary of some of the work carried out on submarine radars from 1945 to 1953 is given below.

3.1 SV-3 Radar

Research and development leading to two models of a modified SV radar designated SV-3 were authorized in July 1947. Improvements included the substitution of a hydrogen thyratron pulser for the magnetron in place of the nonlinear coil pulser to obtain greater reliability. Changes were also made to provide a number of plan position indicator video outputs to repeat the SV-3 display on the SS console and on the standard navy video repeaters located at remote locations in the submarine. Western

Electric was authorized to build 17 SV-3 radars in June 1949; initial delivery was made in November 1950 and final delivery in June 1951.

3.2 SS-1 and SS-2 Radar

Based on experience with the SS radar, the Navy provided a specification in 1950 for the production of new groups of SS radars designated SS-1 and SS-2. The changes were relatively minor and included such items as synchro excitation isolation and a remote error monitor to assure accurate transmission of data output. A production lot of 66 SS-1 and SS-2 radars was authorized in June 1951; delivery began in February 1952 and final delivery was made in August 1953. The radars were produced by Western Electric in a new plant in North Carolina.

3.3 AN/BPS-1 Antenna

The AN/BPS-1 was a replacement antenna for the SJ radar system. In contrast to the parabolic antenna originally used on the SJ, the AN/BPS-1 antenna was a linear array of horns in a streamlined watertight shell whose dimensions were approximately 40 inches by 10 inches. The antenna was on a retractable mast and could be stowed so as to minimize drag in the water—an important consideration since the Navy was looking toward future submarines with a higher submerged speed. Another important feature was a corrugated type of high-pressure Plexiglas[1] cover for the antenna horns that maintained a near constant impedance match when the antenna was under water, partially submerged, or in air. Continuous operation was then possible without waveguide breakdown when the antenna was elevated to just break the surface of the water—but with waves breaking over it—thus providing minimum visibility to the enemy. Production was carried out by Western Electric in the early 1950s.

3.4 AN/BPS-3 Antenna

The Navy became interested in the possible future application of submarines as pickets offshore to detect low-flying aircraft. A number of antenna models were made for use with the SV system. The antenna developed was a vertical array 6 feet high by 2 feet wide and employed an organ-pipe type of scanner to provide a linear scan in elevation with a fast return. Accurate elevation data could thus be obtained on incoming aircraft as far down as the surface. This program was an R and D effort for the Navy—no production was involved.

3.5 AN/SPG-48 Antiaircraft Radar

In a conference held in Washington, D.C., on November 30, 1948, the Navy Bureau of Ordnance asked Bell Labs to assume responsibility for a

---

[1] Trademark of Rohm and Haas Company.

Fig. 9-6.   Console of AN/SPG-48 radar.

major redesign of an X-band radar set, AN/SPG-48, originally designed by another contractor.   Two redesigned models were requested by mid-1950, with production to follow.   This radar was closely associated with the 3-inch 50-caliber, 3-inch 70-caliber, and 5-inch 54-caliber antiaircraft guns and also with a lightweight gun director.   The radar equipment was to be employed with line-of-sight computers designed by C. S. Draper of the Massachusetts Institute of Technology.   One computer would be installed on the gun mount while a second computer would be installed below deck.

In the redesign, Bell Labs had to increase the transmitter power from 50 kW to 250 kW using a transmitter developed for the Mark 25, Mod 3, radar discussed earlier.   The antenna selected was a paraboloid reflector with a spiral scanner similar to that used in Mark 25, Mod 2.   A major effort was required to develop a high-power rotary joint capable of transmitting 500 kW of peak power, with a standing wave ratio of less than 1.5 dB, over the frequency band 8,500 to 9,600 MHz.

The operating console, containing the indicators, receiver, error-detection system, power supplies, etc., was extremely crowded as designed by the original contractor.   The Navy asked Bell Labs to completely redesign the console to make it reliable in operation and easy to maintain.

In addition, the console was structurally weak and did not meet Navy shipboard requirements. A photograph of the redesigned console showing the azimuth-range (A/R), azimuth-elevation (B), and elevation (E) indicators is shown in Fig. 9-6.

Authorization for redesigning the AN/SPG-48 radar was given in May 1949, and two R and D models, assembled and tested at Bell Laboratories, Whippany, New Jersey, were delivered to the Navy in October and November 1950. Western Electric was authorized to start production in August 1950, and final delivery of the production units with various modifications was completed in June 1958.

The AN/SPG-48 radar was essentially a redesign and repackaging of an existing radar that was undertaken for the Navy because key subunits from the Mark 25, Mod 2 and 3 radars then in production could be used to provide the Navy with a reliable and maintainable antiaircraft system for small guns, and one having greater range performance. However, straightforward radar designs of this type were no longer undertaken, since Bell Labs resources allocated to defense work were better applied to new, challenging, broad system programs such as the Nike guided missile system for the Army, the Mark 65 automatic target-evaluation and weapon-assignment program for the Navy, and a fully integrated optical and radar bombing and navigation system (Type K-5) for the Air Force. These forward-looking systems are discussed in other chapters of this volume (see index entries for specific equipment).

Chapter 10

Tactical and Strategic Defense Systems

Based on the results of a 1954 Bell Laboratories study, the concept of radio-inertial guidance was successfully used in the development and production of Thor intermediate-range ballistic missiles and Titan intercontinental ballistic missiles. Through 1974, Western Electric/Bell Laboratories radio-inertial guidance was used in 414 space shots with no failures attributable to the missile-borne guidance equipment. Although a number of these shots were conducted as part of military test programs, most were used to place satellites in orbit. Among the system's achievements: in 1960 it guided the TIROS I meteorological satellite to within one mile of the desired 447.3-mile orbit; in 1960 it guided the Echo I balloon into orbit for the first experiments in "bouncing" telecommunications signals cross-country; in 1962 it guided Telstar I into an orbit with an initial orbit period only 1.12 minutes longer than the computed period of 156.48 minutes; it guided Explorer, Discoverer, SYNCOM, and many other satellites. Thus, the guidance system was an important factor in the United States entrance into the space age.

I. INTRODUCTION

In 1955, the U.S. became greatly concerned that the U.S.S.R. was ahead of this country in the development of an intercontinental ballistic missile (referred to as the ultimate weapon) that would give them a major strategic advantage. Politically this was referred to as the "missile gap." As a result, a major effort was initiated by the Defense Department in both the Army and the Air Force to develop tactical and strategic ballistic missiles. A team of associated contractors was formed by the newly created Air Force Western Development Division under General Bernard Schriever whose specific and urgent purpose was to produce operational Air Force intercontinental ballistic missiles (ICBMs) and intermediate range ballistic missiles (IRBMs) on a crash schedule. Initially the associated contractors

---

Principal authors: T. W. Winternitz and C. A. Warren.

were the Glenn L. Martin Company, developing the Titan ICBM, Douglas Aircraft Company (now MacDonald Douglas) developing the Thor IRBM, and Western Electric/Bell Laboratories for the radio-inertial guidance system. Later, Remington Rand UNIVAC Division was added to work with Bell Labs in providing the ground-guidance computer hardware.

The choice of Bell Laboratories to develop the guidance system stemmed from an earlier Bell Labs study, made in 1954 by S. Darlington and D. P. Ling, on ballistic missile control. This culminated in a two-volume report, dated March 1954, entitled "Command Guidance for a Ballistic Missile," which initiated the concept of radio-inertial guidance. To obtain the precision required to set a ballistic missile on course at termination of powered flight—with an expected miss distance of a fraction of a mile for an IRBM with a 1500-mile range or an ICBM with a 5000-mile range—a rather sophisticated velocity-measuring system was envisioned.

The concept of guiding missiles from the ground during powered flight-command guidance was pioneered by Bell Laboratories in the Nike-Ajax and Nike-Hercules antiaircraft missile systems discussed in Chapter 7. These operationally proven systems, conceived in 1945, provided valuable technological background for the versatile ballistic-missile/space-vehicle command guidance system that emerged from the Titan I development program. A tracking radar similar to those in use for Nike-Hercules, with appropriate smoothing of higher-frequency noise components, would give a good estimate of smoothed velocity; but it must be updated to the instant of missile motor cutoff for adequate accuracy. Such updating was to be performed by integrating-accelerometers located on an inertially stabilized platform within the missile and oriented in an optimum fashion with respect to the trajectory.

A simple inexpensive inertial system was planned, since long-term drifts of the components were not important in the system's velocity-updating mission; the ground radar tracking system provided the smoothing for correcting longer-term velocity-variations. Very early in the development program (about mid-1956), it was recognized that, rather than requiring an additional inertial system, the missile autopilot system already on board could be used for this fine tuning of the motor cutoff commands without loss of guidance accuracy. This resulted in simplified, lighter, missile-borne guidance equipment—the velocity-updating function was transferred to the ground computer.

The inertial system was to be developed principally to work with the Titan ICBM in a hardened underground complex, with missiles and radar antennas in underground silos from which they could be elevated to the surface for firing. In contrast, the Thor IRBM guidance system was planned to be transportable and housed in trailers similar to those of the Nike-Hercules system. The Thor application was a backup system in case the all-inertial guidance system planned for that missile turned out to provide an unacceptable miss distance at the Thor IRBM range. Early in the program, in August 1957, this backup application was deleted from the Western Electric contract; however, test flights on Thor missiles under control of the radio-inertial guidance system were later executed, since Thor was to be the first available vehicle in which the Bell Labs guidance system could be tested.

The Bell Laboratories effort on this contract was initiated in October 1955 in a new department at Whippany under the direction of Julius P. Molnar. Molnar had previously been in charge of the development of microwave traveling-wave tubes and magnetrons at Murray Hill and later was to become executive vice president of Bell Laboratories.

The ground-guidance station, missile-borne electronics, digital computer interface equipment, and special test equipment were developed by Bell Labs. The guidance computer was designed by UNIVAC at St. Paul, Minnesota, under Bell Laboratories technical direction. It was a completely transistorized digital computer specially designed for high reliability and having adequate capability for the Titan guidance problem. A Bell Labs-designed transistorized computer based on Bell Labs experimental TRADIC[1] work had been considered, but was ruled out in favor of UNIVAC'S Athena digital computer in March of 1956, since a preliminary UNIVAC design was already under way as an alternative computer for another Air Force ICBM guidance project. The guidance equations were developed by the mathematical research department of Bell Laboratories and programmed for the computer's magnetic drum by the development department.

In principle, the command guidance system developed for Titan was quite simple. A ground-based radar continuously determined the position of the missile in powered flight. Also on the ground, the Athena, designed by UNIVAC to meet Bell Labs specifications, accepted the radar position data, determined the missile velocity and, by reference to previously stored trajectory data, computed appropriate commands to guide the missile on the desired flight path. The commands, transmitted over the radar beam to the lightweight, expendable, missile-borne units of the system, actuated the transducers that controlled the missile's autopilot and engines.

II. FIELD FACILITIES

2.1 Air Force Atlantic Range

To test the radio-inertial guidance system, a facility was constructed at the Air Force Missile Test Center (AFMTC) at Cape Canaveral, Florida. This facility was staffed by a permanent group of Bell Laboratories and

---

[1] Acronym for Transistor Digital Computer—see Chapter 13.

Fig. 10-1. Air Force Titan ICBM leaving launching pad at Cape Canaveral. Moments later the missile's second stage was successfully steered over the Atlantic Ocean by the Western Electric/Bell Laboratories command guidance system produced by Western Electric.

Western Electric engineers. (Figure 10-1 shows a Titan ICBM leaving the launching pad at Cape Canaveral.) A building of approximately 17,000 square feet was completed in December 1956 to house two complete ground-guidance systems—one was originally planned for Titan and one for Thor. It was located so that the tracking antennas would be in a line of sight with the Titan launchers about one and a half miles away and the Thor pads, which were three miles distant.

One set of guidance equipment was installed in the building in May 1957 and a second in November 1958. Figure 10-2 shows the first ground-guidance antenna ready for installation. This equipment or its successor was operated continuously for Titan testing and space launch guidance until the station was finally shut down in September 1971. The guidance control console and the plotting board in action are shown in Fig. 10-3.

Fig. 10-2. First ground guidance antenna being readied for installation at the Western Electric/Bell Laboratories facility at Cape Canaveral.

2.2 Vandenberg Air Force Base

At the Pacific Missile Range at Vandenberg Air Force Base in California, office and laboratory space was provided in a number of renovated barracks buildings left over from the tank battalion that previously occupied that location. Two quasi-tactical Titan hardened guidance complexes were emplaced nearby—less the elevatable underground missile launchers—with their guidance antennas in a line-of-sight with the various missile test launch complexes. The first installation was the Operational System Test Facility (OSTF), which was a preprototype tactical system. This became operational in early 1960. A Titan missile lift-off at Vandenberg is shown in Fig. 10-4. The second installation was essentially a complete tactical ground-guidance station and was planned for training the installation and checkout teams who would make the emplacement of the final 18 production Titan tactical guidance complexes. These facilities were used for testing various lots of Titan missiles in launch operations and for the guidance of many space vehicles starting in February 1961. One of these guidance stations was still operational in 1976 for space shots, although used at somewhat infrequent intervals. The facility saw its peak activity from 1962 to 1970, throughout which time an average of more than two operations per month were performed.

Fig. 10-3.   The guidance control console and plotting board in action at Western Electric/Bell Laboratories Cape Canaveral test facility.

Fig. 10-4.   Titan ICBM lift-off at Vandenberg Air Force Base under control of the radio inertial guidance system.

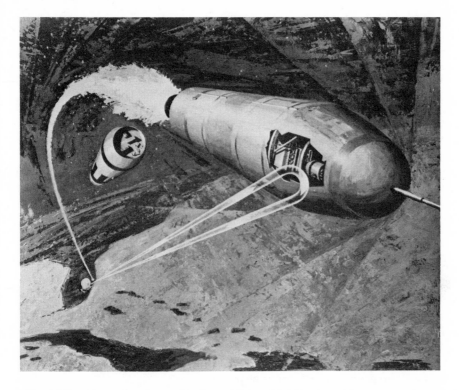

Fig. 10-5. Ground radar maintains contact with Titan's guidance components in ground command of Western Electric/Bell Laboratories guidance system.

III. EARLY MISSION ANALYSIS RESULTS

In 1959, a series of Thor Able Phase II missiles was launched under control of the radio-inertial system at the Air Force Missile Test Center. The guidance system was used to provide close control of performance of an ablating type reentry vehicle at ICBM range. The missile had two stages—a Thor booster, plus a Vanguard second stage—and it could handle a 600-pound nose cone. An illustration of a flight controlled by the Western Electric/Bell Laboratories guidance system is shown in Fig. 10-5. Six flights were performed from January to June of 1959. All of these were completely successful from the guidance-equipment standpoint, and they were extremely useful in checking out the guidance program since they provided the first closed-loop guidance test for the radio-inertial guidance system. Two later Thor-Able II missiles guided Transit 1A (navigation satellite) and TIROS 1 (meteorological satellite) into orbit, as described below.

From August 1959 to August 1960, a series of 16 Titans was launched from AFMTC under control of the guidance system to check out the performance of early Lot B, C, G, and J missiles.   Again, all flights were completely successful from the guidance equipment standpoint.

IV. EXTENSION OF THE WESTERN ELECTRIC/BELL LABORATORIES GUIDANCE SYSTEM TO SPACE APPLICATIONS

In addition to the Titan usage, the Western Electric/Bell Laboratories guidance stations at the Atlantic (AMR) and Pacific (PMR) missile ranges were extensively used for the control of a large number of missions that placed earth satellites in orbit and for the guidance of many space probes, such as the Discoverer and Explorer vehicles.   During the 1960s, almost all U.S. research satellites and space probes requiring accurate orbits to perform their mission were command-guided by the Bell Laboratories/Western Electric test facilities at Cape Canaveral.

Through 1974 there had been a total of 414 missile shots that were guided by the radio-inertial guidance system.   The vast preponderance of these were for the guidance of space vehicles, since only 56 Titan I missiles were flight tested in that program—38 at AMR and 18 at PMR—as shown in Table 10-1.

The first use of command guidance for space research occurred on April 1, 1960, when the TIROS 1 satellite of the National Aeronautics and Space Administration (NASA) was launched by a Thor-Able vehicle, and guided into an almost perfectly circular 447.3-mile orbit with a mean altitude within one mile of the desired altitude.

Launched by a Thor-Delta vehicle on August 12, 1960, NASA's Echo I passive communications satellite (Fig. 10-6), a 100-foot aluminized balloon, achieved a circular orbit that permitted Bell Labs researchers at Holmdel, N.J., to "bounce" signals to, and receive similar signals from, NASA's Jet Propulsion Laboratory in Goldstone, California.

On July 10, 1962, a new era in communications was born when a Thor-Delta placed the Bell System's Telstar I communications satellite (Fig. 10-7) into a planned highly elliptical orbit almost exactly matching the preflight calculated path.   Notably, Telstar I completed its first 42,000 mile trip

Table 10-1.   Missile Missions Using Radio-Inertial Guidance

Mission Period	Number of Missiles	Missile Type	Test Range
Jan '59–May '59	3	Titan A	AMR
Aug '59–Feb '60	2	Titan B	AMR
Dec '59–Apr '60	5	Titan C	AMR
Feb '60–Sep '60	7	Titan G	AMR
Jan '60–Dec '61	21	Titan J	AMR
Sep '61–Nov '63	15	Titan SM68	PMR
Nov '64–Apr '65	3	Titan (Tactical)	PMR

Fig. 10-6.   NASA's Echo I passive communications satellite shown inside a dirigible hangar.

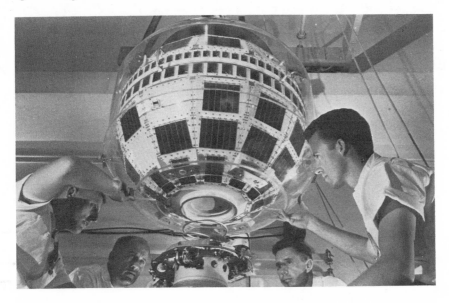

Fig. 10-7.   Telstar I satellite being mounted to a Thor-Delta rocket prior to launching in 1962.

Table 10-2.   Space Missions Using Radio-Inertial Guidance

Mission Period	Number of Missiles	Missile Type	Test Range
Jan '59–APR '60	8	Thor-Able II	AMR
May '60–Sep '71	71	Thor-Delta	AMR
Feb '66–Apr '72	17	Thor-Delta	PMR
Feb '61–May '72	165	Thor-Agena	PMR
Nov '61–Oct '62	4	Thor-Able Star	AMR
Sep '63–Aug '65	8	Thor-Able Star	PMR
Sep '63–Feb '65	6	Asset 2F & 2G	AMR
Jan '65–Apr '66	6	Thor-Altair	PMR
Jul '66–Aug '74	43	Titan (III) B	PMR
Jun '71–Oct '74	9	Titan (III) D	PMR

around the earth in 157.60 minutes, just 1.12 minutes longer than the preflight computed orbital period of 156.48 minutes.

Among the several hundred guidance operations accomplished at Cape Canaveral and Vandenberg are many of historical significance. These include many shots of the TIROS series of meteorological satellites; the Transit navigational satellite; OSO, the orbiting solar observatory; Ariel, the first international satellite; Echo I and Telstar I, as mentioned above; the Explorer series of space research probes; and many security-classified Air Force launches.

A total of 90 space shots were launched at the Atlantic Missile Range and 249 at Vandenberg. The remaining 19 were special operations at remote locations. (Many of the space operations had a military mission for which details are unavailable.) The principal missile systems that used radio-inertial guidance are listed in Table 10-2. A representative but incomplete listing of space vehicles or payloads guided by the system is given in Table 10-3.

In the total course of 414 missile operations using the Western Electric/Bell Laboratories radio-inertial guidance systems there have been no failures attributable to the missile-borne guidance equipment. There were two missions at Cape Canaveral and two at Vandenberg in which malfunctions of the ground-guidance hardware occurred, and six other flights in which human or system errors caused a guidance malfunction. However, in only one instance was a useful orbit not achieved as a result of these problems.

V. SYSTEM DESCRIPTION

5.1 Radar

The basic ground-radar design stemmed from the Nike-Hercules missile-tracking radar. To obtain greater angle-tracking precision, new, more

Table 10-3. Representative List of Space Vehicles Guided by
Radio-Inertial System

Number of Missions	Space Probe or Satellite	Number of Missions	Space Probe or Satellite
20	Explorer	2	HEOS
19	Discoverer	2	Isis
12	INTELSAT	2	NATO
11	TIROS	2	Relay
9	ESSA	2	Skynet
8	OSO	2	Telstar
5	Nimbus	2	Transit
5	Pioneer	1	Ariel
3	BIOS	1	Composite
3	Echo	1	COMSAT
3	OGO	1	Early Bird
3	SYNCOM	1	ERS
2	Alouette	1	PAGEOS
2	Anna	1	Sert
		1	Westwind

precise, higher-ratio antenna azimuth and elevation gearing system were provided. This was achieved at the cost of a reduction in the maximum angle tracking rate of 100 mils per second—an adequate rate for ICBM guidance.

The antenna was a parabolic reflector 94 inches in diameter in a Casse-grainian mount. This was supported by a pedestal that also housed the 200-kilowatts peak, X-band radar transmitter and the detector, local oscillator, and early stages of the radar receiver. Azimuth and elevation angle takeoff was accomplished by a two-stage binary code wheel arrangement—one optical 17-bit binary code wheel and one 4-bit brush contact wheel which provided a combined output of 20 bits of binary data for each angle.

In the tactical system a redundant, switchable, shock-isolated antenna was provided in a separate underground silo with blastproof doors. When the system was to be used, the doors were opened and the antennas were elevated to ground level, locked into position, and checked against location monoliths provided for the purpose. In case a recent near miss had disturbed the site, level-sensing accelerometers were provided to correct the antenna position information.

A novel feature of the tracking system was the completely transistorized digital range unit running at a 6.3-megahertz (MHz) rate. This provided a range-tracking precision of 5 feet out to 700 miles range.

The tracking radar range and angle information was fed to the UNIVAC Athena computer in digital form, and steering and command orders were returned to the missile by the radar via the digital data converter, a peripheral unit of Bell Laboratories design.

Fig. 10-8.   Ground-guidance antenna elevated for action from its underground protective silo after concrete protective doors are opened.   Antenna shown is at the operational system test facility at Vandenberg Air Force Base.

The mechanical design of many of the radar units comprising the ground station was extensively modified for greater reliability and ease of maintenance.   These units were mounted on roll-out frames in standard 36-inch wide cabinets, 72 inches high by 24 inches deep.   Fourteen of these cabinets—two of which were the new digital range unit and digital data converter—and the antenna equipment described above comprised the ground-guidance station.

To provide rapid response to an alert, the radar and system countdown and checkout from standby condition were largely automated in the missile guidance console.   This console communicated radar status information to the main launch console in the central missile control area.

In production systems (manufactured by Western Electric in its North Carolina plants), each dual-antenna arrangement served a complex of three missiles, each similarly elevatable for firing as shown in Fig. 10-8, from the hard base system.   The radar could also, on a backup basis, control several other missiles at remote sites, using a somewhat less automated handover technique.   An artist's conception of a tactical Titan emplacement is shown in Fig. 10-9.

5.2 Computer

The UNIVAC Athena ground-guidance computer was a 24-bit parallel binary machine that used a rotating magnetic drum as the principal programming and constant-storage device.   Instructions and constants were written on the drum after being prepared on punched paper tape and read in by a tape reader.   Provision was made to apply ten sets of specific target constants separately to reserved sectors of the drum, and the selection and

Fig. 10-9. Artist's concept of a tactical Titan emplacement. Ground-guidance equipment is located adjacent to the two antennas (one elevated) and controls three Titans.

use of these were controlled from the Western Electric/Bell Laboratories missile guidance console by a set of hand-set wheels.

All the guidance equations and constants were supplied by Bell Labs. The programs and constant sets used in the Titan test and production programs and all guidance programs required for orbiting and space-probe-guidance missions at AMR and later at PMR were arranged to fit the capacity of the magnetic drum.

Much later in the program—which involved orbiting flights of Titan III research and development missiles in 1966 and later—the Athena computer was found to be inadequate at PMR and had to be replaced by a more capable machine. The new computer consisted of 32,000 words of program and constant memory, and was somewhat more versatile and considerably easier to program than the Athena.

5.3 Missile-Borne Guidance Equipment

The evolutionary development of several versions of missile-borne guidance equipment, first for Titan and later for application to the various orbit and space-probe vehicles, eventually guided by the radio-inertial system, was dramatic. The first fully successful version, Series 300, was used in Titan I production and test systems and in some early space missions. Series 400, shown in Fig. 10-10, was used in 56 later space missions where its reduced weight was important, and the final, lightest and smallest version—Series 600—was used almost exclusively in 278 space missions of various descriptions from 1964 through 1974. A comparison

Fig. 10-10. Series 400 missile-borne guidance equipment installed in the second stage of a Thor-Agena vehicle at Vandenberg Air Force Base.

of size between the 300 and 600 series is shown in Fig. 10-11 and components of the 600 series in Fig. 10-12. All of these highly reliable units were manufactured by Western Electric in its North Carolina plant under stringent quality control considerations.

The basic functions and circuitry were essentially unchanged in the various versions. Mechanically, the equipment was required to withstand at least 15g steady acceleration and 8g vibration up to 2,000 hertz. Since it was required to operate at altitudes essentially devoid of atmosphere, it was housed in hermetically sealed containers to prevent electrical breakdown. The first versions were packaged in three units: transmitter, receiver, and decoder. At first, due to concern about possible high attenuation in the transponder path caused by the missile exhaust plume, a high-power magnetron requiring a high-voltage modulator and oil-filled power supply was used. This proved to be impractical, and after extensive measurement of plume and exhaust attenuation both on the ground and in flight, such high power was concluded to be unnecessary and a low-

Fig. 10-11. Comparison of the series 300 missile-borne guidance equipment used in Titan and the lightweight transistorized series 600 missile-borne guidance equipment used in many space flight vehicles.

power transmitter and modulator were substituted. The receiver employed a ruggedized traveling-wave-tube (TWT) amplifier (at X-band) followed by a crystal detector and video amplifier. The TWT also served as an effective power limiter, providing overload protection for the detector during transmit intervals. It made possible an overall receiver noise figure of about 11 dB.

The Series 300 equipment used vacuum-tube circuitry, and its receiver and decoder were packaged as integrally as possible, each in a rugged cast-aluminum framework carefully designed to avoid severe mechanical resonances below 2,000 hertz. The transmitter, with power reduced to 3 kW peak, used a miniature magnetron modulated by a high-frequency ceramic tetrode vacuum tube, all rigidly mounted in a small spherical unit about 10 inches in diameter. The three units weighed a total of 120 pounds and occupied $4\frac{1}{2}$ cubic feet of space in the missile. Two horn antennas, shown in Fig. 10-13, completed the equipment: a small dorsal horn to provide wide coverage for the early flight pattern and a higher-gain, ventrally mounted antenna for the later stages of the flight. The antennas were covered by fiberglass radomes bolted to the outside of the missile.

So much weight and bulk were a severe handicap for use in the upper stages of space-probe missiles; therefore, Series 400 and 600 transistorized lightweight versions were designed for use in such applications.

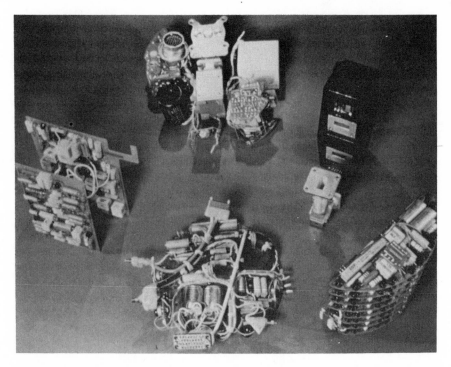

Fig. 10-12. Components of the series 600 missile-borne guidance equipment shown prior to being encapsulated in polyurethane foam. The receiver traveling-wave tube (upper right) and the transmitting magnetron (upper center of photo) are the only vacuum tube devices in the series 600 equipment.

Series 400 equipment was contained in two packages. The transmitter unit was the same as in Series 300, but the receiver and decoder were transistorized and packaged together as a single unit. A polyurethane foam encapsulation technique was perfected to make interlocking subunits that were self-supporting and in which the components were rigidly held and isolated from shock and vibration. The two Series 400 units—transmitter and receiver/decoder—weighed about 52 pounds as mounted in the missile. Two new lightweight Teflon[2]-filled slot antennas that mounted flush to the skin of the missile completed the installation.

Series 600 equipment was contained in a single cylindrical package fully encapsulated in a cannister. The 3-kW magnetron was driven by a newly designed solid-state line-type modulator controlled by a silicon-controlled rectifier. The magnetron and TWT were the only vacuum-tube electron devices in this otherwise completely solid-state design. The finished equipment occupied about one-third of a cubic foot and weighed a mere 26 pounds. Series 600 equipment easily survived steady and vibrational

_____
[2] Trademark of E. I. du Pont de Nemours.

Fig. 10-13. Lightweight flush-mounted missile-borne guidance antennas provided for the Series 400 and 600 systems.

acceleration tests to 2 kilohertz in three axes and stressing thermal cycling and altitude chamber tests.

5.4 The Guidance Function

The intent of the guidance of an ICBM is to terminate powered flight, first of the sustainer motors and then of the vernier motors, so that the missile velocity in range, pitch, and yaw after motor shutdown will permit it to reach its intended target on a ballistic course with the least possible miss distance. For ballistic flight, velocity in range is the most sensitive velocity with respect to miss distance. Therefore, to optimize the measurement of range and the subsequent calculation of range velocity, a radar-centered coordinate system was chosen so that the missile would be flying almost directly down the Y axis away from the radar at the instant of motor cutoff (Fig. 10-14). During powered flight, the missile is restricted almost entirely to the pitch (Y-Z) plane. This same coordinate system was also used for guidance of the various orbiting and space missions in which the Western Electric/Bell Laboratories guidance system participated; however, in these cases, depending on missile configuration, there were different stages to be steered and different motor burns to be cut off (or in some cases initiated), depending on the particular mission to be performed. The basic radar position data in range, azimuth, and

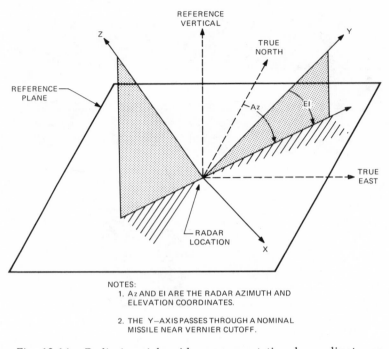

NOTES:
1. Az AND El ARE THE RADAR AZIMUTH AND
   ELEVATION COORDINATES.

2. THE Y—AXIS PASSES THROUGH A NOMINAL
   MISSILE NEAR VERNIER CUTOFF.

Fig. 10-14.   Radio-inertial guidance computational coordinate system.

elevation were input to the guidance function, and from these, range velocity and acceleration and pitch velocity were obtained by appropriately weighted digital filters.

In general, the space shots were flown along predefined trajectories, sometimes called wires.   These were usually defined in polynomial form in position and velocity with constants determined prior to flight by appropriate programs on computers other than the guidance computer. These constants were then checked by flight simulation programs and finally entered into the guidance computer.

In the Titan ICBM case, the steering and powered-flight-termination conditions were determined by solution of the ballistic flight problem in the guidance computer in real time during and just prior to missile flight. In addition to the radar-centered system, an earth-centered coordinate system was required for this computation.   The ballistic solution was valid for a spherical earth and vacuum reentry.   To correct for this, a virtual target was defined such that steering and engine cutoff commands would cause the nose cone to hit the real-world target.   By use of such a solution, the only target inputs required for computation were the latitude, longitude, and altitude of the real target and the offsets necessary to define the virtual target.

System constants dependent on radar location, missile characteristics, the reference trajectory, and a small number of target constants derived from the above target inputs were required for the guidance equations. The principal functions required for Titan guidance were:

Data assembly	From radar data to guidance equations.
Booster guidance	Closed loop only after the missile is in thin atmosphere.
Sustainer guidance	Based on real-time solution of the ballistic flight equations.
Sustainer cutoff	When the required missile velocity and acceleration are attained.
Vernier guidance and cutoff	To compensate for variations in residual impulse of the sustainer engine and velocity errors remaining from sustainer guidance through the use of the ballistic flight equation solution.

In addition to the various steering and cutoff computations, the conditions for transmission of certain discrete orders to the missile (arm, prearm, etc.) were required to be met and execution initiated by the computer. Also, subsidiary computations were performed, such as estimated miss distance for evaluation of mission effectiveness after the Titan vernier motors had been cut off.

The guidance function for the many space shots and other non-Titan missions eventually performed by this system at the Atlantic and Pacific missile ranges was in general similar but tailored to each particular missile and mission type, and, as noted above, normally was characterized by the use of precalculated trajectories.

VI. FOLLOW-ON PROGRAM

Except for a minimum effort in design support, the development and testing of the Titan program was completed in 1960. However, considerable interest remained in various areas of potential improvement including (1) guidance antennas hardened against nuclear environmental effects which would not require lowering into an underground silo in case of attack, (2) a road-mobile ground-guidance system with an attendant lightweight computer, together with targeting and other problems, of such a system, (3) miniaturization, (4) use of celestial radar calibration and orientation sources, plus a host of analytical and developmental problems related to improving radio-inertial guidance systems. This effort continued for approximately two years and produced some significant output but no new systems. All-inertial guidance for ballistic missiles eventually won out for weapon systems because it was proven to have the required accuracy, was self-contained after the lift-off, was less subject to countermeasures, and did not depend on a vulnerable ground guidance station.

However, since ground control was maintained throughout powered flight of the missile, radio-inertial guidance provided an important measure of safety which was missing in all-inertial systems. After vernier motor cutoff and nose cone separation, when the missile is truly ballistic an exact estimate of miss distance could be made, and until then warhead arming could be withheld. If a malfunction of missile or guidance performance should occur at an earlier time, the missile could be intentionally and harmlessly destroyed.

While the important features of command guidance—keeping system complexity, command control, and damage assessment on the ground, and its versatility and programming advantages which proved so successful in space operation—were not considered necessary by the Air Force for use in tactical weapon systems, they did prove valuable (and received much use) in NASA space shots.

Some effort continued until 1963, and in 1964 the entire program was transferred, along with key personnel of the Bell Labs engineering staff, to the Western Electric Company, under whose capable management the support of missile and space operations has successfully continued.

VII. SUMMARY

The technology of command guidance, proven for air defense in the Nike systems, was effectively applied by Western Electric/Bell Laboratories in 1954 in the development of a highly accurate radio-inertial guidance system for the Air Force Titan ICBM. Although later ICBMs adopted all-inertial guidance, the flexibility of being able to continuously monitor the ballistic path by ground radar and precisely set the ballistic path at the termination of powered flight provided the type of guidance system needed for a majority of our space shots.

Through 1974 there were 414 missile launches guided by the Western Electric/Bell Laboratories radio-inertial guidance system, of which the vast preponderance were for guidance of space vehicles since only 56 Titan I ICBMs were flight-tested in this period. An enviable record of reliability was established—the guidance system had no failures with respect to the missile-borne guidance equipment in all 414 missile operations.

Chapter 11

Command and Control

In the period following World War II, one of the weakest elements of Naval defense systems was the area of command and control. Existing systems failed to recognize the shrinking time factor which made it necessary to have machines take over functions that could be programmed in advance. New human-factor approaches were essential for proper display of information so that only high-level decisions would need to be performed by man. Bell Laboratories was a pioneer in addressing the command and control problem in 1945 when it undertook the Mark 65 Program for the Navy. The early Mark 65 studies and laboratory simulation carried out on command and control in the 1945 to 1951 period established principles that have been applied to current Navy systems, to other weapon systems developed by Bell Laboratories like Nike-Ajax, Nike-Hercules, and Safeguard, and to many systems developed outside the Bell System.

I. MARK 65 PROGRAM

1.1 Introduction

During the short period at the close of World War II in which the Japanese launched their kamikaze attacks, the United States Navy lost more of its fleet than it had in all the sea actions of the war. The success of these suicide missions pointed up an immediate need for the Navy to revise its philosophy of defense against air attack. Accordingly, in 1945 Bell Laboratories was asked by the Navy Bureau of Ordnance to study the problem and recommend a course of development. The project eventually came to be known as the Mark 65 Program.

The war itself had brought forth the first evidence that the evolution of adequate air defense was seriously lagging behind that of new offensive weapons. For example, as the war progressed, dive and torpedo bombers greatly increased their speed and maneuverability. But during the same period, improved methods for detecting, tracking, and destroying targets came more slowly. Even with higher radar peak power, designers had used smaller radar beams to obtain improved range and tracking accuracy. As a result of the small fire-control radar beams, excessive time was re-

Principal authors: T. W. Winternitz and W. H. MacWilliams, Jr.

quired for a fire-control radar to acquire an aircraft target using data from a search radar on a rolling and pitching ship.

The Navy contract with Western Electric/Bell Laboratories was for a system study of the entire problem, from search radar detection through to the burst of projectiles against the attacking aircraft, looking forward to a time period of approximately 1960. The Navy forecast that 1960 aircraft speeds would be up to 1500 knots (Mach 2.5), a prediction that turned out to be accurate. The study actually extended over more than two decades and resulted in 100 weapon-direction equipments in some 74 U.S. combat ships for defense against air attack. In the first installation, in the U.S.S. *Northampton,* the defense weapons were antiaircraft guns. However, later installations were adapted to both antiaircraft guns and antiaircraft guided missiles—at first Terrier missiles and then Tartars. Systems were also installed in 20 ships of 7 foreign navies.

The program resulted in an unprecedented amount of analysis, exploratory development, and fundamental data-gathering, which was reported in some 30 formal reports. The program included pioneering work in the automatic dynamic calculation of a defense against a coordinated air attack and in the design of displays and controls, which formed important inputs to design of later systems.

1.2 Initial Bell Laboratories Study of Naval Antiaircraft Defense

The initial Bell Laboratories investigation was carried out in the research area at Murray Hill by a team composed of W. A. McNair, B. D. Holbrook, A. A. Lundstrom, and W. H. MacWilliams.

Studying the requirements and developing a plan of work first required an information-gathering survey to define clearly the defensive elements needed to fight off an air attack. This survey was begun by investigations of the characteristics of such shipboard elements as the surveillance systems—search radars as well as lookouts with binoculars—fire-control radars, and of course, the weapons.

To understand how the Navy's air-defense system was revised requires first a brief description of the methods it had been using. On a typical ship, long-range search radars scanned the skies for targets. Those that appeared on a radar oscilloscope were identified, electronically, as friendly or unfriendly. Unfriendly targets were then evaluated manually as to their potential threat. When these targets reached a certain range, they were assigned to the more precise fire-control radars associated with the guns.

These radars acquired and automatically tracked the targets until they reached a range where the guns could effectively open fire. Information on the continuously changing range and bearing went from the fire-control radars to a computer and thence to the gun-control machinery, which pointed the guns in the appropriate direction.

This defense was coordinated by a shipboard organization, formed during World War II, known as the Combat Information Center (CIC). But CIC was not well equipped for the job. Most threat evaluation and target-tracking from search-radar data were done as grease-pencil notations on a glass screen. Targets were designated by talkers to gun directors over a sound-powered telephone circuit between CIC, far below the main deck, and an officer in the fire-control director, four or five decks above, and as much as 400 feet away.

The Bell Labs study indicated that CIC, although equipped to control interception of threatening targets with fighter aircraft, did not effectively handle the defense with the ship's own weapons. Basically, CIC had no way to give the fire-control radars precise information on the position of the targets they should acquire and track.

This weakness in coordination was one of the major problems to be solved. Therefore, Bell Labs recommended development of a control system to perform this function. The activities to be coordinated included air surveillance, evaluation of the threat of the target, assignment of weapons to targets, and assessment of target kill.

As an aid in achieving this coordination, it was recommended that the new control system include a display of the tactical situation. This display would show (1) the positions of threatening targets about the ship as detected by the search radars, (2) targets being tracked by the fire-control radars, and (3) targets under fire by guns or missiles. Through such a display, the ship's gunnery officer would be able to use his weapons most effectively.

The study also considered new developments both in weapons for offense, such as faster attacking aircraft, and in weapons for defense, such as guided missiles. These, the engineers foresaw, would require quicker threat-evaluation and decision-making when the ship was under air attack.

For these reasons, the study team made a second major recommendation: automate the means of defense. This meant that automatic operation, such as had been used by fire-control computers and tracking radars, was to be extended to the decision-making equipment. The team was convinced that many of the processes and techniques developed through years of work on telephone switching systems would apply in the design of automatic decision-making equipment.

In putting forth these ideas, Bell Labs engineers realized they were suggesting new doctrines for the conduct of antiaircraft warfare. The basic ideas resulted from detailed consideration of the sequence of events, as portrayed in Fig. 11-1. The situation is somewhat analogous to a telephone traffic problem in which the number of customers (attacking aircraft) exceeds the number of available trunks (radars and guns). Thus, the system was designed to provide automatic processing of information to ensure

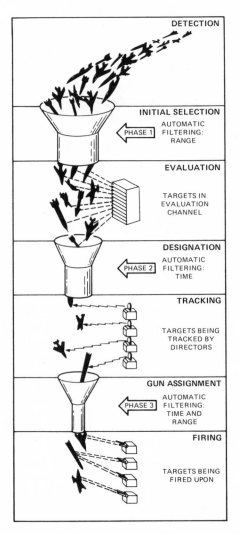

Fig. 11-1.   Fire-control equipment operates to filter progressively the incoming enemy traffic to ensure the ship's defensive equipment—guns or missiles—fire first on the most threatening targets.

that the highest-priority customers (the most threatening targets) would be given first call on the available trunks (the radars and the guns).

In July 1947, after two years of study, a report called "Naval AA" was issued.   Convinced that these proposals were sound, the Navy accepted them, and asked Bell Laboratories to begin to build the control equipment and to study and analyze the approaches in detail by laboratory simulation. The report classified air-defense operations into two groups, damage and predamage operations, that is, the operations concerned with inflicting actual damage to the targets and those concerned with initial detection and analysis. The report charted potential advances in damage equipment, such as guns and fire-control directors, radars, and computers. It then pointed out that the controlling difficulties were and would be in the predamage operations, namely, initial detection of targets by search radars, track-while-scan, threat analysis, and target-to-director designation, plus accounting for differences between radar data coordinate references and those of the antiaircraft directors in relation to a ship's deck that was rolling and pitching.

1.3 Predamage Studies

Understanding of the air-defense problem was clarified by dividing the operations into three phases:

Phase 1 embraced the detection of attacking aircraft by search radars and the establishment of tracks on them.

Phase 2 included the analysis of the attack and the designation of specific targets to specific fire-control directors.

Phase 3 comprised the analysis of targets being tracked by directors and the switching of groups of gun mounts to the directors tracking the most threatening targets.

Although limited gun-to-director switching had been available in the fleet, the practice had been to associate gun groups quasi-permanently with directors, changing the connections only in case of battle damage, since there was a possibility of human error in throwing one of the many switches involved. However, the need to reassign gun mounts dynamically among directors was clear from the fact that gunfire was effective only at short ranges, and guns would be ineffective at long range or when targets were out of range. It was postulated that with automatic or aided-manual tracking of attacking aircraft from search data, proper coordinate conversion, and proper acquisition features in the directors, the Phase 2 and Phase 3 operations could consist essentially of switching and slewing. Clearly, the Phase 2 operation, as defined above, was complex and its time factors were critical, which made it an ideal operation in which to use automatic computation. It was thus proposed that laboratory Phase 2 and Phase 3 computers be designed and tested.

In view of the probabilistic nature of gunfire effectiveness, the testing facilities would have to include means for replicating simulated air attacks, and it was also proposed that a gunnery system simulator be built to represent the rest of the air-defense problem.

1.4 Exploratory Development of Phase 2 and Phase 3 Computers and the Gunnery System Simulator

The Phase 2 operation was shown to have three distinct aspects: (1) determination of which targets were most threatening and thus should be engaged first, (2) determination of which directors had the most suitable

Fig. 11-2.   Control center of Bell Laboratories' ATEWA.

ballistics and arcs of fire (taking into account possible evasive changes of
the ship's course), and (3) designation of specific directors to target tracks
that would maximize the defense of the ship.   Similar considerations
governed the Phase 3 operation.

The combination of attack and weapon considerations was emphasized
in the generic name coined to describe the three-phase attack-handling
operations: Target Evaluator and Weapon Assigner (TEWA).   An automatic TEWA was called an ATEWA.

It was found possible to codify the Phase 2 operation in terms of regions
of high and low priority based on target speed, closing time, proximity
to director and gun-mount limit-stops, and gunfire effectiveness as a
function of range.   Sets of rules of operation were drawn up and relay
computers were designed to implement them.

Some early checks of the first Phase 2 rules of operation were obtained
from a highly simplified setup consisting of three targets and two directors,
with no switching of gun mounts.   This initial laboratory simulation is
shown as the first item in Table 11-1.

From 1949 to 1951, a full laboratory simulation of an ATEWA gunnery
system simulator was designed and installed at Bell Laboratories, Whippany, New Jersey, under the direction of S. C. Hight and A. K. Bohren.   A
photograph of the control center of the system is shown in Fig. 11-2.   This
representation proved to be a substantial undertaking and was probably
one of the largest aggregations of electronic equipment at that time.   The
system represented ten Phase 1 input target tracks, four directors, and four

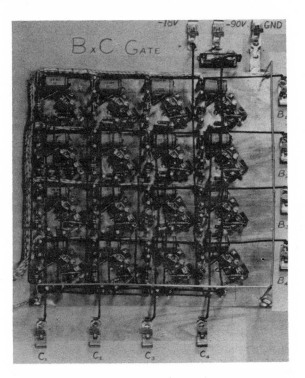

Fig. 11-3.   Transistorized switching matrix.

gun mount groups.   Flexibility was built in so that subsequent switching of gun groups to directors could be added.   Directors and gun groups were represented by the time delays involved in the process of slewing from one target to another.

Each of the ten target tracks was represented by teletypewriter tapes in which increments of range, bearing, or elevation were recorded as punched holes.   The teletypewriter-tape transmitter outputs were fed into integrating dc amplifiers which represented the range, bearing, and elevation coordinates as dc voltages.   A wide combination of target threats was thus made available with the teletypewriter tapes.

A time-to-close analog calculator predicted the time before the attacking aircraft would reach the ship, based on the aircraft's range and closing speed.   The ATEWA used these times to set up a priority for assignment of directors and guns.   The ATEWA computer that carried out the automatic assignment of targets, directors, and guns followed a set of rules discussed earlier.   The computer consisted of multicontact relays wired together to follow the logic set rules designed into the machine.   Once an incoming target was assigned to director and gun, simulated gunfire would start after an appropriate slewing time delay.   The effects of gunfire on the attacking aircraft were simulated as well to permit release of a di-

Table 11-1. Automatic and Manual Target Evaluator and Weapon Assignors.

First Installed	Weapon System	Number Installed	Location Installed*	Type of Weapon	Remarks
1948	3 × 2 ATEWA	1	Bell Labs, Whippany, N.J.	Guns	No Phase 3
1948	10 × 4 ATEWA	1	Bell Labs, Whippany, N.J.	Guns	No Phase 3; Used with gunnery system simulator.
1953	Target designation System Mark 3	1	CLC-1	Guns	Automatic Phase 2 and Phase 3. Included 10 radar channels and 4 optical channels.
1955	Designation equipment Mark 7	2	CAG-1 and CAG-2	Guns Terriers	Phase 2 and 3 automatic for guns, manual for missiles.
1958	Designation Equipment Mark 9	19	CLG-6 to CLG-8; DLG-6 to DLG-15 3 Italian ships 1 Dutch ship 2 Training ships	Guns Terriers	Manual Phase 2 and Phase 3 for both guns and missiles.

1959	Weapon designation equipment Mark 1	59	29 DDG 6 DEG 4 French ships 2 Italian ships 1 Japanese ship 1 Australian ship 3 German ships 5 Spanish ships 3 Training ships	Guns Terriers	Manual Phase 2 and Phase 3 for both guns and missiles. Includes 11 ships with a special digital Phase 1 to go with a digital search radar.
1960	Weapon designation equipment Mark 3	3	CVA	Guns Terriers	Manual Phase 2 and 3 for both guns and missiles.
1961	Weapon designation equipment Mark 4	12	10 DLG 1 CVA 1 Training ship	Guns Terriers	Manual Phase 2 and 3 for both guns and missiles.
1963	Weapon designation equipment Mark 8	4	2 DLG 1 Italian ship 1 Training ship	Guns Terriers	Manual Phase 2 and 3 for both guns and missiles.

*U.S. Navy ship designations used:

CLC Tactical Command Ship
CLG Guided Missile Light Cruiser
CAG Guided Missile Heavy Cruiser
DLG Guided Missile Frigate

DDG Guided Missile Destroyer
DEG Guided Missile Destroyer Escort
CVA Attack Aircraft Carrier

rector and its gun group when the simulated destruction of an attacking aircraft took place. This simulation was performed by an additional computer—the "electronic dice thrower"—which accepted a kill-probability pulse and determined whether or not the particular shot destroyed the target. In effect, it electronically cast a set of dice having the desired (variable) probability of kill and determined for each cast whether the kill had been made. In some of this circuitry, shown in Figure 11-3, very early point-contact transistors were used, probably for the first time in other than component-characterizing circuitry.

A display room was built that included a vertical screen with range and bearing as the coordinates. Small optical projectors were used to project lighted characters onto the screen to represent the 10 target tracks (A through J) or directors (1 through 4). Provision was made for manual as well as automatic designations to permit comparing manual assignments with automatic ones, thus making it possible for responsible officers to override manually the automatic decisions.

Simulator tests of the laboratory ATEWA showed that, given the Phase 1 tracks on incoming aircraft, Phase 2 decisions could be made automatically, quickly, and correctly. Automatic assignments were found to be substantially better than manual ones in heavy attacks. However, for light attacks, manual assignments were very nearly as good, because of the sophisticated displays and controls developed. The ATEWA display room was very valuable in the 1950 to 1951 period in illustrating to a large number of high-ranking visiting naval officers the critical dynamics of a coordinated attack and the advantages of automatic assignments.

II. DESIGN OF TACTICAL COMMAND EQUIPMENT

In 1951, the Bureau of Ordnance asked for a system based on Bell Labs' Mark 65 work—the Mark 3 designation equipment—to be designed for a new ship, the U.S.S. *Northampton* (CLC-1). There were to be eight radar track-while-scan channels and inputs from four optical trackers, four gun directors, and four gun groups, each consisting of two gun mounts. There was also an own-fleet monitor to permit interrupting the CLC-1's defensive gunfire if it appeared likely that it would endanger other ships in the task force. Figure 11-4 is an artist's sketch of the Mark 3 equipment. Three Phase 1 consoles permitted range and bearing tracking from planned position indicator (PPI) search radar data, and an elevation console was also provided to permit elevation tracking when the three-dimensional radar (the SPS-3) was used.

To assure a compatible interface with the SPS-3, tests were conducted with radar consoles and (dc-voltage) track-while-scan channels set up in a trailer at the SPS-3 manufacturer's plant. These tests provided time for changes before shipboard installation. They also confirmed concerns as to the adequacy of the SPS-3's sensitivity and led to a Bell Labs proposal

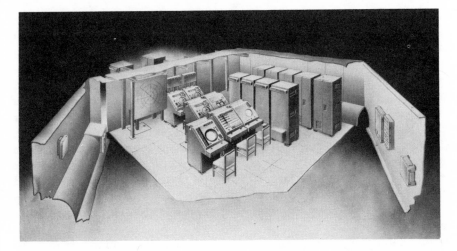

Fig. 11-4.   The first shipboard ATEWA (in CLC-1).

for an improved three-dimensional search radar eventually designed by C. A. Warren and W. Deming Lewis.   This radar was breadboarded, satisfactorily tested, and later installed in the CAG-1 and CAG-2 with the second and third shipboard ATEWAs.

Automatic target evaluation and director and gun assignments were provided by means of relay computers using relays that were dynamically balanced to withstand heavy linear shock.   The Phase 1 and Phase 2 consoles displayed the range and bearing of target track channels and the director range gates by means of symbols for the radar and optical channels and numbers for the directors.

The Phase 2 console included a coordinate switch in which one row of buttons represented channels and another row represented directors; an assignment was made by simultaneously depressing a director button and a channel button.   The Phase 3 display was also a coordinate switch between gun directors and groups of gun mounts.   The function of simulating target kills was also included so that realistic mock attacks could be carried out against the ship without destroying the attacking aircraft.

Ships' personnel need displays that present tactical information clearly. Many human factors are involved in assessing a tactical situation because the information characterizing it is so extremely diverse.   For example, the "blips" on a search-radar oscilloscope indicate the positions of both friendly and enemy planes.   Hence, an operator must have some way of distinguishing between them.   The positions of targets being tracked by the fire-control radars must be precisely known so that when friendly fighters are in the area, fire is directed at enemy planes only.

In addition to the human factors, development of a tactical display required a study of what should be presented and how.   The important objective here was proper interpretation, especially under many confusing situations. Also associated with this work was a way to physically present the selected information to the fire-control operators.

Displays are one of the many devices used for feeding back information—an important function for both manual control and supervision of an air attack. As an example, the activity of each fire-control radar was displayed continuously and automatically, making it possible to monitor the position in space where the radar was scanning or tracking a target. Therefore, when a radar was assigned to a target, operators could observe it slewing to position by the motion of its numeral toward the letter location representing the target. Subsequent field experience confirmed the importance of the feedback of information. This provision was highly commended by the operating people in the fleet who used the equipment.

Bell Laboratories engineers realized early that they had to consider the growth of the air-defense system to meet future developments in air warfare. Thus, early in the development program study effort was directed toward concepts that would be applicable when guided-missile systems materialized. As a result, the rapid decline of the gun and its replacement by the guided missile did not outmode the concepts originally developed under the Mark 65 Program nor materially affect the equipment it used, as discussed below.

During a six-month evaluation of the system aboard the U.S.S. *Northampton*, aircraft flew approximately 1500 mock raids against the ship. In some of these raids, as many as 25 aircraft were employed simultaneously. U.S. Navy personnel operated the equipment throughout this period, and Bell Laboratories engineers on board helped make up test plans and observed and assessed the operation of the equipment. The evaluation indicated that the recommendations of the study were valid and, specifically, that a centralized control system would greatly increase the effectiveness of the defenses of a ship under air attack. These conclusions were wholeheartedly endorsed by the ship's personnel.

The need for high equipment reliability was recognized and also the difficulty in obtaining it in view of the large amount of electronic equipment involved. After the preliminary design had been completed, the entire system was gone over in detail to remove identifiable sources of failure. Specifically, all components such as resistors and tubes were derated for power consumption and rated voltage. In addition, a thorough analysis was carried out on every circuit to show whether the failure of any component—passive or vacuum tube—would place undue voltage or power dissipation on any other component. Circuit changes were made as necessary to remove these potential sources of failure. This emphasis on reliability was outstandingly successful. Shipboard tests showed only one tube failure per 36,000 tube-hours of operation, and the equipment was never down for any scheduled operation period—truly a remarkable record compared to any other Navy equipment then in use.

III. CAG SYSTEMS – GUNS AND GUIDED MISSILES

Meanwhile, ship-to-air guided missiles were scheduled for initial shipboard installation, in CAG-1 and CAG-2 (U.S.S. *Boston* and U.S.S. *Canberra*, Fig. 11-5) together with considerably more guns and gun directors than the CLC-1 (see Table 11-1 for key to abbreviations).

A study of the missile-assignment problem identified differences from the CLC-1 situation. Phase 1 channels could also be used, and director assignments were more complex but less frequent. The director commitment time had to cover not only slewing, acquisition, and prelaunch tracking but also radar illumination throughout a long missile flight. Time-oriented displays were developed, showing for each director the conditions for earliest- and latest-possible intercept. Missile stowage, checkout, and launching were far more complex than the corresponding gunnery operations, and appropriate displays and controls were added.

Fig. 11-5. Operational versions of the Mark 65 gun and guided-missile fire-control equipment aboard the U.S.S. *Canberra*.

The original Navy plans for the CAGs had been for one Terrier missile director and two Terrier launchers. It was apparent that the capabilities of such a ship would be heavily limited by director capacity, and an analysis of attack-handling capacity was performed by Bell Labs showing that the firepower of the ships could be doubled by adding an extra director. After presentations to the Navy, the design of the ships was changed to add an extra director.

A combined gunnery-and missilery designation equipment was designed in which the track-while-scan channels could be switched to either gun directors or missile directors. The system had automatic track-while-scan for Phase 1 and automatic gunnery Phase 2 and Phase 3 computers. The Phase 2 and Phase 3 operations for the missiles were carried out manually using specially developed displays and controls. As indicated earlier, these ships also had the new three-dimensional search radar, designated the CXRX.

IV. OTHER GUN AND MISSILE SHIPS (CLGs, DLGs, DDGs, DEGs, AND CVAs)

Ship building in the late 1950s was concentrated on ships smaller than the CAGs, with much smaller gun complements but comparable missile complements. Weapon-direction equipments were adapted at Bell Laboratories in North Carolina for a number of classes of ships, with Phase 1 track-while-scan channels and manual Phase 2 and Phase 3 consoles for both guns and missiles, as summarized in Table 11-1.

A total of 38 additional Terrier-and-gun systems and 59 Tartar-and-gun systems, in a number of different series, were designed. They were fitted in 71 U.S. combat ships and a number of foreign ships—one Australian, one Dutch, four French, three German, five Italian, one Japanese, and five Spanish. One group of systems was modified to have a digital Phase 1 to go with a special digital search radar. The popularity of the design stemmed from its good human engineering and unexcelled reliability.

V. OTHER STUDIES

In addition to studies directly related to equipment design, a number of other studies were made for the Navy during the Mark 65 Program in the approximate 1949 to 1951 time period. These included:

1. Roughness of Flight Study—This study made accelerometer measurements in specially instrumented aircraft to determine the basic irregularities in aircraft flight that were characteristic and irreducible even when the pilot wanted to fly straight. These measurements were made by the Cornell Aeronautical Laboratory under subcontract to Bell Laboratories and yielded an upper bound to the prediction accuracy for both gunfire and missile fire.

2. Digital Track-While-Scan Study—This study produced equations, flowcharts, and equipment studies for a digital realization of the track-while-scan operation. It included exploratory development in such areas as regenerative quartz acoustic delay lines.

3. Digital Fire-Control Computer Study—This study laid out a digital solid-state fire-control computer. The study indicated the need for large reductions in equipment volume and weight, and in order to exploit these features, the application was changed from Naval gunfire control to airborne fire control, which led directly to the TRADIC development. TRADIC was the first transistor digital fire-control computer (see Chapter 13, Section II).

4. Digital Weapon-Direction Equipment Study—Exploratory development was conducted of a digital solid-state equipment for carrying out the weapon-direction process.

5. Development of Improved Search Radar—Described above.

6. Talos Weapon-Direction Equipment Study—A study that extended the principles of automatic weapon assignment to the longer-range Talos missile.

7. A study combining the problems of missile defense and interceptor aircraft fleet defense.

VI. SUMMARY

The widespread acceptance of the philosophy and concepts developed under the Bell Labs command and control program proved its basic soundness. Subsequently, other defense activities have been organized on the pattern developed from Bell Laboratories' work in this field. Representative concepts from this program were embodied in missile-control systems subsequently developed for the Army and the Air Force, as well as for the Navy.

Chapter 12

Communications

The success of radar, missile systems, and underwater projects, both as technical accomplishments and as military necessities, may have overshadowed other government activities handled by the Bell System during World War II and in the postwar years. Hundreds of critical projects were carried out for both military and nonmilitary agencies in the broad field of communications. The work on these projects ranged from straightforward improvements of existing systems to research on hardware for new systems to exploratory studies of new concepts.

Studies for the Navy included Cosmos—an analysis of communications for command operation with the object of attaining maximum weapon effectiveness by rapidly processing and suitably displaying radar, sonar, and other types of tactical data. Another valuable contribution was Bell Laboratories' studies of methods for the mitigation of electrical interference in project Sanguine, a proposed communications system for transmitting command-and-control messages to submarines.

For the Army, Project COMPASS was an analysis of communications needs posed by the radically new concepts of tactical organization which followed World War II and by the new techniques needed to implement field-army communications. For the Air Force project known as CADS (Continental Air Defense System), Bell Laboratories participated in studies to characterize the type of communications network required for and methods of optimizing rapid processing of radar data obtained from extensive radar early warning systems along the northern approaches to the United States.

Communications system developments in the postwar era included advanced data communications systems for the Navy and the Army. One of these, the AN/TSQ-7, could process and display data on as many as 48 aircraft targets. Another development was an integrated wire/radio 12-channel communications system for the Army, which could provide reliable performance at distances up to 1,000 miles, could be moved and installed quickly, could withstand rough use under tactical field conditions, and could be operated by relatively untrained personnel.

Principal authors: S. E. Watters, J. F. Kampschoer, W. L. Cowperthwait, H. J. Michael, and G. H. Huber.

Specialized systems using vocoders were developed to provide secure speech and data transmission.

One of the largest communications networks undertaken was the development and installation of the Far North Communications and Detection Systems. In addition the Bell Laboratories/Western Electric efforts on such projects as Polevault, White Alice, DEW (Distant Early Warning) Line and BMEWS (Ballistic Missile Early Warning System) were highly successful and were accomplished under the most severe environmental and logistic conditions.

Private-line communications systems were furnished by the Bell System to the military and to government agencies on a leased basis to meet the requirements of specialized missions and important military plans. The integrated structure of the Bell System made it possible for experts to work closely together in the areas of planning, engineering, design, manufacture, and installation of communication facilities, and insured complete compatibility with the switching and transmission equipment of the existing telephone network. Examples of these systems are: SAGE, a network of voice and data circuits tying together Air Force radar, radio, and command-and-control locations; AUTOVON, a worldwide switched network for telephone and data transmission between military bases and command-and-control centers; the SAC Primary Alerting System, whereby a SAC officer could alert all SAC bases worldwide in a few seconds; the Joint Chiefs of Staff Alerting Network (JCSAN); a four-wire switching system used by the FAA at traffic control centers to connect controllers to either internal or external line facilities for effectively handling fast-flying jet aircraft at major airports; a manually controlled switching system, designed for NASA, that permitted a large number of conferences to be set up simultaneously so that in communicating with an orbiting astronaut, a NASA director could establish a voice conference involving hundreds of stations located anywhere in the world.

I. MILITARY COMMUNICATIONS STUDIES AND DEVELOPMENTS

In the years following World War II, Bell Laboratories was asked on numerous occasions to examine existing communications facilities in the armed forces. Sometimes this was done with the intent to recommend needed improvements, and at other times simply to determine the degree of suitability of the equipment at hand.

1.1 Communications Studies — Navy

1.1.1 Cosmos

A study of Naval communications for command operation was started by Bell Laboratories in 1950 for the Bureau of Ships. The study, called Cosmos,[1] was aimed at making marked improvements in systems used by

---

[1] Cosmos, like a number of other code words in this volume, has no particular meaning and was coined so that for security reasons it would not reveal information about the nature of the project.

naval task groups and task forces to keep informed on the immediate tactical status, to appraise the situation, and to direct the combat potential for maximum weapon effectiveness.

This work evolved into studies of radio communications in the HF and VHF/UHF bands and of data handling, culminating in displays suitable for meeting the needs of the users in the command organization. Radio communications and data handling were directed primarily at radar, sonar, and visual tracking between ships and aircraft. As a result of Bell Laboratories recommendations, the Naval Tactical Data System was later implemented.

Bell Laboratories engineers participated in a number of naval exercises as observers . Radio communications traffic was monitored during one large amphibious exercise, and in another exercise, radar tracking of ships and aircraft was investigated.

1.1.2 Sanguine

Sanguine was a communications system proposed by a Navy study group for transmitting command and control messages to fleet ballistic missile submarines and other United States armed forces such as the National Command Authority. The system was intended to provide almost worldwide radio coverage to submerged submarines from a single transmitting location in the United States. As of 1977, it appeared that the transmitter would operate within the frequency band of 30 to 100 Hz and at very high radiated power. About 300 to 400 acres of land would be required for construction of an underground antenna designed to survive nuclear detonations.

Studies and experiments indicated that energy from the high-power Sanguine transmitter would couple into power and telephone lines, causing interference, such as light flicker and noise on telephone lines if no mitigation was applied. And so, early in 1968, the Naval Electronic System Command asked Bell Laboratories to assist the Navy with telephone interference studies, develop mitigation techniques and devices, and demonstrate their effectiveness at a Navy test facility in Wisconsin. Bell Laboratories work under Sanguine started in March 1968 and ended in September 1971.

In 1969, a model telephone plant employing mitigation devices was designed by Bell Laboratories. It was built near the small-scale experimental Sanguine antenna in Wisconsin. Information gained from experiments with this model supported the conclusion that telephone plant could be designed so that it would be operable in the Sanguine environment without interference to communications lines, cables, and central offices.

Bell Laboratories provided the Navy with its solution to the serious power-line interference problem caused by the Sanguine transmitters.

Its implementation permitted uninterrupted operation of the Wisconsin test facility.

As a result of its work on this project, Bell Laboratories prepared and issued an engineering guide for those telephone engineers who were designing telephone plant that might be subjected to a Sanguine environment. Bell Laboratories also contributed to a Navy publication entitled "Environmental Compatibility Assurance Program Summary," which provided information on telephone interference and evidence that telephone systems could be made compatible with this environment.

1.2 Communications Studies — Army

1.2.1 COMPASS

The rapid development of new weapons during the military conflicts that followed World War II caused a radical revision of the concepts of the tactical organization and the maneuvering of armies, with a concomitant revision of the Army communications system. Because of these new tactical considerations, the Signal Corps, early in 1954, requested a study of new combat area communication concepts and equipment characteristics. In August 1954, Bell Laboratories initiated this study under Project COMPASS, an acronym for Communication Planning And System Studies.

The study included extensive analysis and assessment of communications needs. The "Need-Line" concept, which has been extensively adopted in military communications analyses, originated in this study. The concept involves the identification of parties in an organization who need to communicate with other parties.

Radio and cable transmission techniques were assessed, and switching problems were investigated. The object was to identify the most promising techniques with which to implement field-army communications in a 5- to 15-year period.

Other COMPASS projects included a study of a carrier system of 48 or more channels to be used on radio or on a miniature coaxial cable. This study included some preliminary designs of miniature repeaters and tests of small coaxial cables. Another study was of the use of small cables in landing operations, including the laying of two or three small cables in the sea off Sandy Hook, New Jersey, and the measurement of the characteristics of cables in sea water. The potential uses of millimeter waves for certain activities were studied, and the uses of meteor-reflected waves were examined. In addition, some of the first analyses of random access communication systems were made.

As part of this project, completed in 1958, implementation concepts were tested as Project COMPRST in a large army exercise at the Army Electronic

Proving Ground, Fort Huachuca, Arizona. Bell Laboratories engineers participated in planning and observing this exercise.

1.2.2 COMPRST

As a part of Project COMPASS, Project COMPRST (Compass Radio Switching Test) was initiated by Bell Laboratories to simulate the operation of radio-controlled communications. In this communications technique, radio local exchanges with common-user trunk circuits are interconnected by several tandem exchanges. Bell Laboratories developed a system concept akin to telephone practice—but modified to meet military requirements—employing local and tandem exchanges and multichannel common-user trunks.

Employing radio-controlled communications, a field exercise that simulated tactical movement and dispersion was conducted at the Army Electronic Proving Ground at Fort Huachuca by military personnel under the joint supervision of the Signal Engineering Laboratories and Bell Laboratories. Based on the results of this exercise, Bell Laboratories concluded work on the COMPRST project in April 1957, recommending that radio-controlled communications be employed and that a centralized control organization be formulated to coordinate system activities.

1.2.3 ARTCOM

The Army Tactical Communications Project, or ARTCOM, was a Bell Laboratories study of a complete field-army communications system. This study was performed for the U.S. Army Signal Research and Development Laboratory and was started under the COMPASS program.

The main effort, begun in November 1958 and completed in February 1960, included the analysis of the impact of automatic data-processing systems in the field army and the concomitant flow of data over the communications network. System planning studies were based on the work completed under Project COMPASS. However, the assumption of a projected army in a later time frame and a different field-army organization were the major differences in the assumptions made in the two projects.

Need-Line estimates were made to establish the busy-hour voice and data traffic, which included teletypewriter and all other digital information. On the basis of these estimates, a communications system consisting of an area-coverage, long-distance network, supported by a series of tandem networks, was devised to serve the communications needs of the field army. A traffic analysis was made by applying Need-Line traffic to this communications system. The resulting quantitative information formed the basis for a switching plan and a transmission plan that included time-division and space-division electronic switching and an estimate of the number of channels needed in the various networks.

1.3. Communications Studies — Air Force

1.3.1 Global Communications

From August 1955 through October 1956, Bell Laboratories undertook a study of global communications for the Air Research and Development Command of the U.S. Air Force. The ultimate objective was to define and perform the systems engineering required to provide the Air Force with large volumes of rapid, reliable, and secure communications throughout most of the world. Bell Laboratories' effort under this study was spent in four areas: (1) orientation by operational commands and development centers, (2) definition of the type of systems engineering effort that was needed, method of attack, and studies required, (3) definition of systems planning objectives as a guide to more detailed technical studies, and (4) development of factors for defining the scope of service, switching plans, method of operation, and overall communications-system plans.

1.3.2 CADS/SAGE Air-Defense Engineering Services

The development of the long-range intercontinental bomber in the years following World War II posed a threat to the continental United States. The Air Force installed extensive radar early warning systems along the northern approaches to the United States to detect the approach of hostile bombers and installed an additional radar network within the country for interceptor control. For the radar network, Bell Laboratories, during the early 1950s, participated in studies to characterize the type of communications network required and methods of optimizing the processing of radar data. This project was known as the Continental Air Defense System, or CADS.

The development of digital computers in the late 1940s and early 1950s opened the door to the possibility of efficient, centralized processing of large volumes of radar data. Processing capability could far exceed that of human beings, thus providing significantly improved means for conducting air battles.

M.I.T.'s Lincoln Laboratory devised such a system for processing radar data. A prototype known as the Cape Cod System was used for the initial evaluation. In the spring of 1953, Bell Laboratories was asked to assist in the development of a full-scale system, which was first designated the Lincoln Transition System (i.e., a transition from manual to automated operation), and later the Semi-Automatic Ground Environment (SAGE) system.

Ultimately, Western Electric became responsible for much of the implementation of the complete system—site selection, building design and construction, equipment installation and checkout, communications implementation, etc.—under the appellation Air Defense Engineering Services (ADES), as described in Section 2.2. The relationship of the SAGE system to the overall air-defense complex as it existed in the mid-1950s is depicted in Fig. 12-1.

Bell Laboratories' role was more specialized. It was largely an extrapolation of its role in CADS, supplemented by assistance to Western Electric in certain areas. These included collaboration with Lincoln Laboratory in the evaluation of the Cape Cod System, preparation of comprehensive test specifications and computer programs to be used by Western Electric to check out equipment in the field, system studies, preparation of standing operating procedures and job descriptions for all positions in the overall system, field support to the Western Electric test teams, and aid to the Air Force in selecting radar sites.

As part of the ADES task, Bell Laboratories developed both internal and external communications requirements. However, any necessary development of telecommunications equipment to meet these requirements was carried out in specific response to a Western Electric request, similar to the normal Bell System support of Western Electric. Bell Laboratories also participated in a variety of special studies and, largely on its own initiative, coordinated many subprojects for the benefit of the project as a whole.

In the course of this work, Bell Laboratories maintained a sizable staff at Lincoln Laboratory for nearly two years, after which part of the organization was assigned for several months to various field sites. In addition, a traveling force of field engineers visited nearly all Air Force radar sites in the continental United States to assist in integrating the sites into the SAGE system. Most of the activity on SAGE was completed by the end of 1961.

1.4 Communications Studies – Defense Communication Agency

1.4.1 Pile Driver

In 1960, the Defense Communication Agency asked Bell Laboratories to investigate the vulnerability of communications cables to nuclear effects. This information was needed to design cable support and connections for hardened command, control, and communications centers with remote hardened antennas. The study, termed Pile Driver, involved analysis of the effects of blast-induced ground shock, produced by nuclear detonation, on communications cables. Bell Laboratories participated in the design of field experiments to obtain the required data. The results of the experiments, data analysis, and measurements of cable properties proved that with well-engineered structures, cables can survive at very close distance to a nuclear surface detonation. Design information on cable tunnels, vertical risers, and near-surface installations was developed. Also, the geometry of cable routing was analyzed from the point of view

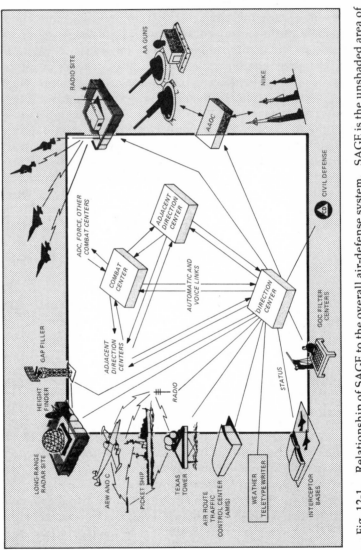

Fig. 12-1. Relationship of SAGE to the overall air-defense system. SAGE is the unshaded area of the figure and includes, as indicated, equipment installed in other air-defense elements.

of the number and yield of nuclear weapons needed to destroy all communications routes. The program was completed in 1970.

1.5 Communications Systems Developments

1.5.1 AN/ USC-2 (XN-1) Data Communications System

Following World War II, it became evident that data-communications systems using coded signals offered many advantages over voice communications for various information and control functions. Bell Laboratories was a pioneer in this field and made fundamental studies that led to the development of the AN/USC-2 (XN-1) Data Communications System.

In 1950, under contract to the United States Navy, the Bell Laboratories/Western Electric team began to develop a data link to exchange information between a surface terminal and a number of airborne terminals. As work progressed, the scope of the program grew to include construction and testing of feasibility models, and later, additional studies and tasks required by the Navy.

Because transistor technology was still in its infancy at the outset of the project, many circuits had to be designed with electron tubes. However, the state of transistor art improved while the USC-2 equipment was developed. After the performance of the initial system was proven to be highly successful, the Airborne Data Multiplex (DMX) was redesigned to be completely transistorized. This redesign afforded a substantial saving in space, weight, and power. A fully transistorized DMX was completed and demonstrated in the summer of 1956.

1.5.2 AN/ TSQ-7 and AN/ TSQ-8 Coordinate Data Sets

The first military equipment with large quantities of transistors to be produced by Western Electric were the AN/TSQ-7 and AN/TSQ-8 Coordinate Data Sets. These sets, developed for the Army Signal Corps, were used in a defense network to transmit radar target data over telephone lines. At the radar, three dc voltages representing position were converted into digital data and transmitted at a rate of 750 bits per second as modulation of a 1500-Hz carrier. At the receiver, the digital information was converted back to dc voltages representing the original position. The TSQ-8 set handled data on only a single target, while the TSQ-7 set managed data on as many as 48 targets.

The TSQ-8 set was designed to do the same job as the earlier TSQ-1, which used 370 vacuum tubes. Although the state of the art would not allow all vacuum tubes to be eliminated and still meet the production schedule, TSQ-8 used significantly fewer tubes than TSQ-1. With 40 tubes and 200 transistors, TSQ-8 occupied one-fifth the volume and weighed only one-fifth as much as the TSQ-1 set.

The TSQ-7 set with 57 tubes and 235 transistors was larger than the TSQ-8. In both sets, all digital operations were performed with point-contact transistors, with junction-type transistors used for linear operation. Vacuum tubes were used only in the encoding and decoding circuits—which changed the dc voltages to digital numbers, and vice versa—and for receiver gain control.

This application of transistors in the early 1950s provided the vehicle for developing various transistor circuit packages. These packages were designed as part of the joint services exploratory transistor development work at Bell Laboratories that began in 1949, as discussed in Chapter 13.

1.5.3 Integrated Wire/Radio Communications System for U.S. Army

Systems for placing several telephone conversations on a single pair of wires or on a single radio channel were not new to military communications. A standard piece of communications equipment in World War II, the CF1 carrier telephone terminal,[2] which was developed by Bell Labs and manufactured by Western Electric, was used successfully with cable, open-wire, and radio in both the European and Asiatic theaters. The CF1 band was limited to 15 kHz so that available radio sets could be used. During the Korean conflict, these carrier telephone terminals were again put into production in substantial quantities. They continued to be produced until the middle of 1953. About this time, the AN/TCC-3,[3] a new version of the CF1 carrier telephone, was placed into quantity production. The AN/TCC-3 terminal gave better transmission in a much smaller package, with components designed in accordance with the latest military specifications (see Fig. 12-2). It provided four telephone-message channels and one voice-frequency maintenance channel. It was a selfcontained, ac-operated, manually regulated carrier telephone terminal. An associated AN/TCC-5 repeater was designed to extend the operation of these terminals up to about a hundred miles. For longer transmission distances, 100-mile "links" were connected in tandem.

While the four-channel system was being planned, a thorough study of military communications needs was in progress. On the basis of this Signal Corps study, it was determined that a longer-distance system with increased channel capacity would be needed. For greater flexibility in difficult terrain, it was also determined that radio-relay links would be required. Bell Laboratories, at the request of the Signal Corps, developed a twelve-channel system for circuits up to 200 miles between terminals

---

[2] O. B. Jacobs, "Carrier System for the Spiral 1–4 Cable," *Bell Laboratories Record* 22 (December 1943), p. 168.

[3] AN/TCC-3 is the designation for the Army-Navy Transportable Carrier Communication No. 3 equipment.

(b)

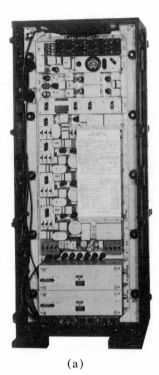

(a)

Fig. 12-2.   AN/TCC-3 telephone terminal (a) compared
in size with CF-1B terminal (b).

and radio equipment suitable for use in either the four- or twelve-channel cable systems.

Each terminal, repeater (except the AN/TCC-11 unattended repeater), and radio set of the twelve-channel system was self-contained and ac operated.   Each was also automatically regulated to compensate for variations in temperature and for cable attenuation.   This regulation was sufficiently precise to permit stable, low-loss operation of all channels, with any type of service in both arctic and tropic conditions.

This communications system met the severe requirements of military use.   It worked satisfactorily with a wide range of supply voltages and line frequencies, in all ranges of humidity and temperature.   It could be moved and installed quickly and could stand rough use under tactical field conditions when operated by relatively untrained personnel.

A new design of four-conductor cable, known as "spiral-4," was used as the wire transmission medium for the four- and twelve-channel systems. This cable, developed for the Signal Corps, was polyethylene-insulated, extremely well balanced electrically, lighter, and more rugged than its World War II rubber-insulated counterpart.   The same band of frequencies was used in each direction of transmission, 4 to 20 kHz for the four-channel system, and 12 to 60 kHz for the twelve-channel system. In addition, a voice channel, operating at frequencies of 300 to 3,000 Hz with the four-channel system and 300 to 1,700 Hz with the twelve-channel system, was provided for maintenance only.

Loading coils were added to the spiral-4 cable at $\frac{1}{4}$-mile intervals for the four-channel application. At 50°F, such inductive loading decreased the loss at 20 kHz from 2.9 dB per mile to 0.8 dB. This allowed the repeaters to be spaced about 30 miles apart. Loading was not effective, however, in reducing loss at 68 kHz, the top frequency of the twelve-channel system, unless coils were introduced at intervals much shorter than $\frac{1}{4}$ mile. This was undesirable because the cable was designed to be readily handled in $\frac{1}{4}$-mile sections. Therefore, to keep the attended repeaters spaced at substantial intervals, an unattended repeater was added to the cable every $5\frac{3}{4}$ miles. This spacing was dictated by cross-talk characteristics in the spiral-4 cable. The unattended repeaters received power over the same spiral-4 cable used for channel transmission and permitted the attended repeaters to be spaced up to 40 miles apart. The gain of the twelve-channel cable system was automatically regulated at the unattended repeaters by thermistors sensitive to ambient temperature. Further automatic regulation was provided at each attended repeater and receiving terminal by thermistors that were guided by a 68-kHz control frequency.

A possible military setup that uses all three types of equipment is shown in Fig. 12-3. At the left are twelve channels—four on each of three short-haul cable systems. For any single telephone message channel, one telephoto channel or sixteen telegraph channels can be substituted. With various combinations of repeaters and terminals, these four-channel systems feed into one twelve-channel terminal (AN/TCC-7). From this point on, the illustration represents the long-haul, backbone portion of the network. The twelve channels are transmitted via unattended repeaters (AN/TCC-11), attended repeaters (AN/TCC-8), and radio (AN/TRC-24) to another twelve-channel terminal at the right. The distance represented in the drawing is only about 180 miles, but additional links can be extended from the twelve-channel terminal to give communications distances of up to about 1,000 miles. At any such twelve-channel terminal, four-channel equipment can branch off from the main route.

The AN/TRC-24 radio sets operated in the upper VHF and the lower UHF ranges from 50 to 400 MHz where antennas could be easily aligned and where fading problems were not serious. Since other services operated in this frequency range, it was essential that the radio-relay system use the minimum radio-frequency bandwidth consistent with good performance. The radio sets used a modified type of frequency modulation to obtain a balance between best crosstalk and noise performance. The

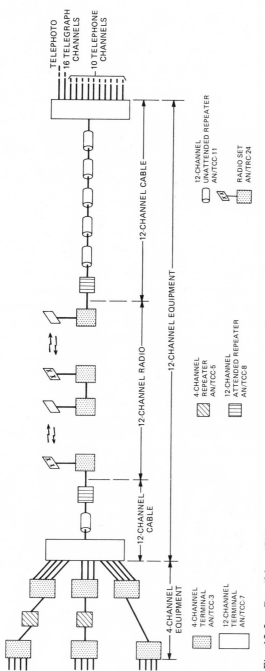

Fig. 12-3.   Possible military-communications setup, using both cable and radio equipment and covering about 180 miles.

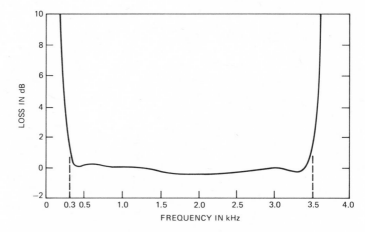

Fig. 12-4. Attenuation characteristic for 100-mile, four-channel system or 200-mile, twelve-channel system.

radio transmitter and receiver were operated on separate frequencies to obtain different channels for the two directions of transmission. The sets could be placed on any of 425 radio-channel frequencies. Radio repeaters could be spaced about 25 to 30 miles apart in favorable terrain. About seven or eight radio transmitters and receivers could operate in tandem with low distortion to form a 200-mile link. Each radio channel carried either the four or the twelve carrier channels plus the maintenance channel.

One of the distinguishing characteristics of these military systems was that 35 radio transmitters and 35 receivers could be operated as a five-link system with five transmitting carrier terminals and five receiving terminals. This system resulted in an overall interference (due to the summation of crosstalk produced by distoration products plus noise) at least 34 dB below the average wanted signal. Equally low interference was present in an equivalent all-cable system with about 170 repeaters.

The 1,000-mile circuits derived from either the cable system, the radio system, or combinations of both, were sufficiently stable to perform as well as the best commercial systems. Each link (100 miles for the four-channel system and 200 miles for the twelve-channel system) could be operated with no overall loss when the transmitting and receiving paths were separately connected, or with a 3-dB loss when the two paths were combined at a switchboard. The band filters that separated the several channels determined the overall attenuation and delay characteristics of the channels. A typical band-attenuation characteristic for one link is shown in Fig. 12-4 and a corresponding delay characteristic is shown in Fig. 12-5.

The development of these carrier telephone systems, together with the

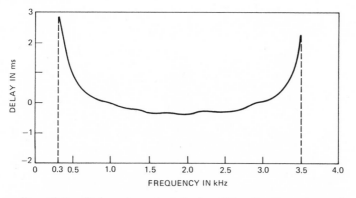

Fig. 12-5. Delay characteristic for 100-mile, four-channel system or 200-mile, twelve-channel system.

spiral-4 cable and new radio sets, formed a basis for a comprehensive military communications network.

The sets were produced in large quantities and successfully tested in the arctic and in equatorial Africa. They were used by the British, French, and Italian armed forces as part of NATO and also by the Signal Corps in Korea. The twelve-channel terminal, AN/TCC-7, is shown in Fig. 12-6, and the twelve-channel unattended repeater, AN/TCC-11, is shown in Fig. 12-7.

Figure 12-8 illustrates the large number of packages comprising the AN/TRC-24 radio set, including alternate tuning units, antenna and mast elements, antenna filters, antenna cables, power unit, and associated gear. Figures 12-9a and 12-9b show the radio transmitter and radio receiver for this radio set, and indicate the compact yet complex designs needed to achieve the overall objective of high performance in portable radio units. Transit cases protected the carrier telephone equipment and the radio set from damage during handling and also sealed and protected them from shock during shipment.

Both the carrier telephone equipment and the radio set were developed and designed by Bell Laboratories people with long experience in these fields. Circuits and operating features were used that had been proven in the Bell System. However, military requirements necessitated the development of new features and designs.

One of the most important requirements for the carrier telephone equipment and the radio sets was that they operate in a stable and reliable fashion under less than favorable conditions, after simple straightforward adjustment. Under military operating conditions this was accomplished by a system of line equalization involving "flat-gain" control at 1000 Hz sent over the "order-wire" circuit for the four-channel equipment, and by equalization and automatic control in the 48-kHz band for the

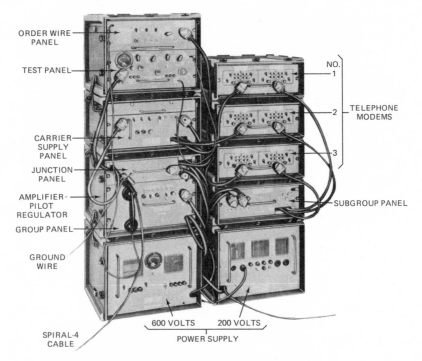

ORDER WIRE PANEL
TEST PANEL
NO. 1
2
TELEPHONE MODEMS
3
CARRIER SUPPLY PANEL
JUNCTION PANEL
AMPLIFIER-PILOT REGULATOR
SUBGROUP PANEL
GROUP PANEL
GROUND WIRE
600 VOLTS
200 VOLTS
SPIRAL-4 CABLE
POWER SUPPLY

Fig. 12-6.   Twelve-channel AN/TCC-7 terminal.

twelve-channel equipment. Great attention was paid to stabilizing the modulator load and carrier-balance characteristics by closely controlling components and their uniformity in manufacture. Attention was also paid to attaining high output stability in the line amplifiers with variations in power and temperature, and with different vacuum tubes. Self-contained transmission-measuring circuits aided in maintaining circuit effectiveness.

In the twelve-channel (wideband) system, the noise on the trunk, including that from interchannel crosstalk, had to meet more stringent

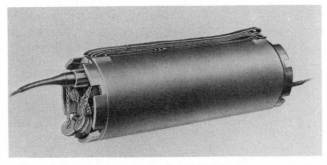

Fig. 12-7.   Twelve-channel AN/TCC-11 unattended repeater.

Fig. 12-8.   Complete complement of packages for the AN/TRC-24 radio (covers are removed from transit cases). (*AIEE Transactions,* November 1954.)

values than in older military systems.   Efficient integration of radio into the system meant that the radio set had to transmit the wide base band of 200 Hz to 68 kHz.   The need for low interchannel crosstalk called for unusual attention to the reduction of distortion in the radio circuits.   This was accomplished by separating frequency-control functions from the modulating/demodulating functions in this frequency-modulated radio set.   The frequencies of the transmitter and receiver oscillators were controlled by motor-driven capacitors operating from frequency discriminators so that the transmitter base band modulator and the receiver base band demodulator would be operated at the center of their characteristics where distortion was minimum.   High-grade components were used to achieve uniformity and stability under field conditions.   Unusual care had to be taken in balancing the receiver demodulator and the transmitter modulator circuits to achieve low distortion.   The receiver intermediate amplifier was designed and tested to produce very low phase distortion over the ±400-kHz modulating band in a 1-MHz passband at a 30-MHz center frequency.

In addition to meeting telephone system requirements, the AN/TRC-24 radio set had to operate near or with other radio equipment.   Thus, it had to be adjustable to deliver 100 watts RF anywhere in the band from 50 to 400 MHz.   This wideband was covered by use of four plug-in tuning units, only two of which (100 to 225 MHz and 225 to 400 MHz) were ordered per radio set.   Interference among closely located radio sets was reduced by the use of sharply selective coaxial tuners in the antenna leads of both the transmitters and receivers.   Special rugged dipole-reflector directional antennas (Fig. 12-10) were developed, along with portable mast sections, to complete the system.

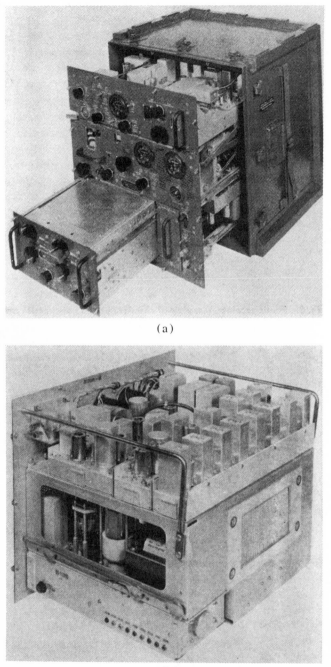

(a)

(b)

12-9.   AN/TRC-24 radio.   (a) Transmitter.   (b) Receiver
(rear view). (*AIEE transactions*, November 1954.)

12-10. Antenna developed for the AN/TRC radio. (*AIEE Transactions*, November 1954.)

This equipment was manufactured from 1954 through 1960 at Western Electric's Marion Shops in Jersey City, New Jersey. Later, manufacturing continued in North Carolina. The records show that carrier telephone equipment was produced in the following quantities:

Designation	Quantity Produced
AN/TCC-3	3,173
AN/TCC-5	1,065
AN/TCC-7	2,324
AN/TCC-8	783
AN/TCC-11	5,654
AN/TRC-24	1,220

1.5.4 Extension of AFMTC Communications System

In 1958 Bell Laboratories was asked by the Air Force to develop and prepare manufacturing information for extending the submarine cable system of the Air Force Missile Test Center (AFMTC) from Puerto Rico to Antigua, and to modify the system, as necessary, between San Salvador and Puerto Rico so that the stations at Mayaguna and Sabana de la Mar could be operated without attendants. As a result, an extensive study was conducted of the physical conditions of the land areas involved and of the marine environment of the underwater links. Numerous system alternatives were considered, such as microwave radio relay versus offshore underwater cable for some of the coastline links. The Air Force preferred the water route and accepted responsibility for the decision.

Some consideration was given to other system alternatives, such as the use of larger cable to span greater distances and thus shorten the route and reduce the number of repeaters, and the use of a twin-cable system with sea-bottom repeaters. The larger cable involved serious development and manufacturing problems, probable schedule delays and no important economic advantage. Although the twin-cable system could provide increased facilities, it was rejected largely because of its greater cost. Bell Labs supplied recommendations for the system to the Air Force in 1960, and Western Electric provided subsequent production assistance.

1.5.5 UHF Radio Communications — Air-to-Air and Air-to-Ground

At the end of World War II, voice communications between U.S. military aircraft and between aircraft and ground stations were conducted primarily in the 108- to 135-MHz band. The airborne receiver-transmitter command sets used aboard the aircraft of the U.S. Navy and the U.S. Army Air Force were AN/ARC-1 sets that were designed by Bell Laboratories. Western Electric manufactured more than half of the 70,000 sets delivered to the military services.

Shortly after the conclusion of World War II, a decision was made to turn over the 108- to 130-MHz band to commercial and general aircraft, and to shift the military air-voice communications to the 225- to 440-MHz band. This decision raised objections in the air services for reasons given in the following paragraphs.

Bell Laboratories developed a radio receiver-transmitter set, AN/ARC-12, for the 225- to 350-MHz band that was physically interchangeable with the AN/ARC-1, providing the same quick selection of any one of ten crystal-controlled channels. One command channel was continuously provided so that commands could be given to and monitored by many planes, even though individual groups were operating on different assignments.

Western Electric manufactured several thousand AN/ARC-12 sets. RCA provided a second source of supply by manufacturing an equal number of sets using the Bell Labs design.

The military services soon discovered that when UHF antennas were installed on ships and on ground locations at the same heights used for VHF antennas, UHF communications to aircraft were quite inferior to those achieved with VHF. This was due to the presence of two to three times as many lobes and nulls in the vertical UHF patterns as in VHF. One of the nulls caused loss of communications from aircraft carriers to aircraft that were flying at altitudes up to 20,000 feet and were at a range of about 125 miles from the carrier. This highly undesirable phenomenon caused the Navy and Air Force to set up an experimental program in May 1948 at the Patuxent River Naval Air Station on the Chesapeake Bay. The program was designed to investigate the problem in detail and to determine remedies, such as different heights for multiple ground antennas. Bell Laboratories participated in these tests and made a number of recommendations for the installation and use of UHF systems that reduced the null problems to a negligible level.

During this same period, Bell Laboratories developed the AN/ARC-19 (XN-1) radio receiver-transmitter. The set provided 876 voice channels at separations of 200 kHz for quick selection by an operator. In a parallel development by the Bendix Aviation Corporation, a set with 1,752 channels at 100-kHz separation was designed. Because of selectivity problems and unusable channels resulting from the methods used for synthesizing the channels from a limited number of quartz crystals, the number of available channels did not differ greatly for the two designs. The sets were tested at the Patuxent River Station (Navy) and Wright Field (Air Force). The AN/ARC-19 project terminated when the development of the set was completed.

The AN/ARC-27 set, designed and manufactured by the Collins Radio Company, was later manufactured by Western Electric at its Hawthorne plant in Chicago to provide a second source of supply.

During World War II, Bell Laboratories started development of an experimental pulse-communication radio transmitter-receiver, designated the AN/ARC-11. This set provided three types of pulse transmission:

1. Frequency modulation of 8,000 pulses per second.

2. Phase modulation of 8,000 pulses per second

3. 8,000 pairs of pulses per second, with the time separation between the pulses of a pair being voice modulated.

Two of the AN/ARC-11 sets were developed and delivered. One was installed in a C-47 aircraft and the second in a ground station. The system was tested by the Navy and Bell Laboratories at the Navy Air Station at Westerly, Rhode Island, in February 1947 and later at Patuxent River Naval Air Station in March 1949. It provided excellent communications to about 75 miles in keeping with the transmitter power, antenna gain, and receiver noise figure.

1.5.6 Far North Communications Systems

One of the largest communications network undertakings in the post-war period has been the development and installation of the Far North Communications and Detection Systems. The radar-detection portion of these systems was described in Chapter 7. In this chapter, the discussion focuses on the unique communications projects undertaken.

The major programs included Polevault, White Alice, DEW (Distant Early Warning) Line with its continental, Aleutian, and transatlantic segments, and the far-flung communications system linking the radars in the Ballistic Missile Early Warning System (BMEWS) to the continental command headquarters at North American Air Defense (NORAD).

These basic communications systems now stretch halfway around the world in the most difficult, barren terrain where wire-line links are essentially impossible to install and maintain and where radio line-of-sight towers are economically impractical. The development of these systems involved the exploration of a new mode of radio propagation—tropospheric scatter—studied by Bell Laboratories in the late 1940s. It employed radio frequencies in the VHF, UHF, and SHF spectrums propagated far beyond the horizon, thus greatly reducing the number of stations required.

1.5.6.1 DEW Line. Knowing of Bell Laboratories work in troposcatter propagation and needing a reliable communications system for its widespread stations on the northern perimeter of the North American continent, the Air Force in 1953 asked Western Electric/Bell Laboratories to carry out two studies on radio propagation. One study was conducted along the northern coast of Alaska and Canada in connection with trial stations of the DEW line. The second study, with the assistance of Bell of Canada, was carried out along the eastern coast of Newfoundland. As described in Chapter 7, the object of the studies was to determine the effects of weather, terrain, and radio frequency on troposcatter propagation. The results of the two Bell System studies, as well as those from propagation studies conducted by Lincoln Laboratories and the National Bureau of Standards, indicated that beyond-horizon radio systems would provide reliable communications.

A crash program was then authorized for a communications system along the Labrador and Newfoundland coasts to link early warning radar stations with continental command centers. This program, called Polevault, showed that satisfactory and reliable voice and digital communications were possible using troposcatter. Polevault, started in 1954 and completed by the Bell System in one year, became a key link in the global communications system of the Department of Defense.

These trial systems were difficult enough, but the real challenge faced primarily by Western Electric and several of its construction subcontractors was to establish the string of DEW Line stations across 3,000 miles of trackless wilderness above the arctic circle. Early survey teams were taken into and out of the prospective sites by helicopter. They lived in heated tents in surrounding temperatures of $-40°$ F with supplies parachuted to them. To begin building the first site, bulldozers were brought in by helicopter, and airstrips were hacked out during the summer months of 1955.

New methods of construction were devised to avoid damaging the all-pervading permafrost. Prefabricated buildings were elevated on piles that were dropped into holes driven into the permafrost by steam jets and immediately were frozen into solid supports. The frozen surface under the buildings was kept stable by protecting it from building heat with a 3-foot cover of gravel, which was in abundant local supply. The logistics of moving the tons of materials and equipment to these remote spots under almost impossible weather conditions for most of the year was a triumph of heavy-construction planning and execution.

The DEW Line lateral communications system, still in service in 1977, operated "beyond-the-horizon" in the frequency range of 800 to 1,000 MHz. This system provided up to 24 voice channels along the Line, some of which were used for teletypewriter service. In general, 1-kW transmitters were used with two 30-foot-diameter parabolic antennas; however, 10-kW transmitters with 60-foot antennas were used on high-path-loss links.

The VHF rearward communications system was of an ionospheric-scatter type that used the ionosphere to reflect radio waves. This system provided several teletypewriter channels in each direction. High-power transmitters were employed with two antennas giving space diversity.

During the first half of 1957, an extensive evaluation was made of the reliability of communications circuits, and of detection and data-handling capabilities. No major flaws were found in the system concept or performance, and the Alaska-Canada portion of the DEW Line began operation about mid-1957.

The Aleutian extension of the DEW line, undertaken by Western Electric in January 1957, provided a westerly extension, reaching 700 miles from King Salmon to Nikolski in the Aleutian Islands chain. Utilizing design, development, and implementation experience gained under the original DEW Line project, the Aleutian extension, consisting of five tropospheric-scatter radio links, was fully operational on March 31, 1959.

The problems of building the eastern extension of the DEW Line from Cape Dyer on Baffin Island to Keflavik, Iceland, a distance of 1,200 miles, rivaled those involved in constructing the original DEW Line. Four of the AN/FPS-30 radars and AN/FRC-39 tropospheric-scatter radio stations were built on the vast, continent-size, ice-covered island of Greenland, and two of these stations were located on the great Greenland ice cap. The problems involved in constructing this eastern extension of the DEW Line were solved by building a simulated site in the United States.

A highly reliable switching center was designed, built, and installed at Cape Dyer by the end of 1960. This center was capable of interconnecting communications from the DEW Line, the rearward communications centers, and Ballistic Missile Early Warning System.

1.5.6.2 White Alice. Activity at Bell Laboratories leading to the White Alice project started with a Department of Defense request to AT&T for a study of an integrated communications system in Alaska. The study, known as Task BJ, was begun in May 1954 by the Long Lines Department of AT&T and was completed in November 1954.

Recommendations of the Task BJ group included the use of troposcatter radio for the long paths (100 to 200 miles) that separate many of the military installations in Alaska and the use of microwave systems for shorter paths where a large number of channels were required. Radio was the preferred medium since it was cheaper and more reliable than cable or wire in the Alaskan climate and terrain. On the basis of these recommendations, Western Electric was granted the contract for White Alice by the Air Materiel Command of the Air Force early in 1955. Bell Laboratories participation started soon after.

The White Alice system comprised a network of trunk routes covering the entire state of Alaska. The Alaskan Air Command assumed operation of the network, which covered 3,100 route miles and employed 23 links of tropospheric-scatter radio, nine links of line-of-sight microwave radio, cables, and all the necessary power plant, telephone, and telegraph terminating equipment. The channel capacity on most of this network has been expanded a number of times since 1958 to meet Alaska's communications growth.

The TD-2 microwave radios and telephone terminal equipment were standard Bell System arrangements; therefore, no special designs were required. For the tropospheric radio links, new designs were needed for almost all of the components, including the radio-frequency equipment, antennas, hardware for transmission lines, dummy loads, and filters. Designs for this equipment and test criteria were prepared by Bell Laboratories or by subcontractors under its supervision. Reliable equipment was necessary in order to meet the high standards of network transmission reliability.

The magnitude of engineering and construction work required for White Alice would have been a huge task anywhere. When compounded by the rugged terrain and weather of Alaska, it became a job that could only be performed by men and women with skill, ingenuity, and courage. Figure 12-11 is a scene typical of the White Alice environment.

An important date in the history of Alaska was recorded when the White Alice network went into operation in March 1958, linking citizens and government personnel of that territory through a reliable long-distance telephone system. After White Alice began operation, its most important job was the transmission of aircraft-warning information from the remote Air Force detection systems to the Alaskan Air Command headquarters and the NORAD installations in Canada and the U.S.

1.5.6.3 Ballistic Missile Early Warning System (BMEWS). In February 1958, Western Electric was named prime contractor for the Rearward Communications System of BMEWS. Under this program, Western Electric was to establish communications links from detection stations at Thule, northern Greenland, at Clear, Alaska, and at Fylingdales, England, to the NORAD headquarters at Colorado Springs, Colorado.

12-11. Tropospheric-scatter radio antenna of the White Alice communications network in Alaska.

Multiple routes were used to provide reliable transmission between each detection station and NORAD. One route consisted of a submarine cable from the Thule, Greenland, site via Cape Dyer on Baffin Island, to Deer Lake, Newfoundland, at which point commercial-telephone-company facilities provided connections to NORAD. Another route linked Thule to Cape Dyer via the DEW Drop radio system, and Cape Dyer to Goose Bay via the Polevault radio system, both of which used tropospheric-scatter radios. Commercial telephone company facilities completed the circuits from Goose Bay to NORAD. The BMEWS program involved the design and construction of three submarine cable stations, land-cable facilities at Thule and Cape Dyer, and the rebuilding of seven tropospheric-scatter radio stations. Figure 12-12 shows two pairs of the UHF "bill-board" antennas at a BMEWS site.

Initially, Bell Laboratories assisted Western Electric in preparing a tentative plan for BMEWS communications, which was submitted to the Air Force in December 1957. This tentative plan was followed by a comprehensive plan specifying the transmission objectives, circuit rout- ings, and underwater-cable and radio-relay requirements. Performance evaluations were made on existing facilities that were of potential use in the BMEWS system. Recommendations were made for upgrading those facilities to enable them to meet BMEWS transmission objectives. As an

Fig. 12-12.   Sixty-foot UHF antenna at a BMEWS communications site in Labrador.

aid in the appraisal of existing tropospheric scatter systems, Bell Laboratories prepared document MCSR-3, entitled "Systems Engineering of
Beyond-Horizon Tropospheric Radio Relay Communication Systems."
Specifications were prepared that covered the criteria for engineering and
constructing radio-relay equipment and antennas, and for retrofitting
existing 30- and 60-foot antennas.   Bell Laboratories prepared studies on
modulation techniques for long-distance transmission of data signals, on
error detection and control systems, on envelope delay and amplitude
response characteristics of line facilities, and on the optimum bit rate for
BMEWS data transmission.

The studies indicated that new data transmission equipment was needed
for BMEWS.   Because such equipment was not available, Bell Laboratories
developed the "custom" BMEWS data sets.

A control and status reporting system was developed for the BMEWS
Rearward Communications System.   This reporting system consisted of
a control console used at the zone of interior (ZI), and several racks of
equipment used at the ZI, and detection and repeater sites.   With this
equipment, operating and supervisory personnel were able to assess
performance of the communications facilities over several routes, to determine optimum routing, and to supervise maintenance so that equipment "down" time could be kept to a minimum.

Bell Laboratories' effort was completed in 1960 with the design of a digital-data-system modification that provided a high-speed alarm-level transmission facility, and assistance with the implementation of Red-Alarm facilities on the three BMEWS routes.

The Far North Communications Systems involved personnel of Western Electric, Bell Laboratories, and the Operating Telephone Companies. The successful completion of these systems was accomplished under the most severe environmental and logistic conditions.

1.5.6.4 Blue Grass.

In March 1959, Western Electric presented the Air Force with a systems engineering plan for the Blue Grass Communications System. The plan included four possible radio-subsystem arrangements comprised of two-link, three-link, and four-link radio configurations, and a combination submarine cable-radio system between Nikolski and Shemya in the Semichi and Aleutian chain.

Primarily because of economic considerations, the Air Force decided to use the two-link configuration and accept the marginal performance that was expected from the long distances between radio repeaters. Construction of the two-link subsystem with high-power amplifiers, 120-foot antennas, and quadruple diversity combiners was completed in March 1962. The Air Force reported unsatisfactory performance shortly after the system was turned over to a maintenance-operation contractor. Consequently, a program was initiated to make all possible improvements, based on knowledge of the system that engineers had at Western Electric and Bell Laboratories. Antennas were reoriented, receiver deviation ratios were optimized, and the terminal equipment was realigned. It was decided at that time that the system met all the design objectives and would perform in a reasonably satisfactory manner if the equipment were maintained in optimum condition.

During 1965, it became apparent to the Air Force that both new and expanded communications facilities would be necessary to meet military and government requirements in Alaska. In 1966, the Air Force requested recommendations from Bell Laboratories for both short-term and long-term improvement and expansion of communications for the Blue Grass network. These recommendations were presented to the Air Force in a three-phase study, outlined in two reports dated March and May 1966.

The first phase of the study was concerned with recommendations for improving the existing two-link, tropospheric-scatter system so that 36 reliable voice channels of toll-grade quality could be provided between Shemya, Adak, and Nikolski. The second and third phases of the study were concerned with requirements to increase capacity between these sites to 60 channels and later to provide 120 channels between Attu and Adak, with provisions for 300 voice-grade channels between Adak and Dimond Ridge. These reports also contained evaluations of systems that utilized tropospheric-scatter radio, satellite, submarine cable, and microwave radio for transmission. Configurations were recommended on the basis of growth capacity, performance, reliability, cost effectiveness, and also maintainability.

1.5.6.5 Greenpine — Phase II.   In June 1962, the Air Force asked Western Electric to perform services needed to implement an improved UHF air/ground communications system and improved tropospheric-scatter radio communications circuits for the Strategic Air Command (SAC) aircraft flying in the northern latitudes of the western hemisphere. Some of the services under this program included the installation of amplifiers and antennas at 14 SAC remote UHF stations and replacement of 30-foot lateral communications antennas with 60-foot antennas at five DEW Line sites.

Bell Laboratories prepared engineering criteria for the site survey team, participated in the evaluation of the test data, and prepared site and antenna layout designs. Bell Labs also prepared antenna-stress analyses for 60-foot antennas, reviews of reliability and maintainability characteristics, and studies on radio interference likely to be experienced by other equipment at a site that might be caused by the installation of 1-kW power amplifiers and 10-dB UHF antennas. (See also Section 2.5.2, below.)

1.5.7 Mercury

Project Mercury, the United States first venture in manned space flight, was made possible by the National Aeronautics and Space Administration industrial team, which included Western Electric and Bell Laboratories.

Bell Laboratories served as a consultant on systems analysis and the test planning associated with the engineering and design of an 18-station worldwide tracking and communications network spanning the continents of North America, Africa, and Australia, and the Atlantic, Pacific, and Indian Oceans. All of the ground station sites, including the control center, were linked together by 140,000 circuit miles of communications channels, which terminated in the Goddard Space Flight Center in Greenbelt, Maryland.

As a technical consultant to Project Mercury, Bell Laboratories helped to solve equipment and operational problems associated with the communications network. Some of those problems included electromagnetic interference between the equipment at each site, design of a system for intrasite intercommunications, selection of boresight cameras for the tracking antennas, redesign of shipboard equipment to avoid effects of vibration, and testing of high-speed data lines between Cape Canaveral and computers at the Goddard Center. Studies were made on data pro-

Fig. 12-13.   Simulator equipment developed for Project Mercury.   Operator console and instrumented capsule are at center.

cessing, computer programming, the geophysical effects on the orbits, and the effects of radar errors on the computation of orbit positions.   In addition, Bell Laboratories developed a simulator for training flight controllers, prepared plans for maintenance and operations, and supervised the design of the command and control centers.   Figure 12-13 is a view of the simulator equipment, with operator consoles in the foreground and an instrumented capsule at the far end of the room.   The monitor consoles of the flight control center are shown in the photo in Fig. 12-14.   The operation-summary display with orbit traces may be seen on the opposite wall.

In July 1961, Bell Laboratories started tests designed to evaluate the completed communications network for Mercury.   Computer simulations were used to determine methods for making optimum use of the communications paths and to determine the accuracy and timeliness of messages during the actual missions.

To determine the operational adequacy of the instrumentation and manning of the communications-range remote sites, a series of tests was conducted at Wallops Island off the Virginia coast during the latter part of 1961, where the passage of the Mercury spacecraft over the Canary Islands was simulated in real time.   The test data provided the timing

Fig. 12-14.   Monitor consoles of the Project Mercury flight-control center.

required for specific events and an evaluation of the overall efficiency of site operations.

Aside from its technical challenge, work on Project Mercury at Bell Laboratories provided contact with the NASA engineers and managers who were responsible for sending astronauts into orbit and landing a team of astronauts on the moon. Bellcomm, jointly owned by Western Electric and AT&T, was later formed to assist and advise NASA on problems associated with the Apollo moon landing project (see also the section on Bellcomm in Chapter 14).

1.5.8 Defense Automatic Integrated Switch System

Security, survival, and flexibility to adapt quickly to changing needs are probably the three most important considerations for a strategic military communications system, in addition to the obvious need for reliability. With this in mind, development of the UNICOM System, later known as DAIS (Defense Automatic Integrated Switch), was authorized by the Army Signal Corps in mid-1959. One of the cornerstones of the DAIS concept was a full security capability for all communications modes through digital transmission, link encryption, and secure signaling. Other aspects of the basic DAIS concept were:

1. Flexibility of stored program control.
2. Integration of data, printed records, facsimile, and voice traffic into a single common-user global system.
3. Provision for store-and-forward and circuit switching in a single switching center.

4. Coordinated design of station, transmission, and switching equipment.

As a result of work on DAIS and on commercial electronic switching, it was concluded that it was feasible to design and build a system that integrates voice traffic with record traffic and circuit switching with store-and-forward switching. Such integration has two important advantages. First, transmission facilities can be used in common with resultant economy, particularly when store-and-forward traffic can be interspersed among circuit-switched traffic. Second, record traffic can be routed by a combination of circuit switching and store-and-forward handling for optimum speed and economy. The DAIS design also provided significant savings by using the same central processor in the switching center for controlling circuit and store-and-forward switching instead of separate, but coordinated, control of both switches.

Foremost among the contributions of this project was the assurance that very large, flexible, real-time, stored-program systems for strategic communications were feasible. There were other benefits as well:

1. Useful data were obtained on high-frequency radio capabilities for handling digital signals at 2,400 bits per second and tropospheric-scatter radio capabilities at 652.8 kilobits per second.

2. Programmed security checks of user authority were demonstrated.

3. Log-differential, pulse-code modulation voice encoding was demonstrated.

4. High-speed digital signaling was employed.

5. The use of any available trunk as a control channel between switching offices was demonstrated.

A functionally complete test model of the DAIS (UNICOM) system was demonstrated to high-level government representatives at the Bell Labs Holmdel, New Jersey, Laboratory in September 1963. This system represented a major technological advance. In fact, many of its principal features have subsequently been realized in operational systems.

II. INTEGRATED GOVERNMENT COMMUNICATIONS SYSTEMS

2.1 Introduction

The United States government is the largest user of conventional local and toll telephone communications. It is less well known that the government—the civil as well as the military areas—is also the largest user of special private-line communications. The services provided run the gamut from the 16-button *TOUCH-TONE®* telephone used at AUTOVON stations to national and global alerting and conferencing systems for the Strategic Air Command and the Joint Chiefs of Staff. While the defense systems discussed in the earlier section of this chapter were usually implemented under government contract, private-line communications have generally been furnished on a leased basis just as conventional telephone services have been. Only when a service provided in CONUS was extended overseas were the necessary terminals sold to the military who arranged for installation at the remote points.

This private-line business was not sought by the Bell System. Rather it was the government's civil and military departments who came to the Bell System and asked for the needed services. Such private-line services, especially those for the military, have departed considerably from conventional commercial systems and have required regular updating to include new and changed features so that they would function properly with current missions and military plans. The systems requested usually have to be extremely reliable and flexible and have to be capable of surviving a nuclear attack.

The Bell System responded expeditiously to the government requests for these services because of a sincere desire to serve the country and because of its unique position in the field of communications. The integrated expertise within the Bell System in the areas of planning, engineering, design, manufacturing, and installation permitted early implementation of systems that were completely compatible with the switching and transmission facilities of the associated telephone network.

Many such systems were placed in service in the quarter century following World War II. Following is a list of some of these systems that were the most interesting and important. Each will be discussed in subsequent sections of this chapter.

SAGE Communications—Network of voice and data circuits tying together Air Force radar, radio, and command-and-control locations (briefly mentioned earlier in Section 1.3.2).

AUTOVON—Worldwide switched network for private-line telephone and data transmission between military bases and command-and-control centers.

SAC Primary Alerting System—Four-wire, dedicated private-line system used to alert all SAC bases simultaneously.

Joint Chiefs of Staff Alerting Network (JCSAN)—Four-wire system that permits all the unified and specified commands to confer with the Joint Chiefs and others.

No. 300 Switching System—Four-wire switching system used by the FAA at Air Route Traffic Control Centers to connect controllers to either internal or external line facilities.

No. 301 Switching System—Key telephone type of switching system used by the FAA in small air-traffic control locations, such as towers and IFR rooms.

No. 303 Switching System—Manually controlled crossbar switching system used by SAC so that CONUS points can confer with their remote VHF radio sites. This system is known as Green Pine.

No. 304 Switching System—Manually controlled crossbar switching system, which was designed for NASA, that permits a large number of conferences to be set up simultaneously.

No. 305 Switching System—Switching system used by the Air Force at SAGE-BUIC installations to provide air-to-ground and ground-to-ground voice-communications switching capabilities.

No. 306 Switching System—Switching system used at remote commander-in-chief locations on the JCSAN network. It provides a four-wire conferencing capability with trunks from the Pentagon.

10A Alerting System—Nonvoice alerting system for NORAD that provides an attack warning to weapons sites under its control.

758 Switching Systems—Four-wire crossbar switching systems providing complete local and tandem switching, secretarial service, wideband switching and full AUTOVON features.

The above is a group of little-publicized private-line switching and signaling systems that have provided, and in most instances, are continuing to provide in the late 1970s, highly specialized, critically needed communications services for various military and government agencies. These systems permitted control of private-line terminations from attendant console equipment in an almost endless variety of ways. For example, in communicating with an orbiting astronaut, a NASA conference director using the No. 304 system could establish a voice conference involving hundreds of stations located anywhere in the world; an FAA traffic controller using a No. 300 system could "hand off" a fast flying jet to a terminal radar- or tower-controller using a No. 301 system; or a SAC officer could alert all SAC bases worldwide in a matter of seconds.

2.2 SAGE

2.2.1 Background

During the 10 to 15 years following World War II, the stronger nations of the world wanted to provide a means for alerting their military defense mechanisms. Fortunately, circumstances at the time allowed the United States to move ahead rapidly and unimpeded in providing a highly efficient communications system dedicated exclusively to the purposes of the military defense structure. At the start, the Bell System was asked by the government to assist in these endeavors. As a result, the Bell System has played a major role in providing the desired system capabilities.

In early 1951, the Air Force requested the Massachusetts Institute of Technology to head up a group to study air-defense problems. The work of this group resulted in a number of recommendations and led to the establishment of Lincoln Laboratory later in the year. Lincoln Lab's work at that time was to be devoted primarily to research and development of air-defense data-gathering systems and was to be supported by the three military services through a contract with the Air Force.

In January 1953, a memorandum was issued by Lincoln Labs that covered a proposed plan for the evolution of an air-defense data-gathering system, which ultimately became known as SAGE. The name SAGE was derived from the words "semiautomatic ground environment." *Semiautomatic* indicated that humans were still used to perform certain functions. *Ground environment,* a term used by the Air Force, encompassed the many forms of electronic equipment strategically located at ground locations to perform various data-gathering and operational services.

A complex project like SAGE required the close coordination and teamwork of both industry and the military. Therefore, the Air Force assigned broad responsibilities, including some to Western Electric. To provide the required support for the project, Western Electric formed the Air Defense Engineering Services (ADES) organization as part of its Defense Products Division. The ADES organization was made up of people drawn from Western Electric, Bell Laboratories, AT&T, and the Bell System Operating Telephone Companies. It ultimately consisted of more than 1,300 people. Bell Laboratories, both directly and through ADES, was asked to develop most of the ground-communications facilities for the SAGE project, including both data and voice, as discussed earlier in Section I.

The SAGE system was created to provide a network of communications facilities to assure adequate air defense of the continental United States. (Alaska was treated separately.) This defense was provided by a vast complex of radar networks, data-transmission networks, and ground-to-air communications systems that not only guarded against surprise air attack but, of equal importance, could direct an aerial fighter offense if necessary. It was not a new defense arrangement, but rather an enlarged modernization of an existing manual-defense setup.

Military communications are unique in having to be tailored to extremely well-defined functions. The success of a plan or mission often depends entirely on the adequacy of the communications facilities available. And frequently a system must be tied or connected to the next adjacent or even higher echelon of command-control arrangements if a situation expands beyond local control. This thinking was an essential part of all military switching considerations, particularly in SAGE.

For defense purposes, the country was divided into air divisions, each of which was divided into sectors. For adequate air coverage, radio sites

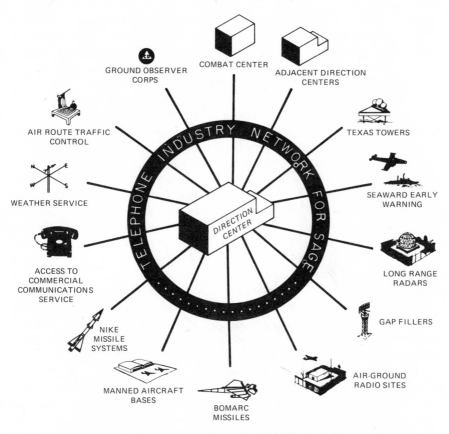

Fig. 12-15.   Components of a typical SAGE air-defense sector.

were strategically placed within the sectors.   Direction Centers (DCs) became the focal point of control communications within each sector where operators, called Intercept Directors (INDs), could selectively communicate with fighter planes through any of the radio sites in the sector (see Fig. 12-15).

2.2.2 SAGE – Voice

There were many units of radio equipment, each on a different frequency, at each radio site.   The numerous Intercept Directors at each Direction Center were connected to this radio equipment over outside-plant telephone facilities.   Since these were vital communications links, the Air Force specified that there be two independent, geographically separated, trunk routes between the Direction Center and each of its respective radio sites.   Two arrangements were developed, one later than the other, to furnish the necessary signaling and switching-control features for these trunk circuits.   In the first, referred to as dual-facility (DF) operation, there were two four-wire circuits, each following a different route, permanently terminated at each end in dual-facility trunk equipment, with one dual-facility connection to each site for each radio channel.   In the second arrangement, which was referred to as common-user-group (CUG) operation, common-control methods were employed to select trunks from a common pool. This greatly reduced the requirements for outside-plant facilities.

To satisfy the requirements for trouble signaling and regular signaling, the 43A1 carrier telegraph terminal was used as the best immediate solution.   This terminal was a three-state system operating on a frequency-shift basis—one state for each of two signal frequencies and a third for the off or no-tone condition.   The two signal frequencies were referred to as "mark" and "space" from telegraph practice, where mark originally meant that current was flowing in the sounder magnet and space meant that current was not flowing.   Since tone was normally present on the line, the absence of tone could be used as an alarm switch-over.   The continuous presence of tone on the line, however, made it necessary to set aside a small portion of the normal speech band for signaling purposes—an arrangement known as slot signaling.   About 250 cycles of the high end of the normal speech band were set aside for this purpose.   This was the first application of this technique in a standard Bell System circuit.

Theory indicated that taking a band of frequencies out of the upper end of the voice channel impairs articulation less than taking a frequency band of the same width from the middle or lower parts of the channel. Therefore, blocking filters were provided to eliminate speech from the signaling channel and to prevent the signaling frequencies from interfering with speech.   In this particular case, the effect on the overall speech-transmission capability of the voice channel was estimated to be no more than that caused by a 2-dB loss.

In both the dual-facility and the common-user-group systems, the signals interchanged between the Intercept-Director position and the radio site were the same; only the manner of establishing the connection was different.   When an interceptor aircraft group was ordered into the air, it operated on a previously assigned radio channel, and an Intercept Director at the Direction Center controlled its operation.   The console position was so arranged that it had access to that particular radio channel at all sites.   The radio set to which it was connected employed the same frequency for receiving and transmitting—one direction at a time.   Thus, when the Interecept Director wished to talk, a push-to-talk (P/T) signal was transmitted to key the remote radio, that is, to switch it into the transmitting condition from its normal receiving condition.   For rapid trouble detection, all trunks were continuously monitored to detect circuit failures.   If one of the lines associated with dual-facility trunk equipment

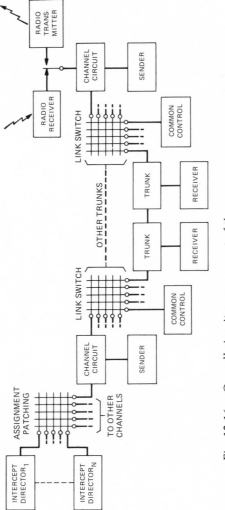

Fig. 12-16. Overall circuit arrangement of the common user group system.

became open-circuited, or if the signaling on it failed, the circuit was switched automatically from the regular route to the alternate route.

Arrangements for sharing trunks through a double-ended form of concentration were proposed and subsequently developed by Bell Laboratories. These arrangements reduced the number of outside trunks required and made the system more flexible without reducing traffic capacity. The Intercept Director could use trunks from a common pool routed over either of two separate geographical paths between the Direction Center and the site to select a particular assigned radio channel. In the other direction, incoming calls could be routed through the same common trunk pool to the particular assigned Intercept Director. This common-user-group arrangement enabled trunks to be used more efficiently (see Fig. 12-16).

The number of trunks required to handle the traffic was determined from a traffic study. Conservative holding times, maximum traffic, and computed circuit-buildup time were used in the study. The results indicated that the size of the trunk groups could be reduced from 15 to 85 percent for the different radio sites.

On the basis of this study, it was decided to employ common-user-group operation with all radio sites, except possibly the one usually associated with the Direction Center; for this site, dual-facility operation would be kept. In the common-user-group system, the normal signals—P/T, acknowledgment, and codan (carrier-operated detector antinoise)—between the remote radio site and the Direction Center were still handled in the same manner as in the dual-facility arrangement. Insofar as the Intercept Director or the pilot in the airplane was concerned, the method of operation was the same whether the regular dual-facility trunk circuit or the common-user-group system was employed.

In the common-user-group system, a method of coding was used that ensured the proper selection of radio channels and contributed to the reliability of the system. (There were 22 radio channels available per system.) A time-division, pulse-length code was used, consisting of a series of long and short pulses. Each code digit consisted of two long and three short pulses separated by short pulses. Any other combination represented a false code and was rejected by the common-user-group circuitry. In addition, parity checking assured that the total number of pulses were received or no operation resulted. Considerable experience had been obtained with this code, and the probability of conversion to a wrong code was considered negligible.

Improvements were constantly being incorporated in the common-user-group system during the development stages and a trial period. A complete common-user-group system that connected Lincoln Labs in Lexington, Massachusetts, with several remote radio-site locations was installed for trial purposes. This trial system was assembled on a plug-in basis at Bell Laboratories in New York City and later shipped and installed at its test location.

For economic reasons, the Air Force found it necessary to reduce further the trunk complements serving the Direction Centers and radio sites. Accordingly, Bell Laboratories design engineers made it possible for Intercept Directors to reach their radio channels at a site, even though there were considerably fewer trunks than Intercept Directors or radio channels. This was accomplished through a scheme that automatically dropped seized trunks in a nontalking condition and made them available to Intercept Directors who needed to talk. This arrangement was particularly effective during busy periods. Somewhat along these same lines, arrangements were provided early in the development that permitted trunks in trouble to be automatically disconnected and made busy while a new trunk was connected.

From a maintenance viewpoint, adequate alarms and line-status indications were provided to both telephone-company test boards and the Air Force. These permitted a high index of system reliability.

2.2.3 SAGE – Data

In addition to the essential air-ground voice-communications handled by SAGE, there was the need to transmit large amounts of data over telephone lines. In the spring of 1956, field trials began on one of the fastest signaling systems ever designed by Bell Laboratories for use on Bell System facilities. Although initially called the SAGE data system because of its first application, the system became officially known as the A1 Digital Data Signaling System. In later years, it was replaced with more modern four-phase data equipment.

A data network was required to transmit information to and from the many computers in the SAGE system. In performing this function, it became the largest data transmission network in the world at the time. The basic requirement of the network was to transmit information at the rate of 1300 or 1600 bits per second, with an error-rate objective of one error in 100,000 bits, or approximately one bit in error per minute per circuit.

The radar sets used with the SAGE system were equipped with a device to convert the radar signals into a form suitable for transmission to data-processing centers. This information was sent over the data network using regular telephone message circuits that had been conditioned for this type of service. At the data-processing centers, the data could be reconverted to radar signals and displayed on an oscilloscope in front of the Intercept Director, or it could be fed directly into a computer.

The computer could continuously relay information from the many radar sites in its area and from adjacent data-processing centers to user locations. The output of the computer was used to identify aircraft as well as to solve complicated problems of navigation and vectoring for interception by fighter aircraft or missiles. The computer kept an active inventory of the status of all weapons. In the case of interceptor aircraft equipped with an automatic pilot, the computer could take over a pilot's job and, being linked to the cockpit via the data circuits, fly the interceptor to its target.

Although the A1 data system had been designed to operate over most message-grade toll facilities, the requirements for data transmission were much more severe than those required for voice transmission. The circuits, in fact, required specialized treatment. As a result, the data system provided satisfactory transmission of the data signals. And it was completely compatible with customer-owned data-generating devices and the computer.

In June, 1958, the first Air Defense Section of the SAGE system became officially operational at McGuire Air Force Base in New Jersey. The Air Defense Command (ADC) of the Air Force became its controlling user.

2.2.4 SAGE – BUIC

As soon as SAGE became operational, plans were generated by the ADC for the integration of a backup system in SAGE. There were many reasons for this. Aside from the military need to provide for contingencies, there was the need to keep up with the rapid advancement of computer technology and with improvements in the communications field. The Bell System was again called upon to play a major role in this new program which, in a short period of time, led to the development of SAGE-BUIC. BUIC was the designation for backup intercept control.

The realignment by the ADC of its air-defense sectors and an expansion of the basic backup system that had been incorporated in the early SAGE program resulted in the creation of NORAD Control Centers (NCCs). These were radio-radar sites that were selected as control points for BUIC. The communications for the NCCs and BUIC were provided by the No. 305 switching system.

The BUIC program, which was started in 1964 and completed in 1966, consisted of the installation of more modern computers, using solid state devices, new customer-supplied display consoles, and associated communications equipment furnished by the telephone companies. At the request of the Air Force, provision was made for future expansion.

The communications control adjuncts used in BUIC at the NCCs were designed with the close cooperation of the Burroughs Company and Bell Laboratories. These adjuncts were attached to the sides of the customer-provided display consoles and permitted the user at the console to control all available facilities.

A number of features were provided which experience with the SAGE program indicated were desirable. Among these was the ability to control the function of a position by operating a key. This scheme activated certain features at a position and permitted more diversified operation with fewer people. *TOUCH-TONE®* dials were provided with access to the newly established AUTOVON system. Also included were connections with conference features to "scramble" lines to fighter bases. Another feature was an arrangement that permitted selectively calling either one of two fighter squadrons at the same base using the same line. Hotline voice-signaling circuits were provided for instantaneous connection with FAA air route traffic controllers. A number of other features were included, one of which created a training and simulator console. This console had all the standard features and permitted the simulated activities needed for training.

Concurrent with the activation of a later phase of BUIC, an addressable data-switching arrangement was implemented on certain SAGE and BUIC services. This arrangement allowed a data user to dial the discrete address of a bridge located in an AUTOVON switching center to obtain desired data. It created a substantial savings in the number of data subscriber lines required from a site location.

SAGE and its companion system BUIC were tested many times over the years by the Air Force through mock penetrations and attacks on the United States defense system. In 1976, the SAGE and BUIC systems were still being used, although on an extremely limited scale.

2.3 FAA Air-Route Traffic Control System

2.3.1 No. 300 Switching System

The 1950s saw a tremendous increase in air traffic, resulting mainly from the introduction of the faster and larger jet aircraft. This aircraft placed greater demands on the communications services used to control commercial and private aircraft that operated daily over thousands of miles of United States airways. In 1956, the Civil Aeronautics Administration, which later became the Federal Aviation Agency (FAA), requested help from AT&T and Bell Laboratories in formulating requirements for a new communications system dedicated specifically for the FAA in their air-route traffic control centers (ARTCC). This system became known as the No. 300 switching system.

The No. 300 system was only one of a number of communications projects undertaken by Bell Laboratories to fulfill the growing needs of the FAA at various aviation-related locations. These projects covered all phases of aircraft control and ranged from the development of specific equipment, such as lightweight headsets, to complete, dedicated switching systems and from dedicated, nationwide voice networks to broadband radar remoting systems. Not to be overlooked were the communications services required for airport control towers and for the more than 300 flight service stations scattered across the country.

The No. 300 system was designed to be extremely flexible and to handle large volumes of calls with no restrictions imposed on the number of calls that could be in progress at the same time. It was a nonblocking system with 100-percent access. Calls through the system were switched on a four-wire basis with all the signaling, switching, and voice-communications facilities required for handling thousands of calls per day. For the most part, the No. 300 system consisted of racks of wire-spring relays and step-by-step and crossbar switches in a separate equipment room. In the operating portion of an ARTCC, there could be as many as 300 attendant positions, each having access through special keys, lamps, loudspeakers, and telephone sets to up to 200 lines of varying types.

Speed was the essential built-in system characteristic so vitally needed for the successful control of aircraft. A single push on a single button by a controller established an immediate connection to the local control tower, a remote Air Force base, another ARTCC, or simply a nearby controller position (see Fig. 12-17). Similarly, connections could be established to customer-owned radio links for contact with the aircraft as it followed its assigned track in the sky. This *direct-access* capability was perhaps the most important feature available to the controller. Of course, it was impractical to have direct access to all lines. Therefore a method was provided that permitted the attendant *indirect access* by seizing a line and dialing a code number to connect to any other desired location.

Associated with the access arrangements was a feature known as "override." This feature was provided due to the urgency of much of the communications in an ARTC. It enabled any controller to reach any line or other position regardless of the amount of traffic in the system or whether the line or trunk was busy. No action was required on the part of the called party to complete the overriding call.

Many other unique features were created, especially for use in the No. 300 system. Because of the semidark lighting in an ARTCC, back lighting of the key control panel was provided and was controlled by the attendant at the position. A position-blanking feature, also controlled by the attendant, was provided at each position. This feature automatically extinguished all other lamp displays at a position upon receipt of an incoming call for which the position had primary answering responsibility. A syllabic lamp was also provided to give a visual indication of speech received on radio channels. The light intensity of the lamp varied with the volume amplitude of the incoming speech. Also, there was an electronic chime that provided for the selection of one-out-of-five fundamental tone frequencies so that adjacent positions receiving incoming calls did not have the same incoming call-signal tone.

To train a controller to operate the No. 300 system, Bell Laboratories was asked to design a training simulator. Such a unit was designed, built, and tested in 40 days. The simulator provided all the basic operating features

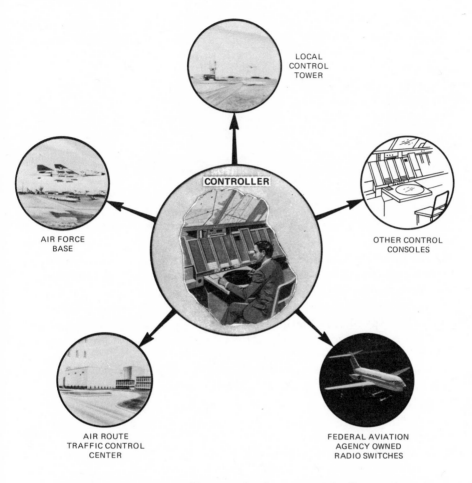

Fig. 12-17. Air route traffic control voice-communications system.

available to an attendent controller in the ARTCC and served as a model for subsequent training facilities used by the FAA.

In the early 1970s, Bell Laboratories, at the request of the FAA, designed a system maintenance monitor console to provide a central monitoring location and continuous status display of all communications equipment used by the FAA in an ARTCC. From this console an FAA engineer and an assistant had access to any position or line serving the No. 300 system, to conference bridging, and to the local PBX.

In 1976 there were 20 ARTCCs being served by the No. 300 switching system and the Bell System within the continental United States. These ARTCCs had been served by this system since 1961. There is also a No. 300 system in Alaska. Several design changes in the system have made it usable in other locations to serve different purposes. It is important to note that the reliability of the system has been outstanding with no system downtime at any installation and with only minor parts replacement. In time, the system will be phased out and replaced by one with more so-phisticated facilities and switching techniques controlled by computers. In view of the record of the present system, this will result in space savings only, a factor which may become significant if any expansion of today's facilities should be required.

2.3.2 No. 301 and No. 301A Switching System for FAA Airport Towers

Closely tied to the No. 300 system were the No. 301 and No. 301A systems. These systems were also designed by Bell Laboratories for the FAA to meet the communications needs of airport towers and other related locations.

The No. 301 system was developed in 1961 to replace existing equip-ment, mainly the key-telephone equipment installed in airport towers that was rapidly becoming outmoded. Its development was undertaken to provide the FAA with a reasonably small communications system that permitted speedier operation, occupied less space, and suited the layout of airport tower facilities. The No. 301 system retained a number of the features of the old arrangements, but incorporated many new concepts of operation, which stemmed from experiences with air-terminal traffic congestion.

One important innovation incorporated in the No. 301 system was a single-lamp-per-key status display—previous displays had two lamps. Another new feature was a multiple-access attendants' telephone circuit that allowed an attendant simultaneously to talk on radio and to override other lines. The override arrangement was a carry-over from the No. 300 system. Because of extreme low-light conditions in a tower, a dark-en-vironment, lamp-control circuit was also made available. Nonlocking pushbutton operation had already become a standard feature.

The No. 301 system was used initially in the control towers as well as in nearby instrument flight control rooms. These were commonly re-ferred to as instrument flight rule (IFR) rooms since they controlled the operation of aircraft flying under instrument-flight, rather than visual, conditions.

A greater emphasis by the FAA on the control of aircraft in the imme-diate vicinity of an airport and the desire to consolidate IFR activities brought about the need to expand the basic No. 301 system. An enlarged, more flexible adaption of the No. 301 system was created. This No. 301A system provided all the features available in the No. 301 with some im-provements and, it allowed for a growth factor that was previously lacking.

2.4 Defense Communications Switching Systems

2.4.1 No. 758 Switching Systems

In the majority of civil government and military requests for communications services, considerable emphasis has been placed on expeditious implementation and reliability. These factors tend to force the adaptation of "tried and true" designs and techniques as the basis for a new system. Innovative arrangements are incorporated on an evolutionary basis. An excellent example of this is the evolution of the No. 758 switching systems, from the manually controlled No. 758A PBX to the complex No. 758C switching system.

One of the main tasks of the newly formed Defense Communication Agency (DCA) was to administer the private-line, long-distance network of the Army, Navy, and Air Force. To monitor this network, a world-wide data network was set up to continuously report the status of the many circuits controlled by the agency. To supplement this data system, DCA asked Bell Laboratories in the Fall of 1960 to furnish a four-wire voice-communications system. It was specified that the system use attended consoles, rather than cord switchboards, provide all normal PBX features plus good conferencing, and be placed in service within six months.

This was a demanding order; but fortunately, the No. 756 PBX was available and was already being used extensively in regular commercial service. The No. 756 was a two-wire PBX that employed two links to complete an intraswitch call; it was a basic system around which the new system could be designed and quickly produced. This new system was developed by adapting the common-control circuits of the No. 756 PBX for direct station selection. The registers were employed with essentially no changes and the marker with only slight modification. The crossbar switch was changed to permit four-wire operation, and the link capacity was substantially increased by circuit modifications so each connection could be established with only one link. The crossbar matrix was single stage with lines and trunks on the verticals and links on the horizontals. Thus, there was no blocking as long as there were links available.

The new system, called the No. 758A PBX (see Fig. 12-18), used a pushbutton-controlled console to handle all traffic, both incoming and outgoing. The system could handle 100 terminations made up of any combination of station lines, trunks, and conference ports.

The No. 758A was cut into service, on schedule, on March 1, 1961. It started more than a decade of very interesting and important work on small, four-wire switching systems.

Although the No. 758A was a manual, pushbutton-controlled system, it had the capability for handling dial operations. So, when the Air Force asked for a four-wire switching system that was completely dial-controlled with no attendant arrangements, it was a simple matter to make the nec-

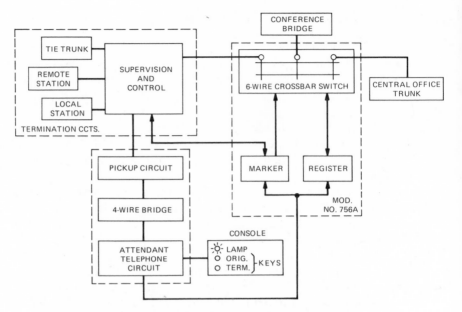

Fig. 12-18.   No. 758A switching system.

essary minor modifications in the No. 758A.   The modified 758A became the No. 758B, which was used to establish calls between stations equipped with 50-kilobits-per-second data terminals.

Not long after, SAC asked for small, four-wire switching systems at a number of ground stations that interfaced with its airborne command posts.   Calls to and from the SAC telephone network, the DDD network, and later AUTOVON (see Section 2.4.4) were handled by direct dialing through these systems.

The No. 758B was also used to switch tandem, long-haul connections around the No. 608 switchboard in the White House Communications Agency.   The No. 608 was a two-wire switchboard.   The circuits were switched through the No. 758B on a four-wire basis, thus permitting a substantial improvement in transmission.   It was possible to integrate the No. 758B into the No. 608 switchboard so that connections could be made simply by pushbutton operation and supervision displayed on the No. 608 board.

In mid-1963, both the civil government and the military indicated considerable interest in a larger-capacity, four-wire system arranged for tandem operation and alternate routing.   Accordingly, the necessary design was undertaken, resulting in the No. 758C switching system (see Fig. 12-19.)   This design involved considerable enhancement of the 758B system.   Two individual markers were provided, instead of the single dual marker, to increase both the reliability and the traffic-handling capability.

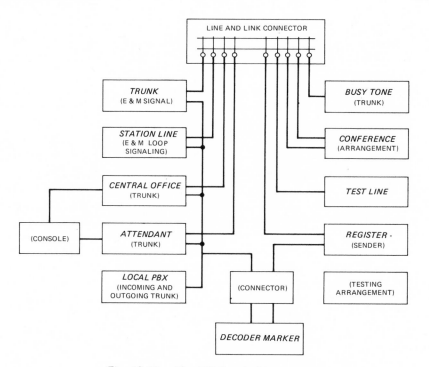

Fig. 12-19.   No. 758C switching system.

The capacity of the system was increased to 560 terminations and 100 links. However, the single-stage XY network was continued to prevent blocking. Senders were added for outpulsing and were integrated with new registers capable of handling ten or more dialed digits, either by rotary or TOUCH-TONE dialing.   A tandem-switching capability and alternate routing were also added.   Alternate routing made it necessary to include route-control digits, since the networks in which the No. 758C was used were normally too small to employ a hierarchical network plan.

Several of the 758C systems were installed for the Tennessee Valley Authority, the Army, and NASA at Cape Kennedy.   About this time NASA, in Huntsville, Alabama, requested a No. 758C that would provide voice and high-speed data switching.   To meet this need, the following changes were made.   The 758C was modified to operate with three separate matrices controlled by the same two marker-decoders. The system was arranged for class-mark screening so that several types of calls could not be connected to the wrong terminations.   Arrangements were included to transmit the class information forward as a prefix to the called address (traveling class marks).   This permitted screening at other switches in the network.

A feature was added that had been patented earlier in connection with a No. 758B project for IBM. This slave-switching feature was employed in connection with TV switching. A normal crossbar matrix handled voice coordination, and a second wider band switch, operating in parallel, accommodated the TV signals.

The ultimate No. 758C switching system was called the "P" switch. Used in the Pentagon, the "P" switch was equipped with two matrices operating from the same two marker-decoders. Each matrix was equipped to handle up to 250 stations and trunks and to accommodate 100 simultaneous conversations. Each station terminated in a wideband encryption device. The switching system worked compatibly with the signaling of these encryption devices. No change was required in the crossbar-switching network to accommodate the 50-kilobits-per-second data stream, only some ingenuity in the layout of the interconnecting wiring. The system was also capable of handling tandem traffic. Trunk groups were available to other similar switching systems in the Washington area, to GFE switching systems in CONUS and overseas, to AUTOVON via narrowband encryption arrangements, and to intermatrix traffic. All of these trunks were equipped with back-to-back encryption devices and compatible signaling devices.

The "P" switch (only) was arranged for multilevel precedence preemption (MLPP) in accordance with the DCA specification for an AUTOVON end office. This preemption could be exercised on station-to-station, station-to-trunk, trunk-to-station, and trunk-to-trunk calls. All AUTOVON incoming and outgoing calls, including calls on the red switch, were handled by an attendant.

So that a red switch could handle classified conversations in the clear, it was necessary to provide better crosstalk isolation than was customary. In addition, the voice bandwidth of the station and switch had to be broader than normal, especially at the low end.

The Navy and Air Force requested red switches, and the Bell System provided them in a combined version of the No. 758A and No. 758B switching systems, called the No. 758A/B. It had an associated console to provide secretarial answering service to certain stations and to handle AUTOVON calls. It also permitted an attendant to set up three simultaneous conferences. The remainder of the stations were arranged for full-dial operation. The system could terminate a total of 100 lines and trunks in any combination and it could accommodate 40 simultaneous conversations.

Stations arranged for dial operation could access any other station by dialing two digits. They could also dial to gain access to the attendant for further call processing or to gain access to the "P" switch. For this switch, the red attendant was dialed, who then inserted the proper precedence digit and completed the dialing for the call. When stations arranged for secretarial service went off-hook, they were immediately routed to the attendant who completed their calls. Incoming calls for these stations were also routed to the operator for manual completion.

Trunks between the red switch and the "P" switch were equipped with wideband encryption devices and compatible signaling arrangements. The same devices and arrangements were also used on trunk connections to GFE switching systems. All connections to AUTOVON were made through the console attendant associated with the "P" switch.

In-and-out dialing was permitted on the red switch. In addition to dialing other stations, a red station was able to dial stations on the "P" switch and to tandem through the "P" switch to other switching systems, including AUTOVON, on a routine basis. Incoming calls could also be dialed directly into red stations.

Since stations on the red switch might encounter vocoders in their connections with the outside world—such as those via AUTOVON—special transmission arrangements were incorporated in the system. The telephone transmitters in the station sets and the overall transmission path from the station set through the line circuit, the switching matrix, and the trunk circuit were essentially flat from 70 Hz to 3,500 Hz. Also, the crosstalk on any line or trunk within the system was below the audible level.

The performance of all No. 758 switching systems over the years has been uniformly excellent. Their flexibility in adapting to particular needs has been outstanding. However, since a single-stage crossbar switching network was used, the 758 switching systems occupied considerable space, especially the larger models. In the mid-1970s it became evident that the systems could be replaced soon with newer, space-saving arrangements with equivalent reliability and flexibility.

2.4.2 *Joint Chiefs of Staff Alerting Network (JCSAN)*

In late 1958, the military asked the Bell System to provide a new, fast arrangement for connecting, in a conference mode, the Joint-Chiefs-of-Staff National Military Command Center (NMCC) in the Pentagon with its ten worldwide Commander-in-Chief (CINC) locations. The arrangements then in existence were incompatible with military operations. The new arrangements replaced manual ones that required the NMCC Emergency-Action (EA) Officer in the Pentagon to call, via a four-wire, private-line network, each distant CINC PBX switchboard and then request connection to the desired party (usually the top area commander). Sometimes this operation took more than 25 minutes. The new automatic arrangement had to be capable of establishing a full conference at all times in no more than one minute.

Bell Laboratories undertook this task immediately and developed the Joint-Chiefs-of-Staff Alerting Network (JCSAN). In JCSAN, special signaling and switching units are permanently associated with each end of certain lines in the existing four-wire, private-line network normally used to connect the NMCC PBX with PBXs at the CINC locations for administrative operations. During an alert these lines (busy or idle) are automatically seized by the special JCSAN circuitry and "switched away" (preempted) from normal PBX terminations and reterminated in conference bridges at each end. Thus, conditions for a worldwide conference are quickly established. This preemptive arrangement obviated the need for new line facilities and permitted the lines used for alert/conferencing to be constantly voice checked by use in normal PBX service.

In mid-1960, the JCSAN system was put into service. By simple pushbutton operations, the NMCC controller could establish a worldwide conference alert in less than 5 seconds. At the Pentagon the NMCC controller could add to the conference hookup special telephones in important Washington locations—among these were the homes and offices of high military and government people. At distant locations, within the continental United States and such far-flung places as Hawaii, Alaska, Germany, and Panama, the CINC duty officer could add the Commander-in-Chief, his deputy, and others through a small, pushbutton-controlled switching system.

The code sending, receiving, and switching equipment used in the JCSAN system had to be extremely accurate in operation. A service-proven, selective-control arrangement was the heart of the system. It provided extremely accurate and fail-safe coding arrangements that, coupled with tone generators and receivers, provided the in-band, single-frequency (SF) signaling for JCSAN. The basic signaling plan for this system is shown in Fig. 12-20. Time-division, pulse-length coding arrangements were employed that were extremely effective, since the distortion or loss of a pulse due to imitation by speech or line disturbances would not result in a wrong order being executed by the switching equipment. To guard against any possible mutilation of codes by speech during the signaling interval, the voice path was cut off from the transmitting leg of the circuit when the coded signals were sent.

To ensure access to a distant CINC location by the Pentagon, a second inter-PBX private line to each location was equipped with JCSAN signaling and switching equipment. If an alert was originated on a primary line and a switch acknowledgment was not received from the remote end in a few seconds, the Pentagon equipment automatically transferred to the alternate line and proceeded with the alert on that line. When the distant switch-acknowledgment signal was transmitted to the Pentagon after the line was preempted from the distant PBX, the CINC duty-officer's console bell would ring to call attention to an alert call. When the duty officer went "off-hook," the remote equipment sent a distinct code to the Pentagon equipment indicating the call was answered. This completed the supervisory signaling and indicated to the Pentagon emergency-action

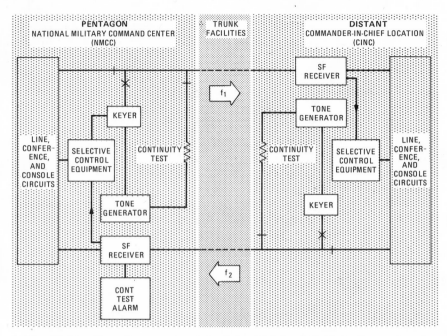

Fig. 12-20. Signaling system of the Joint-Chiefs-of-Staff alerting network.

officer that a CINC location was ready for a conference. The switching plan used to establish connections between the Pentagon and a remote CINC location is shown in Fig. 12-21.

The release of the network (restoration of the JCSAN lines to their proper PBX terminations for regular use after an alert) was controlled by the Pentagon NMCC emergency-action officer. Button operations on the console caused coded signals to be transmitted over the line. At the distant end, these codes caused the line to be switched back to its PBX appearance. Simultaneous with this switching operation, a tone pulse was sent to the Pentagon equipment. This tone pulse automatically restored the Pentagon end of the line to its regular PBX appearance. The line was then ready to be used for regular inter-PBX traffic.

An integrity check of the line facilities associated with the JCSAN system was made when they were idle. A continuous, single-frequency (SF) tone from the Pentagon was sent to the distant end of the circuit over the transmitting path. As long as this tone was received, an SF tone was transmitted from the distant end to the Pentagon over the other wire pair of the four-wire circuit. An interruption of tone for 10 seconds or more on either the send or receive path triggered an alarm at the Pentagon NMCC emergency-action console and in the Pentagon telephone test room. Thus, trouble could be quickly detected and steps could be taken to restore the circuit to normal. Because the lines on which JCSAN op-

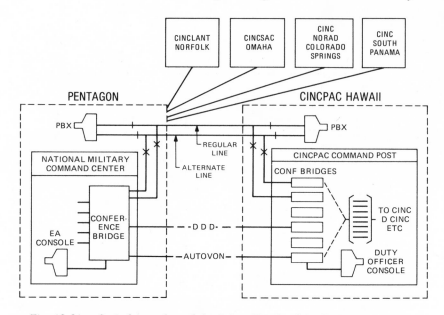

Fig. 12-21. Switching plan of the Joint-Chiefs-of-Staff alerting network.

erated were available for regular inter-PBX operation 95 percent of the time, there were frequent voice checks in addition to the idle-condition tone check. These checks were a valuable asset since marginal voice conditions could be quickly detected, further ensuring high-quality JCSAN operation.

JCSAN system operation was flexible. Particular CINC locations could be alerted individually, or some or all of the locations could be alerted simultaneously. Also, additional locations could be added after a conference had begun. Conversely, all locations could be released at once, or individual locations could be released as desired. If the distant end of the alerted line inadvertently went "on-hook" during a conference, signals were automatically sent to the Pentagon equipment, resulting in an instantaneous indication to the NMCC controller.

Standard arrangements permitted the Pentagon NMCC automatically to transfer control of one or all circuits to an alternate land-based center if the NMCC location became disabled. In addition, to provide as much emergency backup as possible in the JCSAN system, a service was provided so that the NMCC could be connected to the CINC duty-officer location via AUTOVON or the DDD network.

Test alerts were run daily to the distant CINC duty-officer consoles to ensure that all elements of the basic network were intact and ready for use whenever needed. The CINC duty officer could readily establish an immediate voice connection to the NMCC in the Pentagon. This procedure, called reverse preemption, permitted the CINC duty officer to preempt a busy or idle JCSAN trunk from the local PBX by a pushbutton operation that directed coded signals to the Pentagon. When the coded signals were received, the JCSAN equipment automatically preempted the trunk from the Pentagon PBX and connected the line directly to the NMCC console. As soon as this switching occurred, the Pentagon equipment sent an audible signal to the CINC location, confirming the receipt of the call. This signal continued until the NMCC controller answered. If the CINC duty officer did not get through on a reverse-preemption call, either the Pentagon could be signaled again on the same line or the alternate JCSAN line could be selected. Because of the emergency nature of the entire JCSAN operation, calls to either end were always answered immediately. The whole calling procedure (including signaling, switching, and controller answer) usually took only about 4 or 5 seconds.

The basic mission of the entire JCSAN system was to connect the NMCC with the distant-area Commander-in-Chief, his deputy, or a number of other key staff officers in their homes or offices. For this purpose, the distant CINC duty officer was provided with a No. 306 switching system that permitted an incoming JCSAN call to be connected with any of these people by special four-wire telephone sets, which were associated only with the No. 306 system. The number of special telephones varied according to local command requirements, but generally ranged from about 12 to 60. The No. 306 switching system was controlled from a special console by pushbutton operations. Lighted console buttons were used to indicate the status of all lines and trunks terminated at a CINC location. More than one simultaneous JCSAN call could be handled by the No. 306, and local lines could be transferred from one call to another if desired.

The majority of the lines associated with the No. 306 switching system were local, on-base, dc lines. However, if absent from the CINC location, the duty officer could rely on additional facilities to ensure participation in a JCSAN conference. A radio channel could be used if the CINC officer were in a car at the time of an alert. The local on-base PBX could also be used to connect the CINC officer with the duty-officer console. If a location was beyond the dc local-line range, a special long-distance line could be connected.

All local lines served by the CINC console were under constant automatic continuity checks. A discontinuity on one of these lines was immediately displayed on the duty-officer console.

To provide a permanent record of all conversations, a tape recorder was automatically connected to prime circuits whenever an alert was received. The duty officer controlled all other recorder operations with console buttons.

The JCSAN system proved highly successful. A second system, similar to JCSAN, was also installed and served as a conference network between the Air Force Operations Center in the Pentagon and far-flung major Air Force commands.

A number of changes kept the JCSAN system current with military operations. For example, the system was modified so that connections could be included from an airborne command post and a seaborne post if the Pentagon or its land-based alternate became inoperable for any reason.

2.4.3 The 10A Alerting System for NORAD

With the development of the intercontinental ballistic missile, the time available for defense or retaliation could be expressed in minutes. It was with this in mind that the 10A alerting system was designed for the North American Air Defense Command (NORAD) to alert very quickly its various regions, sectors, and weapon sites to an impending action. Known to the military as the NORAD attack warning system (NAWS), it was activated the instant NORAD was notified of a threat, thus utilizing the ensuing short time period during which NORAD headquarters determined a course of action.

The entire 10A system was arranged to operate over narrow-band telegraph facilities with visual and audible signals used to indicate alert conditions at every location. The 10A (NAWS) system greatly reduced the total time required to alert all locations deployed for the defense of the North American continent; previously, a voice alert was sent down the chain of command. The 10A system began operation in December 1965 and continued in service until its function was integrated into the NORAD voice-alert system in 1972.

A fundamental requirement of the 10A alerting system was that its operation be both reliable and secure. Reliability in the system was defined as the ability to transmit and receive signals successfully at any time, and security as the ability to reject false signals. When an alert was received, Air-Defense-Command (ADC) aircraft engines were started, and the aircraft were moved to takeoff positions. A false alert would be extremely costly, and, more importantly, it would seriously disrupt operations at an affected base.

As shown in Fig. 12-22, the overall 10A alerting network consisted of diverse, dual, full-duplex line facilities from NORAD headquarters to each region. Each region was connected by similar facilities to each sector in its command, and each sector was connected via a single facility to each of its weapon sites.

When the alerting system was activated, signal codes were transmitted from NORAD simultaneously to all regions over dual facilities, one code sender being connected to all transmit paths of one group of facilities, and a second code sender connected to all transmit paths of the second group

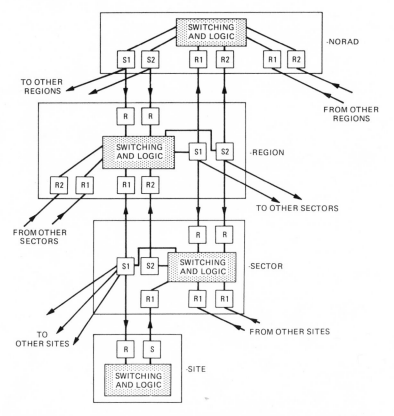

Fig. 12-22.   10A alerting system of the North American Air Defense
Command.

of facilities.   An alert signal consisted of a single code word that was repeated three times.   Two of the three words had to be detected at a region
within a fixed time over both paths before an alert could be registered.   At
the instant of recognition at a region, a console lamp and buzzer were
activated, and alert codes were automatically sent over dual facilities to
each sector location using the exact send and receive techniques that were
used between NORAD and its regions.   Upon successful registration at
the sector, the alert was similarly transmitted to its weapon sites, but only
over a single facility.

The signal codes required to control the 10A alerting system were as
follows:

1.   *Alert Code*—Originated by NORAD and its regions to alert all in-
     stallations in their respective defense areas.

2.   *Test-Alert Code*—Originated by NORAD and its regions.   It was used

periodically to test the entire system but resulted in different console indications than the alert code.

3. *Release Code*—Originated by NORAD or a region. A region could not release a NORAD-initiated alert or a test alert.

4. *Manual Acknowledgment Code*—Originated at a region, sector, or site location to indicate to the upstream location that the controller had noted the alert condition on a console.

5. *Continuity Code*—Automatically generated at NORAD on each set of line facilities and repeated to all locations every 6 seconds as a check of line integrity. Failure to recognize a continuity code word at any location in a 20-second period triggered alarms.

In addition to the dual-facility arrangement, a number of techniques were employed to ensure the accuracy of the entire system. These techniques are touched upon briefly in the following sections.

2.4.3.1 Code Structure. An important feature of the 10A system was the coding arrangement employed. It was the same two-out-of-five pulse-length code used successfully in other military systems such as SAGE and JCSAN, where a very high degree of accuracy was required.

2.4.3.2 Line Continuity Check. A continuity code word was transmitted from NORAD once every 6 seconds. It was received at each region and repeated back to NORAD and down to the sectors. Each sector repeated the code word back to its region and down to its sites. The site in turn repeated the code word back to the sector.

2.4.3.3 Local Test. Console controls at each location permitted the attendant at any time to determine if the local send and receive equipment was able to send and receive alert and test-alert signals. This was especially important for the alert signal, which naturally was rarely broadcast. The local test checked the alert logic, the switching circuit, and associated visual- and audio-signaling capability. Extreme design care was taken to ensure that senders were disconnected from line facilities while this test was in progress

2.4.3.4 Console Lamp Filament Test. This test permitted an attendant to verify that all lamps in a console were in working condition, thus eliminating any possible wrong action during normal operation.

2.4.3.5 Sender Transfer. If one of the two senders at the NORAD regions or sectors became faulty, the facilities connected to it were automatically transferred to the good sender, and the dual-facility operation continued. Alarms were provided to the telephone test room when a sender malfunctioned.

2.4.3.6 Console Button Operation. Two separate button operations were necessary to originate an alert or a test alert. This arrangement prevented false codes from being sent if one button was inadvertently operated.

These arrangements, in total, resulted in a system that had an overall reliability figure that was better than 99 percent, based upon periodic, extensive joint testing by the customer and the telephone companies. (The reliability figure refers to the number of stations successfully receiving the alert indication.) The time to send and receive an alert or test alert, assuming that action occurred after the second code word was registered at a location, was about 3.5 seconds per step or 10.5 seconds from NORAD to a site. This was a dramatic improvement over the previous method of voice alerting.

2.4.4 *Automatic Voice Network for the Department of Defense*

A new era in military communications began in April 1964 when the U.S. Army's Switched Circuit Automatic Network (SCAN) and the Air Force's North American Air Defense (NORAD) network were combined to form AUTOVON (Automatic Voice Network). AUTOVON, the first worldwide switched network for private telephone and data transmission, permitted almost instant contact between military bases that might be miles or oceans apart.

AUTOVON primarily served the Department of Defense and specified government activities, and handled voice, encrypted-voice, and data communications. It served a broad spectrum of traffic, ranging from critical command-and-control communications to everyday administrative calls.

AUTOVON was a global network, which was divided into two parts—the continental United States (CONUS) portion and the overseas portion. The users were spread over hundreds of government installations throughout the 50 states, Canada, Europe, the Pacific, and the Caribbean. The AUTOVON network of trunks and access lines was equal in circuit mileage to the entire Bell System toll network during the early 1950s.

The Defense Communications Agency (DCA), the agency responsible for planning, implementing, and managing AUTOVON, established three major objectives for the network in the following order of priority: ability to survive, quality of service, and economy. The Bell System, upon request, undertook a major role in assisting the DCA in the planning, implementation, and management of the CONUS portion of AUTOVON, and a minor role in the overseas portion. With the exception of Hawaii, the overseas portion of AUTOVON was government-owned and maintained. Bell Laboratories undertook huge development programs to give the military the best communications capabilities afforded by current technology.

The prime objective of AUTOVON communications—the ability to survive, even in the event of severe damage to communications facilities—received intensive study. The result was a new network concept,

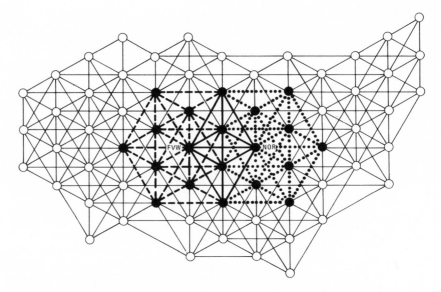

Fig. 12-23. Interconnected switching centers form a hexagonally ordered pattern of AUTOVON trunks across continental United States.

called "polygrid." Switching centers, each of equal importance, were located away from prime target zones. In contrast to the Bell System's Direct Distance Dialing (DDD) hierarchical network, where routing has to follow rigidly determined paths through the hierarchy, AUTOVON's polygrid network provided for alternate routing around disabled centers over any one of many independent paths.

The polygrid system actually consisted of two networks, one superimposed on the other. A basic network formed a geometrically ordered pattern of interconnected switching centers and provided for short- and medium-length connections. A long-haul network was superimposed on the basic network to minimize the number of trunk links required for long-haul calls. After investigating various geometrical patterns, an overlapping hexagonal pattern was selected for interconnecting switching centers in the basic network (see Fig. 12-23). This pattern allowed traffic routing that fully exploited all available transmission paths.

A characteristic of the hexagonal pattern was that it inherently formed home grids for each switching center serving a called party and provided a large number of alternate routes for calls arriving at any one of the surrounding centers. In Fig. 12-23, a typical home-grid arrangement for the center FVW is indicated by dashed lines. Note that each surrounding center is directly connected to FVW, as well as to most of the other surrounding centers. The home grid for NOR (heavy black lines) physically overlaps the home grid for FVW although it is functionally separate.

After the pattern of home grids was established, a pattern of long-haul

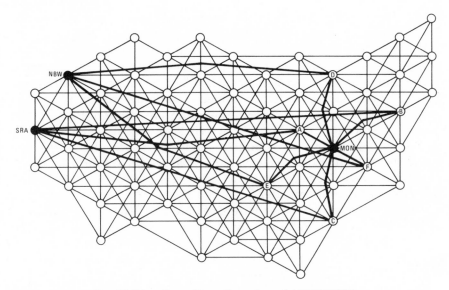

Fig. 12-24.   Overall routing plan of AUTOVON.

trunk groups radiating from an originating switching center toward distant centers was superimposed on the basic network, one center at a time, to determine what long-haul trunks should be provided.   The resulting arrangement permitted points to be reached beyond the practical range of the basic network.   For a call going beyond the practical range, the system was so designed that there would be at least three long-haul trunk groups from the originating center to switching centers in regions beyond the basic-network range.

A sophisticated routing plan was devised for operation with the polygrid network.   This plan included the automatic generation by the switching equipment of route-control digits that were transmitted from office to office as a prefix to the called address.   These route-control digits performed several functions: they exercised automatic control over alternate routing; they prevented "shuttle" (back and forth routing) and "ring-around-the-rosie" (a call returning to an office via another office); and they helped limit the number of trunk links that might be used on a call.

Some idea of the overall routing plan is indicated by the trunking involved on a call from the switching center at Santa Rosa, California (SRA) to the center at Monrovia, Maryland (MON) (see Fig. 12-24).   Three forward long-haul routes are available.   These routes go to centers (designated as A, B, and C) that are connected directly to MON.   If all three routes are in use and cannot be preempted, then a lateral route to NBW, for example, may be available.   In this case, three forward long-haul trunks are provided between NBW and three other centers (designated D, E, and

F) that connect directly with MON. If the direct routes from these points are busy and cannot be preempted, other paths can be seized.

To make AUTOVON possible, Bell Laboratories undertook extensive planning and development in such areas as switching, transmission, station equipment, PBXs, and signaling. Unlike the commercial, Bell System two-wire network, AUTOVON provided communications on a four-wire basis from the originating to the terminating subscriber or PBX. In the switching area alone, development of switching systems and end-to-end, four-wire communications required a sizable effort. Development began in 1959 with the redesign of the No. 5 crossbar system to handle four-wire communications. Development of a four-wire electronic switching system (ESS) followed very soon after.

Connections between four-wire lines are free from echo problems. Stations behind PBXs are practically all served by two-wire lines, however, and connections to these lines require echo suppression. A split echo suppressor—one that controls echoes from one end only—is activated on connections to two-wire access lines.

The primary function of AUTOVON was to complete command-and-control calls rapidly. As a secondary function, AUTOVON handled administrative traffic. The larger network required for administrative traffic permitted more diversified services with greater economy. However, the demand for immediate completion of command-and-control calls required that precedence be given to them. To meet this requirement, a new feature called multilevel precedence preemption was added to permit calls of higher precedence to preempt a trunk or line associated with a call of lower precedence. This feature provided five levels of precedence with four levels of preemption.

Special, 16-button *TOUCH-TONE*® telephones were designed to implement the precedence feature. These telephone sets were the first standard sets terminating both two-wire and four-wire lines on the same instrument. The ten basic buttons of a standard *TOUCH-TONE* set were retained. Two new buttons, marked with a "star" and an "A" were located to the left and right of the "O" or "operator" button, respectively. A new column of four red buttons was added to the right of the existing buttons; these were marked "FO," "F," "I," and "P," from top to bottom, designating Flash Override, Flash, Immediate, and Priority. The "P" button represented the lowest precedence level that could preempt only routine traffic, while "FO" represented the level that could preempt any other level of traffic.

Administrative calls were made on a routine precedence level. They required no special action. Authorized AUTOVON station users placed higher-precedence calls, however, by pressing the appropriate precedence-level button prior to dialing the call so that it would be "tagged" with the appropriate precedence level. Central-office control equipment searched for an idle trunk. If no circuits were available, a call of lower precedence was automatically preempted. A tagged access line or inter-office trunk, however, could not be preempted by a call of equal or lesser precedence. A signal lamp at the called telephone flashed at a distinctive rate to alert the user of a precedence call. A special "precedence" ringing signal also alerted the called party. A unique tone notified users when they were preempted by calls of higher precedence.

In addition to precedence preemption, AUTOVON could set up preset conferences automatically. The best implementation of this feature was at Colorado Springs, where it was employed by NORAD for conferences with its regional subcommands. At Colorado Springs, NORAD head-quarters was close enough to the AUTOVON switching center to make it economical to use an access line for each bridge port. Thus, it was possible to obtain individual switch-hook supervision, a most desirable feature in command-and-control operation.

Other AUTOVON features included (1) dual homing for selected sub-scribers to improve reliability and the ability to survive, (2) "hot-line" service that permitted the caller to be connected immediately with a de-sired party just by lifting the handset, and (3) traveling class indications, which were generated by the user or automatically generated by the switching center, with associated screening to select proper trunk grades, to separate general-use AUTOVON traffic from SAGE traffic, etc.

AUTOVON's requirements were a real challenge to the telephone in-dustry. The Bell System and the independent companies welcomed the challenge and collaborated to provide the most sophisticated communi-cations network possible at the time of its development.

2.5 Dedicated Military Networks

2.5.1 SAC's Primary Alerting System

"Peace is our Profession" is the slogan of the Strategic Air Command, whose retaliatory force is considered to be a major factor in ensuring peace in the world. To fulfill its mission adequately, SAC must be very alert, ready to go into action at a moment's notice.

Under "airborne alert" training procedures, a certain portion of SAC's bomber fleet is airborne at all times. However, a substantial portion of the bombers are on "ground-alert" status. These bombers are always ready to take off, to be airborne within minutes after receiving warning of an attack. After a warning is received, time is precious—every second cut from the interval between the first warning of attack to the command to "scramble" means more bombers in the air, ready to carry retaliatory action to the enemy with fewer vulnerable bombers on the ground.

A vital role in cutting this interval is played by communications—immediate word of imminent attack must be transmitted to all the far-flung

SAC bases. SAC in 1958 asked the Bell System to furnish ready-to-use communications arrangements, with emphasis on voice communications, for broadcasting "alert" announcements to all SAC bases.

Accordingly, the primary alerting system was developed. This was a permanently assembled network, furnished as a Bell System service. Specially designed signaling and alarm arrangements were incorporated to ensure the necessary reliability and continuity. A.T.&T., Western Electric, and Bell Laboratories worked with the customary teamwork of an integrated system to plan, design, manufacture, and put the alerting system into service in less than one year.

The Air Force had two primary requirements: (1) the network must always be immediately available to broadcast alerts; and (2) the network must be reliable. To provide the desired availability, the system used a so-called "hot-line" arrangement. In this way, the voice path was always available directly from a controller to all bases with no intermediate switching required.

A brief description of SAC's geographical organization might clarify the function of the alerting system. SAC headquarters, the nucleus of the command, is at Offutt Air Force Base, Omaha, Nebraska. Major subordinate commands within the continental United States consist of three numbered Air Force (NAF) bases and a missile division. These NAF bases exercise authority and control over all SAC units within three geographical areas covering the eastern, central, and western portions of the United States. More than 60 SAC bomber units are located within these three areas.

As a step in providing the required reliability, system engineers employed dual, four-wire lines throughout the network. This arrangement is illustrated in the simplified layout of the network shown in Fig. 12-25. All outgoing lines were bridged at SAC headquarters. They radiated outward to the NAF headquarters. The incoming line from SAC was permanently connected to other lines going out to its associated bases. Thus, there were two separate lines to each Air Force base, using separate routes and separate equipment; one line went directly from SAC headquarters and one went via the NAF headquarters. (For reasons of economy, overseas bases did not, in all cases, have direct circuits from SAC headquarters, although they could be reached by two alert circuits.) Each line also appeared in a console at headquarters. It was possible to hold a conversation on a selected line without causing interference on any other line.

As a further measure to ensure reliability, all lines, including the circuits on each base, were under continuous electrical supervision with suitable alarms at the originating headquarters end of each circuit. This measure provided SAC with an "up-to-the-second" status check on each circuit.

Because the continuity of all circuits had to be checked, even while they

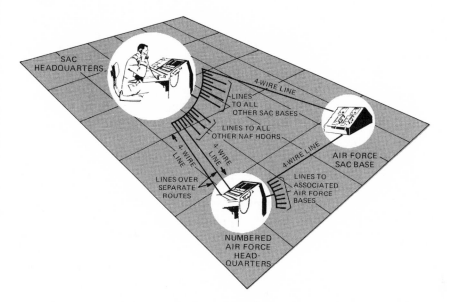

Fig. 12-25.   Primary alerting system of the Strategic Air Command.

were in use, a frequency-sharing, or "slot," signaling technique was employed.   This technique required that a 250-cycle wide band be derived
in the normal speech channel.   All signals were transmitted in this 250-
cycle slot.   The basic talking and signaling path for all circuits is outlined
in the diagram of Fig. 12-26.   As indicated, band-rejection filters isolated
all telephones and loudspeakers connected to the voice circuits.   These
filters prevented listeners from hearing the signaling tones and kept voice
currents from interfering with signaling.

All signals were transmitted over the voice circuits by carrier telegraph
terminals that operated at voice frequencies.   Different frequencies were
used for signaling in opposite directions to prevent confusion in the signaling system if the two sides of a four-wire circuit crossed each other.

The signals passed through the signaling terminals were simple and
highly redundant.   These characteristics helped ensure the reliability of
the system, even under adverse conditions.   The signals included those
for testing circuit continuity in both directions, for sending alerts to the
bases and acknowledgment signals to headquarters, and for sending a call
signal to headquarters for non-alert calls.

Circuit continuity was checked by transmitting a short tone pulse every
three seconds on the "send pair" of the four-wire circuit.   Each Air Force
base had an electronic pulse repeater that returned an answering pulse
at a lower frequency to headquarters on the "receive pair" of the circuit.
The originating end of each circuit was equipped with a receiving circuit

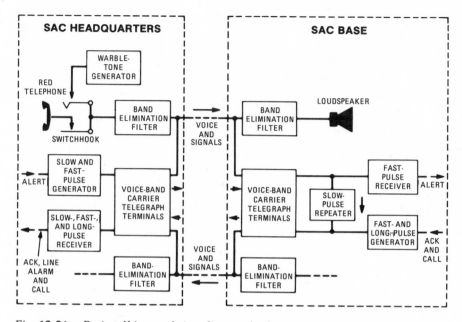

Fig. 12-26.   Basic talking and signaling paths for circuits of the alerting system.

synchronized with the pulse-generator circuit, so that only pulses received at the correct time were accepted as valid reply pulses.   These receivers were arranged to send alarms to both Air Force and Operating Telephone Company personnel if the reply pulses failed to arrive after 10 seconds, or if too many false pulses were received.

Circuits on the Air Force base were also checked for continuity by a flow of direct current.   If this current was interrupted, the tone pulses normally returned to headquarters were blocked.   This caused the circuit to send an alarm.

The alerting and acknowledgment signals, which were sent in opposite directions, were 100-millisecond (ms) pulses, transmitted at the rate of five per second for 3 seconds.   The electronic, slow-pulse repeaters at the bases prevented retransmission of these pulses.

A call signal of about 1 second was used for calling headquarters from the bases.   This call signal and the acknowledgment signals were automatically timed and were produced by momentarily operating the proper key.

All alerts were initiated and all circuit alarms and individual acknowledgments were indicated on specially designed consoles at SAC and NAF headquarters.   The senior controller's console shown in Fig. 12-27 was equipped with a red telephone for alerts and a gray telephone for point-to-point traffic.   All other consoles, at both the headquarters and

Fig. 12-27. Senior controller at SAC underground headquarters in Omaha, Nebraska, places a test call over the "red phone" of the primary alerting system.

the associated bases, had only gray telephones. In addition to the common keys and lamps for alerting and testing, the consoles had individual "appearances" for each line. Each line appearance consisted of two lamps and an illuminated, nonlocking, pushbutton key. The red lamp, which was at the bottom of the line appearance, indicated the status of a particular circuit. If illuminated, it indicated the circuit was in trouble. The pushbutton key above the red lamp was used to select individual lines for point-to-point traffic, which will be described later. The amber lamp above the pushbutton was the acknowledgment lamp. Since these might be illuminated at the same time, neon lamps were used for both the status (red) and acknowledgment (amber) indicators to minimize instantaneous current drain and reduce heat dissipation.

At the Air Force bases each line terminated in a loudspeaker that was always ready to receive alerts, and in a telephone set for point-to-point traffic. There was an "acknowledge" button used to return acknowledgment signals when requested, and a "call" button for ringing headquarters. The base units were suitably packaged and conveniently mounted by the Bell System at each base in a special console, known as the combat wing console. In the 1970s, the primary-alerting-system terminals were being incorporated in new main operating base consoles that were both designed and furnished as a service by the Bell System.

The primary alerting system was very simple to operate. To initiate an alert from the underground SAC command post at Offutt Air Force Base, the senior controller merely picked up the special red telephone and pressed the "alert" button on the alerting console. As a result, both an alerting tone and an alerting signal were transmitted simultaneously over both paths to each base. The alerting tone consisted of alternate spurts of tones at 900- and 1400-Hz, transmitted as long as the alert button was operated. This alerting tone was received on the loudspeakers at all Air Force bases. It served as a warning that an alert announcement was coming. The alerting signal lit the acknowledgment lamps in the consoles at all headquarters and disconnected any point-to-point traffic that might be on the lines at the time. After the voice-alert message had been broadcast, all base controllers were asked to acknowledge receipt of the message by pressing the "acknowledge" button. This resulted in acknowledgment signals being transmitted simultaneously to SAC and NAF headquarters. These signals extinguished the individual acknowledgment lamps. The system was arranged so that a controller at NAF headquarters might also broadcast alerts, including the alert tone and signal, and the acknowledgments, to the associated bases in the same manner.

In the primary alerting system when an alert was not in progress, an individual line could be used for point-to-point traffic between controllers. A headquarters controller, using the gray telephone handset associated with the console, could select any desired line merely by pressing a non-locking pushbutton on the console and calling in the selected remote point by voice. Conversely, a base controller could call headquarters by operating a pushbutton that transmitted a call signal to headquarters. On receipt of this call signal at headquarters, the associated line lamp flashed at all console positions, and an audible signal sounded. When the call was answered at one of the console positions by a controller operating the "line" key, the lamp fluttered at the position, indicating that this was the connected line. At all other positions, the lamp for this line was continually lit.

This connection could be released either by selecting another line or by momentarily operating the common "release" key. If a point-to-point call was in progress at a time an alert was to be transmitted, operation of the alert key immediately disconnected it.

The designers of the primary alerting system made special efforts to assure continuous service and to permit rapid and easy detection of troubles if they occurred. They duplicated equipment in all critical parts of the system and provided adequate alarms. For example, a voice alert could be broadcast from either one of two completely separate, originating red telephone sets with their associated equipment. The designers provided duplicate sending circuits, including amplifiers and signal-sending units. The output was continuously monitored by feeding back one leg of the output bridge to a monitoring receiver. If a single pulse of the alerting signal was missed, an alarm sounded, and the alternate sending circuit, which was also continuously monitored, automatically began operation to replace the regular circuit.

In 1977, seventeen years after cutover, the primary alerting system was still in service, with only minor additions and changes. All the reports from SAC, as well as from the Operating Telephone Companies who provided and maintained the system, indicated that the system was furnishing excellent service. SAC rated the system's overall performance at 99.9 percent.

The primary alerting system is probably a prime example of how the integrated Bell System team, in this case supported by the systems-engineering experience of Bell Laboratories, furnished communications that contributed significantly to the deterrent capacity of SAC.

2.5.2 SS 303 – "Green Pine"

The Bell System also worked with SAC on a system for communicating with bomber aircraft while they were flying through the northern latitudes of the western hemisphere. This No. 303 switching system, implemented in 1962 and referred to as "Green Pine" by SAC, permitted SAC controllers to communicate with their aircraft via remote UHF radio terminals.

Bell Laboratories, under Western Electric contract, prepared engineering criteria for the UHF radio-site survey team, participated in the evaluation of the test data, and prepared site- and antenna-layout designs. Western Electric installed amplifiers and antennas at the 14 SAC remote UHF stations. It also provided and installed the interface and control terminals associated with these radios.

Bell Laboratories devised the overall No. 303 system, including switching, signaling, conferencing, and transmission. The system was patterned after the primary alerting system, but with push-to-talk operation, and included conferencing arrangements. The system was manually controlled by attendants at three locations in the continental United States. SAC controllers, after being connected to one or more UHF radios, could exercise control of the distant radios and communicate directly with aircraft in the remote reaches of the far north.

2.5.3 No. 304 Conference Switching System for NASA

The National Aeronautics and Space Administration (NASA) in June 1962 asked the Bell System to develop a conference switching system to serve the control center of the agency's global satellite-tracking networks.

As a result of this request and a similar one made later by the Air Force, Bell Laboratories developed the No. 304 switching system.

NASA's No. 304 equipment was put into service in October 1963 as the central nervous system of its satellite-communications and tracking networks. Through this switching system passed messages between station operators all over the world who monitored and controlled NASA spacecraft, both manned and unmanned. At the touch of a button the system was connected instantly to foreign project-support stations such as Goonhilly Downs, England, Plemeur Bodou, France, Fucino, Italy, and Woomera, Australia.

In addition to supporting space launches from both coasts, the No. 304 switching system handled daily voice, data, and facsimile traffic from Syncom, Relay, TIROS, and all deep-space probes. It was also used in the Gemini and Apollo lunar missions.

The NASA request was for a system capable of handling a relatively large number of conferences simultaneously, each conference accommodating a large number of parties and offering complete flexibility of assignment. This could have been done with conventional bridging arrangements, but the large number of crosspoints and associated switching needed to provide the desired flexibility would have resulted in a most uneconomical system.

A simple, direct way of conferencing large numbers of four-wire lines had been designed in the late 1950s by Bell Laboratories and Western Electric, and used at the Launch Complex at Point Arguello, California. In that system, all transmitting circuits were connected through isolation resistors to the input of a bus amplifier, and all receiving circuits were connected through isolation resistors to the output of the same amplifier, as shown in Fig. 12-28. With the input and output impedances of the bus amplifier sufficiently low compared to the impedance of the transmitting and receiving circuits, the lines could be connected and disconnected with no idle-circuit termination and with no adverse effect on the transmission bus levels. This arrangement performed well at Point Arguello where all circuits were relatively short-haul circuits.

The NASA network introduced a problem which required a bit more ingenuity. Many of the NASA circuits were extremely long-haul circuits, stretching around the world. In busbar conferencing there is a return path to the talkers through the bus amplifier. On long circuits, the delay from the time the talkers speak until they hear their own voices in the receiving circuits creates an undesirable echo effect. This disadvantage could have been overcome in a variety of ways, but to achieve the minimum desirable degree of cancellation (40 dB), changes greater than one percent in amplitude or 0.5 degree in phase could not be tolerated. This ruled out active elements such as amplifiers, which are subject to amplitude and/or phase drift.

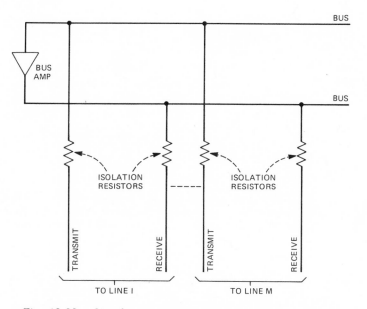

Fig. 12-28. Simple arrangement for isolating transmission paths for use on relatively short circuits.

Good stability was achieved by employing resistors, which are passive elements, for each cancellation and putting the necessary amplification in the line circuit beyond the critical cancellation point (see Fig. 12-29). This design had the added advantage that line amplifiers were required only on long-haul lines and only once per line, regardless of the number of links involved. Short-haul lines (those not requiring echo protection) required only one pair of common amplifiers per link. This arrangement was adopted for use in the No. 304 switching system and is shown in Fig. 12-30.

In the plan adopted, it was possible to connect four different types of lines simultaneously to any conference bus. The first type consisted of those lines needing no echo protection: public-address system inputs, loudspeaker inputs, recorder inputs, and all four-wire lines with round-trip delay shorter than 20 ms. These circuits were connected through isolation resistors to the input and output of the transmit and receive amplifiers, respectively, which were, in turn, connected to the low-impedance transmission bus.

The second type of line was the four-wire line with a round-trip delay of between 20 and 100 ms. It was connected to the bus through line amplifiers and isolation resistors. The phase inverter, low-impedance bus, and isolation resistors made up an all-passive-resistive circuit, which resulted in a cancellation voltage that was very stable and was not subject to any of the drift problems encountered with active circuits.

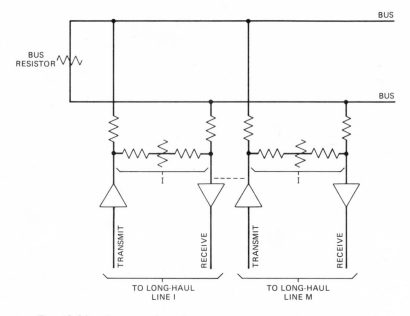

Fig. 12-29.   Improved conferencing system to eliminate echo.

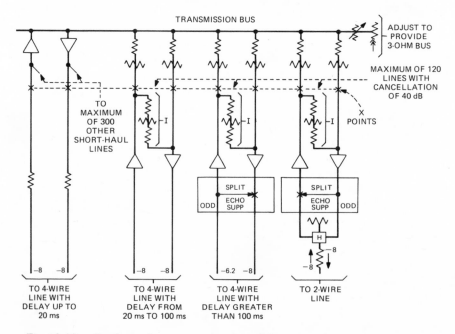

Fig. 12-30.   Conferencing system developed for use in short-haul transmission lines.

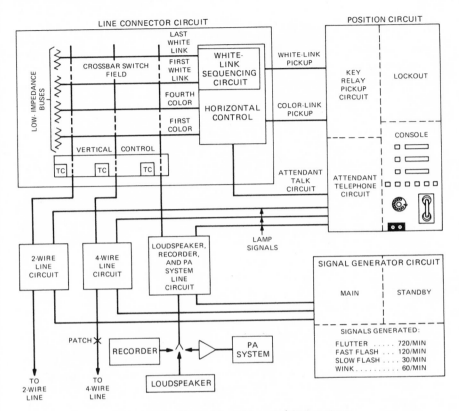

Fig. 12-31.   Basic No. 304 switching system.

The four-wire line with a round-trip delay greater than 100 ms was the third type of line.   Each of these long-delay lines was connected to the bus through a split echo suppressor, line amplifiers, and isolation resistors. The echo protection afforded by phase inversion was not always sufficient for this type of line, so the echo suppressor was provided as an option to increase the protection if it was required.   NASA never used the echo suppressors on their four-wire circuits.

The fourth type of line was the two-wire line.   Each two-wire line was connected to the transmission bus through a hybrid, a split echo suppressor, line amplifiers, and isolation resistors.   The echo suppressor provided suppression for the transmission bus by preventing any speech that was going out on the transmit loop from returning through the hybrid coil to the receive loop.   The phase-inversion circuit provided the distant talker with echo suppression in the same way it did for the medium-delay four-wire line.

The basic No. 304 switching system plan is shown in Fig. 12-31.   A pushbutton console controlled the establishment of connections through a crossbar switch field. In the line connector, lines were associated with verticals of the switch field, and conferences, or links, with horizontals. Each link contained a low-impedance transmission bus that permitted many lines to be bridged simultaneously with no appreciable transmission loss. Multiple consoles were optional; lockout circuits were provided to prevent interferences between positions and avoid false or double connections. By connecting loudspeakers, recorders, and public-address systems to verticals, in the same manner that lines were connected, they could be associated with any conference.

Continuous identification of the lines connected to each of the first four links, which were usually used for the most important conferences, was furnished by illuminating the line lamp with one of four colors. Access to these links was achieved by operating corresponding link-select buttons. The remaining links were accessed through a sequencing circuit that automatically selected the next idle link whenever a new conference began or the attendant answered an incoming call.

The No. 304 system handled as many simultaneous conferences as the number of links provided in the system. Each conference might include a practically unlimited number of conferees located practically anywhere on earth. It could be controlled by a single attendant from a pushbutton console, but additional consoles with attendants could be used if traffic warranted.

While the No. 304 system was originally designed for use by NASA, it was put into service for many of the major command-and-control locations in all parts of the world. These included the main headquarters of the Air Force, Army, and Navy, the National Military Command Center and its alternate, many of the unified and specified command centers in farflung places like Hawaii and Germany, and in numerous nonmilitary applications.

2.6 Summary

In the foregoing descriptions and discussions, the various systems have been treated essentially as isolated entities. So far as the SAGE and FAA systems are concerned, that is substantially the way they have operated. Each control center—DC or NCC in SAGE, ARTCC in FAA—operates with its own satellite radar, radio, and voice terminals. Communications via dedicated lines and DDD with other centers have also been included, but there is no other integration. In more recent years, the SAGE system has used AUTOVON to reduce costs and to enhance backup capabilities.

The other systems were designed primarily to meet the specific needs of the particular customer or customers who requested them. However, transmission arrangements and interfaces were generally designed in accordance with normal Bell System operation. Thus, the Bell System was in an excellent position to respond when the Department of Defense issued a directive in 1971 specifying that communications techniques be implemented to permit the simultaneous transmission of voice alerts to substantially all field forces. The directive also specified that communications be provided to enable the National Command Authority and the Joint Chiefs to confer with any commander faced with a crisis situation anywhere in the world.

Because of the standard nature of the various system designs, it was relatively easy to make interconnection arrangements available. This was usually accomplished expeditiously without additional research and development, and with only a minimum of interfacing circuit design. Figure 12-32 outlines the systems involved in establishing either a worldwide alert or the conference arrangements for handling a crisis management situation anywhere in the world. This is truly an integrated worldwide conference and alerting system.

The emergency-action officer seated at a console in the National Military Command Center in the Pentagon could set up an alert or a conference that included all or any combination of the locations indicated in Fig. 12-30. To illustrate, let us trace the setup of a world-wide alert, indicating the procedure involved and the interconnecting systems employed.

The emergency-action officer could initiate an all-inclusive world-wide alert via the JCSAN system. As indicated, each of the JCSAN circuits terminates in a No. 306 system at the remote, unified and specified service command locations. The duty officer, at each of these locations upon receipt of authentic information, could immediately extend the alert to lower echelons of command. While this "downstream" action proceeds, the emergency-action officer could add the several airborne command posts to the conference. Also, the officer could add all local, important decision-making people to the alert bridge by dedicated lines to their homes or offices, or via DDD or AUTOVON.

At the Omaha, Nebraska headquarters of SAC, the alert could be passed to the lower echelons of command via the primary alerting system. At the Colorado Springs headquarters of NORAD, the alert could be passed to the regions and bases via the AUTOVON automatic conference bridges. At the other major commander-in-chief locations, CINCLANT, CINCPAC, and CINCEUR, the alert could be sent to the lower echelons via the No. 306 systems to the No. 304 systems. In each case, the component commands are reached via existing communications terminating in the No. 304 systems. The time required to assemble most parties in this worldwide conference would rarely exceed one minute. Parties reached via AUTOVON during heavy traffic periods could extend this interval to two minutes. Similar arrangements, on a somewhat reduced scale, are also available to set up worldwide encrypted conferences. A substantial number of these facilities and interconnection systems were furnished

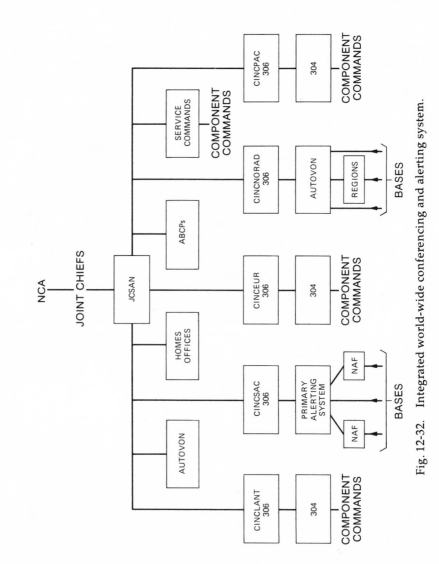

Fig. 12-32.   Integrated world-wide conferencing and alerting system.

by the Bell System. The encryption terminals were, in all cases, furnished by the government.

An attempt has been made in this chapter to provide a representative overview of the special services furnished by the Bell System to the civil and military government. Many services have not been discussed, but the aim has been to give an understanding of the magnitude of these communications systems and the reliability and speed of operation that have been designed into them. Such systems have been a major factor in the deterrent military power of the United States.

Chapter 13

Military Systems Engineering and Research

The application of scientific methods for solving the problems of complex tele-phone systems made Bell Laboratories and other Bell System companies pioneers in systems engineering. After World War II, military weapons grew enormously in size and complexity and in the use of electronics as engineers sought solutions to new defense problems with radars, computers, guided missiles, and advanced communications techniques. These solutions were integrated into systems that approach the potential for automatic, pushbutton warfare.

It was only natural that the Bell System and Bell Laboratories were called upon to apply their systems-engineering background to problems of national defense. The Bell System's work ranged from short system studies to responsibility for complete weapon systems. Some of these systems tasks are described below in Section I (see also Chapters 7, 8, and 11). Another area where Bell Laboratories' expertise contributed significantly to postwar systems was in research and advanced development. One of the most noteworthy examples of this type of pioneering work was the early application of the transistor, invented at Bell Laboratories in 1947. The system planners in the military services recognized the potential impact of this device and supported Bell Laboratories fundamental research and early military application of transistors. Out of this exploratory effort came TRADIC, the first all-solid-state computer. This, and other examples of research and advanced development, were the starting points for major developments undertaken by Bell Laboratories and other companies.

I. MILITARY SYSTEMS ENGINEERING

Although Bell Laboratories was developing various radio communi-cations and sound-equipment systems for the military in the early 1930s, specific involvement with military systems engineering began in 1937 when Bell Labs was asked by the Navy to undertake developments in the field of radar. Rapidly, Bell Labs responsibilities broadened to include

Principal authors: C. A. Warren, B. McMillan, and B. D. Holbrook the design of radar systems for ships, aircraft, and mobile land units, and, by the end of World War II, full responsibility for the design of gun-laying systems comprised of radars and computers.

As in the history of most branches of engineering, it is not easy to determine the particular moment that systems engineering emerged as a discipline or process distinct from development or design for manufacture. In fact, in all of its military projects, Bell Labs has worked with customers to define their needs as completely as possible and to arrive at agreement on objectives. From 1937 to the Safeguard System of 1968, such objectives have grown enormously in scope and complexity. Gradually, the process of defining objectives and of analyzing and evaluating alternative plans for their accomplishment has become an activity separately identified as systems engineering.

There are milestones along this evolutionary path. An early and important one was the study in 1945 of an antiaircraft guided missile system (see Chapter 7). Commissioned by the Army, this study addressed the problem of how to defend ground installations against the high-altitude, high-speed, maneuvering bombers known to be on the drawing boards of potentially hostile nations at that time. The study's report outlined the design of an antiaircraft guided missile system, known originally as Nike (the Greek goddess of victory), and later as Nike-Ajax to distinguish it from its descendants, Nike-Hercules, Nike-Zeus, and Nike-X.

The basic finding of the antiaircraft guided missile study was that it appeared feasible to build an antiaircraft guided-missile system that would be effective against maneuvering bombers flying at near-sonic speeds and at high altitude. The proposed system embodied the central, and at the time most controversial, conclusion of the study: the Nike-Ajax system would be a command-guidance system—radars on the ground would track both attacker (the bomber) and defender (the Nike missile); data from both radars would then be combined in a computer that would issue steering orders to the defender, coded into the pulses of the missile-tracking radar. There were several reasons for the choice of a command-guidance system. One was economy, since the primary computer was not expended with the missile. The overriding reason was that the trajectory of each missile could easily be controlled to optimize the missile's effectiveness. In this way, both accuracy and economy of propulsion (a critical issue in the early days of rocketry) were achieved. Also, the effective field-of-fire of a missile of a given weight was greatly expanded compared to that achieved by using a simpler control system that relied on stereotyped trajectories.

The 1945 antiaircraft guided missile study was a milestone in systems engineering precisely because it was comprehensive enough to address a *whole* system—propulsion, aerodynamic control, steering strategy, warhead design, sensors and computers—to find an economical and effective design. In fact, almost exactly half of the Nike-Ajax report was devoted to the missile, to its propulsion, drag, and control characteristics, and to the design of the warhead. The analyses demonstrated the great economies that result from the use of optimal (low-drag) trajectories. This was a surprising emphasis for a report written by communications engineers and mathematicians, but if was essential to the final success of the project. For the later analyses of aerodynamics and propulsion, Bell Laboratories worked with the Douglas Aircraft Company. The whole team comprised of Western Electric, Bell Laboratories, and Douglas Aircraft was engaged by the Army to develop the system. Not only was Nike-Ajax, when it flew four years later, the first truly maneuverable, supersonic air vehicle, it was also the first air vehicle of any sort designed by a subcontractor to a communications company.

Technical analyses of the kind that characterized the 1945 Nike-Ajax study were continued throughout the development program, and the results were refined in detail and in precision as more data became available. As time passed, new defense threats were examined. Further studies led first to Nike-Hercules, an antiaircraft system that was also developed and deployed, and then to Nike-Zeus, an experimental system, which demonstrated that a guided missile could intercept and destroy an attacking ballistic missile.

Perhaps as a result of the fact that the Nike-Ajax study had stimulated new and successful development, Bell Labs and Western Electric began in the 1950s to receive requests for other kinds of study. Strategic bombing studies were done with the Sandia Corporation for the Air Force. Studies, such as the one for the Mark 65 program (see Chapter 11), were completed for the Navy on the problem of defending ships or task forces against air attack. Problems in air-to-air combat were analyzed, and studies of air defense measures for the United States and Canada continued into the early 1960s. These could all be called planning studies, but most of them were not directed at defining a development program to be followed by Bell Labs and Western Electric. Rather, they were commissioned by the military services to help them identify important technical problems and guide their own development programs.

In 1958 a new vice presidential area, Military Systems Engineering, was organized at Bell Labs. It assumed responsibility for the kind of military-systems studies just outlined, as well as for continuing system studies in support of military development programs in progress at Bell Labs— specifically, programs in air defense, the antimissile program, and communications programs for the military. The Military Systems Engineering organization continued in existence until 1970. Its staff ranged in number from 200 to 400 technical professionals. Although the organization also carried a varying load of design and development projects, the number of professionals engaged in engineering studies was generally more than half the total.

Two other milestones in the evolution of military systems engineering, both of them studies, merit mention. These studies are both similar to and different from the antiaircraft guided missile study of 1945. The first was the Nike-X systems study made in 1963 that, in its general features, resembled the Nike-Ajax study of 1945. Its premise was that the United States faced a threat in the form of a coordinated attack by many ballistic missiles accompanied by decoys and other devices for creating confusion. And the study's design concepts were based on new technology—solid-state devices that allowed the engineer to think in terms of economical phased-array antennas, powerful digital computers, and greatly improved rocketry. A careful balancing of many technical elements led to the concept of the Nike-X system. Specifically, its dramatically new features were (1) phased-array radars, each tracking many attackers and interceptors simultaneously, (2) large digital computers, performing all the functions of data handling, tracking, and control, and (3) a new missile, Sprint, designed to accelerate more abruptly, to travel faster in the atmosphere, and to maneuver more sharply than any guided missile had ever done before.

Consistent with the broader range of problems it addressed, the Nike-X systems study represented perhaps ten times as much technical effort as the Nike-Ajax study. Much more effort than this can be counted if the background of prior studies at Bell Labs were included that were drawn on for data.

Western Electric and Bell Laboratories were awarded contracts to develop an experimental system that was based on the Nike-X study. This system was built and tested on Kwajalein Atoll between 1970 and 1976.

During the development of the Nike-X system, Bell Labs conducted, at the government's request, a sequence of analyses to determine how the elements of the system could be used to defend various kinds of target complexes—military and civil—in the United States. Sample deployments and deployment schedules were postulated and analyzed for cost, and their defensive capabilities were evaluated against postulated attacks of differing kinds and intensities. Gradually, Bell Labs engineers and their counterparts in the government developed a body of knowledge about the capabilities and limitations of a weapons system for defense against ballistic missiles. Based on this knowledge, the Secretary of Defense established criteria for a study to determine exactly what the government might deploy as a defense system. This resulted in the second milestone in the evolution of military systems engineering, the I-67 Study, so named because it was the first study in 1967, following a sequence of studies conducted in 1966. Based in large part on information already accumulated, this study defined a deployment and demonstrated that it met the objectives set forth by the Secretary of Defense. The study established the basis for a system that, in September 1967, the Secretary announced would be deployed.

The I-67 study, though far from unique, offered an interesting contrast to the Nike-Ajax and Nike-X studies. There was little reference to specific technology or technological problems—these had all been covered in the Nike-X study and in subsequent refinements. The emphasis in I-67 was on total cost and on total effectiveness of the deployed system.

It is a long way, technically, from determining the best frequency for a Nike-X radar or the acceleration required by a Sprint missile to estimating the global effectiveness of a defense system. In the I-67 study, more than a thousand man-years of effort went into the many systems engineering tasks required.

An antiballistic missile system, later called Safeguard, was designed and installed. Western Electric and Bell Labs were the prime contractors. The Nike-X test program was subsumed under the test program for the Safeguard system. By 1970, much of the effort of the Bell Labs Military Systems Engineering organization was committed to supporting the Nike-X/Safeguard program. Engineers committed to this effort were transferred to the organization responsible for Safeguard development, which was, in turn, named the Military Systems area. As other engineers completed their military studies, they were transferred to Bell System work, and the Military Systems Engineering area was disbanded.

Although Bell Labs effort for the government diminished from the level of the period 1955 to 1975, its remaining effort was characterized by a strong emphasis on systems engineering and systems analysis, defining, with the customers, the jobs that need to be done and the best ways to do them.

II. RESEARCH AND EXPLORATORY DEVELOPMENT

2.1. Military Transistor Development

Quick to recognize the potential importance of the transistor to future military weapons, the military services made the decision to support research and fundamental development of the transistor at Bell Laboratories, particularly in those aspects that had military significance. This support began with a small contract with Western Electric-Bell Laboratories in June 1949, which was enlarged and later extended through 1958. During this period, approximately $35 million was spent by Bell Laboratories on device development and physical research on materials. Of this amount, the military services provided $8.5 million, or about 25 percent.

On June 23, 1948, at a preview of the public announcement of the transistor, which was held for military-service representatives, the question of security classification was raised by Bell Laboratories. It was decided not to impose a secrecy clamp on the transistor. This decision made it possible for American scientists and industry to push forward freely and unhampered in the development and manufacture of transistors in all their various forms.

One of the important contributions, which resulted from joint Bell System and military support of early transistor research and development, was symposia and written lecture material for the military and its industry representatives. The first such symposium was conducted at Bell Laboratories, Murray Hill, New Jersey, on September 17 through September 21, 1951. Twenty-five lectures and demonstrations were presented by 16 members of the technical staff. The symposium was attended by 121 members of the military services, 41 university people, and 139 representatives of industry. In November 1951, 5,500 copies of a 792-page book on transistors were published and distributed to the military services. This was the first comprehensive publication of material of this nature. It is believed that the book stimulated the marked upsurge starting in 1952 of transistor development for military applications by industry. The book enabled all Bell System patent licensees to get into the military contracting business quickly and soundly. Later, two symposia, which were held in 1956 for licensees and the military, reported in detailed documents the complete diffusion technology developed by Bell System funding. These documents, both those funded by the services and those funded by the Bell System, constituted a very important part of the information benefits accruing to the Services and greatly aided their overall program throughout the country. A summary of some of the development activities carried out as part of the joint service contracts follows.

Initial work in the period from June 1949 to May 1951 was directed toward exploring circuit applications for point-contact transistors in a proposed military application. Specifically, this work was aimed at proving the feasibility of miniature, standardized, reliable, functional, plug-in transistor packages to perform all the critical operations of the military AN/TSQ-1 data set, which used 370 vacuum tubes. The circuit packages developed were: regenerative pulse amplifiers, diode logic gates, one-bit registers, delay pulse amplifier, binary counter, photocell package, and interstage steering packages

System feasibility of these transistor packages was proved by having them perform the majority of the 15 functions of the encoder, adder, modulator, and program generator. Although these transistor circuits were rudimentary compared to today's highly integrated circuit functions, they did show, in that early period, reductions of 4 to 1 in volume and of 8 to 1 in power compared to the AN/TSQ-1 system with its vacuum tubes. The 1689 point-contact-encased transistor (developed with Bell System funds) used in the circuit packages was shown, on the basis of accelerated life tests, to have a lifetime of 70,000 hours. It was also shown to be capable of withstanding a shock of 20,000g and taking 20g over 200 to 2,000 Hz with no detectable modulation in excess of noise. The first two years of work were covered in eight reports, representing the first published work of this nature on early transistor applications.

The second and third contracts with the joint military services covered the period from May 1951 to 1958. Where the first contract did not call for device development, the tasks in these contracts primarily called for device development and characterization. In the belief that the overall military program could be aided by developing devices to the requirements of specific military systems, it was agreed with the services to select those devices that satisfied the general task requirements and that, at the same time, were needed for specific systems development. Some 12 prototype devices were developed during this period for application in military systems being worked on at Bell Laboratories and outside the company. Development of these devices for specific tasks always followed fundamental Bell System research or development that established real possibilities.

As the transistor technology advanced over the eight years of these contracts, there was a shift of emphasis from the point-contact technique to the junction techniques and, thence, from growing and alloying to diffusion. The diffusion technique developed at Bell Labs made it possible to have controlled thin layers and, hence, one or two orders greater frequency response, bandwidths, or switching speed than that proved by any other technique then available. The diffusion technique was also well adapted to the development of high-power devices.

With each of these advances, new military-systems applications became possible. In the period from 1951 to 1954, grown-junction and alloy-junction devices were primarily developed, while from 1955 to 1958 the majority of the effort was concentrated on diffusion techniques. Some of the tasks carried out by Bell Labs between 1951 and 1958 for the joint services are discussed briefly in the following paragraphs.

Bell Labs began development of a new and improved series of transmission- and oscillator-type transistors, which covered the frequency range of 2 Hz to 100 MHz, the power range of 1 microwatt to 10 watts, and had a 2-dB noise figure at 100 Hz as a goal. Designs with these objectives were developed for (1) a general-purpose, low-frequency, low-power transistor with 30 dB gain for the audio-amplifier stages of Wigwam, a mortar proximity fuse, (2) an IF amplifier germanium grown-junction tetrode that extended the frequency to 70 MHz (an order of magnitude over that of previous types) for the Nike missile electronics, and (3) a high-frequency oscillator capable of delivering 25 milliwatts (mW) at 200 MHz for the Wigwam system. The Wigwam oscillator was later improved by the diffusion technique to provide 60 mW of power at 250 MHz.

Although the original point-contact techniques were not suitable for Wigwam, they were used in the design of a high-speed switching transistor for TRADIC, the first all-transistor computer discussed below. The switching time was of the order of a few microseconds. Over 13 million transistor hours of aging indicated a failure rate of less than 0.01 percent per 1000 hours.

Another task undertaken by Bell Labs in the period from 1951 to 1958 was the development of the power transistor. The design, which centered around a hydraulic valve driver for a Nike system, found a number of military applications. An alloy germanium transistor was designed to give 10-watt Class C output at frequencies up to 500 KHz. Later a pnip silicon power transistor was designed as an oscillator for an Air Force crash beacon that produced 5 watts of power at 10 MHz, with its frequency cutoff approaching 100 MHz. A core-driver transistor that was suitable for switching magnetic cores in approximately 1 microsecond was developed for a computer research project. In addition, work on low noise resulted in the design of exploratory transistors with noise figures of 2 or 3 dB at 100 Hz.

These examples illustrate the achievement of the major objectives set forth initially in the joint services contract. Work continued on the design of devices capable of higher frequency operation and higher internal-power dissipation.

As part of this program, the military asked Bell Laboratories to develop transistor-measurement technology that would benefit both the circuit and device designers. The military was faced with the problem of comparing transistors provided by a large number of manufacturers and evaluating the performance of circuits designed around the transistors. Bell Labs' study showed that a more complex set of measurements for parameters was needed in the VHF range than in the low frequencies. Effort was applied to design the necessary measurement instruments.

The objective of another task undertaken for the joint services contract was to provide quantitative definitions of transistor reliability and to explore the possibilities of developing more reliable transistors in terms of those definitions. The results of this work showed that the behavior of transistors during moderately long aging could be predicted from relatively short life tests at elevated temperatures. Work was also directed at determining the environmental conditions and physical mechanisms affecting device reliability, such as moisture, temperature, transient overload, surface ion migration, and contact with ionized gases.

The ultimate results growing out of the invention of the transistor and the fundamental research, such as that described above, are too far reaching to be discussed in detail here, but will be covered as far as space permits in other volumes of this history. However, because of historic interest some of the earliest uses of transistors will be highlighted in the following section. These military applications illustrate the benefits of the early recognition of transistor potential by the military services.

2.2 Transistorized Digital Computers for Military Projects

2.2.1 Transistorized Gating Matrix[1]

The early point-contact transistors, announced by Bell Laboratories in 1948, combined in a single component the logic-gating capabilities of the crystal diode and the amplifying ability of the vacuum tube. Early in 1949, a gating matrix of such transistors was developed by W. H. MacWilliams, Jr. and employed as an essential part of a simulated-warfare computer. This simulator was built to compare, in the laboratory, various possible versions of Naval systems used for optimal control of guns and directors. Such systems would be used by warships as a defense against attack by enemy aircraft.

The gating matrix[2] developed by MacWilliams was an array of 40 transistors (see Fig. 11-3 in Chapter 11)—about all that were initially available—and was used successfully for about 18 months in the study of design aspects of antiaircraft systems. This circuit is believed to be the first to use transistors to perform a practical function in operating laboratory equipment. It proved very useful in the early design of the Mark 65 system for the Navy (see Chapter 11, Section 1.4).

2.2.2 General Considerations

The transistors in this matrix provided gain as well as logical functions. The success of the matrix encouraged exploration of the application of transistors in other computing systems. Until this time, electronic digital computers had almost all used some form of vacuum-tube, flip-flop circuits as basic elements. By 1950, however, the advantages of diode OR and AND gates and similar circuits for the logical manipulation of digital data began to be recognized. These circuits not only simplified the design and maintenance of computers, but since crystal diodes were much smaller and required less power than vacuum tubes, the circuits promised many advantages. Thus, by the end of 1950, several computers were in operation that used crystal diodes for logic purposes and depended on vacuum tube amplifiers only for gain.

The success of this method of separating the logic and the amplification processes in digital computers, the rapid development of crystal-diode-logic technology, and the availability of point-contact transistors in usable quantities beginning in 1950 made it practicable to explore the replacement of vacuum tubes by transistors. As it turned out, the transistors available in 1950 were not well adapted for use as linear amplifiers since they had a tendency to oscillate. This characteristic suggested that it would be simpler to use the oscillation than to get rid of it. A trial of the

---

[1] See also Chapter 11.
[2] W. H. MacWilliams, Jr., "A Transistor Gating Matrix for a Simulated Warfare Computer," *Bell Laboratories Record* 35 (March 1957), pp. 94–99.

transistors in blocking oscillator circuits (monostable circuits in which triggering causes generation of a single pulse) showed that such circuits could be used to provide pulse gain at repetition rates well above 1 MHz. This made it possible, while retaining the available crystal-diode-logic technology, to use such transistor pulse-amplifiers in place of vacuum-tube amplifiers. This was clearly the most direct route to attaining an almost completely solid-state electronic digital computer.

Several possible applications for transistorized digital computers were considered, and two of them were selected for pilot development. The first application was for airborne computers, where major savings in space, weight, and power were of obvious importance, particularly since computational requirements for airborne bombing operations were increasing rapidly. The Air Force asked Bell Labs to determine the feasibility of developing a reliable, all-solid-state digital computer for airborne use. This project, called TRADIC (Transistor Digital Computer) was started in 1951 under the direction of J. H. Felker. The objective of TRADIC's first phase was to show the successful operation, in the laboratory, of a high-speed, general-purpose, all-solid-state digital computer, with input-output equipment, that could be used in an airborne control system. Here "general purpose" implied that the computer could perform addition, subtraction, multiplication, and division of numbers, and that it could transfer the numbers to and from its internal storage and its input and output equipment as required by any program that was inserted into it.

The second application for transistorized digital computers, of primary interest to the Navy, was in handling the track-while-scan problem. In concept, the problem was simple. A search radar, continuously scanning the horizon, provided intermittent position data in three dimensions on a large number of aircraft. These data were used to generate a substantially continuous track for each individual aircraft. This involved (1) the association of new radar data with appropriate stored tracks, and (2) the calculation of rates and the prediction of future positions, which were used to control a ship's antiaircraft equipment for maximum effectiveness. Successful vacuum-tube analog systems existed that provided analog tracking on a track-per-unit basis; but with increasing numbers of attacking aircraft anticipated in the future, it was thought that a considerable reduction in total equipment might be achieved by using time-shared, high-speed digital equipment.

A primary requirement of the digital computer was reliability, and it was this that made transistorized computers of interest to the Navy. Although the memory requirements were much greater than for TRADIC, they could be handled by a serial memory. Such a computer would be basically a special-purpose machine, so that the ease of changing programs would be of relatively minor importance. This project was begun at about the same time in 1951 as TRADIC and was directed by A. W. Horton, Jr.

Fig. 13-1.   TRADIC Phase One computer.

2.2.3 TRADIC[3]

In both the Air Force and Navy projects, the actual computing circuitry consisted almost entirely of pulse amplifiers, crystal-diode gates, and delay lines. In the case of TRADIC, information took the form of 0.5-microsecond pulses, transmitted at a rate of one pulse every microsecond. Each number was handled serially in 16-bit binary form. Amplifiers were synchronized from a central clock. This required about 30 watts of clock power, which had to be furnished by vacuum-tube equipment; at the time there were no transistors that were capable of delivering that much power at 1 MHz.

All of the required logic functions in TRADIC were handled by crystal-diode gates and delay lines. The actual building-block packages were AND, OR, INHIBIT, DELAY, and MEMORY CELL. AND, OR, and DELAY require no explanation. The INHIBIT package transmitted the pulse on its upper input unless a canceling pulse was present on its lower input, while MEMORY CELL stored 1 bit of information until it was requested. Each package also contained a single-transistor pulse amplifier. Basically, the Phase One computer was an assembly of such packages and the necessary interconnecting wiring (Fig. 13-1). There was also a storage

---

[3] J. R. Harris, "TRADIC: The First Phase," *Bell Laboratories Record* 36 (September 1958), pp. 330–334.

unit for numbers consisting of 16 addressable electrical delay lines, each 16 μs in length, and there were toggle switches to introduce any needed constants in binary form. Addition time was 16 μs, with multiplication time less than 300 μs. Programs for the computer were set up on removable plugboards; each plugboard could handle a program of 64 machine steps, together with one subroutine, recallable as needed, also of up to 64 steps. The computer used only about 60 watts of dc power, provided by precisely regulated, all-solid-state power supplies.

The TRADIC Phase One computer was the first large, general-purpose, transistorized digital computer. It contained about 700 early model, point-contact transistors (which were not hermetically sealed), and a little over 10,000 germanium diodes. A major problem was to specify the characteristics of transistors so that they were at the same time suitable for use in new types of pulse amplifiers and could be manufactured to adequate tolerances by techniques still under development. In spite of such problems, the computer was completed in January 1954. After extensive testing to make sure it was working properly, it operated 24 hours a day in a reliability study that continued from May 1954 to May 1956.

During this reliability study, regular checks were made to determine the condition of the computer. As a result of these checks, several transistors and diodes were replaced before they could cause trouble. One transitor and one diode failed without warning, while one transitor and two diodes were accidentally destroyed during maintenance. Even counting *any* removal as a failure, only eight transistors and nine diodes were replaced during this two-year test period. Both the transistor and diode failure rates were remarkably low compared with failures expected at that time for most electronic components. No resistors or capacitors failed in the entire test period, which showed what could be achieved by operating such components at low temperatures and with very low power.

Using the same techniques, a second computer was designed to be tested in an airplane (see Figs. 13-2a and 13-2b). This was known as the flyable model TRADIC, and was designed to operate with a standard bombing and navigation system in place of an existing analog computer. In addition to use in purely computing functions, transistors were used also in a number of circuits associated with the radar, such as the radar range unit. The first of the two computers was installed and operated successfully in a C131 airplane in the fall of 1957.

2.2.4 Digital Track-While-Scan System for Mark 65

The work on the digital track-while-scan project involved the system design of a complete time-shared digital computer. This included several subsystems concerned with (1) data input from the search radar, (2) sorting

(a)

(b)

Fig. 13-2.   (a) TRADIC installed in Air Force C-131-B aircraft.
(b) TRADIC operator's location.

Fig. 13-3.   Digital track-while-scan prediction computer.

input data to match stored tracks, (3) rate calculation and prediction of future positions, and (4) displays to permit optimum control of a ship's defensive armament.[4] Only the prediction computer, which handled step (3), was actually built and tested (see Fig. 13-3), together with enough of the displays to permit such testing.   This decision was made for two basic reasons.   First, the technology of the prediction computer was more complex than that of the other subsystems, but it essentially included their problems as well as some peculiar to itself.   Second, both the available engineering personnel and the facilities for manufacturing suitable transistors were inadequate for doing more than this on an acceptable schedule.

The design of the prediction computer was based on the assumption that a capacity of 50 simultaneous tracks would be adequate.   This required

[4] W. A. Cornell, "A Special-Purpose Solid-State Computer Using Sequential Access Memory," *Proc. Western Joint Computer Conference*, May 6–8, 1958, published by AIEE, New York, March 1959; Q. W. Simpkins and J. H. Vogelsong, "Transistor Amplifiers for Use in a Digital Computer," *Proc. IRE* 55 (January 1956), pp. 43–55; John E. May, Jr., "Low-loss 1000 Microsecond Ultrasonic Delay Lines," *Proc. National Electronics Conference* 11 (March 1956), pp. 786–790.

the transfer of data from the sorting subsystem to the computer at about 50,000 bits per second. The arithmetic operations needed for coordinate conversion, rate computation, smoothing, and prediction of future positions were reasonably simple: a program of about 100 steps sufficed. However, these computations had to be repeated for each track every radar scan, and they had to be done in real time. Memory requirements, though far greater than for TRADIC, offered no real difficulty—for 50 tracks, less than 1,000 words were needed. Overall computing speed was necessarily high, but by operating at pulse rates well over 1 MHz, it was possible to use a serial arithmetic unit with the attendant equipment savings over parallel operation. The specialized repetitive program, which did not have to be changed, together with the serial arithmetic unit, led to the choice of a serial memory; this was also in keeping with the proposed design of the sorting subsystem.

These considerations led to the design of a serial, synchronous computer operating at a 3-MHz bit rate. Except for the threefold increase in speed, the transistor and diode-logic circuitry of the arithmetic unit resembled that of TRADIC. The word length was only 12 binary digits, which was quite adequate for the purpose. The arithmetic operations included addition, subtraction, multiplication, division, shift, and round-off. Addition time was 4 μs and multiplication time 48 μs. About 1,000 point-contact transistors were used, mainly as pulse-regenerative amplifiers, along with about 12,000 germanium diodes for the diode-resistor logic. As in TRADIC, clock power depended on vacuum-tube equipment. Programs were wired into the machine, with provision for automatically sequencing them. Program stepping was controlled by a 168-step magnetic-core stepping switch.

An internal memory comprised of 636 words was provided by two quartz, ultrasonic delay lines driven by transistorized RF circuitry. Input buffer storage provided an additional 318 words of memory. The fused-quartz delay lines were multireflection polygons equipped with barium titanate transducers (see Fig. 13-4). Electrical delay lines were used as temporary storage in the arithmetic unit and as access circuitry for the ultrasonic memories. Major control loops contained single-error-correcting circuits to prevent transient errors in one program from affecting succeeding programs. Output, in the form of aircraft tracks, was displayed on a cathode-ray tube, which could present either an oblique projection of the three-dimensional data or a plan view in ground coordinates. For test purposes, the output data could also be recorded digitally on a pen recorder.

The digital track-while-scan project progressed a good deal slower than TRADIC. This resulted from the greater variety of novel components required for the track-while-scan system, from the much higher pulse rate and its effects on transistor design and procurement and on circuit design,

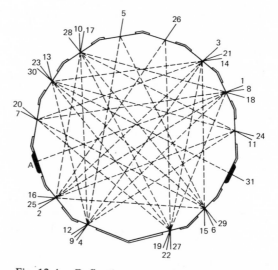

Fig. 13-4.   Reflection pattern for polygon type
of delay line.   (Redrawn from *Proceedings of
National Electronics Conference,* March 1956.)

and also from changes in the Navy's picture of future aerial-defense tactics.
The computer was completed, extensively tested, and demonstrated to a
number of interested groups early in 1957.

Testing and demonstration of the prediction computer presented a
problem often encountered when a piece of special equipment that is part
of a projected larger, but as yet unavailable, system must be operated in
the laboratory.   In such circumstances it is essential to determine how the
testing and demonstration can be done without recourse to a large amount
of auxiliary gear.   In this case, it was necessary to test and demonstrate
the prediction computer without a search radar and without building the
sorting subsystem and extensive display equipment.   This was done by
connecting the computer input to an auxiliary memory that could be
preloaded at low speed and then fed into the computer at the computer
pulse rate.   Since a memory of reasonable size could only keep the computer busy a small fraction of the time, a lot of free time existed between
computer-program runs.   To use some of this free time, a program was
wired into the machine that permitted it to simulate the flight of an airplane, thereby generating a sequence of positions that could be used as
input data for tests or demonstrations.   After it was completed, the computer operated, by such means, for a period of three months on a 24-
hour-a-day basis with high reliability and few component failures.   Although transient errors occurred occasionally in individual programs, the
error-correcting circuitry prevented errors in one program from affecting
the next.   Information was recirculated in the memories for several days
without error.

Work on the computers just described began when the transistor and the electronic digital computer were each only about five years old and when the relevant technologies were still in their infancies. The success of the TRADIC Phase One computer and the high reliability it achieved in its two-year life test, together with the very rapid developments in the following few years in both solid-state devices and computers, led Bell Laboratories to undertake in 1954 a program of research in transistor computers. This was directed toward the exploitation of new techniques in both the solid-state device and computer disciplines.

Most importantly, the new techniques included the use of (1) new alloy-junction transistors with excellent switching properties, which could be operated at lower power levels and with fewer auxiliary components than the point-contact transistors used in TRADIC and the track-while-scan prediction computer, and (2) new magnetic materials and new high-speed, high-current transistors that promised to provide compact, large-capacity, magnetic-core memories. There were two reasons for interest in such memories. First, it was desirable to find out how many cores could be switched by which type of transistor. Second, relatively large core memories would simplify the storage of multiple programs for such purposes as bombing and navigational calculations.

2.2.5 Leprechaun

The "building-block" packages of the early transistorized computers used point-contact transistors to amplify and reshape the signal being manipulated, and germanium diodes to do the switching involved in performing the logic functions. Since the new alloy-junction transistors made first-class switches as well as pulse amplifiers, it made sense to use transistors for both functions, as had been done initially in the transistorized gating matrix. At about this time, the Philco Radio Corporation announced the development of a complete set of simple computer building blocks, called "direct-coupled transistor logic" (DCTL). This logic seemed well adapted to the design of airborne computers because of the great simplicity of the basic circuits.

The principal reason for adopting DCTL circuitry was to achieve maximum reliability. DCTL could help by minimizing both power requirements and the number of types of components. DCTL achieved low power consumption by operating at very low voltage, but at relatively high current. This had two immediate effects: it required careful specification of the transistors to be used, and also extensive study of the noise problem arising from the necessarily complex switching within the computer of the high currents for operating DCTL circuitry. Laboratory studies of noise analysis suggested that a true picture of the noise problem could only be obtained by testing circuits containing almost as many transistors as a complete computer.

As a result of the noise-analysis studies, Bell Labs and the Air Force agreed that construction of a complete computer would be worthwhile, since tests could also be made of two other elements: the use of DCTL for computation and control and the use of a large-capacity core memory of small physical size. Such a computer would also yield basic information for the design of a new bombing and navigation system that was being developed by Bell Labs, and serve as a tool for studying programming and system-organization problems arising in connection with it.

These considerations led to the design and construction of Leprechaun,[5] a general-purpose, transistorized digital computer of the second generation. As would be expected, it differed markedly from TRADIC in a great many ways. Although its word length was still 16 significant bits, it added a sign bit and a parity bit (for checking memory operation) to the word. There were four major differences between the two machines.

1. Leprechaun was designed specifically to be a stored-program machine. TRADIC's programs were on plugboards, an interim expedient to permit early life-testing.

2. Leprechaun operated on the digits of a number in parallel, and its overall operation was asynchronous, while TRADIC was a serial, completely clocked, synchronous machine.

3. Leprechaun provided transistor-driven, magnetic-core storage for 1,024 words, while TRADIC had only electrical delay-line storage for 16 words.

4. Leprechaun's arithmetic and control units, and other units except for circuits directly concerned with the memory, used DCTL, while TRADIC used transistor-gain, diode-logic packages.

In spite of these striking differences, the two machines were comparable in computing speed, although Leprechaun's increased memory and its stored-program operation made it, for practical purposes, a far more powerful machine (see Fig. 13-5).

Leprechaun consisted of an arithmetic unit, a core memory, input-output facilities, and sequence and interunit controls. The computing portion of the machine contained about 5,500 transistors, 3,000 resistors, 50 capacitors, and 40 delay lines. The transistors were packaged mainly in five types of logic circuits. The memory was made up of about 18,000 magnetic cores and 75 associated transistor circuits. Almost all of the transistors were operated at very low voltage (300 millivolts maximum on the collector) and at low power (0.5 milliwatt dissipation). Leprechaun occupied about 15 cubic feet, and its total power consumption was about 250 watts.

[5] J. A. Baird, "Leprechaun Computer," *Bell Laboratories Record* 38 (February 1960), pp. 58–63.

Fig. 13-5.   J. A. Githens (left) and J. A. Baird checking
the control panel of Leprechaun.

Since Leprechaun was to be used primarily in the laboratory, it was
provided with paper-tape input-output equipment. Programs were
punched on tape in machine language, and stored in memory together
with data. The 28 basic operations available to programmers permitted
LEPRECHAUN to handle basic weapons-control problems, and made it
very useful as a general-purpose computer.

Leprechaun was completed in 1957 and was operated under test conditions for about 10,000 hours, over 6,000 of which were devoted to special
error-checking routines devised to check and evaluate machine errors.
During this time, 14 transistors failed. Two became unstable, and the other
12 failed in three separate events when related groups of transistors developed interelement shorts; this suggested that the 12 were damaged by
transient voltages of unknown origin. During the 6,000 hours spent
under the error-checking routines, the machine executed about 160 billion
instructions, and only 22 of these had errors. Such an error rate clearly
showed that although noise and crosstalk had to be considered in the
design of DCTL circuitry, they were not serious problems. In April 1959,
Leprechaun was delivered to the Air Force and installed at the Wright Air
Development Center at Dayton, Ohio.

2.2.6 Other Transistorized Computers

The technology related to transistorized digital computers, continuously improved by new developments, was used extensively in new military systems. One of these was the Nike-Zeus system, developed to control defensive guided missiles, which were capable of intercepting intercontinental ballistic missiles. The amount of computation was enormously greater for the Nike-Zeus system than for earlier Nike systems,[6] and because of the very high speed of ballistic missiles, the time available to obtain a solution was far less. Thus, the analog-computer facilities that sufficed for Nike-Ajax and Nike-Hercules were out of the question for Nike-Zeus. It was necessary to develop transistorized, digital, multiprocessor computing systems capable of 30 million calculations per second. It was also essential to develop and test an elaborate and extensive software system. The computing system was designed and built by Remington-Rand UNIVAC under the general direction of Bell Labs.

The Titan and Thor-Agena systems[7] for the guidance of intermediate and intercontinental ballistic missiles also required large, completely transistorized, digital computers for missile control. The computers were again provided by Remington-Rand UNIVAC.

Almost every commercial computer produced after 1960 has been completely transistorized although today the individual transistors have become almost invisible to the naked eye.

2.3 Millimeter-Wave Radar

There had been interest at Bell Laboratories dating back to the early 1930s in the use of very short waves in waveguide communications systems. When the Office of Naval Research (ONR) asked Bell Laboratories to undertake a research project on millimeter waves in June 1951, considerable background in millimeter-wave technology existed in the Bell Labs (Holmdel, New Jersey) Radio Research Laboratory. Work for the ONR was aimed at advancing millimeter-wave technology, including the development of suitable circuit components, the study of transmission effects associated with propagation through the atmosphere, and the exploration of electron-tube techniques suitable for amplifying or generating power in the millimeter-wave region.

Subsequent to the development of circuit millimeter-wave components, Bell Labs again contracted with the ONR in the field of millimeter waves, this time with the specific intent of assembling a complete radar system to explore the benefits of radar operation in the millimeter-wave region. Following a series of propagation tests in the wavelength range between 3.5 and 5.0 mm, Bell Labs constructed and tested a radar system operating

---

[6] See Chapter 7 for a more detailed description of the Nike systems.
[7] See Chapter 10.

at a 4.3-mm wavelength. This work was carried out at Bell Labs Whippany, New Jersey laboratory with the support of the research people at Holmdel and Murray Hill.

It was believed that the greatest single advantage of a radar operating at very short wavelengths was the high definition possible with antennas of reasonable size. Such a radar could be employed for harbor defense, where good resolution would be of great advantage in the presence of many closely spaced targets, or for station-keeping among ships in a convoy. It also would be valuable for shore-line mapping or for detecting camouflaged installations.

The complete system was first operated on March 4, 1957, and signals were observed out to 8,000 yards. Numerous tests later were conducted from a site at the tip of Sandy Hook, New Jersey, looking toward the Earle Navy Pier near Leonardo, New Jersey, an over-water distance of 11,850 feet. Although the test program was not as extensive as had first been planned, the information gained did show that the unit attenuation along a direct path between two points close to the surface of the sea (3 to 10 feet) was not appreciably different from the unit attenuation of a path over land. The voltage reflection coefficient of the water varied from approximately 0.5 for a rough sea to nearly unity for a smooth one. As a result of the presence of the sea, the radar return from a point target at an optimum height above the surface was increased by about 7 decibels (dB) for a rough sea and by about 12 dB for a smooth sea.

On two occasions it was possible to measure the signal return from an ammunition ship docked at the Naval Pier. It was not possible at these times to vary the height of the transmitting antenna and, hence, no information on such an effect was available. However, on both occasions, the signal return from the ship indicated that the effective radar cross section of the vessel was of the order of 2,500 square meters. These measurements were made on relatively calm days, and the signal fluctuation was about 2.5 dB. At the conclusion of the program, it was recommended that considerably more testing be done to assure that firm and quantitative data would result. Analysis of the collected information indicated that there didn't appear to be any anomalous propagation effects that might seriously interfere with millimeter-wave operation close to the surface of the sea.

2.4. Side-Looking Radar Development

The examination and recording of terrestrial features in a form similar to aerial photography became a field of interest at Bell Laboratories in 1954. This work, generally known as high-resolution radar mapping, was initiated because of a Strategic Air Command requirement for a high-resolution reconnaissance radar system capable of detecting strategic targets, such as airport runways, at relatively long ranges and from high-altitude, high-speed aircraft.

To fulfill the SAC requirements, the Wright Air Development Center selected several possible radar-system configurations for intensive research and testing. One configuration included side-looking, velocity-scanning systems, such as the AN/APQ-56, while the other included normal scanning systems, such as the AN/APQ-7. While the AN/APQ-56 system was evaluated by another contractor, the AN/APQ-7 (discussed in Chapter 2) was employed in Bell Labs tests as a side-looking radar.

The term "side-looking" is generally applied to a radar system that has the antenna mounted parallel to the aircraft fuselage. The antenna is usually not electrically or mechanically scanned. It remains fixed with the scan being provided by the forward motion of the aircraft—i.e., a velocity-scanning technique. When a radar system operates in this manner, a single trace appears across the face of the radar indicator tube. Since significant information cannot be obtained by viewing the indicator visually, the trace is photographed, and the information is stored on a continuous strip of film, which is moved at a rate proportional to the aircraft ground speed.

The film can also be stationary while the indicator trace moves across the face of the tube at a rate proportional to the aircraft ground speed. When a full film frame has been exposed, the film is moved, and the process is repeated. For this type of operation, a series of frames or pictures is obtained, rather than a continuous strip of film.

In general, the longitudinal antenna mounting permits the use of long antennas that are capable of high inherent azimuth resolution without the introduction of impossible aerodynamic problems and complicated scanning mechanisms. Also, because of the slow effective scan, significant signal-to-noise improvements may be realized that, in turn, permit the inherent resolution capabilities of a particular radar to be more fully exploited.

The AN/APQ-7 system is the old Eagle system that was used in the Pacific theater during World War II. Because this equipment had a long antenna capable of good azimuth resolution at X band, it was selected as the test medium for comparing the operation of a system that had a high-resolution scanning antenna with a number of systems that employed the velocity-scanning, or side-looking, technique. For the tests, the AN/APQ-7 antenna was operated in the normal manner and was mounted to look to the side of the aircraft to permit direct comparison with velocity-scanning, side-looking systems. For the first part of the test program, the AN/APQ-7 operated as a scanning system. However, because of the encouraging results obtained both in this country and in England using velocity-scanning systems for reconnaissance, it was decided to also test the AN/APQ-7 as an X band, velocity-scanning system.

Suitable equipment modifications were made to permit this type of operation during the last part of the test program.

The testing effort extended over a 24-month period, beginning in August 1954. Test flights were carried out in a modified B-36 aircraft, which was equipped with both APQ-7 and APQ-56 systems. During the seven months that were devoted to testing the APQ-7 as a velocity-scanning system, the experimental team enjoyed the satisfaction of continually improving results.

2.5 Chirp Technique

The Chirp[8] technique originated at Bell Labs in a proposal by S. Darlington in 1947 that related to waveguide transmission. A by-product of Darlington's idea was a concept for satisfying the requirements of pulsed-radar systems in providing long-range performance and high-range resolution while avoiding the problems associated with generating and transmitting high-peak powers. This concept involved (1) transmitting a relatively long pulse, modulated in frequency over a bandwidth appropriate to the desired range resolution, and (2) collapsing this long pulse, on reception, into a short pulse by means of a network that selectively delayed the signals associated with the various transmitted frequencies.

Early research on the concept started in 1955 with the Project Chirp program, which was to employ frequency-dispersion techniques to improve both resolution and range of the airborne scanning radars discussed in this chapter. An experimental radar system suitable for flight evaluation was developed. The test results, in the form of radar "maps," showed good definition and good halftone print quality.

The real need for the Chirp principle became apparent during the system study of antiballistic missile (ABM) defense conducted from 1955 to 1957 (see Chapter 7). To provide an order of magnitude increase in range on an ABM nose cone about one-thousandth the size of a bomber required about three orders of magnitude increase in radar performance. To meet this requirement, long pulses were needed to provide the necessary large, average transmitter power. Chirp was the only way to form narrow pulses.

The earliest Chirp systems for airborne radars used dispersive networks of distributed or lumped electrical components. A large body of knowledge in network synthesis evolved from the development of these dispersive networks.

In 1957, when the Nike-Zeus ABM development started, it became apparent that the acquisition radar with multiple receiver channels would

---

[8] The designation "Chirp" was first used by B. M. Oliver in a 1951 Bell Laboratories memorandum entitled "Not with a Bang, but a Chirp," which discussed the advantages of this concept.

require so many wired coils for the Chirp networks that the rate at which a system could be deployed might be limited by the ability to produce Chirp networks. A research program was therefore initiated in 1957 at Bell Labs' Allentown, Pennsylvania, laboratories to determine if an acoustic device could be developed that would provide dispersive propagation in an acoustic transmission medium such as fused quartz, steel, and aluminum. As a result of this program, a strip aluminum device was developed that matched the lumped-constant-network design in one-tenth the space and with no serious production problem. Many other compact acoustic devices using fused quartz were developed by the Allentown laboratories to meet the increasingly difficult Chirp requirements for delay and range-lobe suppression for radars that were used later in the Safeguard system.

The Chirp concept stimulated the development of many circuits, Chirp subsystems, complete radars, and special devices to implement the Chirp principle not only in Bell Labs but in other companies and universities in the United States and abroad.

2.6 Electrical Scanning and Stabilizing of Antennas

A project concerned with the electrical scanning and stabilizing of antennas (ESSA) was begun. It was organized in two stages, at the request of the Air Force, in order to cover certain developmental ground before work proceeded on the final contract. The objective of the first stage, which began in 1957, was to develop improved antenna systems for supersonic airplanes. The supersonic airplane, by virtue of its streamlined contours, imposed severe restrictions on the size and shape of the radar antennas that it could carry. Antennas that were scanned electrically, rather than mechanically, were more adaptable to these limitations. Specifically, such antennas permitted flush mounting in the skin of the aircraft, thus eliminating the need for protruding radomes. Electrical scanning promised greater versatility than mechanical scanning because it simplified scanning in two ways: it permitted high scanning rates adjustable within wide limits and it was adaptable to programmed scanning. Furthermore, electrical scanning techniques could be employed to stabilize a radar beam.

Extensive analytical and experimental investigations showed the advantages and limitations of using ferrite-loaded waveguides with biasing magnetic fields in the design of a small, compact, phase-shifting element suitable for introducing a phase delay into the wavefront of a linear array (see Figs. 13-6a and 13-6b). An experimental model of a ferrite scanning antenna operated successfully under transmitting and receiving conditions. The antenna was delivered to the Air Force in April 1958.

It became increasingly evident, however, that the first feasibility model fell short of demonstrating fully the inherent advantages of scanning with

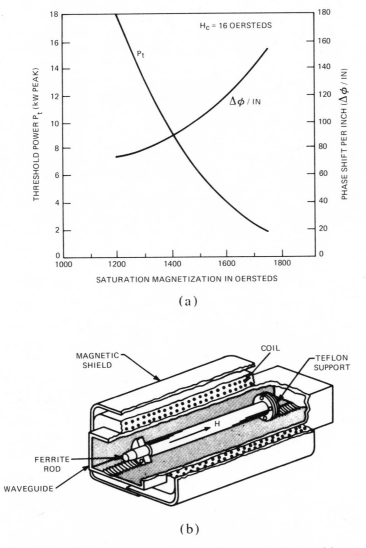

Fig. 13-6. (a) Measurement of magnetic characteristics of ferrite material for L-type phase shifter. (b) L-type phase shifter.

ferrite phase shifters. Hence, the primary objective of the ESSA research program during 1958 and 1959 was to make major improvements in the components of the antenna system and to design and construct an improved, electrically scanned antenna model suitable for operation with an airborne radar set (see Figs. 13-7a and 13-7b). To this end, a new, narrow-beam, fast-scanning antenna system was designed and constructed, featuring:

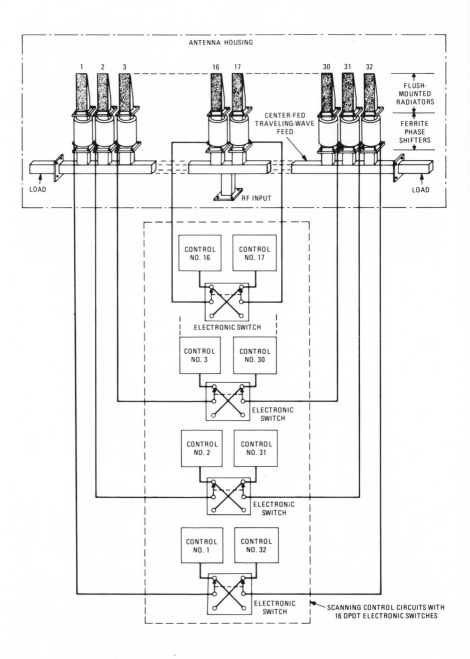

Fig. 13-7 (a).   Improved electrically scanning antenna system.

ELECTRONIC CONTROL
AND POWER SUPPLIES

32 ELEMENT ARRAY
IN WING SECTION

Fig. 13-7 (b). Antenna system used with the AN/APS-23 radar.

1. A flush-mounted radiating system employing tapered-depth radiating elements and a traveling-wave feed.

2. An all-electronic, high-speed switching system that was capable of making an arbitrary change in beam direction in a few hundred microseconds.

3. A lightweight phase shifter employing a longitudinally magnetized ferrite rod mounted in a metalized fiberglass-waveguide.

This narrow-beam, fast-scanning antenna system was completed and began operation as part of an AN/APS-23 radar set in September 1959. The antenna had 32 radiating elements, 32 ferrite phase shifters, and control circuitry that permitted step scanning of the 2-degree beam at the maximum rate of 20 looks per second. There were 20 beam positions covering a scan sector of approximately 40 degrees. Performance of the radar system showed the high degree of resolution commensurate with a 2-degree bandwidth (see Fig. 13-8).

During the entire contract period, considerable effort was devoted to a study of ferrite materials to understand better the physics of the ferrite phase shifter. The emphasis was on theoretical and experimental investigations of optimum geometries for ferrite phase shifters and of phase-shifter characteristics under high peak power loads.

The second stage of the ESSA project, from 1958 to 1959, was concerned with the development of a phase shifter that operated at 35,000 MHz and that could be used in a receiving antenna. By taking advantage of the experience gained in the development of X-band phase shifters with

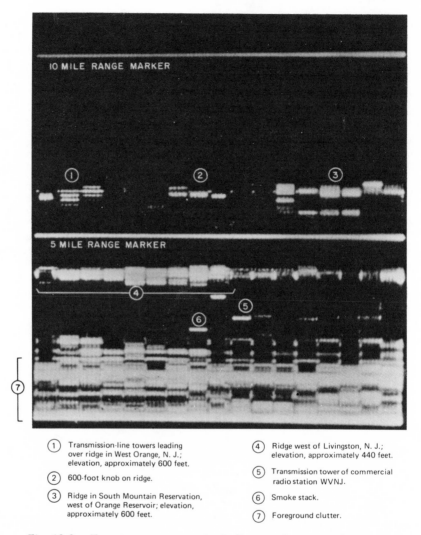

Fig. 13-8. Target returns on radar indicator; elevation of radar was approximately 240 feet above sea level.

longitudinal magnetization, it was possible to develop a high-performance phase shifter with a 1000-MHz bandwidth and low reflections.

2.7. Nuclear Electronic Effects Program

A project, called the Nuclear Electronic Effects Program, or NEEP, was begun in March 1959 to determine the effects of nuclear radiation on semiconductor materials and devices. The work was pursued under a contract with the United States Air Force. The studies included the determination of the interactions and damage centers in germanium and silicon due to electron and neutron damage, and the effects on the properties of these materials.

A selected group of semiconductor devices was studied to determine if they suffered permanent radiation damage and the effects of such damage on their electrical parameters. The results were then employed in evaluating the degradation of circuits incorporating these devices. Several special semiconductor devices, such as four-region devices, diffused-base transistors, Esaki diodes, and compound semiconductor diodes, were studied in a neutron and gamma environment. Surface-effect studies of gamma radiation on semiconductor devices were made after it was discovered that differently designed devices responded in highly variable ways. Some work was also performed to determine the effects of high-intensity transient radiation.

Finally, passive devices such as resistors, capacitors, and magnetic units were studied to determine the changes in the values of their electrical parameters in a fast-neutron environment. For many of these devices, a "performance parameter" was defined from which the performance of similar devices after radiation exposure could be characterized. Other component tests involved the effects of space radiation and radiation from the Van Allen belt on solar cells and satellite electronic components.

For all this work, the necessary dosimetry evaluations were made to characterize the environments used in these studies. The program was concluded in October 1962.

2.8. General Research Support

In carrying out the overall responsibility of major military projects, the broad expertise of Bell Laboratories research departments was called upon to support developments ranging from the basic physics and chemistry to reentry phenomena and operations system research to the problems of stress corrosion, adhesives, etc. Solutions for many of the problems that Bell Labs and its subcontractors faced were critical to the success of the project. For example:

—The peeling of ablative coatings on high-performance missiles required research on adhesives.

—A problem in "sticking" in the start of a missile's gyro brought in lubricating and material experts.

—The large acquisition radar in the Nike-Zeus program employed the largest roller-bearing balls ever developed. A serious problem related to the spacing of the balls developed that was solved by Bell Labs' Metallurgical Department.

—In the Safeguard project, an entirely new type of corrosion developed in the cooling chambers of the very-high-power klystron tubes. Bell Labs researchers carried out a wide range of testing at the operational site and at the tube manufacturer's plant in order to find a satisfactory solution.

—The effects of high pressure on underwater systems were also studied by the research area.

These are only a sample of the problems that occurred in military projects where the wide spectrum of knowledge and experience accumulated in support of the Bell System were called upon.

III. SUMMARY

Bell Laboratories pioneered in applying systems engineering, developed over many years by the Bell System for the telephone network, to complex military and government communications systems. In all its military projects, Bell Laboratories worked with the military to define as completely as possible its needs and to arrive at agreement on objectives to be accomplished.

From 1937 to 1968, the areas of concern grew enormously in scope and complexity. An early, important systems engineering study in 1945 addressed the problem of providing a ground defense against high-altitude, high-speed, maneuvering bombers then on the drawing boards. The final Bell Labs report outlining the design of an antiaircraft guided-missile system was a milestone in systems engineering because it was comprehensive enough to address the *whole* system—propulsion, aerodynamic control, steering strategy, warhead design, and the sensors and computers. The soundness of the study was demonstrated six years later when the system that was developed, with only minor changes to the design suggested by the study, successfully defended against maneuvering, high-speed drone aircraft at the White Sands Proving Ground. This Nike-Ajax study marked the beginning of a whole series of Nike weapon systems.

Because the Nike-Ajax study stimulated a new and successful development, in the late 1940s and the 1950s Bell Labs and Western Electric began to get requests for other kinds of system studies, such as strategic-bombing studies for the Air Force, studies on defending Navy ships or task forces against air attack, studies of the problems of air-to-air combat, ongoing air-defense studies for the United States and Canada, and military-communications studies. In 1958, a Bell Labs vice presidential area concerned with military systems engineering was organized to carry out the responsibilities of these continuing studies. This organization functioned until 1970.

Important results in transistor development were accomplished by Bell Laboratories in its research under the joint services contracts. Discussions with the military services and the patent licensees indicated that the timing of the research, the quality of the results, and the associated technical reports during this early period contributed significantly to military transistor development. The research and reports enabled all licensees to establish themselves quickly and soundly in the military contracting business for solid-state devices. Bell Labs feasibility and exploratory work, backed by Western Electric pilot production carried out in the period from 1949 to 1958 as reported in a number of symposia and in many detailed documents, made very important contributions to the development of transistor technology for the military services.

Bell Labs military research after World War II was, in many cases, a by-product of forward-looking work being carried on for the Bell System. For example, Bell Labs' work on waveguides and microwave components in the 1930s contributed substantially to World War II radar development. And development of millimeter-wave radar, undertaken in 1951 for the Office of Naval Research, drew upon research under way at Bell Labs' Holmdel, New Jersey, laboratory for Bell System communications. The object of the military millimeter-wave program was to determine the benefits and practicality of radar operation in this band. A complete laboratory system was tested in 1957 over water and showed that there were no anomalous propagation effects with millimeter-wave operation close to the surface of the sea.

Another research program on Chirp radars was based on frequency-modulated pulses first proposed in 1947 by Sidney Darlington of Bell Labs' Mathematical Research Department in connection with waveguide transmission. Fundamental work in this field was supported in 1955 by the Air Force for investigation of high-resolution radars. Today, pulse compression is in use in a variety of important radar applications—particularly where long-pulse, high-power radars are necessary to meet range requirements without sacrificing range resolution.

Research on transistors for use in digital-type circuitry began early in 1949 with construction of a transistor gating matrix for laboratory use in studies for the Navy Mark 65 system. Progress in the manufacture of transistors to meet specific requirements made it possible by 1951 to begin development of all-solid-state digital computers. The first one completed was the TRADIC Phase One computer, built for the United States Air Force, which was interested in the savings in space, weight, and power required in airborne applications. A quite different computer was also built for the Navy to test the feasibility of centralized track-while-scan facilities for use in defensive systems such as the Mark 65. Both systems were extensively tested to determine their reliability and maintenance characteristics. Other developments led to the Leprechaun digital computer, which used more advanced hermetically sealed alloy-transistors. Although the circuitry of the early computers using point-contact transistors has long been obsolete owing to rapid advances in transistor technology, transistorized digital computers employing the latest in circuitry and solid-state components are now almost universally found in both military and commercial applications.

Other research projects undertaken since World War II included side-looking radar, which was developed for the Air Force in connection with high-resolution radar mapping, electronically scanned antennas using lightweight phase shifters with a magnetized ferrite rod, and under contract for the Air Force, studies on the effects of nuclear radiation on semiconductor materials.

Chapter 14

Special Projects—Sandia
and Bellcomm

During the post-World War II years, the Bell System carried out a number of special projects for the United States government, two of which are covered in this chapter. These two projects were conducted at the request of high government officials and required the organization of subsidiary corporations.

The first request came on May 13, 1949 when President Harry S. Truman, after discussions with Atomic Energy Commission chairman David E. Lilienthal, wrote AT&T president Leroy Wilson requesting that the Bell System take over the direction of the Sandia Laboratory from the University of California. Mr. Wilson's acceptance of the responsibility in the national interest resulted in the formation of the Sandia Corporation in 1949 as a subsidiary of Western Electric. Sandia was formed with the understanding that research-manufacturing expertise from both Bell Laboratories and Western Electric would be applied to its operation. Section I of this chapter describes the Sandia organization and how its responsibilities have grown under Bell System management.

The second request, which resulted in the organization of a subsidiary company, came on January 24, 1962, in a letter from Roswell C. Gilpatric, deputy secretary of defense—acting for Robert S. McNamara, secretary of defense—to AT&Ts chairman Frederick R. Kappel. Gilpatric asked that Bell Laboratories use its knowledge and experience in systems engineering to assist NASA in its critical Apollo moon-landing program. McNamara coordinated this request with NASA administrator James E. Webb and with Gilpatric. He hoped that Bell Labs could participate without compromising the work it was already doing for the Defense Department. AT&T president Eugene J. McNeely, in a letter to Webb dated March 1, 1962, accepted the responsibility in the national interest and indicated that a subsidiary company within the bell System would be formed. This company would draw on the talents of AT&T, Western Electric, and Bell Laboratories. On March 22, 1962, AT&T organized the new company, Bellcomm, Inc., owned by both AT&T and Western Electric. Section II of this chapter describes the organization and

---

Principal authors: C. A. Warren, J. A. Hornbeck, and Morgan Sparks (Sandia).

responsibilities of Bellcomm in the space program, which continued until 1972 when it was agreed with NASA that Bellcomm support could be terminated and the corporation dissolved.

I. SANDIA LABORATORIES

1.1 Origins[1]

In the final stage of preparing the new atomic weapons that would bring an end to World War II, a Los Alamos group was organized to handle future weapons-development engineering and bomb assembly. This group, the forerunner of Sandia Laboratories, was headed by Dr. Jerrold Zacharias and was called, after the first letter of his name, Z Division. On August 6, 1945, about two weeks after the Z Division was formed, the first atomic weapon to be used in combat, a design called Little Boy, was dropped on the Japanese city of Hiroshima. On that same day, Zacharias wrote to Dr. J. Robert Oppenheimer, head of the highly secret weapons-development program at Los Alamos, and offered some thoughts on Z Division. In his memorandum, Zacharias predicted that the division would grow and proposed that the assembly group and other portions of the division be moved to Albuquerque, 60 air miles south of Los Alamos. Three days later the second atomic weapon used in combat, a Fat Man design, was dropped on Nagasaki, and, within the next five days, the Japanese surrendered.

One week after the surrender, Oppenheimer convened a round-table conference to discuss the future work of Z Division. The conclusions reached at the conference were that the Division should assemble a stockpile of atomic bombs, using components already on order, and should design new weapon models in cooperation with other Los Alamos Divisions. Shortly afterward, Z Division personnel concerned with assembly activities moved to Sandia Base in Albuquerque to begin this work, and procurement specialists from the Ordnance Division accompanied them to redirect deliveries of bomb materials.

The few personnel then located with the military groups at Sandia Base (Fig. 14-1) began the task of identifying usable pieces of Little Boy and Fat Man designs that had been left over from wartime contracts. Although the war had ended, continuation of weapons development was considered essential. Efforts to improve the bombs concentrated on the Fat Man design (Fig. 14-2) because it was believed that the Little Boy design used fissionable materials inefficiently. However, because a test series in mid-1946 demonstrated that the Little Boy design was useful for attack against naval vessels, it was eventually carried into limited production.

---

[1] The Sandia history through 1963 was taken largely from the book by Frederick C. Alexander, Jr., *History of Sandia Corporation Through Fiscal Year 1963* (Albuquerque, N.M.: Sandia Corporation, 1963).

Fig. 14-1.   Sandia Base in 1946.

When B-29 bombers became available at nearby Kirtland Field, additional Z Division personnel moved to Albuquerque.   A bombing range was selected south of Albuquerque for the purpose of investigating bomb ballistics.

Fig. 14-2.   Fat Man atomic bomb.

Because the reliability of the Fat Man weapon was unknown, it became necessary to develop reliable statistical data on the performance of each individual component. Therefore, a program of telemetering bomb-drop data was started. This data included such factors as temperature, pressure, and physical movements of the bomb in flight (roll, pitch, yaw, and vibration). These conditions were then duplicated in a mechanical test laboratory and failure points for each component determined. The components were strengthened if necessary and retested until a satisfactory quality level was reached.

By early 1947, the move of Z Division to Sandia Base was complete. The responsibilities of the division were increasing, and it was assuming a heavier production workload. Personnel increased from 370 in December 1947 to 470 in April 1948, at which time it was announced that the Sandia Base operation would become an independent branch of the Los Alamos Scientific Laboratory and would be named Sandia Laboratory. By the fall of 1948, the personnel roll for the first time exceeded 1,000. But even this rate of growth did not provide the staff needed for the work of the branch.

1.2 Bell System Responsibility for the Operation of Sandia Laboratory for the Government

As a branch of the Los Alamos Scientific Laboratory, Sandia was still under the direction of the University of California. The Regents Committee on Atomic Energy Commission (AEC) projects of the university had become increasingly disturbed by the fact that Sandia's growth involved the university in activities far afield from those of an educational institution. On December 31, 1948, the committee formally notified Carroll L. Tyler, manager of the AEC's Santa Fe operations office, that it wished to divest itself of Sandia because its production, stockpiling, and surveillance were not appropriate for university management.

Meanwhile the AEC management staff in Washington had been observing the Sandia project with close interest. The director of Engineering, Roger S. Warner, Jr., and the director of the Division of Military Application, General James McCormack, Jr., had discussed with several industrial organizations the possibility of taking over the Sandia operation, but had secured only indifferent responses. Among those contacted was Oliver E. Buckley, president of Bell Laboratories and member of the General Advisory Committee of the AEC, who indicated that Bell Labs could not operate Sandia Laboratory because an internal-policy restriction required that defense activity expenditures be held to 15 percent of the total budget.

As a step toward solving the problem, James B. Fisk—later to become president of Bell Laboratories who was then ending a tour of duty as director of research for the AEC—suggested that an impartial authority be secured to survey the entire Los Alamos operation. He suggested Mervin J. Kelly, executive vice president of Bell Labs. The AEC was receptive to this idea.

At the suggestion of General McCormack, David E. Lilienthal, chairman of the AEC, approached Buckley on the subject. Subsequently, the availability of Kelly to review both the Sandia and Los Alamos operations was discussed with Leroy A. Wilson, president of AT&T. Consequently, Buckley advised Lilienthal that Kelly's time would be made available by Bell Laboratories, but that arrangements would have to be made directly with Kelly, who would then be acting as an individual and not as a representative of Bell Labs. In response to Lilienthal's request, Kelly agreed to survey and evaluate the operations at Los Alamos and Sandia and to make recommendations.

Kelly visited Los Alamos and Sandia several times between February and April 1949. He came to the conclusion that Los Alamos was performing its work competently in nuclear physics, chemistry, metallurgy, and explosives, but he felt that Sandia would operate more effectively as a production-oriented organization under industrial management.

Kelly made an oral report of these findings to General McCormack and his associates on May 3, and to the Atomic Energy Commission on May 4, 1949. In accordance with the agreement made when he started the investigation, he did not recommend any specific company to operate the project, but stated that the one selected should have experience in systems work and a high order of ability in scientific fundamentals.

The General Advisory Committee of the AEC, in subsequent sessions, discussed the findings. Several organizations were proposed, but the final decision favored the Bell System. Lilienthal met with President Harry S. Truman on May 13, 1949, informed him that the Bell System had outstanding qualifications for managing the Sandia project, and that the national military establishment agreed.

President Truman dispatched a letter on the same day to Leroy Wilson, stating that the AEC intended to ask the Bell System to assume direction of the Sandia Laboratory, and requesting that the task be undertaken. On May 17, 1949, Wilson replied to President Truman that he had not yet heard from the AEC and that he did not understand the details of the problem, but that prompt and sympathetic consideration would be given to the request. Subsequently, Lilienthal, Carroll Wilson (general manager), and General McCormack of the AEC met with Leroy Wilson on Memorial Day, May 30, 1949.

At this meeting, Leroy Wilson indicated a willingness to arrange to operate the Sandia Laboratory, but said that, first, he had to submit the proposal to his board of directors. He was also concerned about a pending antitrust suit instituted by the Department of Justice against the Bell System and felt that acceptance of the Sandia task, which included the combination of design and production elements criticized by the suit, might be prejudicial to the case. He suggested that if the Bell System were to accept, the operation should not be conducted as a profit-making venture, but should be operated on a cost basis, without fee.

Lilienthal, in his book *Big Business: A New Era* wrote[2]:

> The substantial stockpile of atom bombs we and the top military assumed was there, in readiness, did not exist. Furthermore, the production facilities that might enable us to produce quantities of atomic bombs so engineered that they would not continue to require a Ph.D. in physics to handle them in the field, likewise did not exist. No quantity production of these weapons was possible under the existing "handicraft" setup.
>
> To redesign the bomb so it would be a genuine field weapon, to carry forward fundamental work on new designs, to design and build a plant in which this infinitely complex thing could be put into quantity industrial-type production, and then to operate such a factory required talents in an unusual and remarkable combination.
>
> First of all, this task required *industrial* experience. What we wanted was not something that could be done in a laboratory alone, but in a production center, with factory techniques, factory mechanics (of a high order of skill, it is true) and factory management.
>
> Second, what we wanted done required men of high order of ability in scientific fundamentals, equal to any in the universities but also experienced in dealing with industrial problems and with industrial associates.
>
> Third, this task called for a special kind of operating experience in dealing with the technical characteristics of systems used in these weapons, and others then actively under development, new weapons which have since been proof-tested.
>
> Most important of all, these three capabilities of research, industrial techniques and operation had to be *combined* in the same team, with experience in working together as a unit.
>
> To go out and create such an organization was out of the question. There was not time.
>
> It was our "hunch" that there was such an organization in existence—the Bell System, that is, the team consisting of the American Telephone & Telegraph Company and its associated operating companies, together with the Bell Laboratories, a research and development institution, and Western Electric, the manufacturing arm of the system.
>
> A careful analysis confirmed this initial "hunch." I spent Decoration Day of 1949 with the president of AT&T, the late Leroy Wilson. On behalf of President Truman and the Atomic Energy Commission, I requested that AT&T, Bell Laboratories and Western Electric, as a team, take the heavy responsibility which I have here summarized. Mr. Wilson said that his company was already committed to important defense work, and while it did not relish another great load such as this, the Bell System would accept the assignment as in the national interest.

---

[2] David E. Lilienthal (New York: Harper, 1952), pp. 101–103.

Then he said (and I paraphrase only): the government is asking the Bell System to put its research-manufacturing-operation setup to work on this task because it is a combination of these things that you regard as essential to the nation's security.

On June 24, 1949, Lilienthal wrote to Leroy Wilson, recapitulating the points discussed in the meeting of May 30. The letter outlined the various responsibilities of Sandia and stated that they encompassed work normally done by both Western Electric and Bell Laboratories. Mr. Lilienthal said that the Commission was interested in drawing on the managerial and technical resources of the entire Bell System and suggested that the new operator of Sandia take over the entire operation, including housekeeping and administration.

Wilson replied on July 1, 1949, that the Bell System would agree to manage the project, provided the status of the antitrust suit would not be adversely affected by this decision. He said he understood that Lilienthal had discussed the proposal with Tom Clark, the United States Attorney General, and that Clark saw no reason, from the viewpoint of the Department of Justice, why the commission should not proceed with the proposal. Wilson concluded by stating that, if the above understanding were correct, the Bell System would be ready to send a team of Western Electric and Bell Laboratories people to Sandia to examine the problem in detail.

The AEC issued a press release on July 12, 1949, stating that the services of Western Electric and Bell Laboratories had been obtained to operate the Sandia Laboratory at Sandia Base, New Mexico. The release noted that the new operator of Sandia would bridge the gap between Sandia Laboratory development work and the manufacture of atomic weapons.

A special team then visited Sandia to prepare for the transfer to the new contractor. Members of this group included:

For Western Electric Company:

Stanley Bracken, President.

Fred R. Lack, Vice President.

George A. Landry, Operating Manager, Installation.

For Bell Laboratories:

Mervin J. Kelly, Executive Vice President.

Donald A. Quarles, Vice President.

For the Atomic Energy Commission:

James McCormack, Jr., Director, Division of Military

Application.

The AEC submitted a draft of a proposed contract on August 2, 1949. This contract contained a detailed cost-of-work clause and a fairly broad indemnity, except for "willful misconduct or bad faith." The contract was similar to one that the AEC had just negotiated with Bendix for operation of Project Royal, the first AEC weapon production contract. Western Electric, which was to be the operating agency for the Bell System, felt that the contract was too detailed, and General McCormack suggested that the operation be run on the basis of "good industrial practice." This phraseology was used as a central theme of the contract—an extremely simple, straightforward, and unique one in this respect.

In the midst of these discussions, the announcement was made that an American plane patrolling near the Kamchatka peninsula had detected fission products in the atmosphere. This finding revealed that Russia had built and detonated an atomic device, and underscored the importance of speed in completing the contract negotiations.

The Certificate of Incorporation of the new Sandia Corporation was dated September 29, 1949, and was signed by Western Electric executives H. C. Beal (vice president, Manufacturing), F. R. Lack (vice president, Radio Division), and Walter L. Brown (vice president and general counsel) as incorporators. The stated purpose of the new corporation was

> ... to engage in any kind of research and development, and any kind of manufacturing production and procurement to the extent that lawfully may be done and to enjoy all the powers conferred on corporations organized under the general corporation laws of the State of Delaware.

Western Electric and the AEC executed a contract, designated AT-(29-1)-789, on October 4, 1949, calling for the operation of Sandia Laboratory until December 31, 1953. A feature of the contract, unique at that time, was the provision that the work would be on a cost basis and without fee or profit.

The first meeting of the board of directors of Sandia Corporation was held on October 6, 1949, at AT&T headquarters, 195 Broadway, New York City. At this meeting, Beal, Lack, Brown, and Landry were elected directors of Sandia Corporation. A corporate seal was adopted and the form of stock certificate approved. The corporation endorsed the basic contract between Western Electric and the AEC and formally became a party to the agreement.

Sandia Corporation assumed active direction of Sandia Laboratory on November 1, 1949. Various key people were brought in from Western Electric and Bell Laboratories to round out the management. The initial organization was headed by Landry, with Robert E. Poole as director of development and Fred Schmidt as vice president.

1.3 Sandia Corporation — The Early Years

The change from academic to corporate management on November 1, 1949, created many problems. Some of these were concerned with continuing operation, while others involved the assumption of additional jobs that were not previously handled by Sandia Laboratory. All of these problems were soon intensified by increasing demands for Sandia products and services as a result of the continuing deterioration of international relationships.

The AEC had stated that one of the principal tasks of Sandia Corporation in operating Sandia Laboratory was to provide a smooth transition between the development and the manufacture of atomic weapons. Thus, Sandia Corporation was concerned with applied research, engineering development, and design for production of the ordnance aspects of atomic weapons. Safety, reliability, and quality control were stressed to a degree unprecedented in industry.

Initially, efforts were directed toward completing designs for production of Fat Man (Fig. 14-2) and Little Boy, and releasing these designs for production. At first the weapons were assembled at Sandia, but weapon assembly was later transferred to other facilities in the AEC manufacturing complex. Sandia then concentrated on product definition and design.

In early 1952, a major shift in emphasis from weapons production to ordnance design took place, which was reflected in top-echelon changes at Sandia. Donald A. Quarles, vice president of Bell Laboratories, was installed as president; the director of development, R. E. Poole, became a vice president; and the newly created post of vice president of research was filled by W. A. MacNair, formerly director of military systems engineering at Bell Labs. The design organization was divided into two parts, one concerned with weapons released from aircraft and the other with guided missiles. In May 1952, a vice president and general-manager post was established to supervise those areas not engaged in research and development. The first to occupy this position was T. E. Shea of Bell Labs.

Early difficulties in manufacturing radar devices resulted in a low acceptance rate. A correction-task-force study indicated the need for close cooperation between designer and manufacturer and demonstrated the necessity for adequate manufacturing process control. In May 1952 a preproduction organization was formed to assist engineers in translating engineering designs into products. And as more weapon programs moved into the manufacturing phases, manufacturing planning and inspection assumed a larger role.

Advanced designs for capacitors, spark gaps, electronic tubes, and other devices began to flow from the design boards of Sandia engineers. In time, these items became smaller in size. They also became more efficient, more reliable, and more tolerant of severe environmental conditions. These improvements resulted in weapon systems that required less and less maintenance, and permitted development of so-called "wooden bombs," a phrase used to describe weapons that required a minimum amount of field assembly and testing before use and that could be stored for long periods of time. The atomic bomb thus began to approach conventional ordnance in operational simplicity, resistance to environment, and readiness for combat use.

The increasing pressures of the cold war with the Soviet Union, which had started with the Russian development of the atomic bomb and the blockade of Berlin, stimulated emergency programs to fabricate limited numbers of prototype weapons prior to regular production. The announcement that Russia had detonated a thermonuclear device on August 12, 1953, added to international tension and resulted in even greater design and production burdens being placed on Sandia. In August 1954 the AEC reported that "the nation's atomic weapons stockpile [is] growing rapidly in total number"; the following November Sandia Corporation's annual report read cryptically, but pleasantly, "Production assignments successfully completed."

In the fall of 1953, Quarles was appointed by President Dwight D. Eisenhower to the position of Assistant Secretary of Defense for Research and Development, and J. W. McRae, vice president of Bell Laboratories, was elected president of Sandia, a post that he was to occupy during five eventful years of nuclear-weapons evolution.

A major event in the history of Sandia had its origins in late 1955 and early 1956 when a few engineering and design personnel from Sandia moved to Livermore, California, to assist the scientists of the University of California Radiation Laboratory. This laboratory, now called Lawrence Livermore Laboratory (after Professor Ernest O. Lawrence of the University of California), had been established to compete with Los Alamos in the design of nuclear explosives. The Sandia branch in Livermore was expanded (Fig. 14-3), buildings were erected, and in late 1956 a director of systems development for the Livermore laboratory was appointed. By mid-1957 the increasing activity resulted in the assignment of R. E. Poole as the first vice president to head the Sandia Livermore laboratory.

1.4 Development and Testing

The interval from 1950 through 1958 was a period of dramatic expansion in weapon-development activity: four separate weapon projects were under way in 1950, eight in 1952, twelve in 1956, and sixteen in 1958. By 1958, a total of 53 different weapon designs had been worked on, 36 of which were prepared for production. The emergence of more exotic nuclear designs led to weapons with variable yields and compounded the Sandia work load as matching hardware, components, and electronics were required. Weapon safety continued to receive major attention. Much effort was devoted to design and development of appropriate systems and components. Increasing emphasis on the use of missiles as delivery vehicles made it necessary to solve reentry problems involving heat, shock,

Fig. 14-3.   Sandia Livermore administration building.

and vibration.   Extreme ruggedness was added to safety and reliability on the list of exceptional characteristics demanded of nuclear weapons.

The new weapons being developed were required to survive in environments of varying degrees of severity.   Thus new facilities and equipment were needed to subject the materials, components, and systems to the effects of high temperatures, controlled acceleration, complex-wave vibrations, subfreezing cold, sustained loadings, and impacts and shocks. Groups of engineering specialists were formed to operate the equipment, conduct the tests, and analyze the test results.   Environmental testing capabilities steadily expanded.   By 1958 the additions included a 300-foot drop tower, a climatic test chamber, a high-temperature test facility, and a Van de Graaff accelerator for studies of radiation effects.   In Fig. 14-4, a technician checks the condition of a nose cone at an extremely low temperature.   Although not an item for testing hardware, another important addition was an IBM 704 computer to complement the IBM 705 then in use.

Sandia carried out many bomb-drop and ballistics tests on a variety of weapons at test ranges throughout the country.   New instrumentation techniques and systems were developed, and a variety of data-collection schemes were used, sometimes with unexpected side effects—captive balloons, used for testing instruments and measuring wind velocities over Sandia's S-1 practice bombing range, 25 miles southwest of Sandia Base, created quite a stir in 1956 when they were mistaken for flying saucers by the residents of nearby Los Lunas.

In 1957 Sandia opened the 625-square-mile Tonopah Test Range, located at the north end of the Las Vegas Bombing and Gunnery Range, about 30 miles southwest of Tonopah, Nevada.   Numerous tests at the range would

Fig. 14-4.   Surface of nose cone being checked in the extreme-low-temperature (−100°F) test chamber.

include rocket launches, gun firings, high-performance aircraft tracking, atmospheric sampling, and system-development experiments.

Development and testing were being effectively merged to solve problems and produce designs that could be certified to perform as required.   Late in the summer of 1958, an Air Force fighter, flying fast and low over an abandoned airstrip near Dalhart, Texas, dropped an inert, nuclear test weapon of unusual shape and, as it developed, of unusual significance.   As the delivery plane swept upward, the spike-tipped experimental "shape" struck the 7-inch thick concrete runway and embedded itself like a dart thrown into a cork board.   Telemetry indicated that the components within the casing had survived the shock of impact and were ready to trigger the detonators at the preset time after impact.   This successful test represented a key step in the solution of a multifaceted problem handed to Sandia engineers many months earlier: design—for delivery to a hard target by a low-flying plane—a nuclear weapon containing ordnance systems that would keep the weapon from ricocheting off the target, from failing to detonate because of impact damage, and from detonating before the aircraft was a safe distance away.   Successful solution of the problem was to lead to an entirely new class of weapons, the "lay-down" bombs, designed for delayed-action ground bursts.

Field testing has always played an important part in weapon develop-

Fig. 14-5.   Operation Crossroads series on atmospheric nuclear test—1946.

ment (Fig. 14-5), and Sandia participated in numerous test operations. Fanciful names, hinting at mystery, were used to catalogue the serious business of testing new weapon concepts and investigating the effects produced by nuclear bursts.   Operation Ivy, held at the Pacific proving grounds in 1952, included a test of the design theory for the first full-scale thermonuclear device, and Operation Upshot-Knothole, conducted at the Nevada Test Site in 1953, included military tests and the first demonstrating firing of a nuclear cannon shell.

The shock wave produced by one of the shots during Operation Castle, which was carried out at the Pacific proving grounds in 1954, was clearly recorded at Sandia's microbarograph station in Albuquerque, signaling the development of a practical battlefield thermonuclear weapon.

Other test series included Operations Teapot and Wigwam, which were held in 1955. Operation Redwing took place at the Pacific proving grounds in 1956, with Sandia personnel playing a larger part than in any previous full-scale test series.   Operation Plumbob in 1957 and the Hardtack Operation in 1958 included detonations on the surface, at high altitude, under water, and under ground.   Effects studies measured earth motion, blast loading, neutron output, radiation contamination and fireball phenomena. Sandia-designed instrumented rockets were fired at various distances from the burst point to obtain weapon burst data needed to devise a defense against intercontinental ballistic missiles (ICBMs).

The decision of the United States to declare a testing moratorium on November 1, 1958, resulted in an accelerated series of tests designated Hardtack II. Sandia provided a recording system for the underground shots, performed earth-motion and optical measurements, and monitored the radiation output. A Sandia system using balloons as an aerial platform for instrumentation saved almost $500,000 and shortened the preparation time.

1.5 The Middle Years

Sandia's early years had seen rapid growth, changes in emphasis, intense development activities, and creation of a branch laboratory in Livermore. To keep pace with these developments, organizational adjustments had been made to provide the appropriate management for each responsibility. By the time the organization chart first showed the position of vice president at Livermore (August 1, 1957), the result of cumulative organizational changes was as follows:

President	J. W. McRae*
Vice President and General Manager	S. P. Schwartz*
Vice President, Development	R. W. Henderson
Vice President, Operations	R. P. Lutz*
Vice President, Research	G. A. Fowler
General Attorney, Secretary and Treasurer	K. Prince*
Vice President, Research and Development Technical Services	F. J. Given*
Vice President, Livermore Laboratory	R. E. Poole*

In January 1958, H. N. Snook, from Western Electric's Kearny Works, succeeded Lutz as vice president of operations. In the same month that the United States entered a testing moratorium, November 1958, McRae was elected a vice president of AT&T and J. P. Molnar, a vice president of Bell Laboratories, was installed as Sandia's president.

Resumption of nuclear testing by the USSR on September 1, 1961 terminated the voluntary test moratorium and plunged Sandia and the other nuclear-weapon laboratories (Los Alamos Scientific Laboratory and Lawrence Livermore Laboratory) into a concentrated program of underwater, undergound, atmospheric, and high-altitude tests. The tests in-

* From the Bell System.

Fig. 14-6. President John F. Kennedy being briefed on capability of Sandia weapons by Sandia President S. P. Schwartz, Senator Clinton Anderson, and AEC Chairman Glenn Seaborg.

cluded the 1962 Operation-Dominic series in the Pacific and underground and surface tests at the Nevada Test Site. Full-scale test data were obtained on stockpiled weapons, new weapon concepts, and weapon effects.

A limited test-ban treaty, signed in late 1963, halted testing in space, under water, and in the atmosphere and forced the weapon laboratories to focus their attention on underground testing and on developing means of simulating nuclear-weapon effects in the laboratory. In conjunction with the treaty, President John F. Kennedy enunciated a nuclear safeguard program with provisions for maintaining readiness to resume testing in the denied environments if the test ban treaty were abrogated, for improving systems to detect possible violations of the treaty, and for maintaining viable nuclear-weapon laboratories. Figure 14-6 is a photograph taken during the President's visit to Sandia on December 7, 1962.

Sandia played a significant role in the development of systems to detect violations of the test-ban treaty. These systems included the Vela satellites, designed to detect nuclear tests in the atmosphere and deep space,

Fig. 14-7. Team in underground nu-
clear-test chamber at Nevada test site.

and unmanned seismological observatories to detect underground nuclear
tests. Sandia was responsible for the design, development, testing and
evaluation of the observatories. Sandia also provided logic systems, power
supplies, and some detectors for the satellite payloads.

Early in the 1960s, indications that the USSR was developing an anti-
ballistic-missile capability posed special problems for nuclear-weapon
design. This capability meant that the nuclear-weapon labs would have
to develop missile warheads that could survive exposure to a nuclear burst
in or above the atmosphere, but that could not be fully tested to determine
their ability to survive such enemy countermeasures because of the test-
ban treaty. The result was greater reliance on underground tests (Fig.
14-7) and on simulation of the effects of nuclear radiation. It also meant
much greater use of computers to design experiments and to reduce data
gathered from the experiments. (Between 1960 and 1970, Sandia's computer capacity increased a hundredfold.)

A number of Sandia facilities were constructed in the 1960s to study
radiation damage produced by neutrons, gamma rays, and brief bursts of

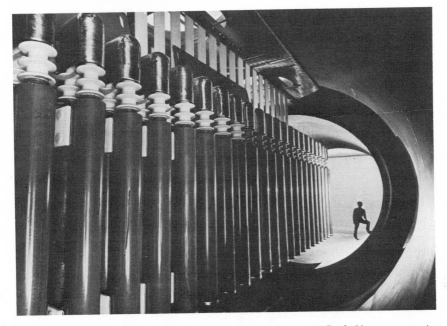

Fig. 14-8. Capacitors mounted in Sandia's Hermes II flash X-ray generator. A bank of 186 of these capacitors was used to store up to 17.5 million volts.

high-energy X-rays. Intense bursts of neutrons and gamma rays were generated by the Sandia pulsed reactor (SPR-I), which was built in 1961 and was superseded by SPR-II in 1967, and by the annular core pulse reactor, which became operational in 1968. The world's largest flash X-ray device, measured at that time in terms of output dose, began operating in 1965 (Fig. 14-8). This device, which produced the X-ray flash by bombarding a metal electrode with very high currents of relativistic electrons, was the first large unit in a series of powerful electron-beam accelerators designed and built at Sandia. These simulation activities equipped Sandia with facilities that would have important energy-research application within a decade.

At this time, major changes in the technical staff were under way to accommodate the needs of an increasingly complex and sophisticated nuclear-weapon technology—a technology that would a decade later prove very helpful in solving some of the nation's energy problems.

By mid-1959 the personnel level (including the Livermore laboratory) had stabilized at about 8,000, but a series of upper-management moves, starting then, resulted in an extensive reorganization over the next 19 months. On September 1, 1960, Molnar returned to Bell Laboratories as executive vice president, and Siegmund P. Schwartz assumed the post of president. Before 1973 the position of vice president of research was held

Table 14-1.   Sandia Laboratories Staff Expansion from 1960–1977.

	1960	1966	1973	1977
Members of Technical Staff				
Degree: PhD	83	245	481	738
MS	334	680	581	729
BS	1,365	1,154	598	647
Other Technical Staff	1,281	1,515	1,562	2,319
Total Technical Staff	3,063	3,594	3,222	4,433
Total Laboratory Staff	7,713	8,110	6,358	7,310

by each of the following Bell Laboratories executives: C. F. Quate, G. C. Dacey, R. C. Prim, R. C. Fletcher, S. J. Buchsbaum, and A. M. Clogston.

Although the size of the staff remained roughly constant, the character of Sandia began to change when the decision was made to expand research activities. Vigorous recruiting of researchers ensued. A second research organization was added in 1962, and in 1965, the research activities were reorganized and further expanded. Late in 1966, John A. Hornbeck, then president of Bellcomm, became president of Sandia and the move to upgrade the staff intensified. The name of the company was changed to Sandia Laboratories, and in 1968 an applied research organization was created at the Livermore laboratory. The changing composition of the technical staff is illustrated by the statistics in Table 14-1, which shows the increase in Sandia's technical staff and the increase in the number of advanced degrees among the staff.

Sandia's research activities attracted high-caliber personnel required to make increasingly sophisticated contributions to weapon systems. Aside from the requirement to develop warheads that were less vulnerable to weapons effects, weapon designers were confronted with the need to develop smaller, more versatile weapons, to continue to develop weapons that were immune to accidental or unauthorized detonation, and to develop weapons that would operate reliably in all types of environments after years of deployment or storage.

The number of weapon-development programs simultaneously under way decreased to four in 1965, which made additional staff available for developing advanced concepts in components and weapons. These development efforts were to have wide-ranging benefits. When Sandia received a commendation in 1972 from the Navy for work on the Poseidon Mk 3 Warhead, President Hornbeck noted that

> . . . the Mk 3 resembles to a marked degree a design developed at Sandia Laboratories in the mid 60's. The product can be considered an excellent example of the payoff from exploratory systems work.

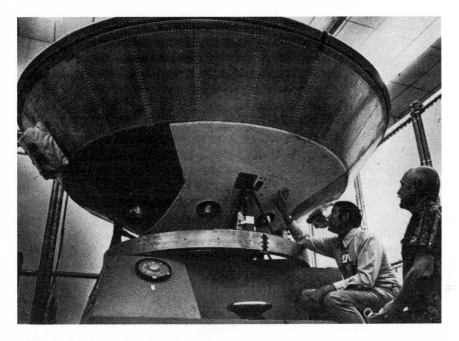

Fig. 14-9. NASA's Viking Lander (now on Mars), which underwent balance tests at Sandia after construction by the Martin-Marietta Company.

Prior to the 1960s, Sandia confined its efforts almost entirely to AEC nuclear-weapon assignments. However, the techniques, skills, and facilities developed during the course of weapons work provided a spectrum of capabilities that enticed other agencies to request Sandia's assistance on several non-weapon projects (Fig. 14-9). These projects, called "reimbursables" because they were not funded by the AEC, included:

1. Space Isotope-Power Program—Begun by Sandia in 1966, this effort provided technical direction for the AEC's program to develop radioisotope-fueled power systems for space missions. The effort included responsibility for the SNAP 27 radioisotope generators that provided power for instrument packages left on the moon by Apollo astronauts.

2. Intrusion-Detection-Sensors Development Program—Begun in 1966 for the Advanced Research Projects Agency, this program was later funded by the United States Army Defense Communications Planning Group in the Department of Defense. Seismic and geophone sensors were deployed in large numbers along the demilitarized zone and the Ho Chi Minh trail during the Vietnam war. The detectors were unique because they were delivered by air drop and used principles developed at Sandia to implant themselves in the ground.

3. Planetary Quarantine Program—Partially an outgrowth of Sandia's revolutionary laminar air-flow clean room, this small program was un-

dertaken for NASA in 1966. Sandia was to develop procedures that would prevent United States space vehicles from carrying contaminants to other planets. This program led to investigations that produced efficient methods for sterilizing sewage sludge and turning it into a useful product.

1.6 Sandia in the 1970s

Reduced funding for the AEC in the fiscal years of 1970 and 1971 created a financial situation that forced a reduction in staff at Sandia. The number of personnel on roll dropped from 8,120 in 1969 to 7,560 in 1970 and, because losses due to attrition were not replenished, to 7,290 in 1971. Continued tight budgets precipitated further AEC force reductions, and in the fiscal year of 1973 Sandia's work force dropped to 6,400.

In March 1974, the Sandia management was as follows:

President	Morgan Sparks*
Executive Vice President	W. J. Howard
Vice Presidents	G. A. Fowler, K. D. Bowers,*
	R. B. Powell, A. Narath, T. B. Cook, Jr.,
	R. A. Bice
Attorney General, Secretary and Treasurer	C. T. Ross, Jr.*

Management remained unchanged until 1977 with the exception that, in 1976, E. D. Reed succeeded K. D. Bowers as vice president.

At the beginning of the decade, warheads were being developed for both the Sprint and Spartan antiballistic missiles. Concurrently, round after round of strategic-arms limitation talks were being conducted. Negotiators viewed limitation of ABMs as a major bargaining point. In May 1972 a strategic-arms limitation was signed in which the signers agreed, among other things, to restrict the number of ABMs that could be deployed. The United States ABM development programs were carried through to completion, but with restricted production.

A Presidential directive issued in 1962 required that all United States nuclear weapons stockpiled in NATO commands be afforded positive protection against unauthorized use. Control and protection concepts that were developed by Sandia evolved from simple, manually operated combination locks to remotely controlled, electronically coded switches and, in the 1970s, to special protective devices and nonviolent destruct systems that prevented unauthorized use of a weapon. Sandia's efforts in protection systems have since been diversified and expanded far beyond use-denial schemes for single weapons. In addition to the established command and control activities, a new organization concerned with nuclear security systems was created in 1974 to address a full range of safe-

---

* From the Bell System.

guards, including transportation and facility protection, as well as threat assessment and response.

The Atomic Energy Act of 1954 was amended in 1971,

> ... to authorize the Commission to conduct research and development activities relating to the preservation and enhancement of a viable environment by developing more efficient methods to meet the Nation's energy needs.

Sandia's weapon-effects-simulation activities had led to the development of some of the world's most powerful lasers and electron beams. In 1972, following some earlier experiments with lasers, the possibility of using ultrahigh-power electron beams in the production of controlled thermonuclear power was recognized, and attention was directed toward that goal. Simulation work was funded by the AEC's Division of Military Application, but in 1973, a proposal for a complementary R and D program devoted to the compression and heating of thermonuclear fuel by electron beams was accepted by the AEC's Division of Controlled Thermonuclear Research. This program became the first at Sandia to be funded as an energy research program.

Meanwhile, an informal committee of Sandia personnel was working to identify energy projects that Sandia could pursue. By October 1972 these discussions resulted in a proposal to develop a solar community engineered to derive essentially all its energy needs from the sun. The proposal was submitted to the National Science Foundation (NSF) for funding but it was rejected by the NSF because it would have used nearly 60 percent of the $1.4 million then available for distribution. Later the NSF did fund a systems study. In July 1974 the project was included in the AEC budget.

As a result of a decision by top management that Sandia could and should play a significant role in helping the nation meet its energy needs, some 21 energy-project proposals were submitted for AEC review in the fall of 1973. The proposals, though addressing subjects as diverse as wind-energy conversion, drilling technology, and combustion analysis by Raman spectroscopy, were all derived, directly or indirectly, from weapons work done at Sandia.

The probability of future fuel shortages was driven home to the American public in 1973 when a fuel embargo by the Organization of Petroleum Exporting Countries forced a nation of automobile drivers to wait in line, sometimes for hours, at service stations to buy gasoline. In October 1974, legislation was enacted that would—on January 19, 1975—abolish the AEC and create two new agencies: the Energy Research and Development Administration (ERDA) and the Nuclear Regulatory Commission (NRC). In the ERDA environment, Sandia's energy research flourished—new projects were started and various ongoing projects were enlarged (Fig. 14-10). Today, major programs exist in lasers, electron- and

(a)   (b)

Fig. 14-10.   Two of Sandia's energy research projects.   (a) Electron beam striking target in fusion experiment.   (b) Vertical axis wind turbine.

ion-beam fusion, solar energy, and fossil energy.   In 1976 the Energy Projects and Systems Analysis organization was formed to direct the work in solar and fossil energy.

Sandia developed and operated nuclear reactors for a number of years to study the effects of radiation on materials, components, and subsystems. Through this work, Sandia gained experience and developed facilities of direct value to programs in reactor safety research.   The value to these programs was strengthened because the reactor work was not oriented toward utility-power reactors.   Thus Sandia had no vested interest in reactor designs and could function as a uniquely qualified, objective investigator of reactor safety.   These qualifications, coupled with its extensive background in the development of safety and security measures for nuclear weapons, enabled Sandia to focus on nuclear-fuel cycle problems in four areas: reactor safety, waste management, security, and transportation.   In 1976 a new organization, Nuclear Fuel Cycle Programs, was created to direct a major program for the NRC.

In 1977 President Jimmy Carter, in a dramatic presentation, called on the country to wage the "moral equivalent of war" on the energy problem. One of his first moves to marshal energy-related forces was establishment

Fig. 14-11.   Sandia Laboratories in 1976.

of a Department of Energy to address the huge task of developing new energy sources and reducing the national energy appetite.   On October 1, three federal agencies, including ERDA, were transferred to the department in their entirety and units from five others were relocated to create the organization.   Sandia's activities continued without interruption: weapons activities were then reported to the Assistant Secretary for Defense Programs and the bulk of the energy activities to the Assistant Secretary for Energy Technology.

That year Sandia's employee population stood at 7,250.   It is projected that by 1981 it will increase to 7,800.   Most of Sandia's work in 1977, about 70 percent, was still related to nuclear weapons.   This effort is a fully matured expression of the purpose for which the corporation was created 30 years ago. (Sandia Laboratories as it appeared in 1976 is shown above in Fig. 14-11.)

The nuclear-weapon effort at Sandia has been a model of a successful technical-development program.   The past three decades have seen a hundredfold reduction in the weight of weapons and a thousandfold increase in their yield.   The technological progress in nuclear-weapon design since World War II has resulted in strategic deterrence forces that are far cheaper and more likely to survive and in a nuclear arsenal that can make a major contribution to the security of the United States and its allies.

Speaking to an Air Force Association symposium in 1976, an ERDA official said,

> Above all we must not allow the nuclear weapons development and production complex to erode . . . . The weapons laboratories represent a combination of trained manpower and physical resources that is available nowhere else in the West.   It would be extremely difficult if not impossible to reassemble this complex in a crisis situation.

In his book of 25 years ago, Mr. Lilienthal described the creation of

Sandia Laboratories and concluded with statements that need only minor modernization to be applicable today:

> The Bell System took over the Sandia operation . . . not long after my meeting with Mr. Wilson. It has been responsible for it ever since. The stepped-up production of atomic bombs and the favorable results in the tests of new weapons, as officially announced from time to time, are, I am sure, in considerable measure due to the unique contribution of the Bell System and of the great scientific talents in the [weapons laboratories].[3]

II. BELLCOMM

2.1 Introduction

On October 4, 1957, the Soviet Union successfully launched the earth's first artificial satellite. Sputnik I comprised four tons in orbit, including 184 pounds of instrumentation. United States plannning at that time, in connection with the International Geophysical Year, was to launch at least one Vanguard satellite with a total payload weight of three pounds before the end of 1958. There followed a period characterized as the "Sputnik crisis."

Concern arising from the Soviet space success caused the government to recognize that space technology had to be given high priority if the United States were to catch up with the Soviet Union. Significant events followed.

On November 7, 1957, President Eisenhower created the post of Special Assistant to the President for Science and Technology. The first incumbent was asked to consider the space problem.

On July 29, 1958, the President signed the National Aeronautics and Space Act of 1958 ". . . to provide for research into problems of flight within and outside the earth's atmosphere, and for other purposes." The National Aeronautics and Space Administration (NASA), created by the Act, began operation on October 1, 1958.

In Section 102 of the Aeronautics and Space Act, Declaration of Policy and Purpose, the Congress declared that the general welfare and security of the United States required that adequate provision be made for space activities, and that these activities be conducted so as to contribute materially to the following objective (among others): the preservation of the role of the United States as a leader in aeronautical and space science and technology. With the passage of this act the United States committed itself to world leadership in space.

The next step was to choose a goal for the space program. At the minimum, the goal had to be such that, by achieving it, the United States would demonstrate the capability to match and excel Soviet space performance. In view of the then existing, superior Soviet booster capability,

---

[3] Lilienthal, p. 103.

the goal had to be a sufficiently large step forward that the United States had a sporting chance of beating the Russians to it.

On May 25, 1961, President Kennedy said,

> I believe that this nation should commit itself to achieving the goal before this decade is out of landing a man on the moon and returning him safely to earth.

It was a goal no one knew in advance was achievable—a magnificent gamble that electrified the nation. To realize the goal required building and organizing the facilities to carry out a vast engineering program that would require the very best our technology was capable of producing. The Apollo-Saturn program that ensued was to grow by the mid-1960s to include 12 prime contractors, 17,000 subcontractors, perhaps 300,000 people, plus three dedicated NASA space flight centers. By far the smallest of the prime contractors was Bellcomm, Inc.

2.2 Bell System Efforts in the Manned Space-Flight Program

Eight months after President Kennedy's announcement of the space-flight goal, Roswell Gilpatric, Deputy Secretary of Defense, wrote Frederick R. Kappel, chairman of the board of AT&T, conveying the request of Secretary of Defense Robert S. McNamara and himself that Bell Laboratories' resources in systems engineering be made available to the NASA space program. But this was to be done without compromising the important work Bell Labs was doing for the Department of Defense.

An exchange of letters followed in 1962 between NASA and AT&T that led to the founding of Bellcomm and defined its job. James E. Webb, Administrator of NASA, wrote a letter on February 21, 1962, to Mr. Kappel, the substance of which is caught in the following quotations.

> It would be a public service of the very first order of importance if the Bell System would undertake to assist NASA . . . by providing an organization of experienced men capable of giving the responsible NASA officials the benefit of the most advanced analytical procedures and the factual basis they need to make the wide range of system engineering decisions required for the successful execution of the manned space flight mission.

The Bell System felt that this assignment could best be handled by a separate corporation to make feasibility studies and operations analyses and, in general, to supply technical facts that NASA's officials needed in making a wide range of systems engineering decisions. Thus, Webb's letter went on to say:

> The form of corporate organization to be employed . . . should be so arranged as to maximize these factors which will make for efficient and effective operation, and we would have no objection to the establishment of a separate subsidiary corporation to do the job.

By 1962, "not-for-profit" and "fee-less" organizations performing technical work for the federal government were receiving some negative reactions from Congress and from the press. In keeping with the times and in contrast to the Sandia no-fee contract agreement, which was working very well, the decision was made to form a profit-making company. Hence, in Webb's letter:

> A cost-plus-a-fixed-fee contract appears to us to be the appropriate basis for defining the business relationships . . . .

And finally, the letter emphasized,

> . . . such arrangement can in no way impair NASA's direct responsibility for all decisions in the planning, engineering, and procurement areas. There will be no delegation of such responsibility to a nongovernment organization. What we are seeking is not a means of diluting the responsibility or authority of NASA's appropriate officials, but rather the most skilled and experienced assistance available to enable us to exercise that responsibility and authority in the most effective manner.

E. J. McNeely, President of AT&T, replied in a letter dated March 1, 1962,

> As you know, it is not our practice to seek work for the Government or for others which is outside the communications area. [However, as a corporate citizen,] . . . we will be glad to assist you in accomplishing the mission described in your letter. . . . we believe we can do this job most effectively through the formation of a separate subsidiary corporation within the Bell System which will be in a position to draw on the talents and experience of this Company as well as Bell Telephone Laboratories, Western Electric Company and our other associated companies.

The new subsidiary corporation of which McNeely wrote was, of course, Bellcomm, Inc.

The founding of Bellcomm and its intended close association with the management of the manned space program, posed a question of deep concern both to the government and to the Bell System—possible competitive advantage to the Bell System, or institutional conflict of interest. There was need for a clear understanding between the government and the Bell System which would exclude the Bell System from providing NASA certain services and hardware and, at the same time, would not unduly restrict NASA from obtaining services that the Bell System might be uniquely qualified to give.

This question was resolved by a letter from Webb to McNeely, dated April 11, 1962. In this letter, the general principle established was that, with the exceptions noted below, Bell System companies would not seek work from NASA in areas related to the manned space-flight program. Also NASA would not call on the Bell System to perform such work except when, in the opinion of the Administrator or the Deputy Administrator, an exception to this general rule was required. The letter suggested that such exceptions would be rare and would arise only when the Bell System was in a unique position to perform a valuable service for NASA, or when the national interest would be uniquely served.

The exceptions to this general rule were stated explicitly. They were communications, including satellite communications, and tracking and guidance. With respect to the communications field, Webb stated that the arrangements between NASA and Bellcomm should not affect the dealings of the Bell System companies with NASA. Such companies would remain free to deal with NASA in furnishing communications services generally, and in connection with the communications aspects of projects such as Mercury, Gemini, and Apollo, on the same basis as if the new arrangements had not been made. Further, the letter stated that there was no reason why the dealings of the Bell System companies with NASA in the communications satellite field should be affected by Bellcomm. (Telstar I communications satellite had yet to be launched, and the Comsat Corporation had yet to be founded.) The treatment of tracking and guidance systems was also quite explicit. Webb's letter recognized the important role played by Bell System companies in the area of missile tracking and guidance (actually by the Bell Labs-Western Electric radio-inertial command guidance system). The letter stated that there was no intention on the part of NASA to disturb Bell System work on existing NASA projects.

In a letter dated April 18, 1962, McNeely replied to Webb's letter on these restrictions and said, "What you suggest is entirely acceptable to us as a satisfactory basis on which to proceed."

To conjecture, there were no doubt several reasons why the Bell System was chosen for this kind of agreement. One was the Bell System's resources in highly competent scientific and engineering personnel. Another was Bell Labs' wide experience in managing the Nike project and in developing tracking and guidance equipment. A third was the willingness of the Bell System to accept a hardware-exclusion provision that denied it the privilege of participating in major dollar contracts. But perhaps the most important consideration was one that was expressed by Webb in his request to Kappel:

> The job of coordinating a world-wide communications network must have presented many of the same kinds of systems planning, engineering and integration problems on a very large scale, that we expect to encounter in carrying out the nation's program of manned space exploration.

2.3 The New Company

Bellcomm was incorporated under the laws of the State of Delaware on March 21, 1962, the month following John Glenn's manned orbital flight aboard Friendship 7. Its initial capital stock of $200,000 was owned jointly in equal amounts by AT&T and Western Electric. Bellcomm officially started business April 1, 1962, under letter contract from NASA, signed three days earlier, with four employees on the payroll, but little else. Bellcomm had no tools to carry out studies, no buildings, furniture, telephones, procedures—nothing but the intent and backing of the Bell System to fulfill a commitment, a very big job.

Bell System news bulletins announced Bellcomm's formation with the words:

> The new company will work with the Office of Systems in NASA's Office of Manned Space Flight. Projects for which it will provide systems-planning support include the Gemini program to earth-orbit a two-man space craft and the Apollo program to land three-man teams on the moon and return them safely, in addition to planning missions beyond the first lunar landing.
>
> President and Chief Executive Officer of the new organization will be John A. Hornbeck, now Executive Director, Semiconductor Device and Electron Tube Division, of Bell Laboratories. Vice President and General Manager will be W. J. Whittaker, currently Assistant Vice President, Personnel and General Service, AT&T Long Lines Department. Mr. Hornbeck and Mr. Whittaker also will be members of the Board of Directors of the new company.
>
> Heading major technical divisions of the new company will be Julian M. West, now Executive Director of the Military Systems Division of Bell Laboratories, and W. Deming Lewis, now Executive Director of the Research-Communications System Division at the Laboratories. Hendrik W. Bode, Vice President, Military Development and Systems Engineering of Bell Laboratories, will serve as a special adviser to the new company and will be a member of its Board.
>
> Other board members will be R. R. Hough, AT&T Vice President in charge of engineering, and formerly a Bell Laboratories vice president; K. G. McKay, Vice President, Bell Laboratories; L. R. Cook, Engineer of Manufacture, Western Electric; H. G. Mehlhouse, Vice President, Western Electric; J. A. Farmer, AT&T General Attorney and J. H. Felker, AT&T Assistant Chief Engineer. Mr. Hough will act as Chairman of the Board of the new company.

Once officially in existence, Bellcomm needed to be molded into a productive operating organization, capable of performing both ordinary and esoteric technical work under personnel practices and procedures and employment conditions that met Bell System standards. A first step was to acquire office space. An empty building, 1737 L Street N.W., Washington, D.C., was rented and fitted out as the company's first headquarters. In staffing the company, it was decided to build from the top down, that is, to provide the essential management and leadership first, and to fill out the organization later. This process was to go on for several years. Services needed to be established: purchasing, travel, accounting, security, and medical. Practices needed to be formulated: normal work week, holidays, employment standards, technical recruiting, education, reporting, definitions of technical report, memoranda and working papers. Insurance protection for employees and the company needed to be secured, a pension plan set up, a Benefit Committee appointed, etc.

As a technical organization, Bellcomm was made up primarily of people who were new to the space field. They worked initially from a rather anomalous contractor position, sometimes in competition with NASA systems engineers, into the spongy impedance of an enormous governmental organization in a state of rapid growth and in the throes of developing its own management structure. Much of the first year was spent in self-education, in developing organizational and personal ties with NASA headquarters and field centers, in developing the tools (e.g., a computer program to compute a trajectory to the moon and back) and concepts necessary to conduct systems studies, and in recruiting a highly competent technical staff. The aim was to be an organization of modest size and high ability; quality of personnel was deemed more important than quantity.

During this period, Bellcomm functioned as a "job shop" and advisory facility to Joseph F. Shea's Office of Systems in NASA's Office of Manned Space Flight, which was headed by D. Brainerd Holmes. Tasks begun included:

1. Formulating and developing the concept of the unmanned space program (Ranger, Surveyor) as a support to the manned program.

2. Identifying and understanding the natural environmental hazards in the lunar mission: meteoroids, radiation, solar flares, and lunar-surface characteristics.

3. Formulating the novel concept of the lunar-excursion-module propulsion system as a backup system to return astronauts safely if the primary-service-module propulsion system failed (Apollo 13 flight).

4. Judging the characteristics of a "good" (safe) lunar landing site.

5. Considering what might comprise a reliability program for manned space flights.

6. Assisting NASA in preparing a comprehensive Apollo System Specification (Figs. 14-12 and 14-13).

Initially these undertakings were reviewed monthly by Bellcomm management and by Holmes and NASA consultant Mervin J. Kelly, retired president of Bell Labs, who took a lively and objective interest in Bellcomm's first tentative steps. This encouragement no doubt helped Bellcomm in its infancy to establish and preserve the principles of independence of judgment in the work it undertook and of technical management of its own people. Forces were strong to treat Bellcomm as a "body shop," that is, an organization that would respond passively to NASA's detailed direction. The body shop, or technical-direction, problem endured as a recurring pressure almost throughout Bellcomm's existence, especially

Fig. 14-12.   Meeting of NASA and Bellcomm representatives in 1962 to discuss Apollo project.   Clockwise from lower center: John A. Hornbeck (Bellcomm), W. Deming Lewis (Bellcomm), William A. Lee (NASA), Julian M. West (Bellcomm), John A. Gautraud (NASA), and Joseph F. Shea (NASA).

(a)

(b)

Fig. 14-13.   (a) John A. Hornbeck points out a possible Apollo landing site on a large scale map of the moon.   (b) Models of Saturn 1, Saturn 1B, and the moon rocket, Saturn V.

on some occasions when NASA acquired new people in managerial positions.

As a fledgling technical organization, Bellcomm faced some questions of immense difficulty and complexity. In the summer of 1962, there was a query from Mr. Webb to Bellcomm's president which might be paraphrased as follows:

> Which is the preferable mode for reaching the lunar surface, earth-orbit-rendezvous (EOR) or lunar-orbit-rendezvous (LOR)? Bellcomm is new to the program and presumably objective. As reported in *TIME* magazine, the President's science advisor (Mr. Jerome Wiesner) favors EOR and suspects that NASA management is deciding in favor of LOR partially for institutional reasons that are not technically supportable. We need your views in a short time.

President Hornbeck appointed a committee of three Bellcomm managers (Sidney Darlington, C. R. Moster, and T. H. Thompson) to address this question. The committee's response was, in retrospect, sound and sensible:

1. The uncertainties in the United States understanding of either of the two modes, EOR and LOR, are greater than the apparent differences between them; thus it cannot be said that technically either is superior;

2. From a program management viewpoint, the interfaces between the already defined NASA management institutions (principally Manned Spacecraft Center and Manned Space Flight Center) are significantly clearer and simpler, and therefore more easily managed in the LOR mission configuration than in the EOR; hence,

3. LOR is a better choice for a mission profile as a basis on which to proceed with development.

NASA chose LOR, and the controversy died. However, the President's Scientific Advisory Committee (PSAC), which raised the question, retained its interest and reviewed the program twice in the succeeding three years asking appropriate and difficult questions concerning its technological feasibility. Indeed, these were questions that Bellcomm Board Chairman Hough also continued to raise.

Another example of the complex and difficult questions faced by Bellcomm involved one of judgment on the design philosophy of electronics in the spacecraft. Should in-flight maintenance and repair be an acceptable path for "solving" subsystem reliability problems? This important question arose early in connection with the design of the spacecraft guidance computer. Even with the assumption of low component-failure rates, the computer design did not meet stated mission requirements, and an elaborate diagnosis and repair scheme, operated by the astronaut, was proposed as an integral part of the design. Bellcomm supported the view of NASA's Dr. Shea, which finally prevailed. This view was that the basic system design philosophy, and therefore a specification requirement on spacecraft systems, exclude in-flight maintenance as a part of the primary mode of operation. This was, indeed, a fundamental systems engineering decision.

The Bell System's entry into the space program did not pass unnoticed by Congress and by some newspaper columnists—Drew Pearson for one. Hornbeck was invited to appear August 31, 1962, before the Subcommittee on Military Operations (Rep. Chet Holifield, Democrat of California, Chairman) of the House Committee on Government Operations. He was asked to describe Bellcomm's job, to explain the Bell System's intentions in the space/military arena, to discuss avoidance of institutional conflict of interest, and to comment on the subject of system development and management which the subcommittee was looking into. In his prepared statement, Hornbeck described the Bell System's intentions with respect to Bellcomm:

> I wish to emphasize that Bellcomm was put together to assist the National Aeronautics and Space Administration, in particular its Office of Systems in the Office of Manned Space Flight, that we are here at their request, and that when they no longer have need for us, we are ready to get out of the picture.

This commitment was, in fact, fulfilled in 1972.

Bellcomm, as a prime contractor of NASA headquarters, was asked to appear before the House Committee on Science & Astronautics' Subcommittee on Manned Space Flight, in hearings on the annual NASA authorization bill. An excerpt from President Hornbeck's testimony of March 20, 1963, before this subcommittee yields insight into the problems of carrying forward the Apollo program under the time pressure generated by the Soviet superiority in space:

> Mr. Roudebush. One final question: I notice on page 10 of your statement you mentioned "depending on what is discovered on the lunar surface." How do you make recommendations and do engineering planning for a mission that involves unknown quantities? For example, how do you design and make recommendations for a lunar mission when we don't really know what we will find on the surface of the moon?
>
> Is it a question of putting the cart before the horse, Dr. Hornbeck?
>
> Dr. Hornbeck. First, I don't think anybody likes to plan with gaping holes in one's information. You much prefer to have sufficiently definite information to do an effective job. One handles this, as we do in the space program, in several ways. One tries to effect designs that are on the safe side from what we expect to find, so that one doesn't have to redesign hardware later.
>
> For example, the landing structure on the lunar excursion module you try to make as rugged as you can afford. Then there is some basis for guessing from what we know, that most probably it will be all right.

But we are not really happy until information comes back from, say, the unmanned program, prior to actually carrying out a landing, which tells us what the nature of the lunar surface is on rather a fine scale, so we know what we are getting into.

Mr. Roudebush. Are you referring to discoveries that would accrue from the Surveyor program?

Dr. Hornbeck. Yes.

Mr. Roudebush. Are we going too fast with the design on the LEM? For example, should we be holding up some of these designs until we do know more about the lunar surface?

Are we perhaps progressing too fast and perhaps designing a vehicle we cannot use?

Dr. Hornbeck. There is always the possibility that when we really know the situation, it will be much more adverse than we expect. This is always the possibility, in which case we, meaning the United States, would have designed the wrong thing.

Mr. Roudebush. Yes. I am not speaking now of Bellcomm, but of the overall effort.

Dr. Hornbeck. Yes.[4]

By April 1963 the company, numbering 160 employees, was consolidated in new quarters in Washington, D.C. at 1100 17th St., N.W. A chart showing the organization in March 1963 is given in Fig. 14-14. Plans for a group life insurance policy and for an extraordinary medical expense policy were announced. A secretarial services organization was established. All supervisory employees completed a statement relating to any possible conflict of interest. The initial benefit committee meeting took place. On June 7 Bellcomm's first open house was held. In July the board of directors declared the first dividend payment with AT&T and Western Electric sharing equally.

In September 1963, the end of Bellcomm's first contract period, negotiations with NASA were completed on the estimated cost for the second contract and related subjects. An IBM computer was installed, a pension plan was adopted, and the first accident under the benefit plan took place. Bellcomm employees became associated with the Telephone Pioneers, and the second annual picnic was held in Rock Creek Park with 475 employees and their families attending. The second United Givers Fund campaign was completed and 204 employees contributed $5,200. Staffing still continued to be of major concern. The original 25 employees of May 1, 1962, had grown by September 1963 to 219—90 administrative and 129 technical employees. For the 18-month period, the Bellcomm contract with NASA amounted to about $8.5 million.

By this time Gordon Cooper had completed the 22-orbit MA-9 mission, which followed the Mercury flights of Carpenter and Schirra; Ranger V,

---

4 1964 NASA Authorization, House Subcommittee on Manned Space Flight, p. 384.

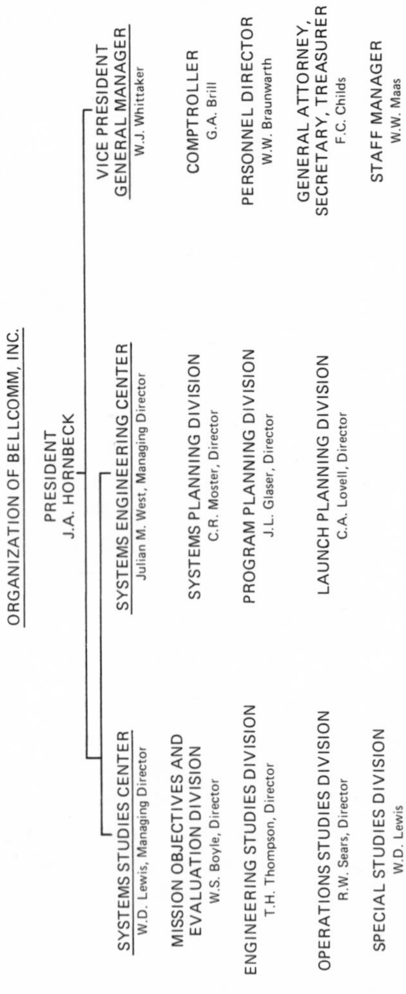

ORGANIZATION OF BELLCOMM, INC.

PRESIDENT
J.A. HORNBECK

SYSTEMS STUDIES CENTER
W.D. Lewis, Managing Director

MISSION OBJECTIVES AND
EVALUATION DIVISION
W.S. Boyle, Director

ENGINEERING STUDIES DIVISION
T.H. Thompson, Director

OPERATIONS STUDIES DIVISION
R.W. Sears, Director

SPECIAL STUDIES DIVISION
W.D. Lewis

SYSTEMS ENGINEERING CENTER
Julian M. West, Managing Director

SYSTEMS PLANNING DIVISION
C.R. Moster, Director

PROGRAM PLANNING DIVISION
J.L. Glaser, Director

LAUNCH PLANNING DIVISION
C.A. Lovell, Director

VICE PRESIDENT
GENERAL MANAGER
W.J. Whittaker

COMPTROLLER
G.A. Brill

PERSONNEL DIRECTOR
W.W. Braunwarth

GENERAL ATTORNEY,
SECRETARY, TREASURER
F.C. Childs

STAFF MANAGER
W.W. Maas

Fig. 14-14.   Bellcomm organization on March 4, 1963.

which was intended for unmanned lunar exploration, had failed; and SA-4, the fourth Saturn I launch-vehicle development test had been completed successfully.

2.4 Evolution to Maturity: The Arrival of Mueller and Phillips

In the fall of 1963, George E. Mueller replaced Brainerd Holmes as head of NASA's Office of Manned Space Flight (OMSF). With him came a new approach to program management, which was taken from the Air Force's experience in managing ballistic-missile-system development. In time a complete reorganization at OMSF also came. Mueller visualized a different role for Bellcomm, similar to that of TRW's Space Technology Laboratory (STL) in the ICBM program. (But, of course, NASA was organized differently from the Air Force, and Bellcomm was much smaller and otherwise different from STL).

Mueller immediately asked for more centralized liaison, a tighter coupling with NASA in systems engineering support. Bellcomm responded as indicated in its organization change notice dated November 13, 1963:

> Mr. T. H. Thompson is appointed Special Assistant to the President. In this position Mr. Thompson will be located at NASA headquarters (OMSF) . . . in Room 429. He will act as a focal point for Bellcomm systems engineering support of the Apollo Program Office."

The concept was that T. H. Thompson would be well informed on program needs and would function as a conduit for loading work into Bellcomm.

Other events took place quickly. Shea, who had come to doubt that the Apollo-Saturn project could be managed from Washington, left Washington for Houston to become project manager of the Apollo Spacecraft project. On January 28, 1964, OSMF issued an organization chart disclosing the new organizational format for headquarters, a format that survived for the duration of the space program. Air Force Brigadier General Samuel C. Phillips was appointed deputy Apollo program director under Mueller. Five organizations were shown reporting to Mueller and Phillips: Program Control, Test, Operations, Reliability, and Systems Engineering. T. H. Thompson, identified with Bellcomm, was named as head of the Systems Engineering function and organization, which was to include only Bellcomm personnel. Mueller's plan was that each of the project offices comprising the Apollo program—Apollo Spacecraft Project at MSC, Saturn IA-V Launch Vehicle Project at MSFC, Launch Operations at Cape Kennedy—would be grouped into five identically titled organizations forming a hierarchy that would encourage, for example, Systems Engineering at the program level to communicate with Systems Engineering at the project level and similarly with the other four organizations:

Test, Program Control, Flight Operations, and Reliability/Quality. (This plan took some time to accomplish.) Also, Mueller conceived that the other large programs in manned space flight, Gemini and Advanced Apollo, would be similarly organized.

By March 1963 the first two Bellcomm/OMSF documents containing systems engineering directives appeared (*Interim Mass Properties Reporting Procedure* and *Interim Control and Design Goal Weights*). They were written by Bellcomm and approved and issued by NASA. Thompson in effect wore two hats, one on Phillips' staff and the other reporting to the president of Bellcomm.

The improved coupling with Apollo quickly exposed (or reexposed) Bellcomm's limited manpower situation. The Program Office demands seemed insatiable, and the organization was placed in a posture of continuous overload. At that time, Bellcomm personnel were engaged in many program activities: investigations of space environmental hazards, scientific exploration of the moon, in-flight checkout, participation in the NASA unmanned program in support of Apollo, study of LOR reference trajectories, etc. Clearly, however, Thompson's NASA function, MAS (for Manned Space Apollo Systems Engineering), needed more muscle. In a Bellcomm reorganization in June 1964, two capable departments were assigned to him. These also were collocated with NASA at NASA headquarters, a decision taken only after much head holding, and with some reservations by a few Bell System officials who feared loss of Bellcomm independence. In practice, both Bellcomm and NASA managers were fully aware of the sensitive nature of the relationship and of the distinction between advice and decision in a chain of command. Through careful attention, the arrangement survived without causing a single major problem.

The MAS function received further strength through a Bellcomm reorganization a year later in mid-1965 (Fig. 14-15). Thompson was promoted to managing director of the Systems Engineering Center and was assigned about half of Bellcomm's technical strength, which was organized under three directors, as shown in the figure. MAS got all the support Bellcomm could supply, and the company survived.

The MAS systems engineering task of Bellcomm was associated both with the level and function of the Apollo program director. Bellcomm took responsibility for a number of studies, many of which formed the basis for program decisions. A major Bellcomm role was to ensure that the hardware and software being developed—the launch vehicle, the spacecraft, the ground control communications and tracking systems, the ground support systems and the astronaut training—were able to perform the planned Apollo mission. It was also Bellcomm's task to help ensure that the missions were sufficiently well identified and described that everyone involved understood what they were and, not incidentally, that

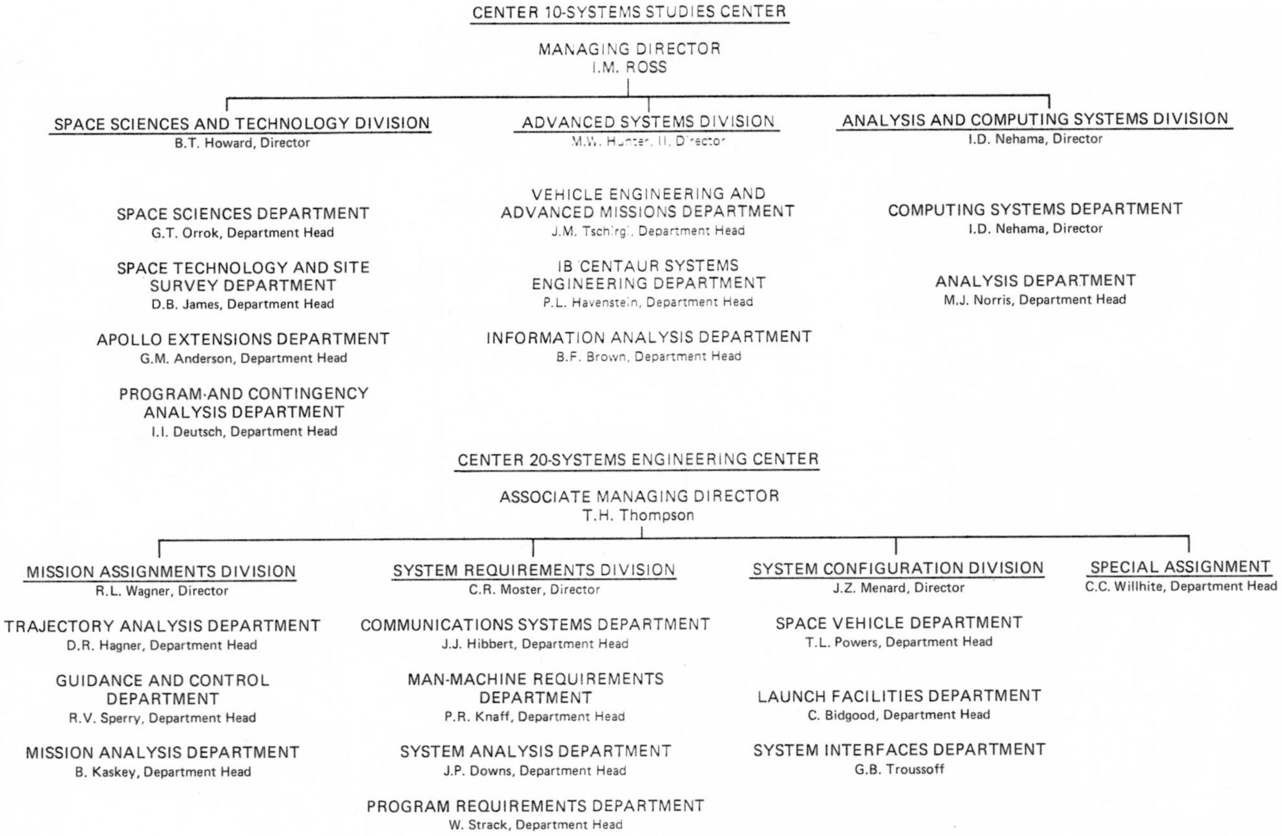

CENTER 10-SYSTEMS STUDIES CENTER
MANAGING DIRECTOR
I.M. ROSS

SPACE SCIENCES AND TECHNOLOGY DIVISION
B.T. Howard, Director

SPACE SCIENCES DEPARTMENT
G.T. Orrok, Department Head

SPACE TECHNOLOGY AND SITE SURVEY DEPARTMENT
D.B. James, Department Head

APOLLO EXTENSIONS DEPARTMENT
G.M. Anderson, Department Head

PROGRAM AND CONTINGENCY ANALYSIS DEPARTMENT
I.I. Deutsch, Department Head

ADVANCED SYSTEMS DIVISION
M.W. Hunter II, Director

VEHICLE ENGINEERING AND ADVANCED MISSIONS DEPARTMENT
J.M. Tsching, Department Head

IB CENTAUR SYSTEMS ENGINEERING DEPARTMENT
P.L. Havenstein, Department Head

INFORMATION ANALYSIS DEPARTMENT
B.F. Brown, Department Head

ANALYSIS AND COMPUTING SYSTEMS DIVISION
I.D. Nehama, Director

COMPUTING SYSTEMS DEPARTMENT
I.D. Nehama, Director

ANALYSIS DEPARTMENT
M.J. Norris, Department Head

SPECIAL ASSIGNMENT
C.C. Willhite, Department Head

CENTER 20-SYSTEMS ENGINEERING CENTER
ASSOCIATE MANAGING DIRECTOR
T.H. Thompson

MISSION ASSIGNMENTS DIVISION
R.L. Wagner, Director

TRAJECTORY ANALYSIS DEPARTMENT
D.R. Hagner, Department Head

GUIDANCE AND CONTROL DEPARTMENT
R.V. Sperry, Department Head

MISSION ANALYSIS DEPARTMENT
B. Kaskey, Department Head

SYSTEM REQUIREMENTS DIVISION
C.R. Moster, Director

COMMUNICATIONS SYSTEMS DEPARTMENT
J.J. Hibbert, Department Head

MAN-MACHINE REQUIREMENTS DEPARTMENT
P.R. Knaff, Department Head

SYSTEM ANALYSIS DEPARTMENT
J.P. Downs, Department Head

PROGRAM REQUIREMENTS DEPARTMENT
W. Strack, Department Head

SYSTEM CONFIGURATION DIVISION
J.Z. Menard, Director

SPACE VEHICLE DEPARTMENT
T.L. Powers, Department Head

LAUNCH FACILITIES DEPARTMENT
C. Bidgood, Department Head

SYSTEM INTERFACES DEPARTMENT
G.B. Troussoff

Fig. 14-15. Bellcomm organization on May 30, 1965.

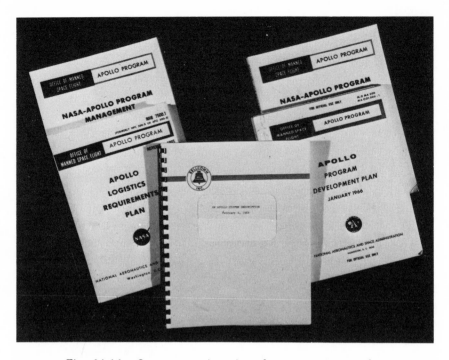

Fig. 14-16.   Systems engineering documents essential to success of Apollo program.   (Courtesy of National Air and Space Museum, Smithsonian Institution.)

the parts fit together in real time.   This work crystallized into a set of Apollo documents that Bellcomm prepared and maintained (Fig. 14–16):

1. *Apollo Flight Mission Assignments*—This document specified the objectives, flight hardware configuration, flight profiles, payloads and on-board experiments on a flight-by-flight basis for each mission in the Apollo program.   It was issued by the Apollo Program Office and approved by the associate administrator of NASA.

2. *Apollo Program Specification*—This was the program-level technical specification.   It delineated the performance, design, and test requirements of the Apollo program.   It was an inch-thick summary, listing every major piece of hardware and what it was required to do.   This document was approved by the Apollo program director.

3. *Apollo Mission Sequence Plan*—This systems engineering document gave a step-by-step account of the first lunar mission identifying what was to happen at each point.

The following documents were provided to control the developing program and to ensure that the interfaces between the Centers and contractors were well defined.

4. *Quarterly Weight and Performance Report*—This regular document summarized the weight and the performance capability of the Apollo space vehicles, giving visibility to interfaces and identifying elements not within planned ranges.

5. *Natural Environment and Physical Standards for the Apollo Program*—Many definitions and natural constants were required in the design of the Apollo system. The constants included meteoroid fluxes, astrodynamic constants, materials constants, lunar soils, geodetic reference systems, and statistically anticipated wind conditions. Bellcomm selected and worked the data into formats and models that would assist engineering judgments. The document provided these data so that all designers were working to the same definitions and standards.

Two companion documents (6 and 7, below) expanded on this theme.

6. *Project Apollo Coordinate Systems Standards*—This document recorded inertial, vehicle, geodetic, guidance and navigation coordinate-system standards used in meshing various mission elements, hardware and software systems, into a unified whole.

7. *Requirements for Environmental Data in Support of the Apollo Program*—This paper outlined the environmental data needed from other NASA offices. The data were related to radiation (solar and Van Allen belt), meteoroids, and lunar surface conditions. The data were to be supplied by other NASA programs—Ranger, Surveyor, Lunar Orbiter—with which Bellcomm worked closely.

These documents provided a focus and an output for much of Bellcomm's efforts.

2.5 Bell Laboratories' Support

The technical assistance of specialists at Bell Labs proved to be a valuable asset in many tasks that Bellcomm undertook. In 1962 Bell Labs began to construct a sizeable trajectory-simulation program that would run on the Bellcomm computer. Based on Bell Labs techniques and experience derived from the Titan ICBM effort, the program generated precision trajectories for Apollo (Fig. 14-17) and became the basic simulation tool used in studies of trajectories, mission and vehicle constraints, navigation, guidance, and control. The trajectory-simulation program required two years to develop, which indicates the complexity of the lunar mission compared with an ICBM targeting simulation. Later, Bell Labs undertook several, smaller, special trajectory studies for Bellcomm.

Bell Labs, on occasion, also assisted in evaluating the status of technical developments. For example, in both the Gemini and Apollo programs, internal electric power in the spacecraft was to be supplied by fuel cells utilizing gaseous hydrogen and oxygen constituents—a relatively new and unproved technology. By mid-1963 there was concern that none of

Fig. 14-17.   T. H. Thompson, center, showing moon-earth geometry to I. M. Ross and R. E. Gradle.   Plastic sheet illustrates orbital plane that will carry space capsule from earth to moon.

the three commercial contractors carrying out development would come through on time, thus seriously delaying flight schedules.   Three specialists from Bell Labs—F. J. Biondi, N. B. Hannay, and Upton Thomas— agreed to survey the different developments and relate their conclusions. In late 1963 they reported favorably on the prospects for success; they were, as it turned out, correct.   Their evaluation tended to remove a serious concern in NASA management, which had plenty of other problems to worry about.

2.6 Growth and Change

In the process of maturing and of acquiring new people and strength, Bellcomm inevitably was to lose some of its strongest people to Bell System companies and to other organizations.   Bill Whittaker, who so personified Bellcomm, returned to AT&T on May 1, 1964.   Shortly afterward, he was replaced by R. E. Gradle from AT&T Long Lines.   Deming Lewis returned to Bell Labs on May 18 and after a short period became president of Lehigh University.   Ian M. Ross replaced Lewis.   On June 22, W. W. Braunwarth returned to AT&T.   He was replaced by N. W. Smusyn.   On July 1, Walter Maas returned to Bell Labs.   Earlier the first employee death, that of J. L. Glaser, occurred.

In the summer of 1964 two General Instructions were issued: (1) General Instruction No. 3 and Administrative Practices 3-1 through 3-7, under which NASA accepted Bellcomm's Purchasing Department practices, and (2) General Instruction No. 5 establishing the formal organiza-

Fig. 14-18.   Dennis James of Bellcomm shows lunar lighting effects on relief map derived from Ranger photograph to Air Force Major General Samuel C. Phillips, the Apollo program director.

tion of Bellcomm's records and procedures.   In August 1964 Bellcomm's president and its vice president and general manager represented the company at a White House ceremony that formally recognized Bellcomm's "Plans-for-Progress" program.   During September, negotiations with NASA for the third contract period, October 1964 through September 1965, were completed, and renovation and expansion of the premises at 1100 17th Street, N.W., were finished.   The Third Annual Picnic was held in Rock Creek Park with 640 people, employees and their families attending. The third United Givers Fund campaign was conducted, raising $5,663.25 from 238 of the 282 employees.

Among other changes, Julian M. West retired in June 1965.   West had been an advisor at Bell Laboratories to Brainerd Holmes before Bellcomm was founded.

At the beginning of the fourth contract period in October 1965, Bellcomm employed 337 people—120 administrative and 217 technical employees.   Of the latter, 22 percent had doctorates, 36 percent masters, 23 percent bachelors, and 3 percent no baccalaureate degree, a distribution in educational experience that remained stable as Bellcomm grew to its peak.

The years 1964 and 1965 brought major advances in the nation's space program.   The Ranger program resumed with a series of successful missions involving lunar photography and exploration (Fig. 14-18).   The Gemini two-man space-flight program enjoyed many successes and established man's ability to endure prolonged, weightless flight in space.

Pegasus spacecraft launched by Saturn I vehicles sent back much-needed data on the micrometeoroid environment in space.

In a briefing for the Business Council on February 1, 1966, President Hornbeck gave his view and Bellcomm's on the status of the space program. The following are quotations from his talk:

> At this time, which I have characterized as one-half way along the lunar landing program, I believe that considered judgment would be that the U.S. is achieving its basic objective of leadership and technological preeminence in space. This follows from the successful completion of the Ranger program, the Mariner fly-bys of Venus and Mars, the launching of weather and communication satellites, the vigorous Gemini program of manned space flight and the existence of large boosters in a nearly completed state of development.

> From this you can see that we are well along in the program. In my judgment there are no unsolved technical or technological problems that will stop us from accomplishing the lunar mission. So far Congress has appropriated sufficient monies so that the program can be done on time. We are left with the only problem being that of execution—execution within the constraints of a fixed time schedule and a tight dollar budget. And this execution rests largely with the industrial team that is engaged in the program. . . The team as a whole includes 12 prime contractors, some 17,000 subcontractors, perhaps 300,000 people . . . plus three NASA Centers and, of course, NASA Headquarters in Washington.

> With such a complex organizational structure to manage, we need powerful techniques to accomplish the work on time and within the budget. . . . In my view these tools are working and the program has achieved the state of maturity such that collectively we are managing the program rather than the program running us.

By the end of the fourth contract period further progress and change took place. Rendezvous and docking were demonstrated in the Gemini series. Surveyor I achieved a soft lunar landing. Lunar Orbiter I began photographing the far side of the moon. Bellcomm became a "mature" Bell System company by providing, for the first time, a total package of employment benefits equal to that provided by other companies in the Bell System. With this, employees with leaves-of-absence from other Bell System companies had their leaves cancelled and became employees of Bellcomm, Inc. Other, improved employee practices were adopted: a College Study Plan providing for tuition reimbursement, an Office Training Program offering (remedial) training in typing and shorthand, and a Special Medical Expense Plan for retired employees.

In May of 1966, Gordon A. Brill, comptroller, returned to AT&T to be replaced by C. Maston Thomas from Long Lines. Effective September 1, 1966, W. C. Hittinger from Bell Labs was elected president replacing Hornbeck, who became president of Sandia Corporation. Shortly thereafter K. G. McKay succeeded R. R. Hough as Bellcomm's board chairman.

2.7 Doing the Job: Fall 1966-July 1969

With a pattern of working relationships and program responsibilities set, Bellcomm continued to provide guidance to OMSF by generating, validating, and coordinating the broad, program-level requirements and standards for Apollo. In such a large development program, these requirements (specifications) and standards were essential management tools. In some cases the requirements were generated directly, while in others they were derived from supporting studies and trade-offs involving many technical organizations and scientific disciplines. Continuity of effort was an important ingredient of this activity.

The fifth contract period, October 1966 to September 1967, saw a shift in program emphasis at Bellcomm with a discernible decrease in effort (29 percent) on Apollo/Saturn and general mission work and a corresponding increase in post-Apollo planning for the Apollo Applications Program and Advanced Manned Missions.

2.8 Apollo Applications Program

Bellcomm studies of post-Apollo earth-orbital activities were initiated in late 1964 as part of the work on the Apollo Extension System. The extension system was designed to conduct long, manned space flights in earth orbit and various experiments—biomedical, scientific, operational, technological—in near-earth space. Work continued during 1965 to develop an interim flight mission plan reflecting NASA objectives for post-Apollo activities utilizing modified Apollo hardware.

In August 1965, the Saturn/Apollo Applications Directorate was established in OMSF, and the Apollo Applications Program (AAP) was formally recognized. By the end of 1966, an important year for AAP, the major hardware modules had been identified and Bellcomm's concept of dual-launch missions had been accepted. In a typical dual-launch mission, a manned module would rendezvous with an orbiting "workshop" after which the crew would direct a second rendezvous with a vehicle holding astronomical instruments and telescopes. This cluster of vehicles would be an order of magnitude larger than previous spacecraft.

In January 1967 the first official Flight Mission Assignment Document for AAP, describing the first four missions, was approved by MSF and issued. In succeeding years, effort and emphasis increased on AAP, the work consisting of trade-offs of various hardware options, analysis of mission modes, further definition of experiment objectives, and also development of the constraints and requirements imposed by potential payloads.

2.9 Advanced Manned Missions

In October 1965 a report was published dealing with entry into the Martian atmosphere. This marked the beginning of advanced mission studies at Bellcomm. Although other work had preceded this report, it was the first product of an organized effort to balance the Bellcomm perspective with an examination of future possibilities. In the late spring of 1966, a significant effort was established to support the NASA Planetary Joint Action Group. This effort was initiated by Dr. Mueller of MSF to examine the feasibility of attempting a 1975 Mars "twilight-class" flyby mission. Planetary work and a separate planetary studies effort in Bellcomm provided the initial focus and a starting point for advanced mission planning.

Advanced missions work proceeded along several lines: a review of intermediate lunar missions, a level-of-effort investigation of planetary-return-trajectory opportunities, assessment of the role of nuclear (solid-core) propulsion in manned space flight, and study of the feasibility of a common space fleet. The latter effort concerned the evaluation of commonality for manned space flight, including earth orbit, lunar orbit and surface, planetary flyby, and stopover missions. (In the particular case considered, four spacecraft were defined which were sufficient to fulfill all missions.) Studies of extended lunar-surface missions included the length of time that the lunar module was capable of staying on the surface, development of an augmented landing capability through modification of the lunar module, and development of alternate landing vehicles from the service module or the S-IVB stage. The nature of the equipment required for these extended missions was also established to assure that realistic mission planning was possible.

In early 1966 the spectrum of manned-planetary-mission opportunities was limited. During the next two years, Bellcomm effort resulted in the discovery of sets of multi-planet flyby and stopover missions.

2.10 Apollo Program Progress

With the very serious exception of the fatal Apollo 1 fire and the accompanying reexamination of the project, the United States manned space-flight program progressed steadily and successfully. November 11, 1966, marked the end of the Gemini flights, which included two unmanned and ten manned flights over a $2\frac{1}{2}$ year period. The longest Gemini flight occurred in December 1965: 330 hours, 36 minutes. The Mercury flights (July 1960–May 1963) consisted of eleven launches, six of them manned. The longest Mercury flight lasted 34 hours, 20 minutes. The Saturn I series of ten unmanned launches concluded in July 1965. The uprated Saturn I (IB) took part in five successful launches. The last launch on October 11, 1968 was a manned earth-orbit flight to test command service module (CSM) operations and was designated Apollo 7 (SA-205,CSM 101). By the time of the Apollo 8 mission, the manned space-flight program had totaled—40 launches, 17 of them manned—a considerable amount of experience for the space-flight team. On the other hand, experience with the Saturn V launch vehicle was limited. It consisted of two launches, Apollo 4 in November 1967 and Apollo 6 in April 1968— both earth-orbit missions. Similarly, experience with the Block II CSM was extremely limited, consisting only of the Apollo 7 mission. Thus, the Apollo 8 mission was daring and unbelievably successful.

On December 12, 1968, the Apollo 8 (SA-503/CSM103;LTA-B) spacecraft rose slowly, majestically from its launch pad at Complex 39 Cape Kennedy, sending Astronauts Borman, Lovell, and Anders through the following flight sequence: (1) flight in earth orbit, (2) by a restart of the S-IVB stage flight into a translunar trajectory, followed by lunar module transposition and docking, (3) injection into lunar orbit by a braking thrust of the service module and (4) by a restart of the service-module engine, emergence from lunar orbit into a transearth trajectory, reentry into the earth's atmosphere, splash down, and recovery—a truly spectacular achievement that thrilled people during the Christmas week. Most of the world saw pictures of lift-off, the earth, the moon, and recovery. The Russians beamed coverage throughout Eastern Europe, and congratulated the United States with the words:

> This event goes beyond the limits of a national achievement and marks a stage in the development of the universal culture of earth men.

There was a pronounced lift in the morale of Space Agency workers with the completion of Apollo 8. This was the second manned flight in nearly two years; the first was Apollo 7, an 11-day earth-orbital exercise. The chances of a lunar landing in 1969 looked better.

Lt. Gen. Samuel C. Phillips, Apollo Program Director, wrote a congratulatory letter January 9, 1969, to Bellcomm president Ian M. Ross (who replaced W. C. Hittinger in April 1968) saying with respect to Apollo 8:

> I would like to especially thank you and the members of your organization who over the past months have contributed their efforts toward making this mission a success. Sometimes the numerous small tasks that go together to make up this total Program may appear insignificant and unappreciated to the individual performing them; I would ask that you take the time to pass on my personal thanks to every one of your people working on the Apollo Program.

In addition, Bellcomm was among the prime contractors recognized by special awards. On January 13, 1969, the NASA Public Service Award was presented to President Ross during ceremonies at Houston, Texas. The citation read:

> The National Aeronautics and Space Administration awards to Mr. Ian M. Ross, Bellcomm, Inc., the NASA Public Service Award for his outstanding contributions as a key leader of the government-industry team which made possible the exceptional success of Apollo 8, the first manned lunar orbit mission.
>
> (Signed) T. O. Paine, Acting Administrator, NASA.

Table 14-2.   Man-Years of Work for NASA by Bellcomm and Its Subcontractors
from 1962–1969.

Program	Man-Years				Program Percentage
	Bellcomm	Bell Labs	Other	Total	
General mission, including mission operations	292	19	20	331	20
Apollo	769	145	117	1031	62
Apollo Applications	140	8	2	150	9
Advanced Manned Missions	149	—	1	150	9
Total	1350	172	140	1662	100

Further Apollo successes followed rapidly and on schedule:

Apollo 9, March 1969, earth orbit, first manned lunar module (LM-3).

Apollo 10, May 1969, a second manned lunar-orbit mission that exercised both the command service module and the lunar molecule.

Apollo 11 (SA506/CSM107/LM-5), July 1969, carrying astronauts Armstrong, Collins, and Aldrin.

On July 20, 1969 Neil Armstrong was the first man to step onto the moon's barren surface, later to return safely to earth, thus fulfilling President Kennedy's national commitment of May 26, 1961—at a cost of more than $20 billion.

2.11 Seven-Year Highlights

Just months prior to the lunar landing, Bellcomm completed its seventh year under contract to NASA.   During this period it billed NASA $56,337,000 in cost and $4,618,000 in fees for a total of $60,995,000 (roughly 0.3 percent of the cost of the Apollo program).   For this, Bellcomm delivered a total of 1,662 man-years of effort with Bellcomm itself providing 81 percent of the effort, Bell Labs 10 percent, and subcontractors 9 percent. For this period, Bellcomm's income before federal taxes was $4,578,000 and after taxes (net income) was $2,395,000, which was paid to its stockholders and made part of AT&T's consolidated earnings.   Incidentally, as of this time only $4,000 in expenses had been disallowed by government auditors.   Table 14-2 shows the man-years applied to NASA work by Bellcomm and its subcontractors during the seven-year period.

At the end of March, the technical staff included 282 people with the following degrees: Ph.D., 34 percent; Masters, 42 percent; Bachelors, 23 percent; no degree, less than 1 percent.   The technical disciplines of the staff were:

Aeronautics	28
Astronomy	1
Biosciences, Geosciences, Meteorology	14
Computer Science, Mathematics, Statistics	56
Electrical Engineering	77
Mechanical Engineering	34
Planetary Sciences	1
Physics	45
Psychology	3
Other Engineering Arts	23
	282

The technical staff was recruited over the seven years as indicated:

Source	Total	Terminated or Transferred	Present at End of Period
Bell System	105	57	48
Advertising media	177	62	115
Recruiting through employees	84	38	46
Bellcomm recruiting	31	5	26
Bell Labs Referrals	34	15	19
Other	72	36	36
	503	213	290

During this same period, the administrative staff was recruited as follows:

Source	Total	Terminated or Transferred	Present at End of Period
Bell System	58	30	28
Other	485	347	138

In July 1968 Bellcomm moved from 1100 17th Street, N.W., occupied since early 1963, to L'Enfant Plaza North Building, situated very near NASA headquarters. Some 450 employees could be accommodated in the available 136,000 square feet. This move represented a significant consolidation of all Bellcomm people under one roof. To foster good communications, the NASA Apollo Program Office occupied space in the same building.

2.12 Winding Down

That the successful completion of the first lunar landing could represent a turning point in the NASA/Bellcomm relationship had been anticipated for some time by Bell System and Bellcomm management. In 1967 Chairman McKay began considering various modes in which Bellcomm might eventually conclude its participation in the Apollo project. The first task that President Ross assigned to new Managing Director D. A.

Chisholm, who left Bell Labs to join Bellcomm in May 1968, was to consider the question: "What path should be followed if current pressures on and in NASA force Bellcomm to reduce its support to NASA, or to shift radically the Bellcomm contractual or operating relationship with NASA?" Using inputs from Robert E. Gradle and others, Chisholm concluded that because of various factors, among them morale, stability, and quality of work, "it was essential to maintain Bellcomm as an entity as long as there is a NASA role." Extensive consideration was given to this issue, and Ross presented his conclusions at the monthly Bellcomm Board meeting of August 1968:

1. Bellcomm must continue support of NASA through the Apollo flight program with the earliest complete phase-out of Bellcomm about March 1972.

2. It would be imperative that Bellcomm support to NASA be of the highest quality.

3. To retain a healthy Bellcomm organization it would be necessary to take on other work partly to compensate for the decreasing NASA work.

4. Bell System technical work that could appropriately be taken on should be identified.

5. Bellcomm might reconsider its policy on assistance to government agencies other than NASA.

By March 1969, the Bell System view had clarified into the following position. (1) At an appropriate time, agreement should be reached between top management of NASA and AT&T that an orderly phase-out of Bellcomm would be in the long-range interests of both organizations. The Bell System would have demonstrated the highly desirable attribute of getting out when the job was accomplished. (2) It should be agreed that a satisfactory way of phasing out of NASA work, while retaining a high level of competence and maintaining a stable and viable organization, would be for Bellcomm to pick up Bell System work. (3) The management of such a phase-out would be eased if it were made clear by NASA that they too found it desirable. In consonance with this, Ross reopened discussions on Bellcomm's future with Dr. Mueller of NASA. These discussions continued for some time.

Meanwhile, during the month of the Apollo 11 lunar-landing success, July 1969, Bellcomm entered into a contract with AT&T Long Lines in support of studies of an econometric nature. In the same month, Bellcomm's Vice President and General Manager, Robert E. Gradle, returned to Long Lines. He was replaced by Gordon C. Bill of Long Lines. A month before, D. A. Chisholm resigned to join Northern Electric Company in Ottawa, Canada. He was succeeded as managing director by M. Paul

Wilson from Bell Labs.[5] To pursue the Long Lines-supported work, two Bell System Studies departments were formed in Wilson's organization. Several months later a Bellcomm Advisory Board was formed for guidance. The board's role was to consider projects that Bellcomm might undertake for the Bell System, to establish priorities and to assure proper coordination. The initial members of the board were J. B. Fisk, A. M. Froggatt, R. R. Hough, H. L. Kertz, K. G. McKay (chairman), I. M. Ross, and A. L. Stott. M. P. Wilson acted as secretary.

Following oral discussions with NASA on phase-out, President Ross wrote NASA Administrator Thomas O. Paine on September 23, 1969, pointing out that with the Apollo 11 success, it would be appropriate to review the role of Bellcomm and its relationship with NASA. He referred to NASA administrator James E. Webb's 1962 letter to the AT&T Chairman seeking assistance, and suggested that the Webb objectives as expressed in the letter had been accomplished. Ross therefore expressed the view that it was an appropriate time to consider phase-out of Bellcomm. Although no abrupt termination of work was contemplated, Ross suggested that phase-out should not extend beyond 1972, a date corresponding to the estimated completion of space flights using then-current Apollo hardware. The letter concluded by asking for NASA's views and recommendations.

Agreement on the phase-out question was reached in March 1970 at a meeting between President Ross and two NASA officials, one of whom was Dale D. Myers, Dr. Mueller's successor as head of OMSF. Mid-1972 was chosen as a target date. The estimated year-end technical staff by work categories for fiscal years 1970, 1971, and 1972 was agreed to in principle. The estimates aimed at an approximately equal effort for Apollo, AAP, and Advanced Missions. Paine wrote to Ross on May 13, 1970, to confirm this planning and to request continued support:

> In response to Mr. Webb's request, Bellcomm was organized in 1962 by the American Telephone and Telegraph Company to provide assistance to NASA in the manned space flight programs. The assistance provided by Bellcomm has been outstanding and is greatly appreciated by all of us at NASA and is, I am sure, recognized by the whole Apollo team throughout the country. Indeed, the success of the Apollo Program is in no small measure attributable to the many significant contributions made by Bellcomm personnel. In your letter to me and in our subsequent meeting, you proposed a planned phase-out of Bellcomm activities. We agree that a gradual phase-out would be appropriate. However, recognizing Bellcomm's established position and the necessity for maintaining continuity in the Apollo and Skylab Programs, the support currently provided to these efforts should be continued. I understand that you are now working with Office Manned Space Flight (OMSF) to develop a plan providing for Bellcomm

---

[5] Two years earlier (July 1967), T. H. Thompson had returned to Bell Labs and R. L. Wagner promoted to managing director in replacement.

support to the Apollo Program, Skylab Program, and some limited support for advanced manned mission planning aiming toward the phasing-out of all support before the end of 1972. Again, let me thank you for the excellent work and outstanding contributions of Bellcomm in assisting NASA to perform its missions.

Behind this agreed-on continuation was a recognition by Myers and Ross of certain factors in the Bellcomm/NASA relationship that needed to be adhered to if the relationship were to be a continued success. First, unique functions of Bellcomm required identification to justify further support of NASA. Second, several conditions of the relationship, which had developed over the years, had to be maintained:

1. To focus the effort, either functional or product responsibility should be identified.

2. Bellcomm should have firsthand access to information in areas important to its assigned work.

3. The principal jobs should be of such size and duration that technical direction at the NASA-Program-Manager level was practicable.

4. Technical direction should come from a level no lower than that of the Program Manager.

Many of the triumphs and tribulations of the NASA/Bellcomm history are associated with these four conditions and their establishment as guiding principles of the relationship.

2.13 Concluding the Work

Bellcomm decreased its support to NASA over a period of three years following Apollo 11, while gradually, and to a much lesser degree, it increased its Bell System activity. The Apollo/Saturn systems engineering work encompassed the remaining lunar exploration program and the support of Skylab, the orbiting workshop. Skylab support consisted of the same formal systems engineering responsibilities as those for Apollo. The hardware failure during the Apollo 13 mission and the mission's subsequent abort diverted effort into analyzing and remedying the failure mechanism. (The abort mode—lunar-module propulsion backup for a service-module propulsion failure—brought back memories of earlier Bellcomm activity in 1962 when, as noted earlier, Bellcomm advanced this useful concept.) Other categories of activity included: Apollo Applications Systems Engineering, Manned Space Flight Program Analysis, NASA Planning System (assistance to NASA's central-planning organization charged with identifying objectives for the space program); Experiment Studies, Technology Studies, and Environmental Studies.

The Bell System decided to dissolve Bellcomm by a corporate merger with Bell Laboratories. This arrangement effectively took care of numerous business problems such as the disposition of Bellcomm's pension funds and other matters involving personnel, continuity of affairs, federal-tax considerations, etc. It was also decided to offer all technical staff members employment at Bell Laboratories and to make suitable Bell System employment arrangements for administrative personnel. A plan for the orderly transfer of people to Bell Laboratories and elsewhere, which was to accompany the decreasing workload, was formulated and implemented.

In September 1970, Donald P. Ling, a vice president of Bell Laboratories, assumed the presidency of Bellcomm replacing Ian Ross who returned to Bell Labs. About a year later Ling retired, and Ross resumed the presidency acting in a dual capacity with Bellcomm and Bell Labs. At closedown on March 31, 1972,[6] the remaining technical personnel became employees of Bell Laboratories and the administrative employees were assigned to Bell Labs and to other Bell System companies. A group of eighteen, working as a Bell Labs department headed by K. E. Martersteck, continued work under a Western Electric contract in support of Apollo 16 and Apollo 17 through December 1972. The Bellcomm systems engineering work for the Bell System was established as a new organization in Bell Labs. Other personnel were assigned to organizations throughout the laboratories. There were no involuntary layoffs as a result of the dissolution of Bellcomm.

2.14 Conclusion

Bellcomm could not have contributed effectively to NASA unless the inherent value of its technical work was recognized, and therefore wanted, and unless Bellcomm was accepted by both the management and employees of NASA, by other space-program contractors, and at least to some extent, by Congress. Factors enabling this recognition and acceptance included:

1. Bellcomm's ties to the Bell System, which gave security and a substantial degree of independence to all levels at Bellcomm.
2. The Bell System's agreement to a space-hardware exclusion clause.
3. The availability of Bell Labs technical management to ensure the establishment and maintenance of the highest technical standards.
4. The availability of Bell System management, both in the company and on the board of directors, to ensure sound corporate policy.
5. Bellcomm's assignment by NASA of program responsibilities at the highest level of NASA manned space-flight management where its work could be effectively coupled in.

Bellcomm employees recognized the importance of their work being technically impeccable, or nearly so, and of carrying it out such that neither

---

[6] Charles D. Briggs amassed the longest Bellcomm service of any employee; it encompassed all of Bellcomm's corporate existence but one month.

NASA nor the Bell System was publicly embarrassed. While working within these constraints, Bellcomm employees enjoyed the satisfaction of performing a public service that contained unusual personal and technical challenges. All of this contributed to a feeling among many that the Bellcomm experience was unique in their Bell System careers.

Postscript:

In Defense of the Nation

In Chapter 6, "Overview of the War Years," the contributions made by the Bell System, particularly the Bell Laboratories/Western Electric team, during World War II were viewed in retrospect. Thousands of scientists and engineers were organized to carry out technical programs of great complexity on very short time schedules. The means for this effort were fortunately inherent in the integrated structure of the Bell System in which design, development, manufacture, and application of technology had a long history. Thus the changes required to make an effective and rapid transition to war work were readily made by trained and experienced management and technical personnel. Equally important in achieving success was the broad base of knowledge in communications technology derived from fundamental research in acoustics and other branches of physics, mathematics, chemistry, and material science. Such research had been skillfully carried out in Bell Laboratories for at least forty years preceding the outbreak of World War II.

I. THE POSTWAR YEARS

After more than five years of intensive wartime effort, the peace, so welcome to all, provided an opportunity to return to the long-delayed expansion of the common carrier network and to provide service to the many potential customers on a long waiting list. Once again it was necessary to reorganize personnel to fit the needs of peacetime communications. This was not simply a return to the organization which had discontinued its work at the onset of war. In the meantime there had been major changes in technology, and priorities for meeting the pent-up service demands were far different from those in an era when the country was emerging from the Great Depression. We need say here only that the management and personnel problems were effectively solved and, as will be related in other volumes of this history, the solution led to a communication network on the centennial of Bell's invention that far exceeded earlier expectations of size, versatility, and convenience to the user.

The coming of peace did not bring a cessation of military effort. Several hundred members of the Bell System technical staff continued work in this area to complete projects that were of high postwar importance. Soon this number increased as the Cold War developed and as the Korean War brought active participation of our armed forces. At this time, Bell Labs personnel participating in military and related R and D grew to several thousand and remained at a significant level until the mid-1970s, roughly 40 years after the first Bell Labs staff had been assigned to prewar radar studies.

Initially the staff involved in the postwar military work came from the pool of experienced personnel built up during the war years. Later it became necessary to supplement this staff through recruiting and transfers within the Bell System, since the demand for technical people for military and civilian projects far exceeded the number available within Bell Labs at the end of the war.

To some extent, the postwar work was a continuation of the work done during the later war years, but a major part of the effort involved new technology and techniques that either were not available or were in a primitive stage during the war. A few of these are mentioned briefly below:

1.1 Transistor and Solar Cell Inventions

The invention at Bell Labs of the transistor and the related silicon solar cell (in 1947 and 1954, respectively) has probably had a greater impact on military and commercial electronics than any other devices appearing during the last 30 years. Without these two devices the electronics necessary for the great advances in space technology would not have been possible, since they lie at the heart of the communication and control systems. The transistor, in addition, has made possible the complex and highly versatile computers used in the design and control of both military and non-military rocketry systems ranging from the series of Nike missiles used as a defense against enemy long-range weapons to the Apollo Lunar Landing System.

The great value of the transistor is too well known to require further elaboration, but it is worth noting that two important decisions played a major part in the rapid development of transistor applications. One was the military decision not to make secret or otherwise restrict the results of transistor application studies. The other was the Bell System decision to make information arising from studies of transistor application, design, and production readily available to everyone.

1.2 Rocketry

The continuation of wartime technology into the postwar years also led to the tremendous advance in rocket propulsion. The Bell Labs/Western Electric postwar effort was much involved with electronic control systems both for guiding rockets into orbit and for controlling rocket-propelled defense missiles. As noted previously, the transistor was a major element in such work, which also included the development of sophisticated antennas, computers, and communications systems.

1.3 Systems Studies

During the postwar years, applications of systems engineering techniques, which had their beginnings in the Bell System in the early 1900s, were greatly expanded in the military area. Systems studies became an essential part of the definition of system requirements and the investigation of potential performance. The large multipurpose computers that became available during this period provided powerful means for conducting system simulation and analysis. Without them much of this work would have been impossible. Consequently, the design and application of computers formed an important part of the new technology applied to the military effort during the postwar years.

1.4 Project Management

The personnel level required to carry out the very large and complex system developments needed for the missile defense systems was far beyond that available in the Bell Labs organization. Consequently, the general plan followed was to use Western Electric as the prime contractor with Bell Laboratories as technical manager. Bell Labs conducted most of the research, systems engineering, and exploratory development. Other work was subcontracted to suitable companies or laboratories, with Bell Labs responsible for direction and coordination. In some cases, this meant a reorientation of personnel from a primarily R and D role to one with considerable emphasis on the skills required for technical management.

II. SUMMARY

It appears obvious that management and organization all played important roles in the Bell Laboratories/Western Electric contributions to military technology. The involvement was for many a long one and, for some, it had its traumatic aspects.

As noted in Chapter 6, F. B. Jewett, the first president of Bell Laboratories (1925–1940), had speculated on the nature of an R and D organization: how it might best be organized and how it might be affected by the changes brought about by the great war in which we were then involved. He emphasized the importance of continuity of teamwork by carefully selected groups of skilled and trained scientists and engineers. He believed that the real power of an R and D organization lay in the ability of people and their training, and not in particular skills; and that groups of such people, accustomed to working as a team, would be flexible enough to adapt to the changing programs required by an emergency situation such as war.

As experience during national emergencies has shown, Jewett's concepts can be extended to the larger team comprising a system in which R and D, manufacture, installation, and operation come under a single management as integrated units.

The policy of the Bell System will continue to be one of serving the public and our government in all ways consistent with its primary responsibility of providing reliable, high-quality, diversified communications services in the nation's network. Where its considerable technological and managerial expertise may be requested by our government for specific projects for which it is particularly qualified, the Bell System has a duty to be responsive. This volume of the *History* is a testimonial to that ability and willingness to serve our country.

Abbreviations, Acronyms, and Designations

AAP	Apollo Applications Program
ABM	antiballistic missile
ABMDA	Advanced Ballistic Missile Defense Agency
ABRES	advanced ballistic reentry systems
ADC	Air Defense Command
ADES	Air Defense Engineering Services
ADP	ammonium dihydrogen phosphate
AEC	Atomic Energy Commission
AFMTC	Air Force Missile Test Center
AGC	automatic gain control
AI	aircraft interception (radar)
AICBM	anti-intercontinental ballistic missile
AM	amplitude modulation
AMR	Atlantic Missile Range
AMRAC	Anti-Missile Research and Advisory Council
ANB	Army, Navy, British
ARADCOM	Army Air Defense Command
ARC	aircraft radio communication
ARGMA	Army Rocket and Guided Missile Agency
ARTCC	air-route traffic control center
ARTCOM	Army Tactical Communications Project
ASV	aircraft-to-surface-vessel (radar)
ASW	antisubmarine warfare
ATEWA	automatic target evaluator and weapon assigner
ATR	anti-transmit-receive (tube)
AUTOVON	Automatic Voice Network
BMDC	Ballistic Missile Defense Center
BMEWS	Ballistic Missile Early Warning System
BSS	time-delay steering board-steered system
BTO	bombing through overcast (radar)
BUIC	backup intercept control
CADS	Continental Air Defense System
CAG	guided missile heavy cruiser
CAMAR	common aperture multifunction array radar
CBI	China, Burma, India theater of war (WW II)

CEP	circular error probability
CIC	Combat Information Center
CINC	Commander-in-Chief
CINCEUR	Commander-in-Chief-Europe
CINCLANT	Commander-in-Chief-Atlantic
CINCPAC	Commander-in-Chief-Pacific
CLC	tactical command ship
CLG	guided missile light cruiser
CODAN	carrier-operated detector antinoise
COMPASS	Communication Planning and System Studies
COMPRST	Compass Radio Switching Test
CONUS	continental United States
COPS	computer organized partial sum (beamformer)
CPR	Chinese People's Republic
CSM	command service module
CSPS	coherent signal processing system
CUG	common-user-group
CVA	attack aircraft carrier
CW	continuous wave
CXRX	three-dimensional search radar
DAIS	defense automatic integrated switch
DBR	double band radio
DCs	Direction Centers
DCA	Defense Communication Agency
DCTL	direct-coupled transistor logic
DDD	direct distance dialing
DDG	guided missile destroyer
DDR&E	Director of Defense Research and Engineering
DEG	guided missile destroyer escort
DELTIC	delay line-time compressor
DEW	distant early warning
DF	dual-facility
DLG	guided missile frigate
DMX	data multiplex
DOD	Department of Defense
DOE	Department of Energy
DR	discrimination radar
DSA	digital spectrum analyzer
EA	emergency action (officer)
ECM	electronic countermeasure
EDL	electrical delay lines
EMP	electromagnetic pulse
EOR	earth-orbit-rendezvous
ERD	equipment readiness data

ERDA	Energy Research and Development Administration
ESS	electronic switching system
ESSA	electrical scanning and stabilizing of antennas
FAA	Federal Aviation Agency
FAR	forward acquisition radar
FEF	(Western Electric) Field Engineering Force
FFT	fast Fourier transform
FM	frequency modulation
FS	frequency-shift
FSK	frequency-shift keying
GPAC	general-purpose analog computer
G/V	ground/vehicular
HF	high frequency
HIPAR	high-power acquisition radar
ICBM	intercontinental-range ballistic missile
IF	intermediate-frequency
IFR	instrument flight rule
IGOR	intercept ground-stationed optical recorder
IND	intercept director
IOC	initial operational capability
IRBM	intermediate-range ballistic missile
ITOR	intercept target-borne optical recorder
JAN	Joint Army-Navy
JCSAN	Joint Chiefs of Staff Alerting Network
LAB	low-altitude bombing
LAR	local acquisition radar
LM	lunar module
LOR	lunar-orbit-rendezvous
MAD	magnetic anomaly detector
MAR	multifunction array radar
MAS	Manned Space Apollo Systems Engineering
MDC	Missile Direction Center
MDI	miss-distance indicator
MDL	magnetic delay lines
MDP	Manhattan District Project
MILS	missile impact location system
MIPS	millions of instructions per second
MLPP	multilevel precedence preemption
MOSAR	modulation scan array radar
MSR	missile site radar
MTR	missile track radar
MUSA	multiple unit steerable antenna
NACA	National Advisory Committee on Aeronautics
NAF	numbered Air Force (bases)

NAS	National Academy of Science
NASA	National Aeronautics and Space Administration
NATO	North Atlantic Treaty Organization
NAWS	NORAD attack warning system
NCC	NORAD Control Center
NDRC	National Defense Research Committee
NEEP	Nuclear Electronic Effects Program
NMCC	National Military Command Center
NORAD	North American Air Defense
NRC	Nuclear Regulatory Commission
NSF	National Science Foundation
OMSF	Office of Manned Space Flight
ONR	Office of Naval Research
OSO	orbiting solar observatory
OSRD	Office of Scientific Research and Development
OSTF	Operational System Test Facility
PAR	perimeter acquisition radar
PARKA	Navy, long-range sound propagation experiments
PBAA	polybutadiene acrylic acid
PCM	pulse-code modulation
PMR	Pacific Missile Range
PPI	plan position indicator
PSAC	President's Scientific Advisory Committee
radar	radio detection and ranging
R and D	research and development
R&E	research and engineering
RF	radio frequency
RMP	reentry measurements program
RV	reentry vehicle
SAC	Strategic Air Command
SAGE	semi-automatic ground environment
SALT	Strategic Arms Limitation Treaty
SAM	Strategic Alloy Materials Lab
SB	submarine cable transmission system; introduced in 1956
SCAN	switched circuit automatic network
SCEL	Signal Corps Electronics Laboratory
SD	submarine cable transmission system; introduced in 1963
SF	submarine cable transmission system; introduced in 1968
	single-frequency
SHF	superhigh frequency
SLBM	submarine-launched ballistic missile

sonar	sound navigation and ranging
STL	Space Technology Laboratory
SWOD	special weapons ordnance device
TACMAR	tactical multifunction array radar
TEWA	target evaluator and weapon assigner
TIROS	meteorological satellite
TR	transmit-receive (tube)
TRADIC	transistor digital computer
TSCS	tactical software control site
TTR	target track radar
TWT	traveling-wave tube
UHF	ultrahigh frequency
VT	vacuum tube
VHF	very high frequency
WHOI	Woods Hole Oceanographic Institution
WSMR	White Sands Missile Range
ZAR	Zeus acquisition radar
ZI	zone of interior
ZMAR	Zeus multifunction array radar

Bibliography

Chapter 1. Introduction

Background

Howeth, L. S. *History of Communications—Electronics in the United States Navy.* Washington, D.C.: Government Printing Office, 1963.

Technology

Radar Systems and Components. By members of the technical staff, Bell Telephone Laboratories. New York: D. Van Nostrand, 1949.
Ridenour, L. N. (ed.). 1st ed. *Radar System Engineering.* M.I.T. Radiation Laboratory Series, vol. 1. New York and London: McGraw-Hill, 1947.

Chapter 2. Radar

Baxter, James Phinney 3rd. *Scientists Against Time.* Boston: Little, Brown, 1946, pp. 136–157, 11–25, and 119–135.
Jones, Philip C. "Bell Laboratories' Role in Victory." (part I). *Bell Telephone Magazine* 25 (Spring 1946): 37–53.
Jones, Philip C. "Bell Laboratories' Role in Victory." (part II). *Bell Telephone Magazine* 25 (Summer 1946): 116–126.
Kelly, Mervin J. "Radar and Western Electric." *Bell Telephone Magazine.* (Winter 1945–46): 283–294.
Watson-Watt, Robert. "Radar in War and in Peace." *Nature.* No. 3959 (September 15, 1945): 319–324.

Background

Tinus, W. C. and Higgins, W. H. C. "Early Fire-Control Radars for Naval Vessels." In *Radar Systems and Components,* by members of the technical staff, Bell Telephone Laboratories, New York: D. Van Nostrand, 1949, pp. 9–55.

Magnetron Research and Development

Collins, G. B. (ed.). *Microwave Magnetrons.* M.I.T. Radiation Laboratory Series. New York and London: McGraw-Hill, 1947.
Fisk, J. B., Hagstrum, H. D., and Hartman, P. L. "The Magnetron as a Generator of Centimeter Waves." *Bell System Technical J.* 25 (April 1946): 167–348.

Technology

Radar Systems and Components. By members of the technical staff, Bell Telephone Laboratories. New York: D. Van Nostrand, 1949, pp. iii, 1–8.

Chapter 3. Electrical Computers for Fire Control

Electrical Analog Computers

Black, H. S. "Stabilized Feedback Amplifiers." *Bell System Technical J.* 13 (January 1934): 1–18.

Blattner, D. G. "Precision Potentiometers for Analog Computers." *Bell Laboratories Record* 32 (May 1954): 171–177.

Bode, Hendrik W. *Network Analysis and Feedback Amplifier Design.* New York: D. Van Nostrand, 1945.

Hagemann, E. C. "Precision Resistance Networks for Computer Circuits." *Bell Laboratories Record* 24 (December 1946): 445.

Lovell, C. A. "Continuous Electrical Computation." *Bell Laboratories Record* 25 (March 1947): 114.

MacColl, LeRoy A. *Fundamental Theory of Servomechanisms.* New York: D. Van Nostrand, 1945.

Och, H. G. "Computer for Coastal Guns." *Bell Laboratories Record* 24 (May 1946): 177.

Pfister, A. C. "Precision Carbon Resistors." *Bell Laboratories Record* 26 (October 1948): 401.

Rippere, R. O. "An Electrical Computer for Flight Training." *Bell Laboratories Record* 25 (February 1947): 78.

Digital Computers

Stibitz, George R. (as told to Mrs. Evelyn Loveday). "The Relay Computers at Bell Labs (Part Two)." *Datamation* 13 (May 1967): 45.

Chapter 4. Acoustics

Introduction

McMeen, Samuel G. and Miller, Kempster B. (eds.). *Telephony.* Chicago: American Technical Society, 1923.

Underwater Applications

Basic Methods for the Calibration of Sonar Equipment. Summary Technical Report of Division 6, National Defense Research Committee, vol. 10, 1946.

Baxter, James Phinney 3rd. *Scientists Against Time.* Boston: Little, Brown, 1946, pp. 172–185.

Felch, E. P. et al. "Airborne Magnetometers for Search and Survey." *Trans. AIEE* 66 (1947): 641–651.

Frank Leslie's Illustrated Newspaper. New York, August 20, 1881.

Gardner, Mark B. "Mine Mark 24: World War II Acoustic Torpedo." *J. Audio Engineering Society* 22 (October 1974): 614–626.

Keller, A. C. "Submarine Detection by Sonar." *Bell Laboratories Record* 25 (February 1947): 55–60.

Keller, A. C. "Submarine Detection by Sonar." *Trans. AIEE* 66 (1947): 1217–1230.

Knudsen, V. O., Alford, R. S., and Emling, J. W. "Underwater Ambient Noise." *J. Marine Research* 7 (1948): 410–429.

Mason, Warren P. *Electromechanical Transducers and Wave Filters,* 2nd ed. Princeton, N.J.: D. Van Nostrand, 1948.

Mason, Warren P. "ADP and KDP Crystals." *Bell Laboratories Record* 24 (July 1946): 257–260.

Mine Mark 24 Experimental Model. Report to Office of Scientific Research and Development, National Defense Research Committee, Division 6, Section 6.1, Contract sr-785-1327.

Practice Attack Meter. Report to Office of Scientific Research and Development, National Defense Research Committee, Division 6, Section 6.1, March 25, 1943, Contract OEMsr-346.

Sternkell, C. M. and Thorndike, A. M. *Antisubmarine Warfare in World War II.* OEG Report No. 51, Office of C&O, Navy Department, 1946.

A Survey of Subsurface Warfare in World War II. Summary Technical Report of Division 6, National Defense Research Committee (NDRC), vol. 10, 1946.

Thomson, Sir William [Lord Kelvin]. *Popular Lectures and Addresses.* Constitution of Matter, vol. 1. London: Macmillan, 1889.

1944 Renegotiation. Report submitted to War Contracts Price Adjustment Board. New York: Western Electric.

Ground and Above-Ground Applications

Erickson, J. R. "Military Telephone Instruments." *Bell Laboratories Record* 23 (June 1945): 193–199.

Johnson, K. S. *Transmission Circuits for Telephonic Communication: Methods of Analysis and Design.* Lancaster, Pa: Western Electric, 1924.

Martin, W. H. "Seventy-Five Years of the Telephone: An Evolution in Technology." *Bell System Technical J.* 30 (April 1951): 215–238.

Worcester Daily Telegram, October 4, 1945.

High-Power Auditory Systems

Cooke, L. B. "The Voice of Ship Command," *Bell Laboratories Record* 23 (July 1945): 241–245.

Giles, L. W. Report on Contract OEMsr-908, April 30, 1945.

Jones, R. Clark. "A Fifty Horsepower Siren." *J. Acoustical Society of America* 18 (October 1946): 371–387.

Lanier, R. S. "What Makes a Good Loudspeaker." *Western Electric Oscillator*, no. 8 (July 1947): 11–13, 34.

Nickel, Frank. "Quality Loudspeakers for Every Use." *Western Electric Oscillator*, no. 8 (July 1947): 7–10, 30.

Vieth, L. "Polly Gets the Japs." *Bell Laboratories Record* 24 (August 1946): 305–307.

Vieth, L. "Beachmaster Announcing Equipment." *Bell Laboratories Record* 24 (July 1946): 261–263.

Chapter 5. Communications

Arnold, General H. H. "Communications and Air Power." *Bell Telephone Magazine* 23 (Summer 1944): 91.

Bradley, Judson S. "The Bell System and National Defense." *Bell Telephone Magazine* 20 (February 1941): 1–20.

Bradley, Judson S. "Telephone Lines and Air Defense." *Bell Telephone Magazine* 21 (February 1942): 4–16.

Buckley, Oliver E. "Bell Laboratories in the War." *Bell Telephone Magazine* 23 (Winter 1944–45): 227–240.

Dudley, Homer. "The Vocoder." *Bell Laboratories Record* 18 (December 1939): 122–126.

Flanagan, James L. *Speech Analysis, Synthesis and Perception.* New York: Academic Press, 1965, pp. 245–247.

"Four-Conductor Cable for U.S. Signal Corps." *Bell Laboratories Record* 21 (April 1943): 251.

Gay, F. Selwyn. "The Role of the Telephone in the Civilian Defense Organization." *Bell Telephone Magazine* 21 (June 1942): 61–79.

Ingles, Major General Harry C. "Electrical Communications in World-Wide Warfare." *Bell Telephone Magazine* 24 (Summer 1945): 54–100.

Jacobs, O. B. "Carrier System for the Spiral-4 Cable." *Bell Laboratories Record* 22 (December 1943): 168–172.

Jones, Philip C. "Bell Laboratories' Role in Victory," (part I). *Bell Telephone Magazine* 25 (Spring 1946): 37–53.

Jones, Philip C. "Bell Laboratories' Role in Victory," (part II). *Bell Telephone Magazine* 25 (Summer 1946): 116–126.

McHugh, Keith S. "War Activities of the Bell Telephone System." *Bell Telephone Magazine* 21 (November 1942): 205–225.

Mitchell, Doren. "History of Speech Privacy Systems in the Bell System." Internal Memorandum, Bell Laboratories (October 2, 1970).

Nichols, Eldon. "Command Circuits." *Bell Telephone Magazine* 25 (Summer 1946): 101–115.

Southworth, George C. *Forty Years of Radio Research.* New York: Gordon and Breach, 1962, pp. 168–170.

The Global Military Communication Network

Electrical Communication Systems Engineering. War Department Technical Manual TM 11-486, April 25, 1945.

Electrical Communication Systems Equipment. War Department Technical Manual TM 11-487, October 2, 1944.

Frequency Shift Keyer—Navy Model FSA. Navships 900754, October 15, 1945.

"Military Teletypewriter Systems of World War II." *Trans. AIEE* 67 (1948): 1398–1408.

Radio Equipment—Navy Model UF. Navships 900223, October 25, 1945.

1943 Renegotiation. Report submitted to the War Contracts Price Adjustment Board. Western Electric. Also *1944 Renegotiation* and *1945 Renegotiation.*

Secure Speech Transmission – Frequency Rearrangement

Dickieson, A. C. U.S. Patent No. 2,132,205; filed June 23, 1937; issued October 4, 1938.

Espenschied, L. U.S. Patent No. 1,546,439; filed January 8, 1920; issued July 21, 1925.

Van der Bijl, H. U.S. Patent No. 1,502,889; filed January 8, 1918; issued July 29, 1924.

Secure Speech Transmission – Time Rearrangement

Hartley, R. V. L. U.S. Patent No. 1,605,023; filed May 19, 1921; issued November 2, 1926.

Mitchell, D. and Wright, S. B. U.S. Patent No. 1,981,114; filed March 3, 1933; issued November 20, 1934.

Secure Speech Transmission – Added Noise

Chapman, A. G. U.S. Patent No. 2,556,677; filed May 10, 1946; issued June 12, 1951.

Emling, J. W. and Mitchell, D. "The Effects of Time Delay and Echoes on Telephone Conversations." *Bell System Technical J.* 42 (November 1963): 2869–2891.

Mills, J. U.S. Patent No. 1, 480, 217; filed December 29, 1916; issued January 8, 1924.

Mobile Radio Systems

Black, H. S. et al. "A Multichannel Microwave Radio Relay System." *Trans. AIEE* 65 (December 1946): 798–806.

Emling, J. W. and Mitchell, D. "The Effects of Time Delay and Echoes on Telephone Conversations." *Bell System Technical J.* 42 (November 1963): 2869–2891.

Koerner, L. F. "Testing Tank Set Crystals." *Bell Laboratories Record* 24 (October 1946): 363–364.

Nordahl, J. G. "Tank Radio Set." *Bell Laboratories Record* 23 (January 1945): 1–5.

Wrathall, L. R. "Frequency Modulation by Non-Linear Coils." *Bell Laboratories Record* 24 (March 1946): 102–105.

Chapter 6. Overview of the War Years

Baxter, James Phinney 3rd. *Scientists Against Time.* Boston: Little, Brown, 1946, pp. 202–206.

Buckley, Oliver E. "Bell Laboratories in the War." *Bell Telephone Magazine* 23 (Winter 1944–45): 227–240.

Harrison, William H. "Service to the Nation in Peace and War." *Bell Telephone Magazine* 25 (Autumn 1946): 159–161.

Jewett, F. B. Memorandum to A. W. Page. Internal Bell Laboratories correspondence, July 10, 1942.

Kappel, F. R. "The Bell System's Part in Defending the Nation." *Bell Telephone Magazine* 30 (Autumn 1951): 141–152.

Chapter 7. Air Defense

ABM Research and Development, Project History. Bell Laboratories for U.S. Army Ballistic Missile Defense Systems Command, October 1975.

ABM Research and Development at Bell Laboratories, Kwajalein Field Station. Bell Laboratories for U.S. Army Ballistic Missile Defense Systems Command, October 1975.

Warren, Clifford A. "Ballistic Missile Defense Testing in the Pacific: 1960–1976." *Bell Laboratories Record* 54 (September 1976): 203–207.

DuCastel, Francois. *Tropospheric Radiowave Propagation Beyond the Horizon.* Oxford: Pergamon, 1966, p. 14.

Misenheimer, H. N. " 'Over-the-Horizon' Radio Tests." *Bell Laboratories Record* 34 (February 1956): 41–45.

Chapter 8. Underwater Systems

Acoustical Research

Balch, H. T. et al. "Estimation of the Mean of a Stationary Random Process by Periodic Sampling." *Bell System Technical J.* 45 (May–June 1966): 733–741.

Cooley, J. W. and Tukey, J. W. "An Algorithm for the Machine Calculation of Complex Fourier Series." *Mathematics of Computation* 19 (April 1965): 297–301.

Fox, G. R. "Ambient-Noise Directivity Measurements." *J. Acoustical Society of America* 36 (August 1964): 1537–1540.

Kaplan, E. L. "Signal-Detection Studies With Applications." *Bell System Technical J.* 34 (March 1955): 403–432.

Labianca, F. M. "Normal Modes, Virtual Modes, and Alternative Representations in the Theory of Surface Duct Sound Propagation." *J. Acoustical Society of America* 53 (April 1973): 1137–1147.

Lauver, R. M. "A Z Transfer Function and Output Spectrum for a Deltic." Internal Bell Laboratories memorandum, September 14, 1962.

Potter, R. K., Kopp, G. A., and Green, H. C. *Visible Speech.* New York: D. Van Nostrand, 1947. 2nd ed. New York: Dover, 1966.

Schevill, W. E., Watkins, W. A., and Backus, R. H. "The 20-Cycle Signals and *Balaenoptera* (Fin Whales)." In *Marine Bio-Acoustics,* proceedings of a symposium held at the Lerner Marine Laboratory, Bimini, Bahamas, April 11–13, 1963. Edited by W. N. Tavolga. New York: Pergamon Press, Macmillan, 1964, pp. 147–152.

Smith, R. A. "A Note on the Frequency Domain Behavior of a Deltic." Internal Bell Laboratories memorandum, September 15, 1964.

Stickler, D. C. "Ocean Acoustics." *Bell Laboratories Record* 47 (April 1969): 113–119.

Talham, R. J. "Ambient-Sea-Noise Model." *J. Acoustical Society of America* 36 (August 1964): 1541–1544.

Walker, R. A. "Some Intense, Low-Frequency, Underwater Sounds of Wide Geographic Distribution, Apparently of Biological Origin." *J. Acoustical Society of America* 35 (November 1963): 1816–1824.

Ewing, M. and Worzel, J. L. "Long-Range Sound Transmission." *Propagation of Sound in the Ocean.* Memoir 27. New York: Geological Society of America, October 15, 1948.

Development Contributions

Baxter, H. A. and Mueser, R. E. "The Development of Ocean-Cable Plows." *IEEE Trans. on Communication Technology* COM-19 (December 1971): 1233–1241.

Brewer, S. T. et al. "SF Submarine Cable System." *Bell System Technical J.* 49 (May–June 1970): 601–798 (nine articles).

Ehrbar, R. D. et al. "The SD SUBMARINE Cable System." *Bell System Technical J.* 43, Part 1 (July 1964): 1155–1184.

Hawley, R. T. "Ocean Cable Laying." *Oceanology International* 5 (November 1970): 18–21.

Mottram, E. T. et al. "Transatlantic Telephone Cable System—Planning and Over-All Performance." *Bell System Technical J.* 36 (January 1957): 7–27.

Peripheral Acoustic Systems

Baker, H. H. "Missile Impact Locating System." *Bell Laboratories Record* 39 (June 1961): 195–200.

Chapter 11. Command and Control

Augustadt, H. W. "The Navy's New Defense Against Air Attacks." *Bell Laboratories Record* 38 (July 1960): 242–247.

Kellogg, W. M. "Slant Range Versus Ground Range in Target Designation Processes," (Radar Mark 65). Internal Bell Laboratories memorandum, December 1957.

Progress reports for Gunfire Control System Mark 65 prepared by Bell Telephone Laboratories on behalf of Western Electric Co. for U.S. Navy, Bureau of Ordnance, under Contracts NOrd-9170, NOrd-10214, NOrd-10422.

Chapter 12. Communications

Baker, E. W. "SAGE in Air Defense." *Bell Telephone Magazine* 37 (Summer 1958): 5–16.

Bidlack, R. H. "The 304 Conference Switching System." *Bell Laboratories Record* 43 (January 1965): 8–15.

Bishop, J. B. "A New Surface-to-Air Data Communication System." *Bell Laboratories Record* 39 (August 1961): 281–284.

Bullington, K. "Characteristics of Beyond-the-Horizon Radio Transmission." *Proc. IRE* 43 (October 1955): 1175–1180.

Bullington, K., Inkster, W. J., and Durkee, A. L. "Results of Propagation Test at 505 mc and 4,090 mc on Beyond-Horizon Paths." *Proc. IRE* 43 (October 1955): 1306–1317.

"Command Guidance Plays Role in Titan Hardened-Complex Launch." *Bell Laboratories Record* 40 (April 1962): 374.

D'Albora, J. B., Jr. "The Cape Canaveral Laboratory." *Bell Laboratories Record* 40 (November 1962): 352–357.

Duncan, C. C. "Communications and Defense." *Bell Telephone Magazine* 37 (Spring 1958): 15–24.

FAA Marketing Handbook. Washington D.C.: Long Lines Government Communications, Summer 1975.

Felch, E. P. "Missile Guidance." *Bell Laboratories Record* 37 (June 1959): 203–207.

Frantz, G. R. "Development of the DEW LINE." *Bell Laboratories Record* 37 (January 1959): 2–6.

Gerbore, A. E. and Walsh, H. J. "The 758C Private Branch Exchange." *Proc. National Electronics Conference* 20 (1964): 454–459.

Gorgas, J. W. "AUTOVON, Switching Network for Global Defense." *Bell Laboratories Record* 46 (April 1968): 106–111.

Gorgas, J. W. "The Polygrid Network for AUTOVON." *Bell Laboratories Record* 46 (July–August 1968): 222–227.

Haury, P. T. and Ilgenfritz, L. M. "Air Force Submarine Cable System." *Bell Laboratories Record* 34 (September 1956): 321–324.

Hibbert, J. J. "Bell Laboratories and Project Mercury." *Bell Laboratories Record* 40 (September 1962): 276–281.

Irvin, H. D. and Cowperthwait, W. L. "Around the World by Simulation." *Bell Laboratories Record* 39 (October 1961): 342–349.

Irland, E. A. "A High-Speed Data Signaling System." *Bell Laboratories Record* 36 (October 1958): 376–380.

"Mercury Communications Network Completed." *Bell Laboratories Record* 39 (June 1961): 224–225.

Michael, H. J. "Selective Signaling and Switching for the SAGE System." *Bell Laboratories Record* 36 (September 1958): 335–339.

Michael, H. J. and Pruden, H. M. "SAC's Primary Alerting System." *Bell Laboratories Record* 39 (July 1961): 234–239.

Monsees, F. W. "Training Simulator for Flight Controllers." *Bell Laboratories Record* 39 (July 1961): 254.

Ozenberger, M. E. "Voice Communication System for Air Traffic Control." *Bell Laboratories Record* 39 (May 1961): 154–160.

"Project Mercury Communications Network Near Completion." *Bell Laboratories Record* 39 (March 1961): 108–109.

Ruppel, A. E. "SAGE Data Transmission Service." *Bell Laboratories Record* 35 (October 1957): 401–405.

Seckler, W. H. "Global Command Post Alerting Network." *Bell Laboratories Record* 42 (November 1964): 370–374.

Tidd, W. H. "BMEWS Communication System." *Bell Laboratories Record* 39 (November 1961): 383–387.

Tidd, W. H. "Demonstration of Bandwidth Capabilities of Beyond-Horizon Tropospheric Radio Propagation." *Proc. IRE* 43 (October 1955): 1297–1299.

Tidd, W. H. "White Alice, A New Radio Voice for Alaskan Outposts." *Bell Laboratories Record* 36 (August 1958): 278–283.

"Titan Guidance System Successfully Tested." *Bell Laboratories Record* 37 (May 1959): 189.

"Tracking and Communications Network Vital to Glenn's Orbital Flight." *Bell Laboratories Record* 40 (March 1962): 106–107.

Chapter 13. Military Systems Engineering and Research

Baird, J. A. "Leprechaun Computer." *Bell Laboratories Record* 38 (February 1960): 58–63.

Cornell, W. A. "A Special-Purpose Solid-State Computer Using Sequential Access Memory." *Proc. Western Joint Computer Conference*, May 6–8, 1958. New York: AIEE, March 1959.

Harris, J. R. "TRADIC: The First Phase." *Bell Laboratories Record* 36 (September 1958): 330–334.

"Leprechaun." *Bell Laboratories Record* 35 (July 1957): 272–273.

MacWilliams, W. H., Jr. "A Transistor Gating Matrix for a Simulated Warfare Computer." *Bell Laboratories Record* 35 (March 1957): 94–99.

May, John E., Jr. "Low-loss 1000 Microsecond Ultrasonic Delay Lines." *Proc. National Electronics Conference* 11 (March 1956): 786–790.

Simpkins, Q. W. and Vogelsong, J. H. "Transistor Amplifiers for Use in a Digital Computer." *Proc. IRE* 55 (January 1956): 43–55.

Chapter 14: Special Projects

Alexander, Frederic C., Jr. *History of Sandia Corporation Through Fiscal Year 1963.* Albuquerque, N.M.: Sandia Corporation.

Sandia—Looking Back. Albuquerque, N.M.: Sandia Laboratories, 1976.

"Project Apollo." *Bell Telephone Magazine* 41 (Autumn 1962): 2–9.

Hornbeck, J. A. "Bellcomm." *Bell Telephone Magazine* 45 (Spring 1966): 44–53.

Credits

Acknowledgment is made for permission to reprint the following copyrighted material:

Figures 2-21 (redrawn), 2-22, and 2-24 from *Radar System Engineering*, 1st ed., M.I.T. Radiation Laboratory Series, Vol. 1, edited by Louis N. Ridenour. Copyright 1947 by McGraw-Hill Book Company, Inc. Used with permission.

Figures 2-1a, 2-1b, 2-3, 2-5 (redrawn), 2-7a, 2-7b, 2-8b,c,d (redrawn), 2-9 through 2-11, 2-13 through 2-16, 2-18, 2-20, 2-23 (redrawn), 2-25 (redrawn), 2-27 (redrawn), 2-28 (redrawn), 2-29, 2-32 (redrawn), 2-36, 2-38, 2-42, and 2-65 from *Radar Systems and Components* by members of the technical staff, Bell Telephone Laboratories. Copyright 1949 by D. Van Nostrand Company. Reprinted with permission.

Figures 4-1 and 4-4 from A. C. Keller, "Submarine Detection by Sonar." *Transactions of the American Institute of Electrical Engineers*, Vol. 66 (1947). Copyright 1947 by the American Institute of Electrical Engineers. Reprinted with permission.

Figures 4-20a,b (redrawn), and 4-22 from R. Clark Jones, "A Fifty Horsepower Siren." *Journal of the Acoustical Society of America*, Vol. 18 (1946). Copyright 1946 by the American Institute of Physics. Reprinted with permission.

Figures 12-18 through 12-10 from V. I. Cruser, "Equipment and Mechanical Features of the AN/TRC-24 Radio Set." *Transactions AIEE*, Vol. 73 (1954). Copyright 1954 by the American Institute of Electrical Engineers. Reprinted with permission.

Figure 13-4 (redrawn) from John E. May, Jr., "Low-Loss 1000 Microsecond Ultrasonic Delay Lines." *Proceedings of the National Electronics Conference*, Vol. 11 (1955). Copyright 1956 by the National Electronics Conference, Inc. Reprinted with permission.

Figure 14-15 courtesy of National Air and Space Museum, Smithsonian Institution.

Index